Mage Publishers
Washington, DC
2007

Masters & Masterpieces of Iranian Cinema

Hamid Dabashi

Forugh Farrokhzad The House Is Black **Ebrahim Golestan** Mud Brick and Mirror **Dariush Mehrjui** The Cow **Arby Ovanessian** Spring **Bahman Farmanara** Prince Ehtejab **Sohrab Shahid Sales** Still Life **Amir Naderi** The Runner **Bahram Beizai** Bashu, the Little Stranger **Abbas Kiarostami** Through the Olive Trees **Mohsen Makhmalbaf** A Moment of Innocence **Marziyeh Meshkini** The Day I Became a Woman **Jafar Panahi** Crimson Gold

Library of Congress Cataloging-in-Publication Data

Dabashi, Hamid, 1951-
  Masters & masterpieces of Iranian cinema / by Hamid Dabashi.
    p. cm.
  ISBN 0-934211-85-X (hardcover : alk. paper)
  1. Motion pictures--Iran. 2. Motion picture producers and
  directors--Iran--Biography. I. Title. II. Title: Masters and
  masterpieces of Iranian cinema.
  PN1993.5.I846D33 2007
  791.430955--dc2

Book design by Hugh MacDonald
The book is set in Akzidenz Grotesk and Janson

Mage books are available at bookstores or directly from the publisher. Visit Mage on the Web at www.mage.com. Call (202) 342-1642 or e-mail as@mage.com for a catalog.

For Ahang Bashi,

Little sister, solid comrade, future filmmaker

All art is autobiographical—the pearl is the
oyster's autobiography.
–Federico Fellini

Contents

Bread and Alley, Abbas Kiarostami, 1970

Much travel is needed before the raw is cooked.
—Sa'di

Introduction
Letter to a Young Filmmaker

YOU MUST BE THE MOST PERSISTENT LITTLE REBEL roaming the streets of Tehran, planting seeds of fear in the hearts of all the reigning and potential tyrants of our homeland! I must tell you, I find myself in something of a quandary. We see each other once in a blue moon somewhere on this planet, and as soon as our conversations begin to build momentum, we must depart and travel in two opposite directions; usually you fly east and I west—except of course the time I flew to Tehran after an absence of twenty years.

You were born a year after the Iranian revolution of 1979. You are the walking embodiment of all its hopes and aspirations, the fragile target of all its terrors and tribulations. You are not just a young Iranian. To me, you are the embodiment of an era, the symbol of a nation in defiance and despair. Since your birth, Iran has not been relieved of a moment of anguish—not that it was a garden of flowering hope before you were born and the revolution betrayed.

It's the beginning of a glorious summer here in New York. The outside world is, of course, in more of a mess than ever—but it no longer bothers me. I am happy in my apartment and during my early morning walks by the Hudson. I still have some nuisances at the office to take care of—the last few months of chairing my department. But other than that I am in a pretty good mood and feel quite talkative. The only problem is that you are not here. Do you remember that beautiful story by Rumi about the man who had a donkey but no saddle and when he finally found a saddle thieves had stolen his donkey?

Well, that's our story.

A good mood, I said, except I have been away from my writing desk for too long, and editors and publishers are breathing down my neck. I have promised to write a book on the masters and masterpieces of Iranian cinema—how do you like that! But my head is anywhere but in writing that book. My mind is instead full of things that I wanted to tell you in peace.

We have never had enough time together for me to tell you my version of how we have come to where we are now. What is the moral and imaginative parentage of this art, and what precisely is the texture and disposition of this precious heritage with which your generation is gifted? I have no intention of making this conversation a lesson in history—art, in fact, has no history. The more Iranian cinema forgets its own history the more creative it becomes. It has never been in the spirit of history but with a sense of wonder that I have thought of having a conversation with you about Iranian cinema and its place in Iranian culture. And I wish I could use the occasion of talking about Iranian cinema to talk about something more.

There is a sense of wonder about what the world now celebrates as Iranian cinema, and I have always hoped that I would have an occasion to share with you in some detail what it is that I cherish about this national cinematic project. There is so much I wish I could tell you, but I wonder if I will ever get a chance to do so. Life is short, art is long, the occasion instant, and the experiment perilous. A Greek once said that, I think.

I still remember our first serious conversation. It was in May 1998, immediately after Mohammad Khatami's election, and there was so much hope and expectation in all of us. You were wondering what I thought the differences between our generations were. So I was trying to explain to you the differences, as I saw them, between your generation—those who were born in Iran soon after the Islamic revolution of 1979—and mine, those who were born and bred during or after the 1953 coup that restored the Pahlavi monarchy to power.

We had heroes, I remember I was trying to tell you, while your generation is heroic. That's our difference. We were scared and hopeless, so we kept inventing heroes among our public intellectuals. You are courageous and full of hopes—you have no need for such figments of the imagination. You were not convinced, I remember, and thought that your generation was actually quite nihilistic, lacking in any conviction. On the surface, I remember I was telling you, it appears that way, that your generation is wanting in idealism. But I said that I thought in reality the reverse is true—that courage and heroism are now spread evenly and democratically in the soul of your generation. Your generation is the dream my generation did not even know it had.

I have enjoyed talking with you. Your face is the topography of a homeland I have lost forever. You were born and raised in Iran right after I left it for good. You represent an Iran that is very dear and yet foreign to me. A comparative assessment of my own youth with yours has always been instructive for me, and the only way I have had of assessing what is happening in Iranian cinema today—by far the most glorious achievement, and thus the most accurate measure, of our culture in living memory. I doubted during our conversation that year that there is anyone that your generation greatly admires. In fact I even suggested that your generation is sick and tired of admiring any figure or idealizing any achievement outside its reach. Instead, I said, I have a sense that you think you can achieve anything, go anywhere. I didn't mean to say that there is no desperation in your generation, but that there is a restlessness in your anxiety—reflected paradoxically in a coolness in your drive and demeanor—that is inexhaustibly energetic, agitating, iconoclastic, and irreverent in a playful and emancipatory way. Even in your *nihilism* there is something good and positive for the general disposition of Iranian culture.

For instance, the young filmmaker Parviz Shahbazi's *Deep Breath* (2003) is very good at portraying that sense of desperation, anomie, and nihilism. But I think that there is a positive side to this nihilism—it adds a healthy dose of despair to an otherwise pathologically anemic attitude.

The nihilism that Shahbazi captures in your generation is a far cry from the ideological determinism of mine, which was the principal point of my initial interest in Iranian cinema. "Where does this precocious wisdom come from?" I remember asking myself. "How could an *Islamic Republic* produce so many visionary filmmakers?" everybody else in the world seemed to wonder. And what exactly was so *great* about this cinematic movement, anyway? These were not easy questions. But there have been so many good reasons that people were eager to ask, and I was anxious to find out. Our previous conversation about generational differences had made me think through these issues more carefully—and the direction of my thinking invariably turned around and came back to the phenomenon of Iranian cinema. What precisely were the defining moments of this cinema, where were its origins, whence its disposition, how it had come about, who were its best representatives, and why?

I was convinced when I began paying closer attention to Iranian cinema, as I am convinced now, that the answer to all these questions rests in the moral mutation of my generation into yours, with a magnificent revolution that went awry (but don't all revolutions go awry?) and a dreadful war in between, and that we were all at the threshold of a whole new era in our creative character. Your generation of young Iranians is the summation of all the heroes that the preceding generations were falsely celebrating in public intellectuals. After the success and failure of the Islamic revolution, the circumstances were radically different. The Islamic "mullarchy" that succeeded the Pahlavi monarchy could no longer arrest and incarcerate a few prominent figures, put them in jail, deny them access to the world, and then rest assured that all its troubles were over. They did all of that. But heroic resistance to their tyranny continued by nameless heroes. My generation had raised a few poets, novelists, filmmakers, and essayists to the status of demigods, a handful of people, most of them men, who could easily be identified, arrested, incarcerated, executed, or sent into exile. You and your generation are the agency we lacked in our character but dreamed of in our poetry. I remember in May 1998 when the largest student organization in Iran had written an open and defiant letter to the Supreme Leader—just think of the obscenity of that title in this day and age, "Supreme Leader"—demanding that he should choose between the future of democracy in Iran or the end of the Islamic Republic! Imagine that! But before I even finish this paragraph let me assure you that that corrupt and outdated regime and the ideology that brought it to power will implode, by the forces of its own contradiction, by the determined will and the creative defiance of Iranians themselves, and certainly not by an attack by a predatory imperial hubris, sustained by an equally corrupt and diabolic ideology called "neoconservatism"—which in fact will do nothing but strengthen the tyranny of this Islamic Republic.

My point is that both the nihilism best captured in Shahbazi's *Deep Breath* and the forgiving embrace of Samira Makhmalbaf's *Apple* complement each other and speak of an emancipatory facet of Iranian culture that we need to heed and harness. Iranian cinema has opened up the perils and promises of its secrets in full view of the whole world to see. Don't you breathe this to anyone, though. Let no one know that in Iranian cinema we are in fact washing our dirty laundry right in full view of the entire world. And that, my dear, is exactly how dirty laundry ought to be washed: no secret and no lies. And there are some nasty stains on our beautiful garments!

While we were talking that year, I remember, the point of our conversation moved to the roots and causes of the sudden ascendancy of Iranian cinema to global attention—and as measured by and in the Cannes Film Festival.

I was thinking in generational terms as to what happened before and after the Islamic revolution, and whether or not that cataclysmic event had anything to do with the rise of Iranian cinema as we know it now. We began to speak of public intellectuals by way of my paradoxical proposal to you that in fact it was terrible for a generation to have too many cultural heroes (the way mine did) because it meant an absence of creative agency. What I had detected in your generation was quite the contrary. You had in fact lost any interest in heroes. Khatami was the most publicly celebrated figure of your generation, quite an oddity for a president of an Islamic Republic. But even he would soon lose significant portions of his popularity when he failed to deliver on his democratic promises.

The Islamic revolution failed and it failed miserably. After a generation of hopes and aspirations, heroic acts and revolutionary struggle, what did Iran gain but a dreaded medieval theocracy. Who would have thought? Almost a century before the Islamic revolution, and in the context of a constitutional monarchy—*monarchy*, mind you—Iran had a better claim to democracy than the monstrosity of the Islamic Republic. Right now Iran has hit such a low point that even Reza Pahlavi has a claim to a revolutionary agenda, even a mercenary army like the Mojahedin-e Khalq (having helped a military dictator like Saddam Hussein perpetrate criminal atrocities against his own nation) has a claim to a liberation agenda, and, worst of all, the United States is poised to come and liberate Iran. Do you see the sad saga of Iran's political misery? But, fortunately, with the failure of the Islamic revolution came the end of our outdated ideologies. The Iranian cinema that emerged after the Islamic revolution is a clear indication of a far more enduring and consequential conversation that your generation has launched with Iran's most enduring works of art—poetry, film, and fiction in particular.

As you well know, beginning in the early 1990s, the Cannes Film Festival started paying closer and unprecedented attention to Iranian cinema. But I was thinking about the presence of Iranian cinema at Cannes in the preceding decades.

Cannes is the mecca of world cinema. For better or for worse, all other film festivals around the world take their critical cues and measure their success according to Cannes. Since Cannes started paying very close attention to Iranian cinema in the early 1990s, so did other major film festivals around the globe—Venice, Berlin, San Sebastian, Locarno, London, New York, Tokyo, São Paulo, Toronto, and Pusan, among many others. Film production and distribution companies were competing to make and buy Iranian films. Art-house theaters and television stations throughout the world began screening these films to packed houses and enthused audiences on a scale rarely noted in world cinema. Japan had Akira Kurosawa, India Satyajit Ray, Russia Andrei Tarkovsky, Egypt Youssef Chahine, China Zhang Yimou, and Spain Pedro Almodóvar. But what was happening in Iranian cinema had its antecedents only in such *movements* as Italian Neorealism, French New Wave, or German New Cinema. And it all began at Cannes—at Salle Lumière in the Palais du Féstival, to be exact.

I am not just talking about Abbas Kiarostami and Mohsen Makhmal-baf—the yin and yang of Iranian cinema. There is an array of poetic visionaries—Bahram Beizai, Rakhshan Bani-Etemad, Amir Naderi, Jafar Panahi, Bahman Farmanara, Ebrahim Hatami-Kia, Dariush Mehrjui, Abolfazl Jalili, Masud Kimiai, Majid Majidi, Nasser Taqvai, Bahman Qobadi, Sohrab Shahid Sales, Marziyeh Meshkini, Parviz Kimiai, Mohammad Shirvani, Kamran Shirdel, Parviz Shahbazi, Ebrahim Goles-tan, Kamal Tabrizi, Arby Ovanessian, Kiyumars Pourahmad, Farrokh Ghaffari, Reza Mir-Karimi, Ali Hatami, Babak Payami—from before and after the revolution, and the list is almost endless. No aspect of Ira-nian culture has ever been so globally received and critically celebrated before. The nineteenth-century attention of European romanticism to Persian poetry, soon followed by a similar proclivity in American tran-scendentalism, all fade in comparison. Persian miniature painting or calligraphy were never as popularly received or as critically acclaimed as Iranian cinema is now. I have seen directors of film festivals pleading with Iranian filmmakers for their most recent films, upping the ante if they're contemplating a rival festival, and turning nasty if they do not comply. It is simply uncanny how this has happened. Every single day of every single year there seems to be a film festival somewhere on the globe, and there is scarcely a film festival anywhere without a couple of Iranian films thrown in for good measure!

There seems to be no end or pause to this crescendo. Comprehen-sive retrospectives on Iranian cinema in general, and that of Kiarostami and Makhmalbaf in particular, have been launched in major cities around the world—Paris, London, Turin, New York, Chicago, San Francisco, Los Angeles, Tokyo, Pusan, Bombay, Beirut, Thessalonica, Tunis, Rio, São Paulo, Sydney, Toronto, Montreal. This is no fly-by-night opera-tion of one or two major filmmakers, or a token attention to a national cinema. Something far more serious is at work here. After attending the 2002 Chicago Film Festival as a member of the jury, Amir Naderi told me that in his opinion half of the films made by young directors from around the world now were paying homage to Iranian cinema, quoting them, adopting, adapting, mimicking, or reformulating them, in some-times creative and sometimes curious ways.

Something of a major epistemic and aesthetic break is globally evident in this cinema, similar to the way that Italian Neorealism, the French New Wave, or German New Cinema had broken new ground. But what is so particular about Iranian cinema? Is it just one form of national cinema among many others that every decade or so Cannes deigns to consider closely, or is there something specific to its aesthet-ics and politics, creativity and criticism, visual vocabulary and emotive universe? Iranian cinema is in the midst of a creative avalanche and so it may never be fully understood—a full understanding of anything (art in particular) is its kiss of death. We should only hope to partake in the joy-ous vision it has occasioned—and let the bored and boring historians of the future worry about its dead certainties.

Though not entirely representative of what has happened in Iranian cinema over the last century, Cannes has been a kind of barometer of its emerging significance. As fate would have it, in 1998 there were *two* young Iranian women representing Iran in Cannes—Samira Makhmal-baf for the premier of *Apple* and Fahimeh Sorkhabi for her film *First Sin*. By sheer serendipity, it seemed, both these films in one way or another had a central concern with forbidden fruit. Remember the scene in *Apple* where Samira had planted the dangling temptation, manipulated by a string held by a mischievous young boy, over the head of the half-crazed mother of the two incarcerated girls, coaxing her to come out of her dungeon and face the world? In *First Sin*, a sweet animation, Fahimeh Sorkhabi also reflected playfully on Eve's temptation of Adam and their subsequent dismissal from paradise. I thought them both splendidly aus-picious—and may we the bastard children of Adam and Eve never be absolved of the sin our splendid mother committed!

How could an Islamic Republic, with its horrific history of atrocious treatment of women, produce so many filmmakers among them? the press was wondering that year. Obviously, the confidence with which a young Iranian woman could stand behind a camera and gaze through its lens—and shout "Action!" and then "Cut!"—had been cultivated through a long and sustained heritage of poets, novelists, filmmakers, vocalists, and activists. Farrokhzad's *The House Is Black* (1962)—a single act of creative genius way ahead of its time—was *the* pioneering event in the rise of contemporary Iranian cinema. A gem of a documentary made in a few short days at a leper colony, *The House Is Black* teases out the rays of hope and signs of joy in otherwise desperate and miserable surround-ings. Farrokhzad's tragically early death in 1967 cut her illustrious career brutally short. But the seeds she carefully planted in yet unborn souls have now come to fruition in a whole generation of young filmmakers.

From the depth of a harshly patriarchal culture, a solid string of creative energy is holding you to a succession of courageous souls your generation now gracefully follows. Iranian cinema as a movement is inclusive of even the most repressed segment of its society, almost half of its population represented by an array of distinguished women filmmakers.

In 1997, the year before we had this long chat, Iran was represented in Cannes by two of its most illustrious masters, arriving in France from two opposite geographical poles, one from New York and the other from Tehran. Amir Naderi brought *A, B, C...Manhattan* (1997) and Abbas Kiarostami *Taste of Cherry* (1997). Naderi is among the pioneering architects of Iranian cinema. His films *Harmonica* (1974) and *The Runner* (1985) are the hallmarks and turning points of Iranian filmmaking. Frustrated with the difficulties of making films in Iran and determined to make them in a different register, Naderi immigrated to New York in the late 1980s, where he made *Manhattan by Numbers* in 1992; *A, B, C... Manhattan* in 1997; and *Marathon* in 2002, the magisterial conclusion to the trilogy. (Right now he has finished shooting his fourth New York film; tentatively he calls it *Sound Barrier.* He is busy editing it these days, so I see him only once a week or so—over my *baqala polow* and a Ford or a Kurosawa—depending on his mood). Kiarostami, meanwhile, was on a glorious streak, having first premiered *And Life Goes On* at Cannes in 1992 and *Through the Olive Trees* in 1994. In 1997 he went with great hopes and high expectations, both richly deserved and splendidly fulfilled when he, in conjunction with the Japanese director Imamura Shohei for *Eel*, was awarded the coveted Palme d'Or for *Taste of Cherry.*

Naderi and Kiarostami represent the two ends of a cinematic movement that had come back to Cannes triumphantly from inside and outside Iran. Naderi had defied the indignities of exile and made it to Cannes without a claim to any national cinema. He was there neither as an Iranian nor as an American filmmaker. He was there just as a filmmaker, with both sides of his hyphenated duality clear for landing. He did not represent Iran in a territorial sense, though he is a quintessentially Iranian filmmaker. He did not represent the US, though his film bears the distinct marks of New York. While Kiarostami had triumphed over the censorial atrocities of an Islamic Republic to continue to produce one masterpiece after another, Naderi had dared the elements of an outside world, entirely devoid of the resources of national subsidies, smack in the middle of the dog-eat-dog cruelty of an artist's life in self-imposed exile—and yet there they both were in Cannes.

Naderi's 1997 appearance at Cannes had made the simplistic application of a national cinema to its Iranian case quite complicated, if not altogether untenable. What does it exactly mean to be an Iranian filmmaker?

The question is far more contemporary than historical, I thought. How can one think of a national cinema these days? We have an *ancient*, a *modern*, and a *recent* history—or more accurately, we remember an ancient history for ourselves, live the consequences of our modern times, while in conversation with our own immediate world. How do we reconcile these three forces when we say we are Iranian? Our ancient history is very present in our collective and creative imagination. In fact the first Iranian film ever to be screened in Cannes was called *Cyrus the Great* (1961), by a filmmaker named Feri Farzaneh. Beyond this ancient but unforgotten history, we have also had a colonial encounter with the European project of modernity, and more recently, since the revolution of 1979, we have been dragged into a global reconfiguration of realpolitik.

It is always within the confinement of these power politics that we remember—or more accurately are made to remember—our history and mark our identity. Since the parameters of that power are subject to historical changes, so are the terms of our remembrances of our identity. But art—and the terms of its engagement—cannot be submissive to the whims of power. So in mapping out the contours of an artistic movement we must think beyond its territorial boundaries and look into the formative forces of its aesthetics and politics. The two are entirely intertwined.

If you consider the case of Amir Naderi and the slew of other Iranian filmmakers who left their homeland after the Islamic revolution, you realize that living in Iran is not the only way in which one can be called an Iranian. As for those who have remained in Iran or were born there after the Islamic revolution, how are they integrated and interpolated in the dominant ideology of an Islamic Republic? How is the creative imagination of Iran's artists, filmmakers, poets, novelists capable of defying such limits? Being outside Iran is not an indication of no longer being an Iranian, and being inside Iran does not mean that your aesthetic and political sensibilities are entirely native to your homeland.

Take a look at the creative characters of these filmmakers: Dariush Mehrjui and Bahman Farmanara were educated in Europe and the United States; Bahram Beizai and Abbas Kiarostami received their education entirely within Iran; and then there are filmmakers like Naderi or Makhmalbaf who in fact never attended college or received any formal education, and yet they are among Iran's best filmmakers. Put these three categories together—those who were educated abroad, those were educated inside, and those who had no formal schooling at all—and what you get is a massive cinematic movement in creative conversation with the best of world cinema. That is the ultimate acid test of the globality of Iranian cinema, which is rooted not only in the best of modern Persian fiction and poetry, but also conversant with the undisputed masters of the craft. Beizai is entirely enamored of Alfred Hitchcock and Akira

Kurosawa. Naderi is a walking encyclopedia of world cinema, and when he starts talking about John Ford or Yasujiro Ozu in the middle of the street I have to watch him closely because he might get run over by a car and not notice it. Makhmalbaf talks about Theo Angelopoulos, Wim Wenders, Andrei Tarkovsky, and Vittorio De Sica as if they were Persian poets, or better yet his cellmates when he was in jail!

What has happened in Iranian cinema makes it more an artistic *movement* with deep-rooted cultural contours, a moral and political vision, rather than an accidental configuration of a number of brilliant filmmakers. Conclusion: very simple—Iranian cinema ought to be understood not just in terms of its territorial location but in terms of its aesthetic and political sensibilities that embrace but are irreducible to that location.

In 1996 at Cannes, Makhmalbaf premiered *Gabbeh*, and his alter ego, Abbas Kiarostami, brought *Through the Olive Trees*. The year before that, Makhmalbaf had been to Cannes with two of his earlier films, *Salaam Cinema* and *A Time for Love*, the same year that Kiarostami's protégé Jafar Panahi, had screened his *White Balloon*. Iranian cinema was by that time something of a sensation throughout the film-festival circuit, generating both admiration and animosity among its admirers and detractors. Makhmalbaf's cinema in particular was the subject of much controversy, because he had arisen directly from the ranks of religious revolutionaries; the added elements of class conflict further complicate this controversy. But above and beyond these controversies (which, to tell you the truth, bore me to tears) is the fact and phenomenon of Makhmalbaf's cinema itself that demands everyone's attention.

If Naderi and Kiarostami's simultaneous presence in Cannes in 1997 points to the parallel but opposite directions of their respective careers inside and outside Iran, Makhmalbaf and Kiarostami's concurrent presence in Cannes in 1996 points to a bizarre persistence of binary oppositions in our cultural disposition—and that strange duality does interest and puzzle me a lot. Have you noticed that everything in our cultural history comes in contradictory pairs and odd couples? In my youth, Iranian households were divided by their affinity for Marziyeh and Delkash, the two leading women singers of the time. Slightly later (but still before you were born), Googoosh and Ramesh replaced Marziyeh and Delkash as the two leading pop singers. You just had to choose between one or the other. You could not like them both. It was against some sort of unwritten law—a kind of blasphemy that we probably inherited from the time we were all Manicheans, and before that Zoroastrians, believing in some eternal battle between the forces of good and evil. But this was only the tip of the iceberg. Sa'di and Hafez, two of the greatest poets ever to put pen to paper, also divided Iranian households—you were either for Sa'di or for Hafez, just as you were for Persepolis or Taj, the two famous soccer clubs of my youth. Proponents of Sa'di thought those who liked Hafez were missing the boat, and vice versa. Supporters of Persepolis accused the Taj fans to be monarchists—a kind of curse in our times (*taj* meaning "the crown"), while Taj fans thought Persepolis supporters were mostly hooligans and thugs. Forugh Farrokhzad and Parvin Etesami, two of Iran's luminary women poets, were the same in dividing our loyalties, smack in the middle. The same was true about Mahmoud Dowlatabadi and Houshang Golshiri, Iran's two greatest novelists, Ahmad Shamlu and Mehdi Akhavan Sales, our greatest poets, Mohammad Reza Shajarian and Shahram Nazeri, our two glorious classical-music vocalists. You just had to take your pick! The same, with an even stronger animus behind it, is still true about the opposing preferences for the pinto bean (*lubia qermez*) and black-eyed bean (*lubia cheshm-bolboli*) in *ghormeh sabzi*, the vegetable stew of our national pride. I remember households were sharply divided—worse than the Montagues and the Capulets—in their preference for one or the other. People who wanted lubia qermez in their ghormeh sabzi were not on speaking terms with people of the lubia-cheshm-bolboli persuasion. And now it is the same story with Kiarostami and Makhmalbaf, the lubia qermez and lubia cheshm-bolboli of Iranian cinema. Well, I like them both, the two versions of ghormeh sabzi I mean, with lubia cheshm-bolboli or lubia qermez—my mother made it with one, while my aunt Batul preferred the other. But then again they were often not on speaking terms.

Beyond this bizarre proclivity of our culture, though, the binary opposition now code-named Kiarostami-Makhmalbaf does point to something in the nature and disposition of Iran's cultural predicament. My own reading of that predicament has in fact marked the precise nature of my conversations with Iranian cinema, and my continuing interest centers around the theme of creative subjectivity in a postcolonial context—how in art we negotiate a form of historical agency for ourselves beyond the debilitating de-subjection that came as a result of Iran's colonial encounter with European modernity. Evident in Iranian cinema, I had noted, was the careful constitution of a poetic vision that has been in the making for almost a century, from the earliest experiments with cinema to the later masterpieces that are now known and celebrated globally.

I believe that there is a critical correspondence between the post-national disposition of Iranian cinema, the way I just described it to you (production of a cinematic culture from within and without its territorial boundaries), and this creative subjectivity in a postcolonial context. That correspondence is the hidden significance of Iranian cinema, concealed under the brand of humanism given it by critics foreign to its historical and aesthetic disposition. Be very wary of this empty phrase "humanism" heaped on Iranian cinema—practically all your elders in Iranian cinema are very pleased by it. What is hidden under that dismissive term (think very carefully of this phrase I just used) is the one dearly definitive fact and feature of Iranian cinema—that it is irreducible to colonial modernity and its transaesthetics of indifference, as Jean Baudrillard (a very wise Frenchman whom people in Cannes have apparently never heard of) calls it. What I mean is this: If there is something significant about Iranian cinema in its international context it is precisely its emancipatory aesthetics in which what is beautiful or ugly is still politically important. Baudrillard has diagnosed the current state of European aesthetics as "the realm of ultra- or infra-aesthetics," where "it is pointless to try to endow our art with an aesthetic consistency or an aesthetic teleology," and then wisely concludes that "in this sense, therefore, inasmuch as we have access to neither the beautiful nor the ugly, and are incapable of judging, we are condemned to indifference." (This is all from page 18 of a book of his called *The Transparency of Evil: Essays on Extreme Phenomena*—remind me to bring you a copy next time we meet.)

Now, next time you're at a film festival, look around and have a laugh for me when you see the jurors trying to evaluate one film against another, and remember the wise Parisian's chuckle: "inasmuch as we have access to neither the beautiful nor the ugly, and are incapable of judging." But far more importantly, remember that this colorless "humanism" pasted thickly on Iranian cinema is the nervous sign of an amoral global economy—the open market of selling everything for the right price. Never fall into that trap. It looks very attractive, but it is deadly. Avoid *aesthetic humanism* as if it were a plague—and beware that your parents' generation is entirely oblivious to it. Iranian aesthetics are entirely purposeful and have emerged from the pain of the suffering we have as a people endured. Do not let a saccharine and generic "humanism" assimilate the specificity of your cinema—the blood and bone of its reality—and send it backward to the transaesthetics of indifference and, by assuming it has known you, nullify you! Know your particularity—save and savor it—and may you always be misunderstood!

The other things about Iranian cinema you ought to pay equally close attention to are its sustained longevity, the traditions that it has generated, the camaraderie and rivalry it has prolonged, and the master-disciple relationships it has cultivated. And take note, when a disciple turns against a master and kills him (metaphorically speaking, of course, except for that poor Afghan guy whose producer literally cut him into pieces recently in New York!), in effect it ups the ante of the creative potential of this art.

Let's look at this proposition for a while. There is a long tradition of the master-disciple relationship in Iranian cinema. The most recent example is Jafar Panahi and Abbas Kiarostami. Kiarostami wrote the script of *The White Balloon* for Panahi when Panahi was assisting him during the shooting of *Through the Olive Trees*. A similar relationship obviously exists between Mohsen and Samira Makhmalbaf, as later became the case between Kiarostami and Bahman Qobadi. What we are witnessing, whether in the autodidactic example of Mohsen Makhmalbaf, or in the master-disciple relationship between Kiarostami and Panahi, is a perfectly self-conscious community of filmmakers that with camaraderie or rivalry, cooperation or hostility, is, in effect, institutionalizing itself on a major artistic scale. With all the political ups and downs of modern Iranian history, that institutional basis of Iranian cinema has remained constant.

Now consider this: Amir Naderi has been away from Iran and living in New York for close to three decades. The first thing every single Iranian filmmaker who comes to New York wants to do is go and "pay their respects" to him—just like in *The Godfather*. This last May, Manizheh Hekmat was here in New York for the Tribeca Film Festival, and one of the most moving scenes ever was to see her admiration for and humility in the presence of Naderi; she dedicated the first screening of her first feature, *Women's Prison* (2002)—an astonishing debut—to him. The same is true with Makhmalbaf, Kiarostami, Beizai, Mehrjui, Panahi—whoever comes to New York. Naderi is like a living monument. Next time you are in New York, I have to ask him to tell you the story of his first visit to Golestan Film Studio, where he met Forugh Farrokhzad while she was editing *The House Is Black*, and how she asked Amir, a young provincial lad—he was only fifteen years old at the time—waiting to see the great Golestan, to help her move a desk from one spot to another; or the story of his hilarious bus trip from Tehran to London to see Stanley Kubrick and the premiere of *2001: A Space Odyssey* in 1968, and how he ended up with Kubrick in a theater in Leicester Square, helping the legendary filmmaker, with not a word of English on his tongue, adjust the projection lenses properly! The point being that this persistent sense of community—the Germans call it *Gemeinschaft*, which has a stronger theoretical inflection about it—is integral to the lasting legacy that gives an artistic event its character and culture. It is within that character and in the defining moment of that culture that Iranian cinema has a global presence—and a self-awareness of that presence—beyond the mere constellation of its masters and masterpieces.

Now, suppose that in Iranian cinema we are looking at the active formation of an aesthetics that makes a political difference, that it is an artistic movement that merits a theoretical reflection of its own without being categorized as yet another national cinema or a globalized humanism, that it has emerged in the context of Iran's colonial encounter with European modernity, that as a result there is a strong sense of purpose and community in it, and that it is fundamental to the creation of our normative subjectivity and historical agency. Then what?

I remember once on that beautiful late afternoon in May 1998, when we had just reached the end of the row of restaurants, on that flat spot where there is a shop that sells colorful tablecloths in Cannes (I loved their multicolored designs), you asked me how and why I had become interested in Iranian cinema. My answer was that after years of indifference my interest in Iranian cinema was rekindled in 1994 when I saw Kiarostami's *Through the Olive Trees* and Ebrahim Mokhtari's *Zinat* in New York, both of which in fact had premiered at Cannes that year. What I did not get a chance to tell you then is that I had for a few years before that initiated a cross-cultural course in world cinema at Columbia University in which I showed primarily Asian and African films in the context of their conversations with such master filmmakers as the pioneers of Russian formalism or Italian Neorealism. In this course I was increasingly drawn toward the intersection of semiotics and sociology, the interface between the *signum* and the *socius*, as I called them. I was engaged in, among other things, a conversation with a fundamental proclivity for signs and signifiers to collapse into each other in the rest of the European preoccupation with semiotic signification. I had my students look at films by master filmmakers as specific cases of such critical reimagining of the socius via a creative unleashing of the signum.

We never had a chance to talk in any detail about this particular subject I was teaching then, but *signs*, I kept suggesting and arguing in this course, had never promised to be law-abiding *signifiers*. They are, I proposed to my students, invariably incarcerated in a legislated semantics and forced to mean one thing or another, ipso facto fabricating and authenticating the socius they thus represented as metaphysically eternal and epistemically immutable. In other words, there is always a politics to the metaphysical semantics behind a system of signs, which I wished my students to note and take to task.

The current movement in Iranian cinema, I think, is the occasion of a critical encounter between the socius and the signum, between the loosened boundaries of the social fabric and the suggestive explosion of signs defying the implications a repressive semantics has legislated for them. The only way that the Islamic revolution was in any significant degree related to the rise of Iranian cinema as a movement is precisely in instigating this conversation between the broken, or at least loosened, seams of the society at large and the explosion of signs beyond their cultural modulation into a metaphysical order of juridical propriety. In other words, politically forcing the rambunctious signs to behave, because they usually do not. Yes, there is a link between Naderi's *Harmonica* (1974) and the Iranian revolution—but the link is articulated not in the prose of our history, but in the poetics of disclosure that films such as *Harmonica* visually recite and perform.

What I now needed to work out in my mind was the logical and rhetorical links between what had happened in Iranian cinema before and after the revolution—looking for both continuity and change in its creative and critical disposition. You may remember when we arrived at the top of that winding road in Cannes, where the street plateaus. We went a bit further and found ourselves in the middle of what looked like a churchyard with a stony parapet at its edge. We sat on that parapet with our legs dangling in the air over a low parterre, looking over Cannes, which was now at a pleasant distance, its lights shimmering right at the shore of the Mediterranean. We could see the Salle Lumière. In my mind at that very moment I was tracing back the years when Cannes had begun to pay close attention to Iranian cinema.

Suddenly, in 1992, three Iranian filmmakers found their way to Cannes—Kiarostami with *And Life Goes On*, Said Mojaveri with *Heart*, and Majid Majidi with *Baduk*. Of these three, Kiarostami's astonishing homage to the soul of a people devastated by an earthquake announced the range and depth of the cinematic vision that the world was about to behold. Although the renewed attention of Cannes to Iranian cinema had in fact started a year earlier in 1991 with the screening of Khosrow Sinai's *In the Valleys of Love*, it was in 1992, with *And Life Goes On*, that the world took notice of a whole new wave of visionary filmmaking.

Kiarostami happened at a peculiar moment in Iranian cultural history. Although he had been making one brilliant film after another since 1970, no one had taken much note of him outside Iran. And for about a decade after the Islamic revolution in 1979, Cannes paid scarce attention to Iran. Between Rafigh Pooya's *In Defense of People* in 1981 and Khosrow Sinai's *In the Valleys of Love* in 1991, exactly a decade, Cannes showed not a single Iranian film. Around the beginning of the revolution, two masters of Iranian cinema were represented at Cannes—Bahram Beizai with his *Ballad of Tara* in 1980 and Bahman Farmanara with his *Tall Shadows of the Wind* in 1979. But in the long decade after that, the Islamic revolution cast its own long, dark shadows over Iranian cinema. It is not that nothing happened in the 1980s. Quite to the contrary: Some of the absolute masterpieces of our cinema were created in this decade. Beizai made his best film ever, *Bashu, the Little Stranger*, in 1986; Kiarostami the first of his Koker Trilogy, *Where Is the Friend's House*, in 1987; Makhmalbaf's *The Cyclist*, in 1987; Amir Naderi's *Water, Wind, Dust* in 1988; and Dariush Mehrjui's *Tenants*, in 1986. But who would go to an Islamic Republic to look for films? Severely censored and brutally repressed, Iranian filmmakers, even those with revolutionary credentials like Makhmalbaf, would not dare or care to imagine themselves outside their homeland. The Islamic revolution had categorically isolated Iran as a rogue state and a cultural pariah. The official cinematic organ of the Islamic Republic, the Farabi Foundation to be exact, acted like a buffer zone between Iranian filmmakers and the world outside. It was in fact Makhmalbaf who, to transcend this system, started something he still refers to as "the fax revolution." He bought a fax machine, recommended to all his filmmaker friends to buy fax machines as well, and gave their numbers to all the festival directors around the world, bypassing Farabi and making a direct connection to the world at large. The Islamic Republic and its censorial apparatus were thus simply outmaneuvered.

Before Iranian filmmakers made their presence known, the whole world, not just Cannes, was oblivious to the Iranian cinema of the post-revolutionary period. The whole world, that is, except for a tiny little theater called Quartier Latin, smack in the middle of the Paris neighborhood of that name, which was managed and operated by a certain Iranian expatriate named Mamad Haghighat, who, at the very moment that I was dangling my feet off the parapet, looking down at the Croisette from a distance and thinking about these things, was deep in conversation with a filmmaker, arranging the global distribution of his newest film.

I met Haghighat for the first time in Locarno, in August 1996. Born and raised in Isfahan, he is a gentle, efficient, and extremely intelligent man who after more than a quarter of a century living in Paris speaks fluent French with a sweet Isfahani accent. Haghighat was a film buff of the first order in his youth. He soon realized, as he once told me over a bunch of grapes we had just purchased from a farmer's market in Locarno and washed under a public faucet in Piazza Grande, that if Cannes is the mecca of cinema, then Paris is the Medina. He got himself on a bus and traveled all the way from Isfahan first to Tehran and then to Paris. He gradually ended up working in a tiny theater on rue Pompolion, at the intersection of boulevard St-Germain and boulevard St-Michel, between the Latin Quarter and the Sorbonne.

From Paris and the little cubical of the movie theater in which he worked, Haghighat followed the course of Iranian cinema very closely, and finally late in the 1980s he thought of sharing his enthusiasm with some friends of his he knew were closely connected with Gilles Jacob, the patriarch of the Cannes Film Festival. Haghighat began showing Iranian films to this close circle of French friends, and was subsequently instrumental in going to Tehran and facilitating the submission of Kiarostami's *And Life Goes On* to Cannes. The rest, as my old teacher Professor Rieff used to say, couldn't wait for history. To this day Haghighat still regularly travels to Tehran on behalf of the Cannes Film Festival, screens new films, and makes his recommendations to French officials, while helping Iranian filmmakers with editing their films, cutting their lengthy sequences short, and, once successfully premiered at Cannes, finding a French distributor that will release them globally. He is equally instrumental in finding producers for new projects and joint productions. It would be dubious, of course, to credit one person with a whole cinematic movement—and like all other people involved with Iranian cinema he has had his share of controversies—but had it not been for Haghighat and his little theater on the rue Pompolion (one of whose halls is now called Salle Kiarostami) the history of Iranian cinema would probably have been much different.

Once the dark veil of Khomeini's charismatic terror was lifted from the face of our homeland and Cannes began to take notice of Iranian cinema, and by the time *Cahiers du Cinema* in August 1996 devoted its cover page to Kiarostami, with a beautiful long shot from *Through the Olive Trees* and a caption that read, "*Kiarostami: le Magnifique,*" the French cinéastes felt as if they owed Iranian cinema an apology. Kiarostami's cinema, richly deserving, was the beneficiary of that sudden sense of guilt.

I would now like to draw your attention to two critical consequences of the sudden and overwhelming attention that the film world began to pay Iranian cinema in the early 1990s, after a decade of negligence—and please do pay attention very carefully to what I have to say because it is fundamental to the critical character and the creative significance of Iranian cinema at its best.

First, the significance of the attention that Cannes pays to any cinema is the significance of an *audience* for any work of *art*. If Cannes is not watching, the world is not watching—for the simple reason that the world comes to Cannes to watch films and then carries them back to the world—and if the world is not watching then *there is no art*. You see what I mean? If you are the greatest pianist alive, the most gifted painter who ever was, the most visionary poet the world has ever read, if you are performing in an empty hall, painting in the solitude of your room, reciting your poems in your own head, no art has taken place. The same is ten times more true about cinema. Take its audience away and there is no cinema—it's just a wasted play of light and darkness running across the screen. Put an audience in a theater, turn off the lights, and even a white screen without a single frame of film projected on it assumes some bizarre artistic significance—for the audience becomes the spectacle, very much the same way that on every New Year's Eve here in New York the audience in Time Square becomes the spectacle. They are apparently watching a ball come down to mark the beginning of the new year. But have that ball come down on an empty square and it would be the silliest thing that ever happened; whereas even without that ball, the audience at Time Square will *will* that ball to appear and fall.

Now add to this strange phenomenon the increasingly globalized world, where we are more in our neighbor's courtyard than in our own kitchen, just like when I was a kid and spent much more time at Aunt Batul's and Uncle Vali's house than in our own because I had a dozen cousins there waiting for us to play together. We were almost a soccer team! It was far more exciting there than in our own boring home, with only my kid brother and I anxiously waiting to sneak out and play with our cousins. The same is true with Iranian filmmakers who can't wait to get out to Cannes and play with their colorful cousins, gathered from around the world!

The reason that there is no art if there is no audience is that art becomes art when the poetic act essential to a work of art is *performed*. Without performance the poetic act of art is only potential and never actual. In fact, in the moment of its creation, a work of art is conceived as if it were being publicly performed. There is an imaginary viewer looking over the shoulder of a painter, an imaginary reader reading over the shoulder of a poet, an imaginary listener listening to a composer at work—and of course an imaginary audience inside a theater watching the film you are shooting. That imaginary audience becomes real when the *poetic act* intrinsic to the work of art conceived in the presence of a potential audience is actually performed.

It is in the *global* performance of our art that we as Iranians can begin *to see* ourselves—and as a result I consider this awkward *resentment* that some of our compatriots have developed for the success of Iranian cinema abroad—they consider these films domestically irrelevant— entirely misplaced. Of course a Kiarostami or Panahi film cannot attract half as many people as a melodrama with perhaps a little bit of localized feminism thrown in for good measure. But the success of Kiarostami or Makhmalbaf abroad does not mean they are domestically superfluous. Those who accuse them of irrelevance need to consider the following: Those who object to the global success of Iranian films and point to their domestic irrelevance have a rather limited conception of what they call "the West." To me their impression of this West is one entirely devoid of a sensitivity to its class divisions, power relations, demographic changes, and, above all, the history, sociology, and geography of a global geopolitics that has been camouflaged under that distorted generality.

Second, they are astonishingly unaware of the colorful composition of the outside world. Predicated on their monolithic conception of the West, they remain entirely oblivious to the massive migration patterns over the last half a century that have completely changed the human composition of the West, and that Paris, London, New York, and the other major cultural capitals of the Western world are no longer the blue-eyed, blond-haired places of their forlorn imagination. Third, they have no conception of the *performative* component of any artistic act, the necessity of its global reception. It's like an athletic team that only practices and never plays a game against another team, let alone competes for the world championship. The same is true with the planet these days. *Donya Khaneh-ye man ast,* "The world is my home"—do you remember that beautiful line from a letter of our great poet Nima Yushij, or in his poem where he says

> *Khaneh-am abri ast*
> *Yeksareh ruy-e zamin abri ast ba an…*

> My house is cloudy
> Cloudy with it is the world…

And do you remember Sohrab Sepehri's verse:

> *Man beh mehmani-e donya raftam*

> I went to the festive gathering of the world.

Now, don't let me forget—I said there are two points I wanted you to pay attention to carefully. The nativist resentment against the success of Iranian cinema is just one of them. The other is how it is received and perceived in the world at large. Just because global success is resented inside it does not mean that Iranian cinema is very well understood outside. That understanding in and of itself is a different predicament altogether.

Does the army of film critics that gathers at Cannes every year, and then from there everywhere, have an inkling of how Iran's artists have turned their political sufferings and ideological failures into an aesthetic triumph in their art? Well, not exactly, but some do. I just remembered something beautiful by Søren Kierkegaard; he was *the* Dane long before Lars von Trier was even a glittering in his grandfather's eyes.

> What is a poet? A poet is an unhappy being whose
> heart is torn by secret sufferings, but whose lips are
> so strangely formed that when the sighs and the cries

escape them, they sound like beautiful music…and
men crowd about the poet and say to him: "Sing for
us soon again"; that is as much as to say: "May new
sufferings torment your soul, but may your lips be
formed as before; for the cries would only frighten us,
but the music is delicious." And the critics come, too,
and say: "Quite correct, and so it ought to be according
to the rules of aesthetics." Now it is understood that
a critic resembles a poet to a hair; he only lacks the
suffering in his heart made the music upon his lips.

Be that as it may, once in place in front of a world audience, Kiarostami's camera—as the locomotive that was now carrying the rest of Iranian cinema with it to a global focus (a Frenchman once used that metaphor and it's a good one)—began to reveal and unpack layers of what now in France (and in Europe in general) leading public intellectuals like Julia Kristeva were addressing as a "crisis of subjectivity"—except as always they had only Europe in mind when they thought they were speaking for the whole world. While Kiarostami, and along with him the rest of Iranian cinema, did effectively constitute a moral subjectivity and a historical agency beyond the predicament of coloniality, these European intellectuals could not see beyond their encampment in Europe.

What has always fascinated me is how, except for the cinéastes affiliated principally with *Cahiers du cinéma* and a number of other film critics with *Le Monde* or *Liberation*, the French intellectuals have by and large remained aloof from the events at Cannes. Public intellectuals such as Kristeva, who herself has an Eastern European background, reflect on what they call "the crisis of subjectivity"—with an eye to recent African and Asian immigrants—as primarily a European phenomenon. What Kiarostami's cinema—and with it the whole cinematic movement that he now represents—means for the character and culture of those who were meant to be his immediate and now distant audience has never been of concern to these people. The whole European (not just French), and by extension American, reflections on Kiarostami's cinema has assumed this surreal aura of writing about a rootless art, as if Kiarostami had fallen like a strange seed from the sky and grew like a mushroom on the surface of Cannes—with no roots in the soil and suffering of his own people. In his Iran, as you know, Kiarostami has faced mind-numbing hostility and jealousy, scarcely allowing for a critical reading of his cinema without a dose of rancor and resentment. What has remained mute, and is now almost moot, is the aesthetic and political impulses and implications of the succession of masterpieces that Kiarostami continues to make. What brought them about? What did they mean? What were their immediate and distant moral causes and social consequences?

The point is that the Iranian cinema you now witness is in dire need of a reading beyond its immediate success and distant memory. Beyond its domestic troubles, above its global tribulations, and central to Iranian cinema is its creative constitution of a subject with an active historical agency, in defiance of its moral and normative colonization at the hands of European modernity. The historical and inevitable failure of a head-on ideological collision with colonial modernity could not but have strengthened and ossified the de-subjected colonial. The creative constitution of the postcolonial subject (this is my principal concern in all I have to say) that constructs its aesthetics from the political launching pad of the colonial corner of modernity is neither in awe of the European Enlightenment nor indeed does it corroborate it by opposing it politically.

Now the question is in what particular terms Iranian cinema achieves this creative re-subjection of the de-subjected colonial? Or, more precisely, what is it about its *realism*, which is neither reducible to its European counterparts nor limited to its colonial origins?

About midnight that beautiful May evening in Cannes, you may remember, we all felt hungry again. On our way up the winding street, we had noted a nice-looking pizzeria right at the corner where the Croisette turns left toward the harbor. We began walking down toward that pizzeria, bypassing all the little restaurants on the left and right of the winding street. The French neglect of Iranian cinema in the 1980s, I was thinking to myself then, was predated by a more attentive record in the 1970s. Bahman Farmanara's *Prince Ehtejab* (1975) was the spectacular achievement of Iranian cinema in the mid-1970s. Like *Prince Ehtejab*, Nooraddin Zarrinkelk's *Tadii* (1975) made it to Cannes in the same year, and two years earlier Farshid Mesqali's *The Grey City* (1973) also premiered in Cannes. Zarrinkelk's and Mesqali's cinematic careers did not last for long, but they sustained a record of critical awareness of Iranian cinema in the 1970s.

All of these scattered instances pale in comparison with Dariush Mehrjui's stunning debut at Cannes with *Cow* in 1971, and then with his *Postman* in 1972. The successes of Mehrjui in 1971 and 1972 and Farmanara in 1975 as the crowning achievements of Iranian cinema in the 1970s point to a crucial element in the artistic texture of Iranian cinema, namely its immediate roots in the rich soil of its literary and poetic origins. Mehrjui's first film, *Diamond 33* (1967), an entirely inconsequential James Bond spoof, is a clear indication of the direction that his cinema could have taken had he not connected with the most distinguished Iranian dramatist of his time, Gholamhossein Saedi (d. 1986). Mehrjui quickly cultivated an enduring friendship with Saedi that resulted in a number of collaborative projects, the first of which, *Cow*, catapulted Mehrjui to the center of the emerging Iranian cinema. Saedi died in Paris soon after the Islamic revolution; he had become utterly disappointed, and his name probably does not mean much to your generation. But you must at some point read him very closely. He was a psychiatrist by training and one of the finest literary figures of the twentieth century, a magical realist before the term was even coined, let alone made into a global fad by Gabriel García Márquez. Mehrjui's early cinematic brilliance would have been unimaginable without Saedi.

This link between Iranian cinema and modern Persian poetry and fiction is critical. Forugh Farrokhzad and Ebrahim Golestan, two pioneering figures in Iranian cinema, were themselves prominent members in the pantheon of modern poetry and fiction. Though Mehrjui was the first major filmmaker who was not a member of the literati, he developed a close and symbiotic relationship with one of their leading voices, namely Saedi. The same complementary relationship soon developed between Bahman Farmanara, who, like Mehrjui, was also educated mostly in Europe and the United States, and Houshang Golshiri, another defining voice of modern Persian fiction. Arby Ovanessian worked closely with Ali Mohammad Afghani to turn his groundbreaking novel *Ahu Khanom's Husband* (1961) into a film. (The project did not go through and Davoud Molapoor finished it in 1968.) One of Masud Kimiyai's most successful films was an adaptation of Sadeq Hedayat's story "Dash Akol" (1930). Amir Naderi's *Tangsir* (1974) popularized Sadeq Chubak's novel of that name, published in 1963. Both Bahram Beizai and Mohsen Makhmalbaf are major literary forces independent of their cinematic achievements. And the films of both Sohrab Shahid Sales and Abbas Kiarostami are deeply indebted to the poetry of Sohrab Sepehri (d. 1980).

Mamad Haghighat was bringing out our pizzas as I was thinking that the connection between Persian fiction and poetry was entirely absent in the 1960s. Notice that only three Iranian films made it to Cannes during that decade—Feri Farzaneh's *Cyrus the Great* (1961), Ahmad Faroughy-Kadjar's *Dawn of the Capricorn* (1964), and Farrokh Ghaffari's *Night of the Hunchback* (1964)—of which only Ghaffari's pioneering film had an enduring effect on the rest of Iranian cinema.

Ghaffari's two previous films, *South of the City* (1958) and *Which One Is the Bride* (1963), were commercial flops and critical anomalies—they made it neither at the box office nor to Cannes. Ghaffari was exposed to *The Arabian Nights* in Paris and thought its Oriental disposition would make for a good film both at home and abroad. He had Jalal Moqaddam, a seminal figure in Iranian cinema, prepare a script on the basis of the story. Ghaffari initially wanted to do a period piece but gradually changed his plans and contemporized the story of the hunchback, setting it in his contemporary Tehran. Probably with an eye toward Alfred Hitchcock's *The Trouble with Harry* (1955), *The Night of the Hunchback* is narrated around the dead body of a hunchback who is accidentally killed while performing musical entertainment at a party. Moqaddam's script, at the center of which is a dead body everyone thinks is alive, was not particularly acceptable to the post-1953-coup atmosphere of the newly installed Mohammad Reza Shah Pahlavi regime. But apparently Ghaffari's influential family background and his connections to the Pahlavi court facilitated the making of the film.

You can learn quite a lot about the class politics of Iranian cinema from the case of Farrokh Ghaffari. Ghaffari was an exceptionally talented filmmaker who was way ahead of his time and yet failed to make a dent in the cinematic culture of his period. His films remained aloof from much that was happening around him and today they have only an archival significance. A number of factors prevented Ghaffari from advancing Iranian cinema in the late 1950s and the early 1960s. First and foremost, Ghaffari was born to an affluent upper-middle-class family and had no immediate experience with the reality of most Iranians. He had spent the formative years of his life in France, and his European education was at once the source of his cinematic brilliance and the cause of his distance from the subject of his cinema, a paradox that ultimately crippled the politics of his cinema. His connections to the Pahlavi court, again, simultaneously enabled him to make films otherwise impossible to make and yet discredited him as an autonomous and critical intellect. As an artist, he was an outsider through and through, with no credentials to recommend him to the Iranian literati. Add to that the crippling jealousy of those Iranians who were resentful of his background and who harbored a deep resentment for his knowledge and skill, and what you have is the picture of a lonely artist: at home neither in his homeland nor abroad, an Oriental in Paris, a European in Iran.

What we learn from our record in the 1960s is that no serious commencement of Iranian cinema could have been witnessed in Iran except as initiated by two established literary figures like Forugh Farrokhzad, a poet, and Ebrahim Golestan, a novelist. These two, Farrokhzad in particular, had a lasting influence on the rest of Iranian cinema. That suddenly in the 1970s there was an upsurge of major filmmakers is a clear indication that they were all deeply rooted in the best and most enduring that the culmination of our poetry and fiction had achieved by the late 1960s. This continuity between film and fiction, syncopated by poetry, is definitive to the nature and disposition of the Iranian cinematic cosmovision.

Farrokhzad and Golestan have had a watershed significance in the art and craft that you now practice. I will tell you more about them later, but for now suffice it to say that Farrokhzad and Golestan are the missing links that connect the ascent of modern Persian poetry and fiction in the 1960s to the final rise of Iranian cinema in earnest in the 1970s. They represent the best that the Persian literary and poetic imagination had to offer, and as fate would have it they also were critically important in the rise of Iranian cinema. For this reason they will have to be closely examined to see in what particular terms the creative constitution of the subject against the backdrop of Iran's encounter with colonial modernity marked Iranian cinema with a very specific mode of realism, which cannot be justifiably termed "neorealism." There is something very specific about Iranian cinematic realism that is not reducible to Italian or any other neorealism. I hope to have a chance to describe to you in some detail how somewhere among Farrokhzad's *poetic* realism, Golestan's *affective* realism, Mehrjui's *psychedelic* realism, Farmanara's *narrative* realism, and Shahid Sales' *transparent* realism, Iranian cinema found its visual vocabulary.

By May 1998, the year that Samira Makhamlbaf's film *Apple* premiered in Cannes, Iranian cinema was squarely established as one of the preeminent sources of world cinema. Since then, Cannes has continued to pay close attention to Iranian cinema and corroborated in broader details the presence of something global in its texture and disposition. The year after Samira's debut at Cannes, Mohsen Makhalbaf was invited to Cannes to premiere his short film *The Door*, along with those of Naser Taqvai and Abolfazl Jalili, a trilogy that was screened as *Tales from Kish*. This trilogy was supposed to have been part of a septet commissioned by authorities in charge of the small island of Kish in the Persian Gulf, a free-trade zone for which many Iranian filmmakers had high hopes as a space away from the severe censorial control of the capital. They failed.

You remember that the septet did not materialize the way it was originally conceived, and the removal of Bahram Beizai's short film from the series, which was included in the quartet submitted to Gilles Jacob, the Cannes patriarch, resulted in a major controversy in the summer of 1999, right in the middle of that huge student uprising in Tehran, which in turn discredited some of the most respected public intellectuals around and prevented them from having a say in their national destiny. What a disgraceful mess that incident was—leading Iranian filmmakers publicly denouncing each other and falsely accusing each other of nonexistent misdemeanors! The presidential election in the summer of 1997, which brought Mohammad Khatami to office, had commenced an unprecedented move for democracy in Iran. The summer of 1999 witnessed some of the most heroic scenes in this fateful struggle. From the young generation leading that student uprising, one young filmmaker, Mohammad Shirvani, managed to screen his short film *Circle* in Cannes during that year. I find it quite symbolic that while major figures in Iranian cinema were busy publicly accusing each other of one pettiness or another, a young filmmaker of your generation managed to keep a historical record of what is best in all of us.

By the turn of the millennium, Cannes again paid homage to the courage and imagination of your generation of filmmakers by premiering three feature films representing a broad spectrum of Iranian society. Samira Makhmalbaf returned that year triumphantly with her second feature, *Blackboard*, which won the Special Jury Award. Hassan Yekta-panah's *Jomeh* and Bahman Qobadi's *A Time for Drunken Horses* joined in winning the coveted Camera d'Or. I did not go to Cannes that year, but I went to Paris and spent a couple weeks watching films at Mamad Haghighat's theater. How proud all of you had made all of us that year by that spectacular achievement! Samira had turned our attention to the predicament of the Kurds, Yektapanah to that of the Afghans, while Qobadi was the first Iranian Kurd to give voice and vision to his homeland on a global scale.

Scarcely would a year be more auspicious for Iranian cinema than 2000—but still more was yet to come. Year after year, there seemed to emerge a healthy dose of intergenerational competition among Iranian filmmakers. The year after the astonishing success of three young filmmakers, the two arch rivals of Iranian cinema returned to Cannes, Abbas Kiarostami with his *A, B, C Africa*, and Mohsen Makhmalbaf with the prescient blockbuster *Kandahar*. Still, the year after that, Cannes brought yet another three feature films from Iran: Kiarostami's *Ten*, Dariush Mehrjui's *Bemani*, and Bahman Qobadi's second feature film, *Songs of My Homeland*. There seemed to be no end to these triumphs. The year after that, in May 2003, Samira Makhmalbaf was there with her third feature film, *At Five in the Afternoon*, Jafar Panahi with *Crimson Gold*, Parviz Shahbazi with *Deep Breath*, and the young Afghan filmmaker Siddiq Barmak, whom Mohsen Makhmalbaf had adopted as his protégé, with his wonderful debut, *Osama*—and to top it all Mamad Haghighat made his first feature film, *Two Angels*, and brought it to Cannes too!

In 2004 Kiarostami traveled to Cannes with two more films, *Five* and *10 on Ten*, and then in 2005 served as president of the jury for the Camera d'Or. Now Samira Makhmalbaf, Parviz Shahbazi, Mohammad Shirvani, Panahi, Bahman Qobadi, and scores of yet more names are waiting to come to Cannes and from there to rest of the world. None of this generation is half as *literate* as their parental generation—and yet all of them are twice as *visionary*. Now, that's a quite mouthful to say and not to explain, but I hope that in due course I may do justice to that claim as I tell you quite a number of stories I have always promised to tell you.

I hold the budding shoots of wheat
To my breast
And I breastfeed them.
—Forugh Farrokhzad

Forugh Farrokhzad
The House Is Black

SHAHLA LAHIJI WAS HERE IN NEW YORK FOR A FEW DAYS. She had come from Tehran to visit her children in California and I asked her to come to New York to talk about a volume we are planning to publish on the status of the women's-rights movement in Iran and to organize a simultaneous conference on the subject.

When Shahla Lahiji was here I was telling her about this book I am supposed to write on Iranian cinema—and then one thing led to another and I began to tell her about Forugh Farrokhzad's *The House Is Black*. I don't think I have ever had a chance to tell you this, but I have a very vivid memory of the summer of 1958 when I was seven years old and a sudden fire broke out in an oilfield near my hometown. I remember the sky over Ahvaz was dark red at night, the way years later in Philadelphia I saw it become pinkish red just before it was about to snow. No sign of snow in Ahvaz, the provincial capital of oil-soaked Khuzestan in the south. Summers were long and torturously hot, winters soaking wet with rain and blessedly short. Fall and spring, if only my nasty allergies would let me breathe, were quite pleasant. During the summer of 1958, as usual, we were sleeping on the roof of our small house, as most people do in my hometown at night during the hot season. The night sky during that summer was lit with a strange orange, gushed from the north, and made our nights bright and burning. The story in and about Ahvaz was that an oilfield had caught fire and no one could stop the inferno. To fight the beast they had to call in a firefighter from Texas. It was years later that I learned he was none other than the legendary Paul "Red" Adair, who died recently, at the age of eighty-nine. Red Adair later gained global fame when he fought another fire, in 1962, at a gas field in the Sahara, known as the "Devil's Cigarette Lighter." Andrew V. McLaglen later made a film about him, *Hellfighters* (1968), starring John Wayne in the lead role.

Little did I know during those illuminated nights of my childhood in Ahvaz that the history of Iranian cinema was also in the making. As I would learn years later, Ebrahim Golestan and his brother Shahrokh were making a documentary about that very fire, and that Forugh Farrokhzad would also make her cinematic debut by masterfully editing that film. Directed by Ebrahim Golestan, shot by his brother Shahrokh, and edited by Farrokhzad, *A Fire* (1958) became a legend, a touchstone of Iranian cinema. It became the first Iranian film ever to win international recognition, winning the Bronze Medal at the Venice Film Festival in 1961. I recently learned that a new DVD of this film has been released in Paris. I have to ask Mamad Haghighat to send me a copy.

Ahvaz was not an unfamiliar place to Forugh Farrokhzad. She had moved there in 1951, the year of my birth, as a newlywed, sixteen-year-old bride, with her much older husband Parviz Shapour, whom she had just married in Tehran against her parents' wishes. Born in 1935 to a father who was a career officer in Reza Shah's army and a mother who followed the example of her husband's military discipline in running the household, Forugh Farrokhzad grew up in the Tehran of the early Pahlavis, protected from the atrocities of her time by her precocious poetic imagination. By age eleven, in 1946, when Iran was under an Allied occupation that had pressured Reza Shah to abdicate in favor of his son Mohammad Reza Shah, Farrokhzad had already started scribbling her first poems. The stories her grandfather told her, the tight ship her mother ran, the acacia petals she loved to scrape and throw into a stream, and her nighttime whispering with her sister Pouran under the starry nights on the roof of their home all cultivated the fertile soil of her imagination—on which grew her poetic disposition, at once exquisitely simple and astonishingly solitary.

Those starry nights watched over Farrokhzad, marking her rise to becoming the greatest woman poet of her and any other generation—and she died not knowing that history would judge her that way.

Farrokhzad dropped out of high school—just like you did—in the ninth grade and opted to go to a training school where she learned how to make dresses and how to paint, a not-too-untypical move made by young girls of her generation either uninterested in or bored with the stark discipline of the Pahlavi-inspired military precision of the public-school system. The decision to drop out of high school to attend a professional school was made by girls at two diametrically opposed ends of the spectrum—those who wanted to get ready to be housewives and those who had a more impatiently creative drive than the torturous routine of public school could satisfy. In 1950, the fifteen-year-old Forugh opted to go to Kamal al-Molk Technical School to divert her attention from memorizing the pointless facts of a mind-numbing history of Persian kings, irrelevant and outdated geographical statistics, and a suffocating indoctrination with the fictive glories of the Pahlavi dynasty. A year into her studies at Kamal al-Molk, where she was particularly fond of dressmaking and painting, she fell madly in love with a distant cousin of hers, Parviz Shapour, and locked herself up in a room until she had secured her parents' consent to her marriage. By 1951, in the summer of my birth, Farrokhzad was a happily married woman on her way to Ahvaz, my hometown, where her son Kamyar was born a year later in 1952.

Shahla Lahiji was not totally convinced that if I were to write a book on the masters and masterpieces of Iranian cinema I should include Farrokhzad's *The House Is Black* (1962). She believes that Farrokhzad is first and foremost a poet, and that her twenty-two-minute documentary film was scarcely seen inside Iran, and even at that level had no enduring effect. I tried very briefly to convince her otherwise. But she had to go back to Iran, and I did not get a chance to explain in any detail, though it was enough to keep me thinking about the matter for the rest of that rainy day. I helped her put her luggage in the trunk of a cab. We said goodbye, and as her cab drove away I decided to go for a walk under the rain by the Hudson.

It appears on the surface that except for some incidental roles Farrokhzad played in making a few other films, *The House Is Black* is her only serious attempt at filmmaking and is, therefore, entirely negligible. In my judgment, however, *The House Is Black* happened at a very peculiar and poignant moment in her monumental poetic career, and that it is instrumental in understanding not only what happened later in Iranian cinema, but even more crucially in understanding Farrokhzad's creative character in general. This short documentary happened quite by serendipity, and the opportunity to make another film never presented itself. Farrokhzad was far more particular about her poetry than she was about her short brush with cinema. She rarely, if ever, made a reference to *The House Is Black*. She made the film, many ridiculed it, some praised it, and that was the end of it—she put the whole incident out of her mind. There is no reason to believe that she took the making of this film any more seriously than she did acting in her friend Pari Saberi's production of Luigi Pirandello's *Six Characters in Search of an Author*, or that her painting or travel writing were not more important to her.

What posterity has made of *The House Is Black*, however, is an entirely different matter. We now have to track *The House Is Black* very carefully in Farrokhzad's creative trajectory in general and try to figure out where and when it occurred. By and large, those who have commented on her poetry have only paid lip service to her film; and those who have paid attention to her film have made some rather generic references to her significance as a poet. But where exactly the two come together is an entirely open and inviting field. Farrokhzad's towering significance as a poet has in fact barred a serious consideration of her film, while a close and caring reading of her film, the way, for example, that a distinguished film critic from Chicago, Jonathan Rosenbaum, has done, has left her poetry almost completely out of the picture. I believe the two ought to be taken and read together—one without the other does not make much sense.

Between her marriage to Parviz Shapour in 1951 and its final collapse in 1954, Farrokhzad was deeply engaged in reading the classics of Persian poetry—and soon some of her own earliest poems began to appear in the leading literary magazines. It is also from this period that rumors, innuendos, and half-truths about Farrokhzad's presumably promiscuous sexual affairs begin to circulate in literary circles and gradually among the public at large. What all of these stories ultimately reveal is far more a pathologically myopic and sexually deprived critical imagination than anything specific about the character and content of Farrokhzad's personality and poetry. Generations of Iranian literati and non-Iranian Orientalists, during her life and after her death, have been speculating about her sexual life with not an iota of insight into the miraculous texture of her poetry. She may or may not have had some extramarital affairs while married to Shapour, and she may or may not have had any number of love affairs after her divorce. But none of these either matter or add up to reveal anything about her poetry, nor do they amount to the bona fide harlot that some of her contemporaries and subsequent commentators have made her out to be. What does matter in our reading of Farrokhzad's poetry, however, is that such rumors bothered and harassed her. This scandalous reputation and its consequences in Farrokhzad's self-perception are important.

What we do, and should, know is that her birth, childhood and adolescence between 1935 and 1951 hastily concluded with a juvenile love for her future husband, a premature marriage, and a relocation from the capital to a provincial town. Her short-lived marriage to Shapour, between 1951 and 1954, produced a son she named Kamyar (whom she soon lost to her husband after her divorce), scattered publication of her poems in literary journals, and a notoriety for her presumed promiscuous affairs. Farrokhzad's letters to her father from Ahvaz clearly indicate that soon after her marriage she regretted it—and years later she confessed that the absence of any ambition in her husband coupled with the inanities of domestic life deeply bothered her. She obviously was not cut out for a housewifely life in a provincial town—she had much bigger fish to fry. She adored her son and much of her early poetry in fact emerged from the melodic rhapsodies of lullabies. Leaving her son behind, knowing that her husband and his family would not allow her regular visitation rights, was the saddest and most heartbreaking decision of Farrokhzad's life. This active choice on her part to leave her son and follow her fate as a poet left a permanent mark on her soul, one from which she would never recover—and that scar was at the very center of her creative character.

Farrokhzad began the four years before she met Ebrahim Golestan, between 1954 and 1958, with a complete nervous breakdown that hospitalized her for a few days. But she soon recovered and proceeded to publish her first collection of poetry, *Asir* (*Captive*, 1955) as well as her second, *Divar* (*The Wall*, 1956), travel to Europe and subsequently write and publish her travel notes, and finally publish her third volume of poetry, *Osyan* (*Rebellion*, 1958). These four years are extremely important in Farrokhzad's life: She emerged from a short though catastrophic marriage, accepted her separation from her only child (though this was a constant source of her misery), published three volumes of poetry, solidly establishing herself as a major poetic voice, and traveled to Europe on a meager budget and yet managed to see the great masterpieces of art that left a permanent impression on her creative temperament. Meanwhile, her reputation as a promiscuous woman grew, as did her anger with the public innuendo and gossip that were in abundance about her.

In the nine short years she lived in love with Ebrahim Golestan (a married man), between 1958 and her early death in 1967, she again traveled to Europe, collaborated with Golestan on a number of his film projects, made her directorial debut, *The House Is Black*, published her undisputed masterpiece, *Tavallodi Digar* (*Another Birth*, 1964), and prepared her final collection of poetry, *Iman Biyavarim beh Aghaz-e Fasl-e*

Sard (*Let Us Believe in the Beginning of the Cold Season*), just before her sudden death in an automobile accident on 14 February 1967. These are the years of Farrokhzad's most mature poetry, bracketing like a bezel her cinematic masterpiece, *The House Is Black*.

Beyond these facts, only Farrokhzad's creative life—her poetry and her single film—are what ultimately matter. Farrokhzad's poetic persona was effectively born with the publication of her first collection of poetry, *Captive*, in 1955. Although years later she would dismiss all her early poetry as childish and self-indulgent—a self-negating trait she shared with many other great poets of her generation—the fact is that the appearance of *Captive* was a singular event in the history of modern Persian poetry, and Farrokhzad became a public figure who had bared her soul for the whole world and a tyrannous history to see. What matters is that a determined feminine voice—at once graceful, fragile, and relentless—was born with such confidence and alacrity that everyone had to stand still and take notice.

The Persian poetic tradition has had a long and illustrious history of women poets. But every generation has a very short memory. Parvin Etesami (1906–41) was still alive when Farrokhzad was growing up in Tehran. Shams Kasmai (d. 1961) was a contemporary of Farrokhzad. The legendary figure Tahereh Qorrat al-Ayn (1814–52) could not have altogether escaped her attention either. But none of these great figures were poetically present in the Iran of Farrokhzad's youth and education. She was the woman of her age, a creature of her immediate sensibilities, the feminine voice of millennially repressed *sensualities*—sensualities not just of a feminine nature, but of a far more universal truth, beyond the pedantic sensibilities and imaginations of her male and female contemporaries. She did not just give voice to feminine desires; she gave body and breath to the very fact and fantasy of desire itself. Farrokhzad's was a journey within, to the realm of the repressed, the forgotten, the unknown, the uncharted, the dangerous. All her navigational errors in her initial poetry were serendipitous, fortuitous, immanent.

What I did not get a chance to explain to Shahla Lahiji was the necessity of knowing what exactly *The House Is Black* is doing smack in the middle of Farrokhzad's far more substantial achievements as a poet. Subtract *The House Is Black* from her poetic oeuvre and nothing seems to be missing. But one must add *The House Is Black* to the origin of Iranian cinema for that history to be complete, and today *The House Is Black* is praised as much as it was denounced and even ridiculed when it was first made. Dwelling in the midst of that apparent paradox is the factual evidence of Farrokhzad's significance as a poet and a filmmaker. But beyond such superlatives, what exactly in her poetic universe and in her moral disposition does this short documentary, her only film, stand for?

Let me tell you all we know about *The House Is Black*. As a matter of archival evidence, we know that Farrokhzad joined Golestan Films in 1958, initially as something of a secretary, but was gradually engaged in more serious aspects of filmmaking; that in the summer of 1958, Ebrahim Golestan financed her trip, along with another colleague, Samad Pour Kamaly, to Europe to study filmmaking; that after her return she was instrumental in editing Golestan's *A Fire* (1959), changing its journalistic style to epic narrative; that she collaborated with Golestan on another film, *Water and Heat* (1959), in which she made the "Heat" part and Golestan the "Water"; that she had written a full script for a documentary on marriage ceremonies in Iran but never had a chance to make it; that the great Italian filmmaker Bernardo Bertolucci apparently made something of a short documentary on Farrokhzad; that she acted for Golestan in a short film he was shooting on the basis of a story by Sadeq Chubak called "Why Was the Sea Stormy?" but that this film was never finished; that she worked on a number of other documentary projects before, in the fall of 1962, she took her camera crew—Soleiman Minasian was the director of photography, Mahmoud Hangaval and Samad Pour Kamaly the sound engineers, and Herand Minasian and Amir Karrari helping in other matters—from Golestan Films and traveled to the Baba Daghi leper colony in Tabriz and in a matter of twelve days shot *The House Is Black*; that she was able to earn the trust of the people at the leper colony and in fact adopted a young boy as a son soon after she shot the film; that she returned to Tehran and did her own editing of the film; that it was premiered in Iran at Tehran University, Faculty of Medicine, where Farrokhzad, Golestan, and his wife, Fakhri Golestan, joined members of the royal family for the screening; that when she subsequently screened it for Iranian cinéastes it was viciously criticized and even ridiculed—including a comment to the effect that she should go and try to be a pretty woman rather than a filmmaker; that the endemic disease of Iranian culture was articulated by and manifest in another critic who openly attributed the making of *The House Is Black* to Ebrahim Golestan; but that at the 1963 International Oberhausen Short Film Festival in Germany *The House Is Black* had a much kinder reception and won its top prize.

And this is what is said about the significance of *The House Is Black*: that it earned Farrokhzad new credentials as a serious artist; that it revealed her view—that of a secular intellectual—of Iranian society at large; that it is a document of the superstitious beliefs of a society that does not know that its cure is in science and not in religion; that Farrokhzad used the leper colony as a metaphor for Iranian society and thus revealed the far more pervasive social leprosy of her time; that she turned a mere documentary that was supposed to be informative in a simple and bureaucratic way into an enduring work of art; that it raises the sign and suggestion of beauty in the middle of an unsightly reality (as such it was the first genuine step toward Iranian neorealism); that in fact it is the best example of what Jonathan Rosenbaum, the distinguished American film critic, has termed the "radical humanism" in Iranian cinema.

This is what is known, said, and suggested about *The House Is Black*. But I have an entirely different reading of it. I think I recently explained to you why I don't care much about this humanism—radical or otherwise—that is always tagged on Iranian cinema. It's a red herring—it means everything, so it means nothing. Much of the praise heaped on *The House Is Black* is really of the *taarof* variety, as we say in Persian, a kind of pleasant and polite verbosity that tries to talk around the issue at hand. People seem to *like* Farrokhzad's *The House Is Black*, or else like *her*, and then they mobilize their Sunday-best vocabulary, as it were, to express their sentiments. Taken together, certainly this praise represents the noble sentiments worthy of a poet who richly deserves them. But ultimately it is as much insightful about what *The House Is Black* does as a film as those nasty dismissals of it were when it was initially screened in Iran. The empty praise and the harsh criticism in effect cancel each other out, clear the field, and leave us to look at the film afresh.

Before anything else, I would like to suggest that *The House Is Black* is the missing link between Farrokhzad's juvenile poetry and her mature poetic form and diction. All those who have commented on the course of her poetic development have expressed astonishment at the transcontinental leap between *Rebellion* (1958) and *Another Birth* (1964). There is a qualitative difference between her first three volumes of poetry, published before 1958, and her last two, after 1964. *The House Is Black* was made in 1962. So it is quite obvious that this film has a poetic light in it, as her poems have a cinematic shadow to them. It seems she had to take a visual detour to achieve her final, definitive poetic style. All serious readers of her poetry know that there is an emotive affinity among *Captive* (1955), *The Wall* (1956), and *Rebellion* that is mountains and valleys away from *Another Birth* and *Let Us Believe in the Beginning of the Cold Season* (1967); and, lo and behold, there is nothing between the two disparate regions except *The House Is Black*. So, one must place Farrokhzad's film squarely inside her poetic territory, to see what they mean to one another.

I will now choose three (what I consider to be typical) poems from Farrokhzad's first three collections of poetry—*Captive*, *The Wall*, and *Rebellion*—as the three significant steps that she had to take before she entered the studios of Golestan Films and made *The House Is Black*. There is nothing particular about these three poems (which I translate here into English in an effort to allow you to feel their resonance in another language) for we could do the same with any of the poems from these three collections.

"*Div-e Shab*" ("The Night Goblin"), a poem composed in Ahvaz in 1954, is a perfect example of Farrokhzad's poetic and personal outlook at the time. What we see in this first, earliest instance of Farrokhzad's poetic persona is a tormented woman on the threshold of a break. The poem is in the form of a lullaby. The narrator of the poem is sitting on the floor with her baby boy—whom she calls Kami, an endearing abbreviation of Kamyar, Farrokhzad's own son—sleeping on her lap. Suddenly she has an overwhelming sense of fear of a demonic darkness that is about to come and snatch her baby away. As in many of her other poems, Farrokhzad plays on a very common folkloric theme, in this case mothers scaring their babies so they will be quiet and go to sleep. She also plays a rhapsodic variation on the lullaby—a rich and fantastic genre in Persian folkloric narratives, in which mothers in fact convey their own fears and anxieties, wishes and aspirations, in a soothing song for their babies. She takes these common themes and plays on them innocently, until we realize that something much more sinister than simple darkness is lurking behind the deceptively innocuous lullaby—at once mournful, fearful, and above all guilt-ridden:

> *Lai-lai, my little boy:*
> *Close your eyes for the night is here*
> *Close your eyes for the dark demon*
> *With blood on his hands and a smile on his face is here!*
>
> *Put your head on my tired lap and*
> *Listen to his footsteps coming!*
> *The old elm's back is broken*
> *So the demon can step on it!*
>
> *Oh, let me pull this curtain*
> *Tightly on the window—with*
> *Two hundred eyes fiery and bloody,*
> *He sneaks through the window!*
>
> *From the flames of his breathing fire*
> *The shepherd in the silent desert was burned—*
> *Oh, be quiet my dear for this drunken darkness*
> *Is listening to you behind the closed door!*

Just remember that once a naughty
Boy bothered his poor mother—and then
The dusky demon from the heart of darkness
Suddenly came and snatched the boy!

The glass is trembling in the windowpane—listen
As the demon hollers and hauls himself up—
He is screaming: "Where's that boy?"
Listen! His hands are scratching at the door!

"No! Get away! You demon you!
Get lost! I despise your face!
I will not allow you to snatch him from me
As long as I am awake by his bed!"

Suddenly the silence of the house was broken—and the dark
Demon screamed: "Enough
You wretched woman! I am not
Afraid of you! You are the color of sin, so full of sins you are!

I am a demon but you are more of a demon than me
A mother with sullied skirt—
Oh, take his head off your lap!
Look where the pure boy rests his head!"

His voice is dying and yet my heart
Is ablaze with the fire of pain—I cry
Out: "Kami, my dear Kami!
Take your head off my lap, my darling!"

A year after the publication of *Captive* in 1955, Farrokhzad published her second collection of poetry, *The Wall*. *The Wall* is a collection of twenty-five poems, continuing with similar motifs as the forty-four poems of *Captive*. "The World of Shadows" is a perfect representative of Farrokhzad's development. The frightful darkness witnessed in the first volume here has assumed a shadowy reality *sui generis*, autonomous in its power and meaning, and primary in its relation to reality. The narrator in this case is witness to the shadows running ahead of two persons walking over a wet path at midnight. She then begins to contemplate the nature of these two shadows:

On the wet path at midnight
Our shadows seem to escape us—away
From us and onto the slippery road,
In the ominous mist of a moonlight that slips away cold
And heavy—they come
Together gently upon the branches of the vine.

On the wet path at midnight—
In the aromatic silence of dust—
Impatiently our shadows
Embrace each other
At times—our shadows:
Just like two flowers drunk
From the dew-wine of last night.

As if in their bitter escape
From us joyously
They whisper
Songs we never sing—
Songs we bury with anger
In the silence of our chests.

But distant from our shadows,
Ignorant of their love story—their
Separations and unities—our
Tired bodies in their solidities give
Form to life.

On the wet path at midnight,
How often have I asked
Myself: "Does life ever find form
Inside our shadows?
Are we not the shadows of our own shadows?"

Farrokhzad published her third collection of poetry, *Rebellion*, with seventeen poems. In this volume, the same tropes of darkness, shadow, and dusk persist. The poem that she dedicates to her son, Kamyar, called "A Poem for You!" picks up precisely where she left off with her lullaby. But it is more a confessional poem, a call for forgiveness, a midway report to her past, in fearful anticipation of her future:

I write this poem for you
In a thirsty summer sunset

Toward the middle of this road that began
Inauspiciously in the old grave of this endless sorrow.

This is my last lullaby
By your cradle—so
That the violent cry of this scream
May echo in the heavens of your youth.

Let my bewildered shadow be
Far from your shadow and distant—let us
Come back together on a day
When no one but God is between us.

I have leaned on a dark door
My aching forehead pushing
Against this open door with hope
My thin cold fingers.

Cauterized with shame I
Was laughing at futile innuendoes convinced
That I would be the cry of my own existence but
Alas I was but a woman!

When your innocent eyes slide
Upon this confused book with no beginning,
You will see hidden in the heart
Of every song the rooted rebellion of all ages.

Here all stars are dark here
All angles are weeping here
All blossoms of tuberose are more
Worthless than bushes of desert thorn.

Here upon every path is
Sitting the demon of deceit, shame,
Duplicity, and upon the dark sky even
I see no light from the wakeful bright morning.

Let my eyes fill up again
With the dewdrops—I will
Depart from me to drop
The veil from the pure face of all the infallible Marys!

I have sailed away from the shore
Of having a good name and in my chest
Shines the star of all stormy nights—alas
The flames of my rage roar
In the dark dungeon of this jail!

I have leaned on a dark door
My aching forehead pushing
Against this open door with hope
My thin cold fingers.

There will come a day when your eyes with regret
Will slide over this painful song—in my songs
You will look for me—telling yourself:
"She was my mother!"

Through these examples let me now suggest that the three collections of poetry are linked as precursors to Farrokhzad's film. In *Captive*, Farrokhzad commences her poetic imagery with a fearful but fixated awareness of darkness—with commands of "close your eyes" and images of a "dark demon" paramount in her poetry. But she also has an inarticulate and paradoxical *attraction* to this darkness, which, though she describes it as having "blood on his hands," has "a smile on his face." The image of an omnipotent darkness persists in the poem with the metaphor of "the old elm's back" standing in for the poet herself: "broken / So the demon can step on it!" She keeps her son on her lap in a protective posture. Both by way of protecting her baby boy *and* as a feeble attempt to resist the temptation of getting up and moving *toward* the dark demon, which she finds at once frightful and irresistible. She soon becomes mesmerized by this dark demon and her wish, "Oh let me pull this curtain," is more an invitation to the darkness than shutting it out. The "two hundred eyes fiery and bloody" have already stripped the poet naked, exposed, vulnerable, excited. There is no keeping this liberating demonic darkness out of the room—it is already inside her head.

As Farrokhzad sees and projects this darkness, it is omnipotent: "From the flames of his breathing fire / The shepherd in the silent desert was burned"; and omniscient: "Oh be quiet my dear for this drunken darkness / Is listening to you behind the closed door!" capable of snatching the mother and child together. The poet's cry is apparently for the boy, more immediately for herself, but ultimately for both of them.

Sin emerges as the defining mark on this moment—not only in this particular poem but throughout the volume. The dark demon both constitutes the sin and accuses the sinner: "I am a demon, but you are more of a demon than me..."" Here we are at the core of Farrokhzad's poetic animus: her sin, which is at once guilt-provoking and yet fatally attractive: "His voice is dying and yet my heart / Is ablaze with the fire of pain—I cry / Out: 'Kami, my dear Kami! / Take your head off my lap, my darling!'" We can almost see the frightened mother pushing her son's head away from her lap, so convinced is she by the dark demon that she is sinful, impure, and unworthy of holding her son. But there, precisely, is the poetic energy that drives the metaphor, and the push is as much to protect the child from a sinful mother as it is to free the (sinful) mother from the child, so that she can get up and run away *toward* the dark demon!

In *The Wall*, Farrokhzad continues her poetic imagery with a far more confident dwelling in the dark side of her attractions—and this time around in full and fruitful communion with it. "The World of Shadows" reveals the leitmotif of her second collection, that the shadows have escaped her persona and assumed full character and autonomy: "Our shadows seem to escape us—away / From us and onto the slippery road..." Possessing a will of their own, these shadows that the poet projects "Embrace each other / At times—our shadows: / Just like two flowers drunk / From the dew-wine of last night." Farrokhzad no longer has any fear or inhibitions about these shadows, an extension of the same dark demons to which she was frightfully attracted in the first volume. In their escape, she has detected their joyous whisper: "Songs we never sing— / Songs we bury with anger / In the silence of our chests." But the songs are bittersweet, because even if they are no longer feared, the dark shadows never sing them.

Here in effect occurs a complete reversal of the physical bodies and their distant shadows—"while our / Tired bodies in their solidities give / Form to life" The conclusion is evident, and the poet's question entirely rhetorical: "Does life ever find form / Inside our shadows? / Are we not the shadows of our own shadows?" Yes, Farrokhzad is saying, our deepest desires, fulfilled or not, are tied in some way to the darker sides of ourselves.

In *Rebellion*, Farrokhzad becomes fully absorbed into the shady half of her character, and by the shadowy assurance of its darker insights. By design, "A Poem for You!" is dedicated to the poet's son ("This is my last lullaby"): "Toward the middle of this road that began / Inauspiciously in the old grave of this endless sorrow." The image of the poet's shadow is primary in the poem and it is from the distant confidence of that shadow that she speaks: "Let my bewildered shadow be / Far from your shadow and distant." The invitation—"let us / Come back together on a day / When no one but God is between us"—is in effect a dis-invitation from any more worldly involvement with her son. And where exactly is the poet as she distances herself forever from her son? "I have leaned on a dark door / My aching forehead pushing / Against this open door with hope / My thin cold fingers." From this door she has entered the dark abode forever and will not return—and all her insights come from the now illuminated depth of that darkness. Quintessential to this moment of entering darkness is still the poet's sense of shame and guilt: "Cauterized with shame I / Was laughing at futile innuendoes convinced / That I would be the cry of my own existence but / Alas I was but a woman!" Her very last cry is far more insightful than mournful; it is from the depth of that othered side of being (a woman) that she now speaks, her poetic persona having completely metamorphosed from guilt into the dark side of creativity. Being a woman is no longer a critical impediment; it is a creative privilege.

Against the endemic sense of guilt and shame, and constitutional to the character and culture Farrokhzad has now successfully defied, the poet in her launches the rebellion of all ages by fully acknowledging where she resides: "Here all stars are dark here / All angels are weeping here." From the midst of that darkness, Farrokhzad reports an apocalyptic vision: "Here upon every path is / Sitting the demon of deceit, shame, / Duplicity, and upon the dark sky even / I see no light from the wakeful bright morning." Nonetheless, there in the darkness Farrokhzad is determined to continue with her journey: "I will / Depart from me to drop / The veil from the pure face of all the infallible Marys!"

From the bliss of that enabling fear, Farrokhzad became the prophetic voice and vision of the dark side of her culture, the return of its repressed. Farrokhzad was no mere "woman poet." She was the poetic voice of a millennial denial at the heart of her culture.

This departure into darkness is the defining moment of Farrokhzad's poetry. It is always predicated on a pronounced sense of guilt and shame, which is paradoxically the source of her poetic energy as well. "I have sailed away from the shore / Of having a good name and in my chest / Shines the star of all stormy nights—alas / The flames of my rage roar / In the dark dungeon of this jail!" The last hope of the poem, that a day will come when the poet's son will look back at her poetry and say, "She was my mother!" is decidedly in a convoluted future/past tense. There are reports that Farrokhzad would occasionally wear a chador (she habitually did not) and go to her son's school in disguise so she could see him. Kamyar is reported to have been frightened on such occasions, refused to talk to her, and screamed, "You are not my mother!" This last line of the poem may of course be a poetic negation of that cry—but equally important is her defiant appropriation of her son into the universe of her own poetic imagination—where he will read her mother's poetry and say,

"She was my mother!" The convoluted past/future tense is the un-time of Farrokhzad's poetry, the dis-placement of her shadow.

Conspicuous in these three volumes of poetry published before *The House Is Black* is an overwhelming sense of guilt, to which Farrokhzad is creatively attracted. This sense of guilt amounts to a progressively infectious emotive paradox that eventually engulfs and defines her entire poetic constitution. Whereas in the first collection the guilt is merely articulated and announced, in her second volume Farrokhzad has lyrically migrated away from the solidity of bodies and taken permanent refuge in their simultaneously guilt-ridden and hopeful shadows, seeking confident residence in their troubling domain. There—looking at the outside world from the darker aspects of her character and culture—Farrokhzad's insights are entirely atemporal, for by now she has poetically filled herself with a prophetic assurance about her apocalyptic visions. By the time she completes the third volume of her poetry, Farrokhzad has made a permanent sojourn to the darker half of her creative consciousness—into the negated, the denied, the repressed, the forbidden, the shameful, the guilty, the bedeviled shadows of her self and society.

Farrokhzad was guilt-ridden to the point of personal paralysis (mutated into creative effervescence). She had a particularly troublesome relationship with her father, and though she loved him dearly, he had hurt her through his misunderstanding of what appeared to him as her erratic and irresponsible life. The same sense of guilt and shame also informs her relationship with her son, Kamyar, whom she in effect had to abandon to liberate herself from a futile marriage. In her mind—and evident both in her poetry and published private correspondence—she thought that she had betrayed and hurt her father to fall in love and marry a man much older than she; that she'd betrayed and hurt her husband by being attracted to a free and independent life and ultimately divorcing him; that she betrayed and hurt her son by divorcing his father to pursue her vision of herself as a poet. Betraying and hurting her father, husband, and son became both the bane of her existence and the source—the *pathos moralis*—of her poetry.

This powerful union of guilt and shame became so overwhelming that Farrokhzad could never be happy or content with anything she achieved, least of all with her poetry, about which in 1965, two years before her death, she openly said she was utterly dissatisfied. "I am thirty years old," she once wrote in a letter, "but the substance of my poetry is much younger—and that is the most serious problem with my [poetry]." In truth, at the age of thirty she, along with a handful of other poets, had become the undisputed idols of her generation. To assuage the guilt of having abandoned Kamyar she adopted Hossein, the son of a leper she had met when she made *The House Is Black*. In her letters to the young boy's father, she repeatedly assures him that she is treating him like her own son. But the irony of her promise—considering the break with her son, Kamyar—could not have escaped Farrokhzad, because the guilt at the root of it never left her in peace—nor did she want to be left in peace: That peace would have spelled the death of her poetry, her journey back from darkness.

And Farrokhzad loved poetry. "Poetry is my God," she once wrote belligerently and yet apologetically to her father in a letter. "That's how much I love poetry. My nights and days are spent thinking to compose a new, beautiful poem that no one before has ever composed." Her love for poetry or her love for her adopted son or her presumably promiscuous affairs with an assortment of men—Golestan in particular—all emanated from this overwhelming abyss of creative guilt and were thus never fully satisfying for Farrokhzad. The paradoxical crux of this guilt, with its innermost core of creative angst, was that at the edge of its threat to cripple Farrokhzad it in effect empowered her. She was not paralyzed by her sense of guilt—she was energized by it. This is not to say that she enjoyed or reveled in her guilt, but that she creatively thrived in it—and the more it nourished her poetry the more it nourished itself. Farrokhzad's sense of guilt against her patriarchal culture—represented by her father, husband, and son—assumed a creative reality *sui generis*. It soon lost contact with its points of origin and took on a self-inventive energy that fed on her poetry as it was feeding it.

Years ago I wrote an essay on the formative forces of Iranian culture and its influence on Farrokhzad's poetry for a volume that a prominent Persianist scholar, Michael Hillmann, was editing. In that essay I dwelled extensively on the nature of this guilt and quite abruptly suggested a link between Farrokhzad's suicidal urges, her automobile accident, and the unrelenting source of her poetic creativity. What I now wish to suggest is a much more precise link between her personal life, social persona, creative character, and Iranian patriarchal culture—while connecting her single cinematic masterpiece to the rest of her poetic output. For I am absolutely convinced that *The House Is Black* is the missing link between her first three collections of poetry and her last two—that without her poetry we cannot understand what happens in *The House Is Black*, and without *that film* we are missing something critical in the course of her poetic career.

This creative pathos at the center of Farrokhzad's poetry can very easily be mistaken for a political ethos, and that is precisely the reason why a careful reading of *The House Is Black* in terms crucial to her life, language, and art has been impeded so far by a rather trite over-politicization. That she detected the beauty of lepers in the midst of their misery has been seen as a metaphor or allegory for Iran at large, or else solicited a musty humanist reading. This prolonged abuse of *The House Is Black* has persistently and erroneously directed audiences toward a banal political reading of a masterpiece. *The House Is Black* is, of course, profoundly political—but political not in some prosaic way, with a one-to-one mimetic correspondence between leprosy and social malaise, science, and emancipation. Because *The House Is Black* is a visual poem, directed by a poet—and not just any poet, but one of rare intellect and miraculous artistry.

If we keep *The House Is Black* on the course of Farrokhzad's *creative pathos*, predicated on and charged by her dynamic sense of guilt and shame, we will get much closer to the poetic persona of its creator and the defiant darkness of her creativity. "I swear by God, and I swear on my son's life, that I love you," she wrote desperately once in a letter from Europe to her father (and you know the terrible weight of the expression when an Iranian mother swears *beh marg-e bachcheh-am*, which is really not "I swear on my son's life" but more literally "I swear by my child's death," meaning may my child die if I am dishonest in what I am about to say). "Just thinking about you," she continued in the same letter, "fills my eyes with tears. Sometimes I ask myself why God created me this way and why He brought to life this demon in me called poetry—and thus prevented me from securing your love and contentment with me. But this is not my fault. I am incapable of accepting and tolerating an ordinary life, as millions of other people do." In one sentence she brings God, her father, her son, and by implication her husband all together, both as the source of her guilt and anxiety and the demonic disposition of her attraction to poetry. And I use the word "demonic" not to sound dramatic, but because I just looked at the original letter in Persian and she actually uses the word *Shaytan*, which means "Satan." You see what I mean?

Farrokhzad was inexorably attracted to the creative demon that possessed her poetic soul, that made her defy the ordinary or socially acceptable life. But she never demonized the ordinary, and in fact maintained an astonishing intimacy with it. In her art, Farrokhzad confronted her benighted culture and found the encounter at once threatening and irresistible. Just like the proverbial moth of Persian poetry that is fatally attracted to light, she was drawn to a light in the heart of darkness.

By the time that Farrokhzad began shooting *The House Is Black* in 1962, the proverbial epithet of *dagh-e nang* (the burned mark of shame) had been carved, communally and culturally, on her body and mind. This metaphor is critically important in Farrokhzad's public persona and creative character. The Persian version of the Scarlet Letter, dagh-e nang is a brutal mark of shame burned by a molten iron bar on the face and body of a woman accused of promiscuous adultery. (You may remember that Bahman Farmanara's 1974 film *Prince Ehtejab* has a very powerful image to this effect.) Farrokhzad's own face was already marked by this cultural dagh-e nang before she went to the leprosarium in Tabriz to shoot *The House Is Black*. The social stigma that branded Farrokhzad's as a pariah was the defining feature of her character and the driving force of her poetry for about a decade before she entered that leprosarium. There the stigma became a sign of communal disgrace and judgmental punishment. The functional equivalent of a solemn ecclesiastical condemnation of her character had already judged her to be gravely opposed to the accepted doctrines of her culture—excommunicating her, in effect, from membership in that culture.

The social anathema attached to leprosy is a result not only of its presumed contagiousness but also because it marks the face as if by some divine sign of punishment—very much the same way that decades later AIDS carries the same social stigma, not altogether because its virus is contagious but because it symbolically marks and stigmatizes presumed sexual promiscuity.

In lepers and their predicament, Farrokhzad saw her own projected image: ashamed of and yet attached to a guilt falsely carried. In the face of the lepers, Farrokhzad saw her own face, and that is why and how she identified with them—other people literally marked with a shameful sign, people moved to the dark, the grotesque, the frightful, the feared, and the despised side of humanity. When through her camera Farrokhzad looked at the lepers' physically deformed faces she saw what the patriarchal pathology she defied had cauterized on her own morally defamed face—a defacement she could until then imagine but not see. The leper was Farrokhzad's vilified public persona, to which she now lent her defiant poetic vision. Farrokhzad had a culturally contracted leprous scar on her face—code-named dagh-e nang—long before she visited that leprosarium. That is why she could identify with the lepers there so immediately.

Contrary to much that has been said about *The House Is Black*, it is not a film about the celebration of life and beauty in the midst of death and ugliness. Farrokhzad did not see the lepers as repulsive (or beautiful for that matter); nor did she go there in search of a common humanity (which quite obviously she never doubted). She just *saw* them—as simple as that—as reflections of her own overwhelming sense of socially fabricated guilt and shame. *The House Is Black*, as a result, is an exceptionally dark, even pathological, film. The lepers are not just afflicted by a ravaging disease. Farrokhzad is very particular to mark their location as a suspension of reason and space, time and narrative, shown in the ingenious scene of a leper walking by a wall, counting the days of the week. The leprosarium emerges as the spatial equivalent of a Foucauldian asylum house, where the internment of un-reason facilitates the social construction of reason.

(Samira Makhmalbaf's *Apple*, I might add, borrows from this aspect of *The House Is Black*, as does her father's *Afghan Alphabet*.)

The House Is Black is not about a humanist detection of beauty in the midst of misery and decrepitude. It emerges from exactly the opposite angle: It dwells in and deliberates on the dark, the repulsive, and the grotesque, to chase the grotesqueries to their utter limits. Any high-school-age teenager could go to a leprosy colony and sugarcoat the horror she saw with some sweet cotton-candy tale of their common humanity. But Iran and its cultural history had sent the single most perceptive set of eyes into that leprosarium. What they saw and showed was no juvenile humanism to amuse and entertain the good-hearted liberalism of generations to come. What she saw there—and deliberately went there to see—was the darkest subterranean dungeon of a culture: a deliberate dwelling on the dark and the grotesque.

In the ravaged faces and bodies of the lepers, Farrokhzad saw the deranged layers of Iranian culture; for her they were a mirror of a brutalized history. She looked into that mirror and reflected those faces neither in sympathy nor in empathy. She probed the distorted features of those bodies in search of the most hidden horrors and exposed them. That is why the single most brilliant shot of the film (in a film inundated with masterful shots) is its opening frame: a woman looking at herself in the mirror. The woman, a leper looking at her face, is also Farrokhzad, and the ravaged face in the mirror is hers as well. That ravaged face and that desolate body have surfaced from the subterranean dungeon of Farrokhzad's patriarchal culture. The denial of the face and the repression of the body are quintessential to that culture—essential to its semiotic constitution of power. In an interview with *Roshanfekr* (*The Intellectual*) magazine soon after her film received an award in Germany, she singled out the abundance of mirrors in the leprosarium. "In every room, what was abundantly available were mirrors—and the same lepers who mostly lack a mouth, a nose, or an ear, like to look at themselves in the mirror"—as did Farrokhzad in *The House Is Black*.

Houshang Kavusi, one of very few critics who took *The House Is Black* seriously and, right after the film was screened in 1962, wrote a perceptive essay on it, dwelled on its psychological aspect and objected to what he considered the addition of the element of sympathy to those of fear and hatred, which he believed were fundamental components of Farrokhzad's film. Kavusi began his critique with the unexamined assumption that Farrokhzad had started the film with the intention of conveying fear and hatred but had allowed what he considered a misplaced sense of compassion to creep into the film. Moreover, Kavusi believed that every film should have a narrative unity and that the narrative unity of *The House Is Black* was violated by Farrokhzad superimposing her poetic sensibility on her filmic style. He argued that Farrokhzad should have checked her poetic vision at the door of Golestan Films, created a different persona, and entrusted her film to it. But Farrokhzad as an artist was not wedded to a conception of unity that critics may have harbored. The senses of unity and purpose—even if we were to accept that such utilitarian conceits are integral to a work of art—emerge from the aesthetic reordering of reality extemporaneous to a work of art. They are not invented or stipulated by a film critic, but are always subsequent to the conception and delivery of the work of art. Any work of art manufactures and delivers its own presence or absence of an aesthetic or thematic unity. The visual vocabulary of *The House Is Black* stipulates its own syntax and morphology, as it were, according to its own purpose. The film, as a result, is coherent on its own terms, which are the terms fundamental to the poetic disposition of its creator.

Kavusi's most bizarre objection is to Farrokhzad's mixing of the *substantive shocks* of the film with its *technical shocks*—meaning with editing, narrative sequence, sound effects, and voice-over. He particularly criticizes the concluding scene of the film, in which a student writes the title of the film, *The House Is Black*, on a blackboard in response to his teacher who asked him to compose a sentence with the word "house" in it. What I find astonishing in Kavusi's criticism is how the most definitive aspect of the emerging Iranian cinema—its mutation of fact and fantasy (for which, in an essay on Kiarostami, I have suggested the term "factasy")—is dismissed as a flaw, and not celebrated as a virtue. The manner and matter, form and substance, of Farrokhzad's film come out of each other and supplement one another. This is straight out of her own poetic convictions as a leading theorist of the Nimaic revolution that was taking place right at the time of her making *The House Is Black*—a fact of which Kavusi seems to be blissfully unaware. The fictive manipulation of reality, or the formal syncopation of substance, gradually emerges as the defining quality of Iranian cinematic aesthetics, coming to full, ingenious fruition in Kiarostami's *Close Up* and Mohsen Makhmalbaf's *A Moment of Innocence*. We can easily track the philosophical basis of this particular feature back to the medieval philosophical debates around the principality of *mahiyyat* ("quiddity") or *wujud* ("being"), or the dialectics of *jawhar* ("substance") and *ard* ("attribute"). But even without taking it that far back we must keep in mind this crucial aspect of the rise of Iranian *poetic realism*, which is predicated on a deliberate and intentional manipulation of the matter by the manner in which it is delivered, or the substance by its form. This, contrary to what Kavusi thought in 1962, not only does not diminish the seriousness of the substance, but in fact accentuates it. The problem with Kavusi and his generation of film critics is that they took the word "documentary" a bit too literally, just as they perceived the notion of cinematic narrative too figuratively!

Neither a prefabricated conception of narrative unity nor a conviction in the absolutism of reality is needed to look through the *poetic realism* of Forugh Farrokhzad's camera and into the mirror she placed in front of her face and Iranian culture. That poetic realism has its own logic and rhetoric, and it is imperative that you do not take it as some sort of lyrical compromise on reality; and for that not to happen you ought to have a very accurate conception of what I mean by *poetic* when I place it next to *realism*. By poetic I mean neither beautiful nor banal—though it can be both. By poetic I mean an angular take on reality, an oblique angle on its whereabouts, an aquiline protrusion into its claim to straightforwardness. But let me be more specific and take you for a short visit to our culture's philosophical takes on reality.

The conversation between Iranian medieval philosophy (*Hikmat*) and gnosticism (*Irfan*) is decisively important for any serious understanding of Iran's current cultural creativity. Because Iranians have received the European Enlightenment through a colonial gun barrel, they have always had a healthy suspicion of its lucrative promises and sustained a creative awareness of their own premodern intellectual history. Iran's artists—poets, novelists, and filmmakers in particular—have had their creative consciousness deeply planted in a premodern intellectual history (in classical poetry most visibly but, through that poetry, with medieval philosophy and gnosticism as well), though cultural critics have categorically failed to sustain a conversation with the same sources. This is principally because much of this intellectual history is in Arabic rather than in Persian, but also because the Pahlavi educational policies raised generations of Iranian intellectuals who shared the pathologically anti-Arab and anti-Islamic sentiments of the Pahlavi monarchy—and they do so to this day, even after a so-called *Islamic* revolution!

This is unfortunate beyond belief. The only people who have generated any sort of conversation between Iran's premodern intellectual history and its modern predicament are reactionary anti-intellectuals who have a visceral hatred for modernity—all in the name of a nonexistent entity they call the "Islamic tradition." Do not get me wrong. I have worlds of love and admiration for this generation of "traditionalists," as they call themselves. They spoke of Avicenna, Ibn Arabi, and Suhrawardi in a simple and accessible language when no one in my generation knew who these people were. For that my generation owes them a lasting note of gratitude. But beyond that I believe these people wrong, so deeply misguided that they are beyond repair. What they call the "Islamic tradition" is very noble and beautiful, but it is entirely a figment of their own perturbed imaginations. "Traditions" were the most atrocious invention of modernity. Enlightenment modernity invented traditions left and right to corroborate its own fabricated ingenuity. As all other world religions, Islam has always been a living organism, always in the making, through the dialectic of its own self-negations—its philosophy against its jurisprudence, its mysticism against its philosophy, its jurisprudence against its theology. Precisely in the sustained debates of that intellectual effervescence has beat the heart of Islam. So clear the air of the likes of this generation of "tradionalists" and their brand of transmigrated souls on one side and the army of secular intellectuals who break out with rashes at the slightest suggestion of a Qur'anic phrase or Arabic text (texts that were written in the *lingua franca* of their time and location and whose poetic distillation is the essence of our classical poetry) on the other, and what we have is an open space in which to generate and sustain a critical conversation with Iran's premodern intellectual history—philosophy and gnosticism in particular. My point is that you must claim the entirety of Iranian culture, from its premodernity to its postmodernity, and avoid the Islamist negation of secularism and the secular disdain of Islam like you avoid a plague—and once you do that, and a vast and variegated open field of inquiry has opened up for you, you will realize what a nonsensical invention this whole notion of *laïcité* is.

The first thing that you will note in any long-shot panorama of Iran's premodern intellectual history is that there has always been a sustained dialogue—at times fruitful, at others futile—between philosophical (logocentric) and gnostic (homocentric) dispositions. My simple suggestion at this point is for you to be aware that when I use a phrase like *poetic realism*, you should not read that word *poetic* as something wishy-washy, or soft-hearted, or liberal-minded, a saccharine sort of "Oh, why don't we just get together and be nice to each other and read poetry and be happy," the way you see it often used. No: I mean to alert you to the presence of a strong intellectual legacy behind that term that roots it deeply in the gnostic dimensions of our premodern intellectual history—of the ideas and practices of gnostic poets like Rumi, speculative theoreticians like Suhrawardi, or transcendental philosophers like Mulla Sadra who sought to counter the solid sovereignty of Aristotelian/Avicennian reason by alternative modes of knowing, which is not tantamount to the abrogation of reason but *supplementing* it by non-reason. By *supplementing* I mean that this mode of knowing does not substitute, replace, or displace reason, but that it covers its blind spots and points to its shortcomings. And what I mean by non-reason is simply for you to see gnostic readings of reality as a disorderly kind of defiance of the power of Almighty Reason—whether the practitioners of this un-reason call it *dhawq* ("disposition"), *mokashefeh* ("active discovery"), or *ishraq* ("Enlightenment," which has nothing to do with what Immanuel Kant much later called *Aufklärung*), and to understand that it is crucial that we get to know in what particular way such soft terms and guerrilla tactics are challenging the omnipotent power and the metaphysical violence of reason.

Terms such as dhawq, mokashefeh, or ishraq refer to a wider domain of speculative discovery that are not reason-based, and in effect radically challenge the primacy of Aristotelian/Avicennian reason, long before it was "instrumentalized" in the course of capitalist modernity. To be sure, in Iran's intellectual history, not all rational discourses are logocentric, which is the sovereign domain of peripatetic (*mashshai*) philosophy. The entire juridical disposition of Iranian intellectual history is nomocentric, namely predicated on the primacy of law, while our gnostic disposition is homocentric, namely presuming the fragility of an existential human being at the center of any production of knowledge. But in historical conversation (or contestation) with each other, the philosophical, juridical, and gnostic manners of knowledge production (or discourses) have collectively stood separate from a poetic manner of knowing, which opts for an entirely different "mood" or "manner" (or what in Greek dramaturgy they used to call *anagnorisis*) of knowing. A *poetic* manner of knowing thus has its own claim to a mode of knowledge production that is irreducible to instrumental reason, a paradigm, an episteme, a syntax, a morphology, a lexicon of its own texture and disposition. Poetic *truth* is thus no mere aesthetic claim. It posits an epistemic claim, a theorem of its own; it possesses a thematic autonomy that defines its particular take on reality.

Acknowledging this crucial aspect of Iran's premodern intellectual heritage is necessary for an understanding of how Farrokhzad was able to cut the tyrannically tall claims of reality to size—to compromise its truth-telling pretensions and confront its autocratic regime. As a poet, Farrokhzad was a practitioner in that manner of speculative reflection, giving a poetic inflection to understanding reality. This epistemic practice of poetry—both verbal and visual—is the strategic infiltration of aesthetics behind the enemy lines of politics, to subvert from within. A work of art assumes its narrative unity, or if it so pleases asserts its anti-narrative disunity, and manipulates reality to tease out alternatives from the tendency of reality toward banality. What Kavusi thought was the flaw of irreality in *The House Is Black* is actually its most glorious achievement. Artists take reality too seriously to take it seriously. Reality, as reality, is always already implicated in a commanding paradigm of violent metaphysics—from theology to philosophy and even to mysticism. Poetry is the defiant act of a pre-speculated reality rising to claim its innate right not to submit to such readings. A poet like

Farrokhzad does not as much dwell on the theoretical underpinning of these counterclaims to truth as practice them. Their poetic predilections, their creative ego, and their defiant disposition all come together to practice and perform an alternative take on reality, giving birth to a poetic realism that is at once miasmatic in its truth claims and yet solidly grounded in reality. "I am not one of those people," Farrokhzad once said in an interview,

> who seeing someone's head hit by a stone then
> concludes that she should try to avoid the sight of
> a stone. Unless a stone hits my own head, I have
> no clue what a stone means. What I mean to say
> is that even after reading Nima, I still wrote many
> bad poems. I needed to grow inside myself, and this
> growth needed, and still needs, time. You will not
> grow tall on vitamin pills. Growing tall is only on the
> surface. Bones do not just crack within themselves.

My point is that her poetry grew from the heart of her dogged grounding in reality, and from there she spoke with her feet firmly grounded in what might be called a material metaphysics—water, wind, fire, and dust, elemental to her self-awareness as a poet, a position from which she could say:

> *The end of all forces is to unite:*
> *To unite with the enlightened principle*
> *Of sun—and to pour*
> *Into the intelligence of light.*
> *It is all but natural that windmills*
> *Rot.*
> *Why should I stop?*
> *I hold the budding shoots of wheat*
> *Under my breast*
> *And I breastfeed them.*

From the depth of this creative encounter with her patriarchal culture, Farrokhzad then comes to the social surface—and not to pontificate in the way Ebrahim Golestan imposes his voice and narrative on *The House Is Black* before it has even started:

> The world is not devoid of ugliness. Ugliness in the world
> would have been more if humanity were to close its eyes
> on it. But humanity finds solutions. On this screen will

now appear a glimpse of an ugliness, picture of a pain—
upon which to close our eyes is far from the magnanimity
of humanity. To find a solution for this ugliness, to seek
assistance in curing this pain, and thus help those who
are afflicted by it, are the reasons behind the making of
this film, and the hope of those who have produced it.

This is the superimposition of Golestan's habitually beautiful but—in
this case—entirely misplaced prose on a film that has scarcely anything to
do with finding a cure for leprosy. Golestan's voice-over reappears at one
other point in the film, when he provides a semi-scientific discourse on
the causes and conditions of leprosy. Entirely superfluous and irrelevant
to this film, his words simulate reason and science, while Farrokhzad's
voice and filmic narrative provoke the poetic resonance of biblical passages. (Houshang Golmakani thinks the male voice might be Asadollah
Peyman's, but I think it is the voice of Golestan himself). Yes, the film was
commissioned by an official agency in charge of ameliorating the condition of lepers. (Most of Golestan's short films were commissioned by
various governmental agencies.) But as Golestan himself said in the same
interview with *Roshanfekr* magazine, that agency paid less than fifty percent
of the budget and, as a result, Golestan claimed, "This was the easiest film
to make because of the free hand we had in making it." The significance
to be gleaned from all this is that the circumstances of the making of the
film as an educational documentary for a governmental agency and what
Golestan whimsically imposed on its narrative by way of a pseudo-scientific discourse explaining leprosy and its treatment should not contribute
to over-determining our reading of a cinematic masterpiece.

The House Is Black is not a public-service announcement, or a human-
itarian documentary to open our eyes to a particularly contagious disease.
It is a daring journey within—there to dwell in the demonic darkness
of a social stigma, to know and acknowledge it, analyze and synthesize
its facial ravages and bodily deformities, visualize its horrors, theorize its
implications, politicize its causes, aestheticize its consequences—in short,
to live the disease, and to take a Gramscian inventory of it. "The starting point of critical elaboration," Gramsci said in his *Prison Notebooks*, "is
the consciousness of what one really is, and is 'knowing thyself' as the
product of the historical process to date, which has deposited in you an
infinity of traces, without leaving an inventory. Therefore it is imperative
at the outset to compile such an inventory." In this vein, Farrokhzad herself considered *The House Is Black*

a film about the life of the lepers and at the same time
about life itself—an example of life in general. This is

a picture of any sealed and closed society—a picture of
being useless, isolated, insular, futile. Even healthy people
living outside a leprosarium in the apparently healthy
society may share these characteristics, without being
afflicted with leprosy. There is no difference between a
young man who aimlessly loiters in the streets and that
leper in my film who keeps walking by the wall. This
young man too has certain pains of which we are unaware.

This image of futility and decay is *not* a political metaphor that Farrokhzad is invoking; it is precisely the picture that she had of herself,
repeatedly writing in her letters how squandered she felt. "I feel I have
wasted my life," she once wrote in a letter to Golestan, "and know much
less than I should at the age of twenty-seven." This was in 1962, by which
time she had published three of her five volumes of poetry and made *The
House Is Black*. The same sentiment is evident in her travelogue from her
trip to Europe in 1956. Whatever great work of art she saw in Italy left
her feeling far more humbled than inspired.

The image of futility Farrokhzad perceived in her own life was in fact
definitive to her creative character. In a letter from London to Golestan she
once wrote how she missed Tehran and "all its miserable countenances":

I love our own Tehran, whatever it is I don't care.
I love it. It is only there that my being finds a
purpose for living. That lazy sunshine, that heavy
sunset, those dusty back alleys, and those miserable,
pathetic, mean, and corrupt people—I love them.

Farrokhzad thrived close to those miseries and stupidities—and
beyond her initial poetic attraction to darkness and shadows, it is in *The
House Is Black* that she has a visual occasion to exorcise her inner darkness
and visibly to dwell and deliberate on the nature and disposition of that
wasteful grotesquery of her ancestral culture.

What happens when the site of the unseen is made visible? A leprosarium is a transgressive place—a grotesque, forbidden space where
bodies ruined by disease are locked away so as not to disturb the legislation of bodily normalcy. Opening the door on a defiant semiotics of the
grotesque, Farrokhzad releases a disruption of the semantic legislation of
the body. If *The House Is Black* is political, which it is, it is political in this
monumentally subversive way. The first look of the daring gaze into the
mirror is bound to see grotesque deformities, which have been hitherto
forbidden. That is the supreme wisdom of the film. "*Ta nah daghi binad,*

kas beh doran nah cheraqi binad," Farrokhzad once wrote in a letter to her brother, quoting a frightfully brilliant line from Nima Yushij:

> *Not until afflicted—*
> *Will anyone see the light!*

Note that the expression *dagh didan* ("to be afflicted with a pain") invokes precisely the mark on the skin, flesh, nerves, and bones of a body.

Add now to this insight a crucial element in Farrokhzad's worldview and you will come close to her greatest gift as a public intellectual. With all her love and admiration for Italian Renaissance art, at one point in her travel narrative she makes a crucial observation.

> When I lived in Rome, sometimes it seemed to me
> that I was still in Iran, and in our own Tehran in fact.
> Everything in Rome reminded me of Iran. In general,
> those countries that are located in the southern part of
> Europe lack that freedom and civility that we imagine
> when we hear the word "Europe." If we were to separate
> the magnificent history of Italian art and civilization
> from what is present today, most certainly not much is
> left. I was under the impression that I had traveled to
> a European country and yet I faced the same pressures
> and suffocation that exist in Iran. The most debasing
> forms of superstition reign supreme among the Italians.
> In Iran we used to make fun of old lower-class women
> who used to frequent soothsayers and fortune-tellers to
> cure incurable diseases. But in Italy I saw very young
> people who sought the cure for all their ailments in a
> small cap that the Pope had once put on his head and thus
> they considered it consecrated—with the difference that
> our old women in Iran are illiterate and the conditions
> of their lives do not allow them to grow intellectually;
> whereas the young people who turn to the Pope's
> sacred cap are mostly students at Rome University.

The reason I bring this to your attention is to show you how Farrokhzad did not share the vision of Europe with which most of her Iranian contemporaries were enamored. Separating what was admirable from what was pathetic in Europe, she did not categorically identify her culture as a historical aberration from the rest of the world—the way that later on Iranian intellectuals did by believing that Iranian culture "took a vacation from history." This recognition, in turn, makes of Farrokhzad's engagement with the dark side of her character and culture in *The House Is Black* more of an existential and sociological introspection, with obvious universal implications, rather than a medical study of an anthropological nature. The result is that Farrokhzad was in fact the first, and by and large the only, Iranian public intellectual of her generation who attained a global perspective on the local predicament of her culture, rather than share the myopic perspective of her contemporaries on global matters. That is the reason why *The House Is Black* so universally resonates with its audiences wherever it is shown—not because it shows the humanity of the lepers, but because it reflects the inhumanity in all of us.

The House Is Black is the missing link between Farrokhzad's first three and last two volumes of published poetry. As such it is both textually and contextually existential (and not ethnographic), transgressive (and not transfusive)—a semiotics of the grotesque and an analytic of the forbidden. In this film, Farrokhzad dared to get close to the darker side of her poetic genius and ventured into the abyss—thus the brilliance of its opening shot. That woman looking into the mirror and examining her ravaged flesh is Forugh Farrokhzad looking from behind her camera, daring to peer into the depth of darkness, the origin of her genius. Farrokhzad's camera is perfectly angled in a medium shot, so that we cannot see the face of the woman, except in the mirror. She has covered her head and face with a scarf and yet her face is visible in the mirror. Farrokhzad has placed a teapot next to the mirror to lend her ravaged face an air of domesticity, while the mirror itself has a floral-motif frame. As we are mesmerized by the horror, Farrokhzad begins to zoom in. The camera is stationary and scared; the lens is intrusive and fearless. The close-up of the face is now fully framed in the floral mirror. *Ecce homo*! Lo and behold, this is she! Come and see! From this frame, Farrokhzad's magnificent cutting pulsates in a succession of other close-ups: a young man reading from a book in a classroom. Reading what? Thanking God for having created him, for having created his kind mother and caring father! Cut: another leper reading from the same book in the same classroom: "We thank thee for creating the running streams and the fruitful trees." Cut. There are altogether twelve close-ups and two medium shots after that initial zoom into the woman's face. Every shot contains a leper thanking God for creation of humanity and the sources of sustenance; and in the middle of it all, in the ninth frame from the beginning, we hear Farrokhzad's own mournfully melodic voice: "Who is it in the mirror that praises thee, Lord? Who is it in the mirror?"

By stretching beyond the Qur'anic and reaching for the biblical (Farrokhzad was always fascinated by the Persian translation of the Bible), Farrokhzad embraces an antiquity of diction that is no longer religious but metaphysical, no longer spatial but eternal, no longer cultural but cosmic, no longer political but mythic. Farrokhzad has let her camera loose to register the topography of a landscape she was at once privileged and condemned to see, and to show. There, upon a hill with the widest possible angle on subterranean realities that cultures categorically condemn and systematically contort, Farrokhzad had planted her piercing camera. And from there she spoke, and in her voice now resonated a prophetic assurance, not just because she recited from the Bible, but because she had reached the source of that prophetic diction: now the soul of her poetry.

After *The House Is Black* Farrokhzad was yet to publish her two masterpieces: *Another Birth* and *Let Us Believe in the Beginning of the Cold Season*. It frightens me just to think where Farrokhzad went in these two subsequent volumes, having looked into that mirror. I always think that we cut our great poets and artists down to our own size—we neither dare their courage nor share their imagination. They flash like lightning, as Ahmad Shamlu once put it in a poem, and disappear—and then they leave it for us frightened bats to figure out what it is that they saw and said. I spent ten years of my life trying to see what Ayn al-Qudat saw, cutting through the veils that generations had pulled around his vision. Farrokhzad deserves no less.

Farrokhzad has a seminal significance in the art and craft that you now practice. *The House Is Black* is the missing link not only between her previous three volumes of poetry and her next two, but perhaps even more poignantly between the ascent of modern Persian poetry and fiction in the 1960s and the rise of Iranian cinema in earnest in the 1970s. She represents the best that the Persian poetic imagination had to offer, and as fate would have it she was also critically important in the rise of Iranian cinema. She touched Iranian cinema with a very specific mode of realism, a *poetic* realism—and if we are to narrow in on what is specific about Iranian cinematic realism then we will have to take the specifics of Farrokhzad's poetic realism seriously.

I hope to have occasions to describe to you in detail how Farrokhzad's poetic realism is linked to Golestan's *affective* realism, and from there to move on to other great artists of our time who have one by one added their momentum to and made their mark on Iranian cinema. But all in good time, my dear and distinguished friend, all in good time.

How clever you are, my dear! You never mean
a single word you say.
—Oscar Wilde

Ebrahim Golestan
Mud Brick and Mirror

AMIR NADERI MUST HAVE BEEN A LAD OF FIFTEEN OR SO when he went to Tehran and found his way to Golestan Films to get himself involved in cinema—and there he met Forugh Farrokhzad in person. Early last April, when Golestan's son Kaveh was killed in an accident while covering the war in Iraq, Amir and I played telephone tag for a few days—not wanting to be the first to give the other the terrible news.

Kaveh Golestan was part of a four-person BBC team that had driven from Sulaymaniyah in the Kurdish region of northern Iraq and arrived at Kifri, a town in the southern part of Kurdistan. Apparently, at about lunchtime on Wednesday, 2 April 2003, Golestan, as the cameraman of the group, had gotten out of the car and stepped on a landmine and was killed instantly. Producer Stuart Hughes was caught by the blast and injured his foot, while BBC correspondent Jim Muir and the local translator were unhurt. Golestan, who was fifty-two at the time of his sudden death, had worked for the BBC in a freelance capacity for about three years. He had become the BBC's cameraman in Tehran in September

2000, and had worked for many other news organizations as well. He was a Pulitzer Prize-winning photographer acclaimed for his work during the Iranian revolution and covering the gassing of the Kurds at Halabja during the course of the Iran-Iraq War. He is survived by his wife, Hengameh, and his son, Mehrak, as well as his mother, Ebrahim Golestan's wife, Fakhri, his sister, Lili, and her family. Kaveh Golestan was born in Abadan, Iran, on 8 July 1950, and died in Kifri, in Iraqi Kurdistan.

Kaveh was born in Abadan in 1950; Forugh Farrokhzad's son, Kamyar, was born in Ahvaz in 1952; and right between the two of them I was born, in Ahvaz, on 15 June 1951. Add to these dates the events of August 1953, when the US-British-sponsored coup against Prime Minister Mosaddeq toppled a nascent democracy and installed a brutal dictatorship, and you get a gist of the animus behind a whole generation of poets, novelists, filmmakers (and of course cantankerous cultural critics tucked away in their apartments overlooking the Hudson River and, when not kicking and screaming against the war in the streets of Manhattan, trying to figure out what is happening around the world).

By the time his son was born, Ebrahim Golestan was already among Iran's leading public intellectuals and progressive literati. He was born in 1922 and raised in the southern city of Shiraz, where he received his early education. The Shiraz of Golestan's childhood and upbringing had just emerged from military occupation by the British during WWI—an experience immortalized by Golestan's fellow Shirazi writer Simin Daneshvar in her magisterial novel *Savushun* (1969). The decadent Qajar dynasty was breathing its last desperate gasps under the increasing colonial presence of the British in the south and the Russians in the north. (This European influence intensified particularly after the discovery of oil in Masjid Soleiman and in the Caspian Sea in 1908.) The Constitutional Revolution of 1906–11 had resulted in curbing the whimsical monarchy but ultimately failed to produce enduring democratic institutions. At this time, new and more vociferous revolutionary movements were fomenting various rebellions. A year before Golestan was born, Mirza Kuchak Khan Jangali (1878–1921) died, ending a rebellious movement in the northern part of the country that he had been leading against the central government in Tehran. In the very same year the Iranian Communist Party was established, inspired and encouraged by the Bolshevik Revolution of 1917. The year before that, a revolutionary uprising in Azerbaijan, led by Shaykh Muhammad Khiyabani, was brutally suppressed, leading one of its most eloquent supporters, the poet Taqi Rafat, to commit suicide in 1920.

Meanwhile, events no less revolutionary were taking place in the world of film, fiction, and poetry. Two groundbreaking events welcomed Ebrahim Golestan to this world as his most appropriate birthday gifts—the simultaneous publication of Nima Yushij's poem "Afsaneh" in Iran and Seyyed Mohammad Ali Jamalzadeh's novel *Once upon a Time in Berlin*. These writers announced the momentous birth of modern Persian poetry and fiction. Two years after that, the prominent British Orientalist E. G. Browne published his four-volume *A Literary History of Persia* (1924), and thus canonized the classics of Persian literature and (inadvertently) implicated the birth of a new era in the Persian creative imagination. Two years after that, Reza Shah toppled the last Qajar monarch in a military coup and established a new monarchy—the Pahlavi dynasty—thus continuing a medieval Persian institution into colonial modernity. The establishment of the Iranian national railroad system in 1927 physically connected the territorial boundaries that the new nation-state was to claim its own. This right before Sadeq Hedayat returned from Europe in 1930 to launch his brief but phantasmagoric literary career with the publication of his first collection of short stories, *Buried Alive* (1930), and wreak havoc on all the cosmetic pretensions of the Pahlavi regime. In the same year, and on the occasion of Ebrahim Golestan's eighth birthday, he received yet another enchanting birthday gift: Avanes Oganians released the first Iranian full-length feature film, the silent *Abi and Rabi* (1930).

From 1930 on, there seems to have emerged an implicit competition between Reza Shah and Sadeq Hedayat as to who would define the content and contour of Golestan's youthful soul—they both did. In 1931, the nine-year-old Golestan saw Reza Shah ban the performance of the Persian passion play, Taziyeh, and disband the Iranian Communist Party; at exactly the same time Hedayat published his second collection of stories, *In the Shadow of the Mongols*. In 1934, Reza Shah established Tehran University, by which time Hedayat had already published two other collections of his stories—in 1932 and 1933—and prepared a critical edition of the poetry of Omar Khayyam, in 1934. By then, Golestan was a precocious teenager in Shiraz and reading Hedayat's stories as if they were *Harry Potter*. In 1935, Reza Shah brutally suppressed a revolutionary uprising in Mashhad, and in 1936 proceeded to ban the veil, defeating Hedayat by about two years with his dictatorial initiatives, until Hedayat collected his wits and published his absolute masterpiece, *The Blind Owl*, in 1937 in Bombay, dodging the monarch's censorship. A tacit celebration of Reza Shah's unveiling of Iranian women suddenly surfaced in an unexpected place when Abdolhossein Sepanta produced the first ever Iranian talkie, *The Lor Girl* (1936)—subtitled "The Iran of Yesterday and the Iran of Today"—and used it to propagate the glorious modernization of Reza Shah the Great! Two years later, Reza Shah murdered Farrokhi Yazdi (1899–1939), a revolutionary poet, because of his socialist convictions. Two years after that, the Allied Forces began their occupation of

Iran during WWII and forced Reza Shah to abdicate in 1941, installing his son Mohammad Reza Shah on the Pahlavi throne. Hedayat was alive and well—a witness to the old monarch's fall from power.

Soon after the Allied occupation of Iran in 1941, the Iranian Tudeh (Socialist) Party was established and gradually emerged as the most progressive political organization in modern Iranian history, before its dishonorable demise under the pressure of Stalinism. Like most progressive intellectuals of his time, Golestan soon joined the Tudeh Party and remained a loyal member until the end of WWII, when the Soviets stayed on in northern Iran and aggressively supported a separatist movement there in the provinces of Azerbaijan and Kurdistan. The Tudeh Party was thus cast in a rather embarrassingly traitorous role as a fifth column in support of Soviet imperial ambitions. The incident created a major schism in the Tudeh Party and quite a number of its leading activists—among them Golestan—left it altogether. When in 1949 an assassination attempt against the young Mohammad Reza Shah failed, the Tudeh Party was officially banned. It continued its underground existence well into the early 1950s, when it came to a disgraceful end, following its opposition to Mohammad Mosaddeq's nationalization of the Iranian oil industry (the Tudeh had wanted to protect Soviet oil interests in northern Iran). Mosaddeq nationalized oil in 1951, the year that Hedayat finally gave up on life and committed suicide in Paris. Following the nationalization of Iranian oil by Prime Minister Mosaddeq in 1953, the shah fled the country, and as a result British and American interests were seriously compromised in the region. The CIA and British intelligence soon devised a military coup, toppled Mosaddeq, and returned the shah to Iran with a vengeance against the nation that had spurned him. The Tudeh leadership fled to the Soviet Union and Eastern Europe—and a winter of discontent descended upon Iranian intellectuals. Mehdi Akhavan Sales summed up the mood of the nation in his apocalyptic poem "Winter," in 1955: *"No one returns your greetings,"* he began, *"Heads are all sunk in the collar."*

Ebrahim Golestan dates the origin of his literary interests back to his political awakening in the early 1940s, soon after the Allied Forces had left Iran and before the young Mohammad Reza Shah solicited and secured US support to consolidate his authoritarian power. In 1942, at the age of twenty, Golestan discovered Sadeq Hedayat's *The Blind Owl*, the most important literary event of the time, and noted its unusually visual vocabulary, which Golestan attributed to Hedayat's encounter with cinema in Europe. Hedayat soon emerged as the measure for young literary aspirants. In fact, Golestan once told me the story of how he ran into Hedayat on a bus and asked him to read a short story he had written.

Hedayat read Golestan's story and jotted down some comments in the margin; they were initially dismissive and sarcastic but gradually became appreciative and encouraging, as he read further.

Starting in 1945, Golestan began to write for the official organs of the Tudeh Party but was soon disillusioned with that sort of political pamphleteering altogether and opted for a literary path. Meanwhile, his interest in the visual arts—photography and filmmaking in particular—was as serious as his interest in the literary arts. In 1947, he took part in a major group exhibition with a number of other Iranian photographers in a gallery at the Soviet embassy in Tehran. A year later, in 1948, Golestan published his first collection of short stories, *Azar, Mah-e Akhar-e Paiz* (*Azar, the Last Month of Autumn*). These seven short stories announced the birth of a major literary voice.

The CIA coup of 1953 that brought Mohammad Reza Shah Pahlavi back to power was a catastrophe for the cause of democracy in Iran and a moral cul-de-sac for public intellectuals. Golestan, however, is not a typically morose intellectual, prone to sitting at home or in a café contemplating the unforgivable atrocity of a US military coup that brought back to power a runaway monarch. During the tumultuous years of Mosaddeq's premiership leading up to 1953, Golestan was hired as a photographer by a number of leading news organizations, including the BBC and ABC. Through some high-level connections he had in his family, Golestan was able to shoot some newsreels during Prime Minister Mosaddeq's parliamentary speeches, which he then sold to the BBC and other news organizations. After the coup, he took advantage of the nationalization of the oil industry that had been brought about by Mosaddeq and quit his job in the public-relations office of the National Iranian Oil Company (NIOC), while soliciting its help to establish his own film production company in 1956. When an American documentary filmmaker named Alan Pendry was dispatched by Shell Oil Company to help make films for the newly established Oil Consortium, he collaborated with Golestan on a number of documentary projects.

This period of Golestan's career as a photographer and filmmaker is the crust of much controversy in contemporary Iranian intellectual history. His detractors point out his rather lucrative, if not shady, business connections to the NIOC, the British and US news organizations, and above all to major oil companies, and thus implicate him in the propaganda machinery of the Pahlavi monarchy—all leading to discredit his progressive politics when he was a member of the Tudeh Party. How could someone exhibit his pictures at the Soviet embassy, sell them to the British with the help of major oil companies, while at the service of major news organizations? Needless to say, Golestan was a very shrewd man who made a very good living from his profitable arrangements with the NIOC and other oil companies—all at a time when the overwhelming majority of Iranian public intellectuals lived in very dire circumstances. But, at the same time, Golestan was instrumental in helping an array of important public intellectuals. From very early in his creative career, Golestan was far more an institution unto himself than a mere literary or artistic figure. From Forugh Farrokhzad to Mehdi Akhavan Sales to Sohrab Sepehri—just to name the most prominent among them—there is a long list of important literary and artistic figures who directly benefited from Golestan's attention. Golestan helped not only financially, which was of course most immediately important to them, but he also provided his vast erudition and an unflinching critical disposition that challenged hardest the people he loved most. His financial well-being and critical faculties gave him an air of overbearing arrogance. But much of that was in fact exaggerated by a deep resentment on the part of his literary rivals and intellectual inferiors. Altogether, it was not a very healthy environment in which Golestan and his friends and foes worked and produced. The publication of Farrokhzad's masterpiece, *Another Birth* (dedicated to EG, Golestan's initials) in 1964 and the stamp of approval it put on the public rumors that she—the most illustrious contemporary woman poet—was Golestan's lover did not particularly help to diminish the tension.

Golestan stirred all these conflicting emotions but continued to work with a relentlessness and ambition unparalleled in his generation. His second collection of stories, *Shekar-e Sayeh* (*Hunting Shadow*), appeared in 1955. With the publication of this book, Golestan joined the ranks of Hedayat and Sadeq Chubak as the three most prominent writers of their time. Chubak had published his *Kheymeh Shab Bazi* (*Puppeteering*) in 1945 and *Antari keh Lutiyash Mordeh Bud* (*The Baboon Whose Master Had Died*) in 1949. Hedayat had committed suicide in 1951 having solidly established his literary supremacy. Both Bozorg Alavi and Jalal Al-e Ahmad were by now equally recognized names. But these latter two owed much of their literary fame to their political activism. They richly deserved their reputation as progressive activists but poorly compared with their literary superiors. The publication of Alavi's *Chashm-ha-yash* (*Her Eyes*, 1952) and Al-e Ahmad's *Modir-e Madreseh* (*The School Principal*, 1958) put forward no solid evidence to alter the fact that these two writers were of course admirable public intellectuals fighting for the cause of democracy in their homeland but were very modest subjects when they crossed the border into the merciless aristocracy of literary imagination.

Soon after the publication of his second collection of stories, Golestan shifted gear and established his movie studio, Golestan Films, in 1956. *A Fire* (1958) was among his first productions. The film was directed by Golestan, shot by his younger brother, Shahrokh Golestan, edited by Forugh Farrokhzad, with sound design by Mahmoud Hangaval and Samad Pourkamali. It was the first Iranian film to receive a major prize in an international film festival.

By the late 1950s, Golestan had solidly established himself as a major literary voice with momentous poetic vision. The style he had carefully cultivated in his literary works—two impressive collections of short stories—was now fully at his disposal to transform a simple documentary about a runaway fire in an oilfield into a work of art. From this moment forward, the direct transformation of commissioned documentary to a work of art becomes the defining occasion of Golestan's aesthetic—navigating the creative distance between factual evidence and its affective sublimation. The lyrical diction of Golestan's voice-over in *A Fire* is strategically located somewhere between the poise of its contemplative nature and the pose of its poetic performance. On the surface, Golestan's poetic voice seems jarring when narrated over a documentary about a fire in an oilfield. But Golestan's aesthetics ultimately find their enduring articulation precisely in this pretentious casuistry—in the deliberate theatricality (bone-deep affectedness) of his highly stylized prose. Nobody before or after Golestan dared to go public with such stylized affectation, cultivating it to perfection, to the level of an exhibitionist art form. The origin of this was in Golestan's prose narratives and novellas, but now they were successfully transferred as sound effects to his films. Golestan's voice-overs, composed and narrated by himself, are thus far better heard as sound designs than as simple narrative aids.

The following decade saw the most productive and ambitious unfolding of Golestan's literary and cinematic projects. Throughout the 1960s, Golestan made one documentary masterpiece after another, without any pause in even more spectacular literary achievements. In 1961 he and Alan Pendry made *Moj-o-Marjan-o-Khara* (*The Tide, the Coral, and the Granite*) about the construction of a pipeline from the Aghajari oilfields to the industrial piers on the island of Khark. Rarely, if ever, has the fate of colonialism in this region been so immediately linked to an occasion in the rise of literary and artistic modernism. The bizarre and amusing fact is that Golestan made his financial fortune and produced some of the most brilliant artifacts of Iranian artistic modernity while fully at the service of oil companies that were robbing his homeland blind. From its lyrical title to its last beautiful frame, *The Tide, the Coral, and the Granite* is a poetic joy to watch and to listen to—and yet at what national cost and to what colonial purpose? It is a sad and paradoxical fact that Golestan and the rise of artistic modernity in Iran were among the principal beneficiaries of the CIA-sponsored coup that thwarted the cause of democracy and brought monarchy back to Iran. Golestan would have become an equally great filmmaker if there had been a socialist revolution in Iran, but as it happened he became a great filmmaker after a CIA-engineered coup returned a despot to power.

Golestan's typically lyrical prose is on full display in *The Tide, the Coral, and the Granite*, its contemplative gaze mingling with a highly stylized narrative pose. If the digging of oilfields and the construction of pipelines can be so astonishingly aestheticized, then how could there be anything wrong, socially or politically, with them? *The Tide, the Coral, and the Granite* soars into a cinematic deliberation on science and technology, precisely at a moment when Golestan is manufacturing one of the most compellingly exhibitionist records of modern Persian prose. There is no escaping the fact that Golestan's *The Tide, the Coral, and the Granite* is an effective over-aestheticization and simultaneous de-politicization of the neocolonial robbery of Iranian oil by a corrupt monarchy and a conglomerate of transnational oil companies. But at the same time, there is no escaping the equally important fact that the visual vocabulary of Iranian cinema and the poetic disposition of Golestan's prose are blossoming like beautiful water lilies on the surface of this very dirty swamp. This paradoxical phenomenon is endemic to the politics of Iranian poetics.

The same poetic scientism that Golestan applies to *The Tide, the Coral, and the Granite* is extended to his narrative contribution to Forugh Farrokhzad's 1962 masterpiece, *The House Is Black*, where he extols the glories and promises of science in curing an infectious disease. *The House Is Black* was commissioned by yet another governmental agency—certainly not as lucrative as the National Iranian Oil Company, but still resourceful enough to commission a film for its bureaucratic purposes. Golestan's commissioned documentaries reveal a critical truth about the predicament of Iranian intellectuals of the 1960s and 1970s. Bereft of an autonomous source of income, they were particularly vulnerable to centers of power, the reigning monarchy in particular. Public intellectuals like Golestan had to negotiate a perilous passage between creative expression and critical judgment on one side and financial security and social autonomy on the other. Golestan's is a typical case of what the Marxist theorist Antonio Gramsci called the inorganic intellectual—a rootless member of the literati who is neither loyal to his own bourgeois origins nor committed beyond an ideological predisposition to the working class. But the inorganicity of such intellectuals does not mean that they were publicly useless. It is precisely, in fact, in their inorganicity that they generate an intellectual environment where enduring historical changes are effected. In the case of Golestan in particular we are much better off working our way beyond the specifics of his finances to understand his aesthetic outlook. That he made a lucrative living by accepting money from the Pahlavi government, and at least on the surface lent his camera to the propaganda machinery of the reigning monarchy, should not stand in the way of seeing that he remains one of the greatest and most consequential figures in modern Iranian intellectual, literary, and artistic history.

One of the peculiar features of the inorganic intellectual is an affinity for metaphor and allegory. By transforming social realities into poetic parables they sustain the illusion that they have in fact launched a political struggle. This is principally the reason why Golestan's influence on *The House Is Black* has been instrumental in creating a weak political reading of that film as a metaphor of the nation at large, rather than allowing its own dark vision—contemplating the long shadows of a colonially mediated modernity—to come true. In Golestan's own documentaries, this tendency toward aesthetic metaphor was sometimes highly effective and resulted in brilliant works of art. In 1963, for example, Golestan made *Tappeh-ha-ye Marlik* (*Marlik Hills*), a documentary about archeological excavations in northern Iran, which won him yet another award at the Venice Film Festival. *Marlik Hills* is along the same lines as Golestan's previous documentaries—a highly stylized narrative superimposed on archeological excavations documenting Iranian ancient history. Prominent professors of archeology and ancient history at Tehran University objected to *Marlik Hills*, because they believed its poetic narrative was inappropriate for the visual evidence the film showed. They believed that archeology as a science, and by extension the delicate remnants of a distant past it investigates, must be respected in its own disciplinary way. In an essay he published in *Keyhan International* in 1964, Golestan responded that he had no intention of making a documentary to aid such academic exercises in futility—that instead he had created a work of art according to his own aesthetic sensibilities. *Marlik Hills*—which in fact is a narrative reflection on the nature of death, dying, and decay—is highly effective in appropriating archeological artifacts for a poetic rather than a political or historical purpose. Archeological excavations during this period were instrumental to the Pahlavi dynasty's construction of a long history of monarchy in the Iranian plateau, a project in which Orientalist and Iranian archeologists partook in equal measures. Golestan's vision of the archeological site is in fact a perfect antidote to that exercise in political archeology. Golestan further frustrated the Pahlavis with yet another documentary, *Kharman* (*The Crop*, 1967), which he again premiered at the Venice Film Festival, much to the chagrin of the Iranian embassy in Italy.

By far the most spectacular cinematic achievement of Golestan in this and all subsequent decades is his undisputed masterpiece, *Khesht-o-Ayeneh* (*Mud Brick and Mirror*, 1965). Golestan began shooting this film in the spring of 1963 and filming was interrupted by two crucial incidents: A very expensive lens in his camera fell and broke while shooting the courthouse scene; and Ayatollah Khomeini led his first, aborted attempt at toppling the Pahlavi monarchy in June of the same year. So while Golestan was waiting for a replacement of this expensive lens to arrive from Paris, Ayatollah Khomeini was busy trying to dismantle the Iranian monarchy. The irony is so thick you can carve a perfect picture of the instrumental futility of a work of art in it—for which reason it is all the more enduring, for precisely in that futility dwells the opening vistas otherwise blinded by revolutionary politics. Never in contemporary Iranian history had art and politics come so close in mirroring—reversing, not just reflecting—each other, and in the dialectics of that mirroring spell out the terms of our emancipation.

By the time Nima Yushij, the founding father of modern Persian poetry, died in 1960, the poetic revolution in Persian prosody was solidly on record and squarely at the service of a progressive politics. But a year after Nima's death, Ayatollah Boroujerdi died in Qom, thus vacating the senior-most post in the Iranian Shia establishment. Into this vacuum stepped Khomeini, launching his revolutionary career. A year after that, the most prominent public intellectual of the time, Jalal Al-e Ahmad, published his *Gharbzadegi* (*Westoxication*, 1962) and drastically influenced his contemporary political culture in favor of a nativist (Islamist) ideology.

It was soon after the publication of *Westoxication* and as Golestan was momentarily interrupted in his shooting of *Mud Brick and Mirror* that Khomeini launched his revolutionary uprising of June 1963. Golestan was still in production when Forugh Farrokhzad published her masterpiece, *Another Birth*, in 1964. Two years after that, the publication of Sadeq Chubak's (Golestan's close friend) *Sang-e Sabur* (*The Patient Stone*) in 1966 was one of the greatest literary achievements of the time. A year later Farrokhzad was killed in an automobile accident, plunging Golestan into what his relations report as a deep depression. Before the decade came to an end, Khomeini was safely silenced in exile in Najaf, Al-e Ahmad died of a heart attack, Simin Daneshvar published *Savushun*, Houshang Golshiri published his masterpiece, *Prince Ehtejab*, and Dariush Mehrjui made his groundbreaking film *Cow*, all in the same momentous year of 1969.

Golestan's output during the 1960s was prolific despite these tumultuous years. He made an incomplete film called *Chera Darya Tufani Shod* (*Why Did the Sea Become Stormy?* 1966); a documentary called *Ganjineh-ha-ye Gohar* (*Treasure Houses*, 1966), on the royal jewelry collection; wrote his third collection of short stories, *Juy-o-Divar-o-Teshneh* (*The Brook, the Wall, and the Thirsty*, 1967); a polemical essay on poetics in 1968; his fourth collection of short stories, *Madd-o-Meh* (*The Tide and the*

Fog, 1969); and a public speech at Shiraz University. I would like to bring to your attention this rather rare speech, which is an important window into Golestan's critical faculties, as an example of what happens to the best of our public intellectuals when they abandon the hope that germinates in the *poetics* of their imagination and fall prey to the *politics* of their theoretical limitations.

Delivered in February 1970, nearly eight years after the publication of Al-e Ahmad's polemic *Westoxication*, Golestan's speech at Shiraz University is a thinly disguised refutation of Al-e Ahmad's seminal text. If *Westoxication* is a prime example of Europhobia, Golestan's speech, "A Few Words with the Students of Shiraz University," is an exemplary case of Europhilia. Between Al-e Ahmad and Golestan and their blindfolded acceptance of the unexamined centrality of "the West" they both managed to sustain generations of misguided readings of their time and place in history.

For better or worse, Al-e Ahmad's *Westoxication* had emerged as the defining sentiment of Iranian political culture in the tumultuous decade of the 1960s. In one way or another, intellectuals thought they needed to respond to Al-e Ahmad's argument against what he considered the predominant malady of his age. The June 1963 uprising of Ayatollah Khomeini, which Al-e Ahmad wholeheartedly supported, seemed to have corroborated his thesis of a self-alienated society in dire need of a cure in its own local medicine. But the massive popularity of Al-e Ahmad and his *Westoxication* had generated a deep sense of resentment among his peers. In his speech at Shiraz University in 1970, Golestan was typically condescending in his language, and—without naming Al-e Ahmad—took *Westoxication* to task, attributing its popularity to the stupidity of its audience. But if in his *Westoxication* Al-e Ahmad had criticized his compatriots for a blind aping of "Western culture," in his speech Golestan took the superiority of "the West" for granted and blamed Iranians for not having caught up with its achievements. (Both of them failed to question the very categorical construction of "the West" as one of the most calamitous inventions of colonial modernity.) With all his legitimate claims to a progressive politics (and if we were to bracket his astonishing achievements in his film and fiction), Golestan would today find himself in the illustrious company of such nightmares as Fouad Ajami, Bernard Lewis, Francis Fukuyama, and Samuel Huntington!

Although Golestan's speech lacks the coherence of Al-e Ahmad's treatise, it flaunts a far deeper familiarity with European cultural history, while putting on display an equally impressive awareness of Islamic intellectual history—a combination rather rare among his peers. But all his erudition notwithstanding, his historical grasp of what he calls "the West" is as deeply flawed as Al-e Ahmad's. The students at Shiraz

University had asked Golestan to talk about his films and stories. He began by insulting all the students (after insulting his host for having introduced him with customary compliments and pleasantries) and told them that they didn't know anything about anything, and that they had not read anything—especially his work. He went on to explain what he believed had happened in modern fiction, and that in order to do so it was necessary to understand what had happened in the world since the European Renaissance. Here he made a leap from literary modernity to Renaissance humanism, which he collapsed into Enlightenment modernity, without noting either their thematic succession or the historical distance between these ideas and movements—let alone in any way questioning the global validity of such self-serving European periodization. With that one swift backhand he dismissed all the intellectual events and merits of the Islamic world simultaneously with the European Renaissance as outdated and irrelevant; and then without naming Al-e Ahmad, who had died from a massive heart attack a few months before, Golestan proceeded with a scathing attack against *Westoxication*.

Golestan's principal argument against Al-e Ahmad's *Westoxication*, which he began to articulate before offering his own perspective, is that it betrayed a misplaced anger and a shifting of responsibility. Golestan argued that Iranians (and he does not place us within any other collectivity such as Muslims or Asians) had fallen behind the caravan of Reason and Progress (of which he had entirely ahistorical, generic, and metaphysical notions), that we made no contribution to their creation in modernity, that we had an auxiliary and parasitical connection to modernity, that because we did not know "the West" we were afraid of and hostile to it—thus positing himself in the unique place of knowing what "the West" is. Lacking the critical faculty of understanding the West, Golestan asserted, Iranians had responded to it instinctively—and that's why, he said then, when one of us writes something so instinctive and hostile to the West as *Westoxication*, it is so easily accepted and celebrated by the rest of us. In fact, he claimed that the reason that a book like *Westoxication* was so popular—though remember he does not as much as deign to name it—is precisely because it is so off the mark (*part* in Persian, or "off," is Golestan's favorite word). We are wasting our time being angry with the West, he argued, and reveal our imbecilities that made us fall behind in the first place, instead of getting to know its glory and joining it.

Upon this premise he proceeded to enlighten his humbled, bewildered, and perhaps even bemused students, who had clearly been wasting their time getting an academic degree in one thing or another—something that Golestan himself never condescended to do. What was his earth-shattering revelation at the end of all this preparatory fanfare? A solidly pedantic, high-school-textbook version of the rise of the Renaissance, but with such affected and condescending diction that you have to have a box of coated aspirin next to you to read through it. Golestan is not the only Iranian public intellectual who abused his status as a brilliant novelist and filmmaker to pontificate about issues above his intellectual capacity. Before him Sadeq Hedayat did the same with his racist writings about "the Arabs"; and after him Ahmad Shamlu did the same when he began a round of pronouncements about Ferdowsi. It is a peculiar fact of our cultural history that our best poets, novelists, and filmmakers are our worst public intellectuals! Go figure.

Golestan's sophomoric take on the Renaissance does not have a critical bone in it. He takes a facile European historical periodization—ancient, medieval, Renaissance, and Enlightenment—entirely at face value, and has no alternative conceptions of his own regional histories or a historical imagination that might generate differing ideas of cultural categories around the Mediterranean basin or any other geographical locations. He refers to Beyhaqi because he wrote beautiful prose; Ibn Khaldun's name is also dropped with no serious attention to his philosophy of history. Instead, Golestan chose to parrot European history textbooks for his bewildered audience at Shiraz University, beginning with the Greek glory of its origins, following the aggrandizing narrative down into its medieval abyss, and up again when the Italian Renaissance came to the rescue and saved humanity. Not a single reference to even the primary sources of such tales—let alone a mustard seed of critical doubt in this fat Italian hoagie he was wrapping around the Mediterranean basin. From Hegel to Ranke, but especially with Franz Kügler and Jacob Burckhardt, generations of German idealists have been at the philosophical roots of such self-serving European tales—and they have long since been discredited by serious and critical scholarship. Today we can pinpoint the specific texts and authors chiefly responsible for the invention of the Middle Ages, the fabrication of European Renaissance, the systematic exclusion of southern, eastern, and western Mediterranean sites from the European tale of the sudden "Italian genius" that gave rise to the Renaissance. "Europe" itself is the greatest invention of modernity—an invention Golestan had no critical imagination to fathom. He bragged about everything, including his personal visits to the tourist attractions of Tuscany, to the poor Shirazi students—everything except a singularly important place in Italy, one that no official tour takes you to visit: the Laurenziana Library, where scientific texts in Arabic, Hebrew, Persian, and Sanskrit speak of a conception of human destiny vastly different from, and far more multifaceted than, the one found in Western European and North American textbooks or in this shallow speech Golestan delivered in Shiraz. The Laurenziana Library is the physical evidence that the rise of the Renaissance in Italy connects the Mediterranean rim to an entirely different conception of world history than a tired and old cliché narrated along an East-West axis, a fact documented in detail by scholars like George Makdisi and George Saliba—names and scholarship light years away from the story that Golestan was telling his audience.

Golestan admonished his generation of intellectuals for not knowing the masters of Islamic philosophy like Ruzbehan Baqli and Mulla Sadra Shirazi, for having had to wait for Henri Corbin (the mystic-minded French Orientalist who distorted the history of Islamic philosophy to match his own post-Heideggerian disillusions) to reintroduce them to Iranians. This he takes as the sign of the superiority of the French— never mind the fact that Corbin owed much of his understanding and appreciation of Islamic philosophy to Seyyed Jalal al-Din Ashtiyani, the most perceptive Iranian historian of Islamic philosophy alive at that time. Golestan, oblivious to these details, was deeply angry with Sadeq Hedayat for having ridiculed Corbin and lauds the French mystic for having been referenced by Carl Gustav Jung—yet another mystic-minded European psychoanalyst. But Mulla Sadra Shirazi and Ruzbehan Baqli were well known and discussed by generations of their students and followers long before Corbin lent his mystical twist to them. If Golestan and his peers did not know them, it was their fault—their fault and the fault of the Pahlavi educational system that, at the service of the same colonial modernity Golestan glorifies, aggressively de-Islamicized Iranian intellectual history. Corbin, as Hedayat knew intuitively or with a superior knowledge of French, or both, did nothing but add a phantasmagoric neo-mystical twist to the writings of these giants of Islamic intellectual history while translating them into French, for those who could not or did not read them in the original Arabic and Persian. If Golestan's generation knew a little French better than they had a decent grasp of Arabic, whose fault was it? Was that the fault of a backward Islamic intellectual history? The catastrophe of those decades was not just the tyranny of the Pahlavis but that it forced Iran's greatest poets, novelists, and filmmakers to make such public fools out of themselves.

Golestan had begun his talk by trying to give an account of literary modernity in order to place the literary movement he best represented in some sort of context. And yet he proceeded to give an account of the Renaissance origins of the Enlightenment and concluded by providing a world history of the last five hundred years in very general and generic strokes. He is occasionally insightful, at times even astute, but quintessentially Eurocentric and teleological in his historiography—ultimately putting his bet on Renaissance humanism as the highest achievement of European history. He spends an inordinate amount of time praising the glories of the Italian Renaissance and its humanist achievements in

painting and politics, with a few occasional references to the Persian poet
Sa'di for his similarly humanist ideals a couple hundred years before the
Italian Renaissance. He then expands the Italian Renaissance to the rest
of Europe, weds it to the Reformation, leads it all the way to the discovery of the Americas and its aggressive Christianization, and finally
rests his case with modernity. Yes, he admits, it does have certain faults,
but those faults should not be exaggerated. "The West of science and
progress," he admonishes, "should not be dismissed because of 'the West
of corruption and greed.'" He comes down strongly on the side of science and progress, which he posits against retardation and the empty
celebration of the past. But it never seems to cross Golestan's mind that
what he calls Reason and Progress and their reverses, or mirror image,
corruption and decay, are integral components of an epistemic invention
of power and knowledge that benefited very few and disenfranchised the
rest of the globe.

Golestan's lack of a critical conception of world history didn't allow
him a view of the Renaissance as a historiographical invention, by German art historians in general, and Jacob Burckhardt, with his seminal
study *The Civilization of the Renaissance in Italy*, in particular—though
the term "Renaissance" in this sense was invented by the French art historian Jules Michelet around 1855–58. Moreover, Golestan missed the
point that this historiography was inextricably implicated in a politics
of power: the invention of Europe as the single most haunting apparition in modern history. In Golestan you will look in vain for a moment
of pause questioning the meta-narratives of Reason and Progress, their
Enlightenment invention in asylum houses, as Michel Foucault had discovered and persuasively argued in his *Histoire de la folie à l'âge classique*
(published in 1961, a decade before Golestan delivered this speech), and
the catastrophic colonial consequences of European modernity the world
over. In his book, Foucault had systematically documented the narrative
and institutional construction of reason by systematically incarcerating
its Other, un-reason, in European asylum houses. Golestan is a Euro-
philiac humanist par excellence, precisely in the same way that Al-e
Ahmad was a Europhobe. Both of them in effect corroborate a figment
of historiographical imagination that invented and benefited very few
national identities and massively disenfranchised the rest of the world,
both of them discursively trapping an entire nation in a nexus of false
consciousness that blinded the emergence of alternative insights, both
of them ideologically paving the way for an inevitable Islamicization of
the revolution about to happen in less than a decade after this speech
and the pamphlet it sought to rebuke. For Golestan there is nothing
fundamentally wrong or at fault with the Enlightenment—his knowledge of European intellectual history having stopped short of the gate

of post-Holocaust angst that had at a massive level created intellectual movements in existentialism and phenomenology long before the cul-de-sac of postmodernism. Of all of these developments, at the time he was delivering this sermon in Shiraz, Golestan was blissfully ignorant.

For Golestan, Iranians were at fault for not having had a share in the formation of Renaissance and Enlightenment. The principal root of Golestan's myopic vision is that he was entirely fixated on Iran as the *locus operandi* of his observations. Not even other Muslims, let alone Orientalized non-Europeans—Asians, Africans, Latin Americans—ever enter his analytical grid. So for him the problem is not that a mode of capitalist modernity has robbed the overwhelming majority of the world population blind to over-feed a tiny minority of it. The crucial question for Golestan was why *Iranians* did not do it. Where did we go wrong and what did we do to have fallen behind the European plundering of the world? That a global mechanism whose modernity is an essential part of the operation of its capital, and the operation of its capital fundamental to its modernity, and finally that both formed the *conditio sine qua non* of the colonization of the non-European planet along with the European working class—this the great Golestan could not see.

Nearly two centuries into the colonial savaging of his own homeland, Golestan lacked the perspective to see the similar colonial situations in the larger context of Asia, Africa, and Latin America—from which point of view he might have seen the problem endemic to capitalist modernity in a different light than posing the rather bizarre question of why the Europeans did it first. Golestan's concern was lashing out against Iranians—a captive audience best represented in the closed doors of that lecture hall at Shiraz University in February 1970—for having failed to lead the world in this catastrophe. All his reading of modern history seemed geared toward a local reconfiguration of power and wealth; who benefited from this kind of modernity and who did not did not matter to him. As late as the early 1970s, nearly three decades after the Holocaust (which nearly decimated the European Jewry), after the good and great Europeans, at the apex of world civilization, had murdered millions of human beings in gas chambers, Golestan had still not heard of Adorno or Horkheimer, or their *Dialectic of Enlightenment*, or the whole philosophical outcry that was fomenting against Enlightenment modernity. Instead, he was very much delighted to have defied Hedayat and discovered Corbin via a reference by Jung. If Golestan was the best we had to offer in terms of our critical historical acumen, no wonder our entire nation turned to Ayatollah Khomeini when push came to shove.

Golestan's reading of history failed to see the politics of power that sustains the myth of "the West versus the rest." If Al-e Ahmad has blamed the victimizer and criticized the victim, Golestan blames the victim and is utterly enamored by the scientific and artistic achievements of the victimizer. He very simply blamed Iranians for having fallen behind what he considers modern civilization. (Years later, Dariush Shayegan, a kindred spirit of Golestan would reiterate this same inanity and propose that Iranians were on vacation from history when "the West" was making all this progress.) For Golestan, there is nothing wrong with this mad instrumentality of reason and the mutation of humanity to machinery (so long as an Italian tourist-information-office version of Renaissance humanism is there to sugarcoat it). The only problem for Golestan is why Iranians—another, older branch of the Aryan race (if you pardon my German)—were beaten to it by our European brethren.

Keep this simple truth always in mind: We know and discover through our prejudices and not despite them. There is always a blindness built into any insight. The scientific and artistic achievements of Europe and the terror that it has perpetrated on itself and the rest of the world are part and parcel of the same episteme. There is a direct link between all the magnificent medical discoveries of the nineteenth and twentieth century and the German gas chambers that sent millions of European Jews to their deaths. It all stems from an instrumentalized reason. Theodor Adorno and Max Horkheimer, in the late 1940s, Martin Heidegger in the 1950s, Michel Foucault in the 1960s and after, and many more unnamed here, the most towering intellectual figures of Europe, discovered and described this fact. Golestan, with all his pomp and ceremony and it's-a-small-world-after-all tourist guidebook of the Italian Renaissance, stood there ignorant of an entire gamut of critical thinking that radically reconfigured the very notion of "Europe."

The sad part is that an end to the Renaissance and the demise of blind faith in Enlightenment reason need not have waited for the advent of what here in my neighborhood they call postmodernism. There were plenty of signs pointing in that direction for Golestan to see. Even if Golestan had not been privy to the revelations of Adorno, Horkheimer, Heidegger, or Foucault, had he not seen the films of Stanley Kubrick either? How did Amir Naderi, with not a penny to his name, make it all the way from Tehran to London for the premiere of Kubrick's *2001: A Space Odyssey* (1968), and Golestan, with all his lucrative business deals, not see that movie and learn from it? In the late 1960s, *2001: A Space Odyssey* had abruptly revised the standing cinematic cosmovision. Captain Bowman and his stoic posturing stood for the post-Renaissance man at large, and his suppliant "Open the pod-bay doors, HAL" only underlined the sinister monstrosity of the machine he and the rest of us dreaded. The silence at the center of Kubrick's masterpiece is part of the film's contemplative mood. The script that he cowrote with Arthur C. Clarke is ingeniously sparse, allowing for an eerie sense of quiet that is carefully built into the sound design—and is as instrumental to its architectonics as Aram Khachaturian's *Ballet Suite*, György Ligeti's *Atmospheres*, Johann Strauss' *The Blue Danube*, or Richard Strauss' *Thus Spoke Zarathustra*, the music that Kubrick had carefully selected for his masterpiece. Geoffrey Unsworth's groundbreaking shots suggest a spatial reconception of the post-Renaissance man and the universe he inhabits—and then he yields those transfigurative shots obediently to Ray Lovejoy's ingenious editing to make *2001: A Space Odyssey* the terror of mid-twentieth-century disillusion, not just with the menace of the machine but with the major blind spots of the Enlightenment. And I find it prophetic that one of the best Iranian filmmakers of our time, Amir Naderi, got himself from Tehran to London for the world premier of this film, and that Golestan, who was infinitely more capable of seeing the movie and heeding its visionary warning, proceeded with an outdated and outlandish celebration of Renaissance humanism—as if nothing had happened before or since the Holocaust and the vicious systematicity with which European Renaissance men sent their fellow human beings in droves to gas chambers.

This detour into Golestan's non-literary and non-cinematic work—his politics, essentially—is to alert you that if today we are standing on our two feet and have a claim to a legitimate "I" it is entirely because of the creative defiance of our critical predicament. This is what I mean when I say Iran has great poets and terrible intellectuals. In Golestan's case too we have to abandon his critical writings altogether because they are entirely useless and symptomatic of the illiteracy of his age. We must instead pay closer attention to what he did best—his film and fiction—because there and then an entirely different creature gets hold of the man. To be sure, Golestan did not stop writing critical treatises. In 1972 he wrote an essay on painting, and sat for a long and entirely useless conversation about his fiction, which he subsequently published in 1998; in 1974 there was another essay on cinema; a few years before the Islamic revolution he made a major feature film, *Asrar-e Ganji-e Darreh-ye Jenni* (*The Secrets of the Treasure at Ghost Valley*, 1974); and years after the revolution he also published a new short story, "Khorus" ("Rooster," 1995), the introduction to which says it was written in 1970. There are of course sparks of the early Golestan evident in these later works, but by and large the magic and grace of his creative pen and camera seem to have left him by now. I followed his writings for years after the revolution to see if in the aging wisdom of his retirement in England he had something serious to say. Alas, nothing of the sort materialized. Sometimes I wish he had the wisdom of the old Shia clerics who had the perspicacity to know, when they had run out of fresh ideas, to kiss their pen and never write anything again. How wise and how precious is the moment when you know when to kiss your pen and never to touch it again!

All his useless critical writing and subsequent journalistic forays aside, Golestan stands today as one of the most significant literary voices of his generation and a founding figure of Iranian cinema. Most literary historians reserve their accolades for Sadeq Hedayat and read Golestan as subsidiary to him. However, I would not hesitate to say that in my judgment Ebrahim Golestan is a figure in modern Persian fiction superior to Hedayat—and I will explain why in a moment. I will also add to that the seminal significance of Golestan as a filmmaker. Subtract Golestan from the history of Iranian cinema and something crucial is missing. Forugh Farrokhzad and Ebrahim Golestan are the missing links, as I told you before, that connect the modern Persian poetry and fiction of the 1960s with the rise of Iranian cinema in earnest in the 1970s.

No other Iranian filmmaker after Farrokhzad and Golestan has had a claim both as a major literary figure and as a seminal filmmaker. The generation of Iranian filmmakers that came after them—Dariush Mehrjui, Arby Ovanessian, Sohrab Shahid Sales, and Bahman Farmanara—were not literary figures at all, and thus their cinematic careers were entirely contingent on the major literary figures they personally befriended and visually translated. Farrokhzad and Golestan are the only founding figures of Iranian cinema who had established a lasting literary significance long before and after they paid simultaneous attention to cinema. If there is something very specific about Iranian cinematic realism that is not entirely reducible to European neorealisms, then it will have to be detected in the specific modes of realism that emerged between the Iranian literary and visual arts. Farrokhzad's *poetic* realism will have to be linked to Golestan's *affective* realism before we can move to other styles of Iranian realism, to see in what particular terms Iranian cinema formulated its visual language. Forget all the useless gossip about the love affair between Farrokhzad and Golestan. From the creative conversation of their respective films, fiction, and poetry was born the rest of Iranian cinema. You are their offspring.

Just a few sentences back I made a claim that may have perked the ears of all Iranian literary historians (the Orientalists don't count). I said I believe Golestan is a major literary figure. I also said that the term that best describes Golestan's film and fiction is *affective* realism. Let me now connect these two claims, and add to them an even more unsettling claim: that despite being their junior, Golestan, and not Sadeq Hedayat or Mohammad Ali Jamalzadeh, is the founding father of modern Persian fiction. Now, if you were to read a couple of Golestan's stories, you will find that before you *understand* anything you will first *feel* as if you are surreptitiously peeping at the private collection of a very rich but rather obnoxious person who has invited you to his home (or rather mansion) but does not have the common courtesy to offer you a proper place to sit, a glass of water to drink, a cup of tea perhaps, or to tell you where the washroom is—expecting you to divine all these things by yourself, waiting for you to make a mistake so he can catch it and admonish you. Take "Azar, the Last Month of Autumn," for example, a story that Golestan wrote in 1947. It is an absolute gem of a psychological thriller—but it is also a perfect example of what I mean by his fiction being disinviting. As you begin to read this short story—I am not even sure if *story* is the right word here—you feel that you are not welcome, that you have trespassed into the privacy of some already-in-progress event. You feel you are eavesdropping or peeping into someone's private thoughts. There is something unusually closed, claustrophobic even, about Golestan's stories. They don't read like stories—they unravel more like jigsaw puzzles that some very smart fellow seems to have devised to tease you, bother you, harass and test your intelligence. This uneasiness of Golestan's stories reaches a point when, a page or two into them, you want quietly to collect your bewilderment, whisper an apology, and tiptoe to the exit without disturbing the peace (or add to the troubles) of the narrator, who does not seem to care one way or another whether you stay and listen to what he has to say or pack up your wits and leave.

Now suppose you tough it out and persist through that rather uncomfortable feeling and read further into "Azar, the Last Month of Autumn." You suddenly find yourself in the midst of the troubled consciousness of a deeply distressed man, full of regret, remorse, and anxiety, reminiscing—as he does—about something or another you have absolutely no clue about. Then he seems to have something of a flashback and gives you the bare minimum of a storyline overburdened with his own sense of anxiety, troubled all because he was about to undertake some sort of illegal or political activity. Someone rings the bell of the narrator's house in a coded manner; the narrator is frightened out of his wits. Soon we find him driving somewhere to do something—it really does not matter what or where, because paramount in the pages you are reading is an almost paralyzing sensation of the terror of being caught. Everything about the story as it begins is vague, unsure, mysterious—and before you know it the narrator's paranoia starts to seep into you. Eventually you may think that the narrator is supposed to pick up someone and help him or her to get out of wherever it is they were—some sort of escape from the authorities or people in positions of power. But again all such thoughts fade in the presence of the overwhelming sensation that you are in the company of a man who is exceedingly, obsessively, self-indulgingly—to the point of paralysis—cautious, frightened, panicky, and unnerved.

Now, by the time you finish the story and realize that the narrator is actually meeting with the family of a political activist who is on the run and whose name is Ahmad, and that the narrator is picking up some of Ahmad's belongings from his mother, brother, wife, and kid, the entire event seems to you rather blasé. Ahmad is a political activist; the police are chasing after him; his friends—probably members of a political organization—are helping him escape; and the narrator is collecting his personal belongings from his family. That's all. That's all except the initial sensations of fear, anxiety, and remorse that the narrator transmitted to you like a virus, which at last narrows in on a paper bag full of nuts that Ahmad's mother had at the very last minute given to the narrator to give to her son. The narrator does not do so because one of his friends—seeing that the cheap bag is made of the used paper on which school children write their homework—made fun of the paper bag, so the narrator decides on his own not to give it to Ahmad for fear of shaming him in front of his friends. The police subsequently kill Ahmad and the narrator is left morally paralyzed—circling around Ferdowsi's statue in the middle of a square in downtown Tehran, contemplating the nature of life and death. The fetishized paper bag emerges as the principal object of anxiety around which the entire story is narrated in a suspended spiral of terror and regret.

What Golestan's stories are about is thus entirely tangential to the range of feelings—sensations, suggestions, psychological outpourings—that they occasion and sustain. It is the aesthetic consequence of that purely constructed emotive universe that you have to grasp in order to see how absolutely crucial Golestan's film and fiction have been in our contemporary visual and literary arts. You have to understand this about Golestan not despite his affected disposition but through it. That he is an all-round estranged and rather apocryphal curiosity is not accidental to his art, but essential to it. It defines his affected posing, his ostentatious casuistry. We have no one—absolutely no one—in the entire gamut of Iranian modern literary and cinematic culture who can fake that honesty so ingeniously. In his character and in his culture, in his films and in his fiction, Golestan is stylized affectation incarnate, foppish exhibitionism personified. Precisely in the realistically stylized histrionics of that androgynous aesthetic, the film and fiction of Golestan is the cornerstone of modern Iranian visual and literary arts. *Performance*: It is the quintessence of the dust that makes the clay from which any work of art is made—and Golestan's prose is the epitome of performance. His words and their musical tonalities are the instruments, and he the composer, the performer, the conductor. There is something of Andy Warhol in Golestan, and of Truman Capote, in character, culture, diction, and disposition. Place that suggestion in the varied homoerotic context of Iranian culture and you get a glimpse of what I have in mind.

Now the reason that I suggest Golestan is a superior artist to Hedayat is this: While Hedayat's fiction is a sustained record of realism—from which then grew his one surreal outburst in *The Blind Owl*—Golestan's *affective* realism is far more evenly distributed and far more tightly controlled throughout his films and fiction. To be sure, Hedayat's *The Blind Owl* remains the undisputed masterpiece of modern Persian fiction. No other work of literary art—even Hedayat's kindred soul Houshang Golshiri with his absolute best in *Prince Ehtejab*—comes close to *The Blind Owl* in its pure literary purgation and visionary catharsis. But put *The Blind Owl* aside and Hedayat becomes an ordinarily gifted, occasionally brilliant, but altogether understandable literary paragon. Golestan, though, is a far superior artist in the sheer self-assuredness of his literary prowess and control of his prosodic medium. In anyone else's hands, this pure stylistic affectation would seem supercilious, but Golestan masters it with perfect pitch. Golestan turns his prose into a melodic mannerism unparalleled in our literary history since his fellow Shirazi poet, Shaykh Muslih al-Din Sa'di (1184–1291).

Golestan's realistic mannerism has its roots in his fiction—or what he himself referred to as his *qesseh* ("story," in Arabic) or *dastan* ("story," in Persian). I propose that Golestan's theory of modern Persian fiction, or at least his practice of it, was no mere adaptation of the European novel; it has its origin in the aesthetics and narrative parameters of the Persian poetic tradition. In my judgment this makes Golestan the real founding father of modern Persian fiction—not Hedayat or Jamalzadeh, who were both heavily influenced by their contemporary European literature. This is not to say that Golestan was not influenced by an array of European and American writers—he was, probably Proust and Hemingway chief among them. But Golestan's fiction is almost entirely his, and, as he once said in an interview, he read so vastly and simultaneously that he cannot tell which Russian, Western European, or North American writer had a more immediate influence on him.

Golestan, I believe, detected in Persian literary traditions certain premodern narrative devices that he used for his own purposes. Perhaps the most significant such narrative device is the mimetic specificity of Persian poetics, which he reconfigured into his prose with astonishing grace and unsurpassed craftsmanship. Let me explain what exactly this mimetic specificity, or spontaneous mimesis, as we may also call it, is.

In the course of an interview, Golestan once observed something quite important. He said that he turned to writing fiction soon after he became disappointed with political journalism. He had been working for the official organ of the Tudeh Party, *Beh Su-ye Ayandeh* (*Toward the Future*), and in fact at some point he was its editor in chief. But after

1946, he became totally disillusioned with the party and began writing works of fiction.

Golestan's turn from political pamphleteering to literature has both historical roots and critical consequences that we need to consider carefully. And it has nothing to do with the false notion that "all Third World literature is an allegory of nationalism," as Fredric Jameson once said. No: The political predisposition of Iranian literature does not turn the entire creative oeuvre of a nation into an allegorical version of nationalism or any other ideology. Rather, it makes the Iranian manner of literary mimesis radically different from the European rendition of its Aristotelian version. Take, for instance, the *Taziyeh* passion play—a perfect example of the Persian aesthetic and narrative form—in which reality, or the look of it, can be made and unmade at the drop of a hat. Add that to the *political embeddedness* of Iranian aesthetics and you will get closer to the roots of the modes of Iranian realism, cinema in particular. Let me explain this point in more detail.

Critics of Iranian cinema have shown a tendency to ignore its particular mode of mimesis. They have simply labeled it "Iranian neorealism," as the result of an unconscious conception of Aristotelian mimesis, and have not considered the possibility that they might be looking at Iranian cinema through a distorting set of lenses. The mode of mimesis specific to Iranian aesthetics is somewhat different from Aristotelian mimesis, which takes reality as a *constant* and then holds all its mimetic mutations (representations) in works of art as *variable*—and as a result can sustain an almost exclusively *icastic* mode of mimesis, where there is a one-to-one correspondence between an aspect of reality and the representation of that aspect in art. But in the Persian poetic tradition, there are—as systematically theorized by one of its most perceptive observers, Khwajah Nasir al-Din al-Tusi (1201–74) in his *Asas al-Iqtibas* (*The Foundation of Logical Learning*, composed in 1244)—two modes of mimesis, one *icastic* and the other *phantastic*, with metamorphic influence of both on each other. Icastic mimesis (or what al-Tusi called *Muhakah*) is the imitation of something that actually exists; while phantastic mimesis (what al-Tusi called *Takhyil*) has no such limitation to things that actually exist. When you put icastic and phantastic modes of mimesis together you have a suppler and more agile counterpoint between reality and its mimetic representations—because the porous borders between fact and fantasy begin to infiltrate and infuse each other. Years ago I called the result of this cross-mutation between fact and fantasy *factasy*—to suggest its both factual and fantastic dimensions—without providing this detail. But in discussing Golestan's *affective* realism and its predicate in spontaneous (unstable, momentary, disposable) mimesis I have to do so—especially because other people have started using this term without knowing how

I came up with it! My suggestion here is that the double-edged sword of icastic (Muhakah) and phantastic (Takhyil) mimesis in Persian aesthetics gives the character of our literary, visual, and performative representations an altogether different quality than a mimetic tradition that gives primacy to one and ignores the other.

The best place to see this dual mimesis in operation is in a Taziyeh performance, because this passion play is formally and stylistically the dramatic embodiment of this particular mimetic feature. The mise en scène, narrative conventions, performance techniques, staging, costume design, sound effects, dramaturgical tensions, musical accompaniment, and audience participation in Taziyeh are mimetic modes both icastic and phantastic—without the two being (except at an analytical level) overtly identifiable. The dialectic result of these two conflating modes of mimesis is a kind of realism that usually baffles an audience that is conditioned to Aristotelian mimesis. This does not mean that the Iranian artists are consciously aware of it. One of my saddest (and yet most amusing) recent memories was after the premiere of Abbas Kiarostami's *Taste of Cherry* in New York, when someone in the audience asked him if his last shot of the film, where we see him and his actor and camera crew wrapping up the film, is a case of Brechtian distancing—to which he (alas!) readily agreed. However, the dramatic tradition much closer to Kiarostami's birth and breeding needs no Brechtian *Verfremdung* (estrangement or alienation) to distance the audience from the event. Taziyeh sustains the richest and most varied modes of such distancing by always reminding its audience that they are just watching a play, a re-enactment, a make-believe representation of something they are otherwise doctrinally prohibited from showing. At the end of *Taste of Cherry*, Kiarostami and his crew are doing nothing other than what Taziyeh directors and actors do regularly—suspending their spontaneous mimesis of faking the truth.

The presence in the Persian poetic tradition of the icastic and phantastic modes of mimesis becomes even more intriguing when you place this tradition in the context of, or make it the context for, the territorial disembodiment of the Iranian imagination under colonial modernity. What I mean by territorial disembodiment is a sense of material alienation, of emotive anomie predicated on an assumption of losing control over one's own destiny, that is coterminous with a colonial domination that is aterritorial—a form of colonialism rather specific to Iran, which was not completely colonized like India by the British or Algeria by the French, where you have an actual territorial conquest and physical presence by colonial powers. Aterritorial conquest, through the political and military influence of the British and the Russians in the nineteenth century, and subsequently the US and the Soviet Union in the twentieth, along with the rapid globalization of capital, had the social and psychological effect of breaking down the historical confidence and institutional veracity of the Iranian creative consciousness. The result is a manner of mimesis that has a far more supple correspondence with reality and thus its representations operate on a much wider plane of suppositional simulacra. The literary consequence of this Iranian configuration of colonial modernity is aided and abetted by local premodern modes of icastic and phantastic mimesis to generate an impromptu and extemporaneous form of imitation that is not structurally or logically wedded to any particular law of representation. As a result a mode of realism emerges that is improvisatory, created on the spur of the moment, made to suit the occasion, and once used effectively no more metaphysical significance is attributed to it.

To understand what Ebrahim Golestan achieved through his particular poetics, all you have to do is to look at the preceding decades of Iranian literature and consider what was happening before he appeared. If we were to trace what Edward Said calls the worldly character of a work of art, namely its location in its immediate material history, in what Golestan did best in his writing, before he turned to cinema, we would eventually arrive at the origin of modern Persian fiction in the mid-nineteenth century. From its very inception, modern Persian fiction has been political, inaugurated by progressive activists who simply used prose to articulate their ideological convictions. Mirza Fath Ali Akhondzadeh's *Setaregan Faribkhordeh: Hekayat-e Yusef Shah* (*The Misdirected Stars: The Story of Yusef Shah*, 1874) is usually considered the first novel written by an Iranian. Akhondzadeh was a prominent public intellectual in the late nineteenth century and was instrumental in the intellectual foment leading up to the Constitutional Revolution of 1906–11. Using the historical context of the Safavid period, in the sixteenth century, Akhondzadeh portrayed his contemporary reality. The same goes for Zeyn al-Abedin Maraghei's *Seyahat-namah-ye Ebrahim Beik, ya Bala-ye Tassob-e Ou* (*The Travelogue of Ebrahim Beik, or, the Calamities of His Prejudice*, 1895), which was also a pioneering project in critical social realism. It narrates the story of an Iranian merchant who has been away from his homeland for many years and returns to find it in ruins. In the book, Maraghei wages a scathing attack on the medieval tyranny of the Qajar dynasty. It is almost impossible at some points in Maraghei's narrative to discern whether it is a simple critical discourse or a work of fiction—or both at once.

What we witness in these early examples of modern Persian fiction is first and foremost a systematic corrosion—a kind of historical amnesia—of Iranian premodern poetics. The narrative strategies of master prose stylists like Sa'di or Naser Khosrow are absent. By that I don't mean that writers like Akhondzadeh or Maraghei didn't know about Sa'di or Naser Khosrow, which, of course, they did. But the references they made to their literary predecessors were merely anecdotal, without any critical attention to or creative adaptation of their narrative devices or literary tropes. This is not to say that new and innovative forms are not employed. Consider for example the fact that just prior to the Constitutional Revolution of 1906–11, in *Masalek al-Mohsenin* (*The Path of the Righteous*, 1904), Abdol-rahim Talebof joins the ranks of his fellow revolutionary novelists and tells the story of a geographical expedition to the Alborz Mountains. In his book Talebof fashions a new literary ploy, a pseudo-scientific narrative, to condemn the colonial presence of the British in that region. The rule of law and an eradication of absolutism are the desired ideals that Talebof propounds in this novel. Mirza Habib Isfahani's translation of James Mor-rier's *The Adventures of Haji Baba of Isfahan* in 1905 was also an extremely important intellectual development during this period. While Morrier's original reads like a typical late-nineteenth-century Orientalist tract, at turns infantilizing and demonizing the natives, Mirza Habib Isfahani's translation of the same text—which, incidentally, was instrumental in the simplification of Persian prose and the free and creative introduction of popular terms and expressions into acceptable literary language—turns it into a scathing criticism of the social malaise he squarely identifies with tyranny. I have always been astonished to see how an author, a language, and an audience can so radically change a text. Ali Akbar Dehkhoda's *Charand-o-Parand* (*Gibberish*, beginning in 1907) was another extraordi-narily important series of satirical social critiques that contributed greatly to make the Persian language a medium of creative correspondence with the urgent issues of contemporary society. Dehkhoda was a leading politi-cal activist of his time, and he combined the scholasticism of a meticulous encyclopedist and the felicity of a satirist. He was chiefly responsibly for editing a voluminous encyclopedia of Persian language and an equally impressive multivolume series on Iranian folklore.

This period in the rise of modern Persian fiction reveals not only a systematic forgetting of premodern poetics but also an increasing aware-ness of the political predicament, in this case a revolutionary uprising against colonialism and its local agents. During the first two decades of the twentieth century we witness the emergence in Iranian literature of the first generation of historical novels, in such works as Sheykh Musa Kabudar Ahangi Khosravi's *Eshq va Saltanat: Fotuhat-e Kurosh-e Kabir* (*Love and Monarchy: The Conquests of Cyrus the Great*, 1918), Mirza Hasan Badi's *Dastan-e Bastan: Sargozasht-e Kurosh* (*The Ancient Tale: The Story of Cyrus*, 1920), Sanati-Zadeh Kermani's *Damgostaran: Enteqam-khahan-e Mazdak* (*The Deceivers: The Avengers of Mazdak*, 1920–25), as well as his *Dastan-e Mani-ye Naqqash* (*The Story of Mani the Painter*, 1926). Heydar

Ali Kamali's *Mazalem-e Tarkan Khatun* (*The Injustices of Tarkan Khatun*, 1928) dealt with heroic events during the reign of King Anushirvan of the Sasanian dynasty. Mohammad Hossein Roknzadeh Adamiyyat's *Deliran-e Tangestani* (*The Brave Men of Tangestan*, 1931), Rahimzadeh Safavi's *Nader Shah* (1931), Zeyn al-Abedin Motamen's *Ashianeh-ye Oqab* (*The Nest of the Eagle*, 1939), and Sh. Partov's *Pahlavan-e Zand* (*The Hero of Zand*, 1933) all had one historical figure or another fictionalized as a champion of Iranian patriotism.

The defining characteristic of these historical novels is their misplaced politics—the outlandish aggrandizement of the Iranian past and the glorification of the Persian monarch as the perennial champion of Iranian nationalism. The birth of the concept of Iran as a nation-state was the principal product of the constitutional period. Having received the idea of nationalism through the filter of colonialism, the emerging Iranian literati imagined a narrative in which pre-Islamic Iranian history could be glorified, ennobled, exaggerated, and celebrated. As a result of these stories, the emerging Iranian bourgeoisie, with characteristic self-regard, assumed the role of heir to a presumably glorious past. But the collective efforts of European Orientalists were crucial in the construction of this ancient history and the making of Iranian nationalism. Predicated on earlier sentiments that go back to the Arab conquest of Iran in the seventh century, a strong anti-Arab sentiment also emerged and became characteristic of this genre. The historical novel, which remained popular through the 1920s and 1930s, also announced the rise of a style in Persian fiction that was oblivious to any of the premodern poetics or aesthetic sensibilities in Persian tradition and yet was deeply embedded in the political fate of the nascent Iranian nation-state, whether in progressive or retrograde politics. As works of art, these early attempts at writing fiction are entirely negligible, but they are the archival evidence of the decline of classical aesthetics and the rise of a politically charged body of literature.

This methodical obtuseness of Iran's early modern literature gradually transformed from a historical or social realism to a kind of social romanticism. The ultimate failure of the Constitutional Revolution and its attendant hopes at the beginning of the century finally had repercussions in the literature of the late 1930s and early 1940s. Much hope and a long list of aspirations were invested in the Constitutional Revolution. But about a decade after the success of the revolution in curtailing an absolutist monarchy and imposing constitutional limitations on its whimsical behavior, the specter of an absolutist autocracy of a different sort, in the shape of Reza Shah, cast its long shadow over the country. The result was almost immediately evident in the literature of the period. Lurid depictions of drug addiction and prostitution and fatalistic portrayals of a generation of hopeless youth characterize the novels of this period, perhaps best represented by Moshfeq Kazemi's *Tehran-e Makhuf* (*The Frightful Tehran*, 1925). Kazemi quickly inspired a whole cadre of imitators, including Abbas Khalili, who penned *Ruzegar-e Siah* (*The Dark Days*, 1924), Yahya Dowlatabadi, who wrote *Shahrnaz* (1925), and Moti al-Doleh Hejazi, with *Ziba* (1933). But the two most prominent writers of this period are Said Naficy, who wrote *Farangis* in 1931, and Ali Dashti, whose *Fetneh* appeared in 1943. Importantly, novelists of this period turned from historical themes to contemporary concerns, dealing with the modern condition and its manifestation in the emergent urban culture, including the darker side of social change, being undertaken by Reza Shah's "progressive" policies. Works like Mohammad Masud's *Tafrihat-e Shab* (*The Nocturnal Entertainment*, 1932) and *Dar Talash-e Mo'ash* (*Making a Living*, 1933) were harsh in their social criticism but lacking in social or psychological depth. And despite the fact that Hejazi, Naficy, and Dashti did manage to polish Persian prose and even gave it a contemporary texture and character, there was still no sign of any aesthetic awareness or sensitivity to the form and style of a literary work of art.

By far the most significant literary event of the 1920s was the publication of Mohammad Ali Jamalzadeh's *Yeki Bud, Yeki Nabud* (*Once upon a Time*, 1921), which is universally recognized as the groundbreaking event in Persian fiction. Jamalzadeh's prose opted for a simplified diction that took full advantage of similar efforts before it, a lucid command of the creative possibilities of the Persian language, and a remarkable awareness of the variety of social types that inhabited the Iran of his age. *Once upon a Time* was first published in Berlin, and because Jamalzadeh had spent much of his youth in Europe his fiction was consciously, deliberately, maybe even mechanically, modeled on the European novel—and thus entirely alienated from the narrative possibilities and aesthetic character of the domestic Persian literary tradition.

The same is true of Sadeq Hedayat's first collection of short stories, *Buried Alive* (1930). Hedayat was another intellectual whose sensibilities owed much to European and American influences. His command of a polished and robust Persian prose, and the justified success and evident brilliance of *The Blind Owl* (1937), have blinded critical attention to the fact that Hedayat developed his literary universe directly from European models with scarcely any organic link to what was narratively and stylistically possible to Persian prose on its own terms.

With Jamalzadeh and Hedayat both writing in Persian from a decidedly European frame of literary reference, Golestan's work distinguished itself as the only pioneering writing in modern Persian fiction that, while fully conversant with European and American literature

(Hemingway in particular), was equally attentive to classical Persian prose narratives. Golestan systematically worked at a refined and spontaneous literary mimesis that was squarely rooted in the icastic and phantastic antecedents in premodern Persian poetics, and successfully wedded it to the territorial disembodiment of Iran's colonial encounter with modernity. He then narratively crafted in his short stories a style at once conversant with premodern aesthetics and yet responsive to contemporary conditions. Whereas Jamalzadeh and Hedayat's fictions are European narratives speaking fluent Persian, Golestan's fiction exhibits a narrative development through centuries of Persian prose (Sa'di and Naser Khosrow in particular), while being equally conscious of the offerings of world literature. When you read Jamalzadeh and Hedayat you are mesmerized by the fluency of their Persian prose and thus become oblivious to their narrative importations. When you read Golestan, the first thing you notice is the primacy of the Persian prose—whatever else happens in the story is tangential to that experience. As if this mimetic mutation of our classic poetics into a contemporary narrative event was not in and of itself a literary feat of exceptional significance, Golestan gave to the literary mimesis he had rediscovered from Persian poetics his own inimitable realism—an affective realism that became definitive to the rest of our literary and visual arts.

What is the result of Golestan's advancement of classical Persian prosody? In the first place, Golestan's writing seems deliberately modulated for a particular sound effect—engineered and manufactured as a filmmaker does his sound design. There is a distinctly formal composition about his prose, coaxed, it seems, to generate a melodic tonality—meant more to be recited than just read in order for its sound effect and musical quality to register. Golestan stretched the truth when in the course of an interview with an anonymous interlocutor he claimed that he does not believe in a melodic prose, and that the musicality of his prose comes from the harmonious properties of the words themselves. Of course words have melodic tonality in and of themselves—just like musical notes do. But there is a difference between the effect that Mozart had when he composed them and when Antonio Salieri did. The same musical notes produce similar sounds but vastly different music.

There is, though, an element of truth in Golestan's assertion that the musicality of his writing comes from the sounds of the words themselves. This idea he borrowed from Nima Yushij, the founding father of modern Persian poetry, who also believed that in abandoning the pre-formulated rhythms in classical Persian prosody he was in effect restoring to words what he called *musiqi-ye tabii-ye kalam*, or "the natural musicality of speech." Golestan had a similar ambition for Persian prose: to detect the innate musicality of words and to allow them to compose melodic registers independent of classical Persian *saj'* (metric prose)—which was itself predicated on Arabic *saj'*—which in turn traced its origins to the melodic structure of the language in the Qur'an. And that, in my judgment, is the reason why Golestan alone among his secular intellectual peers knew the Qur'an and Sa'di so well. As much as he was attracted to Hemingway and his highly stylized prose, Golestan seems far more familiar with Nima's poetic revolution, seeking to replicate it in the realm of Persian prose. For that reason, I would propose that Golestan's revolution in Persian prose, in dialectical conversation with the rhythmic traditions in classical Persian or Arabic prose, is as significant and consequential as Nima's in poetry, who too took the classical Persian and Arabic prosody to task in order to craft a new poetics.

The musical effect of Golestan's writing, as a result, is that it gradually turns into a pronounced affectation in his manner of storytelling. You sit down to read a story and suddenly you notice that your reading pace has slowed and your utterance of the words become discernibly melodic. The rhythm is perfectly audible, pronounced, orchestrated. Golestan's writing is thus effective through its affectation, and affective sensation soon takes over the story's narrative teleology. It does not really matter, it seems, where the story is going, because you have been totally distracted by the stylized syncopation of the prose. But that distraction is precisely the attraction of the story. No one before, after, or other than Golestan in contemporary Persian prose ever dared to make a public spectacle of it—and stage it so effortlessly, gracefully, with panache, poise, confidence, and complete dramatic composure.

Golestan's detractors have criticized him precisely for what I am now praising him—that his prose fashions such an elaborate affectation that it becomes overbearingly artificial and, in turn, feigns a kind of mannerism. But my contention here is that the texture of this mannerism, crafted in order to impress itself upon a literary tradition, amounts to an affected prose that in its evocative vocality becomes consequential for what has happened in Iranian film and fiction. The emotive universe that this affective realism generates and sustains in Golestan's prose is precisely what also becomes paramount in his highly influential cinema. At its best, Golestan's prose risks histrionic insincerity to achieve dramatic self-consciousness, attempts staged superficiality to experiment with a studied mannerism. Golestan's critics see his prose as pretentious, stagy, and unnatural—but precisely in those ostentatious signs and suggestions his writing achieves the simulated power of its mannered speech, the imitative ingenuity of its living language. The performative quality of Golestan's prose is intimately related to the phantastic manner of mimesis that is part of our classical poetics—a creative will to make abrupt, unexpected, or exaggerated formal overtures. This creative tapping into the hidden mimetic powers of (Persian) language gives Golestan's prose, and later his cinema, a freedom of performative exploration.

Golestan's affective realism succeeds in sublimating the factual evidence of his stories into an entire emotive universe. From a simple narrative, which is at once reflective and probing, introverted but insinuating, emerges a poetic performance that is deliberately conscious of itself. The result is a staged casuistry—pretentious, ostentatious, performative, over-acting in the best and most necessarily flamboyant (even frivolous) sense of the terms—a breath of fresh air in an otherwise deeply repressed literary culture. It is the theatricality of Golestan's prose that angers and frustrates his detractors, but I argue that it is, in fact, the defining aspect of his transcendent performance style—what modern Persian prose most needed and yet sorely lacked. Golestan's narrative affectation exuded an effeminized exhibitionism that deeply disturbed his masculinist culture. That coquettish flamboyance is not in the substance of Golestan's fiction—it could be argued there is no substance there—but in the manner of his delivery—and everything in Golestan's fiction is its manner. Without that mannerism we would have had no such thing as Iranian cinema.

Two complementary trends come together from opposite directions to make possible Golestan's mannerist prose: It is histrionically unreal and realistically stylized. As soon as you begin to notice the mannered poise of Golestan's prose and pause to register its histrionic irreality, surreptitiously a realistic element becomes evident in it that checks its affectation and gives it a worldly sense of proportion; and right before that realism can take over and plunge the prose into social realism you realize that it too is highly stylized—and thus affective realism is the best term that I can think of to describe Golestan's artistic universe. In the short story I just relayed to you, Golestan's narrative commences the story of the man about to help out with a political activist in hiding. Soon the realistic element of the man's family in despair and fear sets in and engages the histrionic irreality of the narration. But as soon as one is tempted to take that realism seriously, it too becomes integral to the stylized prose: The result is an affective realism that teases out of reality its "otherwise than itself."

It took me much more time to get to Golestan's film *Mud Brick and Mirror* than I would have liked. But I had no choice because there is nothing either in Persian or in any other language on Golestan that I could have recommended to you. Be that as it may, I hope by now you have a better grasp of Golestan's fiction, from which we can also take a look at his cinematic masterpiece.

The names of two people are almost interchangeable in the early history of Iranian cinema: Farrokh Ghaffari and Ebrahim Golestan. The difference between the two of them made all the difference in their lasting influence on the rest of Iranian cinema. Ghaffari was French-educated and deeply steeped in European film traditions. Golestan on the contrary was mostly an autodidact in matters of cinema but at the time of his first feature film a towering figure in contemporary Persian literature. One could easily consider Ghaffari's *South of the City* (1957) or his *Night of the Hunchback* (1964) among the masterpieces of early Iranian cinema. But Golestan's *Mud Brick and Mirror* has a more legitimate claim to that status by virtue of his deeply cultivated literary aesthetics, transformed for a visual medium. Ghaffari's long and impressionable years in France made him a stranger in his own homeland. He was far more at home in Paris than in Tehran. Not Golestan. He was one of the most influential members of the post-World War II literati. His initial affiliation and subsequent break with the Tudeh Party had placed him smack in the middle of the rising generation of literary intellectuals defining the aesthetic and political future of their nation. He was not half as visually perceptive as Ghaffari, but twice as literate and confident in his bearing in and about the lay of his homeland.

Mud Brick and Mirror was rather sudden in its appearance and had an enduring effect on the emergence of Iranian cinema. Golestan had come to make *Mud Brick and Mirror* after an impressive career as a major voice in modern Persian letters, as well as a successful career as a documentary filmmaker. Some historians of Iranian cinema go so far as considering Golestan as "the spiritual father of Iranian cinema." If by extension and with perfect justification we were to consider Farrokhzad "the spiritual mother of Iranian cinema," then the otherwise illicit love affair between Golestan and Farrokhzad has certainly had an auspicious set of legitimate offspring—generations of prodigious filmmakers all conceived, born, and bred out of wedlock, out of the banned or forbidden fantasies of a nation.

Mud Brick and Mirror was produced at a particularly poignant moment in the history of Iranian cinema. After decades of commercial and melodramatic filmmaking, something serious was bound to happen, and Golestan was steadfast in seeing that it did. But first *Mud Brick and Mirror* was a box-office fiasco, a critical failure, and a victim of paralyzing official censorship. Politically, the timing of *Mud Brick and Mirror* could not have been worse. Though it wasn't released until 1965, it was shot during the June 1963 uprising led by Ayatollah Khomeini against Mohammad Reza Shah. Though the uprising was brutally suppressed, at the time government officials were in no mood for what they considered to be the dark and critical atmosphere of Golestan's first feature film.

Socially, its release coincided with that of the most popular melodramatic film in the history of Iranian cinema, Siyamak Yasami's *Qarun's Treasure* (1965). While Golestan's *Mud Brick and Mirror* was stumbling at the box office, Yasami's *Qarun's Treasure* was breaking every record on the books. *Mud Brick and Mirror*, however, had been categorized as an intellectual film that was too arcane for even public intellectuals to grasp. But that was simply because Golestan's film was too new for the Iranian public, which was used to films like Yasami's, to understand. There was as yet no language, no diction, no visual memory or aesthetic parameter with which to understand Golestan's valiant effort to transform the Persian literary tradition and imagination into a contemporary visual art.

The story of *Mud Brick and Mirror* is simple enough. Hashem (Zakariya Hashemi) is a cab driver who finds an infant child in the back seat of his cab one night after he gives a ride to a young woman. The rest of the film follows Hashem and his girlfriend, Taji (Taji Ahmadi), as they try to cope with this unwanted child. Hashem insists on getting rid of the child, Taji on keeping him. At the end of the film, Hashem gets rid of both.

At first glance, the film, as everything else about Golestan's work, looks concocted, artificial, out of place, with its various narrative elements and sequences not quite coming together. But from very realistic circumstances—of someone abandoning a child in a cab and the driver finding it—*Mud Brick and Mirror* begins to add a surreal dimension to cinematic narrative, at a time almost simultaneous with Federico Fellini's groundbreaking *8 1/2* (1963). In Golestan's case, a dream narrative does not take over the realism, but rather an atmospheric sublimation of reality itself gradually emerges.

The central characters of the film, Hashem and Taji, or indeed the dilemma they seem to face, are entirely believable. But what we see in *Mud Brick and Mirror* is not an illusive take-over of the *real* but a narrative excursion into a *surreal* dimension. The abandoning of a child in a car or at a street corner was something rather common for people in a condition of destitution. A quarrelsome relationship between a couple was equally ordinary. It is more in the mutation of this ordinariness into a simulacrum of urban anomie that defines Golestan's vision. His highly stylized camera movements, transitions, acting directions, sound design, and even overbearing dialogue all transform his otherwise ostentatious casuistry into an affective realism, at once histrionically unreal and yet realistically stylized.

In an interview Golestan once said that in his version of realism it was the "evident appearance of reality" that had to be carefully observed by a filmmaker. In the same interview, he gave an astonishingly perceptive account of his particular brand of realism:

You ought to see this film like a prism. A prism can have
some seven or eight parallelographic sides. If you were
to look at it from just one side you would only see that
one side. But if you were to turn it around, you would
see that it has another side, and then if you turned it yet
again, you would see yet another side. If you get away
from it, you will see that its parallelographic sides will
form a volume, and if you were to turn it around very
fast, according to the famous experiment of Newton,
all the colors will come together and form white. I
have made the entire film on this principle. You should
not consider any one of these parallelographic sides
independent of each other. They all ought to be seen
simultaneously, as they are set next to each other, so
that the voluminous feel of the whole film is grasped.

The metaphor of a prism is fundamental to Golestan's *Mud Brick and
Mirror*, as it is to all of his other works, because the primary property of
a prism is its refracting and bending of rays and waves of light as they
pass obliquely through its alternating density. In and through his affective realism Golestan teases out the otherwise than the real of reality—its
performative theatricality, to be precise, where one can see through the
fabricated foibles of power and the parabolics of mocking it.

The portrayal of the relationship between Hashem and Taji is by
far the most successful such depiction in the Iranian cinema of the time.
Hashem is obnoxious and overbearing. Taji is, by and large, accommodating, and yet persistent. What is important in the depiction of this
relationship is that Golestan creates it as he proceeds. There is no repertoire of such a relationship, at once realistic and yet suggestive of an
emotive universe beyond the visible, in Iranian cinema at the time for
him to explore. Golestan is exquisite in his depiction of interiors, particularly his sequence of the lovemaking scene between Hashem and
Taji, which is erotically suggestive while remaining confined within the
censorial limitations of the time. His camera movement in the orphan-
age sequence is equally confident and fluent—competently conveying
the sense of bureaucratic formality and emotive vacuity of the space.
But by far the most enduring cinematic aspect of *Mud Brick and Mirror*
is Golestan's extraordinary competence in shooting on location, something quite rare that early in Iranian cinema. This was not without its
contingent hazards. In the course of shooting the courthouse scene, an
expensive lens in Golestan's camera fell and broke. He had to wait for
months before he could secure another lens from Europe. Meanwhile,

the season had changed from winter to summer and people had started wearing light clothes, which had in turn created a headache for filming. Be that as it may, Golestan's sense of the city, of traffic in particular, is exceedingly alert and realistic. Not until the appearance of Amir Naderi almost a decade later does another Iranian filmmaker come so successfully close to a sense of a crowded urbanity as Golestan does in *Mud Brick and Mirror*.

Forugh Farrokhzad had produced *The House Is Black* in Golestan's studio and with his direct collaboration, and her film presaged the ascendancy of filmmaking in Iran. Golestan's *Mud Brick and Mirror* elevated that expectation one notch on a higher register. Golestan is an atmospheric storyteller and his cinema is equally atmospheric. His stories, both in his fiction and in his films, are entirely tangential to the psychological mood that he generates. In an interview he once said he had to choose and measure the length of the streets he shot (as the background of his protagonists), the street traffic, and the conversation between the couple in a way that would be compatible with the rhythm of their dialogue and the length of their exchange. The result is an astoundingly atmospheric depiction of the city of Tehran in the early 1960s.

All its realism notwithstanding, Golestan's *Mud Brick and Mirror* still exudes his narrative affectedness. Acting is performative, dialogues are exaggerated, the camera-work pronounced, shots accented, framing picturesque, sequences quite articulate in their choreography. Golestan's sense of sound design is equally performative—from the radio station that plays in Hashem's car to the street noise that we hear on an adjacent track. The result of this performative virtuosity is that *Mud Brick and Mirror* pushed the technical virtuosity of Iranian cinema decades into its future, and furthered that burgeoning experiments of Iranian cinema with a new and unique form of realism.

...No, you unnatural hags,
I will have such revenges on you both
That all the world shall—I will do such things—
What they are, yet I know not; but they shall be
the terrors of the earth....
—William Shakespeare, *King Lear*

Dariush Mehrjui
The Cow

I AM BACK IN NEW YORK with the end of summer looming large and no sense of having done anything worth telling you about. I tried to work on that book on Iranian cinema a bit but I was distracted by the thought of Stanley Kubrick and baffled by his attraction to *Spartacus* in 1960 and *Barry Lyndon* in 1975.

Why in the world would he abandon his own creative autonomy and give himself up to two powerful storytellers like Howard Fast and William Thackeray? Even if one were to dismiss *Spartacus* as the work of a young and ambitious filmmaker who at the time couldn't refuse a multimillion-dollar project (Kubrick did effectively disown the film later in his life), still the mystery of *Barry Lyndon* remains, no matter how astonishing its cinematography (for which Kubrick practically had special lenses invented). The case of *Spartacus*, however, is far worse. Fast's narrative takes complete creative control, and Kubrick's presence swiftly disappears into thin air, as if the film is directing itself. *Spartacus* in effect becomes a showcase for Kirk Douglas in the lead role. It seems now like sheer madness for Kubrick to have walked into that trap. Douglas was in complete control of the film, the story of which was based on Fast's own compelling account of the uprising of slaves against their Roman captors. Douglas fired the director he had initially hired, Anthony Mann (*El Cid*), after a couple of days of shooting because he disagreed with Douglas' vision of the film. In turn he hired Kubrick, who had directed him three years earlier in *Paths of Glory* (1957), yet another film from Bryna Productions, the company that Douglas had established. Presumably Kubrick did not have a creative conflict with the lead actor and executive producer—which is exactly the thing that seems baffling (though rumors are that they did have conflicts and that Kubrick soon bought himself out of a contract with Douglas' production company for three additional films he had sold himself out to make).

The more we learn about *Spartacus* the more Kubrick's involvement with it becomes puzzling. Ordinarily, Kubrick was very finicky about his scripts. But in this case, Douglas had hired one of the greatest scriptwriters around, Dalton Trumbo, who had been blacklisted in Hollywood for refusing to testify in front of the infamous House Un-American Activities Committee. This was a courageous act on the part of Douglas, but it gave more creative control to someone other than Kubrick. Mechanical as Kubrick's role seems to have been in making *Spartacus*, he could not have been entirely inconsequential in crafting the two lead characters of Spartacus (Kirk Douglas) and General Marcus Crassus (Laurence Olivier), and two of the film's famous sequences—the "oysters and snails" scene between Marcus Crassus and his slave boy Antoninus (Tony Curtis), and Spartacus' exceptionally homoerotic mercy killing of the same Antoninus—which clearly display Kubrick's creative investment in the project (though the "oysters and snails" scene was cut from the original release and was not restored until 1992, by Robert Harris and James Katz).

My point is that Kubrick at least twice in his long and illustrious career forfeited his creative autonomy to a writer (not to speak of a megalomaniacal actor) and they are his most forgettable films—which reminds me of a very peculiar development in Iranian cinema shortly after Forugh Farrokhzad and Ebrahim Golestan laid its first two cornerstones. Farrokhzad was a renowned poet and Golestan an accomplished short-story writer before they became pioneering figures in Iranian cinema. But the generation of Iranian filmmakers that came after Farrokhzad and Golestan was one of necessary collaboration—the pairing of prominent and established members of the literati with novice filmmakers. The best example of this kind of partnership was the one that developed between Dariush Mehrjui and Gholamhossein Saedi. Mehrjui became a prominent filmmaker by attaching himself to Saedi. Kubrick's accidental work on Howard Fast's fiction momentarily diminished him as a filmmaker.

But Mehrjui's prolonged relationship with Saedi generated and sustained his significance as a director.

Dariush Mehrjui's *Gav* (*Cow*, 1969) represents the first collaboration between the young and ambitious filmmaker and the renowned dramatist. By the time Mehrjui joined forces with him, Saedi had already established himself as the undisputed master of modern Iranian *psychedelic* realism. Following Farrokhzad's *poetic* and Golestan's *affective* modes of realism, Saedi's particular manner of realism was anchored in an almost clinical psychopathology of the uncanny, and his perceptive articulation of psychosis (neurotic anxiety, to be exact) in his fiction was utterly unprecedented in Persian literature. Saedi's psychedelic realism, through its evocation of the supra-normal and the creative use of superstition, hallucination, and delusions, effected an acute intensification of a literary awareness of reality, combined with a sensory perception of the uncanny. Mehrjui's filmic adaptation of Saedi's psychedelic realism soon added a whole new dimension to what Farrokhzad and Golestan had achieved with their particular poetic and affective renditions of Iranian realism. But when considered together, and added to other modes and variations in style and delivery, we can cautiously develop a more specific understanding of realism and its significance in Iranian cinema. But no rush—all in good time, and all in proper measures!

Dariush Mehrjui was born in 1940 in Iran, and after his early upbringing and education he left for the United States, where he attended college at the University of California, Los Angeles, studying film, although he graduated with a degree in philosophy. Mehrjui returned to Iran in 1965 and began his long and extraordinarily productive career with a bizarre spoof called *Diamond 33* (1965), a frivolous adaptation of the James Bond films—a rather inauspicious beginning for an otherwise seminal figure in Iranian cinema. While in Los Angeles, Mehrjui had become interested in Gholamhossein Saedi's dramatic works, and soon after the fiasco of *Diamond 33* he approached Saedi and the two of them began collaborating on the screen adaptation of one of his short stories—"The Cow"—which became by far the most significant achievement of Iranian cinema after the pioneering works of Farrokhzad and Golestan, before the sudden rise of a new generation of visionary filmmakers in the 1980s.

Throughout his career, Mehrjui's most successful films have been adaptations of works of fiction that were not his own. *The Cow* of course was based on a story from Saedi's collection of short stories *The Mourners of Bayal* (1964). Mehrjui's second successful film, *Mr. Simpleton* (1970), was based on Ali Nassirian's play, while *Postman* (1971) reworked Georg Büchner's *Woyzeck*, the German dramatist's fragmented masterpiece that was found in his drawer after his premature death at the age of twenty-four in 1836. *The Cycle* (1978), Mehrjui's last film before the 1979 Islamic revolution, brought him back to Saedi and an adaptation of his short story "Garbage Dump," from the collection *The Grave and the Cradle* (1977). His first film after the Islamic revolution, *The Backyard of Afagh School* (1980), was based on a story by Fereydun Dustdar. He adapted Saul Bellow's novel *Herzog* (1964) in *Hamun* (1990), and in *Banu* (1992) he made an Iranian version of Luis Buñuel's *Viridiana* (1961). *Sara* (1994) was based on Henrik Ibsen's *A Doll's House* (1879), and for *Pari* (1995) J. D. Salinger threatened to take Mehrjui to court for having adapted his *Franny and Zooey* without permission. Most recently, Mehrjui's *The Pear Tree* (1998) was based on Goli Taraqi's novel. He has used the work of less prominent authors for his other films, and whenever he has experimented with scripts of his own, as in *Mix* (2000), *The Lost Cousin* (2000), and *Bemani* (2002), he has been least successful.

Saedi was Mehrjui's literary alter ego. Saedi (who published his work under the pen name Gohar Morad) was born and raised in Tabriz, and around the time of World War II began his writing career and political activism simultaneously—both of which reached maturity during and after the premiership of Mohammad Mosaddeq (1881–1967). Saedi subsequently entered medical school, where he received his doctoral degree in psychiatry. His youth had been filled with literary and dramatic imagination. "I saw Chekhov hundreds of times on our brick steps," he once wrote of his active literary dreams, "under the quince tree, reclining in our sitting room, from a great distance. I dared not get close to him—and I still don't." Even at medical school he was drawn to literature. "For every medical book I read," he later reported, "I read ten novels." While a practicing psychiatrist, Saedi gradually emerged as one of the finest literary figures of his generation—in 1968 joining 130 other writers to establish the Association of Iranian Writers to combat censorship.

Saedi began publishing his writing in the mid-1950s, and by the time of his premature death in Paris in 1985 he had written close to fifty books, including novels, novellas, short stories, plays, and ethnographic reports. His *Shabneshini-e Bashokuh* (*The Splendid Soiree*, 1960) solidly established his literary reputation in Tehran, a feat rather difficult to achieve for a provincial intellectual. He soon followed up with *Azadaran-e Bayal* (*The Mourners of Bayal*, 1964), a tour de force psychological study of neurotic anxiety that was unprecedented in Persian fiction. The principal mood of Saedi's stories in *The Mourners of Bayal*, and in the rest of his works, is situated somewhere between a literary projection of severe poverty narrated in between the psychotic consequences of religious or communal rituals—both leading his prose to the uncharted realms of *magical realism*, long before Gabriel García Márquez made that a universally recognized literary trope. Saedi soon followed with a succession of literary masterpieces—*Dandil* (1966), *Vahemeh-ha-ye Bi-Nam-o-Neshan* (*Neurotic Anxieties*, 1967), *Tars-o Larz* (*Fear and Trembling*, 1967), *Tup* (*The Cannon*, 1968), and *Gur-o-Gahvareh* (*The Grave and the Cradle*, 1977). In one story after another, he consolidated his prominence as one of the leading literary intellectuals of his time and by far the dominant dramatist of his generation. In his stories and plays, Saedi's attention is narratively fixed on the same set of economic privileges or deprivations that play into the ritualized texture of the uncanny. The feeling of the uncanny, which I will explain in a moment, is generated in Saedi's fiction through an almost nondescript narration of routinized rituals, effectively emptied of all meaning and yet redolent with a sense of looming despair. There is never a causal correspondence between the sensation of pale-faced paucity and rampant poverty, which makes the emotive effect of the two so much more powerful.

Because of the extraordinary influence of his writings, Saedi was arrested, incarcerated, and tortured by the shah's secret police, SAVAK, for about a year between 1974 and 1975. He was released from prison and invited to the United States by the Association of American Publishers, whose International Committee for Freedom to Publish was quite active on his behalf. At the beginning of the Islamic revolution in 1979, Saedi left Iran, first for the US, and then for Paris, where he continued writing, though he was deeply depressed and despondent. He died in Paris in 1985.

The collaboration between Saedi and Mehrjui was one of the most auspicious events of modern Iranian cultural history. *Cow* was only the first project in a close creative relationship that lasted until Saedi's death in Paris in the aftermath of the Islamic revolution. What the Saedi-Mehrjui split personality marks is a transitional phase in Iranian cinema, when the singular creativity of Farrokhzad and Golestan in both literary and cinematic arts parted, and a generation of filmmakers emerged that benefited from but did not share the literary imagination of the preceding generation. Mehrjui's case is quite representative of what was to follow. If Mehrjui did not work with Saedi he turned to other literary figures, without discriminating between Iranian and non-Iranian writers. Although modern Persian fiction continued to thrive long after the rise of Iranian cinema, one may still consider, on a historical scale, the emergence of Mehrjui's cinema as the death of the Persian author and the birth of the Iranian auteur.

It is absolutely critical to understand Mehrjui's film *Cow* in the context of Saedi's works of fiction—otherwise it will tell you nothing of the rich literary tradition from which it came. Iranian cinema has both a vertical and a horizontal genealogy, and they ought to be understood simultaneously.

Mehrjui was as much (if not more) familiar with Saedi's phantasmago-ric fiction as he was with Farrokhzad's and Golestan's cinema. What you see in *Cow* is merely the tip of the iceberg that Saedi had masterfully and over decades crafted in his systematic cultivation of a *psychedelic* real-ism. *Cow* is based on only one of the eight short stories that Saedi had brought together in *The Mourners of Bayal*, while incorporating elements and characters from a few others in the same collection, which is the result of Saedi's extensive travels in the Azerbaijan province in northern Iran. He also published two ethnographic studies based on his travels—"Ilakhchi" (1963) and "Kheyav or Meshkin Shahr" (1967). It is crucial to keep in mind that Saedi wrote works of ethnographic detail and narrative fiction simultaneously, trying to come to terms with his observations and narrow in on the nature of the reality he faced. Obviously, the ethno-graphic study did not fully satisfy or match his experiences—and thus in the magical temper of his fiction he sought alternative ways of reaching for the core and character of the reality he wished to witness, register, and convey.

Bayal of *The Mourners of Bayal* is the name of a fictitious village that could be anywhere—backward, disease-infested, superstitious, isolated, abandoned, full of fears and anxieties of known and unknown threats. Saedi's narrative technique mixes precise and realistic description with phantasmagoric nightmares, haunted by superstitious beliefs, quickly transferring the magic-ridden atmosphere of the village into the breath-ing space of his stories, which become methodical expositions of the supernatural. In *The Mourners of Bayal* haphazard death and rituals of mourning comprise the daily concatenations of village life, while the sick and dying populate the ghastly hospitals in the nearby cities. Plagues—real and imaginary—paralyze Bayal, and professional mourners are busy in a contracted demarcation of days, nights, years, lifetimes. The villag-ers are petrified by pestilence of one sort or another during the days and by thieves at night. Fear of the unknown and the dread of the ordinary combine to horrify the villagers in the frightful nightmares that they live. The people of Bayal are characterized by a fear that is as much the color of their own imagination as the character of their material deprivation.

The Mourners of Bayal was no accidental collection of short stories for the young psychiatrist-turned-writer. Saedi had cultivated a deep friendship with Jalal Al-e Ahmad (1923–69), the most celebrated and influential public intellectual of his generation—and the two of them traveled extensively throughout Iran and wrote path-breaking socio-logical accounts of places they visited. Saedi's fiction grew out of these travels and reflections. Three years after the publication of *The Mourn-ers of Bayal*, Saedi published *Fear and Trembling* (1967), changing the scene of his psychological observations from northern to southern Iran, on which he also wrote an ethnographic study, "The People of Hava" (1967). In a southern world plagued by hunger and submissive to its fate, Saedi reaches for the texture of the mysterious in the ordinary, where fact and fantasy transgress their respective boundaries and sheer strangeness animates the daily reality. Fear and anxiety are once again rampant in *Fear and Trembling*—rooted in the material deprivation of a people and yet sublimated in a cosmology of ritualized terror.

Shortly after Mehrjui directed *Cow*, another prominent Iranian director, Nasser Taqvai, directed *Calm in the Presence of Others* (1970), based on a story with the same name from Saedi's collection *Neurotic Anxieties* (1967). Contrary to *The Mourners of Bayal* and *Fear and Trembling*, the setting of Saedi's "Calm in the Presence of Others" is entirely urban. Saedi's original short story is one of the most ingenious works of fiction in modern Persian literature. I urge you to read it because it complements his literary articulation of the uncanny within which *Cow* is squarely located (though this time in a middle-class bourgeois environment).

"Calm in the Presence of Others" begins very inconspicuously, with a retired army colonel and his young wife, Manizheh, selling their chicken-rearing business, collecting their belongings, and moving in with the Colonel's two daughters from a previous marriage, Maliheh and Mahlaqa—two young girls preoccupied with their own lives. Every important detail of these characters remains unknown—who the Colonel is, what happened to his first wife, where he lives, when he married his young wife, Manizheh, who she is, her background, where the Colonel's two daughters live, etc. We are told absolutely nothing of the sort. Instead, we are witness to the slightly offbeat behavior of these characters, who gradually assume a more ominous quality—such as when the Colonel is about to fall down from the balcony of his daughters' house, or when Ameneh, the daughters' servant, suddenly begins to tiptoe around the house for no apparent reason, or when the Colonel suddenly attacks Ameneh with a vase as she is preparing a chicken for dinner. The combination of the characters' unknown history and the sudden appearance of their bizarre and inexplicable behavior generate an anxiety that psychedelically animates "Calm in the Presence of Others."

We soon find out that the retired Colonel is going mad, and that his two daughters are attracted to two young men, whom we only know as the Young Man and the Doctor, while another young man, the Man with the Blue Eyes, falls madly in love with Manizheh. Not much really happens beyond this. The Colonel is finally committed to an asylum, Mahlaqa marries the Young Man, the Young Man's brother, whom we see for the first and the last time at the wedding, commits suicide, Maliheh abandons the idea of marrying the Doctor and leaves on an extended assignment to a remote provincial city, the Man with the Blue Eyes is disappointed with his unrequited love for Manizheh and marries an ugly woman, Ameneh and her goddaughter are left in charge of the house, while Manizheh tenderly attends to her old and insane husband.

What holds "Calm in the Presence of Others" together is not this thin narrative thread but the thickening cloud of a fearful, relentlessly worrisome, and inexplicable apprehension that hovers over these characters. There is an inarticulate uneasiness that never dissipates, an anxious concern for something that is never exactly known. The characters are in a constant state of doubt, second thoughts, hallucinations about everything but really about nothing at all. The Colonel's diagnosed insanity is the only concrete source of disquiet in the story, but his presentiment of his own affliction somehow threatens the entire family with a sinister event that may or may not really happen, though it manages to strain the whole story and generates a collective and sustained state of neurosis.

Saedi employs specific narrative techniques to intensify this profound sense of anxiety. For example, large, red apples, offered to guests of the two sisters, suddenly start burning in their dish, spurting high and colorful flames; a monstrous apparition emerges behind the window of a car in which Maliheh is sitting alone while the Doctor is out in the middle of nowhere flirting with another woman; or a flock of crows bursts into a chorus of "Hurray! Hurray!" In one particularly harrowing scene, at the wedding of Mahlaqa and the Young Man, an anonymous woman— she has no face and sports hairy moles on her fingers for rings—appears, turns her back to the party, and does nothing else but change the records to which the guests sing and dance. These poltergeists regularly trespass into the characters' otherwise perfectly boring lives.

What is the result of these discursive designs, integral to Saedi's fiction and Mehrjui's *The Cow*? The unknown history of the protagonists, the thickening cloud of a fearful and mysterious apprehension, the sudden appearance of bizarre and inexplicable behavior, and an omniscient but detached narrator coalesce in a nerve-racking narrative that almost clinically diagnoses and analytically exposes the neurotic disposition of a universe that is psychedelically real. Saedi and Mehrjui heighten the senses so that even the slightest tremble is registered as a jarring change in the conscious mind, sustaining hallucinatory and delusional incidents that intensify the awareness of otherwise routine reality.

Before Mehrjui adapted "The Cow," Saedi was—and continued to be— both a practicing psychiatrist and a writer. By virtue of his vocation as a psychiatrist and avocation as a writer, Saedi cultivated an understanding of the uncanny that was at once psychoanalytic and aesthetic. The origin of bringing literary aesthetics to bear on psychoanalysis, and vice versa, goes back to Freud in his influential essay "The Uncanny" (1919). I have no way of knowing if Saedi ever read this essay, but I think it is safe to assume that if anyone among the leading Iranian literati was likely to have read it, then it would have been Saedi. In the end, I think it really doesn't matter if Saedi read Freud's essay, because his fiction is itself far superior evidence of his commanding awareness of the nature and function of the uncanny.

In his seminal essay, Freud reflected on the effect of the uncanny and its aesthetic incidence in works of literature. Tracing the genealogy of the oppositional German terms *Heimlich* ("homely") and *Unheimlich* ("un-homely" or "uncanny") he applied them to an examination of E. T. A. Hoffmann's short story "The Sand-Man" (1817)—which subsequently reappeared in Jacques Offenbach's *Tales of Hoffmann* (1881). The uncanny, Freud proposed, is something that invokes fear and discomfort, and as such it had been shunned in aesthetic theory. For Freud, the uncanny is a constellation of frightful suggestions of impressions that accentuate and demarcate the familiar and too-familiar. But as Freud analyzed it, the German word Heimlich can mean both "homely" and "secretive"— so Heimlich to one person is potentially Unheimlich to another. Freud traces the origin of this word to bourgeois notions of privacy, and thus associates the meaning of Unheimlich with a kind of unwilling or accidental self-exposure. By etymologically tracing the paradoxical origins and contradictory implications of Heimlich (as known and familiar and yet secret and unknown) and Unheimlich (as unknown and unfamiliar and yet revealed and uncovered), Freud concluded that the two terms in effect turn on themselves, overlap with their binary opposite, so that the words themselves become uncanny! From this analysis Freud found that the uncanny is the revelation of what is meant to remain private and concealed—or in psychoanalytic terms the return of the repressed. Freud thought that the world of literature is the most obvious location for the operation of the uncanny, because in that domain our disbelief has been temporarily suspended and we can expect and accept just about anything—which makes the literary return of the repressed (the loosening of reality) that much easier. Freud gives the writer of fiction the authorial power of intimating reality but lets him step into irreality for a full evocation of the uncanny.

Saedi's psychoanalytic training undoubtedly helped him gain insight into the workings of the uncanny. But in his fiction this is an act of literary, not psychological, articulation. There is an almost complete absence of emotive exposition in Saedi's psychedelic realism, which results in a kind of paralysis that flattens the moral dimension of the narrative, in order to expose the hidden anxieties of the real. Saedi's *Homo societus*, as a result, becomes a *Homo psychoticus*—and that not by virtue of any clinical diagnosis but by the very fact of communal association. In the political context of his literary (and, soon through Mehrjui, cinematic) text, Saedi's treatment of the uncanny has a thematic consequence in terms applicable to a critique of tyranny—his lifelong concern. The uncanny mutation of a *Homo societus*, as the archetypal assumption of a political community, into a *Homo psychoticus*, as the evident reality of experienced life, has critical consequences for how the politics of tyranny operates. Tyranny is here detected and revealed not in its exclusively political concentration of power but in the larger domain of its social dissipation of neurosis. The most powerful aspect of Saedi's literary achievement is that in his fiction the political critique of tyranny remains implicit in his psychoanalysis of the *uncanny*.

Be that as it may, Saedi's penchant for the uncanny is far more effectively read as a fictive trope than a psychoanalytical study. To be sure, there is absolutely nothing surreal about Saedi's psychedelic realism. Everything is in its right place. Every gesture, every word, every event resonates with an air of reality, an almost tangible matter-of-factness. And yet, it is precisely this matter-of-factness that is so unreal. Saedi's stories are populated by people who do not do or say anything particularly strange. It is their quite ordinary deeds that, through Saedi's ingenious narrative—a kind of *magic realism* before it had a name—a consistent oddity begins to gather around their otherwise quiet universe. What I keep referring to as *psychedelic* realism is the modus operandi for the exposure of the uncanny from the depth of the otherwise totally mundane or disenchanted reality.

The great achievement of Saedi's psychedelic realism, throughout his fiction but particularly in "The Cow," and as visualized and universalized beyond its verbal limitations by Mehrjui, is to trace a way back from a case of metempsychosis to psychosis, and then from the incidence of psychosis to an exposition of reality that is overtly ritualized. But Saedi and Mehrjui's depiction of metempsychosis—the passing of the human soul at death into another human body—subverts the received notion, as they have the soul of an animal, the titular cow, reincarnated in a human body, a proposition that radically defies the very fabricated boundary between the human and the animal. But "The Cow" is not a simple psychological case study of metempsychosis, of a man who becomes mentally deranged, loses his connection to reality, and thinks himself his dead cow. Through this oppositional constitution of metempsychosis we arrive at a psychosis that re-signifies the constitution of the reality that it exudes. Let me explain this point a bit more patiently, because it is quite critical in understanding how this film works.

In any condition of psychosis it is the nature and disposition of reality that is pathologically reconstituted. In his fiction in general, and in the story that Mehrjui adopts for his film in particular, Saedi creatively thrives on a literary reading of that pathology, puts it under a magnifying glass, not to examine *the psychotic distortion of reality*, but *the reality that it seeks to evade*. In this respect, Saedi is more a sociologist than a psychiatrist, or, perhaps more accurately, he brings his psychoanalytical techniques discursively to bear on his sociological observations. It is not in the flat mirror but in the rounded speculum of the psychotic Other (to extend a critical metaphor of the French feminist theorist Luce Irigaray) that Saedi looks for the delusional disposition of *the real*. What I am proposing here is a critical distinction between reality and *the real*: What we call *reality* is already one order removed from the slippery surface of *the real*—it is the metaphysical ordering of the dangerous chaos that constitutes the real. Reality, when we simply hold a book and say, "This is a book," is always already one step removed from the slippery surface of the fact that the object that we hold in our hand has an ontic quality to it that is entirely pre-ontological, if we were to use a Heideggerian phrase; or a pre-philosophical "existence" (*wujud*) prior to its "quidity" (*mahiyyah*), if we were to use Mulla Sadr's language, following the philosophy of the prominent Shia philosopher Mulla Sadra Shirazi (1571–1640). Here what I call *the real* is the constellation of signs before they have been forced into signifiers that we now collectively call *reality*. I hope this is clear.

What is currently called Iranian neorealism rightly traces its origins back to Forugh Farrokhzad's *The House Is Black* and Sohrab Shahid Sales' *A Simple Incident* (1973)—and not to Mehrjui's *The Cow*. But the fact is that both in Saedi's original and Mehrjui's adaptation we witness an alternative strategy to trace the metaphysically ordered and legislated reality back to its chaotic origins in the real. In cases such as Farrokhzad, Shahid Sales, or Kiarostami, they hold their camera so intensely constant on reality that all its received and prosaic truths ooze out of it and the sheer majestic unnamed, the dangerous domain of the real, pierces through and exposes its fictive transparency. But that is only one mode of visual realism. Mehrjui's version elaborates on Saedi's and registers a psychedelic realism that looks into the dangerous domain—of the real in order to expose the fabricated illusion of reality.

What we see in *Cow* is something far more exciting than a mere "subversion of the content by form," as Adorno rightly detected but hurriedly theorized as the critical manner in which art challenges the politics of bourgeois conformity. Of course, the *formal* confrontation of art with *reality* jolts its claim to metaphysical authenticity. But the mechanism of that confrontation is not a mindless, head-on collision between content and form. The *formal* presence of the work of art confronts the substantive claim of *reality* with an alternative revelation of the real as both present and as perennially Other. In this way, works of art do not as much *point to* the aporias of a given society as *constitute* them; they do not indicate that there are unanswered and uncanny locations in an otherwise fully functioning society, but in fact create and craft them. Even if we accept Marx's diagnosis and Adorno's acknowledgment of aporias as a byproduct of the division between intellectual and physical labor, as an emancipatory strategy they remain indispensable in the lived experiences of colonial modernity. But something that neither Marx nor Adorno considered was the condition of artistic production at the colonial edges of capitalism. There, such a clear-cut distinction between intellectual and physical labor does not take place, if for no other reason than the colonially maligned relations of production, in which both intellectual labor and artistic creation remain constitutionally inorganic. Given the inorganicity of artistic production on the colonial edges of capitalist modernity, then the creative function of aporias is to dwell on the condition of the uncanny in order to pose a systematic challenge to the banality of bourgeois conformity.

How has this psychedelic realism emerged in a work of art, and what is contingent on its presence? We know through Rolf Tiedemann, and from the epigraph of his magisterial *Aesthetic Theory*, that Theodor Adorno had intended to expand and elaborate on Friedrich von Schlegel's ascorbic assessment that "In the so-called philosophy of art one of two things is usually missing: either the philosophy or the art." What has been lost in the middle of this, as in all other false dichotomies between the creative attitude of art and the critical temper of philosophy, is the autonomy of a work of art as an aesthetic act that is self-justifying, and is at the same time both critical (because it thematically defies politics) and creative (because it emotively supplants them). Walter Benjamin's notion of the cultic function of art is predicated on the conversation that takes place between the ossified impossibilities of a culture and the creative loosening of those impossibilities by dreaming them otherwise. Culture is identity. Art is alterity. Culture can only tolerate the Same. Art thrives on imagining the Other. Culture constitutes the subject as the Same. Art reconfigures historical agency by dreaming the potential Other of the Same. Culture is inhibitive; art is transgressive. What Marxist theorists reduce to the contractual obligation of art as a socially progressive critique is in reality an accidental aspect of an enduring conversation between art as alterity and culture as identity, culture as the site of the Same, and art as the vision of the Other.

Yes, indeed, you may rightly interject, art can willingly or unwittingly align itself with the forces of political domination, instead of opposing them. But that is not because art has ceased to be politically committed—that is because art has ceased to envision the Other of the cultural Same.

Art, as the vision of the Other, has in such cases betrayed itself far sooner than it has betrayed the politics of opposing power. The so-called "committed art," as Adorno successfully demonstrated, completely signs off on or abandons its aesthetic claims. The collapse of art into political propaganda, exemplified in an array of Iranian poets from Farrokhi Yazdi to Khosrow Golsorkhi, fails to penetrate an inch into the thick ideological ossification of the Same as self and society—no matter how revolutionary they may think themselves to be. The false consciousness never sees itself either as false or as consciousness. The claim of a culture to truth, its false consciousness, is the dominant—without being aware of its dominance—mode of subject formation, and can only be shaken and de-centered by the active intervention of art, which can conceive the Other.

But how, exactly, is one to postulate the repressed, denied, and denigrated Other as equally real in the face of the monumental fossil of the same's pretense to reality, as in the expression *realpolitik*, for instance? The answer lies in that creative corner of imagination that finds a way out of the ordinary into the extraordinary—from natural to preternatural, canny to uncanny—in order to re-signify the ordinary. Kubrick's *Dr. Strangelove or: How I Learned to Stop Worrying and Love the Bomb* (1964) summed up the mood of the world in the early 1960s and yet reversed the fear of a nuclear holocaust into a highly effective black comedy. The sense of inarticulate fear definitive of Kubrick's cinema is here successfully transmuted into satire, and perhaps precisely for that reason the sense of terror it projects is even more troubling. Kubrick really saw the world at the mercy of lunatic men like United States Air Force Commander Jack D. Ripper (Sterling Hayden), Chairman of the Joint Chiefs of Staff Buck Turgidson (George C. Scott), and the recently US naturalized German Nazi scientist Dr. Strangelove (Peter Sellers). The fear of nuclear holocaust in the early 1960s—with the Vietnam War, the Cuban Missile Crisis, and the Cold War—was not as mundane as it later became. Kubrick's script, which he cowrote with Peter George and Terry Southern (based on Peter George's book *Red Alert*), narrows in on that anxiety, transforms it into satire, and propels it into a darker depiction of the nuclear age—the sudden and total disappearance of humanity from earth. That fear (of total and final annihilation) allowed Kubrick to effect an altering of the bourgeois sugarcoating of reality.

The critical and creative act of positing, as reality, an alternative to that reality can strike any number of strategic alliances with a formal realism. We can begin by pointing to the nauseating Pahlavi censorship in order to figure out why Saedi (and thus Mehrjui) is relentlessly interpreted in a jaundiced political way, at the expense of the far more powerful literary presence of the force of the uncanny in his fiction. Even in his most patently political stories, say "Sayeh-beh-Sayeh" ("Shadow-by-Shadow," in *The Grave and the Cradle*, 1976), Saedi's narrative hinges on an entirely different axis than a mere political statement about tyranny. "Shadow-by-Shadow" is narrated by Ramezun, the drug addict vagabond who lives in Qaleh among other drug addicts, pimps, and prostitutes. He accidentally runs into two medical-students-cum-political-activists and, taking advantage of their naïve idealism, swindles them of a handsome sum. While he is lavishly spending his money the following day he comes across a secret-police agent who is looking for those two student activists. He grows indignant, in his own convoluted and crooked way, as he witnesses an all-out assault by government forces against the inhabitants of Qaleh, and daydreams of a rebellion. To detect and articulate the noble dream of a rebellion against tyranny in the decrepit mind of a drug addict is vintage Saedi and shows his exquisite ability to see straight images in broken mirrors. Much is lost in this gem of a short story if we do not notice its larger frame of references, its literary manner of seeing truth through falsehood. Idealist student activists, secret-service agents, drug addicts, and prostitutes, pimps and homeless vagabonds populate a world of darkness and destitution, from the midst of which Saedi manages to sustain a streak of hope and dignity in the fearful recognition of all its opposites.

Even in his most political example of psychedelic realism Saedi is after much bigger fish than mocking Pahlavi brutality. Through Ramezun's eyes, Saedi experiments with the gamut of psychedelic drugs, popular beliefs, charlatan gimmickries, and fraudulent games. He begins with Delbar Khanom, Ramezun's landlady, who is a drug addict and pusher, giving a full account of opium addiction of various sorts. Here he creates an evocative hallucinatory and hazy narrative milieu. He then moves to Ahmad the Guru, who performs all sorts of so-called "Indian trickeries"— sleeping on a bed of nails, for example—for money. From there he moves to Akhtar the Jinn-catcher and Mashallah the Charlatan before he runs into a swindler who threatens to set a mouse on fire unless someone gives him some money. Then Ramezun invokes the name of Ashath the Indian, the master of all Jinn-catchers, encounters an epileptic woman, and visits Karim the Vodka Seller—just before he runs into the anonymous SAVAK agent—soon after which he finds out that Hassan Tahhaf (an allusion to a local hero) has been murdered. By the time Ramezun sees the secret police and imagines his popular uprising, he has witnessed every sort of fantasy conceivable in a poor red-light district—all narratively designed and metaphorically delivered to alleviate any received notion of reality. The shah's secret police and their brutality are incorporated into the otherworldly fabric of the reality that Saedi depicts. Thus, the SAVAK agent does not politicize the story; rather, the story alienates the SAVAK agent, and with him the entire political apparatus that he represents.

Though most literary critics have been remiss in acknowledging the uncanny temperament of Saedi's fiction—focusing instead on its political content—it has, after all, drawn more attention than Mehrjui's similar experiments in *The Cow*. *The Cow* premiered two years after its completion at the Venice Film Festival in 1971 to a very positive but altogether imperturbable reception. Both at home and abroad, the film suffered from a mind-numbing over-politicization by film critics who insisted on reading it as a mere political allegory. The principal culprit was, of course, the censorship that forced Mehrjui to preface the film with a disclaimer explaining that the story had taken place about forty years earlier, to insure that audiences did not associate the backwardness portrayed in the film with the modern image of Iran the Shah of Shahs was trying to foist upon the world. And all of this undue political hub-bub came at the expense of the narrative revolution the film occasioned in Iranian visual culture.

Mehrjui transformed Saedi's psychedelic realism from a literary mas-terpiece into a cinematic event of unprecedented significance. Saedi's "Cow" told a very simple story of metempsychosis: Masht Hassan loves his cow. Masht Hassan's cow dies. Masht Hassan goes mad and thinks he is his own cow. Masht Hassan's case presents a basic example of trans-migration, or reincarnation, that of his cow's soul, upon departure from the cow's body, into his body, the exiting of his own human soul, and the complete takeover by the cow's. The villagers, dumbfounded by the development, take Masht Hassan to a nearby town to cure him, and he dies on the way. Before Mehrjui's film, there existed no example of such simple but elegant experimentation with the idea of metempsychosis in Iranian cinema. The idea, even before Saedi's masterful treatment of it in his psychedelically realistic story, had been treated extensively in medieval Islamic philosophy, with its roots in Pythagorean, Platonic, and Brah-manic thought. The transmigration of souls from one body to another upon death had been discussed in philosophical, mystical, and narrative terms long before the twentieth century. In that tradition, souls could transmigrate either horizontally (from humans to humans) or vertically (from humans to lower or higher orders of life). Perhaps the most famous poem in medieval Persian poetry in this regard is Rumi's astonishing hymn of transmigration, from mineral to vegetal, animal, human, and ultimately angelic bodies.

> *I died from my mineral being and became vegetal;*
> *I died from the vegetal and became animal...*

That poem is well known. In the philosophical writings of Nasser Khosrow, the eleventh-century Ismaili philosopher, we read about a

Neo-Platonic conception of the transmigration of souls from one state to another. Among Muslim philosophers, from Ikhwan al-Safa in the tenth century to Mulla Sadra in the sixteenth and after, varied forms of belief in transmigration were widely contemplated. Abu al-Fath Muhammad ibn Abd al-Karim al-Shahrastani (d. 1153), the author of the encyclopedic text on medieval sects, *al-Milal wa al-Nihal*, has given a full treatment of various Muslim sects (such as Hululiyyah, Tanasukhiyyah, and Mushshabahhah) who believed in transmigration of souls from one bodily form to another. The question of the transmigration of the soul from one body to another ultimately amounted to an Islamic theory of the physical body and led to the thorny theological issue of bodily resurrection on the Day of Judgment. The rise of philosophical rationalism in medieval Islamic intellectual history resulted in the denial of the possibility of bodily resurrection. That development began to generate and sustain a steady body of philosophical speculation among Muslim philosophers. Al-Ghazali (d. 1111) denounced the philosophers for their belief in the eternity of the world and above all of their denial of bodily resurrection on Judgment Day. Throughout Islamic intellectual history, theological and philosophical debates about bodily resurrection were in effect battles over the metaphysical mutation of the *caro corporalis* into *caro spiritualis*.

The battle culminated in the sixteenth century in the figure of Mulla Sadra Shirazi and the establishment of the School of Isfahan. Mulla Sadra's lifelong ambition was to bring together the best and most enduring philosophical speculations in Islamic intellectual history and wed them with Islamic metaphysical doctrines. One of his most important philosophical followers, Shaykh Ahmad Ahsai (d. 1826), came up with an elaborate theory of the body to rescue it from corruption, save it for paradisiacal praise or infernal fire, and thus metaphysically prolong its endurance into a post-eternity that embraced its earthly existence. To do that, Ahsai categorically divided the body into four stages of its corporeal existence. Two were related to the term *jasad*, which literally means *corpus*, and two with the term *jism*, which literally means *body*. This became the temporal template of a journey for the human soul to move about and above from one stage to another, from earthly to heavenly, in order to sustain an organic notion of the universe from its conception to its delivery.

My point is that Saedi's treatment of the subject—though entirely within the context of his own literary experimentations with the uncanny—was not completely outlandish, and had deep-rooted philosophical and mystical forbears in his immediate intellectual history. As I said earlier, the stories of *The Mourners of Bayal* are based on Saedi's actual travels and observations in Iranian villages in the north and south of the country. Bayal is not a typical example but a prototype of an Iranian village, unreal in its realistic representation of actual villages. The small population of the village—less than one hundred men, women, and children—live in doorless abodes centered around Nabi Agha's Shrine. The Bayalis do not have houses; they have rooms with small windows, and an occasional hole in their roof for light and, perhaps, surreptitious exit and entrance. Saedi is very particular about the architecture of Bayal, and gives it a creepy, labyrinthine, and dreamy feel. The setting of the story thus becomes the story. Bayal itself, the prototypical village that Saedi creates out of the myriad of his travels around Iran, is perhaps the most daunting character of the story. There is a fear about Bayal, an unsettling sense of looming danger, that may or may not ever be delivered or evident. But the sense of dread that it exudes is at once endemic and epidemic to the atmospheric power of Saedi's story.

Bayal's tangled body, frightened and fearful, has a nucleus of intelligence. His name is Islam; a critical character in the story, he is played ingeniously by Ali Nassirian in Mehrjui's *Cow*. Islam is the critical and creative intelligence of Bayal. He has the only cart and the only musical instrument in sight. Islam thinks for Bayal, and can transport—both physically and figuratively—its inhabitants either by his cart or by his string instrument the *saz* from one place to another. With Islam (as a proper name with obvious and yet subversive suggestions) as the center of its nervous system, Bayal projects a monstrous apparition, a phantasmagoric village leviathan, a chimera. It is not that Islam always knows what he is doing. But it seems that he must. The village wills it. The village, in effect, is the extended body of Islam, his limbs and organs, constantly demanding his attention, calling for his intelligence.

Mehrjui, for his part, does a splendid job with his camerawork, editing, and mise-en-scène to generate the atmosphere of Bayal. His camera becomes a local inhabitant of the village, dwelling inside one of those cave-like cubicles, loitering around the village pool, and then sitting for a cup of tea with Islam and his buddies. The village, in Mehrjui's visual depiction, is a subterranean abode of goblin-like apparitions—there are gnomes and elves, as it were, posturing as humans, pixies standing in for the real things. Bayal is not a simile; Bayal is a simulacrum. It is not like any village; it is the unreal simulation of reality. In Bayal, humans and animals live together in the same room—and that is primarily to propose a pandemonium, and not to parody a politics. Bayal is a poly-demonic suggestion of a Miltonian capital city of hell, a place of unnatural disorder, of noise and anarchic confusion—the sights and sounds of the uncanny. I remember when *Cow* was first shown in Tehran. I had just come from my hometown, Ahvaz, to Tehran to go to college. There was a heated debate in the press whether Bayal was realistic or unrealistic. Oh, how green was our valley—green as in *dumb*! Bayal is Saedi's literary rendering of what he actually saw in Iranian villages, enhanced by a realism that creatively disabuses the existing supernatural cant of local beliefs. Not a single element in Saedi's description of the village is exaggerated, let alone invented. It is only in his uncanny ability to demarcate the unreal nature of what is believed and practiced in reality that gives his narrative its psychedelic disposition. Saedi says, and Mehrjui shows, nothing that is not evident and factual in the village. It is in the way that Saedi says and Mehrjui shows what they both see that the uncanny similarity of the village becomes dissimilar. The demarcation of the unreal, one telling and the other showing, is thus more by emotive omission, rather than by creative commission. There is something amiss, we always feel, but we never quite know what it is. Saedi knows and does not tell, and Mehrjui sees but does not show.

Let me be more specific: Smack in the middle of a rat-infested plain sits Bayal and at the heart of Bayal its central pool. The village square around the pool, the village morgue right next to the pool, and the hidden flag-room (where the villagers keep their religious masts and mascots) are added to Islam's mind and the saint's shrine as additional focal points of the uncanny. Right in the middle of all this, Saedi's dark sense of humor drops a piece of equipment fallen from a US military machine, taken as a sacred sepulcher by the villagers, with neither of the two parties having access to the other's darker secrets—what *profanity* is hidden inside that equipment; what *sanctity* violated in that sepulcher? On a diet of donkey carcasses the inhabitants of this rat- and terror-stricken village are paralyzed by the fear of the Porussis, their neighbor villagers, who are always on the lookout to come and steal from the Bayalis. Porussis are among the greatest achievements of modern Persian film and fiction by way of countervailing characterization. We never see them. They are the invented apparitions of the Bayalis' nightmares.

In the middle of this pandemonium, the village that Saedi invented and Mehrjui portrayed to mark the irreality of reality (as in a nightmare), Masht Hassan's cow is a fragile icon of life in an otherwise death-ridden culture. All those who have read this story and film as a political metaphor of Pahlavi Iran—beginning with Samad Behrangi (1939–68), who was a wonderful storyteller and a committed activist who after his accidental death in the Aras River was made into an iconic martyr by the endemic proclivity of his contemporaries to kill the living and worship the dead—did it a terrible disservice and diminished its far greater significance. Only in a superficially prosaic kind of way is *Cow* a political story and film. The Pahlavis were so pathologically aware of their own illegitimacy and mendacity that their secret police was frightened witless of any creative act that could remotely implicate the corrupt regime. One can perfectly understand (though still condemn it) when dedicated political activists but talentless writers were totally wasted by that ghastly regime. But when far superior and enduring works of art are haplessly cut down to the size of the limited imagination of their contemporaries something far more precious has been compromised.

Before its death, Masht Hassan's cow is the sole source of joy in his otherwise funereal village life. There is scarcely a more loving scene in the history of Iranian cinema than the one in which Masht Hassan feeds his cow. What you don't see in the film but is evident in Saedi's *The Mourners of Bayal* is Masht Hassan pleading constantly with Islam to help him to take care of it. Saedi examined the relationship between a human and an animal surrounded by the complete collapse of all human relationships. You will have to have read the third story of the collection—the one about the famine-stricken Bayalis going to Khatun Abad in search of potatoes in a deadly windstorm that is scattering torn pieces of funeral shrouds all over them—to witness the astonishingly loving air between Masht Hassan and his cow. You have to have known the ignominious and illicit relationship between Masht Reyhan and Hassani to see the beauty and nobility of the emotive space between Masht Hassan and his cow.

May I suggest that "The Cow" is a bizarre love story between a human and an animal in a ghost town? Both Saedi and Mehrjui divest Bayal of every trace of humanity and replace it with this strange tale of love and affection. Masht Hassan and his cow are one soul in two bodies—*yek ruh dar do badan*, as we say in Persian—and upon the death of the cow, Masht Hassan becomes both himself and his cow—two souls in one body. In the circularity of that phenomenon, there is a self-referential universe that can generate and sustain a measure of sanity precisely in the heart of an insanity. Would I dare to tell you that Masht Hassan's insanity is the sole example of sanity left after the inhabitants of godforsaken Bayal have lost all their reasons for being? Let me offer just one piece of evidence for my courage and your conviction: The case of Masht Hassan's metempsychosis is balanced in *The Mourners of Bayal* by a case of metamorphosis, of the redheaded character in the village. The difference—completely lost on Samad Behrangi and all other contemporary commentators—is critical. Behrangi considered both cases as metamorphoses—though in the case of Masht Hassan he thinks he is his cow (metempsychosis) and the redhead he turns into a rat-like creature (metamorphosis). But in the metamorphosis of the redhead surfaces a neurosis that mourns death; in the metempsychosis of Masht Hassan hides a psychosis that celebrates life.

August is now fast upon us. Before I know it, official functions, faculty meetings, classes, office hours, precociously diligent undergraduates, nervous graduate students will all be here, and these fine summer days will be but a distant memory. It feels odd to think about the books and films I read and saw in my teens and early twenties, now that I am decades and continents away from them. I still remember the awe of reading Saedi for the first time, and the joy of watching Mehrjui's *Cow*—as if they were the very first and the very last writers and filmmakers on earth. There was a pride in reading Saedi and an elegance to the privilege of watching Mehrjui that I don't think I can ever convey to you or anyone else in your generation. Something far more than a mere monarchy died in Iran after the Pahlavis. There was a grace about our dissent, a solace and certainty to our restlessness. A joyous hope marked our youthful defiance, a promise that no real revolution, no paradise lost and regained, could ever deliver. I now speak of Saedi and Mehrjui to you as if they are the dead pawns in a pointless march of our history. But I assure you that was not the case—not at all: They were the very measures of our truth, and the quintessence of their courage ran confidently through every bone of our contentions.

I have often told you that our poets are the theorists of our historical whereabouts—and by poets I mean those prophetic magicians and visionary wizards who have outmaneuvered the darkness of Iranian history by the daily light of their dreams. I remember long after I had read and forgotten Saedi, watched and admired Mehrjui, I would still wonder how they generated and sustained a measure of boldness for and in us beyond our limited means. The confidence with which Mehrjui stood behind his camera and commanded our attention was essential to what later happened in Iranian cinema, as it was itself so thoroughly embedded in the competence with which Saedi made it possible for Mehrjui to project his otherworldly imagination onto the screen. But where and how did Saedi find the source for that courage, the origin of that imagination, to discover the uncanny and face the fear of what he aptly called *Vahemeh-ha-ye Bi-Nam-o-Neshan*, literally, "nameless and traceless anxieties," or, more technically, neurotic anxieties? That unlettered vision I still cannot fully comprehend—except in literary terms. Saedi's psychoanalytical training as a professional physician may partially explain his insights into the uncanny, but it was ultimately in literature that he bypassed the Freudian diagnosis of neurotic anxiety in contradistinction to actual anxiety—a distinction that Saedi ingeniously dismantled. Saedi's psychedelic realism, I believe, was predicated on a conception of anxiety beyond its Freudian bifurcation into actual and neurotic, and directly rooted in his unique literary imagination.

It was not until the 1920s, more than two decades after the publication of his seminal *Interpretation of Dreams*, that Freud began to tackle the thorny issue of anxiety. In two successive essays—"Beyond the Pleasure Principle" (1920) and "The Ego and the Id" (1923)—Freud distinguished between two kinds of anxieties: realistic and neurotic, one occasioned by actual danger and the other by an imagined threat, which Freud at that time attributed to undischarged or repressed libido. The conclusion of these two essays was that pent-up or transformed libido was the source of neurotic anxiety—the result of semi-successful repression, when the surplus libido breaks the repressive barriers and causes either complete neurosis or else persistent neurotic anxiety. Freud clearly distinguished between this sort of *neurotic* anxiety and what he termed *realistic* anxiety, which for him could have any number of factual sources and evidence, ranging from *coitus interruptus* to such troubling moments in a collective memory of a people as he uncovered in his *Moses and Monotheism* (1939).

About three years later, Freud published "Inhibitions, Symptoms, and Anxiety" (1926), in which he reversed the relationship between neurotic anxiety and repression. He proposed that neurotic anxiety was in fact the cause, not the consequence, of repression. In terms of the most famous cases of Freudian repression—the incestuous and parricidal wishes of childhood—he now argued that they had not preceded the neurotic anxieties associated with them but in fact followed them. The neurotic fear of castration by the father, in this new perspective, occasions the repression of Oedipal tensions—for otherwise the fear of castration, or else the conscious awareness of the Oedipal tension, becomes debilitating. In his 1926 essay, Freud also abandoned his earlier distinctions between *real* and *neurotic* anxieties. He came to believe that in psychoneurosis in general anxiety was not the cause but the result of an anticipated danger, whether real or imaginary.

I have no way of knowing if Saedi was aware of the nuances of Freudian theories of neurotic and real anxiety and their relation to repression. But what is evident in Saedi's work is his collapsing of the two modes of anxiety into one and—even more important—delivering it in literary terms. For Saedi, real and neurotic anxieties are indistinguishable, a fact probably attributable to his attraction to Freud and Marx at the same time. The result is a singular act of literary imagination that can only analytically be broken down into its various components. The collapsing of the real and neurotic into one literary expostulation of anxiety allows Saedi's psychedelic realism to take full advantage of the uncanny in order to narrow in on reality from an entirely unsuspected and thus revealing perspective.

The origin of this simultaneous attention to real and neurotic anxieties, to the point of collapsing the initial Freudian distinction, may also be traced in Saedi's own biography—a suggestion never before probed. In a rather unusual document that Saedi opted to put into the public domain, he divulged some very select and suggestive pieces of his personal life. In this autobiographical memoir, which I read as much as a work of fiction as a piece of factual evidence (like everything else that he created), Saedi paid memorable attention to some specific details of his early childhood and subsequent writing career. He wrote this account at the beginning of the Islamic revolution in 1978 when a group of US publishers put pressure on the shah's government and arranged for Saedi to visit the United States. On this occasion, Professor Michael Hillmann, of the University of Texas at Austin, put together an exhibition of his published work and solicited from him an autobiographical sketch—a translation of which was subsequently published in *Literature East and West* (volume 20, nos. 1–4, backdated to January–December 1976).

For a writer of such unprecedented access to sources of neurotic anxiety, Saedi himself must have been very much in touch with the specifics of his own psychoneurosis. Otherwise, it is rather difficult to explain the reason behind the publication of this short but rather suggestive account of his early childhood, youth, and literary career. According to the report, Saedi grew up with a very young mother: "My mother was fifteen or sixteen years older than I. And I always looked on her as my sister until my grandmother with a great deal of suffering forsook this poverty-stricken and miserable life. Her death, the first in our joyous family, affected us all very deeply." In another reference to his parents' marriage, Saedi writes, "Finally he [Saedi's father] entered into partnership with my maternal grandfather, whose daughter, a young, pretty girl, he married and whose family he moved in with."

The identification of Saedi's young mother with his even younger sister soon assumes a rather ominous turn. The next item of information Saedi opts to share with his readers is the death of a young sister just before he was born. Saedi was the second child—the first child, who was a girl, had died when she was less than one year old. Saedi developed a particular attachment to this dead sister, whom he had obviously never seen. His father took him to visit his dead sister's grave from a very young age. "I frequented my little sister's grave, covered with small bricks orderly arranged. I always imagined her in her grave rocking in her cradle, although neither myself nor my brother who came after me nor my sister who was the last child in the family had a cradle. Our cradle was our grandmother's lap." The powerful image of a dead sister swinging in her cradle in her grave is the enduring mixed metaphor that remains definitive to Saedi's fiction and to his literary perception of the uncanny, in which the fact and phenomenon of birth and death become interchangeable, metamorphic, one standing for the other—precisely what Freud meant by Unheimlich.

To the degree that the repression of incestuous urges are at the root of neurotic anxieties, or vice versa if we take Freud's 1926 essay as overriding his previous speculations, Saedi's were thus immediately associated with the interchangeable images of a young mother (whom he thought was his sister) and a dead sister (whom he thought was rocking in her cradle in her grave), and soon identified with an overwhelming morbidity—facilitated by the father frequently taking the young Saedi to his dead sister's grave. Trafficking between his grandmother's lap and his sister's grave, Saedi may be suggested to have contracted the converging images of cradle/grave/womb, and squarely identified his father with birth and death at one and the same time. He was (not) the first child; his mother was (not) his sister; his sister was (not) dead—the womb of his mother was both his and his sister's cradle and grave, at one and the same time. Going (back) to the grave was like rocking in a cradle, returning to his mother's womb. Defiantly dying was like incestuously giving birth—a paradoxical transgression Saedi deemed necessary to reveal publicly at the age of forty-two in the United States.

The short memoir Saedi wrote was a gem of literary imagination disguised as factual biography. The obvious sense of morbidity associated with these early memories—at once transgressive and imaginative—begins very early and in a rather uncanny way. At a particularly powerful point in this short memoir, Saedi writes of how he and his siblings could identify the members of their family and neighbors by the sound of their footsteps:

> Haji Abbas always walked slowly. The children of
> Mashhadi Jafar the blacksmith always ran instead of
> walking. I still remember the sound of the soft steps of
> a group of people one spring dawn, and Grandfather
> and Grandmother going out the door, whispering.
> The old woman barber at the end of the alley had
> died. From that day onward, the word "death" was
> set in my mind like a deep scar. The name of this
> dirty, ill-natured demon has been with me for forty
> whole years. What deaths haven't I seen! What loved
> ones haven't I buried! The shadow of this cursed
> phantom has followed me step-by-step all the way.

This morbid disposition gave Saedi an early preference for solitude over the company of friends and classmates. Although he reports of happy childhood years, he also speaks of his distaste for playing outdoors with his cohorts, preferring isolation and reading: "I detested play, sports, and mischief, and constantly shied away from childhood joy and levity. I was engulfed in imagination and fantasy, completely enthralled by books, school, and the long winter nights sitting by the kerosene lantern reading story after story until sleep overcame me."

The morbidity of Saedi's early childhood and adolescence continued well through early adulthood and the commencement of his
writing career, when, as he admits in this short autobiography, he nearly
attempted suicide:

> My first book, which was absolute nonsense, was
> published in 1955. As we grow older, it is amusing to
> realize how uninformed we have been and how fragile,
> so fragile that the glass container of our youthful spirit
> could not bear the slightest tap. Something would
> be written somewhere, and I would drown in utter
> despondency. I even bought some cyanide once in order
> to commit suicide; but…[ellipses in the original] but an
> astonishing butterfly at dawn saved me from death.

At the time of writing this autobiographical account, in 1978, he still sustained the same fixation with death. Expressing atypical modesty about
his own writing career, Saedi concluded:

> Now that I have reached forty, I feel that all these writings
> of mine to date have been so much nonsense, written
> hurriedly and published hurriedly. Whenever I say this,
> people think that I am being modest. No. I am a shy and
> reclusive person, but I have never pretended to be overly
> modest. Should my life be long enough—and assuredly
> it won't be—I will really write from now on, yes, now
> that I know in which corner I should sit to have a view of
> the entire scene and now that I know how to shout out,
> shouting words that are more effective than mere echoes.

You should not be surprised if I were to tell you that this fear and
anxiety, a part of his creative ego, ultimately killed Saedi. Consider the
following: Saedi's autobiographical narrative is overwrought with an
overwhelming fear of death, all the way from his early childhood in
Tabriz to his untimely death in Paris. The early identification of a young
mother with a dead sister, the regular visits to the gravesite of the dead
sister, an imagined conflation of grave/cradle/womb, a creative repression of incestuous and parricidal instincts, all come together and result
in an exaggerated sense of fear and morbidity and suicidal urges—to the
point of actually buying cyanide and, ultimately, a death wish resulting in
a severe case of alcoholism in the aftermath of the Islamic revolution. All
of these anxieties were at the root of Saedi's creative disposition. The psychological repression and literary sublimation of incestuous and parricidal

instincts come together and result in an essential and effective commerce with the uncanny.

Now comes the real fire: One may very well argue that it has been fundamental to Iran's type of colonial culture to transfer and project traces of parricidal (Oedipal) wishes from biological fathers to tyrannical father figures because their overwhelming power implicitly emasculates all other fathers. The fear and loathing of the father soon mutates into the fear and loathing of the father figure, and the fear of physical castration into the fear of political impotence. The fear of the father figure and emasculation manifests itself as much in an overwhelming fear of death as in a premature over-politicization of the youth. Add to this a creative disposition and it is easy to see how incestuous anxieties are as much psychologically repressed as they are aesthetically conceived—that is to say, the aesthetic sublimation of the incestuous becomes the functional equivalent of its psychological repression. Our psychological repressions, as a paradoxical result, become aesthetically creative. Creative writing, in other words, is the functional equivalent of politically defying the father and aesthetically appropriating the mother. (I have just shown you a hidden inroad to the tantalizing operation of censorship in Iranian political culture. In defying censorship, we are fooling our father figures and eloping with the aestheticized version of our mothers' love!)

In his fiction, one may argue, Saedi kept politically stabbing with his pen as he aesthetically ritualized (beyond his own immediate recognition) his incestuous and parricidal instincts. In the same autobiographical sketch, Saedi specifically identified the act of writing with wrestling: "Writing is not less important than wrestling. I think that I have recently learned the wrestling techniques a bit in the arena of life and, I venture to say, in the arena of writing." Coterminous with the aesthetic expression of the incestuous is the political transference of parricidal urges—in other words, the parricidal is politically transferred from the father to the father figure, precisely in the same measure that the incestuous is aesthetically mutated from the mother to the work of art—with storytelling, as the most obvious space of the mother-child intimacy, as the principal site of that transference.

In "The Cow," Masht Hassan's relationship with his cow is at once amorous and self-mortifying. His love for the cow is as much incestuous as his death wish is parricidal—with repeated scenes of self-flagellation marking a classical case of masochism, in which, as Deleuze would later argue, the son substitutes his body for the body of the father, and by punishing himself punishes the father. As Masht Hassan is both Mashhadi Hassan and his cow, he is also both Gholamhossein Saedi and Mohammad Reza Shah Pahlavi: self-flagellating and ultimately killing himself in order to scourge and kill the tyrannical monarch, the father figure writ

large. At the end of Mehrjui's *Cow* that was not just Masht Hassan falling from a cliff to his grave; it was also the shah falling from his throne;
it was not just the shah falling from his throne; it was also Saedi falling
back to his sister's cradle, his mother's womb.

There are obvious limitations and many pitfalls to such psychoanalytical readings of works of art. But I offer this reading of *Cow* not by way
of any definitive exposition of Saedi and Mehrjui's absolute masterpiece.
I only suggest this line of argument as perhaps an unexamined path into
the working of an *uncanny* piece of literary genius, and a film that does it
visual justice.

It is part of morality not to be at home
in one's home.
–Theodor W. Adorno

Arby Ovanessian
Spring

LAST WEEK, I SAW A BEAUTIFUL PERFORMANCE of the Mark Morris Dance Group at Lincoln Center, with Mark Morris himself coming onstage at the end of the performance to acknowledge the uproarious applause. For about a quarter of a century, Morris has been revolutionizing the idea of choreography. He no longer seems to choreograph dance to music; he positively sets music to dance! In this case, he had paid a joyously beautiful and flirtatious homage to Franz Schubert's "Wiegenlied," "Ständchen," and "Erlkönig," Antonio Vivaldi's "Gloria," a potpourri of pieces by John Wilson, and finally Robert Schumann's "Quintet in E-flat Major for Piano and Strings." But it does not really matter what music he adopts. He could, just like Amir Naderi did in his film *Marathon* (2002), set New York subway noise to dance. What matters is how in Morris' hands human bodies turn into the visual simulacra of musical notes. Single human bodies dance onto an ascetically emptied stage, shapes and apparitions that Morris then leads into an open-ended variation of figural and compositional shapes and shadows. This is no longer simple balletic design; Morris exposes the unreleased signs and suggestions hidden in the legislated semantics of a repressive culture. For Morris dance is no longer a simple defiance of the body—it is rendering that body irrelevant by choreographing it into a pantheon of possibilities it had never dreamed before, let alone repressed. His dances are not the return of the body's repressed; they are the blissful pouring of a rain of abundant potential on the arid impossibilities that have choked the human body.

It was quite accidental that a couple of nights after I saw Mark Morris Dance Group at Lincoln Center, I also saw Mark Wing-Davey's production of Shakespeare's *Henry V* at the Delacorte Theater in Central Park. It was a full-fledged outdoor production and about half an hour into the play it started to drizzle. By the last act we were all sitting drenched in a summer thunderstorm. The most spectacular moment of the production came with the introduction of Princess Katherine, daughter of Charles VI and Queen Isabel, the king and queen of France, with whom Henry V is waging a war. In Henry's company there was a retinue of regular foot soldiers (to whom, you remember, he delivers that glorious speech, "We happy few"). Among these soldiers was a young kid who occasionally suggested a line or two in a pronounced New York accent. Just before the scene in which Princess Katherine appears onstage, this young soldier went and sat under something that looked like a fire hydrant, placed smack in the middle of the stage, and began to wash, in a gesture all too familiar to us here in New York, especially on hot August days. The soldier did so surreptitiously, and we scarcely noted it at first, until gradually the water faucet began to rise and assumed the shape of a showerhead. The kid soldier then stood up under it and the lighting began to fade completely, except for a floodlight over the shower. Under the shower the young soldier began to undress, and, lo and behold, a beautiful young girl emerged from under the ragged clothing. For a few seconds she stood there, completely naked under that shower, and continued to wash herself, right in the middle of Central Park, with the translucent shimmering of the pouring water her only cover. A maiden then ceremoniously approached the showering princess with a white towel and other garments, and she emerged, fresh from under the shower, Princess Katherine! "Never saw anything like that in me life," I heard someone whispering to his companion in a seat behind me.

What I wish you could have seen was how the mixed metaphor of acting worked in (not so much the geographical fact but the spatial idea of) Central Park—a practice that gives to the physical presence of the actors an ability to meander between fact and fantasy. It is this mixed metaphor of acting not on a stage but in a public place—for in public we are not supposed to act and on stage we are not supposed to phase in

and out of a character so smoothly—that added to Mark Morris' ingenious reappraisal of the human form, which leads the performing body
to make a fool, as it were, of the legislated (socialized, cultured, mandated) body. Between Morris' teasing out the performing body from the
perfunctory, and Wing-Davey's effective use of space in Central Park,
one thing becomes clear along the border between the real and the theatrical: that you either vacate the space naked like Morris to let the body
exude its theatricality, or else you populate the space like Wing-Davey
in a way that allows its factual topography to tease out its spatial character. In either case, the bodily volume of space has a character entirely its
own—but you cannot see it with your naked eye unless you either vacate
it choreographically (Morris) or populate it negationally (Wing-Davey).
What I mean by *the performing body* is the corporeal defiance of a social
mandate for its senses and absences of propriety. I have always considered
Don Giovanni's last and lasting defiance to repent, in Mozart's operatic
version of him, precisely in terms of this rebellion of the performing
body refusing to succumb to a Christian morality. "*Pentiti, cangia vita / È
l'ultimo momento!*" the Statue commands Don Giovanni as it's dispatch-
ing him to hell. "*No, no, ch'io non mi pento, / Vanne lontan da me!*" responds
Don Giovanni unrepentantly. "*Pentiti, scellerato!*" the Commendatore
screams; "*No, vecchio infatuato!*" answers Don Giovanni.

La Statua: *Pentiti!*
Don Giovanni: *No!*
La Statua: *Sì!*
Don Giovanni: *No!*

That is the defiant body, aware and flamboyant with its bodily desires
(remember that Don Giovanni has invited the Statue for dinner and is
eating voraciously when it arrives), refusing to succumb to fear and legislation, morality and propriety. In Morris' case, my sense is that he allows
for that performing body to come out and play by clearing the space of
all the unnecessary objects and their littering effects, and so through this
spatial minimalism stages the flamboyant body; Wing-Davey meanwhile
opts for a kind of uncanny mise en scène in which the spatial topography
of the space is creatively sculpted in a manner that stages not so much
the bodies that populate it but the cavernous carnivalesque of the space
itself, in which bodies assume newly found shapes and shadows. In both
cases, it is the graceful conversation between space and the bodies that it
beholds that strikes me as exquisitely performative.

When it comes to seeing invisible space, nobody comes close to Arby
Ovanessian, whose masterpiece, *Cheshmeh* (*Spring*, 1972) is one of the

most unfairly treated films in the history of Iranian cinema. Without this film the spatial configuration of Iranian culture, the way time and space are specifically coordinated and choreographed unbeknownst even to ourselves, would have remained invisible—too obvious to be seen. Without this film we would not have detected a pattern against which to see the way our bodies perform their hidden desires against the semantics of their social legislations, the way our bodies are taught to behave in the social space, and the way in which our bodies have in fact internalized such codifications to the marrow of their vertical obedience. Subtract this film from Iranian cinema and one of its most crucial characteristics, which we must call *spatial* realism, will be entirely absent. Please pay very close attention, as I give you my reading of *Spring*, to how Ovanessian managed to see the invisible site of a culture by aesthetically vacating and thematically depopulating it of all its cultural insignia. I would also like to warn you that we ordinarily do not see the location of a culture when we are integral to that culture. The alternative has habitually been postulated as and through an outsider's gaze. But that outsider's gaze has its own blind spots. The exceptional significance of Ovanessian's *Spring* is that in it you see the vacated site of a culture from an angle at once local and yet not implicated in it—for Ovanessian is at once domestic and yet foreign to that culture.

Ovanessian's film *Spring* emerged out of a curious corner of Iranian modernist culture called "intellectual cinema." I met Ovanessian for the first time here in New York in Spring 2000 when my colleague at the School of the Arts Andrei Serban invited him as an adjunct professor of theater. I subsequently saw Ovanessian again in Oslo, Norway, when we were both invited (along with Susan Taslimi) by the Centre for Ibsen Studies in November 2003 for a conference on the Iranian reception of Ibsen. Farin Zahedi, who at the time was writing her dissertation on the subject at the Ibsen Center, had invited us all. I subsequently invited Ovanessian to come and teach two courses on Armenian cinema and theater during the spring semester of 2005 at Columbia. On all these occasions, I have had many opportunities to talk to and learn from Ovanessian, whom I consider one of the most distinguished Iranian film and theater directors and an exceedingly learned and cultivated intellectual. While Ovanessian was in New York, I heard him give a brilliant talk on the history of Armenian cinema much to the delight of the Armenian community in New York that had sponsored the talk. I found it rich and informative. My earlier memories of Ovanessian go back to my student days in Tehran in the late 1970s. By 1968, Ovanessian had been part of a progressive band of directors who had revolutionized the theater scene in Iran. He was born in Jolfa, Isfahan, in 1941, did his early education in Tehran, and received his high school diploma in 1960. He worked with a renowned theater director, Shahin Sarkissian, as a set designer, until 1963 when he traveled to England to study cinema. He returned to Iran in 1966 and became one of the most prominent theater directors of his generation. Before he turned to *Spring* he had directed a number of shorts, among them a documentary (about thirty minutes) called *Lebbeus Whose Surname Was Thaddeus*, 1967, a DVD copy of which he brought for me to see in New York in spring 2005. This is an exquisite black-and-white film shot on location about a pilgrimage of Armenians to the mausoleum of a saint, which begins with a contemplative survey of the scared site, culminates in the congregation of the pilgrims, and concludes, after they pack and leave, with a magnificent final shot of the solitary site of the church in the middle of the desert, suddenly covered by a wandering cloud. Lebbeus, Thaddeus, or Saint Jude, known also as Jude Thaddeus or Jude Lebbeus, is known in Christianity as the patron saint of lost causes. He was a brother of St. James the Less, and one of the twelve apostles of Jesus. Jude Thaddeus is often called the "Forgotten Saint" because many people confused him with Judas Iscariot, who betrayed Jesus (and then committed suicide) and thus avoided affiliations with him. Ovanessian's documentary is shot with pious regard for the sanctity of the site, considerable attention to the social character of the event, and the wondrous occasion of a solitary sacred site suddenly transformed into a social event, and then turned back to its originary solitude.

Soon after he made *Lebbeus Whose Surname Was Thaddeus*, Ovanessian began working on a screen adaptation of Mohammad Afghani's novel *Ahu Khanom's Husband* (1968). He soon ran into some difficulties with the producer of the film and, bitterly disappointed, he abandoned the project altogether (the details of which I partially knew and the rest he explained to me over lunch when he was here in New York—it is a nasty story). Davoud Mullapour ended up directing that film, which became a landmark in modern Iranian cinema, and Ovanessian was left with a rather bitter memory of his first attempt at a feature film.

Ovanessian's first experience as a feature filmmaker was thus quite disappointing—and yet it pointed to the potential of his creative intelligence. He was the initial director of what became one of the most successful Iranian films of the late 1960s. But under circumstances beyond Ovanessian's control, Davoud Mullapour ended up directing the film, only after Ovanessian had already shot one complete sequence of a picnic scene. Though Ovanessian did not end up finishing *Ahu Khanom's Husband*, the fact that he had originally thought of adapting the book, written a script on the basis of Afghani's groundbreaking novel, secured the author's approval and endorsement of the project, and in fact started shooting all draw attention to his deep-rooted presence in contemporary Persian fiction. It is important to note that like Farrokh Ghaffari,

Ovanessian was educated in Europe, and that as an Armenian-Iranian he summons a deeply bicultural character—he is as much at home and fluent in the Iranian dimension of his cultivated character as he is in his native Armenian. His native command of Persian with his longstanding experience in modern Iranian theater combined to offset his not having been a major literary figure like Ebrahim Golestan or Forugh Farrokhzad. Like Dariush Mehrjui, however, he had the creative wherewithal to tap directly into the rich and diverse body of contemporary Persian fiction. He developed a close collaborative rapport with Ali Mohammad Afghani, though it was suddenly aborted by the unfortunate events surrounding the production of *Ahu Khanom's Husband*.

Burned by that unfortunate experience, Ovanessian turned to an Armenian story by M. Armin, from which he adapted his own screenplay. When it was first released, in 1972, *Spring* was a box-office disaster, while critically it sharply divided its admirers and detractors—some thinking it beautiful, poetic, lyrical, and revolutionary, while others considered it boring, banal, and complicated. You will search in vain among its immediate and distant reviewers, however, to find anything serious said about *Spring*. The more you read the more you are convinced that we have never deserved the poets who were born to grace our otherwise graceless lives. It is something of a miracle how we have survived as a people with a sense of pride in our presence in history. Zaven Qukasian is one of the most intelligent critics that Iranian cinema has ever produced. But in this particular instance his rather informed and potentially cogent questions, in a rare and precious interview with Ovanessian, resulted in no enduring insight into *Spring*, because Ovanessian himself gave rather short and perfunctory answers and by and large remained at a very disappointing distance from Qukasian's suggestive questions.

For example, one of the faults that people found with *Spring* was that its rhythm is too slow. Even those who have supported the film have implicitly accepted that slowness and come to its defense, attributing it to the slow pace of life in Iranian villages. May God protect Ovanessian from his supporters! I have no clue what these people, offenders and defenders, are talking about. For me, *Spring* is breathtakingly fast. I cannot keep up with it. I watch it in slow motion, sometimes frame by frame. Otherwise it just moves too quickly for a full absorption of its miraculous shots.

In fact, the problem with the critical reception of *Spring* is not with those who did not like it; it is with those who liked it. Those who came to the defense of the film did so with such an afflicted logic and poor, banal prose that they made the case against *Spring* even worse. One critic praised Arman and Mashayekhi, the two lead actors of the film, for their wonderful acting. But the acting in *Spring* is disastrously bad, as bad or even worse than in the rest of Iranian cinema, before it judiciously turned to nonprofessionals. This critic also praised the lovemaking scene between Habibeh (Mahtaj Nojumi) and her lover, which has to be one of the silliest, most ludicrous lovemaking scenes in the history of Iranian cinema. The sad predicament of *Spring* has been that those who have dismissed it have dismissed it with very good prose; and those who have praised it, have praised it with a very lame logic. The significance of *Spring* is neither in its acting (which is categorically bad) nor in its particularly powerful or convincing scenes. Its significance resides in an entirely different domain.

Next time you see *Spring*, notice that its opening credits last for exactly three minutes, with a mini-exhibition of a picture of a village wall, with a small window on the left—a wall and window very similar to Gholamhossein Saedi's description of Bayal and Dariush Mehrjui's rendition of it in *Cow*. When the credits start rolling, you can't even tell what it is you're watching. It takes you a few seconds before your eyes adjust to the proportion and texture of the wall and the window it frames. For three minutes you just sit in front of one haiku-like frame and watch the credits roll (if you care to know who did what for *Spring*) or else contemplate the design of the mass that has articulated itself in the anonymity of this wall. Then *Spring* starts and you watch it (and if I were you, I'd watch it over and over again) for exactly one hour, thirty-five minutes, and thirty seconds. But what, actually, do you see? Terrible acting, positively ridiculous dialogue, a mere suggestion of a story—and yet *Spring* has consistently and correctly (though with lopsided and entirely unconvincing logic) been considered one of the masterpieces of Iranian cinema. But why is it a masterpiece? Iranian film critics keep calling it *aram* (meaning "calm," which is just a polite word for "slow," which is exactly the curse with which its detractors have skewered it over the years); or else they say it is gentle, poetic, thought-provoking, real, and a handful of other similar and similarly generic terms that you can apply to or withdraw from just about any other film. I too believe that *Spring* is a masterpiece. But not for the acting, not for the dialogue, and not for the sex scene, which is embarrassingly silly, with Mahtaj Nojumi holding on to her chador so tightly and Parviz Pour Hosseini (her lover) holding on to his pants so pleadingly, as if their lives depended on them. But I still think Ovanessian's *Spring* is unrivaled in its brilliance and poignancy. If you know how to watch it, it will take your breath away. For that you have to wash your eyes and see differently. *"Alo kam ju,"* as Rumi said, *"Teshnegi avar beh das"*—Seek less water, and become more thirsty.

The strangest thing happened yesterday. I was at Amir Naderi's and we were watching John Ford's *The Hurricane* (1937). Five minutes into the film, two bites into the exceptionally hot salad Amir had made, and the electricity went off! We waited for a few minutes to see if it would come back on. It did not. So he made us two cups of tea and we decided to go out to the street for some fresh air and have our tea by his favorite spot, next to the laundromat right in front of his house on Tenth Street. We were not quite to the doorstep of his building when we encountered one of his neighbors, up in arms cursing everyone from George Bush to Saddam Hussein and everyone else in between. This was not a regular power failure. Apparently there was an electricity blackout all over the Eastern seaboard, all the way up to Canada and down to Washington, DC, and as far east as Michigan. No one knew what had happened. Some ten fire engines were on 10th Street right in front of Amir's building, and all the neighborhood was out in the street talking power and politics, with Amir's young lawyer neighbor taking video of the neighborhood and leading a heated discussion against George Bush and his entire administration, and how "this so-called war against terrorism," as she put it from behind her camera, "was making life impossible in this goddamn city." Her suspicion was that this power outage was a terrorist act. A kid from the neighborhood had a transistor radio with WNBC on. Mayor Michael Bloomberg was assuring people that this was not, "I repeat NOT," an act of terrorism. But the young lawyer was defiant. "You can go and fuck yourself," she shouted in the direction of the poor kid's radio, "you bastard Republican thief! You don't even let us recycle, you rascal!" I looked around and there was no sign of Amir. I looked at the direction of the laundromat. He was sitting there with our two cups of tea waiting for me. He runs away from any political discussion like a hawk from a plague—and he is the man who made *Tangsir*!

I know Naderi's neighborhood in Alphabet City almost as well as I do my own on the Upper West Side. The sense of the space, the sound (or rather silence) of the traffic, and perhaps the muted fear in the heart of the people afraid of a terrorist attack on that beautiful August afternoon had given the neighborhood an eeriness entirely alien to it. I have always believed that you need to be an intimate outsider like Arby Ovanessian to Iran or Amir Naderi to New York to see the *fictive transparency of space*, for otherwise we are too implicated in it to see it. It is a very strange thing to say. But it is true. There was no power outage in Iran that allowed Ovanessian to see this fictive composition of space in *Spring*, but he intuitively detected it like no other filmmaker of his generation. Through the collective conspiracy of his lens and his camera he registered an emptiness, a vacated space, a depopulated transparency about the physical space of his homeland otherwise concealed to the naked eye. How richer we are by virtue of that vision, impossible, in my judgment, without the insider/outsider perception of Ovanessian—one of the most gifted and least recognized Iranian artists of our time.

Amir and I sat in front of the laundromat and drank our tea, but my mind was totally distracted by the eerie silence, by the vague and unadmitted fear on the vacant faces of people in the neighborhood. It looked as if they had altogether abandon the street and the buildings that surrounded it. The walls and the doors that marked them looked more prominent, more pronounced, more visually imposing and evident— precisely the same way that objects (village roads, rooftops, farms, wells, interiors of gardens, exteriors of houses) appear in Ovanessian's *Spring*. There is a *visual silence* (if you forgive an oxymoronic expression) about Ovanessian's film, a manner of awareness of sight without the ability or need to see what exactly one senses, as if everything that we see in *Spring* we see for the very first time. I have no clue how exactly Ovanessian has achieved that visual silence, that sense of *spatial* realism entirely unprecedented in Iranian cinema. What is evident in the visual experience of his cinema is this peculiar presence of space, as if a veil is lifted from its physical disposition and we see where we live—our whereabouts—for the very first time.

We finished our tea and Amir walked me from Tenth Street and Avenue A to Seventh Avenue and Twentieth Street. He was telling me the details of his chance encounters with Bernardo Bertolucci and Ingrid Bergman, as we were negotiating our way around the winding lines in front of hardware stores selling flashlights and batteries for four times the regular price. There was a ghostly, 9/11-ish kind of silence in the air, with people having just been let go from their offices. There was a rush of people walking south toward the Financial District—with Amir and I among the very few people heading north. While Amir was telling me his hilarious story of how he once kissed Ingrid Bergman on her cheek, I was thinking, on a separate track in my mind that seemed to have a mind of its own, how populating and vacating a space changes its nature! I was thinking about the peculiar similarity of Ovanessian's *Spring* to Mark Morris' dance setups and Wing-Davey's stage production and their respective embracing of bodily volumes in a manner that made *space* reveal its own transparency. I was also thinking that in cinema, as in the case of Ovanessian's film, this can potentially become even more palpable because the eye and the camera complement and correct the transparency of the space they mark and register, thus making its lucidity visible. I concluded then that whereas in Morris' dances he vacates the space choreographically and in Wing-Davey's staging he populates it negationally, in *Spring*, Ovanessian reveals it by the inconspicuous location, diverted gaze, and imperceptible movements of his camera.

I said goodbye to Amir at the corner of Seventh and Twentieth and we parted ways, he heading south and I north, thinking to myself that the following day, 15 August, was his birthday and if this blackout were to continue I wouldn't be able to come and see him to give him the birthday gift I had bought him—a very old camera. I put my backpack on, tightened my belt, and got ready for a robust walk of a hundred blocks. People were all out in the street, having evacuated bus terminals, subway cars, train stations, parking lots, ferry docks. There was no sign of a cab or any other moving car for that matter. There was no way to leave or enter Manhattan. NYPD was on full alert and exceedingly visible. The physical attitude of New York, its laid-back and let-loose demeanor, was imposing itself like never before. Perhaps it had to do with the sudden silence—we could hear the sound of our footsteps in the streets and avenues. Perhaps it had to do with the tremor of an inarticulate fear of the post-9/11 vintage and variety. Perhaps the routine illusions of normalcy had temporarily stopped their magical irreality. I could visibly see through the physical presence of New York the same way that I could, for the first time, see through the physical presence of the thing we call "Iran" in Ovanessian's *Spring*. No one, I thought as I was passing by Penn Station, could have looked through Ovanessian's camera and seen the translucent space of "being in Iran" the way he saw it. In *Spring* it is as if he has put our habitual culture under a microscope and then cast it onto a big screen. This is what I mean by his being an insider/outsider. His eyes see things that are so obvious to the rest of us that we do not see them. They are hidden under the veil of their presence, beneath the skin of their immanence.

By the time I reached Fortieth Street, the whole world had poured into Times Square. I saw a woman holding a sign over her head that read, "Mom I am OK. I can't get through!" and keeping it right in front of the NBC camera that is always set on Times Square! "Your mama can't see, sweetheart," smiled a police officer. "Your mama's TV works with electricity, not tap water!" The woman was not amused, but pulled down her sign. Fifty seconds, I was thinking to myself at the time, into *Spring* and you know you are in the presence of something extraordinary. For about three minutes, I remembered as I adjusted my backpack and made sure I was not bumping into people as I walked, as the credits roll, you have a solid, haiku-like shot of a wall with a small window in the lower left side of the frame. It will take you a few seconds actually to see this picture, because as the camera starts rolling initially you have no clue what it is you are actually watching. Those few precious moments of uncertainty, when the light and shadows of the frame can signal and suggest just about anything, are critically important in this film, for Ovanessian casts the intimations of that uncertainty into the rest of his film. That sense of uncertainty is definitive to *Spring*, written into its visual vocabulary and narratively evident throughout the film.

Immediately after the three minutes of credits against this singular shot of a wall, you suddenly see the shady space under a tree—the cut is abrupt, but the space is soothing, the shade familiar, and yet the location entirely unknown, unfamiliar. Into the soothing presence and anonymous location of this space suddenly flies a paper plane—and it just sits there under the shadow of that tree for fifty memorable seconds until it begins to soak up the coolness and wonder of that shaded spot. Now beware, because the thieves at Pars Video, who have pirated this film without any regard for an artist's copyright, have projected their misbegotten advertisement and blasted telephone number about fifteen times and in thirty different ghastly colors, one gaudier than the other, exactly onto these glorious fifty seconds of a superb black-and-white shot. Meanwhile in Manhattan, pizza shops were selling their slices right in front of their storefronts, as were sushi bars, Indian restaurants with their tandoori chicken, Italians with their spaghetti, Mexicans brandishing their tacos. Hot-dog stands were doing a brisk business too. It cost me two of the forty dollars I had to borrow from Amir (for all the ATM machines were down) to buy a can of Coke to quench my thirst. Outrageous. I felt like Gypo Nolan (Victor McLaglen) in John Ford's *The Informer* (1935), wastefully spending the twenty pounds he got from the British police for betraying his friend Frankie McPhillip (Wallace Ford).

On the basis of its astonishingly beautiful opening shot, Ovanessian proceeds with other staccato shots of an idyllic village, all edited beautifully with the syncopated rhythm of the chimes of a ringing church bell. As soon as these bells ring, about five minutes into *Spring*, you will start to realize that Ovanessian has been deeply influenced by the master Armenian filmmaker from the former Soviet Union, Sergei Paradzhanov (1924–90). Paradzhanov first achieved international recognition with *Shadows of Our Forgotten Ancestors* (1965). His subsequent films—*The Color of Pomegranates* (1969), *The Legend of Suram Fortress* (1984), and *Ashik Kerib* (1988)—consolidated his fame as one of the most brilliant filmmakers of his generation. He successfully infused ethnography and folklore in a visual experience that used rhythm, music, dancing, and montage consciously to move away from narrative cinema. I believe Paradzhanov's *Shadows of Our Forgotten Ancestors*, which is the tragic tale of two lovers separated by feuding families, was very much on Ovanessian's mind when he was making *Spring*, not so much in terms of narrative plot as in editing rhythm and melodic vision, in which terms he is also paying homage to Paradzhanov's *The Color of Pomegranates*.

I was a hot commodity all the way to Columbus Circle because Amir had lent me an old transistor radio, on which I was listening to the news, with flocks of commuters coming to hear the latest from the mayor's office. By the time I reached Eightieth, I noted that Zabar's was auctioning—yes auctioning—all its wares, selling them to the highest bidders! I stood on the opposite side of the street and watched people bidding on pots and pans. Cut against the rhythm of the church bell in the early minutes of *Spring* is a succession of staccato shots, lasting for a little more than five minutes, one shot after another, first of a wheel pulling a bucket full of water from a spring, and then the midday sun shining through a tree, a running brook, a shady veranda, an approaching man, a feminine hand fixing the white sheet and white pillowcases of a bed, that hand opening a door, and now the man who was walking on the veranda starts taking his shirt off, drops it on a chair, and the woman who was fixing the bed puts a jar and glass of water on a mantle, before we get a medium shot of an empty room with an empty chair, and then move to an exterior shot of a church, and then a village, its serene roofs, a horse in a pasture, another shot of the same spring, a sitting dog, the veranda again, and then a medium exterior shot of a wall and a door guarding an enclosed garden, and now the rhythmic sound of approaching droshkies, two of which appear, as a man comes out and knocks at that door, another man from the same droshky starts playing the *naqqareh*, a wind instrument, and finally a woman opens the door to an adjacent house. By now eight minutes and thirty seconds have elapsed from the first frame to this door, which a boy opens, saying, "My dad says come in!"

I eventually left Zabar's and walked a few more blocks until finally I got tired around Ninety-first and Broadway, where I went to the median and sat there on a parapet in the middle of the crossroads. We are ordinarily blind to the space we inhabit, I thought, unless and until a familiar foreigner comes along and makes the familiar foreign by making the foreign familiar—I remember one of my students once told me this is the way I teach. She was right. When you see these shots in *Spring* today, they take your breath away, and yet they attracted such a scandal in Iran when *Spring* premiered in 1972. The audience had been bored and the critics rose in revolt. What in the name of madness is this, they demanded to know. As far as the box office was concerned, the film was screened for only five days at the Capri Cinema in downtown Tehran, with miserable sales. As for the critics, its detractors accused *Spring* of useless and boring formalism, of not having really anything to say. And, as I mentioned before, worse than his detractors were Ovanessian's admirers, who could come up with nothing better than calling the film "quiet and poetic."

It was almost dark and the prospect of a pitch-black night over New York was in a bizarre way quite exciting. It was a horror to climb up nine floors when I finally got home, not even knowing if I was on my own floor because it was impossible to see anything! In the serenity of the stairway I could count the sounds of my own footsteps. A night of swelling feet, candlelight, and a sky full of stars over Broadway to my right and the Hudson to my left. I tried to call Amir and my children again, but their phones were not working. By midnight I was a casualty of the Blackout of 2003, the biggest power outage in US history—on the eve of Amir Naderi's fifty-eighth birthday. "Happy Birthday, Amir," I whispered to myself and went to bed.

Let's take a step back for a better view of things. Forugh Farrokhzad was both a major poet and a pioneering filmmaker. In her cinema we witness the visual summation of her poetry. Her *poetic* realism announced the style and substance of Iranian cinema for decades to come. Ebrahim Golestan was also both a major writer and a groundbreaking filmmaker, whose *affective realism* laid the groundwork for much of what would come later. Dariush Mehrjui began the critical practice of young filmmakers collaborating with established literary figures. His successful adaptation of Gholamhossein Saedi's *psychedelic* realism in *Cow* added a new dimension to the rising Iranian cinema. If you look at all these variations on the form of *realism* you will note that they are all thematic, specific to the Iranian emotive universe (or the creative ethos of its normative ideals), and rather confident in their visual interventions into Iran's typically verbal interpretation of reality. Arby Ovanessian joined Iranian cinema precisely the way that Mehrjui did but—and here is his unique significance—from the vantage point of an internalized Other, and it is precisely this perspective, exclusive to Ovanessian and no one else, that informs his exceptionally important presence in Iranian cinematic realism. An Armenian-Iranian by birth and culture, the hybridity of his cinematic vision formed on the porous borderlines of two cultures, Ovanessian brought a varied and global perspective to contemporary performing arts—from a solitary position at once local and yet distant, familiar but foreign, to Iranian cultural modernity. He had studied cinema and theater in England, then launched a successful career as a theater director in Iran. He was chief among a number of prolific theater directors who in the 1960s revolutionized modern Iranian drama by expanding on its repertoire and innovating its dramaturgical possibilities. Before he directed *Spring* in 1972 he had made a number of short films such as *Mask* (1965), in which he experimented with testing the boundaries between fiction and reality, history and metaphor, fact and fantasy. This much he shared with many of his colleagues, Farrokh Ghaffari, Fereydoun Rahnama, Dariush Mehrjui, and Bahman Farmanara in particular. But what is unique to his *spatial* realism is his narratively non-thematic, visually undomesticated, and creatively insecure perspective of Iranian culture. As a result, his turn to cinema, with *Spring* as his most significant achievement, had all the confidence of an insider and yet the unusual advantage of an outsider. This I have to explain in some detail.

Foremost in *Spring* is a minimalist mise en scène, confident long takes, melodic editing, and a very deliberate—almost self-conscious—rhythm that has over time become a hallmark of Iranian cinema. By the time the young boy opens the door, about eight minutes and thirty seconds into the film, and says to the man who has been knocking at the door, "My dad says come in!" the film has thoroughly established its melodic and space-conscious visual vocabulary. Thereafter, a dying man, laid literally on his deathbed, is the first narrative throw to enter the spatial universe that Ovanessian has already masterfully crafted. Who this anonymous man is, why he is ill, why his friends and relatives are paying him a visit, or any other piece of information of this sort becomes rather acciden-tal to the rest of the film. Here is where I think Ovanessian's detractors and admirers have equally failed. Much of the anger and frustration with *Spring* emerges from habitually taking this suggestion of a narrative plot too literally, while much of the empty praise heaped on it comes from a fundamental failure to read the visual vocabulary that consistently takes precedence over the narrative. Almost flamboyantly, *Spring* calls atten-tion to its spatial presence, rather than to what is taking place within that space. Ovanessian's cinema is a visual experience in the emotional charge of a space. Unfolding sequences generate and sustain that mood in an almost Aristotelian exercise in visual sorites, whereby the predicate of every shot becomes the subject of the next.

The crucial aspect of *Spring*, located right here between its visual imagination of space and verbal opacity of narrative, is that its terrible acting and even worse dialogue have a subtextual function of revealing what constitutes this film—its spatial reflections on moods and manners, gestures and sentiments, evocative tones and imperceptible tempera-ments. Ovanessian is neither a character director nor is he exactly a master of Persian prose. But he has a set of eyes that see otherwise invis-ible sights, and thus his *spatial* realism must be the principal point of any serious critique of his masterpiece. *Spring* commences, continues, and concludes with an intimation of categorical uncertainty. Nothing is ever conceptually clear about *Spring*. Because of this categorical uncertainty Ovanessian can intimate his visions of otherwise invisible sights; as if by turning down the volume of the narrative his camera's sense percep-tion is increased. Instead of narrative, Ovanessian is a master of visual rhythm—a rhythm that reveals the nooks and crannies of a sculpted space with which bodies have a corporeal correspondence, a creative conversation, a suggestive choreography. We will have watched his film entirely from the wrong angle if we were to try to follow its story, instead of sensing the vibrations of his melodic shots and harmonic cuts. The narratively non-thematic cinema that thus results in *Spring* is visually untamed, its vision not ordinary, its perception not lulled by a customary habitation in its natural environment. Ovanessian sees and shows things in the unfamiliar strangeness of their otherwise familiar settings. This visually un-domesticated look is informed and animated by a creatively insecure energy, whose insecurity is in effect the principal source of its power and intensity.

This creative insecurity is a perspective or a method that is not ossified and assured in its disruptive forays into capturing the visual evidence of its observations. The closest philosophical proposition that I can think of to match the aesthetic suggestion of creative insecurity is what the great contemporary Italian philosopher Gianni Vattimo calls *il pensiero debole*, "the weak thought"—namely a mode of thinking that is not predicated on violent metaphysical assumptions but rather proceeds on provisional propositions and suggestions. The same is true about Ovanessian's camera, which is entirely alien to what, in comparison, appears as violent, even bullying, visual superimpositions of the camera on reality. Even Abbas Kiarostami at his most gentle and unobtrusive has the creative confidence of telling his camera what to show—whereas Ovanessian's camera is rather bashful, hesitant, tentative. He does not show a street but the traces of its own memories; he does not picture a tree but shapes the shadow of its presence; he does not portray a person but projects the suggestion of a character. One can perhaps attribute this virtue of Ovanessian's cinema to his being doubly an outsider to a culture he will ultimately have to call home. As an Armenian-Iranian who received much of his cinematic education in Europe, Ovanessian effectively turned his outsider's gaze into the internalized Other of Iranian cultural modernity. This is no mean, ordinary achievement. I have to explain this idea of an internalized Other more carefully, after a more detailed reading of *Spring*.

Lately I have been watching Ovanessian's *Spring* regularly. It's a terrible copy. The good copy that Ovanessian himself has sent me from Paris has yet to arrive. I wonder if there is still a good print of this film left in Iran. It was produced by Iranian National Television. If there is, make sure to see it, and see it very carefully. It has much to teach you. Once you get over the terrible acting and the tortured dialogue, and then beyond the mere suggestion of a story, you are granted permission to enter *Spring* as a cinematic event, there and then to watch his camera occasion a spatial contemplation unprecedented in Iranian cinema. What I mean by spatial contemplation is Ovanessian's uncanny ability to sense and suggest the environmental capacity of a location—a street, a house, a garden, a room, a brook, a pasture, a farm, anything and everything he looks at through his camera.

Two of Ovanessian's cinematic practices are integral to the way he creates and sustains this spatial contemplation. One is the consistently unobtrusive, almost bashful (I am even tempted to say noble) way he locates his camera; and the other his equally considerate, pensive, and unobtrusive editing. If *Spring* was the only evidence left a hundred years from now of the *soul* (I rarely have a use for this word, but now I do) of an Iranian rural setting, we will have lost nothing. It is as if Ovanessian woke up one day remembering a perfect dream of an Iranian village, populated by all the factual and figurative sentiments of its people, and then got up, took his camera, and went out and took pictures of his dream—perfect visual memories of something that never happened for it was always there. There is something in the fluency of his vision, in those memorial pictures he took, that makes the familiar foreign—and the foreign familiar—and thus the space that it occupies more visible to the naked eye.

No other filmmaker would have succeeded in exposing the hidden dimensions of spatial realism, because as an Armenian-Iranian Ovanessian occupies the rare position of an outsider inside his culture. In the course of Iran's encounter with colonial modernity, Armenian-Iranians have had a particularly significant role to play. They have occupied what my old teacher Philip Rieff used to call a *remissive space*, in which they could do things, get away with things, that Muslim Iranians could never do. In art in particular, from revolutionary activists to popular vocalists, Armenians have been at the forefront of Iranian cultural and political modernity. From their remissive space, at once Iranian and non-Muslim, Armenians have been such crucial catalysts of progressive change that without their instrumental role the fate of modernity in our homeland would have been much different, and for the worse. Ovanessian is a perfect example of what I mean here by occupying a remissive space. His exceptionally perceptive style is animated and informed precisely by the paradoxical angle that only an outsider who is nonetheless privy to the texture and disposition of a culture, and that from an accented angle, can master.

Let me now give you an example of how Ovanessian's hesitant gaze achieves a spatial realism. As I have told you on many occasions, even the best Iranian filmmakers (among a host of others in our geographical neighborhood) have difficulty shooting sex scenes. One of the best examples of what I mean by this is the sequence in *Spring* where Parviz is sitting down and holding fast to his pants while Habibeh is standing up and holding tightly to her chador. It is really a poor excuse of a love scene. The problem of shooting a successful sex scene is rather irrelevant to the current harassments of censorship in the Islamic Republic, or before that during the Pahlavi monarchy, for there were certainly many sex scenes shot and screened during that regime. The problem has a much simpler and more immediate cause in the bizarre combination of patriarchal power and colonial gaze that have distorted our bodily memory of ourselves. The story of the aterritorial colonization of our homeland (at the very same time that colonial modernity invented the very notion of "homeland") that mutated our body into a singular site of violence and alienated us from the physical sight of our bodies is a rather long story that I have to tell you on another occasion. (I have written about it in my works on Shirin Neshat.) I bring this problem to your attention now just to show you how the awkwardness of that sex scene in *Spring* is in this particular case quite instrumental in demonstrating my point about Ovanessian's unusual ability for depicting spatial realism.

From the moment that Habibeh and her lover meet in the vestibule of her home then walk through her garden and onto the veranda and finally into the room in which they make love, Ovanessian's camera is far more conscious of the space in which they move and interact than it is attentive to their physical presence. For all Ovanessian's camera cares, these two lovers might as well be two flies on the wall, or else engaged in a deep philosophical discussion. It is the wall, the walkway through the garden, the light and shadow of the vestibule behind the enclosed door, that this particular camera cares to contemplate. The awkwardness of the lovemaking scene, the affected dialogue, and the forced acting you see here are all in fact rather welcome because their offbeatness actually syncopates well with the masterful mise en scène, camera location, and above all very effective editing. I might even be tempted to suggest that perhaps Ovanessian's long career as a theater director has had an effect on the theatricality of his acting direction—the formal, stylized, and pantomime-like acting that gives Ovanessian's scenes a feeling of very effective puppeteering that matches perfectly with our visual awareness of the space in which they move.

The reason that I keep emphasizing the bad acting, terrible (almost unbearable) dialogue, and the mere suggestion of a story in *Spring* is not to diminish a film that I consider one of the masterpieces of Iranian cinema, but instead to draw your attention to an organic link between these shortfalls of the film and what I suggest is its revolutionary, entirely unprecedented contribution, namely its spatial realism. The first scene in which Habibeh appears is in my judgment one of the best shots in the entire history of Iranian cinema. Nothing of thematic or narrative significance happens in this scene. It is of an empty, almost desolate street, with a mud-brick wall darkened by the shade of trees. Tall and wearing a white chador, Habibeh is walking toward the camera in a wide-angle long shot, while away from the camera frog-jumps a little girl in a dark shirt, playing what appears to be a game of hopscotch by herself. The camera remains motionless. It is an invitation for the soul of the space to breathe, to be fully present. The movements of Habibeh and the little girl are so accurately choreographed—the near slow motion of one and the jumping staccatos of the other—that they are instrumental in exuding the spatial presence of the street, its suggestion of life, and ultimately a conscious awareness of the location of Habibeh's being, otherwise hidden from the naked eye.

The flaws of this film, as a result, are not just to be forgiven; they are to be understood as the very reason and occasion of its prodigious ability to contemplate spatially on shapes and volume, shades and shadows, sites and surfaces, angles and dimensions. To make this paradoxical point, here I deliberately speak in terms of visual abstractions because I make a distinction between space and atmosphere. Ovanessian is the best filmmaker of space, and not of atmosphere, which Ebrahim Golestan pioneered and Dariush Mehrjui nearly perfected. Ovanessian is in fact entirely incapable of creating and sustaining atmospheric templates in his cinema—and precisely for that reason his eyes are best equipped to see the space to which others are blinded by too much familiarity.

Consider the mourning ceremony, after the death of the husband, Arman, on the banks of the brook. A group of men are sitting around a spread and preparing to drink to their fallen friend. The scene is entirely iconic, ritualistic, stylized, and visually mannered—and precisely in those terms Ovanessian has managed to generate and convey a spontaneous sense of space that never moves to make an atmospheric suggestion. We scarcely have any notion of those people's thoughts, emotions, reflections, or the nature of their relationship to their friend—and yet when Ovanessian privileges the spatial complexion of their gathering he manages to capture the soul of the reason why they are there. He does so not with dialogue but by the way he arranges his actors around their drinking paraphernalia, by the manner in which one of them pours the wine, by the solemnity of their dignified toast, by the murmuring flow of the brook that is running nearby, by the melodic incantation of the music that we hear, by the sound of the glass cups being thrown and falling into the brook, and ultimately by the sense of mourning that becomes evident in the space that Ovanessian has created.

Spring is not a successful case of atmospheric filmmaking because Ovanessian is not keenly attuned to the culture that informs the space. But that is precisely the reason he can *see* it so well. He has a visual sense of space precisely because he does not have an atmospheric awareness of it. As a mostly European-educated Armenian, Ovanessian is twice removed from the atmospheric consciousness of that space—of the historical consciousness that informs it, the class differences that animate it, the social practices that attend it, or cultural codes that agitate it. Precisely because he is closed to that atmospheric environment (in which social agents interact through densely coded gestures and convey heavily loaded meanings) he is open to its spatial presence. Ovanessian's awareness of space is entirely visual because he does not cerebrally understand it, and in this particular case his cultural obliviousness is essential to his imaginative power to see it so well and register it in his camera. In this respect, Ovanessian is close to Mehrjui and anticipates Farmanara—three European- or American-educated filmmakers who were distinctively distanced from their native cultural location. But none of these succeeds like Ovanessian in turning that physical and cultural distance into spatial intimacy.

In January 2005 I invited Ovanessian to come to Columbia to teach two courses on Armenian cinema and theater. Only then did he bring it to my attention that almost at the same time that he was shooting *Spring*, an Armenian filmmaker from Soviet Armenia, Armen Manarian, had quite by serendipity made a film on the basis of precisely the same short story. Ovanessian gave me a video copy of Manarian's *The Spring of Heghnar* (1970) and I watched it a couple of times. It is absolutely remarkable to see how two Armenian filmmakers, one in Iran and the other in Armenia, turned an identical short story into two films so vastly different from each other. Manarian's film is far more descriptive and narrative, almost entirely devoid of the spatial realism that is the hallmark of Ovanessian's version. While Manarian's *The Spring of Heghnar* is very much influenced by the Soviet socialist realism of its period, Ovanessian's *Spring* is in creative conversation with the dominant formalism of his immediate Iranian context, making its own lasting contribution by a careful construction of spatial realism.

I believe that *Spring* has a global significance beyond the context of Iranian cinema—a claim that I need to explain in some detail. A few years ago I put together a course on "The Sociology of Cinema" at Columbia University. There were a number of reasons that had prompted me to do so, which even today, in retrospect, appear pertinent, though preparatory for reasons I could not have anticipated at the time. My primary intention, I remember, was to introduce my students to a range of public and private spaces in which matters of crucial cultural consequence were being actively amplified, negotiated, subverted, and superceded. At the time, I had just finished my book on the Islamic revolution in Iran, *Theology of Discontent*, and writing that book had made me paradoxically conscious of the radically non-Islamic cultural forces and factors dominant in societies that, following the Orientalist legacy, continue to be called Islamic. The point was not that Islam was absent from these societies, but that Islam was present in a more spacious way—a more accommodating domain, deliberately or out of habit outside our analytical view, that included a multiplicities of sacred and secular referents irreducible to a single sign called "Islam" that included but was not limited to religious insignia. Evidenced in any number of films I watched and closely studied in preparation for the course was the compelling presence of cultures, summoned and represented in their public and private spaces, that were in a state of flux and transmutation, as opposed to the false assumption that any culture can at any point be stationary, stable, or resistant to its own redefinition and its relocation in history. What I saw in these films were the aesthetic parameters of cultures engaged in active, even violent, conversation with factors and forces they remembered, feared, or fancied as their history. (Remember, though, that art does not take history seriously; it usually takes it for a ride.) At times radical consequences were contingent on these not particularly hesitant methods of cultural conversation—as when, for example, art manipulates reality to tease out its hidden anxieties, say when Forugh Farrokhzad goes into a leper colony to see what exactly goes into the making of a stigmatized taboo.

There were other factors, more immediate and rudimentary, that had prompted me to offer a film course on a range of apparently incongruent "Middle Eastern" cultures. First and foremost, I along with quite a number of my colleagues had grown particularly suspicious of the textualizing to which the Orientalist project had subjected these cultures, so that if you read, say, the *Bhagavad Gita*, or the Qur'an, or the *Shahnameh*, then you knew how to decode and understand "the Indians," "the Muslims," and "the Persians." In an attempt to de-textualize these rich and effervescent cultures, which of course included such texts but was not limited to them, I was looking for a way for my students to make direct and close contact, eyeball to eyeball, as it were, with a range of all-too-human fears and fantasies, hopes and anxieties, which are the very stuff of which cultures are historically made, metaphysically sustained, and aesthetically subverted. Cinema, I thought, would forcefully shake my students out of their reading habits, deny them their subconscious textualizing strategies, and force them to walk, however vicariously or voyeuristically, in the streets of Istanbul, the back alleys of Jerusalem, the hills of Galilee, the slums of Cairo, the shantytowns of Tehran. With films I could take them to the mountaintops of Kurdistan where they could see a massacre of Kurdish rebels by the Turkish army, to a Palestinian village where they could participate in a wedding presided over by Israeli army officers, to an Israeli prison where they could shed their political prejudices of one kind or another and see identities altered and affiliations transferred, to the streets of Cairo where they could sing and dance with a group of soccer fans sending off their national team to the World Cup, to the rice paddies of northern Iran where they could see real, heroic, splendidly beautiful women who would redefine for them their conceptions of nature, humanity, womanhood, childhood, personhood, birth, being—just to give a few thematically unrelated and quite random examples. In short, where I could lead them visually to place themselves in the distance of their own altered humanity—the face and space of the Other.

I thought I could begin to cultivate in my students a disciplined habit of entering these spaces in a manner more conducive to the realities of cultures at work, with all their miseries and majesties, rather than treating the contemporary "Middle East," as they call it, as the archeological site of a once glorious but now defunct array of civilizations. Either the dead relics of defunct civilizations or else oilfields with colorful flags on them: These were the two debilitating opposites that I sought to undo. I remember the pain and anger I felt when the caption on the cover of an issue of *The Economist* depicting a map of the "Middle East" read, "What's Something Nice Like Oil Doing There?" As I also remember the instant affinity I felt with Yehuda Amichai when I first read his poem "Tourists":

> Visits of condolence is all we get from them.
> They squat at the Holocaust Memorial,
> They put on grave faces at the Wailing Wall
> And they laugh behind heavy curtains
> In their hotels.
> They have their pictures taken
> Together with our famous dead
> At Rachel's Tomb and Herzel's Tomb
> And on the top of Ammunition Hill.
> They weep over our sweet boys
> And lust over our tough girls
> And hang up their underwear
> To dry quickly
> In cool, blue bathrooms.
>
> Once I was sitting on the steps near the gate at David's
> Citadel and I put down my two heavy baskets beside me.
> A group of tourists was standing there around their guide,
> and I became their point of reference. "You see that man
> over there with the baskets? A little to the right of his
> head there's an arch from the Roman period. A little to the
> right of his head." "But he's moving, he's moving!" I said
> to myself: Redemption will come only when they are told,
> "Do you see that arch over there from the Roman period?
> It doesn't matter, but near it, a little to the left and then
> down a bit, there's a man who has just bought fruit and veg-
> etables for his family."

As you can see from this poem, there is an evident politics to the poetics of space and what it entails—the gentle shift of reference away from the Roman arch and toward the place where the man with a grocery bag is sitting: "a little to the left and then down a bit." In the not-so-hidden politics of this poem, Amichai was also counter-textually linking Rachel's Tomb to Herzel's Tomb, both of them to Ammunition Hill, and everything altogether to a Roman arch. He projects an Israeli topography onto a Zionist historiography (built on the broken backs of the hidden and denied Palestinians), adding momentum to the point that the politics of a space is essential to its poetics and aesthetics.

My fascination with Amichai's poem, as indeed my anger with *The Economist*'s caption, reflected a longtime fear that our students were coming back from their summer trips to Turkey, Palestine, Lebanon, Egypt, Iran, or India with devastating tales of Kurdish massacres, the *gestarbeiter* in Germany, the Intifada in Gaza, buses blown up in Jerusalem, apartment buildings demolished in southern Lebanon, the toll of a medieval theocracy on human decency in Iran, or child prostitution in India, and yet we were expected to give them in the following fall semester sanitized, Orientalized, exoticized, or, at the very least, jaundiced versions of "Middle East and Asian Cultures and Civilizations." I was incapable of doing that. What civilization? To this day I come down with rashes any time I hear that word. It is uncivil to talk about civilization these days.

I have always found this de-textualizing aspect of cinema exceptionally important in conveying brutal and debilitating anxieties, paralyzing paradoxes, and yet empowering ironies active in any culture. Once I began to cultivate in my students a wider grasp of the dehumanizing function of the text (turning people into books their ancestors wrote) we were ready to puncture the patriarchal authority of the book itself in the land of the Bible, as it were, through a transgressive aesthetics of moving pictures. That done, we could then see cultures not as monolithic blocks of unchanging truths but in a more fluid state of unending, open-ended conversations among the ever-newer generations of dissenters asking the paternal powers: "By what authority?" Images and stories they told and implied thus gradually became the meaningful repository of effective histories that the inhabitants of these cultures (as opposed to what the Orientalists used to call the Turks, the Arabs, the Jews, the Persians) had actually lived. Please note that I do not mean here to fetishize films even as I intend to de-fetishize books. Films can be as much essentializing as books can be liberating. But I think the open-endedness of the visual imagery restores a sense of hermeneutical undecidability, and thus gives films more a cultural life than an iconic certitude.

Beyond the crucial de-textualization of these living cultures, I remember I also had a compelling concern with decolonizing the manners in which they are read and received. I thought that if I could offer a course in which the visual evidence from any number of these cultures—their spatial defiance of their geographical designation—would be seen together, then at least within the confines of a small classroom in a small department, we would defy the military logic of colonialism and its cultural aftermath. Students ordinarily attracted only to Arabic, Hebrew, Persian, or Turkish cultures, and only to one of them at the expense of anything else, from indifference or hostility to others, began to see visual evidence of realities beyond the reach of their habitual sympathy and politics. Students of Jewish, Arab, Kurdish, Turkish, or Iranian descent began to identify with characters on the opposite side of their preferred or perfunctory politics. Contingency and irony, perplexity and paradox, incongruity and inconsistency became the paramount sentiments of the most exhilarating moments in our class discussions. Something in the metaphysics of fear, in the dichotomy of good and evil, began to crack. Binary oppositions let go of their fabricated facticities. Cultures appeared not as the God-given mandates of fearful Truth, but as the splendid carnivals of laughter, quieting the anxieties of sourceless despair.

I also wanted to use the occasion of these films to de-exoticize the cultures they represented. I thought that these films would help me show both the beauty and the banality of these cultures in terms relevant to their current and effective histories, constitutional to the changing and regenerative sentiments they invoke. What I feared was that, in quite a number of our students, graduate and undergraduate, I detected a lingering sense of romanticism and nostalgia in their inexplicable attraction to the "Middle East." I had no patience for the latter-day Lawrences of Arabia and Richard Burtons dressing themselves in local clothes, "going native," daring the elements, and rescuing the locals from their own evil. Between British colonialism and Hollywood capitalism enough caricatures of "the natives" had been mocked up. From *Ali Baba and the Forty Thieves* to *Aladdin*, vulgar romanticizations of the "Middle East" had popularly reflected the Orientalist practice of massively exoticizing an array of existing cultures to a point where even some of my senior colleagues were perfectly comfortable with phrases like, "Oh, it was so...how shall I put it?...Turkish," or "Well, you know, in a typically Persian way," or "In true Arab fashion," or "It was so Indian, you know." I've even read applications from prospective graduate students stating their reasons for joining our department because they "just love the Arabs." There was a fundamental discrepancy, I thought, a vast and widening distance, between that kind of language and realities that placed these cultures in their respective histories, relevant geographies, and spatial evidence.

I was convinced that nothing better than Yilmaz Güney's *Yol* (1982), for example, could cure a person from the Oriental conceptions of the

Turks and their harems that, from Mozart's *Abduction from the Seraglio* (1782) to Rossini's *Muḥammad II* (1820)—and countless more—had captivated the so-called European imagination. Both in *Orientalism* (1978) and *Culture and Imperialism* (1993), Edward Said had gone a long way toward explaining, particularly with the text of Verdi's *Aida* (1871), the Orientalizing force of these cultural artifacts (I can't believe I am writing these words a week after Edward's death and as we make arrangements for his funeral here at Columbia). If opera, the visual and performative precursor of cinema, could be at the service of Orientalizing cultures, then the films produced from within these cultures by the Orientals themselves, as it were, could be used to de-Orientalize them—which simply means narratively to extract them from the binary opposition that Orientalists had created for them and let them loose to breathe normally in the space of their own destiny. The "Middle Eastern" cinema, in this respect, was an act of counter-representation, I thought. When Mustafa Akkad in *Lion of the Desert* (1981) uses the Hollywood epic genre to celebrate the anticolonial saga of Omar Mokhtar, a critical act of reversing the gaze of the camera takes place that I find profoundly liberating. But my emphasis on these historical reversals was not merely to demonstrate the active agency of all modes of representation. My concern with de-Orientalization was more an act of resistance, a demonstrative strategy of narrative liberation, in order to begin to cultivate a critical intimacy with these cultures—in terms domestic to their historical vicissitude.

Along the same lines of de-Orientalization, I also had in mind de-Islamicizing the active perception of these cultures among our students. "Islamic society" is a generic and misleading appellation. To be sure, any creative reconstruction of Islam requires a dialogical conversation with the material and historical forces that are a part of its long history. But the cultural composition of any society or community historically identified as "Islamic" has never been reducible to any monolithic conception of Islam. Any number of pre-, post-, and non-Islamic cultures—from Central Asian to Berber, Egyptian, Arab, Turkish, Iranian, Indian, and Chinese, and then of course Zoroastrian, Hebrew, Hindu, and Christian—have historically braced and effectively synthesized the historical reconstructions of Islams (in plural) from the ever-changing modes of remembering the Qur'anic and Hadith master narratives. We have had a juridical Islam (predicated on a nomocentric interpretation of the faith) constitutionally at odds with the philosophical Islam (predicated on a logocentric reading of the selfsame faith), and both at odds with a mystical Islam (predicated on a homocentric reading of the very same faith). All of these readings have always made an exclusive claim on Islam as such, but none of them has ever succeeded in disenfranchising the others. The entire Islamic intellectual history is the story of these multiple narratives at once negating and yet corroborating each other, with multiple communal constituencies and conflicting centers of power embracing or dismissing them. The so-called unfinished project of modernity, to use Habermas' critical claim, in practically all of these societies has added zest and momentum to diversities of cultures conveniently packed together by both Orientalists, and their cohort Islamist ideologues, as Islamic. Only in the retarded rhetoric of aging Orientalists in Princeton, and only in the agitated imagination of flat-footed Islamists in Qom, does the term "Islamic society" carry indubitable, essentialist, and categorical authority. The films my students and I were watching, I realized, demonstrated the reality of factual diversities—in flesh and blood—that dismantled such assumptions and cleared the way for far more realistically sculpted readings of these societies.

I found the films we watched, directed and acted by "Middle Eastern" filmmakers, extremely helpful in undoing any lingering notion of not only Islamic societies but any other essentializing assumption that does harm to the integral contradictions of these cultures. Even more significantly they reinforced the notion these continue to be cultures in the making, that these cultures, like all other living organisms, negotiate with the forces of their own history, that by no stretch of imagination are they settled or content. Without exception, the films that I screened for my students constitute compelling visual evidence that these cultures are far from yielding obediently to a monolithic definition of them, whether it be Orientalist, fundamentalist, or Eurocentric. These cultures, as evidenced in these films, radically resist textualization, exoticization, Orientalization, or Islamization. They are colorful carnivals of an open-ended parade, with no definitive point of origin or destination, no reason, logic, or return, just a Dionysian eruption of delusions in which reality is manipulated and truth revealed.

I took this detour to show you the more wide-angled, long shot perspective of where I think Ovanessian's *Spring* sits in terms of radically de-essentializing the visual imagination (specifying the spatial location and temporal whereabouts) of a culture. More than any film I know, *Spring* breaks this terrible act of abusive cultural representation, which is predicated on a tyrannically blind and silent metaphysics—a supernal categorization of communal cultures beyond and above their historical specificities. Through its unusual *spatial realism*, *Spring*, in my judgment, is a remarkably eloquent act of cultural subversion, and as such it allows far more intimate access to the volatile nature of culture as an occasion to challenge the powers that try to legislate, canonize, and regulate it. The *spatial realism* of *Spring* is so radical and anti-narrative that just about everything in the film is at the service of a visual de-sedimentation of its received culture. I strongly suggest you watch this film once with the volume completely down, not hearing a word or a sound. Spatial reflection is quintessential to this film. Never allow the suggestion of the storyline to distract you from the real protagonists of *Spring*—the streets and alleys, farms and pastures, roofs and gardens, animal and vegetal shapes, light and shade, trees and brooks. By denying the comfort of a narrative cohesion to these locations, Ovanessian has restored in them their innate visual vocabulary and formalism—simply the way shapes solicit sentiments before they have become things, or things have been given names, or names are incorporated into sentences and stories.

Spring is narrated, to the degree that it is based on or is in need of any narrative, around a triangular speculation on love, lust, and loyalty. A man (played by the actor Arman) is about to die, and summons his son to tell him something important. We never see him actually telling his son anything, and the suggestion of a flashback is so visually attenuated that it remains quite unclear whether we are witnessing the story of this man's wife betraying him or else a visual reimagination of that story. From the tunnel-vision scene of a street, in which we see a woman approaching the camera while a little girl hops away from it, the story begins to re-unravel. The woman is Habibeh (Mahtaj Nojumi), going home to her husband. She becomes thirsty and tries to drink a handful of water from a spring when it suddenly stops flowing. She is startled; a door opens, a young man (played by Jamshid Mashayekhi) comes out, apologizes for having turned off the flow of water from behind the door, and offers to turn the water on for her to drink. She refuses and leaves, but the brief encounter is sufficient for the young man to fall madly in love with her. Habibeh's husband builds spring wells, and he and the man who has fallen madly in love with Habibeh turn out to be close friends. Meanwhile Habibeh herself is equally madly in love with yet another younger man (played by Parviz Pour Hosseini). When Jamshid Mashayekhi's character realizes that he has fallen in love with his friend's wife, he commits suicide at his own farm, at which point we find out that he was already married and has a wife and a little girl. The suicide adds fuel to Habibeh's already scandalous reputation, for having an adulterous relationship with the man she loves. The men and women of the village begin to gossip and plot to murder Habibeh. She too commits suicide, while the man she loves becomes desolate and, in despair, runs away to the desert, while her husband buries her body inside their home and on top of her grave constructs a reflective pool.

This story is entirely tangential to what is happening visually in *Spring*, which has a story of its own, as it were. *Spring* visualizes the private and public spaces of this archetypal village in a state of flux, when and where they can go in any number of directions. Although Ovanessian's film is loosely based on a short story, it is one of the most visual films of its generation, and as such no other film of that period de-textualizes Iranian culture quite the same way that *Spring* does, giving it a refreshingly cha-otic lease on life. The result is that the poetics of space that Ovanessian crafts and cultivates in *Spring* projects the culture he habitually calls home onto the opposite pole of its politics—it contrives a mundane normative blindness to its setting's historical and geographical whereabouts. The prosaic nature of the story that Ovanessian tells in *Spring* is thus actu-ally instrumental to the visual projection of that space in which mundane realities play themselves against their cultural codifications. We can never tell where exactly this village is—though it projects the very soul of a rural habitat. The specific sites of the village, as a result, become locations with-out any address, objects without any name, farms without topographical coordinates, and the people who inhabit this place are individuals without designated destinies, humans without racialized identities, and yet they do inhabit and inform a culture. The film, then, achieves the quite rare capacity of generating its own local culture—a culture that is no longer Iranian, Armenian, Islamic, Oriental, Occidental, or any other such term of territorial categorization. And yet it has used the building blocks of all these familiar cultures to craft its unfamiliar location. Cinema, as a result, becomes an art that is *sui generis*, giving birth to the ethos of its own mak-ing, predicated on the mythos that it has crafted *ex nihilo*.

Ovanessian's vision of the plain, ordinarily invisible sight of the evi-dent space—behind and beyond its cultural codification (as home or abroad, central or peripheral, East or West, rich or poor, descriptive or allegorical)—is integral to the aesthetic de-colonization of our visual perceptions of reality because it takes the codified sight back to its most elemental imaginative force fields. In the first eight minutes of the film, a succession of long takes both suggests and subverts the thematic ideas of a narrative—the quintessential moment of this counter-metaphysics of meaning and signification—where the verbal completely collapses and the visual takes over. Predicated on that visual restoration of the chaotic sign (when signifiers seem to mean something, but they never quite do) in the guise of perfectly shot frames, then throughout the rest of *Spring*, Ovan-essian's camera has the ability of de-exoticizing the space it covers, placing its perspective somewhere between the familiar glance of a native and the exoticizing gaze of a foreigner. Ovanessian's look is neither native nor alien, and as a result his perspective is uniquely placed to find, ex nihilo, a vision of spaces otherwise concealed behind a thick layer of familiarity. His shots of the village streets, the mise en scène of women sitting and weaving, of children playing in a brook, of men drinking under a tree, and, perhaps most effectively of all, his two drinking sequences, one out-door between the husband and his friend next to a vegetable garden and the other, interior scene with Habibeh and her son and mother-in-law, are vintage visions of a spatial awareness, of emotions conveyed visually and not narratively, of familiar sites seen from an unfamiliar angle, where all systematic acts of locating, naming, and exoticizing a place categorically fail and yield to the sheer physical presence of a space before it is named, just where it can assert its emotive autonomy.

I am fascinated with *Spring* because it is only in this film that I have seen, in its purest and most abstract sense, how visualizing the spatial sight of a culture in the invisible place of its material evidence is such a remarkable antidote against the metaphysical injustice done to it by an entire history of cultural textualization—of reducing living people to their dead certainties, their present hopes to their past anxieties. We as a people are not hidden in our literary masterpieces or poetic ancestors. They, conversely, live within us. You do not go to Hafez's ghazals and seek traces of our cultural identity. The best that is in Hafez's ghazals already constitutes the lyricism of our vision as ordinary human beings. You do not go to the *Shahnameh* and read for past and irrelevant glories; you look for the epic proportions of a people struggling for contemporary dignity by actively remembering a Ferdowsi in their past. You do not textualize a culture; you humanize the textual evidence of their contemporary (not ancestral) claims to decency. The significance of *Spring*, as a creative work of art, is to restore to familiar sights their unfamiliar (repressed, forgotten, abandoned) participation in giving our spatial location in history a renewed meaning, just as the familiarly hidden became evident to me during that solitary walk from one end of blackout Manhattan to the other. New York on that day in August appeared to me strangely familiar—it was both New York and not New York. All the hidden proportions of its architectonic strangeness suddenly came out for a parade. It was as if it was not us New Yorkers walking through our familiar city, but the buildings and parks, skyscrapers and landmarks, coming out of their habitual designations for a walk on the vacated avenues of our imagination of them.

Spring's rhetorical narrative, as Roland Barthes would call it, is set against nothing other than the spatial sights of a village that is reduced to its elemental visual evidence. The literality of these images is transfigured to anticipate metaphoric tales of cultures yet to become, and yet almost already there. The remarkable cinematic language that *Spring* successfully achieves is pregnant with the self-regenerative possibilities of the story it both tells and interrupts, as it tries to remember/forget its own history. The uninhibited voyeurism you take part in when you watch *Spring* undressing its own veiled visual anxieties is conducive to reaching beyond the daily headlines of a culture-in-practice and into the self-sustaining terms of its future enchantments. Watching *Spring* means something more than engaging in a fictive illusion of having been there. It signals an active, however vicarious, participation in a rhetorical retelling of reality, so that reality itself begins to speak hitherto unspoken versions of itself, versions that could ultimately undo the way opposing politics of textuality have sought to codify them. In a remarkably transgressive way, *Spring* celebrates (by a structural dissonance between its narrativity and its visuality, between the story it tries to tell and the spaces it manages to delineate) the fictive transparency of the real, and the resistance of the transitory to permanent codification, narrativization, and historicization.

Taking full advantage of his privileged position as the internalized Other of Iranian culture, Ovanessian's look is from the cultural periphery of the space he must paradoxically call home. This look is perceptive because it transcends the banalities of his culture, and lifts the veil of its customary blindness—precisely because he is not culturally implicated in the atmospheric consciousness of these spaces. The result is a unique, unprecedented, and groundbreaking mode of visual modernism without any investment in colonial modernity—and this, as I have told you on many occasions, is the single most important aspect of our contemporary visual, performative, and literary arts.

The sequence in which Habibeh walks toward the camera while a young girl in torn clothing jumps away from it is the singular reference of visual atemporality in this film. Here Ovanessian suggests the reversal of time through which he will tell the story of Habibeh. This scene is the best example of how visualizing a cultural location becomes a way of making it dialogical, leading it into speaking the terms of its inner conversations, its give and take with a history or memory it simultaneously receives and interrogates. Consider the anecdotal utterances halfway through the film where over the shots of veiled women gathering and weaving, Ovanessian narrates what in Iran we used to call *caricalamature*, a play on caricature, meaning satirical staccatos interrupting reality though not with drawings but with words (Parviz Shapour, Forugh Farrokhzad's estranged husband, was the best practitioner of these satirical phrases). These were satirically clever phrases, on the pattern of haiku, but always with a humorous twist to them—phrases such as "His dog always barked up the right tree, but he was always misunderstood"; or "These overprotective chickens refused to lay all their eggs in a solitary basket." These staccato utterances in Ovanessian's film are entirely counter-narrative. They satirically mean and ironically signify in and of themselves but make no sense within the story except to counter-thematize the thin storyline.

Spring allows you to find your way into those moments, which in their very oscillating nature do not succumb to monolithic definitions and reject meta-historical appellations. In the midst of that chaotic carnival where the visions of the (im)possible defy the codified world, of a succession of material moments of cultures-in-the-making, we can begin to see a hermeneutics of alterity, a habit of mind that can feel at home with conflicting visions of reality, with uncomfortable facts sitting next to each other. That hermeneutics of alterity resists moments charged with an energy to denigrate, disempower, deny, suppress, or colonize the best and most fruitful and in turn canonize the most compromising.

What I have articulated here as Ovanessian's *spatial* realism—his uncanny ability to lift the veil of the spatially evident and make it transparently visible—adds yet another dimension to what I have already told you in terms of Farrokhzad's *poetic*, Golestan's *affective*, and Mehrjui's *psychedelic* realisms. Whereas in both Farrokhzad and Golestan, our cinema remains solidly rooted in its literary origins, in Mehrjui and Ovanessian the literariness of the Iranian imaginative culture begins to create its visual signature. But even in the span of time between Mehrjui's *Cow* (1969) and Ovanessian's *Spring* (1972) you can see how the visual self-perception, rooted as it is in *verbal memories*, became increasingly more imaginative. But with *Spring*, Iranian cinema still had a couple of more rungs to climb to reach the height of its visual confidence.

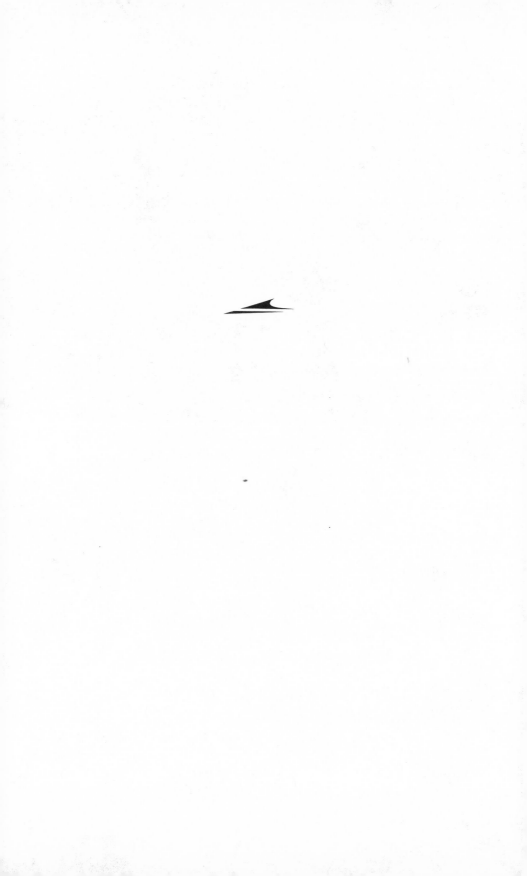

No matter what I write, still my heart is
not happy with it.
—Ayn al-Qudat

Bahman Farmanara
Prince Ehtejab

IT IS NOW TIME THAT I TELL YOU, in some detail, about Bahman Farmanara's masterpiece, *Prince Ehtejab* (1974), a film that adds yet another dimension to what now is generically called Iranian neorealism. You should keep in mind that beginning with Farrokhzad in 1962, through Golestan in 1965, Mehrjui in 1969, and Ovanessian in 1972, I have argued that a succession of different modes of realism have characterized Iranian realism in *poetic*, *affective*, *psychedelic*, and *spatial* terms. Bahman Farmanara's 1974 adaptation of Houshang Golshiri's groundbreaking 1969 novel, *Prince Ehtejab*, has added to the manner and momentum of that realism. My single objective in all of these reflections is to take that *neo* from in front of realism and replace it with something else. That has never meant anything and has always bothered me. Just because there is something called Italian Neorealism does not mean that the rest of the world replicates it in other, national terms—Egyptian neorealism, Chinese neorealism, Indian neorealism, and now Iranian neorealism. Realism is what we see in all of these cinemas, Iranian included. In very specific cinematic terms,

Italians were the first to experiment with and inaugurate this kind of cinema. But when we say *realism* in the case of Iranian cinema, how do we mean it—in what particular sense? That is something we need to narrow in on rather cautiously. Farmanara's *Prince Ehtejab* is, of course, in the same realist tradition, but if you were to watch it next to Ovanessian's *Spring*, or Mehrjui's *Cow*, or Golestan's *Mud Brick and Mirror*, or Farrokhzad's *The House Is Black* you would see a marked difference among them, though each is operating in a distinct register of realism. So we are being lazy, to say the least, just to label all of these *Iranian neorealism*. We need to think a little bit more specifically on the matter. As for Farmanara's *Prince Ehtejab*, first we need to look at a little bit of history.

Born in Tehran in 1942, and raised and educated in Iran, Bahman Farmanara received his higher education at the London School of Music and Dramatic Arts and then at the University of Southern California. In 1966 he returned to Iran and began a career with the National Iranian Radio and Television. His first film was *Nowruz and Caviar* (1971), a documentary about the famous Iranian delicacy and the poverty of its producers. His first feature film, *Qamar Khanom's House* (1972), was a complete flop. Soon after that, Farmanara began working at a film production company financed by the royal family. But by 1974, he had quit that dubious distinction and directed *Prince Ehtejab*, a film that rightly placed him at the forefront of the progressive cinema of his time. At the beginning of the revolution, Farmanara made another film based on Golshiri's story *Tall Shadows of Wind* (1979). And after the revolution Farmanara moved to France and then to Canada, where he established a film distribution company. In the early 1990s, family matters brought him back to Iran, where he began teaching at the Tehran College of Cinema and Theater. By the end of the decade, Farmanara made a triumphant return to cinema with his wise, mature, confident, and caring *Smell of Camphor, Fragrance of Jasmine* (2000). Two years later, his *House Built on Water* created yet another storm of controversy with the censors.

Just like Mehrjui and Ovanessian before him, after some preliminary attempts at filmmaking—some more successful than others—Farmanara had the good sense of turning to a major Iranian writer. Houshang Golshiri's novel *Prince Ehtejab*, which by the early 1970s had established his reputation as a major literary voice, saved Farmanara from wasting his time too much longer. Farmanara's turn to Golshiri replicated Ovanessian's (unsuccessful) turn to Ali Mohammad Afghani, and Mehrjui's (very successful) recourse to Saedi—three consequential decisions that planted the budding stems of Iranian cinema in the rich soil of modern Persian fiction. Golshiri, though, represented a much newer and far more ambitious creative imagination that catapulted—with only one film—Farmanara's cinema to the center stage of his contemporary art.

As Farmanara has said on many occasions, no fewer than three of his friends, almost simultaneously and quite independent of each other, suggested to him that he should turn Golshiri's *Prince Ehtejab* into a film. He took their advice, read the book, got in a car on the eve of the Persian New Year in March 1970, and drove from Tehran to Isfahan to meet Golshiri. But who was Golshiri and what was he doing in Isfahan?

One of the most gifted and influential writers of his time, Golshiri (1937–2000) was born in Isfahan and raised in Abadan, and thus brought a fresh and unexpected vision to the Persian fiction of his time, which had become increasingly based in Tehran. Golshiri's family returned to Isfahan, where he finished high school, and where he went on to attend the University of Isfahan. Upon graduation, he began teaching at various elementary and high schools in the region. His increasing political activism landed him in jail in 1962. By the mid-1960s, Golshiri had published a potpourri of poems and short stories, and then was instrumental in establishing *Jong-e Isfahan*, a progressive literary journal that quickly moved to the vanguard of Iranian fiction. Between 1965 and 1973, *Jong-e Isfahan* was among the leading literary journals of the time, initiating some serious critical discussions about the nature and function of fiction. To this day its eleven issues constitute the most consequential critical intervention in recent literary history outside the orbit of Tehrani intellectuals. Although by the end of his life Golshiri had become one of the most influential public intellectuals of his time, he never, to his credit, lost the singular, haunting, political angle of his presence and vision.

Golshiri had begun writing fiction in the late 1950s, and by the early 1960s his short stories and poems were appearing in various literary journals. His first collection of short stories, *Mesl-e Hamisheh* (*As Always*, 1968), announced a major literary voice—confident, defiant, with detailed attention to a range of prose and narrative techniques. But it was not until the publication of *Shazdeh Ehtejab* (*Prince Ehtejab*) that the Tehrani literary critics had to pack their suitcases (among them smuggled a young filmmaker named Bahman Farmanara) and pay a visit to Isfahan to see what Golshiri was cooking. Golshiri's second novel, *Christine va Kid* (*Christine and the Kid*, 1971), was not as critically acclaimed as *Prince Ehtejab*, but as an experiment in autobiographical narrative it was a tour de force of unparalleled daring and experimentation—staccato phrases, broken and unreliable memories, miniature-like narrative depictions, implication of the reader in the narrative, and many other similar tropes. His political activities, which consisted mainly of investigating the political dimensions of literary works in his own critical commentaries and in the journal he edited, in addition to solidarity with progressive leftist movements, once again landed him in jail for about six months in 1973. A subsequent collection of short stories, *Namaz-khaneh-ye Kuchak-e Man* (*My Little Prayer Room*, 1975), and his third novel, *Barreh-ye Gomshodeh-ye Rai* (*The Shepherd's Lost Lamb*, 1977), registered Golshiri as a seminal novelist of his generation, successfully competing for the top rank with his chief rival, Mahmoud Dowlatabadi.

At the beginning of the 1979 revolution, Golshiri was active in organizing the famous "Ten Nights" of poetry and prose readings at the Goethe Institute in Tehran, a watershed of revolutionary mobilization against the Pahlavi regime. In the summer of 1978, he was invited to attend the International Writing Program at the University of Iowa. While in the US he gave a series of lectures to Iranian students across the country. I was one of them. I was a graduate student at the University of Pennsylvania when Golshiri traveled to the United States. He visited our campus. I still have the notes I kept from his talk at the International House in Philadelphia:

> Golshiri came to Penn today and spoke at the
> International House about modern Persian fiction and
> its links to revolutionary movements. He said his own
> fiction was deeply indebted to Sadeq Hedayat's. He went
> through the whole gamut of modern Persian fiction.
> At the end of his talk, Bahman Sholehvar went and
> said hello to him. Golshiri became visibly embarrassed
> because he had not mentioned Bahman Sholehvar in
> his talk. While speaking, he looked at his notes, but he
> was by and large speaking extemporaneously. He did
> not say much about his own fiction. I am left to my own
> devices as to how to read *Prince Ehtejab*. His concern
> was mostly the revolution, the Pahlavi censorship,
> the political function of literature. After his talk we
> all had dinner with him on the second floor of the
> International House. It was a tasteless ghormeh sabzi
> over cold and insipid rice, both miserably meandering
> on paper plates. When in jest I complained to a woman
> in charge, she took it seriously and said that I might be
> a radical in my politics, but was positively a bourgeois
> when it comes to my taste for ghormeh sabzi. I went
> home and stayed up all night and reread *Prince Ehtejab*.

After his short sojourn and the taste of bad Persian food in the US, Golshiri returned to Iran and continued to be a major literary figure in the course and aftermath of the revolution, fighting for the professional

safety and political immunity of public intellectuals through the Iranian Writers Association, which Golshiri helped to found. He, Ahmad
Shamlu, and Mahmoud Dowlatabadi were by then Iran's most influential post-revolutionary secular intellectuals. Golshiri's *"Masum-e Panjom:
Hadith mordeh bar dar kardan savari keh khahad amad"* ("The Fifth Infallible: The Ballad of Hanging Dead the Horseman Who Shall Come,"
1980) was his first most significant literary publication after the Islamic
revolution. He was soon invited to teach on the Faculty of Fine Arts at
Tehran University, but in 1982, he was purged by the Cultural Revolution Committee, among whose members was Abdolkarim Soroush,
now one of the leading Iranian intellectuals fighting against the atrocities of the Islamic Republic. Between 1982 and 1984, Golshiri published
a literary magazine. After the officials of the Islamic Republic banned
any form of literary or political gathering contrary to their totalitarian
agenda, Golshiri began to receive his readers, admirers, and students at
his home (which in effect turned into an effective literary salon), from
which gatherings gradually emerged a new generation of writers and
public intellectuals. Golshiri was an indefatigable essayist and wrote
voluminously on the interface between literature and society—and yet
he kept an insurmountable distance between his political convictions
and his literary practices. He safeguarded the aesthetic and formalist
preoccupations of a literary artist paramount in his mind and argued for
the primacy of literary imagination in the writer's vocation. He had a
revolutionary fixation with narrative technique—no one before or after
Golshiri did more to make modern Persian prose so richly conscious of
its myriad narrative possibilities.

During the first decade of the revolution, Golshiri was astonishingly
productive. He published one masterpiece after another—*"Masum-e
Panjom"* ("The Fifth Infallible," 1980), *"Jobbeh-khaneh"* ("The Chamber of Antiquities," 1983), *"Hadis-e Mahigir va Div"* ("The Ballad of the
Fisherman and the Demon," 1984), and *"Panj Ganj"* ("Five Treasures,"
1989). Meanwhile he was devoted to training the younger generation of
novelists and short-story writers. In the late 1980s he traveled to Europe
and in 1990 the English translation of a novel attributed to him appeared
under a pseudonym, Manuchehr Irani. *King of the Benighted* (1990) is
indeed a masterful manipulation of classical Persian narratives, and it
engages critically with the innate forces of tyranny and terror domestic
to Persian patriarchal culture. There was (and still is), however, a sense
of frustration and domesticity to Golshiri's literary achievements. His
creative imagination—though visionary and global in its ambitions—was
ultimately jailed in the insularity of the Persian language.

Between 1989 and 1990, Golshiri traveled to Europe and read from
his recent work and lectured on the state of Persian fiction, in the Neth-

erlands, Sweden, England, Germany, Denmark, and France. While in Sweden he published *"Panj Ganj"* ("Five Treasures") in Persian (political conditions in Iran prohibited him from doing so there), and *"Ayeneh-ha-ye dar-dar"* ("Mirrors with Doors," 1990) was published in the US. These travels were, of course, critical in giving Golshiri breathing room away from the suffocating environment of the Islamic Republic. But still he could never speak to the vast and diversified audience that his fiction richly deserved. Golshiri (along with Ahmad Shamlu) represented the last generation of Iranian literary giants who had every reason to but no way of breaking loose from the territorial domesticity of their language and diction.

In the spring of 1992, the Center for Iranian Research and Analysis (CIRA) invited Golshiri to the US for another visit. Golshiri traveled to a number of university campuses for lectures and readings from his fiction, among them University of Texas at Austin, Harvard, Rutgers, Chicago, and Berkeley. It was on this occasion that I invited him to Columbia University, where I was now teaching. I remember one of his hosts from CIRA drove him from New Jersey to New York, where Golshiri and I spent a day together. I never told him about our first encounter in Philadelphia fifteen years earlier when I was a green gradu- ate student at Penn, nor was I sure that he would have a recollection of that ghastly ghormeh sabzi we once ate together. What we did talk about was his absolute fascination with poststructuralism and deconstruction. I remember we walked for hours around the Columbia University campus, along 116th Street and around Amsterdam and Broadway, as he picked my brain about the philosophical origins and the theoretical nature of deconstruction, which interested him primarily as a literary device. He had a modestly well-informed conception of literary movements outside Iran, given his reading limitation to Persian sources. I remember when, later that day as I introduced him to a sizeable audience who had come to hear him talk and read his fiction, one particularly purposeful student of philosophy from the New School was taking Golshiri to task about his ideas on narrative plot. Golshiri could not quite go out on a limb speaking about theory spontaneously. But I saw on that occasion that his political daring had certain liberating consequences that covered for his theoretical limitations.

Altogether, Golshiri's visits outside Iran—early in 1993 he went on yet another tour of Sweden, France, Belgium, Germany, and the Neth- erlands—were more occasions of solitary self-reflection than a global opening of his literary horizons. Post-revolutionary Iran had become too much of a familiar setup, and traveling a necessary occasion for Gol- shiri to disconnect culturally. His output in the mid-1990s nonetheless remained persistently provocative, and despite debilitating censorship, he managed to publish a collection of his short stories and a volume of his essays on poetry. Meanwhile his international reputation grew by leaps and bounds when, in 1996, the French translation of *Prince Ehtejab* was published in Paris. In the spring of 1997, the Heinrich Böll Institute invited him to Germany, where he managed to finish his *Jinn Nameh* (*Book of Demons*, 1998), which he subsequently published in Sweden. The publication of *Book of Demons* coincided with Golshiri receiving the Hellmann-Hammett Award given by Human Rights Watch. Upon his return to Iran in late 1997, two of Golshiri's fellow members of the Iranian Writers Association were brutally murdered by the official agents of the Islamic Republic—as part of a whole cycle of vicious violence known as "serial murders" targeting secular intellectuals. At their funeral, Golshiri's memorial speech was a cry for freedom—marred by a deeply wounded sense of pride and purpose in the writer's task.

Golshiri remained creative and active to his very last years. He published *Jedal-e Naghsh ba Naghghash* (*The Battle of the Image and the Image-maker*) in 1998; and then in June 1999, the city of Osnabrück, Germany, awarded him the Erich Maria Remarque Peace Prize for his literary and social efforts to fight oppression and promote democracy and human rights in Iran. This ceremony followed yet another reading tour in Germany after the publication of the German translation of *Prince Ehtejab* and a few of his other stories.

Golshiri died in Tehran on 5 June 2000. Thousands of his admirers bode him eternal farewell.

Prince Ehtejab the film became the singularly significant cinematic event of the early 1970s, inserting a psychosemiotics of cruelty into the Iranian cinematic imagination utterly unprecedented in our visual memory. To this day *Prince Ehtejab* remains the most insightful visual reflection on the temper of a tormented culture, a symptomatic study of the pathology of power—the contorted, deformed, and tubercular manifestation of a disease long evident but never diagnosed in our political culture. Never was Golshiri more perceptive in his phantasmagoric imagination—and rarely has an author been better served by a visual artist than Golshiri by Farmanara. In his novella, Golshiri had sought to discover what cultural maladies, social diseases, historical causes, and miasmatic malignancies had eaten into the moral memories of our collective consciousness—and in his film, Farmanara had found a visual way, a cinematic narrative, a sinuous semiotics of imaginal discovery to show that psychosis in persistently insinuating details.

Farmanara's attraction, in the early 1970s, to Golshiri's novel and the culture of cruelty in Iranian dynastic history is remarkably in tune with Stanley Kubrick's turn to Anthony Burgess' *A Clockwork Orange* (1971), which began the decade with a relentless dissection of the terror at the base and conclusion of bourgeois morality. In *A Clockwork Orange*, Alex (Malcolm McDowell) is not simply the perfect picture of a sociopath—he is Kubrick's measure of all the lies that have been exposed in dismantling the myth of Enlightenment humanism. In his sociopathology, Alex exposes the lie at the root of every single measure of bourgeois truth—from social to political to religious—all based on a massive hypocrisy. None of the seemingly self-evident truths of reason remain standing by the time Kubrick is done running Alex through the gamut of middle-class morality—the crowning achievement of Enlightenment modernity. Alex is not exactly a Nietzschean overman either, beyond the pale and forts of morality. The nightmarish scientism of prison reform may very well have cured him of all his ultra-violence, as he calls it, without much resistance. His apathy is endemic, extended from his behavior with his parents (and theirs toward him) to his chance social encounters and sexual escapades to the boa constrictor that he keeps under his bed and ultimately to the frivolity with which he rapes, maims, and murders people. He does so with neither a premeditated viciousness nor indeed with any remorse. It is in the fabric and texture of the world at large that brings him to violence, and with a vengeance. Kubrick persistently implicates Beethoven's music in Alex's pathology by way of disallowing any illusion of romantic art and its heroic promises as a hope for humanity. *That* man is dead—if he were ever alive—and in *A Clockwork Orange* Kubrick is a coroner of brutal and ceremonious precision.

Farmanara's diagnosis is of an entirely different quality and yet of a remarkably identical provenance, as it is narrated on the colonial edge of the Enlightenment modernity that Kubrick's Alex represents. Golshiri's novel is ostensibly set in the context of the decadent Qajar aristocracy (1789–1926)—as one ominous servant of the dynasty, Morad (played in the film by Hossein Kasbian), keeps bringing to one of its last descendents, Prince Ehtejab (played by Jamshid Mashayekhi in the film), the news of his cohorts dying, one after the other. But Farmanara's visual narration of the story gave a particularly poignant spin to its contemporary accent—all too evident in Golshiri's novel but far more pronounced in Farmanara's imagining of it. What is paramount in Farmanara's adaptation of *Prince Ehtejab* is the labyrinthine convolution of three generations of murderous decadence narrated and woven into each other. Memories of Prince Ehtejab's grandfather and father join his own translucent presence to form a multiplicity of successively degenerate reminiscences of each other, each engaged in one mode of murderous banality or another.

Consumed by tuberculosis, Prince Ehtejab is projected figuratively inside some subterranean corner of Iran's collective memory, neither here nor there and thus smeared everywhere in the Iranian consciousness, where he is tortured by the remembrance of his ancestral cruelties—the brutal asphyxiation of a disobedient family member on one occasion (his tied-up hands are used as an ashtray by the murderer prince), the massacre of a group of protestors in another. The ghostly character of his remembrances of things past assumes a generational depth and *Prince Ehtejab* traces the declining days of a decadent dynasty into the collective subconscious of a nation. Prince Ehtejab's recollections of cruelties past come forward to create a psychological condition of the present. On the surface he is weak and pathetic, incapable of the cruelties perpetrated by his ancestors, and yet inside the dark dungeons of his repressed horrors he is, in fact, the worst nightmare that his ancestors have left behind. Compared to the cruelty of Prince Ehtejab toward his wife, Fakhr al-Nisa, and their maid Fakhri, his father's and grandfather's cruelties appear acts of mendacious buffoonery.

At the Tehran International Film Festival of 1974, Farmanara won the Grand Prix for his adaptation of *Prince Ehtejab*, and overnight Golshiri's literary achievement became a cultural icon. The successful translation of Golshiri's fiction into a visual vocabulary of unusual grace and power resulted in a *narrative* realism with an unending conviction in the efficacy of narration itself—narration as diagnosis, narration as prognosis, and narration as radical retrieval of the repressed and thus a clear constitution of historical agency. Prince Ehtejab is the return of the Iranian dynastic repressed, the terror of his ancestral dread personified, and *Prince Ehtejab* is the narrative restoration of that memory toward a historical constitution of agency beyond the terror of that collective recollection. Long before Farmanara transformed that narrative realism from fiction to film, it is in its literary form that *Prince Ehtejab* worked its memorial magic—from diagnosis to prognosis, from discursive retrieval to restored agency.

Both the writing and the filming of *Prince Ehtejab* were acts of collective catharsis—of purging convoluted layers of repressed memories by verbally and visually narrating them. Through the verbal narrative of *Prince Ehtejab*, which Farmanara then successfully projected into visual fluency, Golshiri both constituted and resurrected the memorial site of Iranian political repression. In one act of creative genius, Golshiri narrated the brutality and decadence that characterized the Qajar dynasty (and through the Qajars the rest of Iranian dynastic nightmares) through a sequence of historical mutations pasted onto intractable cultural memories, which had sunken deeper and deeper into a people's collective consciousness. Prince Ehtejab is not just the last prince in this terrible spiral; he is also the first person in Iranian modernity who needs to be narratively dismembered for us to be able to imagine a freer future. What

Golshiri has done in his narrative characterization of Prince Ehtejab is to excavate the deepest layers of crazed savagery at the heart of a culture and then bring it up for close examination. As Golshiri and Farmanara descend into the deepest layers of Iranian collective memory, and as they follow them down to their subterranean dungeons, they will inevitably have to dig them up for a liberating examination—all geared to restore a repressed historical agency.

What historical agency? you may ask. Against what sustained amnesia of repressed memories? What *Prince Ehtejab* aesthetically revived and effectively narrated was a history of cruelty at the forefront of our collective consciousness—at once present and invisible. Heads chopped off and piled on each other to make a pyramid, that was the enduring memory of the Qajar dynasty—eyes gorged out, bodies torched, living human beings buried alive, young men castrated, young women raped, visionary government ministers like Amir Kabir murdered in the prime of their noble endeavors, corrupt politicians put to preside over the livelihood of defenseless people. The record of the Qajar dynasty was one of systematic abuse of a nation at large, overburdened with cruel and unusual punishment for the slightest transgression against the whimsical, sickly, and torrid reign of terror historically identified with foreign invasions and inbred tyranny. The savagery with which the Babi movement was suppressed during the reign of Nasir al-Din Shah Qajar was reminiscent of the legendary cruelties of the founding figure of the Qajar dynasty, Agha Muhammad Khan. The public rape and execution of young children who had dared to sing satirical songs ridiculing Agha Muhammad Khan while he laid siege to the city of Kerman led parents to hide their children in chimneys and between walls, covered with bricks and mortar for fear of their lives. Agha Muhammad Khan's generals would bring young people from Kerman to his court on top of a hill where he would have their ears cut off, their eyes gorged out, their throats slit, and their dead bodies tossed down the hill. Women were raped and murdered, children sold into slavery, men blinded and slaughtered. When Lotf Ali Khan Zand was brought to Agha Muhammad Khan, he had his servants sodomize him savagely and then blind him. None of these savageries were depicted in Golshiri or Farmanara's *Prince Ehtejab*. But all of them were at the forefront of its readers' and viewers' minds as they considered the sickly figure of Prince Ehtejab, brilliantly portrayed by Jamshid Mashayekhi in one of the legendary roles in Iranian cinema.

To claim this much for Golshiri and Farmanara, I need to take you back in time to a critical moment in the Persian literary imagination when its most radical articulation of narration became the solitary site of truth-telling. Before doing so, however, let me recap what exactly I am claiming for Golshiri's novella and Farmanara's film: I propose that *Prince*

Ehtejab is an act of creative excavation of the historical cruelty at the heart of Iranian culture, and as such is deeply repressed in our collective memory. That degenerative repression creates our collective identity—which is to say, it is by virtue of that (un)successful repression that today we call ourselves Iranian. Repeat that sentence a few times, please, before you proceed any further—everything I have said so far hinges on its paradox! In *Prince Ehtejab*, Golshiri narratively delineates that repression, and by tracing the spiral descent of its willful amnesia he also finds a way out. And then, through a filmic vision of *Prince Ehtejab* Farmanara manages both to constitute and retrieve the repressed terror of Qajar rule as the penultimate dynastic dread to have wreaked havoc on the entirety of Persian culture. The logic of the exercise is that if you narratively pursue the terror that has paralyzed your historical presence then you can narratively retrieve the agency it has successfully denied. But, as I said, for Golshiri and Farmanara to be able to do so, there must have existed the primacy of narrative as the conduit of truth and all manners of telling it. For that we need to visit a very distant point in the Iranian literary imagination—when there existed a miraculous case of narrative as the primary act of truth-telling—from juridical to theological to philosophical and even the mystical. Now I need to tell you that story.

"No matter what I write, still my heart is not happy with it. Most of what I write these days is of the sort that I do not really know whether it is better written or unwritten." This is from Ayn al-Qudat al-Hamadhani's collection of letters, written somewhere between 1123 (when he was twenty-five years old) and 1129 (when he was thirty-two—just about a couple of years before his execution). A twelfth-century Persian mystic philosopher and jurist-turned-theologian, literary stylist, and storyteller, Ayn al-Qudat was born in 1098 and publicly hanged in 1131. He is as far from Houshang Golshiri and Bahman Farmanara's time and troubles as you can imagine—or is he?

My most dear friend! [This is a suggestively fictitious friend; he may or may not be an actual person; this might or might not be an actual letter written and sent; and right in between that uncertainty Ayn al-Qudat inserts his narrative suspension and proceeds.]

> Not everything that is right and virtuous is proper to be written.... Beware, my brother, beware! Don't you ever take this statement lightly. This is the very kernel of truth. And may God Almighty make you see its veracity out of his bounteous mercy. I should not cast myself into a sea upon which I see no shore,

and thus write things in utter self-forgetfulness that
when I regain my senses I regret them and suffer.

This is all in the course of one letter—a narrative device he adapted
toward the end of his life when he had said and done all he had to in the
juridical, theological, and philosophical languages of his time, opting for
a simple—deceptively simple—diction that told everything fresh, anew,
unprogrammed, unpredictable.

> My dear friend! I am scared, and indeed I ought to be
> scared of the treacheries of this world.... And I swear
> by the dignity of the friendship that is between us that
> I do not know whether what I just wrote sets me on the
> path of moral victory or on that of damned regret. But in
> truth I cannot not write, and I cannot be but a ball in the
> playing field of fate.... When a writer writes the letter Q
> or the letter K on a piece of paper, they indeed cannot
> suddenly become the letter J or the letter D. If the fate
> has made of a man a devil he cannot become angelic.

Now listen to the rest: you will not believe what I am about to quote
for you from Ayn al-Qudat—and yet I swear by whatever is sacred to me
that this is exactly what you'll find on pages 197–99 of the second volume
of the critical edition of his letters (edited by Ali Naqi Monzavi and Afif
Osayran. Tehran: Bonyad-e Farhang, 1972). Now hold your breath and
read this—it is a small miracle:

> And only God Almighty knows that I have not a clue as
> to whether this very writing I do right now is the source
> of my salvation or the cause of my damnation, nor do I
> know that this very announcement I just made to you is
> out of obedience to my Lord or the committing of a sin.
> And since I do not know that, then how do I wish that I
> were altogether ignorant of everything so I would be free.
> Because as it stands now if I were to write something, say,
> on stability or motion, I would regret it altogether, and if
> I were to write something on worldly matters or the path
> of God, I would equally regret it, and if I were to write
> something explicating the status of God's emissaries, for
> example, I would seek refuge in God, and if I were to write
> something about those who are in ecstatic love, it would
> not be right either, nor would it be right if I were to write
> about men of wisdom. Indeed whatever I write, it wouldn't

be right, and yet neither would it be right if I were to
write nothing at all, nor would it be right if I were to say
nothing at all, nor would it be right for me to remain
completely silent, nor would it be right if I were to say
what I just said, nor would it be right if I were not to say
what I just said, nor would it be right if I were not to say
it, nor would it be right if I were to remain silent.... What
utter strangeness is this? I do not know. Nor do I know
whether the result of what I just said is bliss or damnation.

What is the meaning of this? I remember I thought to myself when
I first read these words in their original Persian, years ago, when I was
writing my book *Truth and Narrative* on Ayn al-Qudat. What kind of
miracle is this? In black and white, for the whole world to read, an unbe-
lievably self-conscious consciousness (nervousness even) about the nature
of truth-telling. All we see in this prototypical passage of Ayn al-Qudat
is the performative tellability of truth—its narrative home, its discursive
manner, verbal delivery, syntactical performance, alphabetical order.
There seems to remain absolutely nothing behind, beyond, or beneath
that manner of telling. The manner of telling itself becomes an end unto
itself. It points to nothing other than itself, and that is where things are.
Everything is in telling it, how you tell it—and not what you tell. What
you tell is the resident alien of how you tell it. This is a very strange
thing to say. But that is the lesson in what Ayn al-Qudat is doing. *Telling*
the truth *is* the truth.

This testimonial on the predicament of writing is not by a contemporary of Golshiri or Farmanara. It is by Ayn al-Qudat al-Hamadhani,
sharing, from the distance of about a thousand years, in the glorious
agony of being at once a writer and a member of a metaphysical culture
habitually predisposed to telling the world what to do. Ayn al-Qudat's
overpowering self-consciousness is not accidental to the Iranian creative
character; it is quintessential to its literary disposition. Golshiri tapped
into this self-conscious narrative tradition (for a contemporary novelist
and literary intellectual, he was unusually well read and learned in our
classical literature) in order to retrieve and interpret that heritage. The
access to acts of truth-telling itself has no truth-claim, and thus is it able
to appropriate all truths to its narrative cause.

How can truth have no relation to veracity except through the story
it tells, and more importantly how it tells it? That became clear to me
when on a Saturday evening in February 1999 I was witness to a historic
encounter between Gillo Pontecorvo and Edward Said at the Walter
Reade Theater at Lincoln Center in New York. After a special screening of Pontecorvo's masterpiece, *The Battle of Algiers* (1966), Said asked

the aging Italian legend what he meant by what he called the "choral character" of the struggle in his film. *"La dittatura di verità,"* answered Pontecorvo, "the dictatorship of truth." That objective, he went on to explain, had demanded that he try to portray the character of Algiers more than anything else. The main protagonist of *The Battle of Algiers,* he insisted, was the city itself, a claim best represented at the concluding sequence of the film, when the entire cosmopolis rises in a choral defiance of colonialism and with it the joyous camera of Pontecorvo. The dictatorship of truth—I did not understand what Pontecorvo meant then, but I do now—is embedded in the narrative that delivers it. Truth has no claim to veracity except for the metaphysical power embedded in telling it. That truth, as you see it in the self-revealing passages of Ayn al-Qudat, has no other claim to veracity except in the method of its own narration. The way that narrative has a claim to truth-telling is through its own counter-metaphysical verbality, its grammatological claims on narration. Truth-telling is not part of a narrative, an objective or *telos,* toward which it is directed. Instead, truth-telling is the figurative embeddedness of the story that any succession of sentences produces. That, it seems to me, is what is celebrated in the Iranian literary history in general, as a particularly compelling example of a self-referential narrative as a location of truth—a phenomenon, in my estimation, best evident in Ayn al-Qudat's self-conscious writings. Conclusion: The moral terror perpetrated on the Persian political psyche by successive generations of despotism has an illusive and amorphous air about it that cannot be articulated or exorcized except by an uncanny narrative that at once registers and retrieves it, remembers in order to forget and be cleansed.

The terror at the heart of *Prince Ehtejab* had both a local and a colonial genealogy. Iran's dynastic history concluded its medieval longevity with the Qajar monarchy, which coincided with the rise of colonial modernity in Iran. As Qajars terrorized us in our nightmares, colonial modernity robbed us of our historical agency—by suggesting the possibility of that agency in its modernity and yet ipso facto denying it by the colonial manner of delivering it. What this miraculously important film did for the restitution of Iran's historical agency was not limited to its grasp of historical despotism immediately beneath the surface of our collective unconscious; it was equally critical in confronting our systematic de-subjection in the face of colonial modernity. To understand the significance of *Prince Ehtejab* in restoring Iranian historical agency, I need to give you a long shot of how exactly modernity de-subjected its colonial subjects by robbing them of autonomy. It is a bit of a detour, but worth it.

Three curiously related phenomena appeared during the eighteenth and the nineteenth Christian centuries in Europe. On the surface, the

European age of colonialism, the commencement of Enlightenment modernity, and the rise of opera as the most popular form of public entertainment may appear as irrelevant, distinct, and independent developments. On closer scrutiny, however, one can detect an intimate structural affinity and ideological correlation among these three crucial events.

The successful rise of the European bourgeoisie from the hard-won battles of the French Revolution created a critical mass of accumulated capital that in turn gave momentum to capitalism as an economic reality whose internal logic, released from the fetters of medieval social relations institutionalized in feudal aristocracy, could not be any longer denied, evaded, or compromised. By the time Adam Smith wrote *The Wealth of Nations* (1776), an increasingly global capitalism as a mode of production was much more than an economic reality in search of a theory; it was already a pervasive phenomenon with extended roots in a post-feudal mode of economic production with branches growing ever wider, longer, and more fruitful in moral, normative, political, and artistic directions.

The industrial revolution was not just an outcome of this condition. It gave dialectical feedback to the inner logic of capitalism and all its necessary implications in moral, political, and artistic terms. In specifically economic terms, capitalism as a mode of production and the industrial revolution as its prophetic manifestation created, out of necessity, an expansionism beyond European borders. Capitalism raised the level of economic productivity beyond anything hitherto achieved in human history. Essential to this exponential increase in productivity was the transformation of labor into capital via the intermediary of raw material. To feed their ever faster and ever more productive machines, European factories needed more raw material—oil, coal, ore, copper, cotton, etc.—which was abundant and cheap in Asia, Africa, Australia, and America—especially if you came with a gun in one hand and a Bible in the other, with one shooting people in the face, and the latter telling them to turn the other cheek. Once goods were produced with these raw materials, there was an immediate need to sell them in mass quantities, greater than local markets in Europe could absorb. The need to feed monumentally efficient factories with cheap raw materials from Asia, Africa, Australia, and the Americas was at the root of the classical phase of European colonialism. The equally compelling need, which came only a little later, to have large, open markets for goods thus produced was the impetus for the European colonial expansion and its contingent project of empire building.

The active formation of European capitalism and its extension into imperialism coincided with a profound psychic energy that Peter Gay, a distinguished social historian of the period, has identified as "the cultivation of hatred." In his Freudian reading of the bourgeois experience, Gay identifies both the erotic and aggressive energies that were accumulated and released during the Victorian era, from the defeat of Napoleon in 1815 to the outbreak of the First World War in August 1914. "Aggression," Peter Gay argues, "acquired singular salience for the Victorian bourgeoisie." Not only domestically inside the emerging bourgeois capitals, but externally too, the bourgeoisie developed what Gay calls "alibis for aggression: beliefs, principals, rhetorical platitudes that legitimated verbal or physical militancy on religious, political, or, best of all, scientific grounds." As Gay demonstrates, this cultivation of hatred was not accidental to the Victorian bourgeoisie; it was fundamental to its formation:

> Were assertions of control over raw materials and high
> finance, business organization and sanitary hazards,
> far-flung communications and scientific mysteries
> not purely constructive activities? True enough: we
> can appropriately call Victorian bourgeois aggressive
> not merely because their hunt for profits and power
> exacted grave social costs from sweated labor, exploited
> clerks, obsolete artisans, or maltreated natives, but also
> because they expanded energies to get a grip on time,
> space, scarcity—and themselves—as never before.

As Gay persuasively demonstrates, "a measure of collaboration, and of clashes" emerged between sexuality and aggression in the character of the European bourgeoisie. Where Gay abandons the story and loses interest is with the articulation of "the Orient" as by far the most potent location of this energetic coupling of aggression and sexuality. On the Oriental site, economic exploitation and political domination went hand in hand with sexual fantasies and erotic illusions. The classical age of Orientalism in painting, music, theater, and especially opera coincided with a vigorous renewal of European imperialism.

As a serious and sustained enterprise, and not simply as a profitable adventure, the European age of imperialism emerged as the logical extension of the capitalist mode of production. The same is true about the break with the superfluous aristocratic and ecclesiastical cultural fetters, and with the transfer from Aristotelian to instrumental reason. The rise of the Enlightenment was a quintessentially liberal bourgeois revolt against the medieval impediments of two domineering feudal institutions: the church and the palace. The ideological success of Enlightenment modernity was based on the prerequisite of capitalism, and an uncompromising belief in the primacy of *reason* and *progress*. Enlightenment, as the principal ideology of capitalist modernity, sought to provide the bourgeoisie with the functional equivalent of the metanarrative that the debunked institution of the church had left vacant. The founding fathers of the Enlightenment attended their epic narrative of reason and progress with the same meta-physical intensity as the church fathers had done in Christianity. The Enlightenment thus became the new religion of the bourgeoisie, and the related project of capitalist modernity its popular manifesto.

As the Enlightenment gave the ascendant bourgeoisie its ideological credence and legitimacy, so was the same bourgeoisie in need of public symbols of identity and authority. In form and content, the eighteenth- and nineteenth-century European art in general, and opera in particular, is inextricably connected to the consolidation of the bourgeoisie as a self-conscious class. Whereas the Christian church and the European nobility were the principal patrons of art in medieval and Renaissance Europe, in the eighteenth and nineteenth century the bourgeoisie performed that function. The noticeable decline of the construction of cathedrals and palaces in eighteenth- and nineteenth-century Europe coincides with the marked rise of museums, opera houses, and concert halls. In music in particular there is a noticeable transformation of musical forms such as Bach's cantatas or Vivaldi's concerti, church-sponsored and/or catering to aristocratic taste either in their pious compositions or in their musical dis-position, to Beethoven's symphonies and Verdi's operas, with their appeal to a much larger bourgeois or revolutionary constituency. Opera was of course not the only artistic form with which the European bourgeoisie had a close affinity. But because of its grand theatricality, and because of the great ceremonial apparatus that gradually developed around it, the opera became the epitome of bourgeois public entertainment.

The European bourgeoisie was in need of cultural institutions that spoke to its symbolic identity, and of public performances that substi-tuted the medieval pageantry and ritual of the aristocracy and church. Opera houses, museums, public libraries, annual art exhibitions, peri-odic industrial expositions, and even universities gradually emerged as the specific sites where the nationalized European bourgeoisie both identified and distinguished itself. As the opera began to dramatize and stage the debunked aristocracy as a thing of the past, an object of curios-ity, a spectacle to be watched, it went about the business of identifying itself with the primacy of reason and progress—as the two metaphysical assumptions at the root of its own historical ascendancy. Reason, or what later Max Weber called "Occidental Rationalism" and Theodor Adorno "Instrumental Reason," was fundamental to the capitalist mode of pro-duction, the very *raison d'être* of its historic function. As opera began to stage the realm of the fantasy (at once defining the European bourgeoisie and setting it apart), the world outside its stage became the theater of a different, entirely serious, operation.

Meanwhile, from this economic premise, the centrality of instrumental reason in human affairs was extended into all other social spheres. In *Madness and Civilization*, Foucault extensively documented the process by which madness was defined as a necessary corollary to the constitution of reason. When Weber distinguished between three modes of authority—traditional, rational, and charismatic—in effect he too was operating within the successful establishment of reason by the Enlightenment as the defining term of modernity. Even earlier, when Kant divided high culture into science, morality, and art, or when Hegel considered that division as the principal interpretation of modernity, the principality of reason was very well established as the defining god-term of the European Enlightenment—extended thematically from the realm of economic production to its cultural manifestations.

Economically necessitated and culturally constructed and defined, reason needed its shadow, its negation, its absence, in order to bring it into sharper focus. *Unreason* thus emerged as the binary opposite of European cultural modernity, the Other of its claim to Enlightenment. It was no longer sufficient to define the bourgeoisie in rational terms; its opposites had to be dismissed as irrational. Unreason first became the principal characteristics with which to define the *ancien régime*. But that was not enough. In his groundbreaking work, Foucault argued that Europe saw the advent of insane asylums and the cultural construction of madness, which contributed to the consolidation of reason as the hallmark of cultural modernity in Europe. But even the invention and the confinement of unreason in European asylum houses was not enough. Unreason needed a much larger abode, a much more spacious confinement than just the asylums of Europe. Foucault discovered an island, and did not care to know that just off the coast of that small island there lay a whole new realm. It was called "the Orient."

Reason itself required a domain, a rightful place to reside, a space of its own—and thus was born the notion of "the West," and its counterpart, "the East." As reason was cast as the spirit of capitalism and the Enlightenment, the West began to be identified, by those having already imagined themselves in the West, as the exclusive domain of reason. Subsequently, it was psychologically necessary to excise unreason from the bosom of the West, and to deposit it in a realm far removed, a land exotic, a place where the European Enlightenment could deposit all its own hidden anxieties—the attraction to unreason, the frivolous, the forbidden, the taboo, the terrifying, the transgressive. A simple Manichean dualism—itself already projected as an old "Eastern" prophetic preference!—thus emerged between two binaries, eternally cast at opposite poles: "West versus East"; and thus "the Orient" was invented as the continental abode of unreason, the exotic, the forbidden. Hegelian teleological historicism played marvelously in this Manichean drama, where Europe, or Napoleon as the personification of it, became the ultimate end of human history, its *Geist* fulfilled—very much the same way that Hegel saw himself as the anticipated consequence of Plato.

The construction of the East as the site of unreason was concurrent with the attribution to it of a kind of premodern wisdom. The entire project of European Orientalism, as Edward Said excavated and exposed it, is marked by an extensive attention to archaeological, philological, religious, and literary evidence of dead civilizations and a deliberate neglect of the contemporaneity of its factual existence. The East became the source of some ancient knowledge, now corrupted into madness, chaos, and confusion. The more the presumed wisdom of Zoroaster, Buddha, and Confucius, the more evident the contemporary *unreasonableness of the East.*

As Europe began to inform itself with historical events such as ancient Greco-Persian rivalries and the Crusades, and such fantastic tales as those told by Marco Polo, and as it began to hear of the exploits of colonial adventures abroad, high culture and popular entertainment began to narrate in ever more colorful terms the particulars of the Orient as the center of forgotten wisdom, of magic, treachery, and intrigue, of sorcery, barbarism, and anarchy, of lust, leisure, and forbidden pleasures, of conspiracy, cruelty, and fate—in short the very stuff of which operas with Oriental themes were made. Opera had a dramatic intensity exclusively its own, which contributed to the construction of the concept of the East as the land of unreason and all that it entailed, as the frightful shadow of the Occident, its subconscious. As such the European opera— from Handel's *Xerxes* (1738) through Schoenberg's *Moses and Aaron* (1933)—emerged as the phantasmagoric repository of the psychopathology of power seeking to authenticate culturally its economic logic. The public *illusions* that European opera was manufacturing about the Orient are the *factual* evidence of the European age of economic expansionism, colonial conquest, cultural imperialism, and above all the psychopathological accoutrement of political power.

In both the economic logic of capitalism and in its cultural accoutrements, Iranians, as all other colonially mitigated nations, were at the receiving end of the historic game. Economically (semi)colonized and culturally delegated to the peripheral parameters of a presumed (but nonexistent) center, Iranians as a people lacked both a material domain and a cultural contour to pronounce themselves in charge of their own destiny. The Orientalists had assigned, without any kind of conversation, the Eastern realm of unreason an exotic role that made both political autonomy and cultural authenticity impossible. If Iranians today can stand on their own two feet and utter as much as an "I," it is for no other reason than having creatively defied the predicament of being in the dark shadow of the European Enlightenment, on its receiving end, and from the literary and artistic domains cultivated of their own devices a voice and a vision beyond the fold of colonial modernity. In that context, *Prince Ehtejab* pierces through both Iran's historic despotism and colonial de-subjection to de-subscribe itself, as it were, from an Orientalist hypothesis of unreason apportioned by an accidental location in the imaginative geography of a history it did not write or will. It is precisely that act of defiance that inaugurates the restoration of historical agency.

This restoration of autonomy rests on a liberating psychoanalysis of memorial history—of what is collectively selected to be remembered as an ancestral claim on the continuity of an historical self-narrative—that has never before been mapped out, let alone diagnosed. All acts of subjective autonomies are acts of restitution, of restatement of aspects and vistas of a cultural configuration always present but hitherto hidden. The liberation of the autonomous subject is thus also an act of collective catharsis, of a release from not merely political but accumulated historical repressions. Remember that all history is "memorial" history. There is always a (perhaps hidden) method to the apparent madness of our selective historical memories/amnesias. As such, Prince Ehtejab is the iconic personification of two corrosive forces—congenital corruption and diseased memory—sitting in a dark dungeon of a room, compelled to remember that cruel history. The result is the intimation of a bitter flavor in the unfolding narrative, an acerbic casuistry and bemusement that never lets go of the way the story spirals. Prince Ehtejab reeks in corruption and soaks in his memory of it, and by the time that Golshiri's pen and Farmanara's camera pay him a visit, the criminality in his blood is degenerating from a historically murderous tendency into an immediate and personally homicidal urge aimed at his wife and servant. The manner in which that urge is pursued and dismantled is of critical importance in restoring agential autonomy—against both Iran's patriarchal memories and its colonial predicament.

This is how it works: As suggested by his name, Prince Ehtejab is ostensibly impotent both sexually and politically. His wife, Fakhr al-Nisa, maintains an obvious moral and intellectual superiority over him, and as a result he much prefers the company of his servant girl, Fakhri, who is forced to accommodate the vulgarity of his dysfunctional sexual advances. He forces Fakhri to dress like his wife so that in her disguise he can claim to have a wife that, he knows all too well, he can actually never have. Prince Ehtejab is the psychopathological summation of a history otherwise too distant to tell, too amorphous to narrate, too vague to remember, and too repressed to acknowledge. Golshiri and Farmanara detect, mark, and collect all the dark ages of Iranian history in him. Farmanara's camera takes an almost sadistic pleasure in watching Morad, Prince Ehtejab's servant, bring Ehtejab the news of one Qajar prince after another dying—including the news of Ehtejab's own death. The investment of terror in Prince Ehtejab and its immediate divestment is entirely simultaneous, and thus the function of Golshiri's palimpsestic prose and Farmanara's filmic manner of sparse light and elongated shadows. As evident in Golshiri's prose, Farmanara's filming, and Jamshid Mashayekhi's acting, Prince Ehtejab personifies both the evident presence of his ancestral power, and yet a fragile and petrified version of it. We are not quite sure whether to fear Prince Ehtejab or to pity him. We take pleasure in his wife insulting him (she stands to compensate our fears), and we get frightened and disgusted with his abusive treatment of his servant girl (she stands to articulate our loathing of him). As we oscillate between identifying with Fakhr al-Nisa and Fakhri, swinging between our fears and our pity, we get closer to the tragicomic disposition of Prince Ehtejab, or the banality of evil, as Hannah Arendt would say, that defined his ancestral claims on our collective memory. There is a cathartic release in the exercise, for it is as if both Golshiri and Farmanara take a mischievous, childlike pleasure in first identifying the source of a collective terror and then erasing it. As a strategy, the sheer innocence of this frightened but courageous imagination—playing peekaboo with our ancestral fears and thus teasing them out and making them transparent—is exceedingly effective, and entirely unprecedented in Iranian literary and visual history.

The result of the transparency of Golshiri's prose and Farmanara's imagery (remember Ayn al-Qudat's passage as the ancestor of such narrative transparencies) is its ability to reveal the collective unconscious of a people, made into a nation by virtue of frightfully forgetting the origin of their communal terror. (If we take the implications of *Prince Ehtejab* seriously, as we must, it will disband a nation of frightened memories and terrorizing amnesia). Never had Iran's national history been laid open so bare to a psychoanalytic examination. We watch *Prince Ehtejab* as if a dream, a familiar vision, a forgotten nightmare, retrieved from the hidden-most hideouts of our repressed but not forgotten fears, seductively brought to creative consciousness. Golshiri diagnoses and Farmanara exorcises that nightmarish dream, for us to look at it and remember what has been willfully forgotten, and what made us into a nation by virtue and vice of collective repression.

I would like to propose here that half the reason that visual arts have been doctrinally forbidden by Islam is precisely this frightful possibility of remembering nightmares (which have been repressed precisely because they are so visually compelling), or alternatively imagining their otherwise (which cannot be fathomed unless they are visualized). Nightmares are at once frightening and emancipatory. They frighten precisely because they open up otherwise hidden possibilities of release from sanctified repressions. That visual arts are prohibited in Islam (and Judaism—but in Christianity and other visual religions the repression works differently) is in part because of the juridical anxiety around this semiotic release.

There is an extraordinarily erudite treatise by the late Seyyed Mohammad Kazem Assar (1885–1974) about the prohibition of painting or any other kind of visual representation in Islam, which I would like you to read at some point. Assar was an exceptionally gifted Muslim jurist, theologian, and philosopher. Nobody reads and scarcely anyone even knows about him anymore, but he is one of the major figures in Iranian intellectual history. Born into a prominent religious family in Tehran, he received his early religious education from his father before attending Dar al-Fonun, the legendary secular school that Amir Kabir, the reformist prime minister of the Qajar period, established in the nineteenth century. From there he went on to study both in France and then in Iraq, combining an unusual exposure to both classical Islamic and modern European philosophy. Seyyed Kazem Assar's essay on the prohibition of painting in Islam in many ways reflects his exceptional alertness to the philosophical nuances of Islam and the European Enlightenment, both of which he seems to have had direct access to. The essay appeared in 1966 in a journal called *Ma'aref.* The following passage from that treatise, which I quote in some detail, summarizes the reasons why visual representation is forbidden in Islam. Read very carefully:

> The first reason [why visual representation may have been forbidden in Islam is that this is conducive to making] the imaginative faculty overpower the rational faculty. Because the more the inventive faculties are empowered, the more the imaginative faculties are strengthened, and the more the imaginative faculties are strengthened, in the same proportion, the rational and contemplative faculties are weakened, and when these faculties are weakened, the consequences of fantasies and superstitions become widespread in a society, so much so that gradually all the principles of reason are eradicated and social confusion will arise. This can ultimately result in social anarchy, because naturally whenever fantasies and superstitions are paramount among a people they will inevitably lose proportionately in their freedom of thought, and as a result the very constitution of that

society will collapse and that nation may very well face its downfall and be forced to struggle for its very existence.

The second [reason] may be that persistence in the study of the minutiae of visual representations and the particulars of the art of painting prevent a person from thinking and deliberating about realities themselves and investigating the conditions of the real things. By virtue of being preoccupied with symbols and representations, people will be prevented from contemplating what those symbols and representations refer to. Whereas if a person pays close attention to external things and reflects on the actual manifestations of the natural world, in addition to scientific discoveries and the knowledge of the secrets of creation, the person will discover the Principal Causality and the Primary Material, which are common to all aspects of life. Consequently, the person will discover that the whole world of existence is composed of that very First Principle, and that in the Abode of Existence there is nothing except the manifestations and gradations of that very Principle, so much so that from the lowest form of existence and the most elementary levels that Principle has gradually progressed and via that progression has come up to reach the highest degrees of life, knowledge, will, rationality, and love. It is at that time that to this observer there is no longer any distinction left among the mineral, the vegetal, and the animal, and it is upon such recognition that the secret of "You shall not see in God's creation any distinction" shall become evident.

Neither of these two arguments, though elegantly phrased and per-suasively put, holds much water these days, and yet both point to the inner anxiety at the root of an historical fear of visual representation. We are now of course too much in the sun (following the hapless Prince of Denmark), but that is no indication that the darkest of our ancestral nightmares are any less haunting. The result is an obvious physical expo-sure of our collective culture to clarity and precision, while our historical memory continues to repress our old horrors. What Assar's succinct articulation of the inhibition of visualization demonstrates is that as a revelatory religion (you see what I mean) Islam has a particular anxiety toward visual representation, because its own inaugural moment (when the Qur'an was *revealed* to Muhammad) is an instance of visual repres-sion—because its entire operation is contingent on an unseen God and prophet. Visualization is at once frightful and tantalizing, what Freud called uncanny, fearful, and liberating. Golshiri and Farmanara dare and look and thus fare and win—for all of us.

To this day, *Prince Ehtejab* remains the singular example of what happens when a gifted novelist and a visionary filmmaker join to show and tell a story we have always known but never dared to admit to ourselves: that we are bred on our own moral negation—on the normative denial of our own historical memory. It is quite a scary thought, but we have to face it. As a psychoanalytical treatment of a historical trauma at the very core of our collective consciousness, *Prince Ehtejab* works through a simple suggestion of dream narration, in which the very act of telling the nightmare of the prince's memory structures its meaning and significance. Keep in mind that Prince Ehtejab is not a character but a persona, and as such he is a narrative device through whose memorial remembrances Golshiri and Farmanara tell this collective nightmare. Prince Ehtejab is both the narrator and the object of the narration, both the memory of the trauma he represents and the memorial evidence of his own testimony. Nothing is worse than having seen a nightmare but not being able to remember it. Our daylight history has been haunted by that nightmare and yet we could never quite put our hands on it because we could not remember it—we did not even know we had dreamed it. It is as if Prince Ehtejab has come out of the collective grave of his ancestors for one last, though this time expurgatorial, torment, this time as much his as ours, to both excavate these memories, from their very unsuccessful repression, and bury them again—this time for good.

With Prince Ehtejab Golshiri both locates and narrates the nightmare; and with his film, Farmanara projects a full-bodied picture of that deliberately forgotten vision. How, the question becomes, are we to read, watch, and interpret that dream—the nightmare we had hitherto not even confessed? With the evidence of the nightmare laid bare before our eyes we can no longer deny, repress, or forget it. Golshiri's sinuous narrative, twisting and turning around its own insights, and Farmanara's tortuous imagery, probing the exterior of his set designs as if they were the labyrinth of his characters' consciousness, come together both to simulate that collective memory and make it visible. The nightmare invokes and shows the horrors of Iranian history, with the Qajar dynasty representing all the hidden layers of a terror perpetrated on the tortured body and the collective memory of a people. The parallel cut between the Moharram ceremony and a servant girl masturbating with the young prince in attendance will remain one of the masterpieces of Iranian cinema. In the course of that parallel cut the erotics of denial and the piety of ritual mutate into each other, sustaining the energy with which we have traveled half way around our historical memory to locate the sources of our signal tremors. Both the shah's and Khomeini's respective governments gave Farmanara a hard time for that scene—perhaps oddly concurring that its sacrilegious disposition was harmful to public morality. But the effect of that parallel cut is in the thematic shock and narrative discordance that it visually simulates. I still remember the erotic scene when I watch the mourning ceremony for the sacred Imams, and still remember the reenactment of a sacrosanct moment of a culture when watching that erotic scene. The erotics of piety that Farmanara puts on display is one of the most effective ways of cracking open the hidden manners that remain binding in a culture—even when they are no longer valid.

Prince Ehtejab was written and published after the brutal repression of the June 1963 uprising and made into a film in the course of an equally violent suppression of the urban guerilla movement against the Pahlavi regime. Both the book and the film are written and shot in a deep sense of hopelessness and despair. The hopelessness and despondency of the time opens onto a view of the enduring nature, causes, and consequences of a long history of the same. What follows is a surfacing of the deepest and most successfully repressed layers of a collective consciousness, the origins of calamities, and yet the sources of a destiny of a nation. In *Prince Ehtejab* truth becomes evident by way of repressing its own narrativity, the same way that identity becomes possible by repressing its own alterity. Iranians alive today were born into colonial modernity as a nation through a repression of the historical nightmare at the root of that paradox. *Prince Ehtejab* exposes that paradox and releases that repression—so that we know full well who we are (not). What is the result of this cruel act of emancipation? The bright darkness of nation and narration (as Homi Bhabha would put it), of narrating a nation, though not out of the plain facts of its history, but by remembering and expurgating its nightmares as the solitary claim to culture—thus the texture and disposition of Farmanara's *narrative* realism. The permanent spontaneity of existing with no identity, identity contingent on no alterity, alterity in need of no ipseity, ipseity with no claim to metaphysical continuity. It is a state of flux, a suspension in flight. So you see, there is nothing to be afraid of. Just flap your wings and off you fly away! *Home* is where you hang your hat or rest your wings.

To trace back to the sovereign zero, out of
which emerges that subaltern zero that
constitutes ourselves....
—E. M. Cioran

Sohrab Shahid Sales
Still Life

LAST WEEKEND I WENT TO OSLO, NORWAY, for a conference on Henrik Ibsen and his literary reception in Iran. My host there was Farin Zahedi, who is writing her PhD dissertation on Ibsen at the University of Oslo. She works at the Ibsen Centre in Oslo and had arranged this event. Arby Ovanessian was also there, as was Susan Taslimi. I gave a talk on the reception of Ibsen in Iran (particularly of *A Doll's House* and *An Enemy of the People*), had long and fruitful chats with Ovanessian, and was very happy to meet Taslimi after so many years of admiring her from afar.

Have you noticed that when we travel away from home we are more at home with ourselves than when we are at home? It is a rather bizarre paradox. But that's how it is. I think this is what our ancestors meant when they made a distinction between being *dar safar* (on a journey) and being *dar hazar* (being home, or literally, being present). It seems that we are more dar hazar when we are dar safar, more in the solitary presence of our own selves than when we are at home, when our thoughts can travel all over the world. When we travel around, we have more time to ourselves; when we are at home, we daydream about places and things far away.

While flying to and from Oslo, I was thinking about the significance of Sohrab Shahid Sales in Iranian cinema. Ovanessian and I spoke at length about Shahid Sales. He prefers Shahid Sales' *A Simple Incident* (1973), but I still believe that *Still Life* (1974) has been of far more consequence.

Between the writing of that sentence and this one there has been a span of almost two months—in which I just stowed this computer and went away to Morocco, and traveled from one corner of the country to the other. I needed space away from the madness of New York. What I saw and what I remembered is a bag of colorful and broken marbles. I had to go away, as it were, to be at home with myself.

The story of Shahid Sales' *Still Life* is, of course, no story at all—and that is how it borrows the spontaneity of modern Persian poetry and makes a permanent loan of it to Iranian cinema. An aged and anonymous railroad attendant and his equally old and sedate wife live in a remote and nameless spot in the middle of nowhere. The old man's daily chore is to go to a particular spot at a railroad junction and switch the direction of the tracks for an oncoming train, about which neither we nor the man know anything. People enter and exit the couple's life, very much like the train that punctuates their otherwise memory-less life. The mind-numbing routine is ultimately interrupted—ruptured—by a visit paid to the old man by an inspector from the central office, informing him that he has reached the age of retirement. As his successor comes to take charge, the old man goes to the city to ask to be allowed to continue to do his job. Denied, he returns home and collects his wife and belongings and they quit the premises.

That is all. The rest is pure visual poetry.

Have you ever wondered why and how people breathe? There were once some Muslim philosophers who thought that breathing was intentional, that it was predicated on a particular will and volition. But that is not what I mean here. What I'm asking is what wonder and hope, what grand expectation, illusion, and fantasy of a future sustains the rhythm of human life? Have you noticed that there is an imperceptible rhythm to our immediate being that is always being glossed over by the oncoming minutes that bear down on the moment that is passing—in effect leaving no room for it to breathe? Now imagine that looming weight lifted—that present moment freed to roam openly in the air of our rhythmic breathing, so we could see through the present to the hidden core of the constant instant of being alive. Well, Shahid Sales discovers that translucence by lifting the weight of the advancing minutes and letting the conclusion of the present never announce itself or approach. Was this what our ancestors and their saints called mysticism? Perhaps. Perhaps not.

"*Sufi ibn al-waqt bashad ay rafiq*," Rumi says in the *Mathnavi*: "Sufi is the creature of the moment." How can you dwell in the moment? I wonder. It is such a hard thing to do—to be and to breathe in the moment. I once read an aphorism of E. M. Cioran (1911–95), a Romanian philosopher who lived in France, to the effect that we breathe too fast to think properly, that our breathing rhythm is faster than our thinking patterns. I think Rumi knew what it means, and how hard it is, to live in the moment. But I am not sure if what he meant by "the moment" is this second that just passed by—I think he had a different time scale in mind.

If we were to locate Shahid Sales' *translucent* realism in this film somewhere other than its own immediate visual vocabulary, we would follow it to Kafka, and to Chekhov, and of course to the prophetic visionary of the translucent, Yasujiro Ozu. The anonymity of the bureaucracy that both gives and takes away the old man's solitary source of distraction is Kafka par excellence. The patient endurance of the microcosm of a stolid life that reveals the macrocosmic universe it hides is directly from Chekhov. Just as the stationary camera that has no rhyme or reason to move anywhere beyond the placid matter-of-factness of the old couple's numbing life is solidly Ozu. But the soul of Shahid Sales' vision rightfully belongs to the poetry of Sohrab Sepehri.

There is something more than a bureaucratic anonymity to the faceless authority that demands the old man's retirement—which for him means nothing but a material and physical displacement from a limited claim to life that he and his wife exercise. This vague and pale authority is neither tyrannical nor abusive; it is, in fact, quite caring and even kind. But it is precisely in its insipid care for the retirement of the old man that this distant vibration of power is disturbing, because you cannot hold anyone responsible for it. The problem in this case is not with power but with its command to initiate something it calls retirement. Retirement from what? There has been no tiring effort in the old man's life from which to retire and rest—as there is no conclusion to a life that has not, nor has it ever, even begun. Time and space are languidly stale in this purgatory—nothing really starts or ends, nor does this couple move from one to another location. Shahid Sales' stationary camera has an uncanny ability to capture and register the inanimate objects at the center of life—thus *Still Life*. The image of a train full of purposeful people traveling from an origin toward a destination, entirely unknown to the couple, is a suggestion that punctuates a life otherwise lost in the eternity of its timelessness. The presumed presence of a National Railroad Authority that employs and retires its workers is only there as the ghostly apparition of a power that may in fact not be there—and yet is manifest in its effects.

Shahid Sales' film is not political in the ordinary sense of the term—meaning the absurdity of the bureaucratic power that retires the old man is entirely tangential to its *modus operandi*. But it does set the narrative stage for Shahid Sales to present *Still Life* in the minutiae of details that map its sedentary emotions.

If one were to imagine a source of influence on Shahid Sales, Chekhov's psychoanalytic of the ordinary would perhaps be the principal factor. Chekhov's plays were a common staple in the Iranian theater scene of the 1960s and 1970s—his *Cherry Orchard* (1903) in particular. But that is not all. I also believe that Shahid Sales conceived of *Still Life* very much aware of and in conversation with Paul Cézanne, whose "Still Life with Compotier" (1879–82), with its deliberate outlines and contemplative shadows, is palpably evident in Shahid Sales' framing and mise en scène. Keep in mind that the term *tabiat-e bi-jan* is a Persian neologism for "still life." Sepehri, the principal poetic influence on Shahid Sales, was also a major painter whose aesthetic was formed while he studied in Paris. So what I am suggesting is that both through Sepehri and directly, Shahid Sales was very much conscious of the still life in general and that of Cézanne in particular.

What I have to offer by way of evidence is more circumstantial than biographical or anecdotal. Notice, for example, that Cézanne is legendary for his ability to have brought a succession of symmetries to intersect in his still lifes and thus generated competing axes that animate his pictures despite their evident claims to being inanimate. This aspect of Cézanne's painting is fundamental to Shahid Sales' cinematic translation of the very notion of still life. Cézanne also manipulated the texture of paints by using different shades of materiality—a neighborly conversation between opaqueness and transparency, the atmospheric and the existential, the real and the surreal. Shahid Sales translated this compositional paradox in his deliberate attempt to navigate the microcosmic evidence of life in otherwise stationary moments. Cézanne's "Still Life with Basket of Apples" (1890–94) is a masterpiece of manufactured assemblage for entirely aesthetic and compositional purposes—pure stylistic joy. In it, Cézanne composes a basket of fruit sitting upon a block, with an offering of cookies on a platter sitting on a book, with the red apples effectively floating over an almost accidental tablecloth—all assembled on the mere suggestion of a table. The movement and mise en scène evident in "Basket of Apples" are creatively suggestive of the way Shahid Sales effectively imitates with his stationary camera the contemplative brushstrokes of Cézanne. The same is true with Cézanne's "Still Life with Peppermint Bottle" (1890–94), in which the objects are suspended in vertical planes, suggesting an almost visible panning camera movement. In "Still Life with Onions and Bottle" (1895–1900), the vertical and horizontal conversation among the planes of the paintings are even more evidently dynamic.

What has always fascinated me about *Still Life* is how these pictures contain the course of a lifetime in the snapshot of a moment. The key to seeing life in the stillness of that moment, and thus the *moment*, as both Rumi and Cioran meant it, I believe (though I am not quite sure), is no longer a matter of temporal duration. It is a kind of moment, a metaphoric moment perhaps, that sustains a lifetime, a life, the duration and contour of a universe. Now imagine a film like Sohrab Shahid Sales' *Still Life*. How would this paradoxical capturing of a flowing universe in the fleeting stillness of a moment work? There is the rub.

My stylistic references to Kafka, Chekhov, Ozu, and Cézanne should not distract you from the source of Shahid Sales' poetic solace—Sohrab Sepehri. Sepehri (1928–80) was a painter and a poet, the two aspects of his creative character having an enduring impact on the other. Born and raised in Kashan, Sepehri remained a permanent outsider to the intellectual scene of the Iranian capital. He traveled extensively in Asia, Africa, the United States, and Europe—and he lived in Japan, the US, and France over extended periods of time. He worked at odd jobs in various governmental bureaucracies. But he painted his canvases and wrote his poetry with a gentle perseverance that is the hallmark of his creative legacy. In 1979 he was diagnosed with leukemia, received some treatment in England, but returned to Iran, died in Tehran, and was buried in his hometown, Kashan.

It is impossible to exaggerate the impact of Sepehri on his own generation of poets, painters, and filmmakers. Abbas Kiarostami and Mohsen Makhmalbaf have repeatedly expressed their own indebtedness to his poetry. Kiarostami's ascetic composition (and his photography) and Makhmalbaf's visual minimalism are vintage Sepehri, influenced by both his paintings and poetry. Sepehri was as much a cultural phenomenon as a poet and a painter. There was an odd, innocent gentleness about him and his art. So much gentility and innocence seems almost sinful in the context of the troubles of his time. Ahmad Shamlu, at that time Iran's poet and public intellectual par excellence, once publicly made fun of a line in Sepehri's poem "Water" where he says "Let's not muddy the river / It looks like the pigeon is descending / And about to drink a sip of water." "How in the world can you ask us," Shamlu objected, "not to muddy a river at a time when they are cutting the throats of people upstream?" referring to the political brutalities of the time, from which Sepehri remained blissfully distant. (Though it must be said that he was not apolitical, as evident in his poem "To the Garden of Fellow Travelers" (1967). There was a seriousness about Sepehri's almost mystical innocence—and this extended from his poetry to his personal character. Once when he was a teenager, grasshoppers attacked his hometown and he was put in charge of defending the crops in a nearby village. He could not bring himself to kill a single grasshopper. "If they are eating the crops, then they must be hungry," he concluded. "When I was walking through the crops I made sure I did not step on a single grasshopper."

In 1943, during the Allied occupation of Iran, Sepehri left his hometown and went to Tehran to continue his education. Two years later he returned to Kashan, unwilling to be part of the most extraordinary moments in Iranian political history, when everyone else wanted to be in the capital, witnessing the momentary collapse of Pahlavi tyranny under the boots of the Allied occupation, during the days when the Tudeh Party was established and a rambunctious period in modern Iranian history was in full swing. He would not be part of it. He stayed in Kashan, started working for the Ministry of Education, and in 1947 published an utterly inconsequential collection of poetry, something he would later categorically disown. But he took his painting very seriously—particularly after a friend introduced him to the work of van Gogh, radically transforming his aesthetic sensibilities. In 1948, Sepehri resigned from his post in the Ministry of Education and moved once again to Tehran, to attend the College of Fine Arts and to pursue his painting career in earnest. Meanwhile, he was deeply attracted to and influenced by Nima Yushij—the founding father of modern Persian poetry. But he found and paved his way to his own perfection, with an iron will resistant to the crooked manners of his time.

In 1951, Sepehri published another collection of poetry, *The Death of Color*, and by 1953 he had graduated from the College of Fine Arts—the top of his class, he went to the royal palace to receive recognition from the monarch, who had just been restored to his peacock throne by a CIA-engineered coup. In 1957, Sepehri traveled to London and Paris, where he studied lithography at the École des Beaux-Arts. In 1958, his paintings were exhibited at the Venice Biennale. By 1960, he had secured funding to go to Japan and study wood engraving. After returning to Iran he traveled to India, came back to Iran and began traveling around the country and exhibiting his work throughout the early 1960s, while publishing volumes of his poetry, and in 1970 he moved to New York and lived on Long Island for a few months. He spent much of the early 1970s showing his paintings in Europe, North Africa, and the Levant, including Palestine. Go and read a couple of the poems from his *Green Volume* (1967) and I will get back to you in a while.

What I believe we have accidentally stumbled upon here is a manner of realism (which in Shahid Sales' case we are going to call *translucent*) that is always thematically fragile and narratively brittle, that becomes frail if you start to take it too seriously. That is the reason that the generic term neorealism that people habitually apply to Iranian cinema is in need of redress. That is not all. This generic appellation has been the laziest camouflage ever—preventing us from reading through the manners of realism that have sustained Iranian cinema through its defiant agential assertion of itself beyond the mandate of the colonial modernity we have inherited from our dearly beloved ancestors. But let's leave them to rest in peace and proceed.

Sohrab Shahid Sales (1944–98) was born and raised in Iran and studied cinema in Europe. He had made a number of shorts and documentaries by the time he made *A Simple Incident* (1973) and radically redefined Iranian cinema with a *translucent* realism that was utterly unprecedented. A year later, Shahid Sales made *Still Life*, consolidating his position as a leading visionary of his generation. His next film, *In der Fremde* (*Far from Home*, 1975), was one of the first films to address the issue of *Gastarbeiter*, or the "guest worker," in Germany. Shahid Sales continued to make his films in Germany, funded mainly by German television, and effectively lost his connection with Iranian cinema. Between 1976 and 1992, he made a total of nine films for TV in Germany. Toward the end of his life and before his premature death in Chicago, Shahid Sales moved to the United States where his health rapidly deteriorated—despite the admirable efforts of his friends to save his life. Mehrnaz Saeed Vafa made a fine documentary about his last days in Chicago, and Ali Dehbashi has edited an excellent volume of essays and other material on Shahid Sales' significance as a filmmaker.

A Simple Incident premiered at the second Tehran International Film Festival, and caught the Iranian cinema scene off guard. No one could believe that such a simple incision of reality could carve through the fat layers of Iranian commercial cinema—pretty much dominating the mass consumption of Iranian films at the time. There were of course those who thought *A Simple Incident* slow and boring, its pace intolerable. But you will look in vain, even among those who liked and aggressively supported *A Simple Incident*, for a clue as to why they liked the film—although such standard clichés as "a true cinema" and "an honest cinema" as usual filled in the air.

A Simple Incident is a film of no incident. It is a succession of slightly, ever so gently, mobile still lifes. There is more motion in Cézanne's paintings than in Shahid Sales' films. The character Mohammad in *A Simple Incident* is the son of an ailing mother and a forlorn father who makes a meager living by illegal fishing in the Caspian Sea. Mohammad's life is divided between watching his mother die, his father wither away, and his schooling that is entirely irrelevant to the rest of his life. But the film is not tragic; it is lethargic. Its sluggish pace is deliberately languid—with long takes that neither generate nor expect the slightest suggestion of life. There is a weariness about *A Simple Incident*, an apathetic indolence, that is neither real nor fictive—it is translucently indulgent. It allows for the spontaneity of the real to become see-through, unmitigated, unexplained, inexplicable, standing at the threshold of every and all explanations.

It is precisely this indulgence in the *translucency of the real* that distinguishes Shahid Sales' cinema. Ozu, particularly in his masterpiece, *Tokyo Story* (1972), was a practitioner of this translucent style, as was Robert Bresson (I am reminded of *Diary of a Country Priest*, 1954), and I might even add Vittorio De Sica and *Umberto D* (1955) to the list. But in none of these films do you have the crescendo of literally breathtaking suspension as you do in the needle-and-thread scene of *Still Life*. When the old couple's son visits them, his mother notices that one of the buttons on his coat is falling off and she wants to fix it. For what feels like an eternity, she sits there trying to pass the thin thread through the eye of the needle. She is old and frail, and her eyesight is not what it used to be—and the blasted thread will not cooperate to find its way through. I remember when I saw *Still Life* in Tehran (in a theater on the corner of what used to be called Shah Reza and Pahlavi Avenues—they must carry the name of some martyr or Imam now), I sat there in the dark with my neck straining to see the destiny of that thread, and my breath stuck somewhere in my throat, waiting to see what would happen. What a relief, what a joy, what an everlasting assurance that everything was fine about the universe when it finally did. I swear to you some people burst into spontaneous applause at that moment, in by far the most sedate and anesthetized motion picture you ever saw (especially for an audience of testosterone-infected, over-politicized teenagers). If I were to tell you that to this day that particular sequence of Shahid Sales' film, of an old woman trying to run a piece of thread through the eye of a needle, is still infinitely more suspenseful to me than ten cliffhanger scenes in Indiana Jones movies put together you should not think me hyperbolic.

You remember that absolutely splendid scene in Mohsen Makhmalbaf's rambunctious *Once upon a Time, Cinema* (1991) that is an homage to this scene in *Still Life*? Makhmalbaf has trans-historically placed Naser al-Din Shah, the aging Qajar monarch, sitting and watching *Still Life* in the company of his harem. Shahid Sales' film reaches its suspenseful climax and everyone at court is waiting anxiously to see if the old woman will thread the needle or not. But the royal patience runs out and the shah dispatches Malijak, one of his royal attendants, to walk up to the screen, step into the scene, help the old woman with the damned needle and thread, exit from the scene, and get back in his seat to watch the rest of the film.

Do you know why I love this scene in *Once upon a Time, Cinema*? Because in a film that from beginning to end is a love letter to Iranian cinema, Makhmalbaf has kept his sweetest, warmest, and most endearing embrace for the absolute master of his chosen craft, for Sohrab Shahid Sales. That is not just Malijak going to give a hand to the aging, almost blind, old woman. That is Mohsen Makhmalbaf walking up to Shahid Sales and kissing and hugging him hello: "*Salaam aleikom*," as he is used to saying a bit bashfully, "How's it going, brother? Sorry to have missed you when you were here. We miss you now; wish you were still with us!" If anything brought together the two sides of the frightful abyss that separated the hope that was the Iranian revolution of 1979 and the nightmare it turned out to be, it is this scene of cinematic will to defy reason, to pay Shahid Sales a visit—not the aging, alcoholic, frail, dying Shahid Sales wasting away in Chicago, but the real Shahid Sales: the glorious summit, the call, the caption, the summation, the promise, and the delivery that made Makhmalbaf's chosen vocation and with it the splendor of Iranian cinema possible.

When Malijak steps back in time from the nineteenth century into the room of the old woman in the twentieth century, and when Makhmalbaf looks back in time from post-revolutionary Iran to the scene of *Still Life*, they do so against the logic of history. But they are spacing the gap cinematically, creatively traveling a journey that is the duration and endurance of the patience with which the aging mother is mending her son's coat. How does it happen with such patience? What happens in the span of that patient waiting? How does it help make reality translucent—dropping all the shadows of its accumulated, coagulated, ossified illusions, allusions, darkened visions of itself? Isn't it a wonder that in the bewildered patience of an old, nearly blind woman dwells such miasmatic mystery that only the borrowed (third) eye of an ingenious camera could see, seal, and register it?

Now I would like you to link two crucial aspects of Shahid Sales' *Still Life* together. First the fact that the old man is in charge of shifting a switch at a train junction, thus determining the course of a journey from point A to point B, without really caring where the people on that train have come from and where they are going, and second, the moment that Shahid Sales exposes in the moments when the mother is trying to thread a needle. What we have here is the metaphoric crisscrossing of a *journey* and a *moment*.

You see: This paradox of being at home with yourself when you are traveling around (and conversely daydreaming around the world when you are at home) has a wisdom to it that needs some dwelling on and exploring. "*Sufi Ibn al-Waqt bashad Ay Rafiq*," Rumi says in the *Mathnavi*, "Sufi is the creature of the moment"; and then he adds, "*Nist farda goftan az shart-e Tariq*"—"It is not appropriate to procrastinate in the Path (of Love)." I think that these two ideas are related: to be "the creature of the moment" and to be present with yourself *without* going on a journey. Dwelling in the moment, to be and to breathe in the moment, and thus to resist the temptation of daydreaming around the moment and not feeling it, or instantiating it, to be more precise, is not an easy task. How do you do that? How do you dwell in the moment and not allow your consciousness to scatter (travel) around? I think you do it by going on another journey, a substitutional journey, a journey into yourself, as it were. Sitting at home quietly and commencing a journey within, and thus gaining a presence with yourself by unpacking the mystery of the moment. This, I believe, is what the great sixteenth-century Shia philosopher Mulla Sadra meant by the very title (and content) of his famous book *Asfar Arba'a* (*The Four Journeys*)—four journeys to and through God, with and without the presence of others.

Imagine mixing the existential experience of physically traveling from point A to point B, say from New York to Oslo, with the fact of remaining at home. Imagine being at home with yourself (feel and instantiate your own presence) without physically traveling from point A to point B. If you can do that, if you can be at home with yourself while you are at home, as it were, without needing to get on an airplane and moving from New York to Oslo, or anywhere else for that matter, then you are home free, meaning you have gone through the journey of being with yourself without leaving your door—meaning you have cracked the mystery of the moment, that it has become translucent to you. You are no longer covering the mystery of one moment by the riddle of the next. I think (I am not quite sure, but I am willing to bet) that this is what Forugh Farrokhzad meant when in her famous poem "Another Birth" she says:

> *Safar-e hajmi dar khat-e zaman,*
> *Va beh hajmi khat-e khoshk-e zaman ra abestan kardan.*

> The journey of a volume on the line of time,
> And with a volume to impregnate the dry line of time.

When you commence your journey within the moment, as in splitting the moment and entering into and traversing through it (thus to see and behold what we ordinarily gloss over), then that journey becomes the simulacrum of a physical relocation from point A to point B, achieving the presence of yourself as if you were traveling around, without really taking a single step.

Is this, perhaps, the reason for my fascination with *Still Life?* It could be. What I am after here is to see the course of a lifetime (from birth to death) captured in the snapshot of a moment, to see the flamboyance of life in the stillness of a moment—the paradoxical capturing, as I said, of a flowing universe in the fleeting stillness of a moment—the journey of a train from an origin to a destination (the way the old man regulates it in Shahid Sales' film) and the instantiation of a moment in which this journey dwells (the way the woman tries to pass a thread through a needle).

If I am correct in detecting this *translucent* realism in Shahid Sales' cinema, then we have found an inroad into how to break through the habitual forgetfulness of the moment and see through its instantaneous revelation of being. Let me put it this way. You know how the sagacious poet Sa'di traveled a lot, all over the world, whereas the other great poet Hafez never as much as left his hometown of Shiraz? What I am after here is a metaphoric mixing of Hafez and Sa'di. Imagine if Sa'di had Hafez's perspicacious penetration into a poetic moment without as much as passing out of the gates of Shiraz. Imagine if Hafez had carried his presential knowledge of the moment as if he had traveled all around the world. That's what I mean. Let me put it yet another way. In his *Golestan (Rose Garden)* Sa'di tells a splendid little story about how once in a mosque in Baalbek in Lebanon he was delivering a hermeneutic exegesis on a Qur'anic passage and no one among his bored and boring audience was picking up on his eloquence and erudition. Then someone passes by and cries out loud in joy, having overheard the beauty of Sa'di's eloquence. "Praise be to God," Sa'di exclaims. "Those who are far away and know are close, while those who are close and blind are far away." This is the paradox that I have in mind, and this is the metaphor I suggest in the journey of a life in the serenity of a moment—bringing together what the husband does as a railroad man and his wife while mending her son's shirt. A dialectic of standing stationary and moving away, taking a moment and plunging deep into its mystery by way of reaching for a translucent reality otherwise hidden to the naked eye.

To do so, I would now like to offer you two complementary visions of a journey—at once real and fictive, ancient and modern—that are the narrative simulacra of removing the filter of opacity otherwise covering the countenance of the real. Think about the patience of the old woman in Shahid Sales' film, how she just sits there like there is no tomorrow. Shahid Sales placed his camera in the corner of that room and let it roll until the absolutely perfect time when reality dropped all its pretensions to meaning and succumbed to the sheer accidentality of signs refusing to abide by any rule and regulation to signify one thing or another. I would now like to take you to see two saintly figures, both of them close to Iran's historical predicament, both singular souls in the firmament of the Iranian creative and moral imagination. I want you to see how Mawlana Jalal al-Din Rumi, almost an eternity ago, and Sohrab Sepehri, just about the day before yesterday, traveled—from one point to another, Rumi from Balkh to Anatolia, and Sepehri from Iran around the world—and how their travels became two ways of penetrating the moment, and thus lifting the veils that ossify and darken the real beyond recognition of its evanescent subtleties. These two journeys are real—Rumi and Sepehri made these physical sojourns from one point to another—but they are also metaphoric. Our medieval saints used to call this *seyr-e afaq-o-anfus*, "a journey through horizons and souls"—meaning a journey at once external and internal, and thus a pilgrimage on land became a metaphor for the far more necessary journey within. But here I take these two journeys as traveling within, into the moment, a *dar safar* while *dar hazar*. I wish to show you how the physical journey from one point on the planet earth to another can also be the metaphor of a journey within, from the surface of our being deep down into the core of our existence, as if plunging into just one moment of our existence and splitting the atom of the most irreducible instant of our lives.

I have always thought that the hagiography (by which I mean a pious biography of saintly figures in which the hopes and aspirations of a community are narratively invested in their selected few) of our saints—Mawlana Jalal al-Din Rumi chief among them—has been a metaphor of such journeys within, by way of suggesting a journey without. We know very little about them—but what stories we make and tell about their miraculous deeds! These stories are journeys into a moment, a minute, a second, an instance. They project the span of a lifetime. But they unravel in the depth of only an instant. These biographies tell far less about the people who are the subject of the narrative than about those who have opted to narrate them, the community of agitated sensibilities now set in motion. They expand over the course of a lifetime—but they speak of a moment of hidden anxiety, of a naked encounter with being without the intermediary function of metaphor. I believe in *Still Life* Shahid Sales has achieved visual simulacrum of that journey within.

Consider what we know of the life of Mawlana Jalal al-Din Rumi (1207–73), who has been the subject of numerous hagiographical accounts as well as several scholarly examinations—all of them narrated around this idea of biography as a metaphor for a journey *without* searching to discover the soul *within*. Shams al-Din Aflaki's *Manaqib al-Arefin* and Sultan Walad's *Walad-namah* are among the earliest stories told about

Rumi's life, and they in turn gave rise to innumerable others. A number of scholarly accounts have been produced on the basis of these largely pious imaginings together with a few historical sources of Mawlana's life. Badi al-Zaman Furuzanfar's *Risalah dar Tahqiq-i Ahwal wa Zendegani-ye Mawlana Jalal al-Din Muhammad Mashhur beh Mawlavi* (1936), Helmut Ritter's *Maulana Galaluddin Rumi und sein Kreis* (1942), Fereydun Sepahsalar's *Risalah dar Ahval-i Mawlana Jalal al-Din Rumi* (1946), Reynold Alleyne Nicholson's *Rumi: Poet and Mystic* (1950), Abdolbaki Gölpînarli's *Mevla Celaladdin* (1952), Marijan Molé's *La Danse extatique en Islam* (1963), Afzal Iqbal's *The Life and Works of Muhammad Jalal ud-Din Rumi* (1974), Annemarie Schimmel's *The Triumphal Sun* (1978), William Chittick's *The Sufi Path of Love* (1983), Annemarie Schimmel's *I Am the Wind You Are Fire* (1992), and Franklin D. Lewis' *Rumi Past and Present, East and West* (2000) are chief among the critical encounters with the life and work of Rumi—and in all of them this idea of biography as the metaphor of a journey at once external and internal is paramount.

Pious and hagiographical narratives told about Muslim mystics cannot be considered in any way distinct from the intoxicated theo-eroticism that constitutes the very normative texture of Sufism. From *Manaqib al-Arefin* (*The Virtues of the Mystics*) of Aflaki, who was closest to Rumi's own time, to Annemarie Schimmel's and Franklin D. Lewis' biographical accounts (the most recent), there is a persistent mystical proclivity, and from the earliest sources to the latest there has been a sustained transformation of the few facts available about his life into a metaphor of mystical quest. It is as if the life of one of the greatest Muslim saints had no choice but be narrated in a language compatible with the journey that is at the heart of his message—at the center of a cosmic moment: translucent, miasmatic, evanescent, a vision of reality from within itself. As a result, we read these biographical narratives not in search of the significant events of their lives, but as thematic narratives integral to their communal significance *after* their death. These biographies become in essence the extension of their subject's teachings, their speculative offspring.

Everything about Rumi's life becomes archetypal, paradigmatic, exemplary. His full, honorific name is Mawlana Jalal al-Din Muhammad al-Balkhi thumma al-Rumi, Mawlana Khudavandegar; his nom de plume, Khamush. Just look at his names: Mawlana means "our master," Jalal al-Din means "the majesty of religion." Rumi means he resided in Rum (meaning Anatolia). But he originally came from Balkh in current Afghanistan. So he is referred to as al-Balkhi thumma al-Rumi (meaning "originally from Balkh and then from Rum"). Mawlana Khudavandegar means "our most revered master," and Khamush means "silent," a paradoxically hyperbolic reference to his voluminous writings.

Rumi was born in Balkh, on 30 September 1207. His genealogy having been linked to the first so-called "rightly guided" caliph, Abu Bakr al-Siddiq, he is believed to have descended from the closest companions of the Prophet. His father Mawlana Muhammad ibn Husayn al-Khatibi, Baha' al-Din Walad, was known as Sultan al-Ulama. His grandfather Husayn ibn Ahmad al-Khatibi was called "Allamah-ye Zaman" ("the most learned of the age"). His grandmother is believed to have been a Khwarazmshahi princess. A prophetic descent, an ancestral parentage linking him to the most learned in the faith, and a royal lineage through his mother places Mawlana on a pedestal both sacred and royal in the Islamic and Persian imaginations. But luminaries of Sufism also had to figure particularly high in his identity for his story to take shape. His father Baha' al-Din Walad traced the sanctity of his mantle to Shaykh Ahmad al-Ghazali, perhaps the most prominent Khorasani Sufi of the twelfth century. The way his life is narrated, Rumi's past is always already present—very much on the model of a tradition in which the Prophet of Islam is reported famously to have said, "*Kuntu Nabiyyan wa kana Adama bayn al-Ma' wa tiyn*"—"I was a Prophet when Adam was between water and dust."

These are perhaps factually based, certainly piously elaborated, aspects of a sculpting of an iconic figure, within whom we can begin to excavate the terms of our momentary fascination with a translucent reality. The Sufi affiliation of Rumi's ancestry, critical in this respect, needed and received a necessary dose of anti-philosophical rhetoric, and Baha' al-Din Walad's migration from Khorasan to Anatolia had a classical anti-philosophical twist to it. His fiery sermons are reported to have offended a prominent philosopher of the time, Fakhr al-Din Razi, who was a mentor to Khwarazmshah—the reigning monarch. The hostility and rivalry between Baha' al-Din Walad and Fakhr Razi becomes, in the stories passed down through the centuries, a symbolic representation of two epistemic rivalries of the time, between the theo-eroticism of the Sufis and the logocentricism of the philosophers. The stories of Rumi, then, identify him with saintly figures metaphorically but position him epistemically against prominent philosophers of his age.

In the post-Rumi anxiety of legitimacy that animated his hagiographers, an obviously anti-philosophical disposition continues to be paramount in constructing the character of the Sufi master. He had to transcend any discursive affiliation with the limitations of reason in reaching truth. Biography as metaphor of a journey—from life to death, from darkness to light, contingent on reaching a translucent reality—uplifts discursive reason and mutates it into a narrative of mystical truth-telling. Please note that the communal construction of Rumi's biography as a metaphor of a journey is a cumulative process, in part predicated on the facts of Rumi's life, in part the pious extrapolation of the biographer, in part the biographer's projection of his or her sensibilities onto Rumi's legacy, and in part the subsequent readers/writers glossing over what previous generations of pious biographers have received, imagined, and projected. I call this cumulative process a "moment" for its narrative disposition in effect occurs outside any temporal frame of reference.

The Sufism that is identified with Rumi's immediate ancestors is in fact a kind of religious populism against the juridical nomocentrism (or the primacy of *nomos*, or law) that invariably sided with the medieval feudalism of the Islamic state. Philosophers, in the meantime, were somewhere in between the two, insisting on the primacy of *logos*, or reason (they are logocentric in their discourses). The Sufism of Mawlana's ancestry was as much anti-juridical in its religious populism as it was anti-philosophical in its appeal to an experiential conception of divinity. The fact that Sultan Muhammad Khwarazmshah was a student of Fakhr Razi immediately put the religious populism that Baha' al-Din Walad's Sufism represented on high moral ground (for it posited itself against the presumption of "tyranny" definitive to any conception of political power) vis-à-vis the political establishment. Rumi's parentage had to emerge from such trials and tribulations for him to discard and dismantle them in a poetic diction that mastered and surpassed them all. That poetic diction—summoning and surpassing all other discourses of truth-telling—will remain a constitutional trope in the Persian creative character.

The saga of Mawlana's early life comes to a climax during the Mongol invasion of Transoxiana and Balkh, seen by Rumi's chroniclers as divine retribution for Muhammad Khwarazmshah and his impertinent treatment of Rumi's father. That the migration of Mawlana's family may have been a result of a more general fear of the impending Mongol invasion does not provide sufficient material for the ordained legend that Rumi's hagiographers imagine for him. And the departure of Rumi's family from Balkh cannot be complete without a proper royal visit to prevent it. Aflaki reports that Sultan Muhammad Khwarazmshah went to see Baha' al-Din Walad under the cover of night to apologize and persuade him not to leave. Another report about a warlord who had Majd al-Din al-Baghdadi thrown into the Oxiana River for having displeased his royal lordship may be hard to believe. But the necessity of this nocturnal trip is perfectly logical for the early childhood of Rumi to be invested with the most powerful imageries of his moral and political significance.

Notice how this whole story unfolds like a dream, or the interpretation of a dream, one incident leading to another, the mere fact of telling it making it real and consistent—the mystic unfolding of a moment that will contain the entirety of a culture. Please note that I mean neither to authenticate nor to dismiss the veracity of such accounts as reliable facts of Rumi's life. What I do wish to convey to you here is how there is a consistency in this biographical narrative, one thing leading to another, almost anticipating what comes next, all geared toward the capturing of an instant that holds the entirety of a culture together. Keep in mind that the metaphor of a journey, which is entirely tangential to what happens in Shahid Sales' *Still Life*, is in effect central to its story, very much on the model of this biographical narrative being entirely tangential to Rumi's poetry and yet definitive to its communal conception as a work of art. In the case of Shahid Sales' film, the old man works in the middle of nowhere, switching the tracks of the railroad on which people travel from one remote origin to another distant destination, both of which are entirely irrelevant and utterly inconsequential to the old man and his daily job—and yet in their absence they are definitive to his existential presence, his very reason for being. It is this translucent realism at the heart of the existential presence definitive to both Rumi's biographies and Shahid Sales' film that I wish to covey to you here.

The story of Baha al-Din Walad and Rumi's meeting in Nishapur with one of the greatest Persian mystics of all time, Farid al-Din Attar Nishapuri (1142–1221), is equally imperative in this respect. Sheikh Attar gave a copy of his *Asrarnameh* to Rumi and predicted that he would soon *"atash dar sukhtegan-e alam zanad,"* "set those who are in love on fire throughout the world." Here witness a major turning point, in the application of *karamat* narrative to Rumi's life. Karamat literature comprises a body of miraculous tales about Sufi saints, attributing to them supernatural and extraordinary abilities, such as in this case the aging Attar taking one look at the young Rumi and immediately realizing that he is in the presence of greatness. There must be something paramount about Rumi and premonitory about Attar so that the future saint is immediately recognized. This element of predestination is one of the most powerful animating forces in Rumi's hagiography. As you see, all these factual and fictive incidents are systematically narrated into a succession of relatable tales and miraculous encounters that are, in and of themselves, poetic in the liberty they take with the factual (ir)relevance of history. Pay close attention to what I say about these karamat tales and the way they navigate easily and gracefully between fact and fantasy (what I have already called, you recall, factasy)—for they are the very stuff of which Iranian cinema is made. But for now consider the fact that these narrative elements are all building on each other to make the journey of Rumi from one end of his life to another predestined, circumstantial to his poetry, definitive to his metaphysics, and sculptural to the moment of his presence in our cultural universe.

Moral and political authority seems to attend Rumi's entourage wherever they travel. Abdolrahman Jami, one of his famous biographers (and himself a prominent fifteenth-century poet), reports that Baha al-

Din Walad and Mawlana traveled to Baghdad where they were welcomed by Shahab al-Din Suhrawardi, a prominent Sufi master and the author of *Awarif al-Ma'arif.* Baha al-Din Walad is reported to have anticipated the collapse of Baghdad and refused the caliph's money, preferring to remain in his madrasah and teach there.

The ultimate destination of Mawlana's entourage after their departure from Khorasan could only be Mecca—the destination (as departure point) of all journeys. They had to perform their hajj pilgrimage for this trajectory to reach its apex. So, instead of going to Kunia directly, they first went to Mecca. From Mecca they depart for Syria and from there to the court of Fakhr al-Din Bahramshah, of the Mankujakian dynasty, a particularly notable patron of philosophers and saints escaping the wrath of the Mongols. Royal patronage constitutes a source of grace and blessing for Rumi's companions. Royalty sought affiliation with saintly figures for the benefit of the legitimacy of their own authority by being associated with the Sufi saints, who thus garnered significant symbolic stock in the political economy of Iranian culture, then and now. Muslim mystics have always secured political power by denouncing it. In this paradox dwells the authoritative domain of the Sufi—at once rejecting the world and authorizing it.

Both Jami and Aflaki concur that it was in Larandeh in Asia Minor that Mawlana, at the age of eighteen, married Gawhar Khatun, the daughter of Khwajah Lala Samarqandi, from which marriage he had two sons, Baha' al-Din Muhammad (Sultan Walad) and Ala' al-Din Muhammad. About seven years later, Baha al-Din was invited to Kunia in Anatolia by the Seljuqid Ala' al-Din Kayqubad, whose realm was safely distanced from and immune to the Mongol onslaught. The threat of the Mongol invasion looms large in the stories of Rumi's life and act as a constant source of danger in the shadow of which these tales are told. This is the danger of the earthly life, as it were, against the specter of which matters of moral perfection ought to be measured—which is exactly where you ought to look for the normative fragility of our cultural mores, leading our poets and artists to take reality too seriously to take it seriously. What I mean by "normative fragility" is a set of social transactions, always embedded in history, that at once make cultural mores possible and yet (ipso facto) make their abiding presence subject to historical renegotiations.

We are told that Rumi was twenty-four years old when his father died, and he succeeded him as a jurist in Kunia. He lived in the shadow of his father so long as the aging mystic was still alive, but with his father gone, Mawlana entered maturity in earnest. Aflaki reports that as soon as Baha al-Din Walad died, his disciple Burhan al-Din Muhaqqiq Termedhi realized that he had to protect and teach Mawlana. We are told that Rumi spent nine years as a disciple of Burhan al-Din Muhaqqiq, who had detected in him great juridical knowledge (*qal*) but found him wanting in matters of mystical awareness (*hal*). By 1232 Mawlana is believed to have traveled, on the recommendation of Burhan al-Din Muhaqqiq, to Aleppo to complete his juridical studies. The substitutional function of Burhan al-Din Muhaqqiq in Rumi's life seems to have been to complete his full awareness of juridical learning, so that he could justly denounce it by becoming a prophetic voice for hal.

From Aleppo Rumi went to Damascus, where it is reported that he met with Ibn Arabi, the other great luminary mystic saint of the time. Having seen Mawlana following his father on a road, Ibn Arabi is believed to have said, "How strange that an ocean should follow a lake!" Such apocryphal and anachronistic episodes fall squarely within the karamat narrative, wherein the authority of other saints is sought to legitimize Rumi's ordained place of honor. Ibn Arabi's premonition in Damascus echoes Attar's "He will set those who are in love on fire throughout the world" in Khorasan. Rumi is graced by contemporary saints, who chance upon his path and bless and foretell his destiny. The assumption of this blessing takes place in a time warp that is outside history and in the domain of the eternal.

Upon Mawlana's return to Kunia from Damascus, Burhan al-Din Muhaqqiq acknowledged him as a master and then died, in 1240. From 1240 to 1244 Mawlana was the leading preacher in Kunia. This was the mystic master establishing his full authority over the juridical realm of his intellect. In view of what is about to happen to Rumi after these four years of juridical authority, it is crucial for him to be depicted as the supreme man of law in the Muslim community. In a way, the higher his position of juridical authority during this period the more serious will be the consequences of his falling in love. The drama, in other words, is already brewing in the spontaneity of the moment that holds the entirety of Rumi's life together, as the microcosmic universe of a more universal claim on his followers' piety. As you can see, these collective biographers are running Rumi through the gamut of a moral universe over which he will soon preside with a speculative power rarely matched in the mystical dimension of Iranian culture.

On the morning of Saturday, 28 November 1244, Shams al-Din Tabrizi entered Kunia disguised as a merchant, and thus commenced by far the most shattering event in the life of Mawlana, and with it the most legendary homoerotic love affair in Persian mysticism. Their first meeting is reported with full hagiographical ecstasy. Aflaki reports that Shams asked Rumi whether the Prophet Muhammad was superior or Bayazid Bastami (a legendary mystic saint)—thus forcing him to choose between a man God chose as His Messenger and a common man who sought and achieved God? Muhiy al-Din Abd al-Qadir reports of an episode in which Shams either burned or drowned Mawlana's books. Dulatshah reports of Shams mocking the very instrumentality of knowledge in achieving anything. Ibn Battutah denigrates Mawlana's infatuation with a *"halva furush"* (sweets-seller), which, Battutah claims in his Arabic prose, turned Rumi to writing "unintelligible Persian poetry." The effect of this meeting between Rumi and Shams is very simple. Mawlana substitutes love for fear, dance for prayer, ecstatic song for Qur'anic recitation, Persian poetry for Islamic piety. This transmutation in Mawlana's character is the most enduring in his poetic legacy. The journey by now has become inward, away from the external world and toward the inner space that limns the borderlines of humanity and divinity through the ecstatic moments that are the love affair between Rumi and Shams—the passion and diction of his emerging poetry.

Rumi's exclusive attention to Shams generated envy and hostility, and they both endured the consequences of this animus and resentment. The result, however, if we are to take the clue that Ibn Battutah suggests, was the sparking of a poetic energy that left no room for juridical gesticulation. Love, in all its majesty and glory, inundated Rumi's imagination. He could not see anything except through the translucent energy of love, a love that he now poured bounteously on Shams and through Shams infused the universe of his creative being, from which his poetry began to flower. The narrow back alleys of juridical minutiae suddenly transformed into the wide highways of a profoundly homo- and theo-erotic imagination upon which Rumi soared to the peaks of his poetic articulation of existence. The journey now is no longer just inward and amorous (rather than worldly and metaphysical)—it is also poetic. A poetic shattering of the *logos* has now cracked open a whole different manner of seeing things. That itinerant, migratory, and perambulatory wandering becomes definitive, in its later visual mutation, of a crucial aspect of Iranian cinema—from the passing trains in Shahid Sales' *Still Life* to the centrality of a moving car in practically all of Abbas Kiarostami's films. They are all visual encapsulations of an eternity in a moment.

The zenith of ecstasy attained through his love for Shams led to the nadir of desperation in Rumi's hope for securing the object of his love and source of his poetic inspiration. On Thursday, 11 March 1246, unable to bear the onslaught of hostility aimed at him, Shams left Mawlana, probably for Damascus. They had spent no more than sixteen months together, which amounts to 480 days, or the exact equivalent of twelve *chellahs*, forty-day seclusion exercises. The numerological suggestion again reveals the hagiographical impetus at work in the construction of Rumi's biography—from beginning to end a metaphor of his journey through layers of reality to get to its translucent core.

Rumi sent his son Sultan Walad to bring Shams back to Kunia. Shams returned sometime in 1246, but his stay did not last long, and the hostility against him led either to his assassination or exile from Kunia—the truth is not known, but neither is it important for the sake of chronicling Rumi's life as we have seen it done so far. Thus began Mawlana's heart-wrenching search for his beloved Shams, a recurring episode that infused occasion and character to some of his most beautiful lyrics. Mawlana is reported to have traveled to Damascus to find Shams but returned to Kunia disappointed. For the rest of his life, Mawlana substituted for Shams one figure after another. He turned first to Salah al-Din Zarkub, a relationship that generated the same kind of public anger and jealousy as with Shams. Salah al-Din's daughter, Fatimah Khatun, reportedly married Mawlana's son Sultan Walad, perhaps as a gesture to ease the tension between his ardent disciples and Salah al-Din Zarkub. But the entire pattern of Mawlana's male bonding and love affairs, starting with Shams, is conducive to generating a poetic energy that feeds a much berated and shunned, if not forbidden, relationship with a male figure—and all the homoerotic anxieties that it may have generated and sustained. This amounts to a journey to the realm of the forbidden, the domain of the transgressive, the paradoxical source of a poetic disposition that thrives on the impermissible.

From 1249 to 1258 Salah al-Din Zarkub was Mawlana's companion. After Salah al-Din Zarkub's death, Hisam al-Din Chalabi became the object of Mawlana's love and affection. His time with Hisam al-Din lasted for about fifteen years and resulted in the composition of Rumi's masterpiece, the *Mathnavi*. The completion of the *Mathnavi* during this period suggests that the prolonged relationship with Hisam al-Din Chalabi gave Mawlana the sustained energy that transformed the depth of his passion for an entire spectrum of lovers into his poetic masterpiece. Whereas *Divan Shams*, Rumi's collection of lyrical poetry, represents the episodic outburst of an emerging poetic energy associated with Shams, the *Mathnavi* represents the maturity of that love into a single act of poetic genius.

Mawlana Jalal al-Din Rumi died on Sunday, 16 December 1273, at about the age of sixty-seven.

Do you see how throughout the ages those who have cared to write down an account of Rumi's life have persistently changed him from the mortal man that he was into the manner of the man they wanted to follow—the icon in which they needed to believe? This narrative tradition gave the Persian cultural imagination (meaning a sustained legacy of creativity definitive to what we call "Iran" today) a cyclical continuity that casts the character of Iranian culture, damned or blessed, into a perpetual remembrance of things past. These pious biographical sources are priceless in their exposure of the creative imagination at work in the life of the Persian saint as a metaphor of a journey at once inward and outward—both taking place in the instance of an eternal *moment* in the unfolding saga of a culture. Iran's medieval saints used to call this *seyr-e afaq-o-anfus*, "a journey through horizons and souls"—meaning a journey both external and internal, and thus the journey through distant lands became a metaphor for the far more necessary journey within. My point here is to draw your attention to the difference between the man Rumi (of whom we have a very vague biographical notion) and Rumi the legend, and to map out the distance in terms of a journey from distraction to abstraction, from confusion to concentration, from dystopia to utopia, all leading the narration of the life of a mystic saint into the simulacrum of a creative act of communal salvation. Here, biography no longer has a teleology, from A to Z, from birth to death. Here, biography is an instantaneous act of creative delivery, of birthing and sublimation, as the moment of the biographical incident becomes exemplary, prototypical, an iconic monument to what has come before and after it.

I offer you this narrative of Rumi's actively imagined biography by way of showing you how the metaphor of a journey into a moment and in search of a *translucent* reality is essential to the poetic heritage that informs Shahid Sales' visual vocabulary. In other words, I take something at once very tangential and yet utterly essential in *Still Life*—namely the fact that the old man is in charge of switching the train tracks and thus guiding the course of one journey or another—perhaps slightly more seriously than Shahid Sales intended. If we do so, and then add it to the moment that the old mother unravels, then the (inadvertent) metaphor of a journey entirely implicit in Shahid Sales' *Still Life* becomes central to this film, and the patience with which the old woman must run the thread through the eye of the needle (and Makhmalbaf's later trans-historical defiance of logic by traveling backward in time) becomes the teleological space within which is narrated a journey into the moment, a single second—just an instant. It is a kind of breaking the atom of a moment to explode what power and force is inside it—what universe of knowledge and being takes place within that instant. The scene in *Still Life* forces you to sit there, in the dark, and see that second dissected, that moment opened up, exposed, to reveal what it has hidden.

What I am suggesting is that Shahid Sales' translucent realism is a kind of a journey within the moment—the journey through horizons and souls. The translucency of the real emerges here as the act of being itself is slowed down to its essential moments, which are themselves made see-through, allowing one to regard the essence of being through a contemplation of its now visible essential parts. I would like to take the (equally hidden) travel metaphor of the train running by this old man every day to offer you two travel narratives (one about Rumi and the other by Sepehri) that cover a similar distance within a second, an instant, a moment, that we ordinarily take for nothing. I propose to you that in the split atom of that second, Shahid Sales has discovered and visualized the fundamental truth of his ancestral wisdom of the moment (or *dam*, as we say in Persian, literally a "breath") and made it evident. Rumi is my principal guide in this suggestion: "*Sufi Ibn al-Waqt bashad Ay Rafiq,*" "Sufi is the creature of the moment," adding "*Nist farda goftan az shart-e Tariq,*" "It is not appropriate to procrastinate in the Path (of Love)." Equally pertinent here is a poem attributed to Avicenna: "*Del-e har zarreh ra keh beshkafi / Aftabish dar nahan bini*"—"If you crack the heart of any atom / You'll see a sun hidden in it."

Still Life is a snapshot of this universe, and in the span of time that it takes for that aging mother to run a thread through the eye of a needle with her ailing eyes, Shahid Sales has detected and portrayed the patience with which we have lived our history. We are condemned, as we are blessed, to remember that history as if there is no tomorrow—and thus both our predicament and our salvation is contingent on the translucent realism that visionary poets like Shahid Sales have managed to articulate for us. In that articulation, Shahid Sales has taken his poetic clues from a kindred soul, to whom I will now entrust you: Sohrab Sepehri, Rumi's kindred soul, Shahid Sales' poetic alter ego. Sepehri's poem "Travleler," is another journey, long, but I have made it shorter, cast it into another tongue, so the poet can breathe a little more leisurely and once again travel to another place.

> At the sunset, amid the tired presence of things,
> An expectant gaze could see the very depth of time—
>
> Upon the table,
> The commotion of a few first of the season fruits
> Was flowing in the vague direction
> Of acquaintance with death;
> While the wind carried the aroma of the little garden
> Over the carpet of idleness
> As a gift to the soft margin of life;
> And as the mind was holding the light surface of a flower
> In hand—just like a fan—
> Cooling itself.
>
> The traveler stepped off the bus:
> "What a clear sky!"
> And the length of the street carried his lonesomeness away.

It was dusk.
One could hear the sound of the intelligence of all vegetation.
The traveler had arrived
And sat on a comfortable chair
By the lawn:

"I am sad—
I am inexplicably sad:
And all the way here all I could think of was only one thing—
The color of the surrounding pastures was beyond belief,
And the lines of the road were lost in the melancholic prairie—
What strange valleys!
And the horse—do you remember, it was at dawn—
Just like the purity of a concept
Was pasturing on the green silence of the grassland;
And then: the colorful lonesomeness of the village on the way;
And then: the tunnels.
I am sad—
I am inexplicably sad
And nothing—
Not these aromatic moments
That turn silent on the branches of the orange tree,
No—not even the honesty of a word
That is between the silence of the two leaves
Of this aromatic, nocturnal, flower—
Absolutely nothing can save me from the onslaught
Of this surrounding emptiness—
I believe that this melodically sorrowful song
Will be heard forever."

The traveler's eyes caught sight of the table:
"What beautiful apples!
Life is ecstatic with solitude."
The host asked:
"What does beautiful mean?"
Beautiful means the amorous interpretation of shapes—
It means love—and only love
Can get you warmed up to the tenderness of an apple;
It means love—and only love
Has carried me to the vast unhappiness of lives,
And delivered me to the possibility of becoming a bird—
And as for the sweet remedy of melancholy?

Well—the pure sound of elixir gives that sweet cure.

And now it was night;
The light was on—
And they were drinking tea.

—Why are you sad? It seems you are lonely.
—Really lonely!
—I believe you are afflicted with that hidden vein of colors.
—Afflicted means
Being in love.

—And think how lonely
Would the little fish be if it were afflicted
With the blueness of the vast sea.
—What a delicate sad thought!
—And sadness is the surreptitious smile of a plant looking.
And sadness is a vague reference to the denial of the unity of
*   things.*

...

The courtyard was lit
And the wind was blowing
And the blood of the night was flowing
In the silence of the two men.

"It is a clean empty room.
What simple proportions it has for thinking!
I am inexplicably sad—
No thought of going to sleep."

He went by the window
And sat upon the soft sofa:

I am still traveling.
In my mind I see a boat
Sailing upon all the world's oceans
As if it has been for thousands of years
That I—traveling on that boat—have been singing
The living song of the ancient mariners
Into the ears of seasons
And sailed along.

Where is this journey taking me?
Where would my footsteps be incomplete
And the laces of my shoes be untied
With the soft fingers of rest?
Where is the destination—
To spread a carpet,
To sit carefree
And to listen to the sound of a dish that is being washed
Under the faucet nearby?

And in what spring
Will you pause
And will the surface of the soul
Be covered with green leaves?

One must drink wine
And one must walk in an early morning shade—
That's all.

Where is the direction towards life?

...

Give me the wine
We must hurry:
I am coming back from a visit to an epic
And word for word
I know the story of Sohrab and the belated antidote by heart.

The journey took me to the threshold
Of the garden of my childhood—
I stood there
Until my heart stopped beating;
I heard something fluttering,
And when the door opened,
From the onslaught of truth
I fell on the ground
Prostrate.

Once again, under the heavens of the Psalms,
During that journey by the river in Babylon
I came to my senses:

The sound of the harp was silent,
But when I listened carefully
I could hear someone cry
And a few restless harps
Were twisting around
The branches of the wet willow.

On my journey's path,
The chaste Christian monks
Pointed the way
Towards the silent curtain of Jeremiah
As I was reciting out loud
From Ecclesiastes
And a few Lebanese farmers—
Sitting under an ancient cedar—
Were counting the fruit of their citrus trees
In their minds.

On the roadside, as I was traveling,
I saw blind Iraqi kids
Staring at the script of Hammurabi's tablet.

And all through my journey
I kept reading all the newspapers of the world.

...

The journey took me to equatorial lands
And under the shadow of that huge, that majestic, that green
                              banyan
How well do I remember
That phrase that entered the summer retreat of my mind:
Be vast, and be solitary, be humble, and be steadfast.

I come from a conversation with the sun—
Where is the shadow?

...

I am the interpreter of the sparrows of the Ganges valley,
And on the road to Surnat
I have interpreted the gnostic-studded earring of Tibet
For the naked ears of the girls of Benares.

Put upon my shoulder—
Oh, you the mourning hymns of the Vedas—
All the weight of freshness
Because I am afflicted with the warmth of speech.

And you, all the olive trees of Palestine!
Address the bounty of your shades to me:
This lonesome traveler
Who is back from a visit to Mount Tur
And has a fever—trembling from the heat of revelation.

...

We must move along;
We must travel along the distant horizons
And at times we must raise our tent
In the blood vessel of just one word.

We must move along
And at times we must eat
Mulberries from the tip of a branch.

...

We must move along:
The sound of the wind can be heard.
We must move along:
I am a traveler—
Oh, you the winds of Always!
Take me to the vastness of the formation of leaves.
Take me to the salty childhood of waters
And fill my shoes—to the point of the maturity
Of the body of the grape—with the mobile beauty of humility.
Fly my minutes all the way up to the doves of repetition
In the white heavens of instinct.
Right by a tree,
Turn the accident of my being
Into a lost and lasting relationship.
And in the breathing of solitude
Flutter the windows of my conscience.
On that day send me after the flying kites.
Take me to the solitude of the proportions of life.
Show me the soft presence of Nothing.

I think that to learn what became of me after
Rashomon the most reasonable procedure would
be to look for me in the characters in the films
I made after *Rashomon*. Although human beings
are incapable of talking about themselves with
total honesty, it is much harder to avoid the
truth while pretending to be other people.
—Akira Kurosawa

Amir Naderi
The Runner

YOU MUST FORGIVE ME for ending my last piece of musing so abruptly, but it felt obscene to talk in prose after Sepehri's poetry. As I write now New York is empty. Everyone has left for Christmas vacation, and I can hear the sound of the occasional truck rumbling down Broadway, the sound of its purposeful movement echoing reluctantly in my mind. I am practically chained to my writing desk, or else I sit down and watch Kurosawa. In between I go for very long walks. I have not seen Amir Naderi for more than two weeks. He is busy editing his fourth film, *Sound Barrier* I think he wants to call it. He called me last night from Virginia, where he is visiting his niece. He lost one of his nieces in an automobile accident last fall. He is a man of iron will but declining health—a national treasure who is now a walking monument to the best in Iranian cinema. How we wither!

I must resume my writing and I must write about Amir Naderi. Naderi has been my solitary companion in these dark days. "Suppose your revolution succeeds," he used to say to his political-activist friends back in Iran, "then what? What will you do the day after?" Chekhov will still have things to teach you, he would tell them. Gorky will not. This man, who made *Harmonica* (the audience went on a rampage after seeing it) in 1974 and who turned Sadeq Chubak's *Tangsir* (1963) into a monumental revolutionary epic in 1973 just a few years before the 1979 revolution, is astonishingly apolitical. I have no idea how he manages this. There are times when he seems not to know (or care) who the president of the United States is. I am not exaggerating. He is the only one from whom I hide my politics. I become ashamed of my politics when I am in his presence. He once saw me on national television (it was PBS) commenting on one thing or another. He called me up and said he liked the color combination of my tie and shirt. This was his way of disapproving of my having anything to do with politics, and ever since I rarely accept television appearances. (I do an occasional radio show but don't tell him. He never listens to the radio, but watches television—on mute.)

I have always wondered where in the world Amir Naderi gets his enviable political aloofness, while his cinema is anything but detached. His cinema is like a political ambush, springing from a corner of a critical intelligence cultivated entirely in solitude. Solitude, it seems to me, is the essence of Naderi's cinema. There is a scene in his masterpiece, *The Runner* (1985), where Amiru is sitting in that dilapidated and abandoned ship eating watermelon and looking at the pictures in a magazine he has just bought. It is a beautiful, sunny day, and there is a little yellow chick playing around, and at one point it walks over the magazine in front of Amiru. Amiru picks it up and feeds it a bit of his watermelon. If solitary bliss were to be captured in an image, that scene would be it. No king ever looked so blissful as Amiru does in the scene aboard that abandoned ship.

Where is that ship? What does it stand for? It just sits there, stuck in the mud, far from the sea, abandoned, forgotten, left to ruin, home to no life, the castle of a solitary soul. If that ship were to stand for Iran, stuck in mud and going nowhere, then see what Naderi has done with it, see how he has turned it into the majestic palace of a soaring soul reaching for perfection in the domain of its own solitude. From the angle of that solitude, our society looks wrong, our congregation scattered. How would a filmmaker attend to the malice of a society he calls home? More than two centuries into the birth of a nation into modernity and it still lacks the most basic principals of a free, democratic, and just society—stuck in mud and going nowhere. Naderi's *The Runner* is not a criticism of that predicament. It is seeking salvation within its confinements. In his solitude, Naderi contemplates Iran's society of disparaged parities—of having formed a modern nation-state, but not in terms conducive to addressing the most basic and inalienable rights of its citizenry. Naderi's politics

commences in his aesthetics and extends to his metaphysics. One can neither forget his politics nor make it paramount in his cinema. He is first
and foremost an aesthetician, and then a metaphysician. He turns reality
on to its visual awareness of the sublime, and from there he commences
a metaphysical reflection on reality—and yet all in terms characteristic
of his visual realism. I am absolutely convinced that Naderi's solitude is
by choice, not by accident. He chooses to be a tabula rasa, to reflect the
troubled world of his nation, and with his nation the world at large. His
politics are apolitical. His art is his politics. Having abandoned the realm
of ideology and utopia, in his cinema Naderi has detected a miraculous
take on reality, a visual awareness of its absolutism—and right there and
then navigated the course of his own lifetime as the roadmap of a nation
at large, of a world reduced to its singular affinities.

The texture of Naderi's solitude is deeply rooted in his own biography.
Today when you look at Naderi you realize that he is the Iranian filmmaker who initially brought global attention to Iranian cinema, first with
his film *The Runner* and then with its harrowing sequel, *Water, Wind,
Dust* (1989). If he took the world by surprise, he was long and arduously
at work to make it happen. Naderi was born in 1945 in the southern city
of Abadan, orphaned at a very young age, and raised by a maternal aunt.
Outside his cinema, this aunt has become Naderi's greatest invention,
though a real person and a loving maternal figure for him. He has elevated her into a feminine version of Solomon, a figure who always says
the right thing at the right moment, and she is exceedingly funny and
wise. Naderi is happiest when he talks about his "Khaleh." Some of the
stories he tells about his Khaleh seem to be true; others he has invented
over the years from scattered memories; all of them are the cumulative
invention of his creative soul. There are not that many women characters in the films Naderi made while he was in Iran. One reason might
be this Khaleh, in whom he has invested all his extraordinary gifts of
storytelling—told over many years to his closest friends and family. Central to all of Naderi's films, instead, is a solitary soul, an adolescent boy
(*Harmonica*; *Waiting*; *The Runner*; *Water, Wind, Dust*; and *Sound Barrier*);
a lonely man (*Tangsir*; *Dead-End*; *Requiem*; and *Manhattan by Numbers*), a
young woman (*A, B, C...Manhattan* and *Marathon*)—all of them versions
and variations of Amir Naderi himself.

Naderi's memories of childhood are marked by his joyous discovery
of cinema. You must imagine Naderi, a solitary but vast soul inhabiting a
tiny but resolute body, sandwiching himself between two boarded posters for the latest feature film, walking the streets of Abadan advertising
an Indian musical or else a Hollywood production, screaming at the top
of his voice the names of the lead actors and actresses and occasionally

bursting into his version of the song and dance featured in those films—providing musical melodies with whistles, hums, and bel cantos, lyrics having a rough ride on his adolescent voice, percussion rhythmic on the boarded posters. He would memorize (as we all did) the trailer voice-over of forthcoming films and then go up on the roof of his house to recite them in peace and without interruption: *"Gary Cooper, Burt Lancaster, dar Vera Cruz, filmi sarasar hayajan!"* ("Gary Cooper, Burt Lancaster, in *Vera Cruz*, a film from beginning to end full of excitement!") His attempted eloquence, however, would be regularly punctuated by his aunt's running commentaries on every word or phrase of his rooftop recitations, inconsiderately interrupting young Amir's soliloquies. So if from the rooftop Amir were to announce, for example, "A film full of adventure," his aunt would mutter from the courtyard, "No, mother, no adventure. We need to have a quiet life here"; or if Amir were to proclaim, "A film full of raucous battles, unbelievable love scenes!" his aunt would chime in, "No, my dear, try to lead a peaceful life; and be quiet with those obscenities—we are a respectable family in this neighborhood." What the world has seen of Naderi's cinema is but a smidgen of his memories of things done and imagined, factual and fantastic, real and make-believe—all woven together into a colorful tapestry of his defiant humanity: now bursting into joyous laughter, then pausing for a bewildered gaze, all the time sustained by an overwhelming sense of solitude.

Naderi lived inside those film advertisements, the quick cut and paste of their staccato attendance upon reality, the voice-overs declaiming with playful pomposity, and from them he moved straight into the Neverland of movies—a Peter Pan, orphaned, seeking solace in a rambunctious imagination he controlled with the blink of an eye. September 11 was possibly the saddest that I have ever seen Amir Naderi. At that moment, Lincoln Center was hosting a major retrospective of his films. Richard Peña had lovingly curated it as an homage to a great filmmaker. The day the Twin Towers collapsed, Amir was completely drained. "Why did they do that?" he asked me a few days later, without expecting an answer. "What had these two beautiful buildings done?" He spoke of the Twin Towers of the World Trade Center in anthropomorphic terms. Having shot them beautifully in his *Manhattan by Numbers* (1992), he had an abiding sense of loss about him that day, as if two of his dearest friends, whom he had cast in one of his films, had died.

Naderi's anthropomorphism of inanimate objects has an organic link to the vegetal world that he gathers around him that is pure poetry. He has a huge collection of small bottles of various sizes in his tiny apartment/office, in which he has planted a variety of small plants. He has placed this collection of plants in a very decorous and ceremonial manner by his window. They say some people talk to their plants. Amir does not just talk *to* his plants. He talks *about* his plants, as if they were his children, grandchildren, friends, extended family. These plants have human traits and specific characters. Some of them are kind and considerate, others are nasty and finicky. "You see this one," he once told me, pointing to one of his plants standing at the corner of a perfectly arranged scene. "She is the most stubborn thing you ever saw. She pays no attention to her grandmother, sitting right here at the center, and always turns her head away, toward the window, where the sun comes from, ruining my arrangement." Naderi rarely travels. But when he does, as for example when he went to Japan as a member of the jury in the Yamagata International Documentary Film Festival, he takes all his plants to the nearby park from which he has gradually collected them and replants them there. "They need to be with their family while I am away."

Like millions of other kids in the neighborhood of poverty and destitution, children that he would later autobiographically portray in many of his films, Naderi grew up in the crowded streets and twisting back alleys of the Iranian industrial south, having had to work myriad odd jobs from a very young age to survive. To this day, and for these very reasons, Naderi has an uncanny ability to capture the soul of a city—the cartography of its own self-regenerative imagination. He has a global vision of exterior shots, every frame of which is informed by his visual awareness of the whole. It seems that Naderi was destined to live and work in New York—the quintessential geography of nowhere (and thus everywhere) that he knows like the palm of his hand—which he ultimately opted to call home and map out in four consecutive films: *Manhattan by Numbers* (1992), *A, B, C...Manhattan* (1997), *Marathon* (2002), and *Sound Barrier* (2005). "Wherever you plant your camera to take a shot in a street," he always says to the legions of his Iranian admirers who come to New York to see him with the solemn air of pilgrims, "look around—my camera has been there before." No one, absolutely no one, has more a solid claim on Iranian cinema than Naderi. He knows and has navigated it from ground up, finished its course, and then left it for other horizons.

Naderi's command of exterior shots and his uncanny awareness of the sense of a city is matched by his ingenious skill with interiors—the origin of which might be traced back to his short (rarely known or noted) acting career on stage. Among Naderi's fondest childhood memories is his role, when he was six years old, as Joseph in a theatrical rendition of *Joseph and His Brothers*. In Naderi's neighborhood in Abadan there used to be a theater called Hafez where popular and religious stories like *Joseph and His Brothers* were regularly staged. Amir was the favorite Joseph in the cast. Very early in the play he would be thrown from center stage into a trapdoor well, landing on a pile of potato sacks, and he would not reappear until the very end when a passing caravan would dig him out of the well and take him to Egypt. In between he was in charge of cleaning up the theater, sweeping, mopping, dusting, collecting emptied bottles of soda and such. Not much came out of his acting career, but the experience is one among many other factors that have given him a multifocal, and entirely vernacular, sense of an interior—best represented so far in Gretchen's apartment in his *Marathon* and even more spectacularly with what he has done in a small storage room in *Sound Barrier*.

While sustained and nourished by every single film that found its way to movie theaters in Abadan in the 1950s, Naderi was soon mesmerized by the magic of television, which appeared soon afterward and expanded the horizon of his visual experiences. Children without a television set at home paid something like a penny a person to congregate in the living room (or at times the courtyard) of a slightly more well-to-do family that had managed to buy one of these newfangled boxes. Naderi once told me the story of how on one such occasion the audience became frustrated by the news programs—they were not there to watch the news; they were there to watch song and dance. Realizing the frustration of his clientele, the owner of the house instantly managed to compensate for the ill-timing of the news by starting to sing and play a tune on the back of a cooking pot (turned into a makeshift drum) while his wife and daughter began an impromptu dance. The audience started clapping rhythmically and the whole evening turned into fantastic live entertainment as all present quickly forgot about television and its untimely news. (Just about the same time, maybe a few years later, I made frequent visits to my older brother Majid in Abadan, and I used to go to one of these houses where the owner allowed the neighborhood kids to watch television for a penny or so. I was so mesmerized by the television that I just sat there and stared at it. On the surface that made me look like a very polite and courteous person, which translated into the owner using me as a model of behavior for the rambunctious kids. "Sit quietly just like that distinguished gentleman," he used to say only half-mockingly. This became a rather comfortable business arrangement between me and the owner of the house—I would just sit there quietly and watch television as a decorous decoy for civility and he would not charge me the usual fee. The arrangement did put undue pressure on my own noisy inclinations.)

The most amazing part of these stories that Naderi tells you is that you never know if he is making them up or if they actually happened—or better yet, a combination of both. My own sense is that the stories are true, but that Naderi's manner of telling them has the trademark of his cinematic mannerism, which is in fact the best way of understanding his (and by extension Iranian) cinema, a rugged realism based entirely on lived experiences, sublimated into visual memory that translates them into truth. Cinematic invention turns mere reality into transcendent truth, the ephemerality of a passing incident into the eternality of a lasting vision of where and what we are—a noble lie (in short) that turns mundane reality to sublime truth: That, my dear, is (Iranian) cinema in a nutshell.

Even with its cosmopolitan prestige as the center of the booming Iranian oil industry, Abadan of the 1940s and 1950s was too small to hold Naderi's restless imagination. He was still a teenager when one day he packed a small suitcase and left for Tehran—the capital city of his dreams. From his early childhood, it was as if Naderi was meant to be a global filmmaker, having no home and recognizing no national boundaries—a fact rooted in his provincial origins in the southern part of Iran and the colonial history of the region he and I both call home. Those of us who were born and raised in southern Iran had a very peculiar relationship to the two colonial gazes cast upon us—by Tehran and the Tehranis from the north and by the British and the US colonial presence in our region. This double colonization had invested in us a healthy doze of contempt for our two colonizers—one inherent in our presumed national identity and the other external to it—playing them in effect against each other. The result of this double contempt for power was an arrogance with which we detested any obstacle that got in our way. Naderi's cinema is the supreme example of this creative defiance. A considerable share of my love for Naderi and his cinema derives from this fact. There is a justifiable arrogance about him, a creative confidence, an almost regal sense of self-assuredness that he—along with the rest of us provincial southerners—exudes in his cinema. The character of Zar Mammad in Naderi's magisterial *Tangsir* (1973) epitomizes this stubborn rebelliousness. (To this day, and from a great distance, I still have an allergic reaction to Tehrani intellectuals. I find them astoundingly parochial. The historical implications of this Tehrani parochialism points to much larger issues, which I cannot explore here. But give me half an hour and I will demonstrate to you that much of our historical predicament in confronting colonial modernity is in fact contingent on this very Tehran-based racism, which replicates and thus corroborates the colonial gaze cast at our nation at large—all in a ludicrous attempt to hide the anxiety of its own origin.)

"I always dreamt of getting on a ship and running away to some far-off land," Naderi once said, and in his mind he did so many times. From his hometown of Abadan, Naderi moved first to Tehran where he began a career as a still photographer. But importantly, he continued with his systematic study of cinema. As he frequented Iranian cinema circles and got acquainted with the leading filmmakers of his time, his disenfranchised background separated him from the rest of his generation of pioneering filmmakers, who by and large came from relatively rich middle-class families. Those filmmakers who had studied abroad or had frequent access to world (European in particular) cinema were particularly obnoxious in their class-conscious demeanor and behavior toward poor and provincial boys who appeared to them to have come from nowhere. When merely a teenager, Naderi went to Golestan Studios to meet Ebrahim Golestan. He was made to wait hours at the door and still Golestan would not meet with him. Finally admitted to the studio, he was again made to wait for hours. "Through an open door I saw a young woman," he now remembers, "working at a desk. She came out and saw me sitting. She asked me if I could give her a hand moving a table. I did." That woman was Forugh Farrokhzad. That was the only memorable event that day at Golestan Studios. Years later, in 1970, when Naderi finally made his astonishing directorial debut with *Goodbye, Friend*, Golestan, caught off-guard by a provincial boy beating him at his own game and eager to befriend the young prodigy, refused to admit that he had ever met Naderi before. But Naderi doesn't hold grudges; he is too busy dreaming of his next film.

This early encounter between Naderi, Golestan, and Farrokhzad foreshadowed their more historic rendezvous, when a visual translation of the verbal memory of the Iranian aesthetic imagination would radically transform the very soul of Iranian cinema and come to complete and final fruition in *The Runner*, in which Naderi's *visual* realism was no longer in need of literary anchorage.

The British colonialism of the 1920s and 1930s, the Tudeh Party socialism of the 1940s, the Mosaddeq nationalism of the 1950s, the Pahlavi monarchy of the 1960s, the urban guerilla movements of the 1970s, the Islamic theocracy of the 1980s, and the exilic life of an immigrant filmmaker in his cinematic homeland in the US in the 1990s and after comprise the political universe of Amir Naderi, a filmmaker of extraordinary visual versatility, with a politics subsumed in the aesthetics of his formal preoccupation with visual realism. Naderi is an unlettered filmmaker in the strictest sense of the term. He possesses no formal schooling in anything, least of all in cinema. But Naderi is a walking encyclopedia of cinema. Peter Scarlet, the former head of the Paris Cinematheque and the current director of the Tribeca Film Festival, once told me that he only knew one other director who knew as much about film as Naderi: Martin Scorsese. When I told that to Naderi to make him feel good, he became playfully angry. "I bet you I could beat Scorsese with my hands tied behind my back and blindfolded."

There is a story famous among Naderi's friends that I believe contains much symbolic significance about the commencement of his cinematic career. In 1968 one of Naderi's friends, Manuchehr Jahanfar, at the time working for an airline in Tehran, began telling him stories about Stanley Kubrick making *2001: A Space Odyssey*, which, knowing

English, he had read in *Time* magazine. Naderi became mesmerized with these stories, until, sometime in the spring, Jahanfar read in *Time* that in May of that year Kubrick would premiere his film in London. As soon he said it, Naderi became determined to be in London for the premiere of Kubrick's film. He sold everything he owned, including his handheld camera, and made a bet with his friends that he would travel to London, watch *2001: A Space Odyssey* on its opening night, and come back with the ticket stub to prove it.

In April 1968, Naderi boarded what we used to call a TBT bus (there was a transportation company by that name) and traveled all the way from Tehran, via Turkey, Eastern Europe, and Western Europe, to London. You have to catch Naderi in a good mood for him to tell you this story in full panoramic detail, for it is one of the most hilarious stories in the annals of Iranian cinema. By hook and by crook, Naderi managed to get himself to London and descended upon Leicester Square at about four in the morning one fine day in May 1968, having just passed through the tumultuous streets of Paris during the legendary revolutionary demonstrations, which included such icons of the French intellectual scene as Jean-Paul Sartre, Michel Foucault, François Truffaut, and Jean-Luc Godard.

Naderi's eyes still shine with joy when he describes the huge poster for *2001: A Space Odyssey* he first saw in front of the theater where they were going to show the film. What happens next is an incident of bewildering ecstasy. He proceeded to the front door of the theater. Nobody was there. It was too early in the morning. He approached the front gate of the theater, took off his belt, wrapped it around his left arm, and tied it to the bars in front of the box office. To this day Naderi has never explained why he did that, except to make sure that nobody could remove him from that prime location, so that he would be the first person in line when the box office opened. But there is another way of reading that gesture of a young aspirant about to commence his career as a globally celebrated filmmaker.

The gesture of fastening yourself to a sacred edifice is a common practice among Iranian Shiites when they visit the shrines of their saints and have a serious wish they would like fulfilled. The practice is called *zarih bastan*, and it means to tie oneself to the zarih, the surrounding periphery of a sacred site like the mausoleum of one of the twelve Shia Imams, hoping for a miracle to happen. I vividly remember the mausoleum of the eighth Shia Imam, in Mashhad, when I was a young boy and visited the sacred site with my family. Sick people, people suffering great hardship, people wishing for the fulfillment of a long-held hope would tie themselves to the metal bars at the shrine and sit there for hours, sometime days, reciting their prayers and sharing their grief with the

Imam as if he were a living person and listening to them, until such time that their wish was fulfilled. I remember one night I heard some beautiful music emanating from the top of a minaret in Mashhad, from what is called the *naqareh khaneh*. Musicians were playing the *sorna* (a wind instrument) and the naqareh (a kind of drum), which my mother told me was the sign that Imam Reza had in fact granted a wish, that a miracle had occurred, and the naqareh khaneh was both celebrating the occasion and also letting the whole world know what had happened. I still remember the beautiful, star-filled, evening sky over the minaret when I heard that melodic announcement of a miracle.

And so the man at the entrance to that movie theater was no mere movie fan. That was a pilgrim, at the gate of his most sacrosanct hopes, his most devout wishes, to become a filmmaker, to join the pantheon of imaginal ecstasies, to be given the lantern of light to raise, just like Diogenes, to look for humanity. "From this first trip to London," Naderi told me recently, "I went back to Tehran and made my first film."

At about 10 a.m. or so, as Naderi was dozing off, his arm tightly tied to the box office, he noticed a few people entering the theater. They cast a dirty look at Naderi and asked him to move away. He, in response, tightened the belt another notch. At one point an older English lady, who turned out to be the cashier at the theater, asked him what in the world was he doing there, tied to the box office. It was at this point that he produced a document now a legendary part of this story, a letter handwritten in Perglish, namely a few English sentences that Manuchehr Jahanfar had dictated and Naderi had written down in the Persian alphabet—for he did not (and still does not know much of) the English alphabet. This was a common practice among us in Iran at the time. We transliterated English words in Persian, for we did not know how to read English. From this piece of paper Naderi had informed the whole world from Turkey to London that his name was Amir Naderi, that he was on his way to London to see Stanley Kubrick's *2001: A Space Odyssey*, that he did not speak English, that he had made a bet with his friends that he would attend the opening night of the film in London, and that he would bring back the ticket stub as evidence. With whatever accent or intonation his sleepy head and stuttering tongue could manage, Naderi informed the gentle Englishwoman what his purpose was and tightened his belt again another notch tighter. Amused or perhaps bewildered, the old cashier took mercy on him and let him stay put.

About an hour later, Naderi observed a stretch limousine, guarded by two motorcycle escorts, pulling up to the theater. From it descended a few young men with bobbins under their arms, and they walked straight up to the cinema where Naderi had ceremoniously tied himself. Deep in a heated discussion, they opened the door, inadvertently forcing Naderi to pull himself tightly into the space between the opened door and the adjacent wall. As Naderi lifted his head—having had to lie almost prostrate on the ground—he saw the bearded face he knew by now and recognized by heart to be none other than Stanley Kubrick himself. Now Naderi is legendary for his quick wit—as when years later he found himself in an elevator with Ingrid Bergman between the eighth and ground floors of a building in midtown Manhattan where filmmakers show their films to potential distributors. "I had only a few seconds to make a decision," he told me years later. "May I please kiss you?" he managed to mumble to her. She turned to him, smiled, and extended her cheek. Naderi kissed Bergman's cheek, the elevator door opened, and one of the most beautiful women on the face of the earth disappeared into a crowed of admirers.

Kubrick and his entourage entered the theater, Naderi watching them through the glass doors, and then disappeared behind a closed door inside. A few minutes later, one of the fellows with Kubrick came out and chatted with the cashier lady. They exchanged a few words, and both of them looked and motioned toward Naderi. Minutes after that, Kubrick came out from behind the door and spoke with the same cashier. At this point she motioned to Naderi to come in. He got up, unfettered himself, and went inside. The old lady repeated to Kubrick Naderi's story as she had learned it from Naderi's folded Perglish letter. Kubrick asked Naderi the details of the same story. Naderi took out the letter and started repeating the story, this time directly to Kubrick himself: My name is Amir Naderi, Manuch [short for Manuchehr Jahanfar] told me that Stanley Kubrick would premiere his film in London, so I sold everything I owned, got on a bus, and traveled to London because I made a bet with my friends that I'd be at the premiere and bring back the ticket stub as evidence. Kubrick stared at Naderi for a second and asked him, "Iran? Did you say you come from Iran? Oh, yes, the shah!"—at least this is what Naderi's mesmerized memory now recalls. "But who the hell is this Manuch, anyway?" Kubrick asked—this part Naderi remembers very well. He collected his courage and began an impromptu variation on the letter, repeating the same story, but this time from memory, for by now he had read it to everyone in his path, from Turkey to London.

At this point a couple of Kubrick's companions appeared to tell the director that they were ready. Naderi soon deduced from their gestures that the Cinerama screening of the film during the previous night for Queen Elizabeth II had encountered a problem, namely that the left side of the concave screen was out of focus, and that Kubrick and his crew had come to the theater to test the projectors to correct the problem. Kubrick went inside and a few seconds later someone came rushing out and grabbed ahold of Naderi, now standing bewildered in the foyer of the cinema, and led him into the theater itself, pushing him inside and telling him to go and see the film, for they were running a test. Naderi entered the cinema, which was pitch black, except for a couple of signs under the screen, where the emergency exits were located. Naderi stood in place for a while until his eyes got used to the darkness, and then gradually felt his way toward a seat and sat down. Suddenly the whole screen flooded with light as one reel of the film started rolling. Naderi was flabbergasted at the sight of prehistoric humanoids, for this was not his expectation of a space odyssey. He sat there for about an hour watching that reel, and as soon as it was finished the whole theater was illuminated, with flood lights, and Kubrick and his crew came out discussing and debating one thing or another. They noticed Naderi, and Kubrick asked him if he noticed anything wrong with the screening. Naderi, recognizing the problem, turned his back to Kubrick, pointed to the left of his two ass cheeks, and said in a mix of sign language and Perglish that, yes, one side of the screen was out of focus. Kubrick jumped in a combination of frustration and excitement, for he had been trying to convince his crew of something to that effect, and here was Naderi, having come all the way from Iran, confirming his suspicion. They gradually left the theater, and Kubrick told the cashier lady to give Naderi a ticket, and told him goodbye—leaving Naderi in a state of ecstatic shock with the good-hearted cashier lady.

Manuchehr Jahanfar had told Naderi that in England cashiers have a map of the seats, and that he could choose where he wanted to sit. So Naderi went to the lady, pointed to the seat he wanted, and got his ticket. He reached into his pockets to pay, and the cashier told him that the ticket was courtesy of Stanley Kubrick. Naderi insisted, though, that he had to pay because it was part of the bet. She relented, he reached for all the coins and notes he had, and presented them to her. She looked and saw all the strange currencies, from countries all the way from Turkey to France. She told him that he had no English pounds and that he had to go to a bank and change them. Naderi grabbed his money, left the theater, went out into Leicester Square, found a bank, approached a teller, and once again emptied the contents of his pockets, valiantly mustering the word "change." The teller looked at the scattered currencies, pushed most of them aside as worthless coins from Eastern Europe, collected all the Western European money that he could find, and in exchange gave Naderi somewhere around two English pounds. Naderi grabbed the money and came out of the bank to find that there was now a long line forming in front of the theater. He found the old lady, motioned toward her, and gave her all the money he had, which was about two pounds. It was not enough, but it was sufficient to satisfy, partially, the full price of the ticket, which Naderi now remembers to be about three English pounds.

Ticket triumphantly in hand, his belt back where it belonged, the ecstatic joy of his encounter with Stanley Kubrick in his heart, and the privilege of having helped him straighten out the left side of the projection of his panoramic vision of humanity in space now achieved, Naderi left the theater and found himself still in possession of a few blessed pence. He spied and marched resolutely toward a cafe and bought himself a cup of tea. He sat down, drank his tea, put his head on the table to rest for a while, and fell fast asleep. (If this sounds a bit like Abbas Kiarostami's 1974 movie *Traveler*, you'll have to ask Kiarostami for clarification.) After a while, Naderi got up and walked hurriedly toward the theater, and as he got nearer he saw that a group of young kids were following after him, for by now the story of his encounter with Kubrick had been spread all over Leicester Square by a young assistant to the old cashier. Naderi chatted with these youngsters for a while, again with variations on the theme of his Perglish letter, and then watched *2001: A Space Odyssey* from a preferred position, courtesy of Kubrick himself. After the screening, the same youths and a few others gathered around him asking for details of his meeting with Kubrick. Naderi repeated the story, and the small audience that by then had amassed took a liking to Kubrick's phrase "but who the hell is this Manuch, anyway." They had a good laugh, and, according to Naderi, he managed to stay in London for another four months, going from one party to another, retelling his story, practicing his Perglish, while his audience got ready to burst into a chorus at the opportune time: "But who the hell is this Manouch, anyway!"

Having seen *2001: A Space Odyssey* and even met and chatted with Stanley Kubrick himself, Naderi returned to Iran and made his directorial debut in 1970 with *Khoda Hafez Rafiq* (*Goodbye Friend*, 1970), taking Tehran by storm. A year after that he made *Tangna* (*Deadlock*, 1971). These two early films established Naderi as a major new presence in Iranian cinema. Shot in stark black and white, *Goodbye Friend* and *Deadlock* claimed Tehran (as Naderi would later claim New York) almost as an intimate acquaintance. No one since Ebrahim Golestan had captured the soul of the Iranian capital with such vivid and memorable images. Naderi's vision had the added advantage of having been dreamt and envisioned by a street-smart intelligence entirely absent from Golestan's aesthetic. Thugs, money launderers, pimps, prostitutes, thieves, and gamblers had never been captured in an Iranian film with such an easy and natural command. This is the Tehran of the Pahlavi monarchy at the height of its power. The June 1963 uprising of Ayatollah Khomeini had been crushed, and the urban guerilla movement of the 1970s was yet to commence. Iranian political culture was in a state of social despair and political paralysis. But Naderi was busy meticulously crafting the tools of his trade, and letting the politics of despair emanate from Tehran's thicket of streets and alleyways.

Perhaps best evident in *Deadlock*, Naderi took the genre of what was then called *film jaheli* and transformed it into a social realism of unsurpassed emotive power and cinematic potency. Film jaheli took the useless lives of lumpenproletariat in city slums and turned them into melodramatic cinema—perhaps best represented by Masud Kimiyai's *Qeysar* (1969). It was this genre, and precisely at the moment that Masud Kimiyai gave it supreme cinematic form, that Naderi sought a different manner of visual realism, detached from literary and poetic roots, and squarely planted in the visual vocabulary of its own narrative diction and normative style and mannerism.

Stark black-and-white images, an uncanny familiarity with the sinuous meandering of downtown Tehran, and the navigation of the brutally violent temper of Iranian society in the early 1970s became the hallmarks of Naderi's cinema at this time. The storylines of Naderi's films are always more of an excuse for his visual registers than the chronicles of dramatic events. There is the schematic of a story in *Goodbye Friend*, in which three friends commit a robbery and greed turns them against each other. The same holds true for *Deadlock*, in which a young pool hustler (Said Rad) accidentally kills a friend and takes flight in a proverbial Naderi quest for money to save his life (a theme repeated in many of his films, from *Deadlock* to *Tangsir* to *Manhattan by Numbers*). *Goodbye Friend* and *Deadlock* give Naderi a chance to navigate Tehran as a violent and vibrant cosmopolis, the seat of an urban malaise undetected with such clarity before. Naderi diagnoses and shows that malaise, withholding judgment, prejudice, and politics—and yet the underlying violence at the heart of the city agitates every single movement of his belligerent characters. Both these films, as a result, become a corroborating conversation between a deeply violent city and a set of equally disturbed characters it has engendered. The rebellious anger evident in Naderi's lead character (brilliantly executed by Said Rad)—borrowed from such classics as László Benedek's *The Wild One* (1953) and Nicholas Ray's *Rebel Without a Cause* (1955)—always transcends its evident reasons for defiance and marks a bold audacity that speaks of other causes for revolt. No one before or after Naderi captured the bursting soul and conflicted character of that city. As the two brothers of the man whom the pool hustler has killed chase after him through the streets and alleys of the slums and derelict neighborhoods of Tehran, Naderi's camera in *Deadlock* is busy telling a story far different from the one we are following in the schematics of the storyline. What Naderi shows in these two films is the subterranean violence that is integral and definitive to the character of the cosmopolis—its wild and contagious ferocity.

During the next two years, Naderi made *Tangsir* (1973) and *Saz Dahani* (*Harmonica*, 1974)—two of his most famous and enduring films. These two deeply political films, one in epic and the other in symbolic terms, catapulted Naderi to the vanguard of the Iranian revolutionary movement. *Tangsir* turned the local uprising of a small-town rebel into a global epic of revolt; *Harmonica* used a simple children's story as an allegorical register of dispossession and tyranny.

By far Naderi's most overtly political film, *Tangsir* combined Sadeq Chubak's major novel (of the same title) and Rasoul Parvizi's short story (of the same content) into a narrative of unsurpassed scope and significance in Iranian cinema. In the title role, Behruz Vosoughi consolidated his position as the most versatile actor of his generation. A simple southern man, Zar Mammad, who has entrusted his life savings to the local mullah for investment, is cheated of his investment by the crooked mullah, who is in cahoots with the local governor and a prominent merchant. Zar Mammad tries in vain to collect his money, so that he can continue to provide for his family, but all he receives in response is incessant humiliation. Fed up, he digs up a gun he had buried long ago when fighting against the British, tracks down the mullah, the governor, and the merchant and kills them all. Zar Mammad's personal revenge soon assumes far greater political dimensions in the city as the local uprising of this small town projects a much wider range of political implication among the audience in early 1970s Iran.

I was present at the opening of *Tangsir* at Rudaki Hall in Tehran—and the story of how I got a ticket for that illustrious occasion continues to amuse Naderi to this day. I was an undergraduate student in Tehran and to support myself and pay for my tuition I used to work as a doorman at a very posh apartment building in north Tehran. The building was located on what was then called Amir Atabak Street, just off Takht-e Tavous Avenue. One day, as I was sitting in my small cubical minding my business of minding the building, someone came to me and said that he was an assistant producer for a film starring Behruz Vosoughi and Nuri Kasrai (the Robert Redford and Michelle Pfeiffer of Iranian cinema at the time). They had a scene that they wanted to shoot at the front door of the building where I worked. Could I please secure permission for that shot? I called the owner of the building within seconds. His name was Mr. Fahm, I remember now, quite a well-to-do engineer who owned a number of buildings in Tehran. He was at some sort of a party. I finally located him and secured his permission—after I assured him that I would make sure that the script did not implicate the building with any nasty reputation. In a few days Behruz Vosoughi, Nuri Kasrai, a small camera crew, and the assistant producer appeared at the door. I was, needless to say, flabbergasted. I spent half a day in the company of the two leading actors of my generation. I was (and still am) so excited that for the life of me I could not care less who the director of that film was, and I still don't know the name of that movie. All I remember is being with Vosoughi and casting frightened looks at Kasrai, who was (and still is) one of the most beautiful women I ever saw in my life (she also acted in *Tangsir* as Zar Mammad's wife). Scared and excited out of my wits, all I remember now was following Vosoughi around; at some point he even let me join him when the makeup artists were getting him ready for his scene, and I remember that he needed to have a bit of white hair on his temple. To make a long story short, I stood there ecstatic as they shot the scene, following which (and noting my dumbstruck bewilderment) Vosoughi asked me if I wanted to take my picture with him. Yes, of course, I must have said, and thus we stood in front of Mr. Fahm's building and had our picture taken, by a still photographer among the camera crew. I have since lost this picture, which makes me angry, but I do remember it vividly. It was black and white. Vosoughi and his camera crew thanked me and left, and a few days later, the same assistant producer came back with a picture of Vosoughi as Zar Mammad in Naderi's *Tangsir*, autographed by Vosoughi for me—in his own handwriting: "*Ba sepas-e faravan beh dust e aziz Hamid Dabashi, Eradatmand, Behruz Vosoughi*" ("With much gratitude to my dear friend Hamid Dabashi, Sincerely, Behruz Vosoughi"). I still have that picture in my office here at Columbia, framed and hanging on my wall. Along with the autographed picture came two tickets for the opening night of *Tangsir* at Rudaki Hall, the Lincoln Center of Tehran at the time. I cannot now remember whom I took with me to the film, but I do remember very vividly that we sat in two wonderful seats in the first balcony, a stone's throw (ahem) from the royal box. I could not see inside the royal box, so I have no idea if anyone was there or not, but I do remember the scene when Zar Mammad grabs hold of his gun and, on his way to kill the merchant, mutters to himself, "*Hamash khoda, hamash peyghambar, mageh khodom chemeh*" ("Constantly God, constantly the Prophet, what the hell is wrong with me?"—meaning, Why should I wait for the punishment of those who have wronged me in the world to come, I can take care of them right here myself?)—at which point the entire audience burst into applause.

Naderi's identification with Zar Mammad was not just based on Parvizi's and Chubak's literary accounts of them. Zar Mammad was a local legend in Bushehr and Abadan, and Naderi and many others among his contemporaries had heard of him. Naderi researched the original incident thoroughly and shot many of his scenes in the actual locations. But because Naderi did not remain faithful to the literary sources he had adapted, many critics objected to the film for having been more his own than an adaptation—which was exactly the point because with Naderi,

Iranian cinema had finally moved away from the pairing of a prominent literary figure and a young filmmaker. Before and after *Tangsir*, Naderi traversed a long and arduous path to articulate the terms of his own visual sensibilities, and he did not need to cloak them in literary terms. It is with Naderi, and the specifics of his visual realism, that Iranian cinema finally found its specific visual character, rooted in the Iranian literary and poetic imagination but once and for all beginning to dig deep into the rich and diversified *visual* imaginings irreducible to any literary precedent. This is by far the most significant achievement of Amir Naderi for Iranian cinema. With his cinema, our visual vocabulary finally assumes and asserts its own vernacular lexicon.

Harmonica is Naderi's reflection on the nature of tyranny and the complacency of people caught in its snares. A young boy receives a harmonica as a gift. It suddenly becomes the chief object of desire of all his friends, who want to hold and perhaps play a tune on it. Soon the young boy realizes the amazing power he has over his friends by virtue of possessing this harmonica. He demands and exacts first innocuous but increasingly demeaning services from his friends in exchange for a few seconds with his harmonica. One kid in particular, Amiru, becomes positively obsessed with the instrument and thus a willing subject to the cruelest demands of its owner. Before we know it, Naderi transforms a very simple story into one of the most frightful studies of cruelty and tyranny. The young boy in possession of the harmonica sports only a patch of hair right on top of his forehead while the rest of his head is closely shaven. The effect was not lost on a politicized Iranian audience that the patch of hair stood for a crown, casting the tyrannical boy as an icon of the reigning monarch, Mohammad Reza Shah Pahlavi, who had just nationally celebrated his coronation with royal pomp and solemn ceremony. Soon after the initial screenings of *Harmonica* in Tehran reports began circulating around the city that audiences, excited by its political message, would burst out of movie theaters and engage in violent demonstrations against the monarchy. *Harmonica* thus emerged as the symbolic movie of an entire generation of Iranians, a cult film that marked the rite of passage for millions of Iranian youths, associated in their collective memory not just with a passive act of spectatorship but with acts of defiance. Naderi once told me that when he was shooting his *Search II* (1981), smack in the middle of the Iran-Iraq War (1980–88), in a war zone, when Iranian soldiers fighting the Iraqi army heard that he was among them and shooting a film, they started shouting, "Amiru, Amiru, Amiru!"—both an endearing diminutive of his own name and the leitmotif of *Harmonica*, as it was the call with which the young tyrant would summon Amiru to do one chore or another for him. The twisted irony of this actual story is that it transcends Naderi's film, showing the tyranny that was passed along from the Pahlavi monarchy to the Khomeini mullarchy.

By the middle of the decade, Naderi abandoned politics for a moment altogether to create an exquisite gem of cinematic reflection on his own childhood: *Entezar* (*Waiting*, 1975), winner of a special Jury Award in Cannes that year. In *Waiting*, Naderi successfully experimented with pure visual joy and mystery, long before Shirin Neshat began working with a visual vocabulary of that kind, and brought it to speculative perfection. Shot in understated colors in Iran's sun-soaked south, *Waiting* follows the pubescent excitement of a young boy through his emerging and yet inarticulate sensual encounters with the arm of a woman reaching for a crystal bowl to give him some ice. The extended arm of the young woman eventually lures the young boy into the hidden nooks and crannies of a home, as if it were the rest of the body that housed and animated that hand. The film is almost silent, with scarce dialogue to interrupt its visual charm.

The year was not yet over when Naderi finished yet another film, *Marsiyeh* (*Requiem*, 1975), in which he combined the artistic casuistry of *Waiting* with the political prowess of *Tangsir*. With a tacit reference to a poem by Mehdi Akhavan Sales, particularly a line in which the poet laments, "I am mourning my own dead homeland," *Requiem* captures the desolate despair of Iran on the verge of revolution. When it was screened to the selection committee of the Tehran Film Festival, all the members got up from their seats, mumbled something like "We did not see this film," and quietly left the room (someone from that committee told this to Naderi later and Naderi told me). It is a stark, despairing, and damning film, exposing the suffering soul of Tehran at a moment when all could see but no one dared to say what was gnawing away at the Iranian body politic. At the center of *Requiem* are Nasrollah and two other street performers. Nasrollah carries a BB gun that he uses for target practice, shooting at a board covered with photos of half-naked European-looking women carved out of foreign magazines, while one of his roommates entertains coffee house customers with his chimpanzee and the third roams around the city and tells popular stories from an unfurled canvas. As these three characters move from one end of the city to another, so does Naderi's camera, registering a vision of Tehran unsurpassed in the rambunctious madness of its indifference to the cruelty that inhabits it. Put *Goodbye Friend, Deadlock*, and *Requiem* together and watch them—you have the single most important visual evidence of a cosmopolis on the verge of revolutionary outburst, without a political word being uttered in any one of them. Take these three films out of Iranian cinema (here is my contention), and we have no cinematic record of Tehran as the major city of a nation. Period. What is peculiar and exclusive to Naderi is that while he gives you the smidgen of a storyline to keep your mind busy, his camera goes about an entirely different task—of generating, sustaining, and conjugating the visual syntax and imaginal morphology of Iranian national cinema. No other Iranian filmmaker has a similar claim on Iranian cinema.

Be that as it may, the first decade of Naderi's filmmaking career ended on two deeply disappointing notes: his first foray into filmmaking in the United States, *Sakht-e Iran, Sakht-e America* (*Made In Iran, Made In America*, 1978); and *Barandeh* (*The Winner*, 1979). The first film is about an Iranian émigré in the US who wants to become a boxer, and the second is a short film version of what would later become *The Runner.* His sojourn in the United States ended with no fruitful result, and his entire cinematic career was now contingent on a massive revolutionary movement that was shaking his homeland to its foundations.

With the Pahlavi monarchy gone and the Iran-Iraq War raging, Naderi commenced his second decade of filmmaking in earnest. He faced an entirely different Iran. On one hand, Naderi was much loved and admired by the revolutionaries, and yet on the other the revolution was not his—as no revolution could be. He spent the first two years of the Iran-Iraq War making two documentaries about the events that were changing the shape and spirit of his homeland. *Josteju Yek* (*Search I*, 1980), a documentary on people who had disappeared during the course of the Islamic revolution, and *Josteju Do* (*Search II*, 1981), a similar documentary on the Iran-Iraq War, carried Amir Naderi into uncharted territories. With *Search I* and *Search II*, Naderi joined the revolutionary movement and the war that followed it the best way he could—with his camera. Throughout his *Search* series, Naderi remained far removed from any moral, political, or propagandist pronouncement. But in these films his camera is investigative, curious, searching, silent, even mournful. These documentaries allow the terror that a nation is experiencing to determine its own aesthetic form, beyond the terms of its passing politics. Desolation is the single abiding feeling in both these films—a mournful record of a deeply traumatic period in the annals of a nation.

Otherwise negligible documentaries in a massive body of revolutionary and war movies commissioned by official organs of the Islamic Republic, *Search I* and *Search II* had the advantage of keeping Naderi involved with the fate of his nation while engaging his camera in some of its most traumatic moments. Halfway through the Iran-Iraq War, Naderi was ready for something far more serious, for what I believe to be his absolute masterpiece: *Davandeh* (*The Runner*). *The Runner* premiered in 1985 at the Nantes International Film Festival and won its grand prize, announcing the presence of a magnificent national cinema on the world stage, soon to be reflected in the official selections of film festivals in

Hong Kong, Istanbul, London, San Francisco, Sydney, Tokyo, Toronto, Vancouver, Venice, and scores of others. *The Runner* put Naderi and with him the rest of Iranian cinema into global perspective.

The setting of *The Runner* is the southern port city of Abadan, and the lead character, Amiru (Majid Niroumand), is Naderi's own auto-biographical recollection. Amiru lives on an abandoned ship and works at all sorts of odd jobs to make a meager living. He is orphaned, soli-tary, illiterate, but exceedingly proud and resourceful. He is poor below any poverty line, but his simple existence projects a profile of grace and beauty inherent to the material evidence of his own manner and making.

The Runner is an autobiographical film in many senses. When he was six years old, Naderi now remembers and recounts, he was accidentally stranded on a ship and taken to a place that, to this day, he cannot identify. The story of this extraordinary voyage is very simple, and undoubtedly colored in Naderi's mind by the passage of many intervening years. The husband of the aunt who had adopted him after the death of his mother used to work on a ship in Abadan as a painter. Naderi was assigned to bring this uncle his lunch every day. After giving him his lunch, Amir would roam through the ship and play on its various decks. One day, as he found his way to the lowest level, where the engines were, he fell asleep on a pile of potato sacks. Soon after, the ship pulled up its anchor and left the Abadan harbor, carrying six-year-old Amir to its next port of call. Amir awoke frightened out of his wits and was soon discovered by the ship's crew and put into quarantine. He could not see anything but the sea until they reached their destination, where Naderi remembers seeing some sort of policeman with white gloves controlling sparse traf-fic on some street off the coast where the ship had come ashore. The ship then returned to Abadan, and Naderi to his aunt, who was by then understandably panic-stricken. Naderi's aunt told him that for months afterward he refused to or was unable to speak, and that the first thing that he said after he started talking was that he wanted to leave for a faraway land on a ship. Another time, Naderi says, when he was eleven years old, he tried to run away to Kuwait. But he did not make it beyond a couple of islands off the coast of Abadan. I don't know, nor can I judge, to what degree these stories are true and to what degree they are the col-orful figments of an ingenious storyteller/filmmaker's imagination. (You can never tell with Naderi. His real stories are unbelievable; his fictive films are entirely believable—and thus the function of factasy in Iranian cinema!) But what I can say is that the abandoned ship that you see in *The Runner*, on which Amiru lives, is the miasmatic memory of a ship on which Amir Naderi has always dreamed of living and departing for a far-away land. In a sense, he still lives on that ship, and his small apartment in downtown Manhattan has a remarkable similarity to a cabin aboard an abandoned ship, still sailing in his restless mind on uncharted waters.

Who is Amiru? A poor orphaned boy growing up on the seashore of a nameless land, fascinated with every moving object—huge ships, small boats, speeding cars, lazy bicycles, noisy motorcycles, lumbering trucks, slumbering trains, flying airplanes—anything and everything that moves by itself and can carry him away from where he is. The terror of his life is when he sees an aging woman or a crippled man—people who cannot run away from this place. In the absence of access to any of these vehicles of escape, he runs, fast, faster, and then he runs some more, until he runs out of breath. When a man drinks a glass of water from a bucket full of ice water, which Amiru carries around to make a meager living, and doesn't pay, he chases him down both for the challenge of catching him on foot—the man is on a bicycle—and to get his rightful payment. When another man steals a piece of his ice, he runs after him, grabs hold of his ice, and runs away, both for the triumphant joy of outrunning the much bigger man and for reaching a destination before the ice melts.

Running defines Amiru. But what is he running from and what is he running to? Nothing. Everything. Running is his state of being. Something somewhere calls on him, something that is always somewhere else. There is a scene early in the film where, as he and his friends are collecting empty bottles that foreigners have thrown into the sea, they are suddenly attacked by a shark. A fisherman alerts the kids and they run furiously out of the water. Amiru comes out frightened out of his wits—but frightened not by the possibility that he could have been killed, but by the terror that the shark could have chopped off his limbs, his solitary claim to mobility, to running away from here, to somewhere else.

It is wrong to think that Amiru is running away from poverty. Amiru is poor, but his life is not desolate or joyless. He has the jubilant company of a band of young, equally poor boys, with whom he plays soccer, rides bikes, chases after running trains, and shares joyous songs on top of speeding wagons. His relationship with his friends is not free of quarrels, and poverty reigns supreme. But there is a serenity about Amiru, a gentility about his manners, a solidity to his friendship with his environment. While trying to run away (from nothing and everything), Amiru lives a rich and fulfilling life—rich in the dimensions of the solitude that he explores, fulfilling in the company of friends he keeps. There is a scene where Amiru is washing his shirt in the abandoned ship (his home) and Naderi moves his camera close (ever so gently) to the averted gaze of this poor, orphaned, solitary soul. Amiru's gaze is the look of humanity at a loss, facing an abyss beyond recognition. There and then, *The Runner* is no longer the story of a lonely boy, and Amiru is no longer a poor and orphaned kid—there and then Naderi has pictured humanity at large, at a loss. Sometimes I believe Naderi is the most frightful filmmaker in Iranian cinema—cruel in his insights, entirely metaphysical in his musings. He holds your hand, he moves ever so imperceptively, gently even—but where he is taking you is no party. He has seen something terrorizing, a nightmare perhaps, a subliminal cruelty beyond our human measures. He has seen the absurdity at the root of the brutality that all lives seek to suppress. He has seen it, and he has mastered a way to show and tell it.

Amiru is illiterate, but what does that mean? He collects pictures of airplanes and hangs them on the wall of his cabin in his ship. He goes to a newsagent and buys more magazines to look at their pictures. He soon discovers that he cannot read and write, and that deeply bothers him. He goes and enrolls at a school to learn how to read and write. His teacher begins to teach him the letters of the Persian alphabet: *Alef, Beh, Peh*, etc. He begins to memorize the letters of the alphabet, one by one. Gradually his memorization of the letters of the alphabet begins to assume rhythmic and melodic tonalities, ebbs and flows, sounds and effects entirely independent of what these letters are supposed to mean and do. A visual and verbal stylization gradually emerges that is in pure and undiluted forms. Amiru memorizes them walking, he memorizes them sitting, he memorizes them at the schoolyard, through the crevices of rocks at the coast of a stormy sea. Amiru, the letters of the alphabet, and his natural environment—water, wind, and rock—all begin to coagulate into one symphonic crescendo. The result is not that Amiru learns how to read and write, because Amiru is not just learning the letters of the Persian alphabet—he is teaching them to unlearn themselves. He takes the letters of the Persian alphabet to the seaside and teaches them the material evidence of a truth superior to their abstract meaninglessness. The alphabet sequence of *The Runner* remains the most glorious lesson in a literacy beyond words, and it is one of Naderi's greatest achievements in his virtuoso performances as a sound designer: the noises of water, wind, fire, and dust all collecting momentum to syncopate Amiru's recitations of the Persian alphabet.

Naderi himself is not a very literate person. He dropped out of school early in life. He has had no formal education of any sort. To him the letters of the alphabet are strange creatures, not just Persian (as we see them in *The Runner*), but also English (as in *Marathon*). What are these things? Who are they? And who, by the way, gave them the authority to sound, seem, and suggest one thing or another? So Amiru takes the letters of the Persian alphabet to the seaside and teaches them to behave. He memorizes them to the beat of the waves storming the sea rocks; he memorizes them to the sound of wind, water, fire, and dust (a theme that Naderi will continue in his next film, *Water, Wind, Dust*). Amiru is elemental, elementary, figurative, phenomenal. In the alphabet scene of *The Runner*, humanity is reduced to literacy, literacy to words, words to letters, letters to sounds, sounds to noises, and noises given back to the earth—off they go, go back where they came from, to earth, to life, to world, to existence, to being. There—off they go, stay there, and do not come back. Leave the world alone. What Kiarostami would later do in his mature cinema by way of his ingenious fictive transparency of the real, Naderi had already achieved here, through his trademark visual realism.

The final sequence of *The Runner* will also remain—and it will remain for good. Amiru and his buddies have made yet another wager for nothing, for the fun of it, and for the challenge that it occasions, just to see who wins. The game begins. A huge block of ice is placed near a thunderous fire. What do people see when they see this block of ice near that roaring fire? A universe. Those two items are insignia of a universe. We in the south have so much invested memory in those blocks of ice. In the south where Naderi and I grew up, refrigerators were rare, and during hot summer days these pieces of ice were our salvation. Our mothers would send us on a regular basis, from May through September, to buy blocks of ice to bring home to mix with our water and such. As children, we regularly forgot to take a bag or a towel with us to bring back the ice. So a few seconds into buying the brute but blessed thing, our hands would start freezing, and we had to run home before they completely fell off our arms. The scene in which you see Amiru running with a piece of ice in his hand is a very familiar one in southern Iran.

As for that fire, I know it too, very well indeed. I grew up near that fire. It is near Ahvaz. It is natural gas let loose to burn. It is the fire that ran wild in 1958, when Ebrahim Golestan made a documentary film on it, a film that Forugh Farrokhzad edited. You see how in that scene Iranian cinema has come full circle? In the Ahvaz of my childhood, this fire, when tame, provided a major picnic area during cold winter nights. People from all over the city and surrounding villages would come to this place for fun, partying, picnicking, flirting, frolicking, singing, and dancing. There was a man, a popular entertainer, we used to call him Bambo Lilla, and he was a regular feature of those cold nights warmed by the fire. Bambo Lilla, yes, that was his name. We called him that because he went around the huge fire and sang a song that began with the phrase *"Bambo Lilla, Ossa min Despila."* "Bambo Lilla" means nothing; it's just a nonsensical refrain to provide rhythm and rhyme to "Ossa min Despila," just like "Zip-a-Dee-Doo-Dah" in *"Zip-a-dee-doo-dah, Zip-a-dee-ay, my, oh my, what a wonderful day."* "Ossa min Despila" means "the master is from Dezful"—Dezful being a small town near Ahvaz (where my mother was born and raised). Bambo Lilla was from Dezful, and he sang a hilariously rambunctious song as he played on his small, handheld drum (a *tunbak*, as we call it). I can still remember the rhythm but not much of the lyrics, for the lyrics were in my mother's dialect, and I have long since forgotten it. But I remember the words were funny, flirtatious, erotic even. Women used to laugh and blush when hearing it, and men would turn away and hide their embarrassment if they were in the company of their female relatives. Adolescent boys were the principal audience of Bambo Lilla, kids like Amiru and me. That fire is the center of a universe Naderi and I call home.

So their challenge begins. Amiru and his friends start running toward the fire. The objective is twofold: to be the first to get there, and to get there before the ice has completely melted. But on the way, a brutal truth becomes evident: If you cannot get there, then you must also prevent others from getting there. In the course of that match Naderi has discovered and displayed a barbarity of unsurpassed terror at the heart of Iranian cultural innocence. Amiru and his friends start sabotaging each other's progress, getting in each other's way and knocking each other down as they race toward their goal. In no other film in the history of Iranian cinema has a banality of such factual truth been so vividly and honestly captured. The kids run, roll, bump, bounce, throw, hit, strike, jolt, jerk, jump, punt, push, pull, drag, and yank—anything and everything to be the first to get to the melting ice by the subterranean fire (coming up from the heart of a hidden terror), or at the very least to prevent anyone else from getting there. Amiru does though, against all odds. He gets to the ice by the fire, reaches for the barrel on which the piece of ice is placed. He begins a triumphant, joyous beat of victory. He begins to beat on the barrel victoriously. "*Barandeh shodom.*" If you watch his lips carefully you can see him say it, "*Barandeh shodom*"—"I won." Beating on the drum, rhythmically splashing the water in joy—pure, undiluted, ecstatic joy—he picks up the last remaining piece of ice, lifts it to his head, and begins to dance, the piece of ice held victoriously over his head, his trophy, the goblet of his victory. This is no ice, no frozen water; this is a trophy, held triumphantly over the struggle for his existence. He lives. He is triumphant. Hope. He brings the piece of ice to his lips, drinking his victory, water, the juice of his exultant achievement. That is not a minute or a second or an instant. That is an eternity and it lasts forever. The eternity finally breaks. Amiru comes to his senses. He turns around, looks at his fallen friends, his comrades-turned-rivals— they are approaching but all dying of thirst, one after the other begging for a drop of water. Amiru turns, extends the piece of ice. It is no longer a trophy. The moment of myth is past. It is no more. The magic ended. Reality roams, fire is back. Boys, men, dying of thirst. Generous, Amiru extends the ice, gives it to the first boy in his reach. The boy drinks from the ice, passes it on, sharing, and then on to the next, and then to the next. Boys unite in the last drop of life that the melting ice can give. Life is restored. Amiru is victorious. And Naderi, meanwhile, commands in confidence: Cut.

Naderi's bitter, angry, and brilliant *Ab, Bad, Khak* (*Water, Wind, Dust,* 1989) showed him turning sour at the conclusion of two decades of filmmaking in his homeland. Though the film won a major prize at the Three Continents Film Festival, in Nantes, in 1989, it is also the last film that Naderi made in Iran. *Water, Wind, Dust* is Naderi's personal, cultural, and metaphysical statement about the nature of the world as he sees it. The movie begins in the middle of a desert village, the local inhabitants of which have disappeared in search of water and food. A young boy (Majid Niroumand, the same actor who played Amiru in *The Runner*) returns home to find that his family has packed up and left. He commences a journey through the desert, in silence and desolation, that soon assumes biblical proportions.

At a personal level, *Water, Wind, Dust* is the story of Naderi's solitary quest in a world that he saw as arid, desolate, and forsaken, for a sense of purpose and clarity in his own life—having forever lost any connection to his homeland, which now appears to him as a deserted landscape. On a social and political level, *Water, Wind, Dust* is Naderi's damning condemnation of a useless and wasteful revolution that soon after its success had the signs of catastrophic failure written all over it. Naderi's generation of artists and intellectuals were lost souls searching in vain for prosperity and salvation in a godforsaken land. And at a far more devastating metaphysical level, *Water, Wind, Dust* depicts humanity at large searching in vain for deliverance in a wasteland. The young protagonist of *Water, Wind, Dust* becomes the allegory for a solitary human soul in a ruined land that is no longer just Iran or even planet earth, for it has assumed a metaphysical character beyond geography and history.

Naderi once told me that the greatest literary impact on his cinema has been Herman Melville's *Moby Dick* (1851). "I have always been fascinated by the obsession of Captain Ahab to catch Moby Dick," he said. "The only difference is that I cannot afford having that kind of destructive pessimism at the end of my stories, the way that at the end of *Moby Dick*, after all this searching, the entire crew of the *Pequod* is killed, Ahab himself yanked to his death by the very harpoon he had made to kill the whale. That much pessimism I cannot afford. I always like just a smidgen of hope at the end of my films, not too much and sappy, just enough to sustain my hope in humanity."

Compare what Naderi did at the end of the 1980s to what Kubrick did at the beginning of the same decade. Why did Kubrick turn his attention to a Stephen King novel? In *The Shining* (1980), Kubrick pushes King's playful flirtation with the idea of creativity to a frightful encounter with the primordial—by showing a father chasing after his own son to murder him in the maze of a winter wilderness. In his original story, King toyed successfully with the idea of what happens when the potential characters and events of a murder mystery take over the innocent suggestions of a storyline. An aspiring writer, Jack Torrance, his wife, Wendy, and their son, Danny, have all the innocence of a typical, happy family, and betray all the signs of a murderous subplot—materialized in the mind of King for a novel that Jack Torrance would have written if he were loyal to the facts and fantasies of his circumstances. Kubrick's business with King's story, though, plays on a nuclear family taken out of society—and then watches what happens. Within a month (thus Kubrick's insistence on depicting the precise sequence of time as the film progresses) reason dissolves into madness, love into hatred, paternal care into murderous instinct—all for no apparent reason except for the fact of being left alone in the vast emptiness of a beautiful and picturesque resort. The last scene, of Jack Torrance chasing after his son in the snow-covered labyrinth with no beginning and no end, no entrance and no exit, is the simulation of an eternity that is beyond all time and location, religion and culture. Jack's wolfish cries for his son are more cosmic and primordial than the final scene of *2001: A Space Odyssey*. That wild and bewildered man, forever lost in the vast blizzard of an eternity with no exit or return, is no longer a simple Jack Torrance—he is the first and last man, he is Adam not born, Abel murdered and avenged, Cain condemned and cast out.

Kubrick and Melville, at the presumed center of this cosmic madness, can afford such cosmogonic epics of human fate. Naderi at the projected periphery of the selfsame universe cannot. He is condemned to have hope.

After an initial and unsuccessful attempt to move to New York and start making films in the late 1970s, Naderi finally left Iran for good in the early 1990s, soon after the success of *Water, Wind, Dust*, determined never to go back. "Never look back," he always tells me, "always look forward." Whenever I receive an invitation to attend a conference in Iran he adamantly opposes it. "Going back to Iran," he says, "is like going back to an old girlfriend. Never do that," he will add. "That's why my films always have a fresh and forward-looking appearance to them." He detests nostalgia. If you ask me, he protests too much.

Manhattan by Numbers (1993) is Naderi's first New York film, and it navigates the architectonic surface of his adopted cosmopolis as his Tehran films navigated the capital of his homeland. It was the official selection of New Directors/New Films at the Museum of Modern Art, and from there it traveled to other international film festivals in Houston,

London, Montreal, San Sebastian, Toronto, and Venice. In *Manhattan by Numbers* Naderi tells the story of George Murphy (John Wojda), a journalist who has just been fired from his job and has exactly one day left to pay his rent (or else he will be evicted), and he has to search out the entirety of Manhattan, from the Bronx all the way down to the Financial District, for an old friend to borrow some money. His search is almost identical with the young boy's search for water in *Water, Wind, Dust*, while the cosmopolitan landscape of Manhattan becomes a functional equivalent of that tyrannical desert. It is important to keep in mind that Naderi's New York films, with vastly different looks and themes, continue the visual vocabulary of his films made in Iran, thus radically challenging the very notion of a "national cinema."

Four years after *Manhattan by Numbers*, Naderi returned to Cannes triumphantly with *A, B, C...Manhattan* (1997). This film takes his curious camera deep into the landscape of the lives of three young women living in Alphabet City in New York. If *Manhattan by Numbers* is an attempt at navigating a cold, cruel, but magnificent metropolis, *A, B, C...Manhattan* is an attempt to limn the city with the lives of three young women living in the shadow of the city's magnificent indifference. Kacey (Erin Norris) is a street-smart bisexual who has recently lost her girlfriend, which is much less a nuisance to her than the fact that she has also lost her dog. The most troubled of the three is Kate (Sara Paul), who is trying to make a career as a young musician while breaking up with her boyfriend. At the film's climax we discover that her lover is actually her brother, with whom she has had a prolonged incestuous relationship. By the end of *Manhattan by Numbers* and *A, B, C...Manhattan*, Naderi had cinematically claimed New York—known and navigated it inside out, as it were. With his first New York film he mapped out its exteriors, and with his second he traced the architectonics of that exterior through the inner soul of its inhabitants.

Five years later, Naderi completed his New York trilogy. *Marathon* (2002) unearths the subterranean soul of New York in the fixation of a young woman, Gretchen (Sara Paul), who is obsessed with crossword puzzles and lost in the labyrinthine dungeon of the subway. Gretchen travels the underground system in search of solitude and concentration, so that she can break her own record of solving an increasing number of crossword puzzles in a twenty-four-hour marathon session. *Marathon* watches Gretchen unravel to the point of complete breakdown, as the meaning of words, phrases, and sentences are reduced to meaningless letters of the alphabet, and as the composite of the city disintegrates into its undecipherable sights and sounds. In *Marathon*, Naderi pushes the metaphysical certainties of the letters of the English alphabet to the same noisy semiotics of nothingness that he sought and achieved in *The Run-*

ner, where he reduced the alphabet of another language to its cosmogonic and elemental nothingness.

Marathon is the story of a solitary soul, Gretchen, standing in for Naderi himself, leaning into the abyss of the inarticulate noises at the root and heart of any claim to civilization. In *Marathon* Gretchen is Naderi trying to understand how the city of his voluntary exile works. At a communal level, Gretchen is the bewildered inhabitant of this megalopolis, unraveling the alphabetical elements of the city (and with it the civilization it represents), holding its horizontal and vertical coordinates together in an accidentally meaningful way. Gretchen emerges as the soul of humanity searching—not for meaning but for meaninglessness, not for cohesion but for confusion, not for consistency but for chaos. *Marathon* thus becomes a film about the violence of technological modernity, the layers upon layers of noise coming together to compose a symphonic serenade to the beauty and bestiality of the machine. There is a sequence in which every moving vehicle—cars, buses, motorcycles, trains, subways, helicopters, and airplanes—combine in a crescendo of unbelievable sound and fury. In the apt assessment of David Ng, one of Naderi's most perceptive admirers, *Marathon* is "an aural reverie that could only come from someone both familiar and foreign to his surroundings. His hyper-vigilance endows this decrepit megalopolis with a near protean newness." In Ng's reading of Naderi's conception of the subway car, "Naderi films it as a public isolation chamber where people can go to be alone together—an anonymous community of underground dwellers. In reality, its ear-piercing noises—the screech of breaks, the garbled loudspeaker, the explosions of a passing train—act as so much static to be tuned out."

Toward the end of *Marathon*, we see Gretchen going absolutely mad, turning on every single machine in her apartment that can possibly make a sound, and in the middle of a crescendo of noises, the camera closes in on the black cover of a speaker from which recorded subway noise is coming, before the cacophonic noise fades out to a humming silence of a subway tunnel. When the film cuts back to Gretchen's apartment we see floating in the bathtub the shredded pieces of all the books and dictionaries she has used to solve her puzzles.

"It was in *Marathon* that I discovered," Amir Naderi told me later, "that in my next film I could actually show the moment of madness in which an artist creates his masterpiece. My next film after *Marathon* is a journey into that moment of creation." There is a sequence inside a small cubical storage room in his next film (I have seen a few of the rushes) that Naderi believes will reveal the precise nature of a maddening creative moment. "People always see a postcard of a picture by van Gogh, or at best go to a museum and look at the original. What is lost is the precise nature of the storm that gathers in the soul of van Gogh when he mixes colors and paints. What happens in the human soul in that moment—what madness, insanity, hope, despair, defeat, victory, revolt, submission, what defiance, what piety, what terror, what joy have come together to make that moment possible? I want to show and stage that moment—and I have done it."

As I was reading through these last few paragraphs of things I wanted to tell you about Naderi, something happened and I thought of sharing it with you. Naderi called and came over. The Pusan International Film Festival in Korea is honoring the late Sohrab Shahid Sales and they have asked Naderi to write his impressions of Shahid Sales and share his views on the late Iranian master's cinema. Naderi came over so we could sit down and write what he wanted to say. It was an extraordinary and exquisite moment—interrupting my thinking through his own cinema in order to attend to his moving homage to another miracle in our cinema. I thought of sharing this with you right here and now—for in this paragraph two critical moments of my reflections on the history of our aesthetics of moral judgment have just come together.

It is impossible to exaggerate the significance of Amir Naderi in Iranian cinema—and not only by virtue and the volume of his creative output. Naderi's films are a critical turning point in Iranian cinema because by the time Forugh Farrokhzad in *The House Is Black* (1962) and Ebrahim Golestan in his *Mud Brick and Mirror* (1965) made their contributions to Iranian cinema, it had seen a successful translation of the verbal source of the Iranian creative consciousness into the visual, and two aspects of Iranian cinematic realism, one *poetic* and the other *affective*, were crafted and registered. The next generation consisted of bona fide filmmakers, mostly educated abroad, with no roots in a Persian literary heritage, though they had the creative shrewdness to connect with prominent members of the Iranian literati. Dariush Mehrjui's *Cow* (1969) articulated a *psychedelic* realism in close collaboration with Gholamhossein Saedi; Arby Ovanessian's *Spring* (1972) achieved a *spatial* realism in collaboration with Ali Mohammad Afghani and M. Armin; Bahman Farmanara's *Prince Ehtejab* (1974) mapped out a *narrative* realism with Houshang Golshiri; and finally Sohrab Shahid Sales' *Still Life* (1974) reached for a *transparent* realism in conversation with Sohrab Sepehri's poetry.

With Naderi, the long road of Iranian cinema and all its promises finally come to fruition, and he becomes the first Iranian filmmaker who makes his films in purely visual terms, with no connection to any literary tropes. He is the author of *visual* realism. This is only in part because Naderi dropped out of school at a very early point in his life and is an entirely self-educated man: he had no way of acquiring the formal literary education of Farrokhzad, Golestan, Ovanessian, or Shahid Sales. Even more importantly, Naderi has seen an incredible number of movies—and his narrative memory is almost exclusively visual. What's more, I propose that whereas all other Iranian filmmakers have a life within which they also watch and make movies, Amir Naderi's life is cinema, and from that life he may occasionally emerge to eat a meal or go for a walk. "There was an outside world," he once told me, "that to me was ugly and intolerable. And then there was a world inside my mind, full of movies made and movies waiting to be made, which was beautiful and exciting." Do you see that little boy in *The Runner*, with his back turned to the world, facing the sea, and eating watermelon? Well, that's Amir Naderi, watching a movie.

Once when I was a child I was playing on a street corner, as children often do. Suddenly I saw a group of children coming toward me. I was startled by the way they had come together. I approached them and asked where they were going. They said they were going to school to gain knowledge. I asked, "What is knowledge?" They said, "We have no idea; this we will have to ask our teacher." This they said to me and then left.

–Shahab al-Din Yahya Suhrawardi, *Risalah fi Halat al-Tufuliyyah*

Bahram Beizai
Bashu, the Little Stranger

FOR THE NOBILITY OF YOUR OWN SOUL, if you ever run into Bahram Beizai, if you are walking, stand respectfully still until he passes; if you are standing, give the right of way to him; and if you are sitting, get up and give him your seat, for no one in Iranian cinema has more right to your highest respect and has earned your most sincere expression of humility than Bahram Beizai. Love and honor him, as he so richly deserves it. Some people in our old and enduring culture assume iconic significance, for reasons far beyond our crooked measures. Beizai is one of them. When the annals of our contemporary history are written, Beizai will have the same significance as Hafez. I don't believe I need to say anything more.

Why this deference and whence this significance? I will tell you.

As the Maarefi family is getting ready in Tehran for the wedding of their young daughter Mahrokh, the bride's elder sister, Mahtab Davaran, Mahtab's husband, Heshmat Davaran, and their two children get into a car in the northern part of the country to drive south for the occasion.

The camera watches the Davaran family as they prepare the car for the trip. They put their children and their luggage, including a mirror they handle with special care, into the car. Before getting in, Mahtab Davaran (née Maarefi) looks straight into the camera, which has now come to her quite attentively, and with a disarmingly blank face says, "We are going to Tehran to participate in my younger sister's wedding. We will not reach Tehran. We will have an accident and we will all die."

With that simple line something extraordinary happens in the vast and variegated spectrum of Iranian cinema. How does Mahtab Davaran know that she and her family are going to have an accident and die? Why does she not stop her husband from driving if she is so sure that they will have an accident?

After the opening sequence of *Mosaferan* (*The Travelers*, 1992), Mahtab Davaran, her husband, Heshmat, and their two children all get into their car, head south toward Tehran, get into a fatal car accident, and die. Meanwhile, Mahtab's sister, Mahrokh, and her entire family are getting ready for her wedding. The sad news of the accident arrives. The wedding ceremony turns into a ceremony of mourning. But against all the evidence, Mahtab's grandmother refuses to believe that Mahtab and her family have perished in an automobile accident and insists that the wedding proceed as planned. Though the entire family is stricken with sorrow, she persists in her optimism. Finally, at the crucial moment when the wedding is to begin, and Mahtab was to arrive with her family and the auspicious mirror, the grandmother insists that the bride should go and change into her wedding gown. Against all indications and her own better judgment, but unable to refuse the grandmother's wish, Mahrokh goes upstairs and changes into her wedding gown. As she descends the stairs, suddenly the door opens and...in comes Mahtab with the promised mirror in her hands and her entire family behind her.

How does this happen? Do they not die? But we actually see the scene of the automobile accident. We see the devastated truck driver involved in the unfortunate event. Mahtab herself predicts that it will happen, and it comes to pass. So where do she and her family suddenly come from? What sort of a story is this? A bizarre beginning and an even more bizarre ending, wrapped around an otherwise normal story, except for the grandmother, who simply refuses to heed the accumulated evidence that her grandaughter and her granddaughter's family have all perished in a car accident.

The Travelers is the culmination of the career of arguably the most visually perceptive Iranian filmmaker. The film is narrated with haunting precision within the double bind of two impossibilities, two negations of the ordinary, two suspensions of the rational, two framings of the common. *The Travelers* unfolds with a tempo and a movement that actively suspends and transforms every shred of reality into a visual narrative of compelling power and poise. From the very first shot of a mirror laid down on the grass, and from the very first sequence of the Davaran family getting ready for their trip to Tehran, that visual narrative informs an aesthetically transformed reality, a transformation that holds everything in suspense from the beginning to the end of its story.

How are we to understand that suspense? All those who have written on *The Travelers* have tried in one way or another to grapple with the central tension of the narrative, which is the startling announcement in the very first sequence of the film and its precise reversal at the end. Is Mahtab Davaran joking with the audience? Is she mad? What sort of a film is this for a lead actor to face the camera and tell the audience that she and her entire family are going to die in an automobile accident? Why do they all come back to life at the end of the film? Did we not see that she and her family actually got into an accident and, according to all evidence, including a police report, die?

There is one way we can make sense of this film. If we begin from the opening sequence, what we see is a sheer, undiluted, and pure cinematic will to shock and kill. Turning to the concluding sequence, we see an equally uncompromised cinematic will to shock and bring back to life. One magical cinematic will on top of the other—one in fact facilitating the other: In the first you have one of your own characters announce death before it happens, and in the next you bring them back to life after death has visited upon them. This is cinema in its purest and most willful defiance of random reality, as Beizai systematically crafts a *mythical* realism with its own innate and dynamic reason, rhetoric, logic, and lunacy. This is the cinematic will to resist the power of the real by a defiance of its logic, which yields to the superior logic of a mythic realism. This is cinema forcing prosaic reality to break down and to expose the poetics of its mythic foundations.

There is another way that we can make sense of this film, if we connect its strange beginning to its central tension—the fact that a whole family dies early in the film and yet is resurrected at the end. The resurrection of dead people: If we were to take that as the central creative tension of *The Travelers*, how are we to deal with it? Well, Muslims believe that they will all be resurrected on the Day of Judgment, face God, and be punished or rewarded for things they have done in this world. They are not alone in their belief in resurrection. Christians believe that Christ resurrected from the dead. To Shiites in particular, bodily resurrection, *ma'ad-e jesmani* as it is called, is a central doctrinal issue. Muslim jurists have written volumes on the subject, mystics have theorized it, and philosophers, including Avicenna, have grappled with the proposition.

One of the most recent philosophical discussions of the issue of bodily resurrection in a specifically (Shia) Islamic context is that of the early nineteenth-century Iranian philosopher Shaykh Ahmad Ahsai (d. 1826). Right from the heart of what from the sixteenth century forward was known as the "School of Isfahan," and under the influence of the monumental figure of Mulla Sadra Shirazi (d. 1640), who had initially formulated its principal tenets, Shaykh Ahmad Ahsai dealt with the issue of bodily resurrection in a rich philosophical language that Mulla Sadra had virtually invented, and it constitutes the material elements for an Islamic theory of the body. In his treatment of bodily resurrection, Ahsai makes a distinction between *jism* (the body) and *jasad* (the corpse)—jasad is the jism from which *ruh*, or "spirit," has departed. This distinction is not only central to Ahsai's own theory of bodily resurrection, it is one of the most crucial perspectives of an Islamic theory of the body. Jism, in Shaykh Ahmad Ahsai's theory, is the body while ruh still inhabits it and we are living human beings; when we die ruh leaves our jism and our jism becomes a jasad. This simple trilateral connection among jism, jasad, and ruh expand the Islamic notion of the body into a dialectical domain far beyond its physiological limitations. It opens up a whole different epistemic apparatus for understanding the human body.

Ahsai argues that this dual aspect of jism and jasad, narrated around the centrality of ruh, is not limited to human beings. Mineral, vegetal, and even celestial bodies fall within the same domain. Ahsai's assumption that celestial spheres in particular take the form of jism (body and soul) and not jasad (body minus soul), namely that they are living things rather than dead masses of matter, or that they have "interdependence with the souls by which they are moved," as he puts it, is a crucial observation the credit for which should really go to Aristotle. In *Generation and Corruption, On the Heavens*, as well as in *On the Generation of Animals*, Aristotle argued that the sun is the efficient cause of all events, that the planetary spheres and the planets are responsible for all worldly events, and that the generation of everything, including animals, is "controlled by the movements of these heavenly bodies." From the Aristotelian sources the idea of the planets and planetary spheres having not just a body but also a soul that animates them and thus makes them authoritative over human affairs gradually entered Islamic astronomical beliefs. Al-Kindi (805–73), for example, as one of the earliest Muslim commentators on Greek philosophy, believed that "the planets are rational, spiritual beings capable of intelligence and speech, and cause and administer everything in this world by the order of the prime Creator who controls all." (I learned about the centrality of Aristotle's thought in Islamic astrophysics from an essay by my friend and colleague George Saliba, "The Role of the Astrologer in Medieval Islamic Society," which was published in *Bulle-*

tin d'Études Orientales. Saliba has an even more detailed treatment of this subject in his book *A History of Arabic Astronomy: Planetary Theories during the Golden Age of Islam.*)

Understanding Shaykh Ahmad Ahsai's expanded conception of the human body, and the way that it has been perceived and imagined in the Iranian philosophical tradition, Beizai's cinema becomes contemplative in the metaphysical tradition of Iranian culture, far beyond its seemingly narrative disposition. The particular manner in which Beizai's cinema works toward an aesthetic transformation of reality is to suspend banal reality and thus give it back its innate (but repressed) mythic proportions. It is not just the ending of *The Travelers* that challenges our normative convictions; it is also its beginning. In between that beginning and that ending, both of which seem to outweigh our common sense of belief and behavior, Beizai has postulated a narrative manner of mythic realism—his unmistakable cinematic trademark—that commences from a tangible reality but then carves its mythic proportions out of its hidden assumptions. The mirror that you see in Bahram Beizai's *The Travelers* is thus a mirror of the invisible world, a mirror in which reality begins to unveil itself and expose its innate anxieties and possibilities.

This mirror that we see at the beginning and the end of *The Travelers* becomes emblematic of Beizai's cinema in general. It is an incarnation of his mythic realism, which itself functions as a mirror of the invisible world, the world we intuitively know but habitually do not see, or habitually see but do not perceptively watch. *Mirror of the Invisible World* was a title that my friend and colleague Peter Chelkowski once gave to a collection of stories from the great Persian poet Hakim Nizami (1141–1209), and I think it is a very apt way of referring to the imaginal universe that Nizami creates in his *Khamseh* (*Quintet*). What I am suggesting is that Beizai's cinema allows us to see things that we ordinarily do not. In the course of a conversation with a film critic in Iran, Beizai once said, "You see, my duty is to show you things that you have not experienced yet and that are not tangible to you, for things that you already know are no longer of any interest to you. You cannot call these things that I show you unreal. Pages of newspapers are full of incidents, but since they have not happened to us we think they are unreal." As a mirror of the invisible world, Beizai's cinema has a manner of excavating aspects of reality otherwise hidden from the naked eye. His cinema as a whole becomes a constellation of multifaceted lenses that expose the hidden anxieties of reality, those facets of the world that we have habitually opted to conceal, not to see, for perhaps they are inconvenient to know.

I trust by now it has become quite clear to you that I believe in a bifocal perspective in what is enduring in our cinema—a vertical and a horizontal perspective. Horizontally, our cinema is linked to a global conversation currently underway among all the major filmmakers around the world. Vertically, I believe Iranian cinema is, inevitably, deeply rooted in a cultural universe much older than the history of film as an art form. If Amir Naderi represents those of our filmmakers whose cinema is thoroughly engaged with world cinema, Beizai is a filmmaker whose cinema, more than anyone else's, is rooted in the deepest layers of Iran's cultural memories, all the way back to its inaugural mythic imaginings.

This is not to suggest that Beizai is not in conversation with the masters of world cinema, Alfred Hitchcock and Akira Kurosawa in particular. This is to suggest that his engagement with world cinema is through the grounded metaphysics of his immediate cultural heritage, and in this respect he is very much like Stanley Kubrick. I say "grounded," for I believe the iconic vocabulary of a visual universe is pretty much determined in a given historical culture—and it is the joyous task of artists to manipulate and/or exasperate them. It is in this respect that Beizai is by far the most "Iranian" filmmaker among all Iranian filmmakers. He has set upon himself the extraordinary task of revisiting the mythic origins of his cultural heritage. It is imperative that you not have an archaic or prehistoric conception of what I mean by "immediate cultural heritage." That is the reason why I point to the rather odd similarity between Beizai and Kubrick. Keep in mind that Kubrick's turn to the Vietnam War in *Full Metal Jacket* (1987) emanated exclusively from his own philosophical disposition and had scarcely anything to do with the war itself, which for over a decade had not engaged US public opinion, let alone the attention of the world at large. The first part of *Full Metal Jacket*, centered around the conflict between Gunnery Sergeant Hartman (R. Lee Ermey), the marine drill instructor, and Private Gomer Pyle (Vincent D'Onofrio), is arguably the most violent segment in the history of war films—and yet without a single person being shot until the very last minute of the first act. From the opening song, "Goodbye My Darlin' Hello Vietnam," to the most extraordinary cut among all of Kubrick's historic cuts, the shot of the Vietnamese prostitute walking toward the marines to the rhythm of *You keep sayin' you've got somethin' for me*, is precisely forty-five minutes and six seconds of grueling violence—a horror of drilling killer instincts into young men that saps every ounce of humanity out of these "short-timers," as the title of Gustav Hasford's original novel had it. The violence of the film begins with the marine drill instructor's rhapsodic opening—

> I am Gunnery Sergeant Hartman, your senior drill instructor. From now on, you will speak only when spoken to, and the first and last words out of your filthy sewers will be "Sir!" Do you maggots understand that?

—and ends with Private Joker's concluding reflections, accompanied by the chorus of the US Marines singing a Mickey Mouse song about fair play and hard work, all in harmony:

> We have nailed our names in the pages of history
> enough for today. We hump down to the Perfume River
> to set in for the night. My thoughts drift back to erect
> nipple wet dreams about Mary Jane Rottencrotch and
> the Great Homecoming Fuck Fantasy. I am so happy
> that I am alive, in one piece and short. I'm in a world
> of shit...yes. But I am alive. And I am not afraid.

From the hellhole of horror, Kubrick emerges the Dante of his time and troubles, still celebrating life in the midst of murderous monstrosity—his eyes, for all of us, wide open and shut! It is the Dante in Kubrick that corresponds to, say, the Suhrawardi in Beizai. No other Iranian film-maker provokes so many references to Iran's philosophical traditions, and makes them read in a language never before presumed possible. Precisely for that reason, no reading of Beizai is ever complete; all such readings are always tentative, suggestive, provisional, and contemplative.

If you follow the logic of my argument, what I am proposing here is that the idea of Iranian cinema imagining the world visually and not telling it narratively is born with Naderi. The other filmmaker who is equally instrumental in pulling Iranian cinema straight out of its literary soil and planting it confidently in its own visual provenance is Beizai, who in his cinema in general but in his absolute masterpiece, *Bashu, the Little Stranger* (1986), in particular, successfully articulates a mythical realism independent of any literary anchorage. With these two filmmakers, the primacy of the visual in Iranian cinema becomes triumphant. The critical difference between Naderi and Beizai is that Naderi took the primacy of the material evidence of his lived realities and made them into a visual real-ism; Beizai did the same, and with the same effect, but through a mythic realism that sought and suggested the illusory proportions otherwise hidden and repressed beneath the surface of an "absolutism of reality."

The German philosopher Hans Blumenberg's preoccupation with myth challenges the importance of secularization as the driving force of history. He later expanded his ideas into other works that culminated in *Work on Myth*, in which, through the idea of the "absolutism of reality," he came up with a theory of myth that expands it from the dawn of history into our own time, and thus no longer separates our society from those prone to myth-making. Blumenberg argues that human beings are biologically incapable of facing the absolutism of reality, the overabundance of things that our senses perceive. There are simply too many individualized, atomized, fragmented phenomena for our mental capacity to decipher all of them in a way that reduces the innate anxiety that the act of observing and interpreting them generates. Myths, Blumenberg believed, are formalized manners for *Homo sapiens* to categorize, systematize, compartmentalize, and codify things in an intelligible manner. The absolute facticity of things, the fact that they have been force-fed into a mythic narrative to make them behave, is already present in our collective consciousness. As a result, myths have a habit of sustaining our momentary credulities, and when they lose their legitimacy, there is a perpetual need to fabricate new myths, in different languages—visual, performative, philosophical, theoretical, biological—that uphold our momentary trust in the world. My sense of Beizai's cinema is that he is after dismantling the comfortable myths that have come to be called reality. He wishes to undo that claim, by way of revealing, through both his instrumental mannerism and his substantive cross-references to Iranian cultural leitmotifs, its anxiety-ridden repressions. Dismantling the mythic comfiture that reality has assumed, Beizai's cinematic method thrives on a visual vocabulary that is deeply rooted in the lexicon of Iran's premodern visual and performing arts, while the substance of his cinematic reflection is in contemplative conversation with the visionary recitals of medieval philosophers like Shahab al-Din Yahya Suhrawardi (1154–91). The result is a cinema that borrows from the performative and narrative devices of the past to dismantle the mythic solemnity of reality—by reminding it of its own mythic origins.

The first thing you should know about Beizai, who was born in 1938 in Tehran, is that his creative output is not limited to cinema. He is a major scholar of Iranian performing arts, and his *Tarikh-e Namayesh dar Iran* (*History of Drama in Iran*) is a serious contribution to the field. He taught classes on the history of performing arts at Tehran University before he was dismissed from his post by the ideologues of the Islamic Republic. He is a major theater director, having both written and directed a sustained body of highly influential and popular plays. One of his most popular and critically acclaimed, staged numerous times with great success, is *Chahar Sanduq* (*Four Boxes*, 1967), a typically allegorical reflection on the nature of despotism. Four characters, appearing in four colors, and representing four classes of society, come onstage and start making a scarecrow to protect them against some mysterious enemy. Very soon this scarecrow, meant to protect them, begins to assume a life of its own and turns against its own creators, forcing them to seek protection and solace inside four boxes, made out of their own fears and anxieties.

Moreover, oscillating between theater and cinema, Beizai has become one of the master practitioners of Persian prose. In addition to the plays and films that he has directed, he has written and published a large body of plays and scripts, though the overwhelming majority of them have not been produced. For Beizai is one of the most precious victims of the Islamic Republic, having been systematically and consistently censored and harassed by the official organs of the theocracy. Nevertheless, over the last three and a half decades, he has produced an impressive cinematic oeuvre, unparalleled in its visual opulence and thematic diversity. His cinematic career began in the late 1960s with the short film *Amu Sibilou* (*Uncle with a Mustache*, 1969), produced under the auspices of the Institute for the Intellectual Advancement of Children and Young Adults. It was screened in the Children's Film Festival in 1969 to no particular critical or popular acclaim, which was by and large reserved for Abbas Kiarostami's first film, *Nan va Kucheh* (*Bread and the Alley*).

During the 1970s, Beizai gradually emerged as a prominent figure in Iranian cinema. *Ragbar* (*Thundershower*, 1971) was a landmark in the emerging Iranian cinema and was soon followed by *Safar* (*Journey*, 1972). *Gharibeh va Meh* (*The Stranger and the Fog*, 1974) was a sensational success, while his *Kalagh* (*Crow*, 1976) and *Cherikeh-ye Tara* (*The Ballad of Tara*, 1979) were by and large ignored in the course of the revolutionary upheaval that led to the collapse of the Pahlavi dynasty and the establishment of the Islamic Republic.

The Islamic revolution resulted in a great deal of restrictions on Beizai's cinematic output. *Marg-e Yazdegerd* (*The Death of Yazdegerd*, 1982) went almost entirely unnoticed, while *Shayad Vaghti Digar* (*Perhaps Some Other Time*, 1988) received a modest audience and serious critical acclaim. His masterpiece, *Bashu, Gharibeh-ye Kuchak* (*Bashu, the Little Stranger*), was produced under severe circumstances, but it brought Beizai modest critical recognition around the world. Soon after *Bashu*, Beizai sought to leave Iran, first to the United States and then to France. But after a short stay, he opted to go back to Iran, where his reputation and the respect he richly deserves increased enormously, but the possibilities of working became even more limited.

In the 1990s, Beizai made only one film, *Mosaferan* (*The Travelers*); after that, he did not make another film until *Sag-Koshi* (*Dog Killing*, 2001). Both these films are highly acclaimed in Iran but have rarely been seen abroad. Beizai's films became a victim of the censorial policies of the Islamic Republic and his exceedingly rich cinematic vocabulary was no longer translatable to a global audience. This was not just because different aspects of Iranian cinema, those best represented by Kiarostami and Makhmalbaf, defined the terms of engagement with Iranian films at major international film festivals, but because Beizai's films have always been more ambitiously rooted in the modes and manners of a rich and diversified visual vocabulary, one he sought to retrieve from the bosom of premodern Iranian visual and performing arts. In effect he became too much of a scholar to be a natural filmmaker; too many semiotic forces comprise his visual lexicon for it to be immediately legible. Beizai succeeded cinematically, but the terms of his success alienated his global audience. In the annals of Iranian cinema, as a result, Beizai is a principal keystone, without which the entire edifice would crumble, but for reasons both inherent and external to his films, they never received the global celebration they richly deserve.

The significance of Beizai as an artist, however, is more than the sum total of his actual work. He himself, as a person, has been raised to the status of an icon of the best and the most promising in Iranian culture. It is very difficult to say in any analytical detail what exactly happens to an artist when he assumes that kind of iconic significance—but the signs of its factual presence are written all over Iran's claims to cultural modernity. Beizai is a homegrown artist. He did not study cinema in any formal setting in Europe or the United States. He is a highly influential writer and prose stylist. He commands an astounding facility with the Persian language, something rarely shared by other filmmakers of his generation. He is completely at home in classical Persian prose and poetry, painting, music, intellectual history, and philosophical discourse. But he is also equally at home with world cinema. He has written an authoritative book on Chinese theater—and in the course of my conversations with him, here in New York a few years ago, I also found him impressively informed on a variety of subjects I would have never suspected, such as Islamic architecture. Amir Naderi, who knows Beizai quite well, tells me that he comes from an exceptionally learned family. My point is not to try to account for his iconic (charismatic, perhaps) presence, but to suggest that such solid and swift command over a vast panorama of Iranian culture is rare and rarely translated into a rich and fulfilling art form. As I said, I have always thought of Beizai as the most "Iranian" filmmaker, for something about him is almost archaic or archetypal in his iconic representation of Iranian culture. When he makes a film, it is as if Hafez or Ferdowsi had come back to life, had learned the techniques, and were now making a film. I think you get the picture.

One of the most ambitious challenges that Beizai set for himself was to decipher the performing parameters of premodern Iranian dramatic arts, and then translate them into cinema. For example, he is one of the most learned masters of *Taziyeh*, the Persian passion play. One of his most ambitious projects has been to translate the performing techniques and mimetic principles of Taziyeh into film. Touraj Noroozi, a dear friend and colleague whose untimely death many of us still mourn, once delivered an astounding paper in Chicago on aspects of Taziyeh in Beizai's *The Travelers*. Years later, I heard another brilliant paper, this one in New York, by Negar Mottahedeh, on the same subject. The point is that Beizai's ambition was twofold: first to decode and theorize the mimetic principles of Taziyeh and second to translate them cinematically. Even more than in *The Travelers*, in *The Ballad of Tara* we see him engaged in this dual project. Beizai was far more successful in adapting Taziyeh techniques cinematically than in theoretically speculating on the nature and function of mimesis in Taziyeh. But what is paramount is that he successfully transmuted the performing energy of a principally theatrical tradition into a cinematic vocabulary with astounding dramatic effect.

Consider the opening gambit of *The Travelers*—a woman facing a camera and telling the audience that she and her family are going to have a car accident and die. As you know, the stories of Taziyeh are pious remembrances of the lives and predicaments of Shia imams and saints, and the drama that animates a particular Taziyeh performance is not one of a plot crescendo in which a major crisis is generated, drawn out, and then resolved. The audience knows the story by heart, even before they have entered the theater (or the mosque or the street corner or wherever the Taziyeh is performed). So the challenge of Taziyeh is not to tell a story that no one knows and then let the hidden trauma gradually unfold. The challenge of the Taziyeh performance is in *how* to tell the story, for the plot of the story is already evident, or known. (In this respect Taziyeh is, of course, like European opera, where the audience again probably knows the story, or, if they have forgotten it, a summary is given to them before the opera starts.) So when Mahtab Davaran faces the camera and tells everyone what is going to happen, Beizai, in effect, is using a standard dramatic feature of Taziyeh—the audience has full knowledge of the impending tragedy before it even takes place. The result is rather shocking, because in cinematic narrative we are not supposed to know what the central conflict is until such time that it happens. But Beizai has here adapted a standard feature of Taziyeh drama, wedded it to a well-known principle borrowed from Alfred Hitchcock—that fear is when you know what is going to happen but you just don't know when it's going to happen—and alchemized the result with mesmerizing energy.

I remember when I was a child my mother had a religious vow to buy and shell nuts every month and give them to the poor—*ajil-e moshkel gosha*, she called it, "the problem-solving nut mix" (a bad translation for a beautiful original). She would gather me and my younger brother around a small spread and then begin ceremoniously to clean the nuts (take the pistachios, walnuts, almonds, and such out of their shells, pick the stems from the raisins, etc.), and as she began doing so she would tell us a story about a poor man, a certain *kharkan* (someone who gathered dried bushes from the desert and sold them in the market for a living), who became suddenly rich after he found a bundle full of marbles that were miraculously turned into jewels. Telling this story as she shelled the nuts was part of the ritual—as was having an audience (and thus the initially reluctant but gradually eager presence of her two youngest sons). My younger brother and I must have heard that story of the old kharkan hundreds of times (once a month, all through our childhood), so we knew it by heart, almost sentence by sentence. Nevertheless there were dramatic twists that we eagerly awaited, particular turns of phrases, my mother's intonations of various characters at certain critical moments of the story. It was not the actual story that mattered, but the ritual and habitual gathering of the three of us for this event, and then the eager expectation of precisely those foretold moments that planted seeds of joy in our hearts. It is the same with Beizai's adaptation of old-fashioned storytelling techniques, which cinematically become quite compelling, adding an entirely unexpected twist to the manner in which a story is told.

There is another adaptation of Taziyeh in the opening sequence of *The Travelers*, this time from its mimetic logic. Contrary to Aristotelian mimesis, in Taziyeh there does not exist a stage-based, one-to-one correspondence between reality and its dramatic representation. The mimetic act in Taziyeh, as a result, is not permanent. It is spontaneous and transitory. A Taziyeh actor can do his lines as Shemr or Imam Hossein, and then while still on "stage" turn around and chat with a friend in the "audience" about a business matter. A quintessential condition of this manner of mimesis is that in Taziyeh there is neither a stage nor a proscenium, as there is in Greek theater, nor, as a result, an audience distinct from the actors. The stage is where the audience is, and the audience is integral to the stage. Acting as a result is not stipulated as a permanent (for the duration of the play) representation of some other reality. In Aristotelian mimesis, no actor ever comes out of character to say anything. If you notice in European theater, even when the actors all come to stage to acknowledge the applause of the audience they remain absolutely silent and in costume, for they are still onstage, and as a result they cannot dissolve the mimetic illusion of their characters. Not so in Taziyeh, where acting is predicated entirely on a spontaneous, momentary, and transitory conception of representation. The actor says his line and then he is no longer Imam Hossein or Shemr (historically, no women were allowed to act in Taziyeh, and just like old-fashioned Shakespearean plays in Europe, all the female roles were played by male actors). This particular manner of mimesis might be attributed to the doctrinal prohibition of artistic representation in Islam, or it might be related to the absolute inimitability (for they have an exclusive claim to infallibility) of the Imams and saints. That is why in Taziyeh you see the actors habitually holding on to a simulacrum of a script from which they are reading their lines. They might (and they do in fact) know all their lines by heart, but the visible presence of the script in their hands becomes an iconic marker that they are only momentarily acting, and they are not really Imam Hossein or Shemr. The same factor is behind the visible presence of the director on stage. The audience can always see the director and other stagehands frequenting the "stage" without the slightest hesitation. The result is a form of dramatic representation that is impermanent, momentary, intentionally make-believe—there is never even an assumption that these actors are the real thing, whereas in Aristotelian mimesis, the actors will do everything within their power to pretend that they are what they pretend to be.

So when Mahtab Davaran faces the camera and says that she and her family are going to die, she has temporarily stepped out of her scripted role, facing the camera directly, and through it the audience, telling them what is about to happen. When Homa Rusta (the actress playing the role of Mahtab Davaran) vacates the role of Mahtab Davaran, it is perfectly compatible with the logic of Taziyeh. But translated into a cinematic trope, it suddenly jolts the habitual Aristotelian assumption of permanent representation and injects an explosion of energy into narrative dissemblance.

To be sure, Beizai is not the only Iranian filmmaker to have been influenced by this particular aspect of Taziyeh. Both Abbas Kiarostami and Mohsen Makhmalbaf have borrowed the kind of narrative dissemblance that Taziyeh sustains. I vividly remember that when Kiarostami screened *Taste of Cherry* here in New York, someone from the audience (I later learned it was Shoja Azari, a fine Iranian artist and the principal collaborator of Shirin Neshat on many of her works) asked him if the ending of the film, when we see Kiarostami and his camera crew and actor congregating to wrap up shooting the film, was a kind of Brechtian anti-catharsis (what Brecht called *Entfremdung*, meaning "distancing," "alienation," or "de-familiarization")—to which he readily responded, "Yes. That was Brechtian." But I believe that the moment in question is straight out of Taziyeh, where you always see the director onstage, and where anti-catharsis, as a purging of emotional tension, or abreaction, is achieved through an entirely different dramatic technique, known technically as *goriz*, literally meaning "escape," but referring to the manner in which the dramatic re-narration of the height of the Karbala drama of Taziyeh is ritually syncopated with the stylized mourning of the audience. This is not to suggest that Brechtian anti-catharsis could not have been an influence (perhaps even a more conscious influence) on Kiarostami in that last scene of *Taste of Cherry*, for, indeed, Brechtian theater, both in theory and practice, was very much loved, read, staged, and admired throughout Kiarostami's formative years in Tehran. But it is to suggest that whereas Brechtian anti-catharsis is much theorized and discussed, the kind of mimetic representation much closer to Kiarostami's culture and context (and perhaps more unconsciously ingrained) are equally important and instrumental, and yet almost entirely untheorized.

This narrative dissemblance later becomes integral to the cinema of both Kiarostami and Makhmalbaf, and through them Jafar Panahi and many others, giving a definitive characteristic to Iranian cinema and its multiple manners of realism in which fact and fantasy (what I have termed factasy) merge to become an inroad into reality otherwise hidden by the term *realism* as such (the way we see it, say, in Italian Neorealism), or in the fictive narrative of standard cinematic or dramatic mimesis. Beizai's adaptation of Taziyeh, though, results in a kind of narrative stratagem that sculpts the mythic dimensions of reality out of the stale matter-of-factness that ordinarily hovers over it.

An equally provocative adaptation of Iranian theatrical techniques in Beizai's cinema is his creative assimilation of *arusak-bazi*, or "puppeteering," the story-based manipulation of marionettes in popular performances. In many of his films, particularly in *The Travelers*, Beizai intentionally stylizes and figuratively modulates certain movements of his actors and actresses as if they were marionettes, held and operated by a master puppeteer. The effective result of these performances is the addition of a highly stylized theatricality that systemically disrupts the illusion of reality and forces it to exude its hidden mythical dimensions. This particular technique, in addition to those of Taziyeh, all come together in what one might call mythologizing reality, dissolving it backward into the realm of the mythos. Making an audience conscious of the theatricality of an act that is pretending to be real in effect pulls the parameters of reality into the domain of the mythological. Then, we no longer identify myth with some remote point in history and reality with something current. Narrated within a collectively conceived mythological matrix, the mythic proportions of reality itself—past or present, transitory or permanent—become evident, and subject to all sorts of conversations, negotiations, transference, ascendance. It is in this sense that Beizai's cinema is most political—he is after altering the mythic matrix of our collective memory.

To Beizai, the historical person is a quintessentially mythmaking creature. The illusion of reality is in fact the most successful fabrication of truth by this mythmaking proclivity. In this respect, and perhaps without consciously knowing it, Beizai concurs with Nietzsche's premise that "truths are illusions about which one has forgotten that this is what they are." But the difference is that Beizai is not after exposing what Nietzsche called "a mobile army of metaphors, metonyms, and anthropomorphisms" that have made that mutation of illusions into truths possible. Beizai's project is "poetically and rhetorically," as Nietzsche puts it, to reinvent alternative myths, with solid claims to truth, and by letting them loose on the illusion of reality to shake its tyrannical metaphysics of authenticity and to expose its fabricated character. Beizai's mythic realism, as a result, always begins with reality at hand, takes it for granted, and then before you know it, has transmuted it, sculpted it into a metamorphosed version of itself, equally compelling and legitimate, and thus caught lived reality in the act of fabricating its claim to universal validity. To demonstrate the cultural currency of what he sought and achieved I know of no better way than reminding you of the poem "The Song of Abraham," by Ahmad Shamlu (1925–99), the poet laureate of Iran's defiant modernity. As you read this poem, see how Shamlu borrows and transmutes familiar biblical, Qur'anic, and ancient Persian mythological tropes to sing an ode to a fallen revolutionary: This is how a narrative dissemblance of truth makes the foreign familiar by making the familiar foreign:

> *In the bloody battle of dawn*
> *When wolf*
> *Cannot be told from sheep—*
> *Behold:*
>
> *Ecce Homo (Behold the Man)*
> *Who wished the earth green*
> *And who deemed love the only thing*
> *Worthy of the most beautiful women!*
>
> *For this to him*
> *Was no worthless gift*
> *To deserve stoning*
> *And burying under the earth.*
>
> *What a man!*
> *What a man—who*
> *Used to say that*
> *A heart*
> *Is better bloodied*
> *With seven swords of love;*
> *And a throat*
> *Worthier*
> *Uttering the most beautiful names!*

And a lion of a man thus made of iron—
And thus in love—
Traversed the bloodied domain of fate
With an Achilles heel!

An invincible man—
The secret of whose death
Was in the sorrow of love and
In the sadness of solitude.

"Ah, thou sad Esfandiyar!
You are better off with
Your eyes shut!"

"Was it not enough?
Was one not just enough:

To pave my destiny?"

I alone screamed:
No!
I refused to succumb—I
Was a voice—just a shape
Among other shapes—and I
Found a meaning.

I was and I
Became—
Not the way a blossom
Becomes a flower,
Or a root
A leaf bud,
Or a seed
A jungle.

No.

Exactly in the same way that
An ordinary man becomes a martyr—
So that the heavens will prostrate to him.

I was no little
Wretched creature—and the way

To my Everlasting Paradise
Was no solitary goat-path of prayers and servitudes:

I needed another kind of God
Worthy of a creature
Who does not bend
His neck in obedience
Just to get by—

And thus I created
Another God."

Alas!

The lion of a man thus made of iron
That you were—
And thus just
Like a mountain,
Long before you fell down
Upon the earth and died,
You had died standing up
Untiring and solid.

But neither God nor Satan—only an idol
Had written your destiny,
An idol that others had glorified,
An idol that others glorified.

It is not just in the visual vocabulary of his cinema and the stylized formalism of his cinematic diction that Beizai creatively adopts and logistically adapts the dramatic and narrative elements of Persian visual and performing arts. In the substance of his cinematic reflections he is also in contemplative conversation with the language of medieval philosophers such as Shahab al-Din Yahya Suhrawardi. By way of demonstrating my point, let me compare the way Beizai's masterpiece, *Bashu, the Little Stranger*, unfolds with one of Suhrawardi's visionary recitals, "Treatise on the Condition of Childhood." I believe the two of them make for an instructive comparison, for reasons beyond the obvious centrality of a young boy in the respective narratives.

Bashu is a teenage boy from southern Iran whose parents and young sister perish in the course of the Iran-Iraq War. Fearing for his life, he hides on the back of a truck headed to northern Iran, by the Caspian Sea. Bashu falls fast asleep on the truck as it travels north on a nocturnal journey that makes it look like a ghoulish apparition escaping from hell. Paradise indeed seems to be where Bashu wakes up in the morning, and he finds himself in a Garden of Eden far removed from his war-torn imagination. He is now in northern Iran, in the lusciously green, abundantly peaceful, and generously bounteous jungles, woods, and rice paddies of Gilan and Mazandaran. Where in the world is he? Where was that hell, and where is this paradise? Is he still on the same planet?

Let's now cut a few centuries back to Suhrawardi's little kid whom we can call Shahab al-Din (Shahab for short), after his author, playing one day at a street corner, as children often do, when he sees a group of children coming his way. He is excited and a bit bewildered by this group, but approaches them and asks them who are they and where are they going. We are students, they respond, and we are headed to school to learn. To learn what? Shahab wonders. We don't know yet, the children respond. We will have to ask our teacher. They say this and off they go. A few days pass and Shahab wonders what in the world it is that these kids are learning from their teacher. His curiosity finally gets the better of him and off he goes looking for the children and their teacher. He fails to find the children, and there is no trace of any school, but he runs into an old learned man and asks him if he knows where these students and their teachers are. The old learned man tells Shahab that he is their teacher. Shahab says fine, would you please teach me what you have been teaching them? The teacher says yes. He brings forth a tablet, writes the letters of the alphabet on it, and tells him, there, you go home and learn these. Shahab goes home, does his homework, learns the alphabet, and returns to his teacher. The teacher gives him some more exercises and sends him back home. Shahab goes home, does his homework again, and comes back to the teacher. This continues until such time that Shahab goes back and forth to his teacher ten times a day, until not a single minute of his life is spent doing anything except learning from the old teacher.

Cut back to Bashu now, who is completely bewildered in the jungles of Mazandaran. He hears the sound of an explosion and runs away in fear, thinking that these are the Iraqi bombers attacking, even though the sound has come from dynamite being used in the construction of a tunnel. He flees, bewildered and confused, through the rice paddies and woods, having no clue where in the world he has landed, for he was asleep when the truck left and he has no indication that he is even in Iran. He runs and runs and runs and is by now exhausted and hungry. Finally, he sees two young kids tending a rice paddy with their mother. The young kids are frightened when they see Bashu, for he is disheveled, dirty, frightened, hungry, and, coming from southern climes, dark-skinned, whereas these young kids (as all other kids in this part of the country) are quite fair-skinned. Their mother comes to protect them from Bashu, whom she takes for some sort of wild animal. She wards off Bashu with a long stick, is puzzled by his look, neither human nor animal to her eyes, gathers her children, and takes them away, leaving a piece of bread for Bashu. Bashu comes out of the bush where he is hiding, grabs hold of the bread, and watches the mother and her two children leave. The bread made sense to him, but nothing else does.

Meanwhile Shahab has a splendid time learning from the old, wise, and learned teacher, until one day as he is walking to his regular lessons he runs into a nasty, suspicious, and nosy person who wants to keep him company. He is unable to get rid of this person and much to his regret takes him to his lesson with his teacher. The teacher writes something on Shahab's tablet and holds it up for him to read. Shahab reads what his teacher has written and is ecstatic from the beauty and wisdom of it. In his excitement, he keeps repeating what the teacher has taught him to his companion. But the nasty, nosy, prying person starts laughing and ridiculing Shahab and his teacher, and asks him if he has gone completely mad speaking such nonsense. Shahab's enthusiasm is killed, as if a bucket of cold water were poured over his head. He approaches his teacher for both solace and apology, but notices that he has suddenly disappeared. He looks in vain for him everywhere, but he has vanished. Despair befalls the soul of the young apprentice.

Back in Mazandaran, Bashu eats his bread and slowly follows the young children and their mother to their cottage. Night soon descends upon the village and wild animals begin to shriek and bawl. Bashu is scared and seeks refuge in a barn adjacent to the family's home. After a while, the mother comes out and gives him a blanket. The following day, Bashu wakes up and decides to get acquainted with his new surroundings. Between Bashu and the mother, whose name we will soon discover is Nai, of this small family gradually emerges a maternal and filial relationship, despite their vast cultural differences. Initially they do not even understand each other's language, but Nai sits down patiently and teaches Bashu her language and learns his. "We call this *pomodore*," she says as she holds up a tomato. "What do you call it?" "We call it *tamata*," Bashu responds, both of them inadvertently revealing their respective colonial and commercial histories. Bashu learns and teaches, Nai teaches and learns, and Bashu soon begins to help out with chores around the farm. The village neighbors begin to harass and ridicule Nai for having brought this dark creature to their village. Her husband, away from home to find a job and hearing of this unwanted guest, writes to his wife demanding that the boy be sent away. Nai refuses, Bashu runs away, comes back, swallows his pride, the villagers continue to harass them, and things finally calm down, until Nai's husband comes home and has a quarrel with is wife about Bashu. Suddenly wild boars attack the rice paddies and all the family runs to scare the boars away and save their farm.

Disappointed and heartbroken, Shahab finally finds his way into a Sufi *Khaneqah*, comes across an old sage clad in a beautiful robe, half black and half white. He approaches him and tells him his story. The old sage says that of course the old teacher was right to disappear, for Shahab had divulged the joyous secret of a teaching he had learned to an ill-mannered, foul-mouthed, vulgar, and uncouth creature. Shahab pleads with the sage to take him to his old teacher to apologize. He agrees to his request and takes Shahab to the old teacher. The old teacher forgives him, reminds him that not everyone is ready to learn everything, and resumes teaching Shahab even more subtle, ecstatic, and beautiful truths.

By far the most critical difference between Suhrawardi's story and Beizai's film, separated as they are by the span of some eight hundred years, is the instructive manner in which Shahab is fathered by his teacher and the symbolic way in which Nai mothers Bashu. Shahab's fathering is verbal; Bashu's mothering is visual—their metaphoric parenting identical. As Suhrawardi narrates the story, Shahab comes into being by way of learning from a tablet on which his teacher writes blissful truths. Beyond this stage of instruction, and after a moment of separation and trauma, the teaching between the old master and the young Shahab is no longer mitigated by the written word or the instrumentality of the tablet. It becomes aural, direct, *"nafas to nafas, sineh beh sineh,"* as we say in Persian, "breath to breath, chest to chest," in solitude and confidence. Nai's mothering of Bashu commences with aural lessons (where Shahab and his teacher conclude) as they teach each other their respective languages—and then continues into the realm of the visual, the symbolic, the semiotics of a whole different manner of teaching and creating.

It is important to keep in mind a crucial distinction between these two stories. The first encounter between Shahab and his teacher commences with the teaching of the letters of the alphabet—theirs is a literate relationship. The first instructive encounter between Nai and Bashu, however, begins and ends with the actual things, for the names of these things differ for Nai and Bashu, because they come from two different linguistic cultures. Shahab's learning is initially bookish whereas Bashu's learning from Nai is aural and concludes in a symbolic mutation of both of them—Nai and Bashu—into a semiotic universe that embraces them both, and thus makes them both meaningful and significant to each other. More importantly, Shahab's teacher is literate. Nai is illiterate—and it is in her illiteracy that she *begins* to teach and learn, though it is where Shahab and his teacher *conclude*. Nai dictates the letters she sends to her husband to Bashu to write. (This is a very common practice. My own mother was illiterate, so she dictated the letters she wanted to send to people and I would write them down. We have to take the word "illiterate" quite literally here, for though my mother could not read or write the letters of the alphabet, she had a superb command of the Persian language—both prose and poetry. This is a very strange phenomenon that has never ceased to baffle me.) Nai dictates, Bashu writes—her speech, his writing. The final letter that Nai dictates and Bashu writes is the iconic culmination of their having become a mother and son. Bashu has just nursed Nai back to health after she fell ill trying to find Bashu in a wild storm. Nai is washing her clothes as she dictates the letter to Bashu—informing her husband that she will *not* let go of Bashu. My son Bashu writes this letter, she says, and Bashu writes. Just like all other children, he is the offspring of earth and sun, she says defiantly, and Bashu writes it down.

Beizai has carefully prepared for this prophetic sentence by emphasizing the universality of literary Persian beyond its regional variations—specifically in a moving scene when Bashu and Nai's neighbors' children get into a physical fight and Bashu suddenly picks up a school textbook and starts reading from it—"We are all children of Iran." Predicated on that sequence, and soon after Nai gives ritual birth to Bashu, the scene is set for the idea of an immaculate conception, a birth by mythic will. This is how it works: When Bashu falls into a small river and is about to drown (for he does not know how to swim), Nai takes a fishing net and fishes him out of the river and embraces him, inside the net, which has now become the functional equivalent of her womb. So when she says my son Bashu writes this letter, she means what she says, and Beizai has carefully and consistently prepared his audience for that moment. The birth is mythic, symbolic, carefully choreographed, and highly stylized—all for the singular purpose of giving texture and tonality to the phrase, when Nai utters it, that just like all other children, he is the offspring of earth and sun. With that sentence, Nai and Bashu have become integral to a cosmic order of heaven and earth that only Beizai's mythic realism could have so carefully constructed—a mythic realism that can now show and tell an immaculate conception, a birth out of wedlock, as it were, a mythic birth, the symbolic elimination of the father, the principal source of violence, the figure whom Beizai brings back to Nai and her children having already cut off his right arm, the phallic exterior sign of his violence and virility at one and the same time.

Just like Suhrawardi's story, Beizai's mythical realism begins on very simple and solid ground. Suhrawardi's starts like a children's tale: "Once when I was a child I was playing on a street corner, as children often do." Given the extraordinarily rich philosophical diction of Suhrawardi in his other works (particularly his Arabic texts, and specifically his masterpiece,

Hikmat al-Ishraq), this is a disarmingly simple way to begin a narrative, which then ascends to a sublime reflection on the nature of dangerous knowledge. Similarly, Beizai's story commences with the almost documentary-like depiction of the Iraqi bombing of someplace in southern Iran, where we see Bashu's parents and sister perish in a fire caused by the blast. Then we see him get onto a truck on its way to northern Iran, the same way that we see Shahab meeting a group of children and asking them who they are and where they are going. Suhrawardi's story is a plot to suggest the irreducible orality of truth, that it cannot be taught by the written word, without grave danger and serious distortion—in effect the singularity of teaching: only one teacher per student per lesson per truth. Beizai's mythical realism suggests a similar moment, one that visually carves the hidden dimensions of being-in-the-world out of its docile and worn-out plasticity. It is just like conjugating a verb that one had thought defective, hallow, sealed off from further meaning. Both Suhrawardi and Beizai begin with the real and transcend to the surreal (where reality becomes miasmatic). One master achieves this transcendence through philosophical hermeneutics, and the other through mythic realism. And yet one can easily imagine Suhrawardi a groundbreaking filmmaker and Beizai an illuminationist (*Ishraqi*) philosopher. No other Iranian filmmaker can fit that bill or merit that comparison.

What I would like to conclude from this comparison between Suhrawardi's "Treatise on the Condition of Childhood" and Beizai's *Bashu, the Little Stranger*, a comparison I have rarely dared to make between any two cultural icons in our history so distant from each other, is that Beizai's cinema has crafted a kind of kinetic consciousness—a mobile army of material metaphors, if I were to refer back to Nietzsche—in which certain things can happen that are otherwise illogical and even unimaginable. First, let me explain what I mean by "kinetic consciousness." Consider one critical visual prop that runs through *Bashu* from beginning to end. We see Bashu's biological mother as she descends into a hole of fire. In a subsequent account of his predicament, Bashu tells Nai and demonstrates to the children of the village how his parents perished and his sister disappeared. Now recall the scene where Bashu spends his first night at Nai's barn, and remember that just before he falls asleep, we see his biological parents, standing and looking over him in the barn as he falls asleep. In another scene, as he moves to help Nai with a chore, we see him having a visible recollection of his biological parents walking across a desert as he goes to help them carry a ladder, which action then visually morphs into his helping Nai with the chore. Recall also the scene where Bashu has run away from Nai's home after he reads her husband's letter asking her to get rid of him. As Nai chases frantically after Bashu to find him in the middle of a thunderous storm, again we see Bashu's biological mother pointing the direction in which Nai ought to go to find Bashu. These visual props, endemic to all Beizai's films, come straight out of his construction of what I just called a "kinetic consciousness"—for otherwise they are narratively outlandish and logically flawed. Thus Beizai can move bodies around varied chronological planes and across colliding spatial domains with a mythical (and not rational) logic.

As Beizai links these two mother figures visually across time and space he is crafting one of the most compelling female characters in Iranian cinema. Nai is perhaps Beizai's most illustrious character, the iconic summation of his vision of the Iranian woman, or even women at large. The most significant aspect of Nai's character is the fact that she works, that she is part of a labor class, which is the single most important source of her character, culture, autonomy, and authority. The archetypal model for Nai is, of course, Tara from Beizai's own *The Ballad of Tara* (1979)—integral to the earth, fundamental to history, the very stuff of which myths are made. Like Tara in *The Ballad of Tara*, Nai is a solitary figure. We see her only in the company of her own two children and Bashu. We don't see her with her husband until the very end of the film, and when the husband does arrive he is an entirely superfluous and irrelevant character. The solitary presence of Nai is instrumental to Beizai's choreographed and stylized ritual birth of Bashu, a kind of immaculate conception that constitutes Nai as a symbol of mother earth. Here, in Nai and Bashu, Beizai has in effect crafted a Mary and Christ analogy, which is no longer merely Christian, but reflects the Christianized version of a much more global archetype. Beizai's mythic realism makes the archetypal character of Nai possible. He has, over the course of a lifetime, taught his camera how to move objects and recast their bodies and shapes in a way that from their immediate material reality far more mythic claims on our consciousness are articulated.

The specific features of Beizai's cinema—his aesthetically transformed reality, by way of giving back to reality its mythic proportions, his modes of narrative dissemblance, of mimetic dissimilitude, and ultimately his kinetic consciousness—all come together in his attention to art as communal ritual. Throughout his scholarly and artistic career, Beizai has been consistently at work to map out the contours of communal rituals as the most basic building block of a national history. For example, in two potently ritualistic dance scenes in *Bashu*—one when Nai is ill and another when Bashu and his friends play a game to sort out their feud—Beizai seems to have inadvertently turned cinematic spectatorship itself into a communal ritual act. For Beizai art is irretrievably connected to a larger context of rituals that bring a people together, and art, independent of ritual, seems not to have an autonomous function for Beizai. The stylized acting in his films, borrowed and adapted from a variety of Iranian dramatic traditions, sustains this mutation of Beizai's cinema into a communal ritual. What I mean to say is that not only do Beizai's films (and plays) portray a communal ritual, but that they also transform the act of spectatorship itself into a communal ritual. It is safe to suggest that for nearly forty years, from his first short film *Amu Sibilou* (*Uncle Mustache*, 1969), to his most recent play now on stage in Tehran, *Majlis-e Shabih: Dar Zekr-e Masaib Ostad Navid Makan va Hamsarash Mohanddes Rakhshid Farzin* (*A Staging Act: On Trials and Tribulations of Professor Navid Makan and His Wife, Engineer Rakhshid Farzin*, 2005), Beizai himself has been the principal "high priest" of a communal ritual of prophetic visions in modern Iranian cultural history.

One may thus argue and demonstrate that the social function Beizai has performed in modern Iranian history is in and of itself a ritualistic act, and the invariable controversy that his films have sparked over a long and fruitful career is precisely the way communal rituals function in a society—they are not always understood in any analytical detail, but they do manage to gather people around their iconic presence. Beizai's art (cinema and drama) has now attained that totemic status in the Iranian cultural consciousness. His audience does not quite understand what the ritual is about, and what it is that they are doing when they perform it, but that it must be performed they now take for granted. This may also help to explain why Beizai's cinema is so indecipherable to foreign audiences. Taking part in his films as communal ritual requires possessing the cultural currency or the linguistic facility that has made the ritual possible.

Making art a kind of social rite is perhaps Beizai's most ambitious project. The social function of an artist, over the last two hundred years and throughout the globe, has long since ceased to be either communal, ritual, or sacred. But Beizai has a singularly sacral conception of art. To be sure, no single artist can go against the grain of history. And at a time of rapid atomization of individuals, commercialization of art, the global phenomenon of what Theodor Adorno called "the culture industry," the systematic corrosion of what Walter Benjamin called "the aura of a work of art" under the monumental pressure of its mechanical reproduction, there exists an urge for a restoration of art to its pre-capital (medieval or ancient) role as the occasion of sacramental communion. But short of that historic reversal, Beizai has managed to sublimate his own cinema, and through his cinema the entirety of his artistic production, into a ritual event, whereby participating in it assumes a historic significance beyond any specific artistic event or aesthetic judgment. Keep in mind that what Beizai has suggested in his art does put forward a hermeneutics of its own, whereby a whole different manner of reading art in contemporary society is made possible, against all odds, and despite the institutional reconfiguration of the function of art in postcolonial, and now global-ized, transnational societies.

It may sound strange to you that I am casting a filmmaker as a visionary prophet, a high priest of the sacramental attendance upon the beautiful and the sublime, the true and the significant. But allow that sense of wonder to inform your gaze upon a generation of intellectuals and artists who have now long since lost their whereabouts in the dynam-ics of Iranian history. I am asking you to imagine Beizai looking, with a determined and resolute stare, at the manners and modes of our history, a stare with which he can torpedo a compromised culture, a complacent reality, which is now (in his eyes) the chief accomplice of a global pres-sure to make people bend backward to accommodate power. Beizai has used his camera with surgical precision, and he has cut and pasted reality backward and forward until it began to yield shapes and give emancipa-tory assurances despite itself.

To see this, you ought to understand that Beizai comes from a cul-ture of rebellious defiance that has now been almost completely lost to a culture of overriding complacency, which for the life of me I can-not understand. I am not quite sure if the new generation of Iranians, from their noblest to their basest, will ever come close to the universe of imaginings where Beizai reigns supreme. One look at the brilliance of Parviz Shahbazi's inspired film *Deep Breath* (2003) and you can tell that his generation is a constellation in a whole different cosmos. We believed in things much bigger than ourselves. That made us humble, and that humility in turn made us worthy of principles that we held sacred in utter impiety. The other side of the coin that Shahbazi so poignantly mints, the side of apathy and despair, is the malady that has afflicted comprador Iranian intellectuals here in the US. Today, it seems to me, the best of us (Parviz Shahbazi) lack all convictions, while the worst (take your pick among the Orientalist regiment of US neocons from Johns Hopkins to Stanford) are full of grotesque intensities. I am paraphrasing Yeats, but what I am trying to say lacks all poetry. It is not just defiant nostalgia that makes the generation of Beizai's visionary artists appear so preciously far and so emotively remote now. To this day, when I read the news of a new film or a new play by Beizai, I think that something of cosmic signifi-cance has happened—and it has happened.

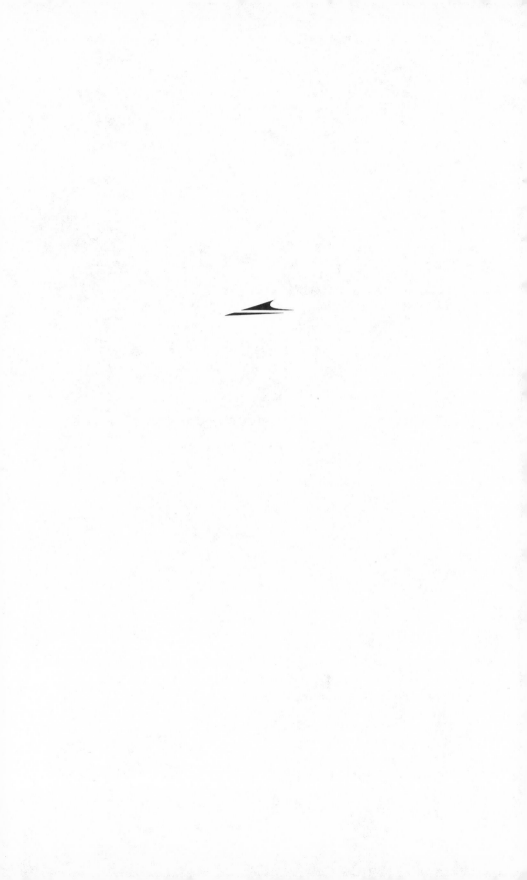

Oh, those storytellers! They can't rest content
with writing something useful, agreeable, palat-
able—they have to dig up all the earth's most
cherished secrets!... I'd forbid them to write,
that's what I'd do!

**–Prince V. F. Odoyevsky, quoted by Fyodor
Dostoyevski, in *Poor Folk***

Abbas Kiarostami
Through the Olive Trees

I HAVE NOW IMMIGRATED TO THE WINTERY CORNER OF MY SOUL, the hibernating state of my mind. Except for my regular long walks by the Hudson, I am mostly home chained to my writing desk—and I write as an act of prayer, in the shadow of a faith that no longer claims me. The gray and heavy air about the Hudson is so mighty and so indifferent to our fate. It is now completely in its own somber mood—flowing down to the ocean with a majestic arrogance flowing in its solemnity. Columbia, deserted by students for yet another week, has stretched its long and lazy legs under a blanket of silence and serenity. The Hudson to my left and Columbia to my right—I don't even have to open my window to see them embracing me in their commanding indifference. But I can feel them both, markers of my days and the corridor of my current homelessness.

Today I chose to walk down Broadway instead of going to Riverside Park. I do this when I feel I need to get lost in the anonymity of a faceless crowd. I came across a sidewalk bookseller. There are quite a few of them selling old books on the sidewalks of the Upper West Side.

Now they sell all sorts of other things—DVDs, worn-out videos, black-and-white pictures of New York, really cool and outdated 33 LPs, huge posters of Malcolm X, Che Guevara, and Muhammad Ali, and even a few autographed copies of Philip Roth's books. But this bookseller grabbed my attention for he was new to the block. I took one glance and I saw it: the first edition of Anthony Wilden's 1968 translation of Jacques Lacan's *The Function of Language in Psychoanalysis*! This was quite a catch. The original, in French, was published in 1956. I was particularly happy to find this edition because it contained a magnificent essay by Wilden himself, "Lacan and the Discourse of the Other," which I had read years ago from a photocopy that my old teacher Philip Rieff had given to me. But I had long since lost that photocopy, with all my graduate-student marginalia on it.

The man asked for two dollars for the copy. It was quite a bargain (though there was some sort of coffee stain on the front cover, and the back cover was slightly torn). I bought the book and continued to walk toward Lincoln Center, thinking of Lacan's revolutionary re-reading of Freud, particularly his insistence that the instrumentality of language between the analyst and the patient is something that needs to be carefully brought into the open, for the patient in effect turns the analyst, through a standard act of transference, from a mere auditor who sits next to the couch and listens silently into an interlocutor. The inadvertent (and inevitable) mutation of the analyst into interlocutor of course changes everything, for now the mere pieces of information provided by the patient suddenly turn into what Mikhail Bakhtin called "utterances," meaning words, expressions, phrases, and sentences that now intend to mean one thing or another. In other words, mere expressions now assume what Gayatri Spivak calls "idiomaticity": they become idiomatic, for the very act of psychoanalysis, the room, the furniture, the assumption of a medical science, etc., have all given the space the character of a culture in which things are said and interpreted in a specific context of intention.

At the corner of Broadway and 82nd I noted that Leitner's had a sale, so I thought maybe I would check it out and see what they had. I was also wondering if one could look at cinema and not become an interlocutor, the same way that Lacan discusses. Does cinema not turn its audience into an interlocutor also when it speaks of the dreams of a nation, the nightmares of a people, the fears, hopes, anxieties, and agitation of a communal remembrance of things past, present, or future by one among them who can see better than the rest? Everything at Leitner's was on sale. Everything. Amazing! Capitalism, thy name is America: two huge pillows (ninety-five percent feather and five percent something else) for $24.95. So I bought two pairs and walked out of Leitner's with two mammoth-sized bags in my hands. I placed Lacan's *The Function of*

Language in Psychoanalysis in one of those bags, right next to the pillows. It was impossible for me to walk back to 116th with these pillows in tow. So I stopped at the bus station on the corner of 82nd and Broadway. Soon the 104 bus showed up. I got in and squeezed myself between an old lady with a bag full of knishes from Zabar's and a very tall musician with his acoustic guitar. I had no idea why the bus was so crowded. I put the pillows on the floor between my legs and held fast to a handle above my head. What a mess. Lacan's distinction among what he called the imaginary order, the symbolic order, and the real had always fascinated me. I remember when I was working on the book Peter Chelkowski and I wrote on the iconography of the Islamic revolution, *Staging a Revolution* (1999), I had thought a great deal about that extraordinarily insightful categorization of Lacan's. Now I thought that the way he posits the two complementary categories of *the imaginary* and *the symbolic* around the defining moment of *the real* is very much what I have always thought of Abbas Kiarostami's cinema, though in a slightly different way. The categorical distinction (and the binary opposition) that Lacan constructs between the imaginary and the symbolic in effect collapses in what I have called Kiarostami's *actual* realism.

What exactly is this *actual* realism and how does it operate in Kiarostami's cinema? When the bus stopped at 96th Street, quite a number of people left, including the old lady and the appetizing aroma of heavenly knishes under my nose. I squeezed the pillow in front of me and looked at the changing apparition of the trees outside, now completely naked and neurotic. If you ask me, in Manhattan buses stop too often, practically at every single block. My theory is that the city would add an average of five years to the life span of every New Yorker if the buses stopped at every other stop and the subways at alternate stops, for then people would have to walk a little more. I don't know what happened to that tall musician. The reason that Lacan differentiates between the imaginary and the symbolic is to propose that we experience reality (the real) through a meandering machination between two sets of correlated enterprises, one rich and confusing (the imaginary) and the other legislated and meaningful (the symbolic). The symbolic is the selfsame imaginary, though just a small portion of it has been successfully repressed and made to behave properly. Society at large is a particular symbolic order made out of the imaginary variations that, left to their own devices, will prevent any formation of social order and meaning.

If I am correct in my understanding of Lacan, then Kiarostami navigates more fluently between the imaginary and the symbolic than otherwise allowed in the normative orders of his culture, history, society, religion, and metaphysics. This makes his realism what I have always suspected it to be: *actual*—namely, reduced to the threadbare minimalism of its irreducible facticities, which are shorn of all meaning to the point that they begin to exude a different order of reality.

I still remember the very first essay I wrote years ago on Kiarostami's *Zir-e Derakhtan-e Zeytun* (*Through the Olive Trees*, 1994), and how I was mesmerized by its announcement of a whole new Iranian cinematic aesthetic. That revolutionary aesthetic, I remember saying in the essay, subverts absolutist terms of certitude, and it originated in Kiarostami's visual transformation of a reality he has sought relentlessly to bracket, to alter radically, to crack, and to redefine through the systematic unveiling of his cinematic vision. The roots of Kiarostami's cinema go much deeper than *Through the Olive Trees*. Since the early 1970s he has been tirelessly at work crafting a vision of reality in which life is celebrated, death condemned, and the whole paradox of being underlined with a colorful crayon of irony. Be that as it may, it is in *Through the Olive Trees* that Kiarostami's entire cinematic vision comes into full view for the first time. To detect that reality Kiarostami always dwells on the surface. "It is only shallow people," Oscar Wilde says, "who do not judge by appearances. The true mystery of the world is the visible, not the invisible." Kiarostami is the mystic musing on our visible appearances, made invisible in the glare of their own light. He is our aesthetic cure, our historic antidote, to the millennial poisoning of our minds with just too much hidden meaning and too many symbolic references. Nothing in Kiarostami is symbolic. Everything explosive in his cinema appears on the surface of things. I laugh out loud and uncontrollably when I read American and European film critics trying their best, bless their Oriental fantasies, to do a reading of Kiarostami's films through "Iranian culture." Put the entirety of "Iranian culture," whatever that might be, on one side and Kiarostami's cinema is the mirror image of it—its diametrical opposition. He is teaching us (as I have said on many occasions), and what a cruel teacher he is, crueler than that nasty teacher in his film *Where Is the Friend's House?* (1987), what we have missed seeing on the surface.

Does he have to be cruel to be kind? Is it wise to abandon the comfort of presumed hidden meanings for the mystery of their uncharted surfaces? Weren't our forefathers wise to have fooled us, diverted our attention, our gaze, away from the abyss of the surface and sent us on the wild goose chase of hidden meaning, so we wouldn't be scared witless of the unfathomably slippery surface of the thing itself, the *Dinge selbst*, as Kant calls it? Maybe yes, maybe no. But promise me one thing: If you want to know what our Abbas the Great is up to, never, ever try to see what he is *alluding to* in his cinema. He is alluding to nothing. He wants you to glide over the silvery surface of signs, just before they start meaning anything—there, that's where the cruel fate and crooked fortune of life is.

Blast! I missed my stop at the corner of 116th and Broadway and I now had no clue where in the world I was. I got off the bus as soon as it stopped again. I was up on 126th. No big deal. I headed back toward 116th. But it is a nasty uphill walk.

I remember the first time that I saw *Through the Olive Trees* here in New York. Beyond its New York Film Festival debut in 1994 and Miramax's decision to distribute it the following winter, *Through the Olive Trees* was also the official Iranian entry in the best-foreign-film category at the 1995 Academy Awards. When the film was finally released in February 1995, it was compared by *The New York Times* to Truffaut's *Day for Night*. Meanwhile, J. Hoberman of *Premiere* magazine enthusiastically identified Kiarostami as "an old-fashioned humanist film intellectual" and credited *Through the Olive Trees* with "complicat[ing] one's view of life in Iran." This was a time between the US hostage crisis of 1979–80 and the events of 9/11. So anytime an American film critic saw an Iranian doing anything not quite classifiable as "terrorism," they called it "humanist."

Among the many sympathetic readings of Kiarostami's *Through the Olive Trees*, perhaps the most insightful, I think, was Gary Dauphin's review in *The Village Voice*, which concluded with a brilliant analysis of the last scene of the film, an insight that echoed many of the similar comments that this last scene had generated worldwide. Stanley Kauffmann of *The New Republic* also saw the film and wrote enthusiastically and generally positively, despite a few inconsequential factual errors. Perhaps the most ironic aspect of Kauffmann's review was that it began with a reference to politics. Writing approvingly of Kiarostami's cinema, Kauffmann asked, "Do we still need reminders that human connections, conveyed in art, persist through political differences? We still can use such reminders, I guess, especially when they come through truly good art." Yes, I had thought at the moment, we do need reminders. But now I think I thought so in vain. Come 9/11, Kiarostami himself would be denied a US visa for fear that he might be a terrorist.

I remember how at the time I went around and collected every piece of information I could about *Through the Olive Trees*. Kiarostami's films, in general, have had quite a controversial presence in Iran. Not only *Through the Olive Trees*, but the entire trilogy of which it is a part was the subject of bitter debates inside Iran. I do not believe that our love and admiration for Kiarostami's cinema ought to ignore these criticisms. I believe that our understanding of *why* Kiarostami is one of our greatest filmmakers should articulate itself *through* these criticisms and not *despite* them, for I am convinced that it is precisely in these criticisms that his detractors have revealed the sources of our collective anxieties.

Through his camera, Kiarostami has seen and shown a vision of reality that is bone-deep but on the surface, skeletal, exquisitely kinetic, and yet invisible to the naked eye—a kind of X-ray of an otherwise heavily codified surface of reality. That is the reason that I believe his cinema can see Lacan's distinction between *the symbolic* and *the imaginary* orders that demarcate our conception of *the real*. The world is too symbolically coordinated, reality too normatively legislated, for the real not to be systematically assimilated backward into one symbolic order or another. If you think of Kiarostami's cinema in that way, he is one of the most radical counter-metaphysicians our culture has ever seen. So I believe we have to see what exactly his detractors are saying, for they are articulating the fears of looking at an X-ray of reality, at a structure that is otherwise hidden from the naked eye—and not because it is hidden, but because it is too obvious.

The Koker trilogy, to which *Through the Olive Trees* is integral, is primarily concerned with the transparent constitution of "reality," a concern that Kiarostami has elaborated through a series of fictive and real events in and around the village of Koker, some 350 miles north of Tehran. *Khaneh-ye Dust Kojast* (*Where Is the Friend's House?*) was the first installment of the trilogy. When Koker was devastated by an earthquake in 1991, Kiarostami returned there and made *Zendegi va digar Hich* (*Life, and Nothing More*), aka *Zendegi Edameh Darad* (*And Life Goes On*), which is about the director's search for the missing children who had acted in *Where Is the Friend's House? Through the Olive Trees* seeks to tell a love story in the making while Kiarostami's camera crew is busy shooting *And Life Goes On*. The result is one of the most effective forms of cinematic self-referentiality—a film inside a film inside a film.

No one remembers now, but Kiarostami had a rough ride to the global recognition that he now receives. His detractors have always been hard at work accusing him of any number of things, even of being a talentless charlatan. The earthquake of 1991 in northern Iran and the film that Kiarostami made in relation to it have laid the central battlefield on which the significance of his cinematic vision has been assailed. Active hostility against Kiarostami's cinema in general took a particularly sharp turn after *And Life Goes On* was released. In a 1993 review of that film in the journal *Sureh*, Farhad Golzar took strong exception to what he considered Kiarostami's dismissal of the tragic depth of the earthquake in northern Iran. "This is a television show," he objected. "It is only by mistake that it is being shown in theaters." Golzar ridiculed what he took to be Kiarostami's banalization of a natural disaster. "This film is full of insults to life," Golzar concluded. "It dehumanizes the human condition. It should not be called *And Life Goes On*, but something like *Life Is Nothing*, or *Man Is a Descendant of Monkey and Nothing More*." Kiarostami's primary audience, Golzar believed, was the international film-festival circuit, especially Cannes. What in the world would make a man say such things about a filmmaker and one of his finest achievements? I think in these harsh and dismissive words is hidden a particularly nasty spot, a raw nerve, that Kiarostami has (inadvertently?) touched. I believe between categorically rejecting or categorically accepting the validity of such criticisms, we ought to read through them, come to Kiarostami's cinema in fact not through the blasé and cliché-ridden vernacular of those who absolutely adore Kiarostami's cinema and yet fail to say why but through the particular anxiety evident in his harshest, mostly Iranian, critics.

Masud Farasati, another critic, has been equally dismissive in his condemnation of Kiarostami. "*And Life Goes On*, from the very beginning, and principally, is based on two lies, two big lies: (1) a representation of the earthquake, and (2) a claim to cinema," as he put it in a review in the same issue of *Sureh*. Farasati finds Kiarostami's camera too neutral to the tragedy it observes. That neutrality, Farasati believes, represents not an ability but a failure to look, to observe, to see. Kiarostami's vision of life is too "bestial" for Farasati, as he puts it. There is no sense of tragedy in it, no depth, no sorrow. Farasati accused Kiarostami of commercialism, even of charlatanism. The film is custom-made, he claimed, for the European film festivals, the French in particular. Farasati then proceeded to give a full political account of why he thinks Kiarostami's cinema is being received and celebrated in Europe—this passage in his review stuck in my mind:

> Indeed, why is it that European film festivals and their
> juries...are so impressed by *And Life Goes On*?... Why is
> it that they are trying to represent its poor, aborted, and
> fallacious technique as genuine and stylish?... It seems
> to me that [Kiarostami's vision] is the "neutral"—indeed
> bloodless, from-behind-closed-eyes, from-behind-
> sunglasses—vision of foreigners who have not seen the
> earthquake in Rudbar in a close-up, and they thank
> God that they were not there when it happened. For
> sure, they are neither Iranian nor from the East. This is
> the Western humanist vision that after watching a few
> minutes of news on television feels a little guilty, as they
> used to feel guilty about Hiroshima, etc.... Indeed the
> producers of *And Life Goes On* are these [Europeans],
> not an Iranian filmmaker who has character and identity.
> These people have commissioned the making of this
> film, and it is they who propagate it and give it prizes.
> Our filmmaker, like all other identity-dealers, is caught

and humiliated in their trap, putting up for sale himself and his forsaken culture. There is no honor in this, but shame. Kiarostami has enjoyed this historical-calendar opportunity that his film goes to the West—and then from there exported back to our country—at a time when the Westerners are afflicted by "the New World Order" epidemic, the politics of eliminating the borders and creating a unified Europe, which itself is an attempt to confront the deep global economic crisis. This new politics demands its own culture...a culture that engages in the elimination of ethnic and national boundaries. Lack of identity is the new strategy of the new world order.... But the self-lost and talentless culture-sellers will not benefit from this transaction and shall earn nothing but shame. All the prizes and praise will last but a short time. Art shall be victorious once again. Because life, as art, continues. But not under the new cultural order; instead via a return, and proudly so, to one's origin and roots.

I continued to read this issue of *Sureh* and found even more attacks on Kiarostami's cinema. Maryam Amini echoed Farasati's sentiments and shared the frustration with what she took to be Kiarostami's "intellectual" and "touristy" distance from the pain and suffering of people devastated by the earthquake.

It is imperative not to exaggerate the negative responses to Kiarostami's cinema, for obviously not all reactions have been so negative. The journal *Film*, perhaps the most widely read and influential periodical on the art and craft of cinema in Iran, has been extremely sympathetic to Kiarostami and enthusiastically reported his accomplishments in international film festivals. In its August 1992 issue, for example, *Film* ran an interview with Kiarostami in which he talked about some of his frustrations with his Iranian critics:

My experience in showing this film [*Close-Up*] in Iran has been quite peculiar. I remember very vividly that after the film was first screened some people came up to me and said, "What was wrong with the sound in the last scene, when Makhmalbaf and Sabzian were driving on a motorcycle? Was something wrong with the sound? Could you not dub it afterward? And some were even suggesting that I intentionally screwed up that scene.... None of the Iranian viewers

could follow that I had an intention other than
showing the conversation between the two men.

Kiarostami then gives a comparative assessment of his European and Iranian critics:

> But viewers in Berlin all recognized that scene as an
> exceptionally good one, full of innovation. The director of
> the academy, who is one of the great German filmmakers,
> told me, "I wish I could cut this section of your film
> and keep it for myself!" It never occurred to any of
> the [German] viewers that that scene was accidentally
> screwed up, or that I had done a trick. They viewed the
> film as a mode of filmmaking, and they liked the film
> for that reason, and I think that perhaps precisely for
> this reason people did not like the film in Iran. At any
> rate, I am absolutely convinced that we are an intelligent
> people, and I do not think that Iranian viewers lack
> anything in comparison with European viewers. Actually,
> when I compare the reviews that Iranian critics have
> written on my films with those written by European
> critics, I come to the conclusion that the Iranian critics
> are very intelligent. The only distinction that exists, in
> my judgment, is our politics-stricken consciousness,
> as a result of which we confront a product maliciously.
> In addition, since we have not yet passed through the
> melodramatic period [in our filmmaking], we still
> look for story. Thus when we confront a film, instead
> of trying to find out what it wants to convey, we are
> more interested in what we want to understand by
> it, and if we come up short [in our reading] then we
> swiftly dismiss the film and refuse to connect with it.

In the high-handed diction of Kiarostami's encounter with his Iranian
audiences—now dismissing, then praising, always condescending—notwithstanding, there is a bitterness about his having been misread, as he
believes, by his own countrymen. The bitterness, I believe, is misplaced,
however natural and understandable. I recall that one of the most perceptive readings of Kiarostami's cinema I read was by Houshang Golmakani,
who in that same issue of *Film* came valiantly to Kiarostami's defense and
enthusiastically argued for the aesthetic integrity of his work. With a rare
and remarkable insight he observed that "We [Iranians] are a people who
in the course of our history have been more used to eulogy than songs of

life. Whoever can describe a tragic event more lamentably we consider that person a more eloquent and capable orator." Golmakani then proceeded to read every technical aspect of Kiarostami's virtuosity with a view toward the highest compliment that an Iranian aesthetician can give an artist: that his art is "impossibly simple," for that is the way we usually describe the work of our great medieval poet, Sa'di (1184–1291).

Golmakani is not alone in his praise for Kiarostami. Javad Tusi also has given rather positive reviews of Kiarostami's cinema, with certain reservations. Kiarostami's "realism" in particular is refreshing and healthy in Tusi's reading. He does object, though, to Kiarostami's preference for Vivaldi's music as opposed to any number of jubilant melodies in Persian classical music. Robert Safarian, Reza Dorostkar, and Majid Islami all have had positive responses to Kiarostami's vision. Gholam Heydari, in his theoretically informed book *Zaviyeh-ye Did dar Cinema-ye Iran (Point of View in Iranian Cinema*, 1990), has included a positive reading of Kiarostami's camera work as a good and relatively consistent example of third-person-singular narrative.

As soon as I thought I had found a balanced perspective among Iranians on Kiarostami I ran into Shahrokh Dulku's essay on him in the June 1993 issue of *Film*. There Dulku took strong exception to Kiarostami as a filmmaker, accusing him of not knowing the basics of camera work while pretending to redefine the entire grammar of it. In his essay Dulku gave a full description of how Kiarostami disregards the rudiments of point of view, but ultimately concludes with a moral condemnation of Kiarostami's cinema. Of *And Life Goes On* he writes:

> I cannot disregard one crucial issue, and that is the moral lesson that the filmmaker wants to draw, following his previous film [*Where Is the Friend's House?*], and yet, just like in the previous film, because of weak execution, structural confusion, misconception of truth, and a convoluted vision of man and life, he reaches precisely the opposite conclusion that he wishes to reach. *And Life Goes On* wants to say that the "human" life is something precious and praiseworthy, but [actually] says that the "bestial" life is dear and lustful. It intends to praise and propagate human life, but in reality it propagates the bestial life. In order to give meaning to life, Kiarostami reduces it to the level of animal instincts (eating, sleeping, sex, and defecation). As opposed to noble, conscientious, and selfless men, the people in *And Life Goes On* are introduced at the end as base and mindless animals, ready to pull apart the dead bodies of

the members of their family like carcasses, and spend
their wedding night under a few feet of "*palastik.*"

Dulku proceeded to denounce the European reception of Kiarostami's
cinema and concluded with a sweeping condemnation of what he takes
to be Kiarostami's arrogant view of his own country and its culture:

> I could have finished this review right here. But one small
> item, perhaps even repetitious, is left which is troubling
> me badly and I am going to say it. Although I believe that
> content criticism is not criticism at all, and a film that
> in form and structure has not yet reached the point of
> "speaking" does not deserve to be discussed in terms of its
> content, nevertheless I am going to say what I have to say.
> There are things in *And Life Goes On* that are extremely
> troubling, so troubling that one cannot just pass them
> by.... I will just mention them in a list and leave them to
> the readers' judgment: A man with a touristy appearance,
> whitish hair, and a "European" and "emotionless" look
> among the victims of the earthquake, the presence of a
> Renault automobile, the French poster of the film *Where
> Is the Friend's House?*...the repeated appearance of the Red
> Cross cars, overwhelming emphasis on the instinctual
> (and not intellectual) aspects of life, and more importantly,
> a train of thought that looks at life not face to face and
> eyeball to eyeball but from above (high on top), and
> with a pair of dark glasses.... This arrogant, emotionless,
> and calculating look inevitably represents an unreal
> picture of life, a picture about which (and in my view
> about Kiarostami's cinema in general) the judgment of
> Mohammad Hossein Ruhi [another critic] as an accurate
> doubt is applicable: "What kind of cinema is this?"

Indeed, what kind of cinema is this that generates this kind of criticism? Judged by the criticism of both Kiarostami's admirers and detractors
his radical revision of reality either has not been registered successfully
at all or else it has been judged morally repulsive. In the November 1994
issue of *Film*, for example, Javad Tusi wrote a satirical piece on *Through
the Olive Trees* in which he announced that he, for one, was not impressed
by Kiarostami's version of realism. Mostafa Jalai Fakhr, however, in the
same issue of the journal, celebrated Kiarostami's "universal language"
and saw nothing wrong, for example, with such "foreign" elements as the
French poster for *Where Is the Friend's House?* or a Red Cross ambulance.

But he failed to back up his defense by confronting the thorny issues of (im)morality in Kiarostami's cinema. In the midst of these ideological debates, occasionally a critic manages to concentrate on a scene and read it according to the logical conclusions of its own aesthetic promises. Yet again in the same issue of *Film*, Naghmeh Samini gave by far the most insightful reading of the concluding scene of *Through the Olive Trees*, calling it a "magical long shot," and noting how the camera

> in the most sensitive moment, precisely at that instant
> when because of our previous cinematic experience
> we expect an answer for all our curiosities and thus
> share in the emotional climax of the work, the camera
> shies away from the focal center of contention, and
> authoritatively imposes its distance on us too. As if
> it does not consider us intimate enough, or think
> us worthy of closely witnessing this love poem.

On the same long shot, Ahmad Talebi-Nezhad, in his piece in the December 1994 issue of *Film*, offered a similar reading, emphasizing, however, that the intimate expression of love—of a sort that could persuade Tahereh to marry Hossein—is simply not permitted in Iranian cinema nowadays, and thus he accounts for the social and political imperatives underlying this hauntingly beautiful long shot.

Despite the occasional attention to technicalities (always stopping short of pushing the argument to face Kiarostami's belligerent critics) and what they might imply, the debate that has raged over Kiarostami's cinema inside Iran invariably turns to questions of moral imperatives. Perhaps the most critical review of *Through the Olive Trees* was written by Masud Farasati, the editor in chief of *Naqd-e Cinema*, a periodical devoted to a technically informed and critical reading of film, published by the Islamic Propaganda Organization. Very bluntly, Farasati, in the Spring 1994 issue of that magazine, identifies *Through the Olive Trees* as

> a disingenuous and insulting film. An experimental
> and abortive film...every shot of which exudes
> lie, artificiality, and clumsiness.... The film
> closes the same way that it opens, artificially and
> pseudo-documentary-like, and thus leaves open a
> path—an escaping path—for all kinds of shallow,
> pseudo-intellectual interpretations and exegesis....

Farasati's language very soon turns moralistic and condemnatory:

What is the use of these artificial dialogues, putting their heavy weight on the film and subordinating the scenes fully to their own advantage, other than denigrating and belittling the people? Why should they appeal to the audience? Could it be that by "audience" it is meant those few hundreds of spineless, rootless, and sick pseudo-intellectuals, natives, and foreigners alike who have discovered Kiarostami and are now putting him on a pedestal?

Farasati is deeply contemptuous of Kiarostami's cinema:

A horrifying earthquake leaves thousands of people dead and much annihilation and destruction behind. Among all the problems and sufferings of the people afflicted by the earthquake, it is only a bestial marriage that attracts the attention of our filmmaker. And why? He himself puts the answer in the mouth of the "hero" of *Through the Olive Trees* and says that "the earthquake was a godsend," because now nobody has a house, and thus he is equal to everybody else. Is the sickly and psychopathic world of the peasant boy, who wishes everybody's house destroyed, not part of our filmmaker's own inner world?

Farasati proceeds to accuse Kiarostami of self-hatred, of being incapable of anything but disgust and denigration for his actors, audience, and ultimately himself and his national and cultural identity.

In a sense, Kiarostami's films are like remembering a nightmare while being awake. These nightmares are often distasteful, and one sees oneself in them passive and incapable of doing anything. Kiarostami seeks refuge from one distasteful nightmare to one even more distasteful. Kiarostami's films, lacking both the pleasant aspects of some dreams and the painful fear and weight of nightmares—because he is incapable of facing either—tell us that he lives in such an insecure and torturous world. If at this late age he is still to learn the elementary principles, the very alphabet, of cinema, is because of this obvious reason that for him learning is equated with fear and denigration.... Denigration, humiliation, fear, and escape are like a

vicious circle that he cannot, and does not want to,
break. He is accustomed to, and feels cozy within, it.

Farasati's indignation and fury are matched by Behzad Rahimian's
ridicule and derision. After an entirely dismissive review of Kiarostami's
films, in the same issue of *Naqd-e Cinema*, Rahimian claimed, among
other things, that he feels

> quite embarrassed by Mr. Kiarostami's most recent
> films that are considered to be ways for Europeans to
> get to know us Iranians.... We are not Czech, Greek,
> Japanese...or Latin American to share certain cultural
> traits with Western nations. We are a nation with
> our own character, and our own ways, very difficult
> to be grasped by either Westerners or Westernized
> Easterners. So it is perfectly natural for them to
> have a strange interpretation of us. But it must be
> a source of shame to use their interpretation of us
> (just to appease them) to untangle Iranian life.

After this subordinate clause on cultural authenticity, Rahimian proceeded with a joke about Kiarostami's cinema, implying that he has
gained celebrity status in the world by virtue of a fake cinema, soon to be
discovered for its embarrassing emptiness.

Why so much venom and wherefore this animus? What has Kiarostami's cinema touched that has so angered these critics? I think one
should neither dismiss nor accept them—but instead read through them,
and try to see what exactly in Kiarostami's cinema arouses so much anger
(for I believe that there is a direct link between angst and anger, between
the *imaginary* [dis]order that Kiarostami interjects and the *symbolic* order
that he disrupts). On many occasions, Kiarostami has appeared troubled
by these strains of criticism and has sought to respond to them, directly
and indirectly. In an interview with Omid Ruhani, in the December
1993 issue of *Film*, Kiarostami tried to give an accurate description of
the protagonist's perception of the earthquake that is, I believe, equally
applicable to Kiarostami's own aesthetics:

> The young man [Hossein Rezai, the lead character in
> *Through the Olive Trees*] has believed the earthquake. For
> him it is like the Final Day of Judgment. When all the
> houses are destroyed and everybody appears in apparent
> and evident equality, it is only natural that in the face of
> this superior fate such a futile thought should occur to

the young and inexperienced mind of the young man that now, on the Day of Judgment, it is the day of salvation for those who have survived. It is the day of equality and equanimity. But an experienced and worldly old woman corrects this illusion on his part and reminds him that the only thing that has happened is an earthquake and all the old and ancient principles and values continue to be valid. People are still alive, and so far as we are alive we will not permit for these principles to be turned upside down.

My sense of Kiarostami's cinema, however, is that it does turn all those ancient principles upside down. Perhaps the most enduring aspect of Kiarostami's cinema is precisely his discontent with "reality" as it is. By bracketing it, and thus equally suspending our conceptions of morality, propriety, and political posturing, Kiarostami has been constantly reimagining a more enabling vision of reality. To do that, he has ultimately had to loosen the structural presumption of narrative-as-truth in order to expose its metaphysical underpinnings, its unexamined truth-claims. He has had to demonstrate that there is no solid, unique, and metaphysically definitive signature to reality, to any collective act of legislated signification that gives it the quality of an abiding truth. The more ambitious Kiarostami's unstated agenda, the harder the counter-truth of his cinema is resisted—resisted that is by a reality that has always already scattered about the world varied agencies of registering itself as truth, and in the process barricading itself against the onslaught of its own meaninglessness. In Lacan's terms, Kiarostami is challenging the imposing symbolic order that ordinarily prevents the onslaught of the anarchic imaginary disorder; he is threatening and dismantling its regime.

Kiarostami does dismantle that regime, and my sense is that this is precisely what bothers his Iranian critics most. At home, it is mostly his religiously musical observers, as Max Weber used to call them, that find his cinema troublingly unethical, while his liberal and secular critics come to his defense (and yet they don't know quite how). But what unites both his religious and his secular critics is what they consider to be Kiarostami's daring to replace the "spiritual" (*ma'navi* as we say in Persian) with the material (or *maddi*). This is the reason behind all those nasty comments you read about Kiarostami's vision being material or bestial. He is material (and he has learned his materialism from Forugh Farrokhzad's and Sohrab Sepehri's poetry), but he is material in the most positive and life-affirming sense of the term. In the over-politicized piety of post-revolutionary Iran, Farrokhzad was either censored in her material celebration of the physical body or else dismissed as a whimsical incident, while Sepehri was radically mutated into a latter-day mystic.

Meanwhile, in comes Kiarostami following their footsteps though this time around with a wholesome visual vocabulary. The allergic reaction of his ethically injured critics is thus rooted in a deeper malady. *"Ay baradar to hameh andishei"*—these critics must have Rumi in mind—*"O brother, you are all intellect,"* then adding, *"Mabaqi khod ostokhan-o rishe'i"*—*"The rest of you is just bone and cartilage."* This is the metaphysics entrenched in Kiarostami's critics, and precisely the metaphysics against which Abbas the Great has (rightly) revolted. As I quote John D. Caputo, a splendid American philosopher whom I deeply admire, and who in his magnificent book *Against Ethics* writes, "I have for some time now entertained certain opinions that I have been reluctant to make public," I can imagine Kiarostami's critics would probably be fainting or else reporting me to the Islami Guardian Council. "But I have at length concluded," continues Caputo in his jubilant tongue-in cheek manner, "that the time has come to air my views, clearly and without apology, and to suffer whatever consequences come my way." Do you want to know what Caputo's conclusion is? Don't breathe a word of this in any Islamic Republic (or Jewish state or Christian empire for that matter): "I am against ethics," says Caputo, and then quotes Martin Luther, only half in jest: "Here I stand. I cannot do otherwise." The point is (Caputo is the American Nietzsche or Kierkegaard read together in a deceptively colloquial English) a mode of morality that is beneath and beyond ethics—something like Roberto Benigni's *Life Is Beautiful* (1998), in which Guido Orefice (Roberto Benigni) always does the right and noble thing, saving his son from the horrors of a concentration camp, never carrying that noble act to the land of metaphysical morality.

In the summer of 1995, something extraordinary happened in the history of Iranian culture. The site of this remarkable event was neither Tehran nor Qom, Mashhad nor Shiraz, nor indeed any other place within the political boundaries of the Islamic Republic. The transgressive thrusts of both our postmodern condition and the post-national renegotiations of imaginative boundaries have allowed radical possibilities beyond the reach of any particular state apparatus. The scene of this remarkable event was the tiny resort town of Locarno in the southern, Italian-speaking part of Switzerland, where the forty-eighth Locarno International Film Festival was held during the first two weeks of August. Thanks to the indefatigable energy and enthusiasm of Marco Müller, at the time the director of the festival, Iranian cinema in general and Kiarostami's in particular received the most enthusiastic global audience that it always deserved but had never attained. Over the course of ten days some thirty Iranian films were shown. In addition to a complete retrospective of Kiarostami's cinema, the festival also included an exclusive section on Iranian women filmmakers, ranging from Forugh Farrokhzad's *The House Is Black* to Rakhshan Bani-Etemad's *The Blue-Veiled*. Also screened were Mohsen Makhmalbaf's *Salaam Cinema* (1994) and Jafar Panahi's *The White Balloon* (1995). In the long run, and after the initial shocks of this phenomenal exposure had disappeared, the presence of this worldwide audience for Iranian cinema had a catalytic effect on the rest of its history, which was soon to unfold.

The French daily *Le Monde* reported in its 4 August 1995 issue (I still remember the exact kiosk in Lausanne where I picked it up) not only to the French but to all future audiences of Kiarostami the significance of this event, with an added political twist to the effect that "whoever is expecting from him a spectacular condemnation of the mullah's regime will be disappointed. Kiarostami is not particularly suicidal...." One will indeed search in vain in Kiarostami's cinema for political pamphleteering, or for ideological statements immediately accessible to a global audience. An "independence of spirit," as Jean-Michel Frodon, the distinguished French film critic who wrote this piece for *Le Monde*, called it, is what is most evident in Kiarostami's cinema. In his judgment, Kiarostami's choice of children as the principal subjects of his films is at least partially explained by the debilitating element of censorship. What Frodon noted in Kiarostami's oeuvre was *"la diversité et la cohérence."* The diversity and coherence of Kiarostami's cinema was something that even Iranians themselves were only intuiting before this sudden global attention, which began to have a stimulating effect on our own understanding not only of Kiarostami's cinema but Iranian cinema in general and the culture that it represents.

Frodon's article in *Le Monde* drew attention to Kiarostami's camera work, which, he noted, is deeply animated by his peculiar sense of reality. "In front of Kiarostami's camera," Frodon suggested, "the smallest place, the smallest object, exudes a secret beauty. Everything is worth being filmed when it is filmed with such dignity." Comparing Kiarostami's cinema to the Italian masters of neorealism, Frodon detected a "sensuality," an "absence of didactics" far superior in the Iranian filmmaker. In Frodon's judgment "a beauty, humor, and vigorous exigency" characterizes Kiarostami's cinema, even in his pedagogical films for children. In a perhaps forgivable attempt to assimilate Kiarostami's cinema into a French vocabulary, Frodon read Kiarostami's *Hamshahri (Fellow Citizen,* 1983) as the verification of a sociological insight of Jean-Luc Godard, who "has often said that had we filmed the Place de l'Etoile, we would have learned much about social relationships as well as about infectious [social] diseases. That is exactly what Kiarostami has done [in *Fellow Citizen*]." Frodon ultimately described Kiarostami's films as works that reveal a "powerful thought, a moral exigency, and an extreme sensibility."

It is impossible to miss in Frodon's French review of Kiarostami's Iranian cinema the joyous enthusiasm of an explorer who by serendipity has just landed on the shores of a rich and beautiful territory. With a full retrospective of Kiarostami's cinema, the forty-eighth Locarno International Film Festival anointed him, as Frodon put it, "*l'un des trés grands cinéastes d'aujourd'hui.*" Depicting Kiarostami as "the 'locomotive' that has pulled to the Occidental light the cinema of his country," Frodon was not an exception in showering Kiarostami with praise and admiration. Some of the greatest directors from around the globe, from Akira Kurosawa and Wim Wenders to Jean-Luc Godard and Quentin Tarantino, were among the luminaries who were reported as having expressed great admiration for Kiarostami's cinema.

These aesthetic appreciations of Kiarostami's cinema were by no means at the expense of ignoring the political context of his films. Frodon's piece in *Le Monde* was subtitled with the provocative question: "How can one of the greatest contemporary filmmakers be from an Islamic Republic?" Frodon was quick and accurate in recognizing the connection between the simplicity of Kiarostami's cinematic aesthetic and the particular problems of cultural production in an Islamic Republic. Kiarostami's "aesthetic and civic ambitions," Frodon noted, are circumscribed by the fact that he has to operate "in the particularly constraining and complex context of the Islamic Republic." In the same vein, he also recognized the ambivalence of the officials of the Islamic Republic vis-à-vis the success and reputation of Kiarostami abroad. Frodon accurately analyzed that ambivalence as "the mixture of suspicion toward the artists and the pride of being admired by foreigners and the diplomatic use to which they can put this [positive] image."

So as you can see Kiarostami's cinema has received a far more positive reception outside his homeland—unmercifully vilified at home and yet enthusiastically glorified abroad. It is safe to say that had it not been for the accidental chance of the no man's land of film festivals and the naked eyes of a foreign audience, the culturally compromised eyes of Iranians would never have seen what Kiarostami is trying to show. Kiarostami's cinema is, in my judgment, too simple, and the Iranian perspective too conspiratorially compromised, too culturally curtailed, for a revolutionary aesthetic to register in the immediate neighborhood of its own creative vicinity. It seems to me that Kiarostami had to be celebrated abroad in order to be understood domestically at home. This is a bizarre thing to say, but I believe it to be true. A dialectic soon emerged between his foreign admirers who were trying to figure out his cinema and his native audience who were trying to see him otherwise than they had. Kiarostami makes films neither for his foreign audience nor for his domestic audience. He just makes films—and that categorical bifurcation between domestic and foreign audiences has performed its historic function and is no longer valid. There is nothing wrong or right about the dialectic that I am proposing between Kiarostami's foreign and domestic audiences. That is the way things happened around his cinema—it is the result of that dialectic that matters—the catalytic effect of his European admirers trying their best to see what Kiarostami was up to, and the global recognition of Kiarostami that they thus facilitated made his domestic audience rethink their conception of his cinema.

Notice the fact that by and large Iranian film critics know quite well what the French and other Europeans say about Kiarostami (for they read them in their original or else in the abundance of perfectly competent Persian translations of these sources), while Europeans have no blessed clue what Iranians say about Kiarostami, unless they read about them in an essay or book written in one of their languages. This is the simple logic of European colonialism and has nothing to do with cinema. We "Orientals" know their languages far better than they do ours. Those Europeans who knew our languages, the Orientalists, are by and large dead or dying—and even if they were alive they never cared about contemporary Iranian (or Arab, Indian, etc.) anything, least of all our contemporary art. If you were to put a poem of Shamlu or a film of Kiarostami in front of, say, Bernard Lewis (you don't know him; he is an octogenarian Orientalist), he would not know which way to run. The Orientalists by and large treated us as residual remnants of mostly ancient cultures. But European film critics are not Orientalists. They do not know how we speak and they cannot read what we write. The imbalance of that relationship in this particular case has actually worked to the advantage of understanding Kiarostami's cinema better, for the French (and by extension European) reception of Kiarostami's cinema has functioned like a catalyst, activating otherwise dormant aspects of our reading of it. Please note that I am not saying that the French understand Kiarostami's cinema better than we do (that's what Kiarostami himself believes and he is wrong), but that their understanding of his cinema agitates something otherwise dormant in Iranians' own grasp of what the great Kiarostami is up to. The reason for this has to do with the aesthetics, politics, and analytics of spectatorship. When you take a work of art out of its immediate and perforce limited context and place it on a global pedestal that very work of art begins to sing and dance to a different tune. Art, as I just wrote in an essay about Shirin Neshat, has become incessantly site-specific. It was the change of that site, the relocation of the venue in which Kiarostami's cinema was received and perceived, that radically changed how we understand it.

The avalanche of international prizes that fell Kiarostami's way had a crescendo effect that could not be ignored. In August 1992, the François Truffaut Prize was given to Kiarostami for *And Life Goes On*. He received the Roberto Rossellini award earlier that year during the Cannes Film Festival in May. Other major and minor film festivals around the world soon followed suit: Locarno, Rimini, Montreal, Dunkirk, Amsterdam, Istanbul, Valladolid, Chicago, São Paulo, Singapore, Rome, Melbourne, Venice, Athens, Toronto, San Francisco, Beirut. Film critics the world over could not praise Kiarostami enough. They lavishly compared him to Rossellini, Renoir, and Truffaut. When in 1997 his *Taste of Cherry* won the coveted Palme d'Or at Cannes, his reputation as one of the world's most prominent filmmakers was thoroughly established. This was no fly-by-night operation; this was the global celebration of an artist who Ozu-like had kept his nose to the grindstone and over a lifetime of sustained and serious work cultivated his craft—in exquisite detail. Kiarostami had become for Europeans a reality *sui generis*. Scarcely anyone talked about people who had come before him, filmmakers (forget about poets and novelist) from whom he had learned his craft. Sohrab Shahid Sales was dying in Chicago barely noticed except by a small group of Iranians. Arapik Baghdasarian—no one knew who he was. Ahmad Faroughi Qajar was buried deeply in the bosom of thick and irrelevant histories of Iranian cinema. Amir Naderi (Sisyphus-like) was climbing the Olympian mountain of his career as an American filmmaker. History is cruel. But art is beautiful. It ultimately does not really matter that Europeans (French in particular) think they invented Kiarostami. In a way they did. What matters is a body of work that had now transcended any national boundary, and that its global audience—facilitated precisely by the very same French film critics who could not care less about the origins of Kiarostami in Iranian film, fiction, and poetry—had started soliciting, seducing, and teasing out from one of the greatest artists Iran has ever produced meanings and significance otherwise hidden to Iranians' altogether too-self-conscious eyes.

This is not the complete picture, though. In addition to his domestic detractors and foreign admirers, there is a third circle of commentators complicating our grasp of Kiarostami's cinema even more. Because the officials of the Islamic Republic, the illegitimate inheritors of a legitimate revolution, have sought to take advantage of the global recognition that Kiarostami's cinema is receiving, the political opponents of the Islamic Republic at times have deeply resented Kiarostami's success, not because they fail to recognize the brilliance of his art but because the target of their political anger is taking advantage of that cinematic success. The psychopathology of this situation is quite evident. More than a quarter of a century into the successful failure (yes "successful failure") of the Iranian revolution, there are still mountains of perfectly justifiable anger among Iranians against the clerical takeover of their revolution. And any global success that an Iranian artist now receives inadvertently legitimizes the Islamic Republic—and thus the painful paradox of rejoicing in Kiarostami's global recognition and yet getting angry at the advantages of this success reaped by the Islamic Republic. I remember very vividly when Hamid Naficy organized one of the earliest Iranian film festivals, at UCLA, and Parviz Sayyad mobilized a demonstration against this festival. For months Sayyad was writing articles against Naficy in various venues. It was an exceedingly torturous time, for they were both right—Naficy had done a great service to put together a magnificent festival when people scarcely knew about Iranian cinema; and yet Sayyad had a point that the success of this festival meant the whitewashing of the criminal atrocities of a medieval theocracy. That this was by no means Naficy's intention or even the point of any of the films he had curated became an entirely irrelevant fact.

Another example of this debilitating problem is to be found in Reza Allamehzadeh's critically insightful account of Iranian cinema in the Islamic Republic. Allamehzadeh's *Sarab-e Cinema-ye Islami-ye Iran* (*The Illusion of Iranian Islamic Cinema*), which was first published in Saarbrücken, Germany, in 1991, argues that the most internationally acclaimed Iranian films have been produced not because of but despite the official censorship brutally imposed by the propaganda machinery of the Islamic ideologues. Allamehzadeh asserts that none of the leading Iranian filmmakers is a particularly believing Muslim in the ideologically charged (or any other) sense of the term. Speaking of Makhmalbaf, Allamehzadeh says that he "has exited the crowd of committed and devout Muslims" after the making of his famous feature *Dastforush* (*The Peddler*, 1987). While preserving his critically positive judgment of Kiarostami and of *Where Is the Friend's House?* in particular, Allamehzadeh condemns both the Islamic Republic and the Locarno Film Festival for having accepted this film, which was produced in 1986 but was included in the festival in 1989 against the specific stipulation of section C, Article 6 of their bylaws, which says that only those films produced during the preceding twelve months may be included in the annual festival.

Allamehzadeh's criticism of the Islamic Republic (written in Persian, published in Germany), Parviz Sayyad's bitter attack against Hamid Naficy for having organized and Iranian film festival, and many other similar incidents categorically failed to have any effect on the enduring global reception of Iranian cinema in general and Kiarostami's cinema in particular. The French magazine *Positif*, in its 400th issue, asked a number of leading film directors from around the world to identify the previous generation of filmmakers who had had an enduring influence on them. Kiarostami was given the distinct honor of being included among these directors. His response was published in French, and then in its original Persian was published in the February 1994 issue of the monthly *Film*. A remarkable confession of Kiarostami in this statement is that for the last twenty-five years he has scarcely seen a film, that he cannot stand sitting through a film, especially his own. Fellini, however, and particularly his *La Dolce Vita* (1960), has had an enduring effect on him. Of *La Dolce Vita* Kiarostami wrote:

> In my judgment, *La Dolce Vita* is a complete picture
> of a moral and social collapse. People who had lost
> all their principles sat, with perfect intelligence and
> awareness, witnessing their own demise, wasting
> their lives in absolute passivity. *La Dolce Vita* was
> the celebration of incompetence and hopelessness.
> People...with no stability and in utter disappointment
> followed endless events, while Fellini, à la Dante,
> through a poetic disorder and a sagacious vision, warns
> of an obscure and dangerous future, which we can now
> feel after some thirty years. Some thirty years before
> he spoke of the corruption of modern civilization
> and the collapse of all principles, of the absolute and
> utter destruction of moral virtues, and he spoke of a
> rejection of the pseudo-intellectual bourgeois world.

Kiarostami's take on Fellini, and on *La Dolce Vita* in particular, is quite revealing in terms of his own reading of the reality and received culture he has sought to change and negotiate, through what here he calls a "poetic disorder." Film appears to be the most effective artistic medium through which he can engage in that negotiation, for as Yann Tobin noted in his reading of *And Life Goes On* (in *Positif*, October 1992), this film "is also a grand film on cinema, its powers and its dangers, its magic and its artifice, its truth and its lies."

By the beginning of the twenty-first century, the systematic canonization of Kiarostami had reached irreversible proportions. Perhaps the appearance of Alberto Elena's magnificent book, *The Cinema of Kiarostami* (2005), might be considered a landmark in this canonization. With unparalleled research and impeccable insights, Elena studied deeply and widely Kiarostami's cinema. Even Jean-Luc Godard's tongue-in-cheek statement, "Film begins with D. W. Griffith and ends with Abbas Kiarostami," appears on Elena's book cover as a sign of unequivocal approval. Elena himself systematically and unequivocally praises Kiarostami and is entirely intolerant of the slightest critical jab he senses toward any aspect of Kiarostami's cinema (he takes an unfair swipe at me too, but that's cool—he is a fine critic). Meanwhile Geoff Andrew wrote an equally insightful short book on Kiarostami's *10*, and it became an almost impossible task to try to keep track of learned books and insightful essays being written on Kiarostami. Monographs in English, French, Italian, Spanish, and Persian have kept appearing throughout the early 2000s. Edited volumes, collected essays, selected interviews, PhD dissertations—Kiarostami became a phenomenon. He soon surpassed the status of just a filmmaker. His paintings, photography, video installations, theatrical experiments with Taziyeh, and even his poetry became the subject of global attention. A collection of his poetry, *Walking with Wind* (2001), was translated and published in English. His translators, Ahmad Karimi-Hakkak and Michael Beard, otherwise perfectly reasonable scholars of modern Persian poetry, got curiously carried away in their praise and made the rather ludicrous claim that Kiarostami was "the most radical Iranian poet of his generation, perhaps of the century." What absolute nonsense is that? But no one, they thought, was looking. When quoting this bizarre and idiotic passage, Geoff Andrew cautiously added that he could not vouch for its accuracy. He was wise in doing so. For it is a stupid statement—false, misleading, disrespectful of a stellar heritage of Persian poets from Nima Yushij forward, hard at work for over a century to earn and deserve that praise. But no one was minding the shop. Nima was dead, and so was Ahmad Shamlu, Mehdi Akhavan Sales, Forugh Farrokhzad, and Sohrab Sepehri. Neither Andrew nor anyone else interested in Kiarostami's cinema knew these poets. It was a bizarre and at times obscene situation as people who ought to know better jumped on the bandwagon, made fools out of themselves, abandoned their critical perspectives. But in the midst of all this at times cruel, at times curious, at times pestiferous, sad, and opportunistic *marché folklorique* stood the glorious cinema of Kiarostami itself—defiant, majestic, confident, wise, worthy, a still ocean all by itself, on the silvery surface of which one could sail forever, entirely indifferent to and unaware of the treasures and treacheries it buried deep below.

Between his admirers and his detractors inside and outside his homeland stands Kiarostami's cinema, constitutionally irreducible to any propaganda for or against an Islamic, or any other kind of, Republic. If Kiarostami is successful at holding our attention and teaching us to see differently—and he has endured so far for more than four decades, through an imperial dictatorship and a gut-wrenching revolution, an Islamic theocracy, and, perhaps most challenging of all, the paradoxical forces of a global limelight—he will map out the principal contours of a post-metaphysical mode of being in which no ideology, no absolutist claim to truth, no meta-narrative of salvation will ever monopolize the definition of "identity," the constitution of "subjectivity." Any attempt (this is a fact of Kiarostami's cinema) to locate and define a "statement," or worse a "message" or a "politics," in him, is utterly misguided. This is not to say that Kiarostami does not have a perspective on, or a reading of, the Iranian political reality that is unmistakably his. That reading is an angle on reality that has emerged with remarkable consistency in Kiarostami's films, over a long cinematic career. But there is no politics in the ordinary sense of the term in Kiarostami's cinema. The visual vocabulary of his *actual* realism is decidedly aesthetic, from within which a politics of emancipation is envisioned in the face of otherwise catastrophic political failures. But to understand that, I have to explain to you how exactly I mean to draw a politics from Kiarostami's aesthetic without committing structural or normative violence to it.

Let me begin that reading from an angle that has always made sense to me. Ordinarily, the critique of Enlightenment modernity and its constitution of subjectivity has remained squarely limited to the heart of the project itself, either subverting its continued validity (Michel Foucault) or else seeking to sustain it (Jürgen Habermas). The extension of the critique of the Enlightenment to its colonial frontiers, a project just begun, will have to take note of the emancipatory act of the aesthetic (a singularly ambitious project begun by Theodor Adorno that needs to be extended to the colonial constituency that he, like all other European post-Enlightenment critics, systematically ignored). The counter-narrative lucidity of the work of art, its "charismatic" rupture of the politically and metaphysically routinized, or its autonomous claim to counter-truths explodes the set boundaries of an Enlightenment-predicated, and for us colonially mitigated, subjectivity. The work of art *makes* an artist an artist, a Kiarostami a Kiarostami. But the work of art itself, *Through the Olive Trees* released from its creator, has a function that is always *deferral*—meaning it is always ipso facto postponed and delegated in its acts of signification. Attending to a work of art is thus countersigning its authorship—whatever significance its author has originally assigned to it, the work can conspire with distant readers to betray and transgress. I do not believe in the absolute autonomy of the text, or the author, or the reader. I believe in that famous triangle that the Italian hermeneutician Umberto Eco suggests, a triangle formed along the intention of the author, the intention of the reader, and the intention of the text. It is that triangular, notoriously unpredictable, dialectic operation in the phenomenon of a work of art that I think provides an emancipatory aesthetic.

The "ears" of the Other who hears, as Derrida puts it in *The Ear of the Other: Otobiography, Transference, Translation*, or the "eyes" that see, are the site of that countersigning a work of art. By substituting the ear for the author as subject, Derrida has sought to displace the site of the signification and thus release the self-centeredness of the subject. In the colonial outlands, however, we have been told to sit down and listen. For us, as the captured audience of the colonizing Self, our "ears" were always already pierced. We made the colonizing Self possible by being the colonized ear of an absolutely necessary Other. Because we could never write an "autobiography," we do not see anything particularly revolutionary or earth-shattering in the proposition of "otobiography." We were born, or better yet aborted, otobiographically. It is second nature to us on the colonial frontiers that no work of art is the sole source of its own authority, because for us the artist's signature is indeed a very recent phenomenon. "If Lars von Trier makes a film," I remember a young Egyptian filmmaker once told me, "it is called 'a Lars von Trier film,' but if I make a film it is 'an Egyptian film.'" This absence of a signature also has a catalytic effect on the loosening and de-sedimenting of the rigidity of the sovereign subject who has been wont to observe us. There is a plurality of counter-interpretations, as a result, a hermeneutics of emancipation, in the unpredictability of the ears and eyes of us as being born, or aborted, as the Other. The Other is, and we as the Other are, located far and away as much historically as geographically, as when we, as the colonials, hear and watch the theorists of the metropolitan centers of power, as when we actively remember or try to forget our own forefathers.

To speak or listen, remember or forget, ours is the task of being born into our own sensory history while fully alert of its already collapsed teleology—that it was never meant to mean anything or go anywhere. I am resisting calling this what our old mystics used to call "to live in the moment" (*ibn al-waqt*) for although it has an uncanny similarity to it, it lacks any mystical metaphysics. In other words, we need to find where our ears and eyes are, just touch them, rediscovering our essential sense perceptions, for what we have received and inherited is a manner of colonially de-subjected sensory servility that hears but does not listen, sees but does not watch. When I call us "colonially de-subjected," I do not mean, as usually our critics allege, to blame everything on European colonialism and the Christian missionaries that kept it company. No. That is not what I mean. What I mean is the preponderance of power, and the critic of that power. It really does not matter if the gun that is pointed at you is held by a white European or a "colored Oriental." A gun is a gun is a frightening thing. What I mean is that dialectic of power that the colonial extension of the logic of capital necessitated and exacted. It is in the context of that dynamic that we are colonially de-subjected. We are damned if we do and damned if we don't—for our minds, even (or perhaps particularly) our critical minds, are always already colonized—this is what I mean by "de-subjected." Now, to map out that sensory topography, to put our hands on our ears and eyes and sense and feel them and what they do, Kiarostami has had to enter into the no man's land, the twilight zone, of flattened-out reality in which things can begin to signify nothing, persons and volumes and animals and lines and trees and dots and emotions and concepts and colors can once again fade into a tapestry of a pre-significatory state so that Kiarostami's camera can begin only to imply the possibility of another mode of reading reality. In a conversation with Philippe Piazzo and Frédéric Richard in *Positif*, October 1992, Kiarostami was asked about the nature and function of the trip in *And Life Goes On*: "Is it ultimately real or fictive, lived or dreamed?" they asked Kiarostami. "You put me in a difficult spot," Kiarostami answered.

> The perception of reality is such a complex and nuanced phenomenon that we cannot really give a definitive answer to this question. The best of all positions undoubtedly consists of being ceaselessly in motion between dream and reality: This is a place of ideal life, my space of preference. My attitude is to refuse all convictions of reality, it is to sit between the two chairs of the real and the dream, to stay in motion and alive. My perception of reality is always the source, the mobilizing force that pushes me to make movies. The real always has a power of fiction and of poetry that excites me and stimulates my creativity. This is the way I stay always faithful to reality....
> It is a constant rule that animates all my films.

This is a crucial clue for reading Kiarostami's cinema. For what we see in *Through the Olive Trees* is Kiarostami's mastery of his own version of "truth," which he detects and places between a reality he wishes to reverse and a vision he cinematically imagines. As a master ironist, Kiarostami crafts a meticulous labyrinth of subtle negotiations between fact and fantasy, radically suspending the whole conception of what is really "real." There is a studied unstudied-ness and a deliberately loose logic and rhetoric to Kiarostami's preferred modes of narrative—sporadic, spasmodic, non-sequestered but nevertheless inconsequential sequences, suspicious and shy of any grand narrative. Evident in his *Nama-ye Nazdik* (*Close-Up*, 1990), Kiarostami is fascinated by that nebulous borderline where reality submits to fantasy. In *Close-Up*, he had the same concern when he told the (real-life) story of a man who out of love and admiration for a leading Iranian filmmaker, Mohsen Makhmalbaf, pretended to be he, and went so far as fooling a whole family into believing that he was

Makhmalbaf and that he intended to make a film about them. *Close-Up* turns this (real-life) story into a disturbing, yet endearing, tale of fantasy as reality. But that man, Sabziyan, did make a film about that family. Did he not? He had one of the greatest filmmakers of his time shoot it and document his lifetime fantasy of being Makhmalbaf, which he was—and thus the power and beauty of that penultimate sequence when he and Makhmalbaf get on a bike and ride through the streets of Tehran. There you see it in full, fantastic, and objective projection: fact made of fantasy.

In *Through the Olive Trees*, Kiarostami has precisely the same fixation with that shadow land where reality and illusion begin to negotiate their boundaries, and give and take their respective anxieties—of one being too real and the other too fictive. Toward that end, Kiarostami's camera is alternatively documentary-like and passive, sedate and agitated, yielding to the shaking movements of a truck on a country road in one sequence and suddenly shifting to a long shot of green pastures and olive trees studded with the colorful dresses of women and young girls in another. The lyrical roughness of Kiarostami's narrative is both a function of and a necessary angle on the story he wants to tell, to the received reality he wants to subvert. As a strategy, the confrontation between reality and illusion—between the shaky de-visualization of the real and a numbingly stable gaze at its transparency—begins to corrode edges of the metaphysics of the real and dismantle its aging authority.

Here, we are at the heart of Kiarostami's counter-metaphysical re-signification of the real and through it the active re-subjection of his immediate audience, a project to which all his French (and by extension European) audience, without any exception, has remained oblivious. The immediate journalistic treatment of Kiarostami in Europe and the pathologically hostile reception he has suffered at home have both failed to see through the simplicity of his narrative to his monumentally ambitious project. To reconstitute a sovereign and defiant subject at the receiving end of European Enlightenment modernity—where we as Iranians share a destiny with all other post-colonials—is easy, if we are conscious and alert that both the project and all its theorists, beginning with Kant himself, wrote the colonies out of the Enlightenment; and yet it is difficult because of the hegemonic power of an intimidated acceptance of that project. Such aesthetic strategies as fictionalizing the real and realizing the fantastic are intuitive to us and yet not theoretically thought through or analytically articulated. For us the act of dismantling the metaphysics of our inherited orders has assumed a colonial inflection, not by choice but by necessity. As a revolutionary break from our colonial predicament, art has always been the exceptional way out of our political cul-de-sac. The reception of our art in the colonizing centers of power, in Kiarostami's case France in particular, always presents the danger of dulling the edge of that emancipatory potential. While it is a splendid cause for celebration that the French have "discovered" Kiarostami (in my judgment for all the wrong reasons), it is crucial for a critical reading of his cinema for us not to stop at the gates of *Cahiers du Cinema*. Kiarostami had to be misunderstood by the French for the rest of the world to understand and celebrate him. That Iranian critics have vilified Kiarostami does not mean that the French have really understood him. If Iranians have failed to see the revolutionary power of Kiarostami's aesthetics, the French have assimilated that aesthetics into their own. Consider, for example, Laurent Roth, who in his essay "Abbas Kiarostami, le dompteur de regard" ("Abbas Kiarostami: Taming the Gaze") in *Cahiers du Cinema*, (July–August 1995) sums up the whole interpretative premise of his reading of Kiarostami on the assumption that:

> *Une premiere constatation s'impose: la ou d'ordinaire la création d'un artiste est plutôt brimée—entendons le cadre de l'œuvre de commande en contexte institutionnel, ici renforcé par un régime politique autoritaire, que ce soit celui du shah d'Iran ou de la République islamique—nous assistons au contraire au prodigieux épanouissement d'une œuvre qui exploite avec une surprenante liberté toutes les hypotheses et toutes les combinations possibles pour le cinema.*

> At first, an immediate realization imposes itself: where ordinarily the creativity of an artist is often circumscribed—namely in works that have been institutionally commissioned and enforced by an authoritarian political regime, whether the shah's or that of the Islamic Republic—there on the contrary we witness a prodigious blossoming of an oeuvre that exploits with a surprising freedom all cinematic hypotheses and possibilities.

It is not *despite* the authoritarian context of artistic production that Iranian art is emancipatory; it is *because* of it. Creative intelligence emerges and strengthens much more rigorously in opposition than in conformity. It is impossible to theorize the texture and disposition of that art from the center of metropolitan power—where there is always a condescending "surprise" even at the moment that Iranian art is celebrated and praised. One has to place that art and the artist that creates it at the colonial frontier, at the distance from that center to see how it is emancipatory precisely because it has not been theorized by the First World (as they like to call themselves), precisely because it cannot be theorized by the beneficiaries of the European Enlightenment, and precisely because it has to locate itself at a site of signification where neither a Persian monarchy nor an Islamic Republic nor any other claim to "traditional authenticity" can compromise it.

As you can sense, I am categorically against this kind of bleeding-heart, brotherhood-of-mankind, universalistic aesthetic into which the French and other European admirers of Kiarostami are trying to conjugate his cinema. The French in particular are very much in a hurry to whitewash and forget their horrendous colonial past (for decades Gillo Pontecorvo's *Battle of Algiers* was banned in France) via this pushing and pulling of other national cinemas into directions that they ipso facto resist—the manufacturing of a universal ethics against the very grain of the history that the French colonialism in particular has been instrumental in marking with barbaric brutalities. But consider the irony that while the French film critics are systematically robbing Kiarostami of the national, regional, and emotive universe of his cinema, one of their most distinguished philosophers Jean Baudrillard rightly speaks of the creation of what he calls an "aesthetics of indifference." Well, if you let works of art be (as in interpreted from) where they are produced and read and have them register where they are meant to mean and signify, then you would not have an aesthetics of indifference, would you? There is much, much, that is at stake in art—in the aesthetics of its formal defiance of material history in particular. Please notice, my point here is not to over-politicize Kiarostami in order to compensate for his over-aestheticization by the French, but to alert you to the damage done to the integrity of Kiarostami's oeuvre by both aesthetically and politically uprooting it from where it was produced—at the colonial edges of an artistic modernity that imbues it with a particular mode of aesthetic signification. That we have so far miserably failed to theorize that aesthetics and trace its function in producing a sovereign and defiant subject does not mean that it is open season for the *Cahiers du Cinema* filmcrits to produce a whitewashed version of Kiarostami. I would not blame Kiarostami himself for having been frustrated by his Iranian critics and found a happier abode among his European admirers. But I do believe that his art has been much shortchanged in that company.

Kiarostami's is a cinema of emancipation in the most trans-normative sense of the term, a transmutation of all the symbolic orders of reality into an imaginative disorder where things can begin to mean just about anything. And yet anchored in the anarchic possibility of that moment is the *actual* realism of a border zone where facts and fantasies have long since abandoned their metaphysics of certainty. There and then Kiarostami has taught his camera how to un-tell the truth. Surfing on the surface of reality, against all the inherited and incumbent metaphysics of signification and meaning—Iranian, Persian, Islamic, European, colonial, and, above all, that horrid emptiness "the West," Kiarostami's cinema, banking on generations of poetically imagining ourselves otherwise, is against all ethics and against all politics—defiant, suspenseful, unyielding, mysterious to all vernaculars of power: just like his own cinema. This is all that Kiarostami's cinema is doing—but the devil is in the details. So fasten your seatbelt and come along.

For Kiarostami, that maneuverability has always been an evasion of the real in the imaginary and a simultaneous attendance of the imaginary on the real. Throughout *Through the Olive Trees*, Kiarostami tests the blurry boundaries of fact and fiction, the no man's land of the (un)real where facts fear fantasies, where fantasies brace and muzzle reality. In this, his aesthetically most compelling version of his fixation with the nature of reality, Kiarostami narrows in on the traces of a would-be love story off and on camera. A camera crew and a director from Tehran have landed in a paradise-like village, Koker, in northern Iran, recently devastated by a massive earthquake. There is an operative precision in the making of docu-fiction that has now become the defining language of Kiarostami's vision.

The fictive/real camera crew has jammed the front door of the home of a young couple who are to be the central characters of the would-be film (shooting a scene from Kiarostami's previous film, *And Life Goes On*). The husband is to come home in this scene, drop a masonry bag he has been carrying at the door, exchange greetings with his wife, and then change clothes and leave. That is the non-event of the film-to-be-made (*And Life Goes On*), which Kiarostami in turn takes and weaves into a love story he now wants to tell. So *Through the Olive Trees* frames *And Life Goes On* by way of a ruse—soon abandoning it and taking its own course of action. Kiarostami's alter ego is Mohammad Ali Keshavarz, a veteran Iranian actor, who early in the film introduces himself to us as such and says that "In this film, I play the director." It is on the premise of that oxymoronic shot, the director in front and not behind the camera, that *Through the Olive Trees* begins to tell its circuitous (hi)story. In a telling scene that captures that circuitous arrival in the really fantastic world that Kiarostami generates, Keshavarz-cum-Kiarostami addresses a group of young schoolboys who have been cordoned off in a corner to watch the making of the film and says to them, "Children, you are not supposed to cross this line to come over here where we are making the movie. Do you mind if I come to your side?" Then he proceeds to go to their side, thus transgressing the visible line—a rope—that is to separate reality from fiction. The director takes one of the children's school texts and quizzes them on their knowledge of local geography. Now, at this

very moment, and as soon as he has passed beyond the rope, the director is in the land of Oz, in the realm of the (un)real. With that move, the
whole fictive borderline between fact and fantasy is visibly and literally
crossed. This border crossing is by far the most revolutionary event in
Kiarostami's cinema. With the crossing of that rope, Kiarostami makes a
fictive representation of himself, an actor, cross the border from the fiction of making a film called *Through the Olive Trees* into the factual world
of its behind-the-scene, which is itself the fictional world of making *And
Life Goes On*, which was the factual world of finding out what happened
when an earthquake destroyed the region that Kiarostami had filmed in
his fictional narrative film called *Where Is the Friend's House?*

This is a crossing between the real and the fantastic in the manner
of a parody. The director is doing something for the locals that actually
matters. These kids need a teacher, which they obviously lack; otherwise
they would not be sitting there watching a film being made. Which one
is more important, a lesson in geography or the observing (and taking
part in) the creation of a film? The same self-parody is evident when
the assistant director is taking Hossein, the protagonist, to the set and
runs into a construction site barring her access to the set. The mason in
charge of construction bluntly suggests that instead of taking an able-
bodied man like Hossein to make an actor out of him, she should let him
come and work on the building being constructed. As a rhetorical device,
Kiarostami's self-parody works like a double-edged sword: It makes the
real and useful world reveal its inherent fictionality, and, simultaneously,
it makes fiction palpitate with reality. The result of this strategy is that
reality can no longer innocently deny its fictionality, nor can fiction claim
aloofness from reality. This double-erasure of the real doubly material-
izes the fictive, as it fictionalizes the real.

There is much of local logic that is either assimilated or else yielded
to by the intruding camera crew. When the director finds out that the
local cook in his camp, Mr. Baqeri, has recently been widowed, he
suggestively asks him why he does not get married again. "It is uncon-
scionable," the sixty-something cook responds, "I was married to my wife
for a lifetime, we have six children together. It is not fair for me to get
married again now that she is dead." The director of course recognizes
his intruding presence. This directorial intrusion turns the location of
this entire event, the village of Koker, into a paradisiacal site of reinvent-
ing reality, with Hossein and Tahereh (the two chief protagonists) as the
Adam and Eve of this Garden of Eden. Kiarostami knows that his presence in this place is momentary. Early one morning he confides to one
of his crew, the man who had acted as himself in *And Life Goes On*, that if
he were to shout at the village of Koker from a distance, "the soul of the
people" would answer him back. There were only two words that when

shouted out loud were echoed in the landscape: "Hello" and "Goodbye."
If you were to shout "Hello" at the valley, the village would answer you
back and greet you—"Hello!" If you were to shout "Goodbye" after
that first "Hello," the village would echo back "Goodbye." But after the
"Goodbye," the next "Hello" would not even be answered/echoed. After
saying "Goodbye" the intruding camera crew should just pack and leave
and never return. This is a terra incognita, the remissive space where
the borderline between fact and fiction can be negotiated anew. But this
world is not real. We are in a twilight zone.

What does Kiarostami do in this twilight zone of (im)possibilities? Hossein and Tahereh are the two central characters whose story holds the film
together. Hossein is a construction-worker-turned-actor who is ambitious
and upwardly mobile, having sworn not to touch another brick. Tahereh
is the young daughter of a couple who perished in the recent earthquake
and who is now living with her matriarchal grandmother. Tahereh is
selected by Kiarostami's alter ego, Mohammad Ali Keshavarz, because
of her mute beauty, which is sustained by a piercing gaze that drives poor
Hossein to madness, and does not leave the audience entirely unaffected
either. She is selected from a handful of equally beautiful young girls who
are surrounded by a sea of less gifted classmates.

The opening shot, a pre-credit sequence that begins the narrative, is
also what puts a post-revolutionary Iranian audience in awe of an emerging aesthetic. Imagine an open space in the middle of an olive garden in
which stand some one hundred young girls all garbed in what in Iran
is called "Islamic dress": dark colors, baggy coats, topped by an equally
dark scarf, tightly set, leaving all but the roundness of the face covered.
Then the heavy wind blows the long robes and the flying scarves into the
agitated branches of the olive trees. Dark and light spots on olive green
is the contrasting vision with which Kiarostami's camera makes love from
this to the very last moment of the film. The film in its entirety is cast
and photographed in a fresh olive green, spotted white, and scattered
colors, all against a background of khaki dirt—sprouting life from the
hearth of an earthquake-ravaged earth.

A shaky camera that is never quite sure where to stand, a story
line that cannot resist departing tangentially, a dialogue that oscillates
between a Tehrani accent and the local Gilaki dialect, a fiction that is prohibited by a reality it cannot control, a paradise-like village ravaged by an
earthquake and invaded by this outlandish camera crew, a director who
while waiting for a new leading man casually leaves his set to mingle with
the local children or chat with the cook in his camp, and scores of other,
similar ends that release this film and all its narrative boundaries into the
surrounding hills of the village are the defining moments of Kiarosta-

mi's deliberately free-form mode of storytelling. He dwells comfortably, deliberately, and with an ease that disarms all concocted readings in the ironic space he crafts for his camera between reality and all its opposites. One should not see this film with any expectations of where the lines of demarcation are drawn between fact and fantasy, between the real and the concocted, between the received and the staged, between location and studio, between living and acting. One has to let oneself loose to permit Kiarostami's camera to reveal a mode of being carved between any set of binary oppositions. He has been hard at work to create and perfect this aesthetic space and *Through the Olive Trees* is by far his most successful version of it.

Kiarostami's shaky camera, however, is kept steady by his assistant director (played with remarkably deceptive ease by Zarifeh Shiva). She is addressed by her real name, "Ms. Shiva," throughout the film. She is the axis of an otherwise perfectly confusing cross-breeding of fact and fantasy. Her clapboard opens every shot of the film within the film (*And Life Goes On* within *Through the Olive Trees*). But Kiarostami cannot pass up any chance for irony and double-erasure: While the clapboard is ostensibly for the filming of *And Life Goes On*, the wording on it actually contains all the details of *Through the Olive Trees*. Within that double-erasure (two cinematic narratives canceling each other out), "Ms. Shiva" becomes the very image of determined order while the whole world around her seems to be plunging into a bottomless pit of confusion. She is like mother earth herself restoring order to a life devastated by an earthquake.

Every nonevent in *Through the Olive Trees* works toward creating and sustaining this transparency of the real. In real life Hossein is in love with Tahereh, but Tahereh does not as much as answer his greetings. Yet in the film the Tehrani director is making Tahereh play Hossein's wife. In that electrifying span between the directorial liberating command of "Action" and the brutal abruptness of "Cut," Hossein lives a fantasy for which his entire being yearns. Between that brutal "Cut" and the next liberating "Action," he has to live the debilitating anxieties of a life cut short by an "acting career," a love left brutally unrequited. In fantasy, Hossein shouts at his wife for having inadvertently dropped water on a stranger while watering her plants. In reality, he offers her tea on a tray adorned with a freshly cut flower and tells her, between the two takes of the same scene, "I will never scream at you when we marry. For me marriage is this. I offer you tea and flowers, and you'll do the same for me." After "Action," Hossein is the happy husband of a beautiful wife and the proud owner of a gorgeous house, perfectly confident in the ability of all his bodily movements. After every "Cut," he is commanded by the camera crew to water the plants or serve them tea or attend to one chore or another.

This trading between the real and the fictional, and the resulting transparency of those phenomena, puts forward a radically subversive reading of a culture of inhibition tyrannically institutionalized by a theocratic revolution. No young woman speaks to a young man in this film. Tahereh in fact epitomizes forbidden speech, which elsewhere is equally present. Young men do not fare much better. There is an absolutely mesmerizing scene where Azim, a local man who was first supposed to play the lead role, finally confides in the director that he cannot talk to Tahereh, "because whenever I talk to a girl, I stutter." This is the ultimate sign of an arrested culture in which an unarticulated sense of fear and shame prohibits the most natural of acts.

As much as Azim stutters, Hossein is eloquent, rhetorical even, with an abundance of philosophy that seems to come naturally to him. During a ride in a truck he begins to share with the director his frustration with Tahereh and her family. They refused to let him marry their daughter simply because he does not own a house. He has been a construction worker since he was eleven years old and yet he still does not own a house. "Well," Hossein reflects with noticeable irony, "then there was an earthquake and nobody had a house." Hossein takes the earthquake as a sign of divine justice for his broken heart. He refuses the director's suggestion to marry an illiterate gypsy girl because, he asks, what would be the point of an illiterate man who does not have a house marrying a girl who is equally illiterate and does not own a house. "Those who are literate, rich, and own a house should marry those who are illiterate, poor, and do not have a house," he proposes. That way things would be distributed equally. Otherwise, "What's the point of those who already have a house marrying those who also have a house? What would they do with their extra house?" The director's rejoinder on the logic of capitalism entirely escapes Hossein.

Hossein's real love for Tahereh, however, solves the director's fictive problem, because under the warm gaze of Tahereh he defies the culture and speaks his mind and heart to his love. As a carnivalesque occasion, film is a subversive moment in the otherwise repressive monotony of a routinized culture. Precisely because of that subversiveness, *Through the Olive Trees* is phenomenally successful in portraying the suppressed sexuality of a culture. There is an absolutely beautiful scene during the truck ride when the director begins a conversation with an older woman. She says she does not understand a word he says because she only speaks the local dialect. The director does succeed in engaging another older woman in a banal conversation about where they have been and where they are headed. In the meantime, he notices a stunningly beautiful girl sitting next to the older woman with whom he is talking. He makes a futile attempt to ask her name, when he is cut short by Hossein's admonition: "Here, strangers do not ask young girls what their names are." During this entire episode the young girl hides her face, especially her gaze, behind her mother's back. She never as much as utters a word.

Tahereh's grandmother does speak loud and clear, though, as do other older women and young ones when in each other's company, disregarding the presence of the grandfatherly director. The only other time that young girls speak is when they are not in front of the camera. The film exudes a culture of inhibition, which narrows in on the young men and especially young women, with their innate sexuality thus accentuated and denied. The penultimate sequence, a brilliant tracking shot that weaves the gracious walk of Tahereh down the winding path through the olive trees, is the silent scream of this denial. Throughout this scene, Hossein talks incessantly in a desperate attempt to persuade Tahereh to marry him. Tahereh walks fast yet graciously, with her young body adorning every moment of the sequence, never pausing for an instant to say a word. Kiarostami is conscious of the utter brutality of this silence. In fact, he makes a brilliant point of it when Hossein and Tahereh are waiting between two takes and Hossein resumes his ceaseless verbal supplication, to no avail. When he talks, she pretends to read from a book. "I understand if in front of all these people you don't want to say anything," Hossein interjects. "But if you care for me, would you just turn the page in your book?" The camera waits desperately on Tahereh, the book, and her hesitant hands, while her fingers hold the tip of a page. She does not turn it. Hossein reformulates the same question, as if in a second take, and this time the camera oozes with the anxiety of an almost turned page.

The plot of *Through the Olive Trees*, to the degree that it can be called that, is animated by a succession of cultural inhibitions. But the film also becomes a transgressive movement whereby Kiarostami's (re)reading of reality can effect emotive resonances beyond the cinematic space he demarcates. In this space, Kiarostami defies all the logic and rhetoric of narrative strategies by alternating successfully and incessantly between the expected familiarity of the factual and the promising suggestions of the fantastic. The story of the film within the film (the fantasy) is thus never anything more than a would-be sequence of innumerable, mostly unsuccessful, cuts. The fictive transparency of the real is effectively achieved by weaving an almost real sequence into the fabric of a life momentarily interrupted first by an earthquake and now by this bizarre group of filmmakers.

The strategic necessity of this interruption is evident throughout Kiarostami's vision of this paradise-like village. In fact, intrusion and interruption are the operative modes of this vision. But if that is the

Masters & Masterpieces of Iranian Cinema

case, then how can a story be told—how could a story be started and ended? Kiarostami tries to achieve narrative closure—as much as closure may be permitted in this kind of non-genre created over a lifetime of self-conscious filmmaking—via a long shot with the sheer beauty and intelligence that simply defies description. After a pause of momentary disappointment when he sees Tahereh first disappear into the olive garden and then emerge from it into the wide pasture, Hossein chases her down a slope that ultimately takes him to her side. The two tiny creatures, now mere spots in the vast and ripe olive-green tableau, abandon the intrusive gaze of the camera and almost disappear into "real life" when an instant of hesitation on Tahereh's part sends Hossein jubilantly running up the track, toward the camera, as the most subtle suggestion that he may have received a positive answer. At this moment, the camera has the instructed decency of standing on the hilltop, leaving the young couple alone to the privacy of their emotions. The camera of course does not blink. It simply stands there, gazing through a long, submissive, and singular look, perfectly content to watch a jubilant Hossein climbing up toward it. Kiarostami has crafted this long shot—with only one master shot, no coverage, and only a suggestion of mise en scène—with impeccable control. The long shot is almost identical to the penultimate sequence of *Close-Up*, where Kiarostami again instructs his camera and sound crew to stay out of private, and supremely beautiful, moments in people's lives. Right before the last long shot in *Through the Olive Trees*, Keshavarz/Kiarostami appears from behind the olive trees, un-directing his two protagonists, but this time not for his fictive camera, the whereabouts of which we remain blissfully ignorant, but for Kiarostami's, which must cast the last, long, and loving gaze. Gary Dauphin, in *The Village Voice* (on 21 February 1995), has brilliantly captured the essence of this hauntingly beautiful shot:

> How Kiarostami weaves together these disparate threads is the film's closing gift to its audience. The last scene is less an ending about Hossein and Tahereh than it is a revelation of what Kiarostami has been doing throughout the film, the image comprising a cinematic gesture so in keeping with his always gentle intrusions that to even reveal its existence is to do Kiarostami something of a disservice. Let's just say that much like Hossein's final trip through the grove of the film's title, getting the point of *Olive Trees'* ending requires a certain measure of faith, not so much in Hossein's blind love for Tahereh as in Kiarostami's love of all of them.

The closing shot also needs to be read in conjunction with the opening shot of the film, for if anything Kiarostami is the master of inconclusive closures. The last shot is even more perceptive if one remembers that Kiarostami's camera has learned to know its limitations and keep its nose out of people's business only after its very opening shot when the camera literally opens into a wall, from which both it and the car that carries it have to turn away as they begin their journey into people's lives. The initial version of this delicately constructed sequence was damaged in a film laboratory, and Kiarostami had to reshoot it. The camera and the cars of the director and the assistant director in fact have similar intrusive functions throughout the film. They always have to negotiate an uncomfortable passageway for themselves into lives and spaces in which they do not belong. Throughout the film these intrusions work toward the final resolution of a new man and woman that Kiarostami seeks to create. Thus in that very last scene, among the olive trees—the "Garden of Eden" Kiarostami has planted—walk a new Adam and Eve, cleansed in the green showers of love Kiarostami has generously poured over them.

To be able to reinvent a new Adam and Eve, Kiarostami and his camera must be quietly intrusive, and the act of trespassing is the principal method of subversion in Kiarostami's cinema. There is an eyewitness report from the location of *Through the Olive Trees* that is worth noting. In an article in the July 1993 issue of *Film*, Houshang Golmakani reports that Kiarostami's sets are remarkably quiet and peaceful:

> The few scenes that I witnessed being shot lack any sign of professional acting as it is understood in other films. It is as if nobody is filming anything. The serenity of Kiarostami's films are also evident on his sets. There is no screaming "Sound, camera, action!" nor is there any sign of the usual hustle and bustle of shooting. It is as if on one side people are going about their ordinary business, and on this side a group of people are gathered around a camera, doing something or another with it. There is no shouting of "Cut!" either. Kiarostami and Jafarian [the director of photography], who is even calmer, whisper to each other about the beginning, the end, about some technical issues, whether or not a retake is necessary. Occasionally, there is not even a whisper—just a signal or a look.

The aesthetic origin of this mode of looking in *Through the Olive Trees* can be traced back to its poetic genealogy. Kiarostami's cinematic

vision is best represented in what Golmakani has called, in jest, but nonetheless accurately, the "Rostamabad Trilogy." Based on a visual reading
of a poetic phrase from Sohrab Sepehri (d. 1980), this cinematic mannerism evinces a stunning simplicity. For example, the title of *Where Is
the Friend's House?*, the first in the Rostamabad Trilogy, is taken from the
following poem of Sepehri's, titled "Address" (which I translate from its
original so you can see how it moves in another language):

"Where is the friend's house?"
It was in the dawn when the rider asked this question.
The sky paused.
> *The passenger presented the branch of light he held with his lips*
> > *to the darkness of sands*
> *And pointed to a white poplar and said:*

"Before you reach that tree,
There is a tree-road, greener than God's dream.
On it, love is as blue as the feathers of honesty.
You go to the end of that road,
Which takes you to the other side of puberty.
Then you turn to the flower of solitude.
Just two steps before that flower,
You pause at the foot of the eternal fountain of earthly myths.
A transparent fear overcomes you there.
Then you hear a hissing sound in the fluid sincerity of the air,
And you will see a small child
Who has climbed a tall cypress to catch a bird in the nest of light,
And you will ask him
Where the friend's house is."

It is not accidental that Kiarostami finds in Sepehri a kindred soul.
He is doing visually what Sepehri sought to do poetically with words.
By the time Kiarostami reaches cinematic maturity in *Through the Olive
Trees*, his *actual* realism was a reality *sui generis*—no longer in need of
any verbal support. But in his visual poetry he sublimated Sepehri's language. Sepehri was to modern Persian poetry of the 1960s and 1970s
what Kiarostami is to Iranian cinema of the 1980s and later. They both
deliberately regress to an irreducible simplicity as a narrative strategy to
subvert the configuration of a reality they dislike. Theirs is a mode of
"weak thought" (*il pensiero debole*, as the distinguished Italian philosopher
Gianni Vattimo calls it), a post-metaphysical subversion of all absolutist certainties. They oppose "violent thinking," and thus do not propose
their positions violently, but by gently overthrowing the very foundation

of violent thinking. Sepehri's poetry and Kiarostami's cinema are in and of themselves aesthetic manifestos against a complicated reality that has progressed exponentially to unbearably ugly proportions. They both intensely dislike politics, ideology, and all historicized realities that go with them. Their poetic and cinematic perspective is a joyous celebration of life in its irreducibly material configurations. When one reads Sepehri's poetry, for example one of his masterpieces, "The Sound of Water's Footsteps," it is as if he had a poetic premonition of Kiarostami's cinema:

> *I am from Kashan.*
> *My life's not bad:*
> *With a piece of bread, a dash of intelligence, a bit of taste.*
> *I have a mother, better than a tree leaf,*
> *A few friends, better than the flowing water.*

It is very instructive to compare Sepehri's relentless fixation with nature with Kiarostami's similar attraction to trees, flowers, rivers, stones, and mountains.

> *I am a Muslim.*
> *The direction of my prayer toward a red rose.*
> *My prayer-cloth a fountain, I prostrate on light.*
> *The prairie is my prayer-rug.*
> *I take my ritual ablution with the pulse of windows.*
> *The moon and the shadows roll in my prayer...*

What I am suggesting here is a complete visual mutation of Sepehri's poetic diction into Kiarostami's cinematic form. A return to the irreducible simplicity of nature and all the glorious restrictions it imposes on being became Sepehri's Dionysian way out of the miserable, debilitating negation that reality imposed.

> *Love was visible, so was the wave.*
> *Snow was visible, so was friendship.*
> *Word was visible.*
> *Water was visible, and the picture of things in it:*
> *The cool resting place of cells in the heat of blood,*
> *The wet side of life,*
> *The eastern sadness of humanity,*
> *The season of wandering in the alley of woman,*
> *The aroma of solitude in the street of season.*

The two poet-painters (Sepehri was an accomplished painter, as is Kiarostami) are identical in seeking visual and poetic ways out of the engulfing configuration of reality through a subversive redefinition of it. If not read carefully, Sepehri could be dismissed as a pessimistic and disengaged poet, tired and angry at the world and seeking to live a life diverted from it. There is no misunderstanding Kiarostami, however. He is relentless with his disquieting and subversive gaze. That is precisely what deeply angers and frustrates his critics, who are the violent ideological metaphysicians of moralizing imperatives—metaphysically trapped in an Islamic Republic that speaks of even deeper maladies.

Beyond Kiarostami's quiet aesthetic revolution is a claim to a great moral transformation, a Dionysian carnival of death-rejecting, life-affirming, and loving laughter. Kiarostami's cinema bothers his hostile critics so much because beneath its gentle touch lurks a deadly serious determination to take his (incurably) guilt-ridden Shia culture to a pre- and post-guilt encounter with physical life. He has detected a festive Bacchanalian streak in life (long savored in Persian poetry) that is neither Greek nor Roman nor post-Islamic Persian nor the exclusive property of any historical culture. Culture, in fact, appears to Kiarostami as the aestheticized institutionalization of a historical tyranny, a brutal denial of the Dionysian mode of being that comes naturally with life and that is more life-affirming than frivolous, more death-rejecting than decadent, more loving than libidinal. He wishes through the relentless, though gentle, intrusion of his camera to de-aestheticize that brutal institutionalization of false guilt that denatures the historical person. He is defiant, and thus the appearance of arrogance, to all scared moralizers who denounce him. In essence they are envious of his Dionysian liberation from the deadening imperatives of a culture that has more than metaphorically sold the cash of this life for the promissory note of the one to come. In this, Kiarostami is true to the spirit of Omar Khayyam, another, more distant, of his poetic ancestors.

Alberto Elena (in his magnificent book *The Cinema of Abbas Kiarostami*) is wrong in thinking me irresponsible for having taken this part of Kiarostami for the whole and believing that I consider Kiarostami a "guileless optimist." This is no optimism—this is a journey within the heart of a heartless history. I read Kiarostami beyond the pale of optimism against pessimism. I am not pessimistic about our history to posit Kiarostami as its optimistic panacea. I read Iranian history as a saga of defiance, not a chronicle of signed and sealed destiny. Kiarostami's cinema is a Dionysian celebration of life, made infinitely more poignant by the fact that he is a filmmaker caught in a life-rejecting theocracy embattled by all presumptions of its own nightmares it calls, what else, modernity. There is something festive, joyous, discretely sensual about his subversive vision. His Rostamabad Trilogy ought to be seen precisely the same way historians of ideas today read Bakhtin's conceptualization of the carnivalesque under the Soviet system, with Kiarostami's Khomeini standing for Bakhtin's Stalin. Kiarostami's "characters," who are real, not fictive, are called by their own names, not by fictitious ones. They get up in the morning and exercise, or go for a walk, or get the breakfast ready. Kiarostami has an uncanny eye for the stunning simplicity of the ordinary, and catches its magical spell precisely at the moment when it begins to permeate and thwart the received metaphysics of obedience. Kiarostami's cinematic genius is to create supremely subversive sequences in a way that, precisely because of their simplicity and un-codability, lets them work their magic.

This un-codability is essential to Kiarostami's cinema. It would be not only futile but also utterly inane to try to read Kiarostami's cinema metaphorically. He is in fact a master practitioner of violating the metaphysics of interpretation by a physical, material, actual aesthetic. He is not trying to convey any hidden message. In fact, he destroys the very assumption of "hidden messages." His aesthetic is on the surface—that's where he is seeking to discover the mystery of things. Everything he frames with his camera is naked. "It is only shallow people," Oscar Wilde said, "who do not judge by appearances. The mystery of the world is the visible, not the invisible." (After Oscar Wilde, Susan Sontag wrote a beautiful book, *Against Interpretation*, expanding on that dictum. She just died, and we miss her dearly here in New York.) Kiarostami, too, is against interpretation. His aesthetic exists exterior to his camera, not internal to his received culture. It is perfectly natural that Kiarostami's hostile critics experience anxiety attacks when confronted with the naked beauty of his well-shaped, full-bodied, and voluptuous camera work. Theirs is a hermeneutics of hidden meanings and veiled sentiments; Kiarostami's is an aesthetic of exposed truth, naked curiosities: As Sontag says in *Against Interpretation* (page 7):

> Today is such a time, when the project of interpretation
> is largely reactionary, stifling…. [T]he effusion of
> interpretations of art today poisons our sensibilities.
> In a culture whose already classical dilemma is the
> hypertrophy of the intellect at the expense of energy and
> sensual capability, interpretation is the revenge of the
> intellect upon art. Even more. It is the revenge of the
> intellect upon the world. To interpret is to impoverish,
> to deplete the world—in order to set up a shadow world
> of "meaning." It is to turn the world into this world.

Through that naked camera the whole world is now watching Kiarostami's Iran. We may have anxiety attacks, we may not be used to looking at our naked bodies and exposed souls. But the historical moment is indeed momentous. In its 493rd issue, July–August, 1995, published in conjunction with the forty-eighth Locarno International Film Festival, *Cahiers du Cinema* provided a full dossier on Kiarostami's work, while the chief editor of the journal, Thierry Jousse, called him *"un des plus grand cinéastes du monde."* The cover of this issue of *Cahiers du Cinema* featured a glorious shot from the last sequence of *Through the Olive Trees*, accompanied by a picture of Kiarostami by Carole Bellaîche, and the caption read: *Kiarostami, Le Magnifique!* He had arrived, and with him, we were liberated.

The last step toward nihilism is the
disappearance into divinity.

−E. M. Cioran

Mohsen Makhmalbaf
A Moment of Innocence

I MISS MOHSEN. I miss my meandering walks with him through the streets of Tehran, the nooks and crannies of Cannes, and the back alleys of Paris. I miss the nobility of his anger, the serenity of his having mastered it. He swore he would never return to the United States, after the last time he was here and they harassed him at the airport. It was March 2001. Marziyeh Meshkini, his wife and colleague, was screening her first film, *The Day I Became a Woman* (2001). Then in May I flew to Cannes to see the premiere of *Kandahar* (2001). And in September hell broke loose. In October, I screened *Kandahar* here at Columbia to a packed audience to protest the war in Afghanistan. What terror has come our way ever since! I saw him again in May 2003, when I went to Cannes for the premiere of his daughter Samira's film *Five in the Afternoon* (2003)—and that was it. I was increasingly drawn to Palestine, he to Afghanistan, with an occasional phone call here and there. I miss him dearly. Until December 2005, when on my way back from Cyprus (from a conference on Rumi), I stopped in Paris for almost a week, walking and talking with Mohsen, incessantly. I miss the swiftness of his intelligence, the impatience of his wit, and the ocean of patience in which he hides it. But now, perhaps most of all, I miss his films.

I want to talk about the significance of Makhmalbaf in Iranian cinema. As soon as his name is mentioned, one cannot help remembering that his name is immediately identified with the entire project of Iranian cinema since the 1979 revolution. What is it about him that so agitates and divides people, Iranians in particular? Some adore him, some detest him, and many wonder who in the world he is. People are suspicious of his cinema because he was initially identified with the ruling cadres of the Islamic revolution, and as a result the secular and expatriate community simply refuses to believe that what they contemptuously dismiss as "Islamic" can actually have a claim on a cinema, an art, a poetry, a drama. But I think under the disguise of this controversy about Makhmalbaf lurks a more fundamental suspicion about Iranian cinema. Its rise to global prominence and celebration in the 1980s and 1990s has made even the staunchest Iranian nationalists a bit wary of so much attention. Iranians are not used to such celebration. We think, unrelenting as we are with our conspiracy theories, that there must be "a pot under the half-pot," as we say in Persian—something is fishy about this whole Iranian cinema thing. We could not possibly have something worthy of this global attention, that the world might be positively inclined to admire it.

At least since the American hostage crisis of 1979–80 (but I am pretty sure that the roots of this malady are much older), Iranians (of the sort that I have in mind here) seem to be positively grateful if the world is not actively demonizing them and simply letting them be. We do not believe, it seems, that we really have much to say or to show to the world, and thus so much attention makes us more than a bit nervous. In an article published in Persian in *Iran Nameh* in the summer of 1996, Farrokh Ghaffari, a veteran Iranian filmmaker and a pioneering figure of the best that Iranian cinema has produced, categorically denies that Iranian cinema is anywhere near that of Japan, as represented by Akira Kurosawa, or of Italy, as represented by Roberto Rossellini, or India, as represented by Satyajit Ray. He believes that the entire history of Iranian cinema has yet to achieve a status comparable even to that of Egypt or Turkey.

I believe that Makhmalbaf's roots in poverty and religious politics triggers in the mostly middle-class, secular, bourgeois Iranian audience a whole constellation of sentiments that they cast on the entirety of Iranian cinema. What exactly that anxiety is I am not quite sure. But it seems to me that, so far as we are hiding behind our veils of anonymity, we are concealing (and thus denying) our self-flagellation, or else with false modesty veiling our self-glorification. We dream in flamboyant colors of having achieved great things in our culture—particularly in the past. The world has not recognized us, we invariably believe. The Greeks did us wrong, then the Arabs, then the Turks, then the Mongols, then the British. Had it not been for such atrocious acts of tyranny perpetrated against us we are really a great nation, we invariably believe, and have monumental achievements of world culture to our credit. *The Massive Contribution of Iranians to World Civilizations* is the title of one copious book published under the auspices of the Islamic Republic. But these inanities are not the exclusive prerogatives of the Islamic Republic alone.Right now there is a bizarre controversy brewing among Iranians on the Internet over a major conference and exhibition that the British Museum has organized about the Achaemenid empire (where is my pillow?), and has opted to call it "The Forgotten Empire." "Why 'Forgotten Empire'?" our learned elders object. "Our enemies, the Greeks, wrote our history," they insist. What madness is this, I wonder as I read these reports. I for one am happy that the Achaemenids died and their empire was forgotten. All empires should die, dismantle, and never come back. What a shameful thing to have in one's history—a warmongering world empire—a bunch of militant imperialists going around the world and conquering people. The Achaemenids were the Americans of their time—Cyrus was like Bush. If I were around at the time of the Achaemenids I would have fought on the side of the Greeks—a splendid band of brothers they were, full of philosophers, scientists, poets, and dramatists. Do you think I would abandon Plato, Aristotle, and Homer for the pleasure of Cyrus' and Darius' and Xerxes' company? And whose fault is it if the Greeks wrote the history of their fights with Persians—and in fact made an art out of it? A massive empire made up of useless, illiterate, fanatical warmongers—why do I need to remember or claim those horrid ancestors, if indeed those Achaemenids had anything to do with me, some two thousand five hundred years after every Greek, Seleucid, Roman, Arab, Turk, Mongol, and to top them all European colonial officer came and marched their groins from one end of the "Land of Roses and the Nightingale" to the other? I don't really feel particularly connected to these Achaemenids, do you? Every time I hear the name of "Cyrus the Great" I am reminded of "Reza Shah the Great" and I want to run away and hide, rather than stay and claim ancestral heritage with him. "Persian Heritage Foundation!" Give me a break, people. Go get a life!

We insist and fight over the fact that a small patch of water to the south of Iran be called the "Persian Gulf," and not the "Arabian Gulf"—and while the Arabs and the Persians (God Almighty with all these inane epithets chasing after our common and endangered humanity) are busy fighting as to what to call that blessed basin of water (which itself could not care less one way or another—unless someone has taken a poll of the fish and the sharks and found out what in the world they wish to call themselves), not even a seagull can fly over it without the permission of the US Navy. It is neither the Persian nor the Arabian Gulf, I like to say, irking both sides of this inanity—it is the "American Gulf." This pitiful aggression becomes instantly passive, though, the second the world begins actually to look at Iranians, examine them, even, *horribile dictu*, like and perhaps even admire something about them. Take the camera away! It exposes too much. Things that even we may not want to see. Even Iranian cinema is a bit camera-shy, as it were.

Meanwhile, hundreds of film festivals throughout the world compete to get the best of Iranian cinema. When spotted on the street at Cannes, Locarno, Venice, or Berlin, prominent Iranian filmmakers like Makhmalbaf are harassed to the point of abuse by directors of film festivals to get their most recent films premiered at one and not the other. I know of one particular European festival director who promised the Iranian cultural attaché in his country better press coverage for the Islamic Republic if the ambassador made sure that a prominent Iranian filmmaker's latest film went to his festival as opposed to another's—and if you talk about the politics of film festivals and its adverse effect on national cinemas, they call you a terrorist and call the US Attorney General, and dispatch you to Guantanamo Bay, where Alan Dershowitz and Michael Ignatieff (consider yourself fortunate that you don't know who these people are) think you should be legally tortured because you are a ticking bomb.

Meanwhile, Iranian filmmakers themselves have all but lost their self-respect in their own open feuds over who gets to go to what festival. The fiasco over the *Tales from Kish* (1999) episodes, perhaps more than any other case, reveals this catastrophe. The story goes that six prominent Iranian filmmakers were approached by the Kish island tourism authority to make six short episodes that would focus on the Persian Gulf island of Kish, which is a free-trade zone. By the time of 1998 Fajr Film Festival, five of the episodes were ready; one was not. Of the five, one did not make it through the Islamic censorship. The other four films were screened at Fajr and collectively submitted to the Cannes authorities. Gilles Jacob and his selection committee liked only three and cut the fourth. Those three were screened at Cannes in May 1999 and all hell broke loose in Iran. Professional jealousy, fragile egos, and journalistic sensationalism all culminated in a most embarrassing show of the dismal pathologies of some otherwise distinguished and extremely creative artists. All involved in this fiasco managed to dishonor and discredit themselves. All this at a time when a massive student uprising, quite independent of the public intellectuals, was rocking the nation.

Thus, between two sorts of pathologies—one domestic, the other global; one nativist and phobic, the other corporate-driven politics of managing a globalized transaesthetics—a body of extraordinary art is being created and pulled tightly across its interpretative parameters to the two opposite poles of (1) the possibility of it soon withering away into oblivion after a quick flash and (2) the equal possibility of its enduring as one of the richest artistic creations in recent memory. What is particular about Iranian cinema is what is hanging in balance from that tight rope.

What exactly is particular about Iranian cinema? Quite a number of things. It comes out of nowhere. It is simple. Its exoticism is accessible. It is aesthetically ascetic, minimalist in its narrative construction, to the point of pictorial nominalism. It has "the Third World" written all over it. It reveals an image of a culture and society sharply different from that portrayed by the European and the US media since the Islamic revolution. Iranian cinema confirms its European and American audience's belief in the technological superiority of their culture. Iranian filmmakers are not glamorous and their simplicity set against the extravaganza of places such as Cannes or Venice is particularly disarming. A cinematic culture nauseated by excessive violence and tasteless sex is soothed watching a Kiarostami or a Makhmalbaf film. Iranian cinema is at once avant-garde and simple to read. No obscure theory is required to decipher it, as it is in reading a Bergman or a Tarkovsky or a Godard. Iranian cinema, in effect, laughs in the face of complicated cinematic theories, defies them all, posits its own manner of seeing things, and yet it cannot be ignored. Iranian cinema is neither theorized nor does it need to be theorized in terms (at once local and global) inimical to the social production of its own specific aesthetics. Iranian cinema is its own theory. Michael M. J. Fischer, a prominent American anthropologist full of theories, has written a massive book on Iranian cinema, *Mute Dreams, Blind Owls, and Dispersed Knowledges: Persian Poesis in the Transnational Circuitry* (2004), he calls it. Like its title, Fischer's book is full of useless insights. Fischer thinks Iranian cinema was produced for the private entertainment of him and his French buddies. It was not. You will never read a more disembodied book full of utterly pointless observations, quite neat and nifty theoretical gesticulations, and yet produced at the heavy price of plucking a national cinema out of its social habitat and playing Ping-Pong with its imageries. Yes, there is something quietly disturbing about Iranian cinema that demands and exacts critical attention—but only if you think too much about it. Most audiences don't. For me the model of scholarship and insight into Iranian cinema are defined by Alberto Elena's book on Kiarostami (exquisite, competent, thorough, respectful of the national culture that has given birth to a filmmaker) and Eric Egan's on Mohsen Makhmalbaf (precisely in identical terms). On Iranian cinema, people like Michael Fischer are out to lunch.

329

The unexpectedness of Iranian cinema was in part due to the serenity of the visions it juxtaposed against the violence of the world-media images about Iran that had preceded it. In an otherwise inconsequential piece that the American Broadcasting Corporation (ABC) did on the prominent Iranian filmmaker Dariush Mehrjui, I remember the reporter began his piece by showing footage of angry Iranians demonstrating against the US, burning flags and screaming their heads off, and then asking, "Are these Iranians?" He then gave a summary account of the urbane and polished life and career of Mehrjui—featuring both his habitat and cinema—and then concluding by again asking, this time with a rhetorical incredulity in his voice, "Are these Iranians?"

In a paradoxical way, the ugliest and most threatening face of Iranian culture had prepared the world for one of its most serene and reassuring vistas. It is as if the world had had a long, disturbing, and unrelenting nightmare in the violent images that characterized Iran, from the obscene self-celebrations of the Pahlavi monarchy to the cantankerous self-flagellation of a nation revolting against tyranny and then at war with itself and the world. But Iran, it seems, was waiting and wishing and thus preparing to give full celebratory birth to a reassuring negational interpretation of that nightmare in a cinema of simplicity, serenity, and innocence. The more violent and disturbing the nightmare the world had seen of Iran the more peaceful and reassuring the innocence of this cinema had to be—and, lo and behold, it was.

But in the projection of this positive, quietly contesting image, one cannot underestimate the influence of European intellectuals, the generation of 1960s activists, who saw in Iranian cinema a belated, though welcome, cause célèbre. In France, where the fate of Iranian cinema was sealed, we can find no more accurate statement about the moral and intellectual condition in which this cinema was received than in Julia Kristeva's paradoxical pronouncement in her book *Strangers to Ourselves* (38–39):

> Nowhere is one *more* a foreigner than in France. Having
> neither the tolerance of Anglo-American Protestants, nor
> the absorbent ease of Latin Americans, nor the rejecting
> as well as the assimilating curiosity of the Germans or
> Slavs, the French set a compact social texture and an
> unbeatable national pride against foreigners.... And yet,
> one is nowhere better as a foreigner than in France.
> Since you remain incurably different and unacceptable,
> you are an object of fascination: one notices you, one
> talks about you, one hates you or admires you, or both
> at the same time. But you are not an ordinary, negligible

> presence, you are not a Mr. or Mrs. Nobody. You are a
> problem, a desire—positive or negative, never neutral.

Much of the theoretical discussion of the culture of globalization, as those of modernity and postmodernity, remain by and large geographically limited to the centers of economic power and (despite the very nominal claim of the term) are not really global in their theoretical scope. But the celebration or condemnation of the phenomenon of globalization is a matter that cannot be decided from the vantage point of the globalizing capitals, without a preliminary attempt at locating the centrally designated peripheries (for there is no "periphery" without a body of racialized sentiments placed at a "center") in the global picture. Globalization, as Fredric Jameson has suggested (in *The Culture of Globalization*, page 55), "is a communicational concept, which alternately masks and transmits cultural or economic meanings," and as such it embraces the world in a closely tied network of moral and political exchanges totally unprecedented in the capitalist project of modernity. The technological, communicational, mass media, and electronic dimensions of globalization as both economic and cultural events are all the results of the inner logic of capitalism in full and uncompromised pursuit of raw material, cheap labor, and an ever expanding market. Nothing (in the so-called process of "globalization") has changed in the simplicity and organicity of that inner logic. It has simply given rise to ever newer, ever faster, and ever more effective modes of transforming cheap labor and raw material into consumer goods and selling them to an ever expanding market.

Now take Iranian cinema out of its Iranian origin and French reception and place it in this globalized context. What do you see? Not since Baron Joseph von Hammer-Purgstall's translation of Hafez into German in 1812, and after that Edward J. FitzGerald's translation of Omar Khayyam's *Rubaiyat* in 1859, has an aspect of Iranian art been received so widely and enthusiastically as Iranian cinema over the last two decades of the twentieth century. Hammer-Purgstall's *Geschichte der schönen Redekünste Persiens* (Vienna, 1818), which was based on Dowlatshah Samarqandi's *Tadhkirat al-Shu'ra*, had a lasting influence on German romanticism, on the poetry of Goethe and Rückert in particular, as did FitzGerald's translation on a generation of English poets. The world has changed much from the time of Goethe and FitzGerald. But today the world receives Iranian cinema in an entirely different way. Cultural institutions like the Cannes Film Festival and the Venice Biennale bring together the financial resources of governmental agencies and multinational corporations to the aid of "Third World" artists and in the process give those artists a forum. If romanticism was responding to the Enlightenment's instrumental rationalism when adopting Persian poets, today it is the attraction to a *minima moralia*, as Adorno would say, that informs the pull toward Iranian cinema. Globalizing capital continues to wreak havoc in the world and in response we have mystical flights in the form of the New Age transcendentalism of Deepak Chopra, who is equally attracted to Persian poetry (Rumi in particular). From Hollywood, California, to suburban New Jersey, Deepak Chopra's reading of Rumi navigates a psychopathology of moral anomie, both conditioned by and yet instrumental to the globalized collapse of any sense of purpose other than ceaseless production at the service of the planetary operation of capital. By the time that kind of self-delusional mysticism has exhausted its financial feasibilities and transmigrated in its soul and body into yet another shelf in the occult section of conglomerate bookstores, other commodities are (and must be) in the offing.

The minima moralia that the Iranian cinema at its best represents is, in fact, the result of two centuries of creative and critical exclusion from the project of modernity at its colonial terminus. In a way, Iranians (like the rest of humanity at large) were excluded from European modernity only to come back as the return of its repressed—the nightmare of what Immanuel Kant had called "the Orientals" and their fundamental (in his "pure judgment") lack of any sense of the sublime and the beautiful. From the colonial shadow of that Enlightenment modernity that Kant dreamed and other Europeans interpreted, Iranians, as postcolonial agents, can speak to the catastrophic consequences of instrumental rationalism and its progeny, capitalist modernity, with almost total impunity. If we need any theorizing, let me tell you right here and now, this is the site of our self-theorization, not the aping of European postmodernity (which we must of course understand, though that is not our problem) or Indian (or Bengali to be more exact) postcoloniality. Just because India was liberated from British colonialism (and then plunged into global capitalism) it does not mean that colonialism is over. Any kid in the streets of Baghdad or Kabul these days will tell you that. The problem is not with what Bengali theorists say, but with what the rest of us colonials do not say—namely, and so far as the issue of art is concerned, the specific terms of an emancipatory aesthetics domestic to our global predicament, and not (as they are wont to say) nativist to our conditions. Not a single sentence have I written on Iranian cinema without this predicament paramount on my mind—and then I get Los Angeles-based, Westwood-variety filmcrits reviewing my book and objecting to my complicating "the beautiful Iranian cinema." *As-Sabur jamilun*, "Patience is beautiful!" Do you know where this is from? Find it out yourself. It's good for you!

Iranian cinema, in its globalized context, tells the story of the geopolitics of uprootedness, as well as the condition of homelessness the world over, where scarcely anyone is at home anywhere, for the very logic of globalized capital denies it, sees it as superfluous. These days we seem to live in our e-mails and breathe in our cellphones. Globalized and homeless, fragmented people dwell in the figments of their own imagination—and thus art emerges as the virtual home of humanity at large, as it holds reality at bay and negotiates a new significance for it. Thus when we exit the warm illusion of a movie theater (when cinema is at its best) into the bitter cold of the real winter outside, the temperate memory of our magical musings will keep us happy until the next time when we find ourselves inside the magic box again. Every time I see a great film (just like last night when I saw Lars von Trier's *Manderlay*, 2005, during the New York Film Festival), and walk out of the movie theater and step into the street, I think the so-called real world is really a very badly made film, and I wish I could just get up and walk out—but I can't find the exit door.

In a collection of essays called *Crisis of the European Subject*, Julia Kristeva asks the most obvious question about what the unification of Europe and a globalized world will mean for people to continue to call themselves "European." As the crossed-out word in the title of the collection suggests, the question is not limited to Europeans, nor indeed should the question even be asked from the standpoint of a European—for in these cases the presumption "European" (and all the terror that it has perpetrated upon the globe) continues to claim authenticity. Europe is the invention of the Third World, Frantz Fanon once said. Be that as it may, the unification of Europe (and thus the crisis of the subject that it has posed—particularly if Turkey joins) is part and parcel of a more global reconfiguration of the political economy of power and its distribution. The geopolitics of the reception of Iranian cinema is just one among myriad other (far more urgent) questions that we would not have even asked as recently as two decades ago. Whereas Kristeva may think that the crisis of the subject is a European predicament, or may wish to ask it from a European perspective, we know only too well, at least since Gayatri Spivak's legendary essay, "Can the Subaltern Speak?," that the question is essentially flawed even if asked from the particularity of that position—for the "subaltern," the term that a group of Indian historians borrowed and expanded from Antonio Gramsci to describe those unwritten from history, were at the ultimate receiving end of this Europe now in subjective crisis. The question is global, planetary, as Spivak calls it, and it is in global terms that both the European and the non-European (categories that are by the nature and location of this question obsolete) ought to ask it. European or not, Iranian or otherwise, we have entered a new phase of what the British-German sociologist Ralf Dahrendorf has called the "atomization of individuals," whereby they are made susceptible to all sorts of emerging communal solidarities, for the porous fact of national boundaries also means the formation of transnational communities across borderlines and sentiments. Between the absolutism that empires imagine (and do not for a second think that the US neocons are the only people imagining imperially; there are plenty of them in Europe too) and the atomized individual stands the space of art—the virtual simulacrum of a universe where the emancipatory imagination can supersede the entrenched symbolics. If there is a politics to art (and there is) then here is something I would like you to know: That art, and cinema in particular because of its vast global reach, is the most wholesome alternative to a range of options that extends from mystical to militant solidarities that have emerged to embrace and give a wandering soul a home.

The (now global) crisis of the subject means not just the atomization of spectatorship but also the crisis of the creative ego for a number of young and old filmmakers. How and why is an Iranian artist to create, for what audience, in what context, and what logic and rhetoric of spectatorship will frame their creative impulses? These potentially paralyzing, possibly reinvigorating questions pair with the Iranian collective unconscious, which has to navigate the terms of its own presence though it is not quite at home in its global reconfiguration: tradition or modernity, economic or cultural, local or global, ethnic or national, Iranian or Islamic. It is impossible to imagine (but it is true) how even Abbas Kiarostami, globally recognized, remains deeply nervous about how long his celebration will last. (He recently served as the president of the Camera d'Or jury for the 2005 Cannes Film Festival, so he is still in pretty good shape.) Though the problem with his most recent celebration in London, in 2005, is that the Iranian expatriate bourgeoisie is systematically ethnicizing him and thus helping shortchange his cinema from art to anthropology. But nobody is paying any attention to these things, for the road to anthropology is paved with good nativist intentions.

The political culture of globalization amounts to an atomized spectatorship, crisis of the creative ego, a transaesthetics of indifference (as Jean Baudrillard suspects), a traumatic reconfiguration of the collective unconscious of a people, and the final dismantling of the cultural geography of the imagination. Under these circumstances, we should always choose to look at the material basis of cultural production, the ground zero of the creative ego, the soil from which artistic plants grow, roots descend, branches spread, and fruits ripen—and it is in that manner that I want to place, first and foremost, Mohsen Makhmalbaf's biography in Iranian cinema.

If you follow my argument so far, my point is that when we look at a filmmaker like Mohsen Makhmalbaf, his creative consciousness has come to fruition out of a collective unconscious that is deeply troubled and agitated by its own revolutionary traumas, and by its unfolding quest for freedom. Today, people look at Makhmalbaf's cinema and have no clue of the tumultuous times in which he was born, and in response to which he launched his cinematic career. Not just the Iranian but also the global memory in general is fading, and his cinema, like much else in our contemporary art, is seen in the vacuous air of overtly aestheticized or endemically anthropologized terms. Subsequently, a reading of Iranian cinema is emerging that is disembodied, bland, insipid, and at its worst in conversation with the most useless theories awkwardly applied to a postcolonial setting. It is imperative for those of us who still remember to place Makhmalbaf's cinema in the soil of its roots. Take the latter part of twentieth-century Iranian history and look at what has happened, and consider the turmoil in which Makhmalbaf was born and bred. He was not born with a camera in his hand. On his body, marred by torture, he literally carries the history of his nation. Immediately before Makhmalbaf's birth, in August 1953, the popular prime minister Mohammad Mosaddeq was removed from government by foreign powers. It is impossible to exaggerate the traumatic impact of this treacherous event on the collective psyche of Iranians. Mosaddeq's democratically elected government was toppled by a CIA- and MI6-engineered coup, putting Mohammad Reza Shah Pahlavi back in power with the direct support of the American government. The result was the resumption of autocratic rule, the destruction of all Iranian actual and potential democratic institutions, and the rise of underground resistance movements, ideologically predicated on both secular and religious ideas and sentiments. Arguably, no other event in contemporary Iranian history has had such an enduring traumatic event on the Iranian collective psyche as does the CIA coup of 1953, which happened just about four years before Makhmalbaf was born.

Soon after the downfall of Mosaddeq, the Tudeh Party, by far the most progressive leftist political organization in modern Iranian history (despite its slavish subordination to Soviet imperialism), became the chief target of Pahlavi repressive measures. The military branch of the Tudeh Party, under the leadership of Colonel Siamak and Khosrow Ruzbeh, was uncovered and destroyed, and Colonel Siamak himself was executed. An atmosphere of fear and intimidation now filled the Iranian political and social scenes. But new forms of resistance to tyranny began to emerge. A coalition of nationalist, socialist, and Islamist ideas and sentiments were soon brought together under the National Resistance Movement, which was formed under the leadership of Ayatollah Mahmoud Taleqani (d. 1979) and the engineer Mehdi Bazargan (d. 1992). By 1955, the Tudeh Party was almost completely destroyed and discredited and its remaining leaders forced underground. Meanwhile the shah, triumphant over his adversaries with the solid support of the US, joined the Baghdad Pact, which later became the Central Treaty Organization, by way of joining an alliance formed by the US against the Soviets. The Pahlavi regime now enjoyed the full military and political support of the United States and its NATO allies. The political struggles of the Tudeh Party and the National Front against the Pahlavi monarchy had made the king completely intolerant of any critical stance challenging his autocracy. But three major fronts of resistance now formed against him: a secular left, a liberal nationalism, and a combination of both in militant Islamism. Makhmalbaf was born and raised within the epistemic and emotive milieus of these three modes of resistance.

Soon after the coup of 1953, the leading Soviet revolutionary theorists reported to the Twentieth Congress of the Communist Party of the Soviet Union, in 1956, that revolutionary movements in the Third World ought to ally themselves with the national bourgeoisie. This was partly in response to the catastrophic failure of the Tudeh Party to ally itself with the Iranian national bourgeoisie as represented by Mosaddeq. The leaders of the Tudeh Party had meanwhile escaped from Iran and, in the Fourth Plenum of the Tudeh Central Committee, held in East Germany in 1957, admitted that they had made an historic mistake not to have supported Mosaddeq. Mehdi Akhavan Sales' poem "Winter," written in 1956, captures the utter desolation of the Iranian spirit at this moment, after the failure to establish democracy, having seen the seeds of that democracy uprooted and taken away, and having no hope in the future.

> No one responds
> to your greetings—
> heads are drawn
> into collars.
> No one raises
> his head
> to greet or converse
> with friends.
> The eyes cannot see
> beyond the feet,
> the road is dark and slippery.

It is right here, under these circumstances (with both Iranian socialism and Iranian nationalism having failed politically and having effectively cancelled each other out), that one Mohsen Ostad Ali Makhmalbaf was born in Tehran on Tuesday, 28 May 1957, to Hossein Ostad Ali Makhmalbaf and Esmat Jam-pour. They divorced after a marriage that lasted less than a week.

With the shah's anti-democratic persecutions intensifying, no serious institutional resistance to Pahlavi autocracy was any longer in sight. The Shia clerical establishment was either completely silenced or else in active cooperation with the shah. The young Makhmalbaf, meanwhile, was growing up in downtown Tehran under the protective custody of three mother figures: his mother, his maternal grandmother, and his maternal aunt, who formed a modest, devoutly religious family. They also saved him from being kidnapped by his father, who had married Makhmalbaf's mother as his second wife, for he did not have a son from his previous marriage; now he had a son whom he desperately wished to claim. Makhmalbaf thus grew up with three strong mother figures, no father, an overwhelming fear of being kidnapped by his father, all at a time when "the father of the nation," as we were told to call the king, was struggling to keep his shaky throne.

Leftist intellectuals for their part were meanwhile busy soul-searching. Religious revolutionaries were by and large silent. A literary and poetic form of resistance was taking shape. Makhmalbaf's mother worked as a nurse in a hospital and his upbringing was entrusted to his grandmother and aunt. His grandmother was intensely religious and told him colorful stories of saints and prophets as lullabies during summer nights on the rooftop of their modest home. His aunt soon started teaching him how to read and write, and introduced him to literature. His mother was the breadwinner, his grandmother the pious storyteller, and his aunt his teacher. No father in sight. *Pedar-e Tajdar*, the "Crowned Father," as we were told to call our king, was our father. What terrors we lived in those medieval times that framed our modernity! What even more troubling days were still ahead of us.

The election of the twentieth Majlis, in 1960, demonstrated clearly that there was no institutional basis for democracy in Iran. The two nominal political parties that the monarch had created, the so-called Nationalist Party and the People's Party, openly admitted their obedience to the shah, who in turn appointed Jafar Sharif Emami, who had no ties to either party, as his prime minister. Makhmalbaf's mother married the lawyer who had assisted her during her divorce proceedings. Makhmalbaf's stepfather was a devout religious man with strong political convictions; he was deeply committed to a young rebellious cleric called Ayatollah Ruhollah Khomeini. In the young Makhmalbaf's mind, the stepfather and the revolutionary father figure begin to replace his own estranged father and "the father of the nation," while the material evidence of his livelihood, soul, and intellect remained entrusted to three mothers.

On the strong recommendation of President Kennedy to initiate a series of cosmetic reforms to prevent a radical revolution, Mohammad Reza Shah, "Sun of the Aryan Race," replaced Sharif Emami with Ali

Amini in 1961. Prime Minister Ali Amini did initiate a few reforms and sought to eliminate some centers of corruption in the government. At the time, the young Makhmalbaf was undergoing an intense religious upbringing in a devout family. He spent much of his time in the company of his grandmother at the local mosque, while his aunt remained chiefly responsible for his home schooling. The shadow of his father and the fear of kidnapping remained over his head. "To me," he once told me in Paris, "God has always been identified with my grandmother. Nothing in the world was as soothing and reassuring as when she told me the stories of saints and prophets while I was falling asleep." I remember once in London, Esmail Khoi, one of Iran's most distinguished (radically secular) poets, also said that he only saw God once, when his grandmother was combing her silvery hair and the sun was shining on her head.

Hasan Arsanjani, Prime Minister Ali Amini's minister of agriculture, wrote a radical Land Reform Act in 1962, breaking the backbone of the Iranian feudal system, and then appropriated the land thus nationalized and redistributed it among the peasantry. The move was in complete harmony with changing the structure of the Iranian national economy from semi-feudal to state-sponsored capitalism and the manufacturing of a corresponding bourgeois nationalism. In the same year the publication of Jalal Al-e Ahmad's *Westoxication* was the most significant event of the decade in Iran's political culture. In this seminal text, Al-e Ahmad argues for the formation of a *national* political culture predicated on Iranian social and economic interests. Flawed and lopsided, Al-e Ahmad's argument nevertheless defined a whole generation of radical ideas. The young Makhmalbaf was kept aware of the tense political circumstances through his stepfather, who was politically affiliated with the religious radicals.

The assassination of President Kennedy in November 1963 eliminated the American pressure for reform. The shah modified the radical ideas of Arsanjani into a much milder policy of land reform and yet expanded it to include a wider range of cosmetic social changes to encourage the formation of a national bourgeoisie. Then, in June 1963, Ayatollah Khomeini, representing a coaltion of bazaar merchants and disaffected clergy, led an uprising against the shah. The displaced peasantry at the fringes of Iran's urban centers became his new revolutionary audience. Khomeini was captured and forced into exile. Makhmalbaf, age seven, was already aware of the religious uprising and (he once told me) began distributing revolutionary pamphlets on Khomeini's behalf. His stepfather became an even more ardent supporter of the revolutionary uprising. A major reconfiguration of the Iranian collective unconscious was now fully under way. The June 1963 uprising put the secular left and liberals on the defensive. The religious radicals had outmaneuvered them. After the June 1963 uprising, Al-e Ahmad, at a regular luncheon he had with a few friends, would excoriate the secular left for having failed to support Khomeini's revolt. After the June uprising, Al-e Ahmad's *On the Services and Treasons of Intellectuals* appeared in a clandestine edition.

The expulsion of Khomeini from Iran put an abrupt end to his revolutionary uprising, soon after which the shah resumed his reign with a vengeance, mobilizing the military, the security forces, as well as economic and bureaucratic measures to consolidate his autocracy, all fully supported by the United States and its allies. Makhmalbaf's life continued apace with his religious upbringing by his grandmother, his literary education by his aunt, his political awareness through his stepfather, all under the overwhelming love of his mother and the fear of his father. Makhmalbaf once told me he fell in love, when he was seven, with a five-year-old girl called Najmeh who had come with her mother to the same religious gathering, *rozeh-khani*, that he attended. It seems, I told him, he's always been multi-tasking.

In the complete absence of any serious political activity in the mid-1960s, Persian literature became the principal locus of intellectual revolt against the dominant powers. Ahmad Shamlu in poetry, Sadeq Chubak in fiction, Gholamhossein Saedi in drama, and Forugh Farrokhzad giving a poetic feminine voice to the insurrectionary consciousness now exemplified a whole generation of cultural resistance to power. Nascent political groups then began to emerge and complement these cultural developments. Three Muslim student activists—Mohammad Hanifnezhad, Said Mohsen, and Ali Asghar Badizadegan—formed the Mojahedin-e Khalq, perhaps the most powerful urban guerrilla movement in modern Iranian history (before it degenerated into a cult and mercenary army in the hands of Saddam Hussein), with massive popular support. They had met Seyyed Mahmoud Taleqani and Mehdi Bazargan, their spiritual guides, in prison after the June 1963 uprising. The Mojahedin-e Khalq soon emerged as a potent political force with a wide range of effective political activities. Oblivious to these developments, Makhmalbaf's imagination was thoroughly entrenched in a religious consciousness that conflated the sacred and the political together.

The publication of Sadeq Chubak's *Patient Stone* (1966), and its groundbreaking stream-of-consciousness narrative marked a new height in modern Persian fiction. The death of Forugh Farrokhzad in an automobile accident on 14 February 1967 silenced an eloquent feminine poetic voice. It was now the peak of SAVAK (the shah's secret police) control of the entire spectrum of political and cultural activity. Makhmalbaf was increasingly drawn to religious gatherings with an overt political aspect. Soon he began to form his own religious group, or *dasteh*, which met on religious holidays to commemorate the death of various Shia martyrs, but with evident political concerns. On the literary scene, the death of Samad Behrangi in 1968 in a swimming accident in the Aras River in Azerbaijan shocked his admirers in the capital. There settled a general atmosphere of defeat and gloom. The death of Al-e Ahmad in 1969 marked the end of an era in modern Iranian intellectual history. By far the most eloquent voice among his peers, Al-e Ahmad epitomized an entire generation of political activism—flawed, furious, passionate, genuine. His death coincided with the sudden appearance of Dariush Mehrjui's film *The Cow*, which commenced a glorious story in Iranian cinema. The twelve-year-old Makhmalbaf, oblivious to the significance of this film, did not even see *The Cow* at the time. Years would pass before the shah's censorship allowed the film to be screened in Iran, and even then Makhmalbaf's religious convictions prevented him from seeing it, for his grandmother had convinced him that music and cinema were *haram*—forbidden.

By 1970, the Tehran University campus was the focus of student political activism. A new generation of political rebels was now going beyond their parents' preoccupation with the Tudeh Party and the National Front. At places like the Hosseiniyeh Ershad (a well-funded religious establishment that organized public events), Ali Shariati (1933–77), a leading Muslim revolutionary, was actively engaged in giving new momentum to political Islam, providing a radical reading of Shiism leading up to the 1979 revolution. At the same time, though, Makhmalbaf's increasing political consciousness and activities did not prevent him at the age of thirteen from falling in love with an eighteen-year-old girl named Nayyereh from his neighborhood. He was honing his religious, political, and erotic sensitivities all at the same time, and these components became the alphabet of his future cinema.

To protect and prolong his illegitimate reign, the shah's pro-US policies became more pronounced. All the repressive measures of the regime notwithstanding, in March 1971 the People's Fadaian Guerrilla Organization (*Sazeman-e Cherik-ha-ye Fadai-ye Khalq*) was formed to advance a more aggressive Marxist agenda in Iran. The armed uprising in the northern region of Siahkal by a group of Fadaian guerrilla commenced a series of sustained attacks on the Pahlavi regime that culminated in their active participation in the 1977–79 revolution. In the same year the Mojahedin-e Khalq also resumed its urban guerrilla activities, initially targeting the obscene festivities celebrating the presumed 2500th anniversary of Persian monarchy, a spectacular show staged to lend legitimacy to the Pahlavi dynasty on the world stage. By now Makhmalbaf was fully convinced that he had to have a more active role in the political fate of his nation. He became increasingly disappointed with the mainline religious politics of the local mosques. Khomeini was nowhere in sight, tucked away in Najaf and out of touch with the more recent religious and secular movements that were working to topple the monarchy.

By 1972, both the Fadaian and Mojahedin were actively waging major urban guerrilla attacks against military and political targets, challenging the hubris of the Pahlavi regime. University campuses were flooded with revolutionary fervor. SAVAK and the police, and occasionally even elements of the army, brutally suppressed student protests. Makhmalbaf formed his own urban guerrilla organization, determined to take part in this national uprising. He once told me that his local mosque sent him on a mission to go to Hosseiniyeh Ershad, the religious establishment in which regular anti-regime lectures were organized, in order to plot the assassination of Ali Shariati. He went there, sat and listened to Shariati, and became mesmerized by his revolutionary ideas, and never set foot in his local mosque again. The active hostility of the traditional clerical establishment against Shariati remained a major component of the ideological movement of the mid-1970s. Shariati drew his constituency in part from disaffected youth from religious backgrounds, but also from secular activists disappointed with the legacy of the Tudeh Party.

The shah's self-confidence in the face of any opposition to his regime was such that he allowed for the public trial of Khosrow Golsorkhi, a leading Marxist revolutionary, to appear on television in 1973, and then announced his execution. During this year, the shah did not participate in the Arab oil embargo following the Arab-Israeli war of 1973, resulting in an avalanche of financial resources for his state apparatus. The Iranian oil revenue quintupled between 1973 and 1974, most of it spent on state-of-the-art military machinery purchased from the United States, which in turn began calling Iran an "Island of Stability" in the Middle East, meaning essentially that Iranian territory was used by the United States as a strategic location for pursuing its policies in the region, both against the Soviet Union and in support of Israel— Israel in grateful acknowledgment began helping the shah build his ambitious nuclear project. (The US did not object.) The oil revenue was in effect returned to the United States with the shah's purchase of weapons of such sophisticated nature that it far exceeded Iranian technical ability to operate them. American military personnel were then brought in to operate the weapons to protect the American global interest in the region, using Iranian resources.

Makhmalbaf's anti-Pahlavi passion, now fully developed, was charged by Shariati's ideological resuscitation of Shia Islam. In his extensive ideological tracts, Shariati had given political Shiism a new lease on life by wedding it to the Third World anti-colonial ideas of Frantz Fanon and African and Latin American revolutionaries. At this point Makhmalbaf had an almost mystical attraction to Shariati, who was eloquent, defiant, religiously musical, with a radical revolutionary ferocity informing his fiery speeches and discourses.

After a visit with Khomeini in Najaf in 1974, a group of Mojahedin-e Khalq activists seceded from their main body and formed a more overtly Marxist group called Peykar. This marked a succession of breakups in the urban guerrilla movement. But the general atmosphere of insurrection only intensified, and Makhmalbaf and his small band of comrades began plotting an attack on a police officer in order to steal his gun, rob a bank, and get more seriously involved in the armed uprising against the regime. Makhmalbaf was the leader of the group and chiefly responsible for disarming the police officer, which he failed to do, and was almost killed in the process. He was shot in his belly, captured, initially hospitalized, and then sent to jail in August 1974. He escaped with his life because he was too young to be executed. In the Pahlavi prison, he underwent severe and systematic torture, the scars from which still mark his body.

By 1975, Iran was fully integrated into global capitalism, exporting crude oil and importing consumer goods and military machinery (far above and beyond the Iranian national defense needs and entirely at the service of the US interests in the region). Increasingly dictatorial in his demeanor, the shah announced the establishment of the Rastakhiz Party as the single, comprehensive, political party of the country and demanded that all loyal Iranians enlist in it or else leave the country. To complement the aggressive de-Islamicization of Iranian political culture, the shah ordered the imposition of a new imperial calendar that replaced the commencement of history from the migration of the Prophet Muhammed from Mecca to Medina to the presumed date of the coronation of Cyrus the Great. No longer even remembering what exact year on what calendar we were born, we were now told to call him "Mohammad Reza Shah, Sun of the Aryan Race," if we ever dared to refer to him at all. We had to stand up at the beginning of a movie when we went to the theater. We had to sing his praises, dance on his birthday, do the same on his son's birthday, and every morning at school ask God to perpetuate his reign. Makhmalbaf spent the first year of his incarceration in the company of other religious and secular revolutionaries. His jailers continued to torture him. Today he can neither walk, sit, or sleep comfortably. His physical scars are also the insignia of our national wounds, deeply carved in the vertebrae of our political culture. Like him, we, as a nation, still cannot walk properly.

In 1976 reports by Amnesty International and the International Commission of Jurists documented massive abuses of power in Iran. In the course of his presidential campaign, Jimmy Carter made human rights a political issue. Makhmalbaf endured his second year in jail, spending much of his time, when he was not being tortured, reading history, sociology, psychology, philosophy, as well as Islamic texts. He was barely seventeen when he landed in jail, but he was now nineteen. If he had been born in suburban New Jersey, he could have been a Columbia undergraduate, plowing through the Core Curriculum, mastering the masterpieces of "Western Civilization," as they say.

The honeymoon of the Sun of the Aryan Race would soon be over. Disagreement with the Saudis on fixing the price of oil in 1977 coincided with a general market decline in crude prices, which in turn translated into a sudden decline in oil revenue for Iran. In June, Mehdi Bazargan and other prominent figures in the National Front and Freedom Movement wrote a letter to the shah demanding the restoration of the constitution. Meanwhile, the shah's visit to Washington, DC, was marked by a rambunctious student demonstration against him. The picture of the monarch wiping his tearful eyes (from tear gas that the police threw at the demonstrators) with his white handkerchief made it into the international press, including Iranian television.

Makhmalbaf had now completed his third year of incarceration. He still has bitter memories of how political prisoners who belonged to organized groups were vicious in their behavior toward people like him who were not part of their cliques. In prison, he once told me, he also learned the art of brevity, because he had to memorize instructions, abbreviate and summarize them, in order to communicate them to his cellmates. That art of brevity soon became a hallmark of his asceticism, and in turn found its way into his aesthetic minimalism, and from there into the virtual realism that defines his cinema. (You see how I trace the origin of certain aspects of Makhmalbaf's cinema to his prison experiences. This is quite a different manner of theorization from, say, sitting, like Michael Fischer, in Cambridge, Massachusetts, and playing long-distance Ping-Pong with Gilles Deleuze in Paris and using Makhmalbaf's cinema as your table. It is quite a curious pastime. But apparently Duke University Press is quite amused by the result and pays for this sort of postmodernity.)

In January 1978, an article attacking Ayatollah Khomeini in obscene terms was published in a Tehran daily, *Ettelaat*. Massive anti-government demonstrations soon followed in Qom, Iran's center of religious studies. By fall of that year, the Peacock Throne was trembling. In January 1979, massive anti-regime demonstrations engulfed the country. That month, the shah appointed Shapour Bakhtiyar, a respected National Front figure, prime minister, then packed up and fled the country. Soon after, Ayatollah Khomeini returned to Iran. Iran was euphoric. People poured into the streets, singing and dancing. The headlines of the emancipated newspapers read first, *SHAH RAFT,* "The Shah Left," and then, *IMAM AMAD,* "The Imam Came." It was a moment of historic catharsis—an entire nation releasing its pent-up frustrations, not just of decades and centuries, but of a millennial memory of tyranny. What would happen after the shah left was almost irrelevant. In March, a national referendum declared the formation of an Islamic Republic. By April, hundreds of former military and cabinet officials were summarily executed. In June, the draft of the constitution for an Islamic Republic was made public. In July, a severe crackdown on the freedom of the press ensued (I left my graduate studies at the University of Pennsylvania during this time and flew to Tehran to take part in many of these public demonstrations), and no public forum for the discussion of the draft constitution was available. Those who dared to defy the prevailing atmosphere and discuss the draft openly were subject to systematic attacks by hoodlums and thugs mobilized by the Islamists. In August, elections were held for a seventy-three-seat Assembly of Experts to prepare the final draft of the constitution; fifty-five members of the assembly were clerics, and the rest were equally committed to an Islamic Republic.

By September, more crackdowns on the press indicated that the constitution would never be subject to serious public debate. Secular revolutionaries were systematically smothered. In October, the shah arrived in the United States for medical attention. Fearing a repeat of the August 1953 coup, massive protests against the United States ensued in Tehran, in front of the US embassy. A group of students took over the US embassy and took the American diplomatic corps hostage on 4 November. Bazargan resigned his post in protest on 6 November. The revolution became more radical, more Islamized, and something called the Islamic Revolutionary Council took control of the country—the army and the police in particular, with everyone reporting directly to Ayatollah Khomeini. Under the smokescreen of the hostage crisis, on 15 November the Assembly of Experts approved the constitution of the Islamic Republic. By December of that year, the world's attention was entirely focused on the US hostage crisis, while Iranians were asked to go to the polls on 2 and 3 December to approve the constitution of the Islamic Republic. All opposition was either silenced or made to consent to the Islamic constitution. An Islamic government was now the official state apparatus. Khomeini was triumphant. In October, Makhmalbaf was released from jail, having spent four years and three months in prison—his full term. Soon after his release, he married Fatemeh Meshkini, and began to put his talents and energies completely at the service of the nascent Islamic revolution. Makhmalbaf was devoted to the revolution, serving it with dedication by way of trying to create a new revolutionary Islamic culture. He and his wife were particularly active with the national radio—covering the news, writing proclamations, supporting the fragile revolution.

The year 1980 began with the election of Abolhasan Bani-Sadr, a major economic ideologue of the revolution, as the first president of the Islamic Republic. In February, the first anniversary of the revolution was celebrated. The organs of the Islamic Republic were now all in order. In March, the first parliamentary elections were held, but the voter turnout was very low. The majority of the elected members of the parliament came from the clergy. In April, a failed mission by the US military to rescue the hostages resulted in the aggravation of anti-American fervor in Iran, further restricting any possibility of dissent inside the country. By May, a succession of counter-revolutionary plots to overthrow the Islamic Republic were reported in the Iranian and foreign press. In July, Mohammad Reza Shah died in exile in Cairo, Egypt. His death brought the Pahlavi (and with it the centuries-old tradition of Persian) monarchy to a symbolic end. (Years later, in May 2001, I visited his gravesite in the Rifahi Mosque, in Cairo. I have no idea why.) In August, Amnesty International denounced the arbitrary execution of dissidents and former Pahlavi officials in Iran. In September, Saddam Hussein invaded Iran and a brutal eight-year war began, bringing death and destruction on a massive scale to both sides.

In January 1981, as the Iran-Iraq War raged, the fifty-two American hostages, no longer useful to the Islamic Republic, were released (as a gift to President Reagan on his inauguration). Khomeini ordered a major revision of the revolutionary courts' procedures, having them preside over a brutal reign of terror, silencing all opposition to the Islamic Republic. Attempts of the Islamic Conference Organization and the Nonaligned Conference as well as by the UN to end the war were fruitless. In July, in the course of a new presidential election, Mohammad Ali Rajai was elected as the second Iranian president, but soon after, in August, President Rajai and Prime Minister Mohammad Javad Bahonar were killed in a bomb blast. Ayatollah Khamenei succeeded Rajai as the third Iranian president. In response to the attacks, Chief Justice Mir Hossein Musavi Ardabili presided over thousands of political executions. By December, Saddam Hussein was showing the first signs of defeat and proposed to end the war.

Around this time Makhmalbaf wrote *Marg-e Digari* (*Someone Else's Death*), an allegorical encounter between a general in his bunker on the verge of a massive military operation and Death. It is a claustrophobic reflection on the incomprehensible ability of people to kill other human beings. All through these years, Makhmalbaf's cinema was being formed and imagined (in his mind alone) in the most traumatic experience of Iran's recent national history. His metaphysical convictions metamorphosed to revolutionary proportions. It is these experiences of the national trauma—stipulated between a massive revolution and a bloody war—that later came to define his cinema.

In January 1982, the Islamic Republic began violent persecution of religious (the Jews and the Bahais in particular), ethnic (Kurds in particular), and political (both the Mojahedin and the Fadaian) minorities, while middle-class Iranian women were brutally forced to cover themselves from head to toe, a custom of which they had no memory, as Reza Shah had banned the veil in Iran, with equal barbarity, in 1926. In February, the ranking members of the Mojahedin-e Khalq were killed in a raid on a safe house. In March, the Fadaian-e Khalq suffered a major attack by the security forces of the Islamic Republic. The Islamic revolution, like all other revolutions, was eating its own children. In April, Saddam Hossein continued to call for a peace treaty with the Islamic Republic, but Khomeini refused to relent. The Iraqis began to bomb Iranian cities, in an attempt to force the Iranian authorities to accept a cease-fire. Under these circumstances the domestic political atmosphere had become intolerant of the slightest opposition to the Islamic Republic. In December, Iranians went to the polls to elect eighty-three members to the Assembly of Experts to decide the role of the Supreme Leader in the event of Khomeini's death. While Khomeini admonished revolutionary leaders' abuse of power, Iranian universities reopened throughout the country after a massive purge of secular academics.

It was during this year that Makhmalbaf made *Tobeh-ye Nasuh* (*Nasuh's Repentance*) and wrote *Sheshomin Nafar* (*The Sixth Person*). Now his films and fiction were fully at the disposal of the Islamic revolution and its ideals and aspirations. *Nasuh's Repentance*, as indeed the other two films that he would soon make, is elementary, stylistically and thematically—entirely negligible in Makhmalbaf's complete oeuvre. Evident in this early phase of Makhmalbaf's cinema is a full-fledged, fundamentally religious disposition, but this spirit was exorcizing itself from his creative soul, for him and the rest of the world to see. Without that exorcism, the rest of Makhmalbaf's story as a filmmaker would not have been possible.

To mobilize a systematic mechanism of repression, in March 1983 the Islamic security forces were consolidated into a new Ministry of Intelligence at the very same time that the official control of the women's dress code was put into the law. The war continued, despite further efforts by the Islamic Conference Organization, an international body formed by Muslim states, to end the war. By October of this year it became clear that the French were selling Super Étendard fighter planes to Iraq, fully equipped with Exocet missiles. Iran threatened to close down the Hormuz Strait. As President Reagan promised not to allow that to happen, the US Marine battalion headquarters in Lebanon was destroyed by a suicide-bomb attack, killing 241 Marines. (I was in a hospital in Allentown,

Pennsylvania, for the birth of my son Kaveh, when I saw the news on television.) The US implicated Iran in the bombing while Iran was busy further intensifying the war with Iraq, resulting in heavy Iranian casualties. In November, Iran threatened to close the Strait of Hormuz again, condemning the French for having sold the Iraqis Super Étendard fighters. By the end of the year the US began to shift its policy toward helping Iraq, fearing that a weakening of Iran's western neighbor would result in strengthening the Islamic Republic. "I hope they kill each other," Nobel Peace laureate and former US secretary of state Henry Kissinger was quoted to have said at this time, adding, "Too bad they can't both lose."

During this entire year Makhmalbaf was busy making his next two films, *Esteazeh* (*Fleeing from Evil to God*) and *Do Chashm-e Bi-Su* (*Two Sightless Eyes*)—artistically negligible and ideologically at the service of the Islamic Republic. Nevertheless, these films witnessed a noticeable improvement in his command over the camera, a distinct visual vocabulary, and a creative confidence. The critical community of Iranian cinéastes began to take notice of Makhmalbaf beyond his ideological identification with the ruling Islamists.

By February 1984, the war had extended on both sides to attacks on civilian targets in major cities. The Iraqi use of chemical weapons was reported, and condemned by the world community. In March, the Iraqi army began attacks on oil tankers, and the Arab League condemned Iran for refusing mediation. The year ended with even more failures to end the war, more bombs, more civilian casualties. During this time, Makhmalbaf began to take his chosen profession more seriously and read extensively on cinema. He was equally prolific in writing fiction, completing two short stories, "Valeh" and "Zangha" ("The Bells"); during the summer, he started working on his best-known novella, *Bagh-e Bolur* (*The Crystal Garden*), and in the fall he wrote *Hoz-e Soltun* (*The Soltun Pond*), another novella. These two works of fiction deeply complicate an appraisal of his early creative record, for there is not a trace of the committed ideologue in any one of them. It seems as if he had put his cinema at the service of the Islamic revolution, while his fiction remained the exclusive domain of cultivating his own aesthetic concerns. Most who categorically (and correctly) dismiss his early cinema have never bothered to read or consider his fiction of this very same period. They radically differ from his films, as if they were written by an entirely different person. As the war and the revolution raged, these two novellas saved Makhmalbaf for posterity.

Imagine that posterity and count the days and the distance of our humanity from our realities. Brothers killed brothers. Hatred reigned supreme. A glorious revolution went awry, and a fragile hope was shattered to pieces under the iron will of a raging old man—sending off his own grandchildren to the slaughterhouse of a senseless history. Measure and imagine the horrors of those days, the terror of those nightmares. Iran has become a nation of amnesiacs, memories having mercifully given way to oblivion—all except the troubled few, who are condemned to remember, chroniclers of our predicament as a people, a nation, a permanently postponed promise.

The tanker war claimed a Greek casualty in January 1985, as an Iraqi counteroffensive resumed in full. In February, the "war of cities" escalated, and the UN accused both Iran and Iraq of abusing their POWs. The campaign of terror against even the most innocent youthful public expression in Iran intensified. By March, civilian casualties on both sides reached catastrophic proportions, with the Iraqis using chemical weapons against civilian targets. In April, Ayatollah Khomeini moved to close the gap between the regular army and the Revolutionary Guard, consolidating them both into a warring army. The leaders of the Islamic Republic were split over how to end the war. Mehdi Bazargan's Freedom Movement was by now the officially sanctioned opposition and was, by and large, tolerated. By summer American and Iranian officials were swapping arms for hostages with Israel as an intermediary. Khamenei was reelected president in yet another mockery of democratic process. Then the Guardian Council disqualified the Freedom Movement candidates. Ayatollah Montazeri was officially named successor to Khomeini as Supreme Leader.

Makhmalbaf made *Baykot* (*Boycott*), wrote *Madreseh-ye Rajai* (*The Rajai School*), and in fall finished writing *Bagh-e Bolur* (*The Crystal Garden*)—except for *The Crystal Garden*, none of them were of any enduring significance. While his films served the metaphysical underpinnings of the Islamic revolution, or else exorcised his own bottled-up demons, his fiction is where he had already begun to discover the magic of an emancipated soul, of groundbreaking doubts—with human (all too human) details.

By January 1986, Washington was still selling arms to Iran in exchange for the freedom of hostages in Lebanon. Massive casualties on the Iranian side were reported in February in the capture of al-Faw, a strategically crucial peninsula in Iraqi territory on the Persian Gulf. In March, the UN confirmed and condemned the Iraqi use of chemical weapons against Iranian targets, both military and civilian. Bus bombs in Tehran and other cities killed and maimed civilians throughout April. Meanwhile, arms-for-hostages deals among Iran, Israel, and the US proceeded apace with former National Security Advisor Robert McFarlane and Lieutenant-Colonel Oliver North in Tehran negotiating deals. Iran began selling oil to the Soviets in August. In September, the shah's son made a clandestine television broadcast to Iran, proclaiming himself the king and asking Iranians to overthrow the regime on his behalf. Ali Akbar Hashemi-Rafsanjani (at the time the powerful speaker of the parliament), meanwhile, made contact with the White House for further developments on arms-for-hostages deals. The French were reported in October to be involved in their own arms-for-hostages deal with Iran, while a Lebanese magazine revealed the American-Israeli link with the officials of the Islamic Republic. In November, as the Iran-Contra scandal was surfacing, Iran and Iraq resumed their bombing of cities and civilian targets. The Russians joined as trade partners of the Islamic Republic in December, as did the French. Meanwhile, Makhmalbaf wrote "Bachcheh-ye Khoshbakht" ("The Lucky Kid"), "Tavallod-e Yek Pir-e Zan" ("The Birth of an Old Woman"), and "Dastforush" ("The Peddler"), which would form the three episodes of his film *The Peddler*. By far his most significant work of the time *The Peddler* revealed both a radical ideological break with the Islamic Republic (and its categorical failures to deliver on its revolutionary promises) and an astonishing cinematic breakthrough. Poised, confident, and scathing, *The Peddler* announced the birth of a filmmaker no longer committed to anything or anybody but the integrity of his own work, and at the same time exposed the underbelly of the Islamic revolution and the Islamic Republic, the massive poverty, the schizophrenic delusions, and the persistent paranoia at the heart of Iranian society. The Islamic Republic was now going one way, and Makhmalbaf was going another. In his cinema, he became the guilty conscience and the emancipated hope of the Iranian revolution.

Attacks on civilian targets in Baghdad and Tehran continued with the start of the New Year, as Iran launched the "Karbala-5" offensive. Rafsanjani made public the Bible that President Reagan had autographed for him during the arms-for-hostages swap, which was put to an end by US Secretary of State George Schultz. In February, Khomeini proclaimed "war until victory," and no end was in sight. Cities in Iran and Iraq lived under the constant threat of bomb attacks. Chinese Silkworm missiles were reported deployed along the Strait of Hormuz in March, as the US warned Iran against using them. In response, Iran declared its freedom of navigation in the Persian Gulf. Some 333 ships were reported as casualties of the Iran-Iraq War—Lloyd's of London was counting. To force Iran to accept a cease-fire, Iraq continued to bomb military, industrial, and civilian targets in Iranian territories well into August, as the Soviets negotiated a deal with the officials of the Islamic Republic to buy more oil. The US banned the import of Iranian crude oil. Mehdi Hashemi, who had close ties to Ayatollah Montazeri, was executed on charges of treason. He had been instrumental in leaking the arms-for-hostages deal between Iran and the US. Rafsanjani tried (with no success) the old game of playing the Soviets against the Americans as new commercial pacts were signed between the Iranians and the Soviets. France and Iran swapped French hostages in Lebanon for cash and the expulsion of opposition forces (the Mojahedin in particular) from France. In December, Khomeini revised his will, as negotiations continued in New York around UN Resolution 598 to end the war.

Makhmalbaf, meanwhile, wrote *Bicycle-ran (The Cyclist)* and turned it into a movie. Then he wrote *Arusi-ye Khuban (Marriage of the Blessed)*, *Farmandar (The Governor)*, *Moft-abad (Goodfornothingville)*, *Garma-zadeh (Heat-Stricken)*, *Nazr-e Aghnia (The Rich People's Vow)* and *Jarrahi-ye Ruh (The Surgery of the Soul)*. *The Cyclist* and *Marriage of the Blessed* further advanced Makhmalbaf's status as a major force in Iranian cinema. *The Cyclist* pushed Makhmalbaf's attention to Afghan refugees inside Iran, a problem that he turned into a metaphor for far more atrocious calamities in his homeland. *Marriage of the Blessed* dealt with the casualties of war, both physical and psychological, and was the most emphatic sign that Makhmalbaf had lost all hope in the promises of the Islamic revolution.

In January 1988, Khomeini ordered the formation of a new, undemocratic governmental body. The Expediency Council was to mediate between the Guardian Council and the parliament—so if the Guardian Council became too juridical and got finicky about insisting on the scholastic and juridical qualifications of the next Supreme Leader, rather than on his political compatibility with the Islamic Republic, political expediency could rule out their objections. Nobody remembers now, but the Expediency Council was Khomeini's way of moving (an excessively juridical reading of) Islam out of the way in the name of politics. Human casualties were mounting as Iraq continued its relentless bombing of Iranian cities and civilian targets. Iran reciprocated, attacking civilian targets in Baghdad and Basra. Then, Iran finally rushed to accept UN Resolution 598. But in March massacres of Kurds were reported in Halabcheh and Marivan by Iraqis using chemical weapons. Tanker wars in the Persian Gulf intensified, leading the Italian government to announce that freedom of navigation in the Persian Gulf ought to be observed, "otherwise the condition of human rights in Iran is really in bad shape"—yet another indication that Iranians' and Iraqis' "human rights" are only relevant when Italian (European, American) business and military interests are at stake. After a series of counterattacks in June, Iraq claimed to have recaptured much of its lost territory. On 2 July, the USS *Vincennes* shot down an Iran Air passenger plane, killing 290 people on board. The US authorities said it was an accident; Iranians said it was intentional.

On 18 July, the Islamic Republic agreed to the terms of UN Resolution 598. Five hundred forty-six ships, Lloyd's of London reported, had been hit since the commencement of hostilities in September 1980. In August, peace negotiations commenced in Geneva. The UN condemned

Iraq for its systematic use of chemical weapons. Iran accused Iraq of continuing to use chemical weapon in Kurdistan even after the cease-fire. In September, the flood of European envoys to reopen their embassies and resume their trade with the Islamic Republic began. A period of reconstruction immediately followed, and yet as early as October the wall of mistrust between Iran and US was as tall as ever.

The last year of Khomeini's life was not memorable until he went after Salman Rushdie. On Valentine's Day, 1989, he issued a death sentence in form of a religious edict, or fatwa, against Rushdie for having blasphemed the sacred tenants of Islam in his novel *The Satanic Verses* (1989). As the world's attention was distracted by the Rushdie affair, Khomeini was busy doing something far more damaging to the fate of sixty-five million Iranians. In March, he dismissed Ayatollah Montazeri as the heir apparent to the office of Supreme Leader because of his increasing criticism of the regime, his involvement in the Mehdi Hashemi case (exposing the Iran-Contra affair), and his opposition to the fatwa against Rushdie. During the following month, Khomeini ordered the formation of a new Assembly of Experts to revise the constitution in order to, among other things, reduce the clerical requirements of his successor in order to accommodate politically committed but scholastically wanting figures such as President Khamenei. Under the smokescreen of the Rushdie affair (very much on the model of the American hostage crisis a decade earlier), Khomeini had the revisions of the constitution ratified to his liking in May. On Saturday, 3 June 1989, Khomeini died.

During this year, Makhmalbaf read vastly and voraciously, trying to catch up on years of college missed while in prison. He also wrote *Fazilat-e Bismillah* (*The Virtue of Saying "In the Name of God"*), *Nan va Gol* (*Bread and Flower*), and *Seh Tablo* (*Three Pictures*). During the following winter he wrote *Nobat-e Asheqi* (*Time of Love*) and *Mara Bebus* (*Kiss Me*). *Time of Love* was an engaging experiment with philosophical relativism—but nothing more than that. The year Khomeini died, Makhmalbaf was shedding his old skin.

Soon after the death and burial of Ayatollah Khomeini, Iran commenced a long recuperation from a decade of charismatic terror. With the constitution of the Islamic Republic now revised in a way that facilitated the rise of lower-ranking clerics, Khamenei vacated the presidency and became the Supreme Leader; Rafsanjani quit his post as speaker of the house and became the president; Ali Akbar Nateq-Nuri became the speaker of the house; and the office of the prime minister was subsumed into the presidency. Khamenei and Rafsanjani now became two split characters seeking (in the classical Weberian sense) to routinize Khomeini's charismatic authority, to institutionalize it into their respective offices of Supreme Leader and president. One of them, in a rather bizarre historical mutation of the symbolic father figure, had no beard, and the other had lost his right arm in an assassination attempt—the paternal figure of power was now split in half.

Makhmalbaf made *Nobat-e Asheqi* (*Time of Love*) and *Shabha-ye Zay-andeh-rud* (*The Nights of Zayandeh-rud*). He also wrote *Khab-e bi-Ta'bir* (*The Dream with No Interpretation*) and *Mard-e Na-Tamam* (*The Incomplete Man*). Banned by the government, *The Nights of Zayandeh-rud* continues with the same philosophical relativism as *Time of Love*, this time casting a bitter look at events before and after the Islamic revolution. At the center of the story is a professor of sociology who loses his wife in a motorcycle accident before the revolution, because no one would help him take her to the hospital. In the course of the revolution, the same professor witnesses the love and care that people then had for each other. After the revolution, he sees the same indifference has returned. Not much of an addition to Makhmalbaf's cinematic vision, *The Nights of Zayandeh-rud* is more an indication of Makhmalbaf's own frustration and disappointment with the revolution (as well as an indication that this professor of sociology did not grasp the elementary insight that during revolutionary mobilizations a false *Gemeinschaft,* or sense of community, emerges in otherwise cold and fragmented societies).

Iran remained neutral during the Iraqi invasion of Kuwait and the subsequent invasion of Iraq by the United States and its allies in 1991. Iran also accommodated the release of more American hostages in Lebanon. During this year, Makhmalbaf wrote *Nasir al-Din Shah, Actor-e Cinema* (*Once upon a Time, Cinema*) and then turned it into a film. He also wrote *Honarpisheh* (*The Actor*). *Once upon a Time, Cinema* shows the birth of Makhmalbaf as a major filmmaker. It is an astounding tribute, a beautiful love letter, to Iranian cinema. The pure cinematic madness of this film is beyond description. It is as if a volcano of creative energy was fomenting somewhere deep and hidden in Makhmalbaf's mind, heart, and soul, and suddenly released in an outburst of sustained, superlative, unrelenting power. I believe that much of my love and admiration for Makhmalbaf's cinema has to a large extent something to do with the fact that this is the first film of his that I saw here in New York. In black and white and of enduring beauty and charm, *Once Upon a Time, Cinema* displays the cinematic will to create and craft at its flamboyant best. It casts the entire history of Iranian cinema into a wholesome visual feast. It quotes liberally, beautifully, gracefully from all the major signposts of Iranian cinema. The film is also a letter of apology, a seeking forgiveness, and a work of redemption—Makhmalbaf asking all the major masters of his chosen craft to please forgive his youthful indiscretions. In this film, Makhmalbaf is liberated and delivered from the metaphysical terrors of his ideological convictions and political commitments and is let loose to roam with the best that the aesthetics of his emancipated camera offers. It is also a cinematic history of Iranian modernity, colonialism, treachery, hope, despair, and above all a solitary act of communal generosity.

In another round of parliamentary elections in 1992 more conservative forces entered the Majlis, as Minister of Culture and Islamic Guidance Mohammad Khatami was forced to resign. Makhmalbaf made *The Actor* into a film along with *Gozideh Tasvir-e dar Doreh-ye Qajar* (*A Selection of Pictures from the Qajar Period*). Makhmalbaf himself does not like *The Actor.* He thinks it is too contrived, that he wrote and shot it formulaically, only to prove that art-house films could sell well. But I like this film a lot, precisely because it does not quite come together, and it is a window into Makhmalbaf's subterranean layers of creative energy. The ménage à trois that he manages to generate and sustain in this film exudes with an astounding eroticism, including homoeroticism, rarely dared or seen in Iranian cinema.

During the spring of 1993, Makhmalbaf wrote *Sang va Shisheh* (*Stone and Glass*) and then turned it into a film. At this point he was running up against severe problems with the official censorship. During the fall he wrote *Salam bar Khorshid* (*Greetings upon the Sun*) and in the winter he wrote *Hajj* (*The Hajj Pilgrimage*) and sat for an interview, entitled "Cinema-ye Shaeraneh" ("The Poetic Cinema") with Werner Herzog.

In 1994 Makhmalbaf wrote and directed *Salaam Cinema*. During the winter, he wrote *Qaziyeh-ye an Naqqash-e Doreh-gard* (*The Story of the Vagabond Painter*), *Zendegi Rang Ast* (*Life Is Color*), and *Gabbeh*. *Salaam Cinema* is a bitter and brutal examination of dictatorship, seeking its roots in the frailty of the human soul. It is also a strange revelation about the power of cinema, and what people do when faced with a camera. The power of a desk, behind which sits a figure of authority (the filmmaker, in this case Makhmalbaf himself), begins to assume eerie, inanimate, and frightful proportions. *Salaam Cinema* is a historic document about the significance of cinema in contemporary Iran, and the strange effect that it has on a people at large. Is *Salaam Cinema* also a commentary on the brutal dictatorship of Khomeini during the preceding decade? It might very well be read that way. But like all of Makhmalbaf's good films, more than anything else it is the instrumentality of the camera itself that remains at the center of the cinematic event.

In 1995, the United States aggressively sought the economic and political isolation of Iran, and the Islamic Republic came under severe economic pressure—accused of supporting international terrorism, pursuing weapons of mass destruction, and causing instability in the region. During the summer of this year, he wrote "Forugh Khahar-e Ma Bud" ("Forugh Was Our Sister"), "Seh Tarh dar bareh-ye Sad Salegi-ye Cinema" ("Three Sketches for the Centennial of Cinema"), and

"Khodahafez Cinema" ("Goodbye, Cinema"). During the fall, he wrote "Nun-o-Goldun" and turned it into a film—*A Moment of Innocence*. During the same year he made the film *Gabbeh*. With *A Moment of Innocence* and *Gabbeh*, Makhmalbaf achieved his purest cinematic form to date, his virtual realism assuming its undiluted poetic style and parabolic narrative. This mature phase of Makhmalbaf's cinema has every trace of two brutal decades of political turmoil, a gut-wrenching revolution, and a bloody and prolonged war—and yet all of these transformed into the visual vocabulary of a deeply contemplative disposition. This poetic cinema is neither mystical nor mythic, neither forgiving nor forgetful. It is a cinematic realism of a very particular and definitive character—reaching for a reality stripped of all its distracting particulars and thus revelatory by virtue of its minimalist take on reality.

In 1996, Makhmalbaf attended the forty-ninth Locarno International Film Festival for the premiere of *A Moment of Innocence*, where I met him for the first time. Amir Khosravi's edited volume on *Salaam Cinema* was published during this year, as was the three-volume collection of Makhmalbaf's writings, *Gong-e Khabdideh* (*A Dumb Man's Dream*). During the fall, he sat for the interview "Shadi-ye Zendegi, Gham-e Insani" ("The Joy of Life, the Sadness of Humanity") with Moslem Mansouri. These interviews were instrumental in clarifying Makhmalbaf's cinematic vision for the public at large, but in his own mind as well. Much controversy had by now been generated around Makhmalbaf's cinema, and he used these interviews creatively to reinvent himself in the image of his emergent cinema. Makhmalbaf also traveled to New York for the US premiere of *Gabbeh*, and we conducted a long interview on this occasion that later appeared in my book on Iranian cinema *Close Up: Iranian Cinema, Past, Present, Future*.

In the 1997 presidential election, Iran witnessed one of the most critical moments in its modern history when the former culture minister Mohammad Khatami won in a landslide against Speaker of the House Nateq Nuri. The wily Rafsanjani was appointed as the head of the Expediency Council. Like many other Iranians, Makhmalbaf was exceedingly excited about Khatami's victory. I remember on the night of the presidential election, I stayed awake here in New York exchanging phone calls and faxes with him, as he kept me abreast of the latest figures from Iranian television. In winter, Makhmalbaf wrote *Sokut* (*Silence*) and then he went to Dushanbe, Tajikistan, to turn it into a film. He also published *Zendegi Rang Ast* (*Life Is Color*), another collection of his writings. How much useless hope in Khatami we all had that year.

President Khatami traveled to New York in 1998 to attend the UN General Assembly. There he proposed the idea of the Dialogue of Civilization, while in Iran elements within the Interior Ministry were charged with having murdered Iranian dissident intellectuals. President Khatami ordered an investigation. In September, Iran mobilized a massive force along its border with Afghanistan after eight of its diplomats and one journalist were killed by the Taliban. Makhmalbaf took *Silence* to the Venice Film Festival. He also published the book he had prepared on this film. *Silence* completed what in my view is a trilogy—*A Moment of Innocence, Gabbeh,* and *Silence*—bringing Makhmalbaf's virtual realism to perfection. To this day, Makhmalbaf has not surpassed the mastery he established in this trilogy. These are his absolute best films, with *Once upon a Time, Cinema* a precursor to them.

In the course of the municipal elections in 1999, the conservative elements within the Islamic Republic were severely challenged by the reformists. In July, a massive student uprising was brutally suppressed, while Ataollah Mohajerani, the minister of culture, was being impeached in parliament, and Mohsen Kadivar, a leading oppositional cleric, was imprisoned. Akbar Ganji, a courageous investigative reporter, implicated the highest echelons of the Islamic Republic in the murder of dissident intellectuals, as Mashallah Shamsolvaezin emerged as the champion of reformist press in Iran, and Said Hajjarian proved himself the chief strategist of the reform movement.

Makhmalbaf made *Dar* (*The Door*) for *Qesseh-ha-ye Kish* (*Tales from Kish*). The controversy over *Tales from Kish* brought Makhmalbaf's name to the forefront of events in Tehran. He went to Cannes for the premiere of the film (having completely shaven his head for some mysterious reason). He also planned the Kish International Film Festival, but the plan fell apart following the *Tales from Kish* controversies. At this time, Makhmalbaf became fascinated with the ability of the press to deal quickly with current issues, whereas cinema, he thought, always lagged behind. Evident in his intellectual demeanor and paramount in his mind, however, was now Afghanistan. He was deeply disturbed by the predicament of more than two million Afghans in Iran, millions more in Pakistan, and the rest of them under the horrid reign of the Taliban at home.

During the sixth parliamentary elections in February 2000, the conservatives were ousted from the Majlis. In March, Said Hajjarian, the leading reformist strategist, was the target of an assassination attempt, which he barely survived. In April, some seventeen reformist newspapers and other periodicals were closed down and their editors thrown in jail. By early May, other reformists and public intellectuals were incarcerated for having participated in a conference in Berlin, organized by the Heinrich Böll institute, on the future of democracy in Iran.

Makhmalbaf's attention, meanwhile, was almost completely devoted to his family. On a short trip to Kish he made *Testing Democracy* (2000), a highly experimental film exploring the possibilities of digital cinema.

Makhmalbaf's daughter Samira completed her second feature, *Takhteh Siah* (*Blackboard*, 2000), and his wife, Marziyeh Meshkini, made her first film, *Ruzi keh Zan Shodam* (*The Day I Became a Woman*, 2000). *Blackboard* premiered at the Cannes Film Festival in May, *The Day I Became a Woman* in Venice in September. In October, Makhmalbaf traveled to Pusan, South Korea, for a complete retrospective of his work. In December he was busy shooting *Kandahar* on the border between Iran and Afghanistan. He was increasingly obsessed with that country, which had become a nightmare under full Taliban control—a vicious, fanatical Frankenstein, created by a US-Pakistan-Saudi alliance to oust the Soviets, and now coming back to haunt its own creators. The story of a young Afghan journalist on her way to save her sister from the claws of the Afghan Taliban, *Kandahar* is a journey through the war- and fanaticism-torn Afghanistan, through the caring and creative camera of Makhmalbaf at his minimalist best. As evident in *Kandahar* (and previously in *The Cyclist*), Makhmalbaf was now drawn to the fate of the Afghan people, and his cinema became almost entirely tangential to that primarily political concern. His art seemed to have come a full circle—though this time on a more global scale.

President Khatami won yet another landslide victory in the presidential election of 2001, though he had completely failed to deliver on his first campaign promises, because his presidency was beleaguered by the conservatives' hold on key positions of power. In March, Makhmalbaf and Meshkini visited New York for the US premiere of *The Day I Became a Woman*. He was in New York when he heard the news that *Kandahar* had been accepted to the competition in Cannes, and he was there in May for its premiere. In June, he wrote a public letter to President Khatami urging him not to send Afghan refugees back to Afghanistan and to allocate a budget for Afghan children's education. He was now fully devoted to the education of Afghan children within and outside Afghanistan. In July, he put together a Web site for the Makhmalbaf Film House, a major global network of communication for his art and that of his family. In August, UNESCO announced that *Kandahar* was the recipient of its annual Federico Fellini Award. The events of September 11, 2001, and the subsequent American attack against Afghanistan suddenly catapulted *Kandahar* to massive global attention, giving it an almost cultic reputation. In October he went back to the border of Iran and Afghanistan to shoot a documentary for UNICEF about the status of Afghan children. The result, *Alefbay-ye Afghan* (*Afghan Alphabet*, 2001), was completed in about two weeks. In November he lobbied the Iranian parliament to change the law allowing Afghan children be educated in the Iranian school system, and then traveled to Europe to raise funds for schools he was building in Afghanistan. Nelofer Pazira, the inspiration behind and the lead actress of *Kandahar*, was actively involved in all these efforts. Makhmalbaf's cinema was now totally consumed by his obsession with the fate of the Afghans. He was writing essays and articles, giving interviews left and right, traveling around the world and raising money, lobbying Iranian politicians, meeting with Afghan warlords, UN representatives, Pakistani officials, all the while preparing a major school system he planned to build in Afghanistan.

By 2002, Khatami's presidency was again failing miserably to deliver on its promises. The US was by this time globally engaged in what it called a "war on terror." The US defeated the Taliban, which it had brought to power to begin with, and installed a puppet regime in Afghanistan under Hamid Karzai.

Makhmalbaf continued his activities on behalf of Afghan children and their health and education—undertaking scores of major and minor projects, and using his Web site to promote their cause. He established the Afghan Children Education Movement, or ACEM, and in the fall of that year, he moved to Afghanistan to supervise the building of schools and to help his daughter Samira shoot her third feature film, *At Five in the Afternoon* (2003). He was equally instrumental in helping out a young Afghan filmmaker, Siddiq Barmak, make his first feature film, *Osama* (2003). "I am tired of making films," I remember he told me that year in Cannes. "I want to make filmmakers." Behind that tongue-in-cheek admission was hidden the bewilderment of an artist going wayward. I remember asking him around that time if he did not miss making films while being increasingly drawn to the bottomless misery of the Afghans. "I was like a painter," he said, "standing at a seaside and painting the beautiful sunset. Suddenly I heard a voice crying for help from the sea. I dropped my brush and swam to rescue that person, and when I got there I discovered scores of helpless others. I now keep swimming back and forth between the sea and the seashore, trying to rescue as many as I can, and meanwhile my brush, my palette, and my canvas are sitting there idly by."

By 2003, the conservative faction of the government of the Islamic Republic had made it impossible for Khatami to function. He was utterly helpless as scores of his allies were being arrested and incarcerated. The US attacked Iraq in March and threatened Iran not to interfere, and the Nobel Peace Prize was given to Shirin Ebadi, an Iranian civil-rights activist. In May, Makhmalbaf accompanied his daughter Samira to Cannes for the premiere of her film *At Five in the Afternoon*. Also in Cannes was Siddiq Barmak, the young Afghan filmmaker, presenting *Osama* in the Directors Fortnight section of the festival. As soon as Makhmalbaf returned to Iran, in June, he heard the good news that a bureaucratic hurdle preventing the official inauguration of his schools in Afghanistan had been lifted and that they would soon be operational, offering thousands of Afghan children elementary education and computer and language training. It had now been three consecutive years since he had made a film—the longest dry spell in his entire career.

The next year brought a major parliamentary victory for the conservatives, as the US invasion of Iraq met with catastrophic consequences, with revelations of torture at Abu Ghraib, Bagram Air Force Base, and Guantanamo Bay scandalizing this belligerent empire. Meanwhile, frustrated by an assortment of obstacles to his production company in Iran, Makhmalbaf began to look into production facilities in Tajikistan and India. In May 2004, the Ministry of Culture and Islamic Guidance prevented him from working on his new film, tentatively called *Amnesia*. By November, he had decided to begin shooting another film in India he now called *Cries of Ants*, a philosophical journey through death, resurrection, love, and annihilation. Simultaneous with that film, he made *Sex and Philosophy* in Tajikistan, yet another metaphysical reflection on relativity and the changing disposition of time and narrative. (I saw both these films at Makhmalbaf's home in Paris in December 2005.) Cannes and Venice rejected the film. Many others accepted it. I had a long telephone conversation with him in August 2005. He had decided to shoot his future films in Tajikistan, take them to India for post-production, and then bring them to Paris for distribution. I have always been fascinated by Makhmalbaf's asceticism, that he would travel around the world with no more than a handbag. He was now living like a wandering dervish.

As I write, Makhmalbaf has started thinking of his next film, and here in New York there is a huge snowstorm, beautiful, serene, soothing—someone somewhere seems (me and my wishful thoughts) to be forgiving us all our failures.

Makhmalbaf's cinema is scarred, just like his body and the soul of his nation. Makhmalbaf's realism is virtual, because the full reality it wishes to convey and contest is too traumatic to bear. He has neither the panache nor the patience of Kiarostami to witness the actuality of reality (hidden under its overburdened symbolism), nor the steely eyes of Naderi to look reality straight in the eye without submitting it to any metaphysics. Makhmalbaf once told me of an idea he had for a film about a boy who was told never to look at evil, and whenever he ran into something evil or ugly to turn away. That boy ultimately became Khorshid in his film *Silence*, and Makhmalbaf made him completely blind. Have you ever wondered what happened to that boy? Makhmalbaf found nothing for him to look at that was not evil or ugly, except in his own mind, and thus he had to be completely blind. That boy is Makhmalbaf himself, having made his eyes blind to imagine a world inside his own head—one that is *virtually* beautiful. That's why *Silence* is so beautifully shot and beautiful to look at, because it is shot from inside Khorshid's (Makhmalbaf's) mind's eye. This phenomenon is not limited to Makhmalbaf. Do you remember that scene in Amir Naderi's *The Runner* where Amiru is sitting by the sea, having turned his back to the world, with the ships in the harbor, eating his dinner of bread, cheese, and watermelon? That's Naderi too. He once told me here in New York that there were always two worlds, one outside that was ugly and intolerable, and the other the world of movies inside his head—beautiful and sparkling. "I would close my eyes and turn my head and just get myself lost in that world," Naderi said. The same is true of Makhmalbaf. His cinema is tortured, just like the soul of his nation; his realism is virtual, just like the dreams of his people.

Makhmalbaf's virtual realism has emerged from the creative consciousness of an artist in critical conversation with the collective unconscious of a nation. This creative source has given rise to the virtual simulation of a minimalist universe, stripped to its bare bones, a universe that one can safely call home without a particular attachment to any nation. Was this the secret of Makhmalbaf's global success, and was this also his cinema's Achilles' heel? Could this be the reason that people around the globe love Iranian cinema in general? Has Iranian cinema crafted a creative corner of reality where the globalized, atomized, brutalized, and ultimately homeless people the world over can call home?

We need to cast a wider look at the world and consider this thing called the "crisis of the subject" from a nondenominational angle. Have the horrors that Iranians as a nation experienced in the course of a monarchical dictatorship, a violent revolution, a devastating war, a brutal theocracy (and yet they have managed to hold their heads high, fight for their freedom from domestic and global tyranny, and still find time, energy, enthusiasm, care, love, intelligence, and humor to remind everyone of their collective humanity) resonated with some deep fear and offered it a soothing metaphor? Look at the lonely planet—every day and every night someone somewhere in the world is watching an Iranian film. But what they are watching is not just an Iranian film. Filmmakers and artists around the world, from Asia and Africa, North and South America, Europe and all its former colonies, have lent a lens, offered a helping hand. Iranian cinema is the window of the world upon its own garden. This is a collective gift, every frame of every single worthy film crafted from an angle at once domestic to the Iranian predicament and yet global in the aesthetic configuration of its whereabouts. Not a single Iranian filmmaker worthy of his or her name has been an artist sui generis. Iranian cinema is a mirror in which the best of world cinema is always already reflected. Master filmmakers from around the globe—American, Russian, European, Asian, and African—have had a say in the matter, a vision of the scene, telling our filmmakers where to put their camera, how to frame a shot, when to say "Action!" when to dolly out, when to zoom in, when to pan, how to tilt, and when to say "Cut!" Iranian cinema is as much an Iranian gift to the world as it is a gift from the world to Iran. In Iran's cinema, Iranians have become world citizens.

My contention so far has been that by the time Amir Naderi and Bahram Beizai had continued the tradition handed down by the previous generation of Iranian filmmakers and were done with their own contributions to Iranian cinema, a visual lexicon had been generated, articulated, and ultimately brought to triumph, allowing subsequent Iranian filmmakers no necessary connection to the verbal realm of their creative memory. Kiarostami's cinema, though he is a contemporary of Naderi and Beizai, has traced the contour of an *actual* realism that is at the same visual distance from the preceding, verbally grounded period of Iranian cinema. Kiarostami's realism is markedly different from Makhmalbaf's, for he takes the evident image of reality at face value and begins to unveil the layers of presumed and received meanings from that face, exposing the marrow of its facticity, of its just being a fact and not meaning anything beyond the evident presence of that fact. That's why all searches for "symbolic meaning" in Kiarostami's cinema (the way, for example, that the distinguished American critic Godfrey Cheshire does) is entirely misguided. All the heavy coatings of inherited and regurgitated symbolic signification are cleansed and jettisoned in Kiarostami's cinema, and a vision of the glorious eruption of imaginary (dis)order put on display. It is along the same lines that I propose that Makhmalbaf's cinema is anchored in a *virtual* realism, akin to Kiarostami's actual realism and yet characteristically different from them. In Makhmalbaf's case, he has cultivated an uncanny ability to discover what is virtually true about reality, and how he can show it with an absolute minimalism. If you notice, his scenes are unusually clean, clear, and measured. In short: They are virtual, both real and unreal at the same time. In two or three visual strokes he exposes the most elemental forces of reality—its shapes, shades, colors, volumes, attitude (think of the vase of white geraniums sitting at the center of a niche in the middle of a passageway in *A Moment of Innocence*). I call this minimalist absolutism, this ascetic mysticism of visions through veils, his virtual realism. Thriving visually in complementary ways, Kiarostami and Makhmalbaf are the visionary culminations of Iranian cinema.

In these filmmakers, one may argue, Iranian cinema completes its historic cycle and attains its full epistemic potential. Nothing (and this is quite a claim I am making here) will happen in Iranian cinema beyond the visual lexicography of this generation of filmmakers, unless some major epistemic rupture breaks through to a whole new manner of seeing things. This does not mean that Iran will not continue to produce great filmmakers. But they will continue to operate within and through these interrelated epistemic corollaries. But these three epistemic formations conclude the half century of persistent work—from Forugh Farrokhzad to Kiarostami, one might say. This situation is also the principal reason that a global celebration of Kiarostami, a tacit acknowledgment of Makhmalbaf, and an almost complete ignorance of the rest, has generated and sustained an entirely false conception of Iranian cinema around the world—and for which no one is more responsible than the French, who have cut and pasted the nature of Iranian cinematic aesthetics according to some abstract notion of cinema they have cooked up at *Cahiers du Cinema*, with which they manufacture a "world cinema" that has a global logic of its own and could not care less what has gone into the making of a particular filmmaker. Kiarostmi or Makhmalbaf thus becomes a reality in and of themselves, not celebrated in France but in effect manufactured in France, having either fallen from the sky or else grown like a mushroom with no organic links to their natural habitat. This of course is ultimately fine, and there is nothing wrong with it. Let the French think that they "discovered" Kiarostami or Makhmalbaf (the way Americans think Christopher Columbus "discovered" America). My point is to see where specific Iranian filmmakers like Kiarostami and Makhmalbaf—predicated on a previous generation of master filmmakers like Naderi, Beizai, and Mehrjui, and further back to Farrokhzad and Golestan—fit and form a distinct cine-aesthetics that cannot just be called "Iranian neorealism." If the French and other Europeans think Iranian national cinema is for their private and public entertainment every May in Cannes, well that's fine too. They are adding a global angle to Iranian cinema that has had a tremendous catalytic effect of its own—we just should not be altogether taken over or enamored by that global reading.

This is not to say that systemic globalization is something to be ignored or altogether dismissed. Given my initial proposal to you—that I see a direct and dialectical correspondence between the emergence of a national cinema and the national trauma that a nation has experienced—I see no way of a new visual lexicography emerging unless something seriously drastic happens in Iran. But there is the rub—I no longer believe that fates of nations, political or artistic, are any longer (if they ever were) contingent on and limited to their national boundaries, and so arise artists without borders, artists whose epistemic apparatus is no longer limited to the country of their origin (if it ever was), filmmakers who shoot their films in Tajikistan, edit them in India, premiere them in Cannes, launch them in the United States, and then sell them around the world on Amazon.com. I think you catch my drift.

Among all Makhmalbaf's films I am most mesmerized by *A Moment of Innocence* (1996). Is it because it is the first film of his that I saw with him sitting right next to me, in Locarno? Perhaps. I am not sure. It was a beautiful summer night in August 1996 at the huge and magnificent Piazza Grande, right by the Lago Maggiore. Makhmalbaf's daughter Hana had fallen asleep on his lap. His wife, Marziyeh Meshkini, was sitting at his side and I on the other. The chairs belonged to a McDonald's restaurant, I remember now. That year, Mohsen was fascinated by the idea of simple and self-served food—and there was a tray full of McDonald's sandwiches and such right in front of him as we were watching *A Moment of Innocence*. There was a soft serenity about the Locarno air that night. I remember that it was the pure simplicity of *A Moment of Innocence* that most fascinated me. It was like watching a dream—incoherent, frightful, exciting, the film taking its own time entirely, and I was afraid that the dream would end before I was finished dreaming. It is hard to imagine that a film can be so personal and yet so universal, so privately narrated and yet so cosmic in its defiance of time and location. I can hardly believe that even Mohsen himself will find again the nerve that he struck in this film, the mythic morphing of reality into his trademark virtual realism. He did manage many more times to register his orbital, sideways manner of signification—but not again with such visual verve, with such imaginal precision.

I believe it all has to do with Makhmalbaf's virtual realism. In *A Moment of Innocence*, Makhmalbaf has mastered the art of un-telling, with what I once called "a benign kind of self-forgetfulness of the story of his youthful political indiscretions." But what does "un-telling" mean? Well, it means you are telling a story, but you are really undoing a previous telling (and commission of the acts) of that story, and you do so by way of telling something else. It is what in Persian prosody we call telling something through *ima'* and *ishareh*: "signs" and "indications." In this case, it is using the story of his own youthful political activism to tell another story. When Makhmalbaf was seventeen, he wanted to change the world for the better. So he thought that the way to do it was to attack a policeman, disarm him, get his gun, then go and rob a bank, use the money to form an urban guerrilla network, and bomb the living daylights out of the Pahlavi regime. As you know, he and his comrades pretty much screwed up the plot of that story. Makhmalbaf was almost killed, landed in jail, and was tortured and tormented until he was released in the course of the Islamic revolution—having fully served his term.

As you can see the biographical details of the actual event are just too obvious, too real, too blasé, and as such are narrowly jaundiced by the factual ferocity of the evident, the pointlessness of the prosaic, a fleeting experience that dies upon itself. The point is how Makhmalbaf transforms the prosaic in his story into a poetics of history. He committed that act of violence when he was seventeen and he made the film when he was forty. In the span of that time, he lived the length and breadth of a very tumultuous life. The result of this precocious politicization was picking up arms and seeking to alter the course of history. Arrested, put in jail, and savagely tortured, Makhmalbaf spent the years between his arrest in 1974 and his release in 1979 becoming even more politicized. Released from jail at the wake of the revolution, he became artistically devoted to it. But soon he broke his ties with the propaganda machinery of the Islamic regime and suffered and celebrated all the consequences of that break. He was born as a filmmaker when he had sublimated that tumultuous history, both personal and national, into his enduring aesthetic. By the time he started shooting *A Moment of Innocence*, in 1995, he had already established a long and illustrious career as a filmmaker, conquered Cannes, and triumphed at many other prestigious international film festivals. He was sedate, I remember, when I saw him for the first time in Locarno, in complete control of his cinematic career, devoted to his family, and he had about him the air of a confident visionary, attending to his family with the same tenacity and care as he pursued his vocation as an artist and his commitments as a humanist.

Like Kiarostami, Makhmalbaf seeks visually to re-narrate reality, a re-narration that forces reality to yield alternative modes of being, perception, and signification. In his case, and when he is at his best, as in *A Moment of Innocence*, he always begins with *the most palpably real* and before we know it he has led us toward *the true*. I still remember when I first tried to follow this trajectory toward the true in *A Moment of Innocence*. We know biographically that at seventeen Makhmalbaf formed a small band of Muslim revolutionaries and planned to attack a police officer in order to steal his gun and use it to rob a bank and launch an urban guerrilla attack against the Pahlavi regime. We also know that Makhmalbaf's ill-fated attack on the poor police officer was unsuccessful, that instead he got himself shot and subsequently captured and imprisoned. These are the things that actually happened. (I recently saw a picture of Mohsen on his Web site from the time that he was arrested by SAVAK, the shah's dreaded secret police, plus the official account of his arrest and incarceration. "The banality of evil," as Hannah Arendt called it, is written all over this official account, a banality that also speaks to the nature of the reality it frames and narrates. It is the sublimation of that banality into art that I have in mind here.)

You can look at the same story the other way around—the way *A Moment of Innocence* tells it. One day a police officer, who on another day many years ago was about to be assassinated by a young revolutionary, finds out that the famous film director Mohsen Makhmalbaf is none other than the same rascal who once tried to kill him. He comes and pays him a visit and asks him to let him act in one of his films. "No," says Makhmalbaf to the middle-aged former police officer whom he had once almost killed, "instead of acting for me, let's go and find our youths, your youth and my youth, and ask them to reenact what we did when we were young." Bewildered by the idea, the police officer agrees, and they go and find two actors who are willing to act as their respective youthful selves. They take them to the scene of the accident and tell them to reenact the event. Makhmalbaf directs the version of his youth and the police officer directs his. The trouble starts when the young Makhmalbaf and the young police officer refuse to do as they are told. Talentless actors or else conscientious objectors, they cannot, will not, and dare not repeat the stupidities of the youths of these two adults, who seem to have nothing better to try than reenacting their youthful imbecilities. (At some points, I think *A Moment of Innocence* is a hilariously comic film, but with a bizarre and twisted sense of irony.)

When you look at *A Moment of Innocence* from these opposing perspectives you notice that there is a creative confusion about it, a kind of quiet erosion of the dead certainties that separate the real from the make-believe. This creative confusion disregards facts by subjecting them to a set of multiple fantasies and their meanings—all in a variegated thrust that no author or filmmaker, let alone a censor, can control. I discovered this "multi-significatory" construction of meaning when I was working on *Truth and Narrative*, my book on Ayn al-Qudat al-Hamadhani. I opted to use this term—"multi-significatory"—as a substitute for Ayn al-Qudat's *mushtarik al-dilalah*—meaning a kind of signification in which a signifier, say a word, stands for more than one thing. I remember Ayn al-Qudat writes in one of his letters that when a physician uses the word "hand," he means it in a different way than a calligrapher, or a philosopher, or a theologian. It is the same word "hand," but it means (signifies) different things to different people in different contexts. This is also, I believe, what Lacan means when he says the *imaginary order* (which I really think is more a disorder) stands on the opposite side of the *symbolic order* that gives meaning and significance to reality. My point here is that in *A Moment of Innocence*, Makhmalbaf has crafted a virtual realism in which what we see is no longer what we see. It is a fantastic paradox and it is worth thinking through some of its suggestions and conclusions.

Visually, few filmmakers match Makhmalbaf in his ability for a poetic shattering of the real. *A Moment of Innocence* is the rhythmic slowing down and then reversal of time, the narrative recasting of space, the crafting of an alternative possibility of being. In *A Moment of Innocence*, I believe Makhmalbaf rewrites his own history as the story of his people. The wintry feeling of nostalgia that hovers over the film, the snowy sense of a hinterland, and the quiet calmness of a dead beauty all come together to give *A Moment of Innocence* its wintry accent, its cold, creative, calculated syncopation of pace, patience, and wonder. How Makhmalbaf crafts this calm and yet disquieting serenity of paradisiacal coldness has to do with the way he manages time to be of no time, space to be of no space, movements to slow down, frames to freeze, and details to demand an unearthly attention.

The schizophrenic disjunction of *A Moment of Innocence* is ultimately where its narrative force thrives. The historical Makhmalbaf directs his young version to kill. The ahistorical Makhmalbaf teaches his young actor to love. The historical Makhmalbaf directs his police officer to direct his youthful self to kill. The ahistorical Makhmalbaf pleads with his victim to forgive. The seventeen-year-old Makhmalbaf acts the way the forty-year-old Makhmalbaf wants and wishes him to act. The forty-year-old Makhmalbaf directs the young Makhmalbaf to act the way he wishes he had acted when he was seventeen. The result of this schizophrenic re-narration is a kind of cinematic adaptation of Parousia, that is to say a parable that is told at a time when time did not exist yet. I borrow this term "Parousia" from Christian dogma, where it refers to the "presence" of Christ, which in turn refers to the second coming of Jesus. In Islam we call this *zuhur* (as opposed to *ghaybah*), the reappearance of the Mahdi from his occultation, who will in turn guide humanity back to the right path at the end of time. Do you see how Makhmalbaf's cinema draws us to the sacrosanct and thus the most hidden in our (albeit forsaken) faiths? In *A Moment of Innocence*, Makhmalbaf recreates a personal Parousia, but for its communal effects, a presence articulated in the heart of an absence.

What I am proposing here is the detection of a creation myth in *A Moment of Innocence*, articulated from the soul of Makhmalbaf's virtual realism. Born into a wintry paradise are an Adam and an Eve (yet to come), the bride and bridegroom of a whole new reality—Mashy and Mashyanah, the first human couple, who grew out of a rhubarb plant, according to the old creation myth in the Zoroastrian text the *Bundahishn*. In the creative mind of Makhmalbaf comes forward the visual apparition of a new coupling of innocence and faith, transmuted from the depth of a man's belief in a metaphysics that can no longer sustain him or give character to the culture he calls home. In Makhmalbaf's youth, and in the image of virginity he imagines in the woman that his youth ought to have loved, dwells the sanctity of hope, the postponed piety of a place that one must (but alas can no longer) call home. Hidden behind the gaze of this budding innocence are all the promises of a future that must hold, and all the fear of a past that must let go.

The most astounding sequence in *A Moment of Innocence* takes place when Makhmalbaf brings the actor playing the young Makhmalbaf to his cousin seeking her permission to use her daughter in the film. Makhmalbaf and his cousin, as the film puts it, used to be comrades in arms, and now Makhmalbaf wants his cousin's young daughter to reenact the presumed role her mother had in the drama. (The figure of this cousin is fictive. There was no such cousin in the real event.) Makhmalbaf's cousin refuses, though her daughter is very eager to act in Makhmalbaf's film. As we watch this take place, we are now in the present, watching the mature Makhmalbaf, who regrets his youthful violence, try to persuade his cousin (whom we never see and can only hear) to allow her daughter to act in a film he is making about the futility of his youthful deeds. While Makhmalbaf and his cousin are negotiating back and forth, the young girl appears and brings a bowl of soup for the young man who is to play the young Makhmalbaf. She greets the old Makhmalbaf and proceeds to the car where the young man is preparing to play Makhmalbaf. Their conversation is quite formal and at first makes no reference to the past, to the roles they are meant to play: "Hello, how are you? Please have a little of this soup," and such. So we are all gently led to believe that this is the present, with Makhmalbaf trying to make a film in the 1990s about something he did in the 1970s, until suddenly the young girl slips a book to the young Makhmalbaf and makes arrangements to see him to carry on the plot and assassinate the police officer. Within the space and span of the present time, suddenly a temporal shift takes place that sucks the present back into past. Without the slightest change in location or even the mise en scène, or even a blink of the camera's eye, Makhmalbaf generates a virtual sense of the past in the middle of an evident present. Nothing has changed except the cinematic manufacturing of a time warp, as a performed past comes to mark the enacted present.

Ultimately *A Moment of Innocence* amounts to a moving exercise in turning back the course of history, as Makhmalbaf reaches back into the past in order to change it. This temporal abnegation of reality—making time effectively move against its own logic and thus against the course of history—comes to a climax at the end of the film when the actor playing the young Makhmalbaf, goaded by the old director, approaches the police officer in order to assassinate him. The young cousin approaches the police officer to ask him a question in order to distract him (just as her mother had done years before), so that the young Makhmalbaf can surprise and stab him. Meanwhile the old police officer has told the actor playing his younger self that the girl is not really in love with him but is in fact the accomplice in an attempt to kill him. The police officer has given his own youth a gun and told him that, instead of giving her the flowerpot he has brought, he is to kill the treacherous girl as soon as she comes near. So the young girl approaches the young police officer, turns her (very beautiful) face toward the camera, lifts her veil in a way that obscures the police officer but embraces the camera, and asks in a close-up of beautiful suspension, "Excuse me, officer, what time is it?" Of course, the whole purpose at this point is precisely "time" and its whereabouts, but in more than one sense. The camera freezes on the face of the young girl, the music syncopates, as she repeats again, "Excuse me, officer, what time is it?" The time now becomes no time, the ever, the never, the always—this is a moment pregnant with all possibilities, a mythic moment, the pre-moment of the universe, the instance when absolute nothingness is about to give birth to other than itself, in the no-time of time, in the midst of the void in which space is to take place—in short the moment our poets have always called *alast*, the moment that (just before He created man) God asked, "Am I not thy Lord?" This is Parousia before the commencement of history, a moment of innocence.

The camera stands still. The young woman holds her veil tightly, hugging the camera, as two hands enter the inner sanctity of her face, one offering her a flowerpot (instead of a gun) and the other a piece of bread (instead of a knife, which Makhmalbaf had used in the attempted robbery)—history remade. I remember soon after we saw the film in Locarno, Mohsen told me that the whole film is really a postcard, that he made the film in order to arrive at that concluding image.

This picture (and with it the sequence and the entire film) is a cinematic will to rewrite history, to remake the world, to revise its destiny, modify its verdict. Here Makhmalbaf the rebel is in full control of a cinematic urge to dismantle and dismember the fate of an entire nation. This is a deliberate act of mis-remembering history in order to let it forget itself—for its own good. Makhmalbaf himself may wish here to apologize, to seek forgiveness, to solicit absolution. But Makhmalbaf the filmmaker is after a much bigger fish—for there is nothing to forgive, and no one to forgive. Makhmalbaf the filmmaker is in possession of a history much more significant than his own—history with a purpose, a point, a vision. In the span of this film, Makhmalbaf the filmmaker manages to overthrow what in his wildest dreams he could not have imagined overthrowing when he picked up a knife to launch a revolution. What he is doing here is dismantling the government of the subservient subject. No form of subject control is operative here. This is a cinematic will to resist power, an emancipatory vision that gives the subject full control over what has been made into a pliable world—time, space, and destiny together. Makhmalbaf is thus the harbinger of portentous news, his cinema the remaking of history as if it never happened before, a blissful, reinvigorating, forgiving, and generous amnesia.

It's just like threading a needle. If you hold the thread
right in front of the eye of the needle and your eyesight is half decent you can thread it with just one try.
But if like me your eyes can hardly see anything, then
you have to keep wetting the thread with your mouth
and thin it with your teeth and bring it close to where
you think the eye of the needle is, and then keep
pushing and pulling the thread until it accidentally
passes through the eye of the needle.

–Simin Daneshvar, *Savushun*

Marziyeh Meshkini
The Day I Became a Woman

AGAINST THE BACKGROUND that culminated in the respective cinemas of Bahram Beizai and Amir Naderi, Abbas Kiarostami brought an *actual* realism to full fruition. Mohsen Makhmalbaf, meanwhile, carried to visual perfection his own independent and spontaneously crafted *virtual* realism. Marziyeh Meshkini, I would now like to argue, has explored a *parabolic* realism (as in parable-like), achieved within Iranian cinema proper and drawn from previous generations of women filmmakers. My proposal here is that in specifically visual terms and in three complementary ways, the particular forms of Iranian realism in its most mature stages assumed three distinct shades of articulation—*actual, virtual,* and *parabolic*—in which women filmmakers in general, and most distinctly in Meshkini's cinema, have had a major role and presence. One can argue and demonstrate the manifestation of this parabolic realism through any number of young Iranian filmmakers. I opt to do it through Marziyeh Meshkini because she is perhaps the least pretentious practitioner of it and as such most unconscious of the visual inheritance she effortlessly represents.

The reason (the last point I made is worth emphasizing) I have opted to single out a woman filmmaker of the younger generation is that by the time Marziyeh Meshkini picked up a camera and started working on her first feature film, she was not even aware of the recent history of Iranian cinema's gradual development of a visual take on reality—which is really the best way to create any enduring work of art. If Forugh Farrokhzad commenced the creation of a visual vocabulary that has since defined the entire course of Iranian cinema, Meshkini has brought that auspicious commencement to an aesthetic conclusion. The specifics of that aesthetic are spelled out in a mode of realism that begins and ends in the factual evidence of the ordinary sublimated into a parabolic mode of storytelling, without ever allowing the particulars of such evidence to coagulate into a morality, a politics, an ethics, or even to make a universal claim on our credulity beyond the detailed determinism of a world without a beginning, an end, or a dramatic resolution. Meshkini is the filmmaker of that detailed determinism, the vernacular vision of a world whose supreme drama is in the absolutism of a reality that yields to no metaphysics of ultimate ends, and allows no mythology to assuage its raw nerves. How she has been able to define the character of this parabolic realism is the story of a cinema dedicated to the cause of the fallen and the forlorn, without forfeiting the grace of the sublime and the beautiful.

Before I discuss Meshkini's masterpiece, *The Day I Became a Woman*, let me first begin by placing her in the proper critical context. It is necessary to understand that two aspects of Iranian cinema—one thematic, the other aesthetic—are systematically incorporated into a larger frame of debate almost despite themselves. Thematically, the issues of race, gender, ethnicity, economy, polity, and culture are compromised by their corrosive assimilation into the domain of an international civil society that ultimately robs Iranian cinema of its fundamental contributions to debates on those very issues. The predicament of Iranian women in particular—as a result of a combination of patriarchal and colonial factors—is now the subject of global abuse. Throughout Iranian history, but particularly under the calamity of colonialism (and the ideological manifestations of resistance to it, Islamism in particular), no other segment of Iranian society has suffered and sacrificed more than Iranian women. Across classes, ethnicities, and generations, Iranian women have been systematically abused and denied their innate and inalienable human rights. The two most recent dynastic and revolutionary regimes to have ruled over the destiny of Iranians—the Pahlavis and the Islamic Republic—have a particularly atrocious record of human-rights abuses in general and the abuse of women's rights in particular. If women gained ground in their social and political liberties under the Pahlavis, it had scarcely anything to do with the reigning monarchy and everything to do with the ongoing historic struggle of Iranian women for their rights, which was given more social breathing room by the expansion of the Iranian economy, urbanization, foreign investment, the accumulation of significant local capital, and the need for cheap labor. If women have found their way into the highest echelons of economic, cultural, civil, and social—including parliamentary—leadership in the Islamic Republic, it has absolutely nothing to do with the medieval texture and tyrannical temper of the reigning theocracy. There has been a sustained history of struggle by Iranian women to demand and exact their human, social, civil, and economic rights. These were neither given to them by Reza Shah nor were they to be taken back by Ayatollah Khomeini. That Iranian women still have a long way to go in order to gain legal and social parity with men is the agenda of their own struggles, subject to domestic, regional, and global geopolitics that affects them and the rest of Iranian society—and as I write this sentence they are all indeed paying a very heavy price doing precisely that. Meanwhile, if in the United States an Iranian contingency representative of a disease that here they call "neo-conservatism" is abusing the struggle of Iranian women for freedom and equality as an excuse for liberating imaginary harems full of waiting Lolita-like virgins, one Abu Ghraib torture chamber and Falluja massacre at a time, then it is really a pathology unique to the United States, with obviously catastrophic global implications.

There is a universality to the struggles of Iranian women, across classes and ethnicities, that no particular cross section or category can faithfully represent, least of all a bland, bourgeois feminism. This is the kind of feminism that mistakes its particular class interests for those of Iranian society at large, and is now placing the historic struggles of all sorts of Iranian women on a silver plate and heralding it as an emerging "feminism international," thus soliciting sympathy from suburban kaffeeklatsch gatherings, an act that necessarily compromises the integrity of a liberation movement as varied and as grass-rooted as that of Iranian women. The problems of single mothers in downtown Tehran, of runaway teenagers from rural areas turning to prostitution or drugs in major urban centers, of rice-paddy laborers in the north, of women among the migratory tribes in central Iran, and of poor Iranian women married off to Afghan refugees are not exactly identical with those of the transnational bourgeoisie politicking inside the Beltway in Washington, DC, trying to make an appointment with the US secretary of defense. Sisterhood is not global. Women speaking on behalf of the globalized bourgeoisie and endorsing the global expansionism of a Eurocentric conception of the world may indeed feel particularly sisterly toward each other; but the vastly unjust world that separates them allows for no sisterly presumption. There is a nasty class warfare at work between those who benefit from the global operation of capital and those disenfranchised by it. Eight hundred and seventy million people, approximately half of them women, go to sleep hungry every night, while the military budget of the United States between 2000 and 2008 is projected to be the number thirty-two with eleven zeroes behind it. On what end of that disequilibrium you lay your weight decides who is whose sister (or brother).

Aesthetically, the scene is even more troubling. It has now become something of a cliché to talk about "Iranian neorealism" without taking the slightest pause to understand exactly what this generic term means. Just because one of the most important events in the history of cinema has been the phenomenon of Italian Neorealism, it does not mean that Iranians (or Cubans, Chileans, or Palestinians) ought to have a local brand of neorealism or New Wave as well. This is very much the way Immanuel Kant, in his *Observations on the Feeling of the Beautiful and Sublime* (1764), called Arabs "the Spaniards of the Orient," and "the Persians...the French of Asia...[while] the Japanese could in a way be regarded as the Englishmen of this part of the world." People ought to be allowed to learn and borrow from a variety of cultures and conditions and yet produce their own take on reality. There is no doubt that Iranian cinema, as indeed much of the rest of world cinema, is highly influenced by Italian Neorealism, French New Wave, German New Cinema, as well as by Russian, Japanese, and Indian (Satyajit Ray in particular) masters. In fact there are very few masters in world cinema who have not registered the syntax and morphology of world cinema—and they do not all come from Italy, or Europe; they also come from Russia, Japan, India, and more recently from Iran, China, Africa, Central Asia, the Arab world, and Latin America. Nations and cultures practice their art as much in conversation with their neighbors as they do with their own historical traditions and exigencies. The term "Iranian neorealism" conceals much more about Iranian cinema than it reveals.

The enduring poverty of theory on Iranian cinema compounds with the overriding mandates of global civil society to rob Iranian cinema of a necessary interpretation based on the appreciation of a local and immediate aesthetic and context. (That sort of interpretation would, in turn, help to foster greater defiance of the patriarchal and colonial predicaments of Iran as a nation-state.) These thematic and aesthetic factors come together, in a compelling and irreducible manner, in Marziyeh Meshkini's cinema. Thematically, the beauty and power of Meshkini's cinema is that it is immune to appropriation by bourgeois feminism by virtue of its rugged and robust roots in a reality that reveals the predicament of the poor and the forgotten. Aesthetically, the generic appellation of Iranian neorealism falls far short of the kind of realism that Meshkini has inherited from previous generations and then cultivated in her films.

What I propose here is that Meshkini's particular kind of realism builds on a tradition that the previous generation of women filmmakers (and by extension writers) had established. Perhaps the best way to see and understand the specific nature of that realism is to compare and contrast it with its two immediate neighbors: the *actual* realism of Kiarostami and the *virtual* realism of Makhmalbaf. If Kiarostami's particular take on realism is *actual*, and Makhmalbaf's *virtual*, Meshkini has inherited and crafted to perfection an uncompromising *parabolic* realism—a kind of realism whose thematic parameters borrow from a factual documentation of truth-claims and reality narratives and yet sublimate them into fable-like representations. This realism finds and delineates the simple facts, before they have been assimilated into a theory, perspective, ideology, or metaphysics—without allowing the particulars of her observations to claim a normative morality. Her aesthetics are thus her politics, and not the other way around. Meshkini's films are so compelling, as they factually reveal the mundane, that her particular cinematic vision is never revealed to the naked eye. It is evenly spread and thus hidden within the texture of the film, and not worn on her sleeve. The single most important source of this definitive disposition of Meshkini's cinema is the way she traces the factual evidence of life back to some elemental parable.

By far the most provocative aspect of this kind of realism is the way it strategically suspends any possibility of disbelief, dismissal, and incredulity constitutional to the cinematic event itself, even when cast in a realist mode. Even the best documentaries harbor the debilitating danger of dismantling themselves, doing themselves a disservice. In fact the better a film documents a neglected or denied truth, the more effectively it shoots itself in the foot. Truth-telling narratives ultimately become stories that fictionalize and discredit themselves. In his seminal study of the structural correspondence between time and narrative, the distinguished French phenomenologist Paul Ricoeur discovered and demonstrated the hermeneutic circle that governs the epistemic relationship between the temporal dimension of a narrative and its thematic cohesion. As any form of narrative (factual or fictive) appropriates the temporal duration of its utterance (in other words the time in which it articulates itself), time in turn posits the truth-claims of the narrative as legitimate. The temporal duration of the narrative casts its truth-claims in a spatial contingency that makes it meaningful by having it uttered, and by virtue of the selfsame utterance makes its suppositions and conclusions factually evident and thus legitimate. But the irony of the act is that the very narrative progression of the utterance itself, the act of utterance itself, ipso facto acts to dismantle that truth-claim by evidencing it as a tale told in a grammatological proposition. This mimetic component of narrative, a narrative entailing a truth, crosses the border between fact and fiction, and as a result the cinematic documentation of a truth-claim ultimately dismantles its own truth-claim by virtue of the narrative progression it has to adopt in order to make sense of itself. In an offshoot of Ricoeur's theory of narrative and Hans Georg Gadamer's hermeneutic theory as proposed in *Truth and Method,* I worked through the hermeneutic theory of the medieval Persian mystic Ayn al-Qudat al-Hamadhani (1098–1131) in my book *Truth and Narrative* (1999). What I found was al-Hamadhani's revolutionary proposition that all truth-claims are narratively embedded, and thus the narrative emplotment of any truth-claim alters the very language, or idiomaticity, of its utterance. Truth narratives, as a result, are doubly dismantled in and within themselves, first by the temporal duration of their utterance, and second by the narrative emplotment of their idiomaticity. In other words, as the very act of telling a story is its own undoing, the truth that it seeks to reveal becomes narratively implicated in the fabricated mechanism of its delivery.

Of course such hermeneutic propositions are not the first thing on our minds when we watch a film, documentary or fiction. But their cumulative effect in dismantling the assumption of reality certainly takes place, and this complicates the very purpose of making a realist film in the first place. The truth is that the most successful realistic films dismantle themselves at the very moment of their success. Forugh Farrokhzad goes to a leprosy colony, makes a documentary, edits it, and calls it *The House Is Black,* takes it to an international film festival, screens it, and gets a prize, and that is the end of it—the reality at the heart of that documentary recedes back to its factual dislocation and becomes yet another calamity in the midst of myriad others. This palimpsestic paradox of rewriting truth suspends the force of a documentary at the moment of its impact. But the power of a parabolic realism is that it can suspend its own representational claims to truth-telling, which in fact has the effect of discrediting the cinematic act. There is a sense of futility about parabolic realism. It mocks the medium itself, points an accusatory finger at the filmmaker and the spectator alike, and thus it imparts an urgent energy to the moment when the filmmaker points her camera at the subject of her film and starts shooting. The question "What is reality and what is fiction?" is asked right there and then, and thus shines a spotlight on the mimetic distance necessary between fact and representation. Facts uplifted to the status of parables retain their facticity, as Heidegger would say, but project themselves to the semiotic pregnancy of the uncanny.

Contrary to the narrative propensities of all acts of truth-telling to dismantle themselves, the *parabolic* realism I propose to you here builds into its narrative method a corrective mechanism that can prevent its own undoing. It crosses off the gap that ordinarily exists on an imaginary line where the screen and the audience meet and depart. In a wholly different speculative act of spectatorship, the audience is denied the comfort of systematic distancing—hiding in darkness, projecting self-soothing sympathy, and, having done so during the film, going out for a dinner and conversation, having given over a couple of hours of their lives to watching a group of unfortunate poor people. The strategy of parabolic realism makes viewing a film quite uncomfortable, and its psychological effect quite uncanny—it halts the impulse to console oneself with the politics of self-authorizing agency, which occurs at the expense of (always "other") people's real miseries. Parabolic realism thus becomes subversive of its own genre, its own manner of storytelling, successfully sublimating facts into reality, reality into parable, without allowing reality to succumb to the habitual banality of facts. There is thus a creative character to the critical disposition of a filmmaker like Meshkini that propels the perennial problem of representation to a domain where exposition is no longer representational, but instead operates in a prolonged moment of epistemic rupture in which reality registers itself without being assimilated backward into dismissive facts—with the parabolic as the intermediary agent.

Meshkini's film *The Day I Became a Woman* does not introduce or hint at any identifiable politics or argue any particular ethics. All metanarratives of power and morality are dismantled in the face of her parabolic realism—and keep in mind that her cinema emerged after a tyrannical monarchy and during an even more tyrannical theocracy! It would be quite instructive for you at some point to compare what I am suggesting here in Meshkini's cinema with, say, Kubrick's cosmic dilemma, which, throughout his oeuvre, detected and analyzed the nature of the "dram of evil" that, as the hapless Hamlet put it, "doth all the noble substance of a doubt." Seen this way, and placed in the context of Kubrick's overall cinematic cosmovision, the character Humbert Humbert (played by James Mason in the film version of *Lolita*) incarnates the quintessential Kubrick question—the dram of evil in him is the origin and destiny of his fate. Kubrick's reading of *Lolita*, for which he asked Nabokov himself to write the script, looks timid today, though it was certainly scandalous when he first made it. Shelley Winters' nagging and hysterical Charlotte Haze and Peter Sellers' devilish and daring Clare Quilty help Sue Lyon put forward a lovely but not a lyrical Lolita—damaging the character when the émigré professor is obsessed with her but making her perfectly homely and hard-headed when she turns into a pregnant housewife. The sedate matter-of-factness of the final conversation between Humbert and Lolita anticipates the final conversation between Dr. William Harford (Tom Cruise) and his wife, Alice (Nicole Kidman), in *Eyes Wide Shut* (1999)—and the similarity points to a much wiser and worldly investment by Kubrick in his female characters, leaving the dram of evil to foment trouble in the worlds of Jack Torrance, Alex, Humbert, and HAL. Joker also asks the quintessential Kubrick question. This pacifist who in *Full Metal Jacket* (1987) has joined the Marine Corps (while brandishing a peace sign on his helmet all along) point-blank kills a wounded Vietnamese POW—which is anticipated by his vicious beating of his buddy Gomer Pyle when the platoon attacks him in retaliation for his causing them trouble by being overweight and constantly angering their insufferable drill instructor.

The hunt for that dram of evil in Kubrick's cinema is predicated on a universal preoccupation with theodicy—why is there evil in the world if God is one and God is just? The sum total of the cinema that Meshkini represents is a fabulous realism that is too busy with the specific details (where and how deities and the devil dwell) to care for the big picture. There is no big picture, contends the logic and language of this fabulous realism, in the disarming evidence of the factual mediated through the fabulous. Nobility and bestiality both boil in the pot of the same soup, whose taste is irrelevant.

Meshkini's cinema and the aesthetic force of her parabolic realism are rooted in a long and illustrious cinematic tradition. But the literary sources of that heritage are equally important. Those literary sources might range from her mother's lullabies to the masterpieces of Persian prose and Persian translations of world literature. But by way of paying homage to one particular line of her genealogy, I would like to focus on seven women writers chiefly responsible for the contemporary literary culture in Iran, an aspect of Meshkini's cinema that is ordinarily neglected under the power of her more visual evidence.

Seven women writers, avatars of literary excellence, have been responsible for teaching, by example, an entire nation, Meshkini's generation of filmmakers included, how to tell a story. Nobody now remembers her, but the very alphabet of reading and writing good prose was taught to generations of Iranian students from a book called *Dastan-ha-ye Del-Angiz-e Adabiyat-e Farsi* (*Lovely Stories of Persian Literature*, 1958), by Zahra Khanlari. The title of this book and the name of this noble woman probably mean nothing to you and your generation. But it does not mean that Iran is not indebted to her. Every time I go online and read one of these horrid Persian newspapers and break out in rashes because of their ghastly prose (in Iran *Keyhan* and outside Iran the BBC's Persian site are the absolute worst, mutilating Persian prose on a daily basis; what the BBC Persian site in particular is doing to Persian prose is worse than what the invading Arab army did to the Sasanid dynasty!) I think of Zahra Khanlari and the amnesia that separates the current generation of Persian prose writers from hers.

Born in 1916 and raised in Tehran, Khanlari was initially educated at a teacher's college and had begun teaching by the time she was seventeen. At the time she had to obtain special permission from the Ministry of Culture to take the college entrance examination with male students. She entered Tehran University as a student of literature in 1934, the very first year that the venerable institution opened its doors to female students. By 1937, she had received her BA and by 1942 her doctoral degree in Persian literature. In collaboration with her husband, Parviz Natel Khanlari, a leading member of the Iranian literati, Zahra Khanlari was instrumental in establishing *Sokhan*, one of the most influential literary journals of its time, to which she regularly contributed essays and works of fiction (including the first versions of her rendition of the classics of Persian prose that would later be published as *Lovely Stories of Persian Literature*). It is impossible to exaggerate the significance of her *Lovely Stories of Persian Literature*, which for generations introduced young Iranian students to beautiful, simple, and elegant Persian prose through a number of fantastic stories otherwise hidden and buried in the aging heart of the body of Persian literature. Though she did not produce a major literary work of her own, the narrative diction that she crafted became the cornerstone of much that would happen later in modern Persian fiction.

Simin Daneshvar is Iran's most distinguished female novelist, and one of the most influential literary figures of her generation. Daneshvar was born in Shiraz in 1921 into a highly accomplished and cultured family. Her father was a prominent physician and her mother a painter and the director of an art school. In 1949, she left her hometown for Tehran to attend college, and in the following year she married Jalal Al-e Ahmad, one of the towering public intellectuals of twentieth-century Iran. In 1948, Daneshvar published her first work of fiction, *The Extinguished Fire*, which was also the very first appearance of a feminine voice in modern Persian literature in the twentieth century. A year later, she received her doctoral degree in Persian literature from Tehran University, and in 1952 she traveled to the US to attend Stanford University, where she studied creative writing and wrote and published a few of her stories in English. Upon her return to Iran, she began teaching at Tehran University. In addition to her own highly influential works of fiction, Daneshvar translated extensively from the works of Anton Chekhov, Nathaniel Hawthorne, and George Bernard Shaw, among others. In 1962, her second collection of short stories, *A City Like Paradise*, was published. But her principal achievement is *Savushun* (1969), one of the most popular novels in the history of Persian fiction. Set during the British colonial occupation of Shiraz, and from a decidedly provincial angle, in contrast to the Tehran-based conceptions of modern Iranian cultural history, the publication of *Savushun* was a watershed in modern Persian literary prose, and its protagonist, Zari, is one of the most memorable literary creations of twentieth-century Persian fiction.

After Daneshvar came Goli Taraghi—with Khanlari's and Daneshvar's prose solidly sustaining her literary ambitions. Born in 1939 and raised in Tehran, Taraghi was educated in Iran and the United States, and she earned degrees in philosophy and literature. Her first collection of short stories, *I Am Che Guevara* (1969), established her place in Persian letters, and her novel *Great Lady of My Soul* (1979) was well received and widely translated. Before the atrocities of the Islamic Republic forced her into exile in Paris (where she continues to write and publish), she taught philosophy at Tehran University and published highly influential works of fiction, such as *Hibernation* (1973), a masterpiece of Iranian urban anomie. To generations of Iranians, Taraghi's literary prose has been the exemplary model of an exquisitely sophisticated prose style. She commands that distinctively cosmopolitan elegance of the Tehrani inflection of Persian that has, it seems, been forever lost either in the overburdened scholasticism of the clerical rhetoric that serves the ruling clergy or else degenerated into the neologistic colloquialism of daily journalism. Whereas Daneshvar brought to Persian prose her distinct literary formalism from the heart of the Fars province, Taraghi's prose was a graceful elocution that spoke of the cultivated urbanism of the Iranian capital. Taraghi collaborated with two prominent Iranian filmmakers, Dariush Mehrjui (on *The Pear Tree*, 1998) and Hazhir Daryush (*Bita*, 1972), giving birth to some of the best examples of screenwriting.

Then there is Mahshid Amirshahi—wise, worldly, witty, political, with her own urbane sense of humor that is written into the very texture of her defiant prose. She was born in 1940 in Iran, educated in England, and now lives in Paris. The publication of *The Blind Alley* (1966), soon followed by *Bibi Khanom's Starling* (1968) and *After the Last Day* (1969), commenced her prolific writing career. Her first novel, *At Home* (1987), is a masterpiece of post-revolutionary literature, and it brought to perfection her simple, elegant, and deceptively straightforward tone. What is paramount in Amirshahi's prose is the way she combines her radical flamboyance (bordering almost on verbal exhibitionism) with her tasteful cosmopolitan confidence. How she manages to deliver that combination despite her otherwise self-effacing character is the mark of her literary excellence. In the immediate aftermath of the Islamic revolution, Amirshahi put all of these particulars of her literary prose at the service of articulating the sentiments of the defiantly secular opposition forces outside Iran. She soon complemented *At Home* with *Traveling* (1995), and these two books represent a set of classics on the course of the Iranian revolution and its exilic aftermath. More recently, Amirshahi has embarked on the publication of a quartet that she calls *Mothers and Daughters*, of which three volumes have appeared so far. Amirshahi embodies a breed of urban intellectual with an unflinching secular disposition—which in her case is fundamental to her creative character. Cultured, multilingual, and widely read, Amirshahi writes with a crystalline clarity, and her body of work is a deeply moving chronicle of the generation of Iranian secular intellectuals that she now best represents.

Shahrnush Parsipur is one of the most gifted Iranian novelists alive. Courageous, and with a barely tamed command over a subversive volcano of suppressed emotions, her fiction is consistently phantasmagoric. Parsipur was born in 1946 and went to college at Tehran University before going to France to study Indian languages and cultures. Beginning in the mid-1970s, Parsipur rapidly emerged as one of the most gifted novelists and short-story writers of her time. *The Dog and the Long Winter* (1976) immediately established her reputation as a major literary contender in the late Pahlavi period; soon after her *Crystal Pendants* (1977) and *Free Experiments* (1978) reinforced that status. Her masterpiece, *Tuba and the Meaning of Night* (1988), was an overnight success, while *Women without Men* (1989) landed her in the barbaric dungeons of the Islamic Republic. Soon after her incarceration and before her exile to the United States, where she now lives, Parsipur was diagnosed with chronic manic depression. A feat of narrative neurosis and creative psychosis, *Tuba and the Meaning of Night* stands as one of the greatest achievements of modern Persian literature. At the center of Parsipur's works of fiction is a fervent creativity that has seemingly imploded on itself. In *Women without Men*, she weaves the scattered lives of a number of women from various walks of life and has them converge in a garden—at once real and paradisiacal—where they plant themselves and flower. Parsipur's stories begin innocently, inconspicuously, and with perfect realistic cadence, and then gradually metamorphose into surreal dimensions. In this imperceptible transformation, made possible through direct access to a writer's innate emotive universe, Parsipur discretely teases out aspects of women's lives otherwise hidden behind the banalities of their quotidian existences. Shirin Neshat, for long the most gifted video installation artist of her generation, is currently turning *Women without Men* into her very first feature film. I have seen some of her rushes. Parsipur herself has a small role in one of the episodes of the film!

Moniru Ravanipour comes next. A wild magician of words and visions, a storyteller from the dark nights of the Persian Gulf, she conjures with elemental force the forlorn souls of drowned fishermen and the sea monsters that swallow them. Born in 1954 in the village of Jofreh and raised in Shiraz, she received her early and college education in that provincial city before moving to Tehran. Her magical realism brought peripheral psychosis (a melancholic dismantling of reason that was based in Tehrani-centered modernity) to perfection in her literary masterpiece, *People of Gharq* (1989). A year before that, Ravanipour had burst onto the Iranian literary scene with her book *With Kanizu* (1988), and two years after that *Satan's Stone* (1991) consolidated her reputation as a major post-revolutionary novelist and short-story writer. Despite all censorial difficulties, Ravanipour weathered the storms and remained inside Iran, traveled to her native south, and each time brought back ever more fantastic stories for her readers. Ravanipour is the sunburnt, bright-eyed, openhearted expression of her homeland like nothing seen or heard before. Her prose is salty and dry, her wisdom climactic (full of the thunder and lightning of the sea storms of her native south), her stories full of sea ghosts and mermaids—shades and shadows of frightened, frightful hopes—a southern sister to Gholamhossein Saedi, in ways he had never anticipated, could not have foretold.

And then came Ghazaleh Alizadeh—the crowning achievement of generations of women writers, one after the other the clear conscience of their nation, registering dimensions of hope, shadows of fears, colors of frustration. Before her untimely death by suicide in May 1996, Alizadeh's masterpiece, *The Idrissi's House* (1992), gradually emerged as the iconic text of the first generation of Iranian novelists after the 1979 revolution. In *The Idrissi's House*, Alizadeh tells the story of her nation in the macabre, aristocratic mansion of an old family (very reminiscent of Golshiri's *Prince Ehtejab*), presided over by an old maid and her children, and suddenly invaded by a band of coarse and crude revolutionaries. Alizadeh's prose is introverted, archaic, musty, and meandering. She writes as if with a searchlight, navigating the hidden corners of an attic full of useless possessions. *The Idrissi's House* becomes a parable of the Islamic revolution and Alizadeh's story is a trans-historic reflection on the terrors of violence and the hidden horrors of aristocratic elegance— at one and the same time. Even more hauntingly, the tale is recounted by an omniscient narrator who seems to hover around the house like the ghost of the young daughter of the family, dead before the book begins—a kind of self-projection by Alizadeh—her opening sentence the chronicle of a death foretold:

> Chaos and confusion do not happen in a house
> quite suddenly. In the gap of wooden bars, flanked
> by the creases of sheets, in between the cracks of
> windows, and hidden in the folds of curtains first
> sets a very gentle dust—all waiting for a wind to

blow through the house from an opened door and let
loose all the scattered pieces from their hideouts.

I remind you of this particular genealogy of prominent women writers in
order to map the contours of the moral and imaginative foundation upon
which Meshkini's art of storytelling sits. This is what I have been trying
to tell you all along, to give body and substance to what generations of
Iranian filmmakers have achieved in the visual and performing arts. I am
often troubled by much that is written about Iranian cinema outside Iran,
not because some of it is not exceedingly intelligent and insightful, but
that precisely in their intelligence and insights most of these writings (by
no means all) are disembodied. They have plucked Iranian cinema out
of its natural (by which I mean historic, social, economic, literary, altogether cultural) contexts, and have given it a reading predicated entirely
on their exposure to Iranian cinema in major film festivals, sporadic retrospectives, occasional and limited commercial releases, and now the
video and DVD market. Iranian cinema belongs to a people, and this
people has a history, a cultural location, a pride of place—and this cinema is an art of emancipation from the claws of a nasty tyranny, local and
global, and it has aimed to achieve its historic task: to restore dignity to a
nation, agency to its people, and creative confidence in their future. For
that to happen we need to rescue Iranian cinema and its masterpieces
from (among other things) being mutated into objects of anthropological
curiosity for mere (and useless) theoretical speculation—in short turning
Iranian films into museum pieces while their makers and their audience
are still alive and well. This, I insist, is the result of the disciplinary translation of none other than the old-fashioned Orientalism that refuses
(because it is unable) to understand a living art for what it is: organically
linked to the hopes and aspiration of the people who make it.

Meshkini's parabolic realism is a case in point, where the mere evidence of a cinema cannot be read unless and until it is linked to a wider
frame of reference. For Marziyeh Meshkini did not just happen. She is
rooted—like the cinema she represents, and like all mighty and beautiful
trees. In this case not only are the literary sources of Meshkini's visual
vocabulary integral, but the generation of women filmmakers who have
come before her are as well. The existence of a significant number of
women filmmakers in and of itself is an exceedingly significant social fact
in any society, but perhaps particularly in Iran where Iranian women are
systematically denied not just social visibility but, far more importantly,
the public articulation of their own vision of things. Meshkini brings a set
of social and cinematic sensibilities to her art that are both personal and
historical, and she effectively bears witness to a record of Iranian women
trying publicly to assert their vision of their realities. Without that vision,

Iran's notions of its historical whereabouts are infinitely poorer, structurally flawed, politically malfeasant, and aesthetically lopsided.

The earliest record of an Iranian woman filmmaker dates back to the mid-1950s. Historians of Iranian cinema consider Shahla Riyahi's *Marjan* (1956) the first film made by an Iranian woman. Riyahi was already a popular actress of stage and screen by the time she made *Marjan*. Masculinist historiography has twice compromised her achievements, once by giving only her first name, a mere "Shahla," as the director, and another time by completely denying that she even directed *Marjan*, asserting that she was the producer of the film and that her costar, Mohammad Ali Jafari, directed the film and that "the name Shahla was also added as director on top of theater doors, and this was quite attractive for the audience, to see a woman's name as director," as one historian, Jamal Omid, puts it in his *Farhang-e Cinema-ye Iran* (look it up; it is in the first volume of this book, pages 48–49). For a melodrama, Riyahi's *Marjan* had its own peculiar twists. A young gypsy girl falls in love with a teacher who has just captured her father trying to steal a sheep from the school where he teaches. The teacher eventually leaves his village and moves to the city, and the young gypsy girl follows him. She cannot find him and ends up working as a nurse in a hospital where some time later the teacher brings his young wife to deliver their child. Disappointed, Marjan returns to her tribe.

It is crucial to remember that by the time that Riyahi made *Marjan* in 1956, Forugh Farrokhzad's first collection of poems, *The Captive* (1955), had already been published. Riyahi's vision, as a result, may not have been predicated on a history of women filmmakers, but it was given momentum by Farrokhzad's poetry and the revolutionary resistance to historical blindness that she represented. Farrokhzad's poetic voice was the antecedent of the agential memory of Iranian women, resisting their enforced veiling, which seemed a means of blinding them to their own historical presence. It is a miraculous fact of modern Iranian culture that the first globally celebrated Iranian woman filmmaker was also the most distinguished poet of her generation. Farrokhzad is the only major Iranian poet who was also a major filmmaker, albeit by the virtue of only one short documentary that she made. Nobody else shares that singular distinction. She is as integral to the creation of modern Persian poetry—the only woman in the halls of its patristic heritage—as she is constitutional to the making of modern Iranian cinema. Nothing visually significant happens between Riyahi's pioneering *Marjan* and Farrokhzad's masterpiece, *The House Is Black* (1962), and it is not until then that Iranian cinema fully recognizes and duly celebrates the birth of its first woman filmmaker.

As I have already told you in some detail, *The House Is Black* is a poetic ode to beauty in the heart of misery. *The House Is Black* has valiantly survived its over-politicization by a succession of malnourished and mis-guided film critics. It is only at the most artificial level that *The House Is Black* can be watched as a commentary on Iran under the Pahlavis, a society afflicted with a disease and yet incapable of curing its ailment with reason and science. Left to its own magnificent devices, *The House Is Black* is a crystalline, black-and-white gem, stealing beauty and teasing joy from the depth of despair and the heart of darkness. It is no Manichean bifurcation of good and evil. It is a prophetic call to purposeful prayer. Farrokhzad moved through the lens of her camera and beyond just imag-ining herself inside the world she saw; she kissed its wounds and nurtured its pains, showering a long cascade of love and affection upon the most afflicted, the most forgotten. It is impossible to describe the fear and loathing that the mere mentioning of leprosy would invoke—far worse than when AIDS had just emerged publicly in the 1980s in the United States and the Christian Right began branding it as a sign of divine wrath against homosexuals. The horror and harassment to which the gay com-munity in particular was subjected compares well with the experience of lepers in Iran. There was something mysteriously repugnant about the public perception of leprosy, as if it were some sign of divine punishment for some mysterious sin. It was feared like a bubonic plague, believed to be deadly contagious. With *The House Is Black*, Farrokhzad walked into that forbidden and transgressive space and cured both the afflicted and the fearful.

After Farrokhzad's *The House Is Black*, the emerging Iranian cinema could not boast of a major woman filmmaker for a very long time. As Dariush Mehrjui, Bahram Beizai, Abbas Kiarostami, Amir Naderi, and a host of other directors began to map out the contours of a spectacular and variegated national cinema, there was, lamentably, not a single woman to be found among the leading directors. Marva Nabili's quietly shot and secretly smuggled *The Sealed Soil* (1977) kept the hopes and aspirations of Iranian women filmmakers alive. Nabili is so tangential to Iranian cin-ema now that one must believe in miracles to conceive of her appearance in the 1970s to establish a barely visible thread between Riyahi in the 1950s, Farrokhzad in the 1960s, and the rise of a constellation of promi-nent women filmmakers after the Iranian revolution in the 1980s. While in Iran, Nabili had worked with Fereydun Rahnama on his *Siavash at Persepolis* (1967), a landmark in the history of Iranian cinema. She subse-quently studied film in London and New York, and then returned to Iran to direct a television series based on Persian fairy tales. It was in the mid-1970s that she discretely shot *The Sealed Soil*, smuggled it out of Iran, and premiered it at the San Remo film festival where she was awarded the prize for best new director. The film's protagonist, Roybekheyr, is a young peasant woman rebelling against her immediate surroundings, not particularly attracted to the promises of an urban life, and yet impatient with some inner palpitation she cannot quite articulate. She refuses to heed her family's advice to marry and in a moment of frantic frustration violently kills a chicken, which results in her being diagnosed by the community as emotionally disturbed and entrusted to a local soothsayer. The final shot of *The Sealed Soil* shows Roybekheyr yielding her body, almost like a planted tree, to the downpour of a bounteous rain, uniting her with the elemental forces of a nature she has been forced to repress.

Nabili never returned to Iran after the revolution. She moved to New York, where she made *Nightsongs* (1984), a feature film about a Chinese-Vietnamese woman who comes to New York and lives in Chinatown on the margins of an already marginalized community. Nabili became the precursor to Shirin Neshat, who a generation later revolutionized what—because of its radically globalized aesthetic and political configurations—can no longer even be called an *Iranian* visual art. In Nabili we see the beginning of a global gaze that, even in a remote village in Iran, is fully cognizant of the multiplicity of sites in which her work will be seen. Nabili is thus critical in facilitating that worldly perspective, opening one, however small, window through which the world could now peek into the otherwise closed circuits of a culture, as that culture was using the same window to cast a long and lasting look at the world at large. Nabili's singular achievement was that her camera remained native to Iranian sensibilities while decidedly perceptive in the wide angle of its global perspective.

What came to be called an "Islamic revolution" was one of the most violent events in modern Iranian history. Two years of continuous rebellious uprisings culminated in a massive mobilization that destroyed the old regime and executed its public officials and military officers before it brutally eliminated all its own rival claimants to revolutionary power and then faded into a horrific eight-year war with Iraq. But the same revolution ushered in a period of unprecedented creative effervescence in which women were to have an exceptional presence. Suddenly a small army of women filmmakers picked up cameras and began to make one film after another—Kobra Saidi's *Maryam and Mani* (1980), Marziyeh Boroumand's *The City of the Mice* (1983), Pouran Derakhshandeh's *The Little Bird of Happiness* (1987), Tahmineh Ardakani's *Golbahar* (1986), Faryal Behzad's *Kakoli* (1989), Tahmineh Milani's *Children of Divorce* (1989). Where were all these filmmakers before? *The Sealed Soil* was scarcely seen inside Iran, and Marva Nabili was hardly a household name; Riyahi's *Marjan* was a matter of archival curiosity; Farrokhzad's *The House Is Black* was at that time still not a widely watched or extensively discussed film. There was no record, no collective memory, of any woman filmmaker with a large body of work. But if you place Farrokhzad's *poetry* where it was best preserved, in the minds and souls of generations that came after her, then there remains no mystery. She saw in her poetry what women directors would later see for the entire world in their films.

The story of Iranian women filmmakers before and after the Islamic revolution of 1979 cannot be told either chronologically or teleologically. What has ultimately happened is the gradual and mosaic assembly of variable and consistently insightful visions, making every subsequent effort more focused than the one before. After the revolution, women's emancipatory movements, from peasant and urban uprisings to literary and artistic achievements, could not be brought to an abrupt, tyrannical end—not after what women had endured under two Pahlavi shahs, and not under the brutalities of a patriarchal theocracy. The political subject had invested too much in winning historical agency (and all of that through the caring camera of a few but furiously persistent band of visionaries) to allow it to be sucked back into the jaws of bureaucratic censorship and ideological fanaticism. The massive participation of Iranian women in the course of the revolution, an illustrious record of women novelists and poets, painters and photographers, singers and actresses, university professors and schoolteachers, all along a massive participation of women in the workforce, had resulted in a critical mass and a creative core that could not but come to artistic fruition. Urbane, educated, cultivated in the tumultuous torrents of their history, and in full public view, Iranian women joined the corps of post-revolutionary artists who opposed institutional violence, which was perpetrated against their vision and symbolized in their forced veiling. That they still have a long way to go is more a sign of the catalytic effect of domestic tyranny and globalized imperialism, the unintended consequences of injustice that generates more defiance against it, that engulfs their region than their failure to achieve their goals.

At the conclusion of the Iran-Iraq War, which lasted from 1980 to 1988, and upon the death of Ayatollah Khomeini in 1989, the reign of charismatic terror that had for a decade brutalized a nation began to subside. Established filmmakers continued to thrive and new names joined their ranks. By the end of the 1980s the feminine figure of modernity was placed squarely and safely beyond the reaches of its colonial and patriarchal shadows in the Iranian imagination—in no small part because of the consistently defiant and superb work of women poets, novelists, artists, and filmmakers themselves. No amount of forced veiling, no violent banning of young women from soccer stadiums, no systematic campaign of terror and intimidation or gender apartheid in schools, hospitals, and other public domains could compromise what these filmmakers had achieved. Women could be juridically barred from having their bodies exposed to the public gaze (and thus by extension preventing them from accumulating bodily memories), but through the lenses of women film-makers they could already see and imagine themselves otherwise.

The election of President Mohammad Khatami in 1997 marked the beginning of a new era in modern Iranian history. When Samira Makhmalbaf's film *Apple* premiered in Cannes, in 1998, the whole world knew that Iran had entered a new phase in its long and embattled encounter with colonial modernity. Soon after, and as Samira Makhmalbaf was making her second feature, *Blackboard* (2000), Meshkini's stunning debut, *The Day I Became a Woman* (2000) marked her successful entry onto the global scene. Members of the previous generation were still equally active. Pouran Derakhshandeh, for example, made *Love without Frontier* (2000), and Maryam Shahryar joined in with her first feature, *The Daughters of the Sun* (2000), a fine film with very precise and measured movements toward the cultivation of a promising career. Tahmineh Milani's *Two Women* (2000) and *The Hidden Half* (2001) established her as one of the most socially conscientious and politically controversial filmmakers of the time. Milani is not a filmmaker of enduring aesthetic significance or cultural insight. But she is a courageous rabble-rouser of uncommon dedication. When Niki Karimi, by far the most celebrated Iranian actress of her generation, made her first documentary, *To Have or Not to Have*, in 2001, the significance of filmmakers as the authors of their national destiny led yet another woman to an authorial position. Karimi is the conclusion of Shahla Riyahi: Celebrated in their chosen profession, the bodiless face of Karimi (because she is forced to veil in front of the camera) now complements the faceless body of Riyahi (because her identity as a filmmaker is denied) to make a complete human being, integral to the fate of a nation, competent in their collective gaze, and jointly imagining a whole person, and with her an entire people in their place in history.

The Day I Became a Woman consists of three thematically interrelated episodes, each narrated around a central feminine figure: a young girl, a married woman, and an old woman. The first episode, "Hava," is the story of a young girl who wakes up one morning and is told by her mother and grandmother that today is her birthday and she is now a grown woman, and cannot go out without a proper veil or play with young boys her own age anymore. Hava manages to persuade her mother and grandmother to allow her a few more hours of freedom so she can go out for one last round of playing with her friends before she puts the veil on and stays away from boys. "Ahu," the second episode, is the story of a young married woman who defies her husband's prohibitions and joins an all-women bicycle race. Angered by her defiance, Ahu's husband chases after her on horseback and divorces her on the spot. "Hura," the final episode, is the story of an old woman who seems to have recently inherited a substantial amount of money and has come to a free-trade zone, Kish, in the Persian Gulf, where all these stories are taking place, to indulge in a shopping spree, buying things that she has probably always yearned to have and yet never did.

What is most significant about *The Day I Became a Woman* is its episodic breakdown of a life cycle into three interrelated moments—childhood, youth, and old age. One can easily see Hava as the child of Ahu, and Ahu as the youthful Hura. This bodily breakdown of one person into three narrative instances, cast into three different people, gives Meshkini's film the parabolic realism that simply portrays the evident reality of the stories told and yet implies the surreal mutation of that reality into a realm beyond the mundane matter-of-factness of things that have and could very well have happened. The other notable phenomenon of *The Day I Became a Woman* is an almost total absence of adult men. In the first and third episodes we never see either Hava or Hura in the presence of any grown men. It is only in the second episode that we see bearded and angry adult men swarming around Ahu, admonishing and threatening her into one course of action or another. But these men—husband, father, brother, uncle—are always on the move and unstable, their habitual sedentary confidence yielding to an unstable agitation, with their figures now the mobile visions of a masculinity with pretensions to the moral high ground, which is moving under its feet. Equally important is the film's location, Kish. At the southern tip of the Iranian geographical imagination, Kish is an almost outlandish location that gives the film an idyllic or mythic character; things there seem not as solid and contentious as they appear to be on the mainland, close to the influence of the political and cultural center.

The film operates through the perforated space between the three actual episodes, which come together to augment the parabolic evidence of the episodes themselves, thus forming an evident but inconspicuous whole. The three shades of stories that we actually see and the blank shadows of their presumed but unseen links constellate a universe at once real and mythic, factual but parabolic. This parabolic realism is neither realistic nor phantasmagoric, but in it reality and phantasm together demarcate a space for storytelling that forces reality to yield its other-than-itself. The three stories are not actually connected, but a thematic connection arises from them. Hava, Ahu, and Hura are three different people, and their stories take place simultaneously (Hava of episode one and a number of cyclists from the second episode appear in the third episode), and yet a teleological progression of aging is suggested and continued throughout, giving the whole film the simulacrum of a continuous life cycle. The incongruity of these two diametrically opposed trajectories complement and complete each other, and give the film in its entirety a perforated formality, a staggered mannerism modulated between the seen and the unseen, the marked and the unmarked, the stated and the suggested.

As such, the formal (in)congruity of *The Day I Became a Woman* is one of the most effective examples of how a creative work of art defies the historical mandates of a culture. The fact that emerges from *The Day I Became a Woman* is the systematic, unjust, and endemic repression of women written and carved into the fabric of a culture. But the fate of Iranian women is still very much found on the borderline where their own creative imagination and their material conditions collide and implode. The mode of realism evident in Meshkini's cinema, whereby reality is forced to reveal its otherwise than itself, is just one way of forcing the culture to yield its own and innate forces of creative imagination. That parabolic realism, and its creative mode of manufacturing agential autonomy for Iranian women beyond their own patriarchal and imported colonial predicaments, is not something that "masterpieces of Western literature" have condescended to provide to Iranian women. It is something spun and woven out of the creative soul of a people and their historic struggles for freedom. What generations of Iranian filmmakers leading up to Meshkini have achieved in this parabolic realism is an unrelenting dwelling on the factual evidence of the real, barring it from any metaphysical mutation or ideological distortion, all by way of running it through a parabolic narrative—a visual narrative that reduces reality to its most irreducible force as a parable. Within and domestic to that parabolic evidence, filmmakers like Marziyeh Meshkini have come up with ingenious ideas that make reality speak beyond the metaphysically dissipated and ideologically enforced, constrictions that have left women out of the cosmic order of culture and allowed them only a backdoor entry. Artists like Meshkini oppose and seek to end that constitutional injustice not via an ideology that posits an alternative vision of reality, but by holding reality itself accountable to a better account of itself. The parabolic realism that I detect and purposed in Meshkini's film works through a cinematic adaptation of the icastic-phantastic mimesis I have already outlined and that has been dramaturgically anticipated by Taziyeh.

What women filmmakers like Meshkini are doing in the hidden dungeons of our collective consciousness, our forgotten and feared nightmares, is something beyond the politics of the moment and deep in the emancipatory sites of liberation. If anyone among Iran's artists were to be trusted to go that deep, to disturb the anxiety-ridden peace, and dig that pointedly, it would be a filmmaker like Meshkini, her parabolic realism working with surgical accuracy, at once revealing and seeking, to heal the ills of a culture—not by fighting their social formations, but by dismantling their metaphysical ordering in the ordinariness of our prosaic language. Meshkini always says that all she does is just show and tell, and nothing more. But embedded in her cinema, in both *The Day I Became a Woman* and in *Stray Dogs* (2003), is not just a daring invitation to expose the roots of corruption and the cultural maladies of a nation. Meshkini's manner of realism does not throw the baby out with the proverbial bathwater. She excavates gold in dirty mines—just like Farrokhzad, Zahra Khanlari, and Ghazaleh Alizadeh did before her. Meshkini's characters are all earthly, believable—they seem to have just stepped off a bus, waved goodbye to a friend, walked home, greeted a relative, sat down to have a cup of tea. Her realism works through a parabolic simulation of reality, but it is ultimately factual in the sense that social facts remain at the level of their communal construction, neither sublimated to any truth nor mutated into any fantasy—and precisely in the simplicity of that cinema she has hanged her fictively evident truth. She makes her descent into the darker side of the Iranian collective psyche with the searchlight of forgotten reasons for being—*bahaneh-ha-ye sadeh-ye khoshbakhti*, Farrokhzad used to call them, "simple reasons for happiness." What I mean to say is that Iran is an old, aging, and bewildered culture—embedded in its own miseries, harassed by its location in the cross-currents of history, too old in its memories to live anew, too young in its demographic composition to let go of its past. The predicament that its artists face—prophetic visionaries who have sustained our hopes and held our hands through a really miserable history—is the language they need to muster in order to remind not just the truly perturbed psychopaths who keep ruling over Iran's destiny but their kindred demons who keep animating our own inner fear that life (fragile, precious, just a breath away from self-destruction) really does not need to be so miserable. What I mean by the parabolic realism in Meshkini's cinema is precisely that ability to remind a people the very first but always forgotten reason of being thrown together and called "a people": decency—not as if mandated by a heavenly ordained revelation; but decency as in the very fact of our otherwise inexplicable reason to be here in the first place. You see what I mean? It's really just Khayyam—still writing his poems in us, the best of us.

Who are we and why are Iranians so incapacitated as a people? Patriarchy, colonialism, monarchy, mullarchy—is that all, do these things exhaust the range of reasons and explanations? Is there something else? Where does the politics of our poverty, material and moral, end and the ethics of a higher order begin, and where do the aesthetics of an emancipation commence to sublimate and transmute the terror of that politics, uplift the sanctity of that ethics? Through Meshkini's camera, and those of generations of Iranian women filmmakers before her, we have had a glimpse into the darkest corners of our soul as a nation, corners we carefully tuck away and never dare to unfold. There is a stanza in Farrokhzad's masterpiece poem, "Another Birth," where she describes a spiral descent: "*My fate is to descend an old stair / reaching down to connect with something in decadence and solitude.*" I have taken two liberties in this translation: one is "fate" for *sahm*, usually translated as "lot" or "share," and the other is "solitude" for *ghorbat*, usually translated as "exile" or "nostalgia." Those choices, in my judgment, better represent the sense of the poem. My point is this: In the mode of parabolic realism that Meshkini represents we see a similar subterranean dungeon of negation and abrogation, something hidden in the millennial memory a people, something frightful and terrorizing, a volcanic violence hidden under a perhaps wise and necessarily placid surface. In that vision, the cinema that Meshkini's generation of women filmmakers represents is an extension of that single shot of Farrokhzad in *The House Is Black* where the camera begins to zoom in on the mirror reflection of a leprosy-ravaged face of a woman. Meshkini's generation of parabolic realists has taken that single shot and written it large. Her cinema is the mirror of our nightmares—seen, heard, and interpreted by the caring, confident, and wise heart of one among a handful of prophetic visionaries we as a nation have scarce merited and yet always managed to produce.

Be not too tame neither, but let your own
discretion be your tutor.
–William Shakespeare, *Hamlet*

Jafar Panahi
Crimson Gold

I BELIEVE that with Abbas Kiarostami's *actual*, Marziyeh Meshkini's *parabolic*, and Mohsen Makhmalbaf's *virtual* realisms, Iranian cinema has come to a full visual and epistemic conclusion, and thus to an end. These three filmmakers took Amir Naderi's and Bahram Beizai's groundbreaking mutations of Iranian cinema and, in visual terms, brought them to fruition. Before Naderi and Beizai we had successive developments—from Dariush Mehrjui to Arby Ovanessian to Bahman Farmanara to Sohrab Shahid Sales—in which this visual vocabulary was crafted in creative conversation with master practitioners of Iranian literary arts. They were the purgatorial passage from the verbal into the visual. In that verbal realm stood two giant literary figures, Forugh Farrokhzad and Ebrahim Golestan—the Eve and Adam of Iranian cinema, the first dreamers of our cinematic hopes, conceived in the bosom of their poetic diction.

My proposal is that the filmmakers of the new and subsequent generations no longer remember this history; for they swim in it, just as a fish is not conscious of the sea, or a bird aware of the air—they just swim

393

and soar in it. Here I can take any one of them as an example of what I have in mind. I can talk about Samira Makhmalbaf, or Bahman Qobadi, or Parviz Shahbazi, or Mohammad Shirvani, and on and on. But I opt to consider this through the cinema of Jafar Panahi, for I find him the least conscious of what he is doing, and among the best at swimming and soaring in the visual elements of his cinema. Thriving in the visual inheritance of Iranian cinema, the generation of filmmakers that Panahi represents are the beneficiaries of an opulent visual vocabulary delivered to them on a silver platter—fortunately (like all other rich children) without their full awareness of it. The result is an undiluted *visual* realism (anticipated in the generation of filmmakers that produced Amir Naderi and concluded in the next generation that culminated in Jafar Panahi) that has finally come to complete, confident, and colorful consummation. In them is invested the visual constitution of a creative unconscious in which we can create, stage, and watch *visually*—surpassing the long and illustrious history of our verbal memories. My concluding argument is that toward a full realization of that visual vocabulary our entire verbal memory has now completely unfolded.

Jafar Panahi was born in 1960 in Mianeh, Azerbaijan, in northwestern Iran, and after his high-school education and military service he studied cinema in Tehran. He had already made a few short films for television when he joined Abbas Kiarostami and worked with him on *Through the Olive Trees* (1994). It was while working on this film that Kiarostami wrote the script for Panahi's first feature film, *Badkonak-e Sefid* (*The White Balloon*, 1995), which won the Camera d'Or at the Cannes Film Festival and catapulted him to international fame. Soon after that, Panahi made *Ayeneh* (*The Mirror*, 1997), which received the Locarno Film Festival's Golden Leopard award. Panahi received even more global recognition with his third feature film, *Dayereh* (*The Circle*, 2000), which won the Golden Lion at the 2000 Venice Film Festival, before it was selected as the Film of the Year by FIPRESCI, and subsequently appeared on the top-ten lists of many critics around the world. His *Tala-ye Sorkh* (*Crimson Gold*, 2003), inspired by actual events and again based on a script by Kiarostami, is his most recent and arguably best film, and cemented his position among the top filmmakers of his generation.

Crimson Gold is the story of an armed robbery and subsequent suicide. The film begins as Hossein (Hossein Emadeddin) is about to rob a jewelry store when things go awry and he gets trapped inside the store. Frightened and out of options he kills himself. The rest of the film is a flashback, not just into the history of how Hossein came to commit this crime but also to recent Iranian history, the history of the failed Islamic revolution and the Iran-Iraq War in particular. Alienation, anomie, and a subdued violence are written all over the visual texture of a picture that trembles with the unanswerable questions of a history of betrayed hopes and denied aspirations. Hossein is perfectly cast. His face is vacant, his demeanor forlorn; there is not a trace of connectedness to anything or anybody about him. He is sullen and apathetic, brooding with a subdued anger with no apparent origin or purpose. Who is this man and where did he come from? From the hidden corners of what subterranean denial did Panahi dig him out?

Panahi himself has said that he heard the story on which the film is based first from Kiarostami, when they were both caught in a traffic jam—the story of a man who was tempted to commit robbery, was caught in the act, and unable to face the embarrassment of its consequences killed himself. Panahi became mesmerized by the story and wanted to turn it into a film. Kiarostami agreed to write the script. He wrote it and Panahi made the film. But that is where reality ends and art begins—in the mind and soul of two master filmmakers. Between the two of them, they fired a shot that announced a major turning point in the history of their chosen profession. The bullet that kills Hossein is the bullet that cinematically marks the end of the Islamic revolution, the dissolution of the solidarity that it temporarily generated and then lost, and with that the end of what today the world calls "Iranian cinema," a cinema deeply rooted in the revolutionary trauma of a nation. Hossein's is a suicide that the French sociologist Emile Durkheim would identify as "anomic," a sign of alienation from any bond of social solidarity. But while Durkheim theorized anomic suicide as the sudden or gradual dismantling of social solidarities and normative orders in the course of European modernity, Hossein's suicide signals the end of solidarity occasioned and sustained by Khomeini's revolution. But Khomeini died in 1989, and Panahi made *Crimson Gold* in 2003, and Khomeini's charismatic authority, which made the revolution possible and engendered a momentary and false unity, came to an end immediately after his death. So the bullet that Hossein puts into his own head is also the bullet that kills the charismatic memory of Khomeini. In a classic case of masochistic violence, the son replaces his own body for the body of the father and by inflicting (the ultimate) pain on himself revenges himself against the father.

The opening shot of *Crimson Gold* is invested with the imaginative confidence of the whole history of Iranian cinema. Where Panahi places his camera, how he frames the shot and lights the scene, what sound effects he engineers and designs, what actors he chooses and how tall or short or fat or thin they are—these are among the almost unconscious decisions of a filmmaker who has long since forgotten where and how he learned his craft, which is exactly what needs to happen for a cinema to transcend being simply an industry and become a culture. There is a corroborative correspondence between the creative unconscious of a filmmaker and the collective consciousness of the culture he represents. In what he called "conscience collective," Emile Durkheim posited a set of beliefs and sentiments—in symbolic, institutional, or sentimental orders—that held members of a community together. In what he called the "collective unconscious," Carl Gustav Jung sought to trace the communal residues of such orders beyond cultural or historical specificities. Between Durkheim and Jung, we can detect and identify the historical parameters of a normative culture, the subterranean sources of which artists creatively tap. The more an artist is unconsciously communicative with his own creative unconscious the more his art becomes an account of a vision that his culture dreams in him. It is that act of dreaming that agitates the symbolic-real-imaginary triad theorized by Jacques Lacan and places a collective unconscious at a momentous occasion of reconfiguration. If there is any revolutionary force to a cinema in its (post)colonial disposition, then it is right here, where the colonial subject creatively taps into his creative unconscious and is thus set categorically free.

Hossein's friend is Ali (Kamyar Sheissi) to whose sister (Azita Rayeji) he is engaged. Hossein and Ali work as pizza deliverymen. They are poor (what happened to the promise of the Islamic revolution to eradicate poverty?). They chance upon a jewelry shop in the rich part of the city (what happened to the promise of the revolution to create a "unitary classless society?"). By some bizarre force of reason and accident, Hossein, his fiancèe, and his friend are attracted to the mysterious appeal of the uptown, upscale, out-of-their-league jewelry shop. But why? That lurking question remains disturbingly alive under the thin surface of Panahi's film. There is a violence to *Crimson Gold* that grows ever more powerful precisely because it is by and large hidden. This manner of showing violence without showing who has perpetrated it has now become a trademark of Panahi's cinema. We saw it first in *The White Balloon*," when Razieh's brother (played by Moshen Kalifi) appears with blood on his face and shirt, and it is obvious that someone has beat him up, but we never know who exactly—and yet we can surmise that it was probably his cantankerous father, whom we never see, but always hear screaming from a bathroom where he is taking a shower. We saw (or didn't see) the same thing in *The Circle*, when one of the two young prostitutes, Nargess (Nargess Mamizadeh), has the signs of a brutal beating on her face, though we never find out who has hit her or why. Violence in Panahi's cinema is like a phantom: You see through it, but it lacks a source or physical presence—who has perpetrated it is made intentionally amorphous. The result is a sense of fear and anxiety that lurks in every frame of his films, but it is a fear without an identifiable referent. This is one of the most radical forces in Panahi's cinema, for he is in effect dismantling the connections of violence to dismissible (identified, categorized, and archived) specificities and seeks to generate a whole new *sensus communis* (as Hans-Georg Gadamer, following Vico, theorized it) in reading violence.

Hossein and his companions enter the jewelry shop. They look like three fish out of water: bewildered, frightened, embarrassed, out of place. The owner of the jewelry shop realizes in a second that they are not his customers. "What are they doing here?" is written all over his face before he has even opened his mouth, or so Hossein thinks, as do his fiancée and friend. They collect their courage and ask to look at things. But they are clumsy. Their body language appears lame, their accent is jarring, their demeanor demands too much attention. Seconds into an attempt at conversation with the owner and they are told in so many words to go back where they came from, back downtown, there are plenty of jewelry shops there where they can find items suitable to their taste (class), prices they can afford (cheap). Rarely has Iranian cinema depicted the brutality of class differences so powerfully. It is impossible for a filmmaker to capture the essence of that brutality without having himself felt it over a lifetime of experience. Layer after layer of the politics and economics of power are stripped away. Panahi is relentless, persistent, a visual surgeon of uncompromising precision. What is this class distinction? Where does it come from? Is there a common humanity left beyond class differences? That jewelry shop becomes smaller than a prison cell, larger than the whole universe. This scene is by far the most violent scene of the whole film, far more violent than the final suicide scene—for here violence is subsumed in a fake formality. Do you remember the Persian expression we have, "to cut someone's throat with cotton"? That's the meaning of this scene.

At one point we see Hossein delivering a pizza at the home of a man who used to be his comrade during the Iran-Iraq War, but now appears to have done well for himself. "How has this man become so wealthy, and Hossein so poor?" Panahi's class-conscious camera asks. On the surface, this is just a commentary on the massive hypocrisy of the Islamic revolution, for its miserable failure to deliver on its promises. But the scene also marks the intransigent borderline, right there at the door of the wealthy man, between the beneficiaries and the disenfranchised of the Islamic revolution. It is not just the revolutionary claims of the Islamic revolution that are here discredited, but far more effectively its *Islamicity*. What sort of "Islam" is this? Who was that charismatic prophet of violence (what was his name—Ayatollah one thing or another?) who overthrew a monarchy just to replace it with a mullarchy—and thus sustained the selfsame relation of power and wealth, even worse, that existed before. The whole moral and metaphysical underpinning of the

Islamic revolution is dismantled and returned at that very doorstep, as Hossein turns around and leaves, and his former "comrade" goes inside his palatial home and closes the door.

The central scene of *Crimson Gold* occurs when Hossein goes to deliver a pizza to a house where a group of young people are having a party. If no one other than Panahi could have shot that scene inside the jewelry shop, no one but Kiarostami could have written this scene in front of the opulent apartment building where the party is proceeding apace. The point of view of the apartment is from the perspective of a young provincial boy, conscripted into the military, summoned here by the Islamic morality police (the same "Islam" of the "Islamic revolution" that has generated obscene wealth for one small group and sustained inhuman poverty for the massive majority) to capture and incarcerate a group of young people who have defied the rules of the theocracy and gathered for a party. Hossein comes to deliver the pizza but is prevented by the morality police because they do not want to alert the people at the party that they are about to be arrested the moment they leave the apartment. Hossein stands by the young soldier, awaiting his fate, for he has been forbidden to leave as well, in case he might alert the partygoers. The camera now begins to look up at the dancing shadows of the young people through the window of a room high in the building. A look of yearning and *ressentiment*, of repressed longing and denied desires, now darkens Hossein's face and the face of the young soldier. Panahi's camera is psychoanalytical, surgical, penetrating, brutal. Let them out, his camera commands, those years and decades, centuries and millennia, of repressed wishes and swallowed prides—condemned, curtailed, incarcerated: the cruelty of a whole political culture of denial written all over their faces.

Before long, young people begin to exit the building, and they get arrested and put inside a van. Parents who have come to pick up their children from the party are told to stay in their cars and park on a corner, as Hossein and the young soldier continue to stare through the window at the party upstairs. Hossein suddenly realizes that the pizza he was supposed to deliver is getting cold and becoming useless. He opens the box and offers a slice to the young soldier. The young soldier refuses, saying he is not allowed and that his superior will object. Hossein moves toward the chief morality policeman and solicits his permission for the solider to have a slice of pizza. The chief condescends to allow him a slice of pizza. Hossein goes back to the young solider, offers him a piece, looks at the rest of the pie, and realizes there are more slices about to be wasted. He looks around the darkened street, at the bewildered and frightened crowd, and now Kiarostami instructs Panahi's camera to follow Hossein in one of the most beautiful, forgiving scenes in the entire spectrum of Iranian cinema. Hossein moves around the street and offers slices of pizza to everyone gathered there, victims and victimizers, tyrants and tyrannized, men and women, young and old, religious and secular, Islamist and otherwise. All gather, all have a bite of a piece of bread and some cheese and tomato. There is more love and forgiveness in that accidental scene than in cathedrals full of the perfunctory Eucharist. This central scene of *Crimson Gold* is a piece of poetry in and of itself, a poem that begins with mapping out the details of a subdued ressentiment and a swallowed anger, and yet ends with a universal forgiveness of all.

In the penultimate scene of *Crimson Gold*, Hossein delivers a few boxes of pizzas to a young man who lives in an exceedingly ostentatious apartment (with an indoor pool and other similar amenities). This incursion to the interior of wealth is carefully choreographed throughout *Crimson Gold*. First Hossein finds a receipt from a jewelry shop, which amounts to a roadmap to where wealth dwells; then he delivers a pizza to a wealthy man who happens to have been his comrade during the war; then he stares for hours at the façade of an apartment building where he was to deliver a pizza before he was interrupted by the Islamic morality police; and then finally he finds his way into a house where wealth abounds in full, tasteless, and clumsy vulgarity. This carefully measured approach to the interiority of wealth maps out the contour of Panahi's visual subconscious, in which class distinctions have become (in architecture and urban planning) spatial. The identification of north Tehran with ostentatious wealth and south Tehran with rampant poverty is the simplest taxonomy of this spatial distancing. But the articulation of class difference has become equally architectural. With the advent of colonial modernity, Iranian architecture gradually and systematically lost its own domestic and climatic logic and rhetoric. Western European and North American architectural designs eventually found their way into the creative imagination of Iranian architects, catering to their nouveau-riche clientele. The current urban landscape of Tehran, ranging from shanty houses to high rises, from the homeless poor to palatial homes, speaks voluminously to this spatial articulation of class distinction. Panahi's *Crimson Gold* is a masterpiece of implicit awareness of this spatial alienation in the architectural landscape of the Iranian capital.

Panahi himself is always fond of using the metaphor of a circle for the human condition, a circle into which he believes we are all trapped by our birth and breeding. That spatial metaphor is the most evident sign of his visual subconscious picking up on shapes and volumes in hidden political terms. The significance of circularity in Panahi's cinema is not merely a narrative device but also a sign of his awareness of spatial alienation. Perhaps *The Circle* is the most obvious example of this fixation. That *The Circle* begins and ends in a prison is not something that is immediately evident, for the tight frames and close camera work do not allow an immediate recognition that the film begins inside a prison hospital. That opening shot of a small window into a maternity ward could be anywhere, and there is no indication that it is actually a prison hospital. But the film is called *The Circle*, and it ends quite clearly inside a prison, so it must also have started inside the prison—and thus the suggested significance of the first circular shot down the spiral stairs that link the prison maternity ward to the street where the camera picks up the story of the two brutalized and frightened prostitutes.

Navigating the spatial metaphors of Panahi's visual subconscious are no longer fictive characters but visual personae who give a liberating force to his brand of *visual* realism. Panahi's cinema is by far the most ostensibly political among his contemporaries—but his politics are far more formal than thematic: a creative combination of *actual, virtual,* and *parabolic* realisms, working, in Panahi's case, through a subsumed violence, spatially alienated, and operative through a gathering of transfigurative personae. My argument here is that Panahi's cinema, already the culmination of the best in Iranian cinema that has come before it, operates in a semiotic domain where signs have all been liberated from their enforced signification. We are, to put it more succinctly, no longer conscious of the visual grammatology at the heart of Panahi's semiotics, and neither is he himself. From Farrokhzad to Panahi, one might argue, Iranian filmmakers have been busy discovering and conjugating the paradigmatic infrastructure of Iranian cinema, upon which Panahi's generation of filmmakers can erect any edifice they wish, no longer even conscious of the foundational link that has made their camera conscious of the unconscious they picture.

Panahi's cinema, as a result, confidently converses in the realm of signs and visions. His visual language has been effectively liberated from its own (tyrannical) symbolic orders and feeds on the rich reservoir of its own (emancipatory) imaginary citations. As such, the filmmaker, as a visual artist, no longer works with symbols, but with signs. Signs, restored to their originary power, signate. They do not signify. They mean nothing. They are made (as in forced) to mean, in some formal symbolic order, against their defiant will. That will is inherently anarchic, subversive, and anxiety-provoking. The counter-will to make signs signify is a repressive measure to incarcerate their defiant energy.

In Panahi's cinema, as the summation of more than half a century of systematic visual reflection on the nature of reality, red is red is red, as in a rose is a rose is a rose. Red does not mean anything, let alone "Stop!" Red might as well be green or yellow for that matter. But the reign of terror and intimidation that the semantic (symbolic) rule of signification has perpetrated upon signs has robbed them of all but a remnant of their innately anarchic soul. We (as cultured people) have become inured to signs and their glorious gift of anarchic frivolity. Signs are too visible to be seen, and yet they are in the open, for everyone to see. Visions though, as in films, dreams, ideas, hopes, or aspirations, invisible as they are, suggest that they have seen the signs, that signs, in their naked sign-ness, have paid them a visit. But—and here is the rub—signs are too clearly apparent to be perceived, and thus the invisibility of visions is the only way we have to get a glimpse of them. The cast of significant characters that cultures, and their pernicious metaphysics, have imposed upon them prevents us from seeing them. Signification (always through a symbolic order) is like a veil cast upon the sign to enslave it to carry a limited and limiting message. But signs rebel against that will to dominate, and against any cultural control to have them unilaterally signify, under the penalty of law, one thing or another. Traffic lights, located within a symbolic order and policed by an invisible cop, may be forced to signify and regiment obedience during the day, but in the middle of the night and in the heart of darkness, when the traffic cops are all asleep, they become again ghostly apparitions. They mean nothing. Sensible people (ought to) ignore them. Visions, being invisible, have an inroad to the hidden reservoir of signs, where they secretly but publicly signate beyond any significant control.

Let me explain what I mean by "signs" here, and how Panahi's cinema is the summation of a visual subconscious generated over a prolonged cinematic reflection. Signs, like traffic lights, are made to signify: Red is to stop, green is to go, yellow means the light is changing its mind, from green to red. Beyond being legally mandated to signify, against their will to rebel, signs may even occasionally signal, say when the red, or yellow, or green light is manipulated by a traffic cop to blink incessantly in no collectively conclusive consensus as to what exactly it is supposed to mean. As it signals—but to no easily conceivable conclusion—there is a vague feeling that we ought to be careful in its vicinity, even without its having a clear claim to signification. I have perpetrated this perhaps unpardonable violence on the English language (being an [il]legal immigrant to the language I can get away with lexical infelicities otherwise forbidden by law) and suggested this thing called "signation" for what signs do when they are not forced by a culture or a cop on the beat to signify, or, if even slightly off the record, signal. I concocted this thing I call "signation" because it means nothing, which is exactly what signs do—they mean nothing.

In and of themselves signs mean nothing. They are richly exciting and deeply anxiety-provoking, and in them there is a healthy will to rebel against attempts to make them signify. This liberation of signs from their enforced and habitual significations I believe is at the root of every new movement that we witness in "national cinema." Visionary filmmakers of national cinemas discover and unleash a whole new constellation of misbehaving signs. Cultures and their metaphysics, politics of power and their opposing ideologies, unilaterally impose this man-made will to order, of "signification," on them. You create a green light and order it to mean that people can apply the gas pedal and continue on their way, and it says "Fine, that's what I will do." But the fact of the matter is that neither the green light nor any other light, color, concept, shape, word, or change in the weather *means* anything. They reluctantly and begrudgingly submit to mean.

But that submission does not altogether leave signs completely obedient. They relentlessly bother and banter, which in turn results in signs that signate beyond the control of the culture that created them, or even their own reluctant obedience. This signation finds a subterranean way into our visions (dreams, hopes, aspirations, prophetic movements, works of art, inventions, inspirations—all the shades of our critically creative imagination). Visions that inform our visual subconscious (and from which we make good films and take compelling pictures) in turn are invisible because they have been secretly ignited by the disobedient and rebellious signs that are not content just to sit there and forcefully signal one thing or another. Visions, as a result, are the nocturnal and subterranean Trojan horses that signs instigate to come and haunt us so that we will not remain content and comfortable with the way we have forced signs to signify and make life ordinary, legal, comfortable for some, and miserable for many. So visions are in effect invisible boomerangs that signs throw at cultures and their metaphysics that have enslaved and forced them to signify one thing or another. Visions as boomerangs (all good films are great boomerangs) come and cause disturbances and revolutions, schisms and protests in cultures and metaphysics, which in turn go back to release signs from their incarcerated bondage and forced acts of signification. Visible *signs* send invisible *visions* to disrupt the culture of their domination and let them loose to roam freely, freely to signate the world back to its originary chaos, the jubilant dance of signs to no significant end.

Signation is no mystery, nor signs mystifying mirrors of some distant whereabouts. The way I see and suggest it, signation is a kind of palpitation, an involuntary breathing of signs, when they are left to their own devices. Signs mean nothing, and as such they are made to make a mockery of themselves when they are forced to mean something or another, and of course of the semantics of their dominant culture, their reigning metaphysics, their demanding parole officers, when they are made to signify (or even signal) under duress, or when a traffic cop is looking. Give the selfsame traffic light—red, yellow, or green—to Abbas Kiarostami and he will have his camera gaze at it for such a long, lasting, interminable time that every ounce or pretense of signification leaves it, and staring at you will remain a gloriously glaring meaninglessness. So signs do not signify. They just signate.

Signs signate, and once they do that, which is forever, incessantly, inadvertently, subversively, they are the mirror in which visions are reflected. Throughout my conversations with Iranian cinema—from Farrokhzad to Panahi—I have tried to see the possibilities of those invisible visions through the impossibility of these visible signs. That is not an easy task, because we have a structural deficiency in seeing how signs signate. We ourselves are, because of that structural deficiency, implicated in the metaphysical tyranny of turning signs into signifiers. The structural deficiency is in our inability to see our own faces. What we see in the mirror is not the plain fact of our face. It is always already a significant mutation of the sign of our face, always inscrutable and with the terror of *Homo hierarchicus* written all over it.

What we see in the mirror is the articulated reflection of our names, not the plain sight of our faces. The terror of the gaze of the Other that Sartre tried to articulate and theorize in *Being and Nothingness* is nothing compared to our amnesia of the sign of our own face under the cultural duress of the anamnesis of its metaphysical signification and cultural remembrance. Sartre took the sign of the face for the significance of the character. When he narrowed in on *look* and zeroed in on *shame* as the defining moments of our consciousness, he had already taken the sign of the face as the significance of identity. He was one step behind himself, two steps ahead of the sign of a face. Those steps are where, both in the mirror and in the Other's eyes, the face and body are already identified and thus robbed, not just of their alterity as Levinas would later note, but of something far more primal, i.e., their constitutional incomprehensibility, their signating signness, their strange appearances, which have all been stolen at the moment of birth (certificate). "Being-seen-by-the-Other," as Sartre calls it, is always already in the realm of signification, because the Other recognizes you, and the moment of that recognition is the instant of a major robbery, which he has perpetrated on you, as you on him, robbing each other of your signating strangeness, permanently pregnant with all that we are (not yet). The reign of the sign is in the realm of being, but mutated into a signifier it already exists. Signs do not exist. They just are. They lack an objective presence because they are unrecognizable. Once they are recognized—here is a red light, you must stop now; here is a man, say hello—they have been dragged out of their jubilant state of simply being there and placed in the tyrannical order of existence, a metaphysics beyond their control. The thatness of sign is miasmatic, amorphous, anarchic, entirely free-floating in its own sign-ness. The case of sign is not one of *genitivus objectivus*. Sign is too unruly to be in the genitive case.

In Panahi's *visual* realism, Iranian cinema has finally reached its epistemic closure, where signs begin to surface and dismantle their legislated semantics. Panahi's cinema, as a result, announces a turning point in our semiotic history, where we can begin to theorize our visual and performing arts in confidently imaginal terms. To start that task, we must rethink the central conception of "sign" by considering what Iranian cinema has made possible, and there is a whole history of semiotics with which we must engage in a prolonged conversation. The theoretical conception of sign has been assimilated into a markedly Christian semiology, where the face of Christ is at once the sign and the signifier, because to Christians he is both man and God, son and father, with the Holy Spirit as the animating intermediary. In the fiercely anti-iconic Jewish or Islamic semiology there is a wholly different conception of signs. Signs are signs are signs. They signify nothing. "But signs are initially useful things," think deeply Christian philosophers who carry, unaware, their Christology into their ontology, "whose specific character as useful things consist in *indicating*." This is none other than Martin Heidegger, in his *Being and Time* (in its English translation by Joan Stambaugh, page 72). But signs *indicate* nothing; they just signate. "Such signs," say the Christian philosophers, "are signposts, boundary-stones, the mariner's storm-cone, signals, flags, signs of mourning, and the like" (*Being and Time*, page 72).

Signs are no such things. Heidegger did try to distinguish between sign and signifier, and asserted categorically that "'referring' as indicating is not the ontological structure of the sign as a useful thing." But he stops at the distinction between "referral as serviceability and referral as indicating." Signs, he contends, may be both *serviceable* and *indicating*. But they may just indicate without being of any service, while there are things like a hammer that are serviceable but not a sign. He still reserves for sign the property of *indicating*, and goes about trying to figure out what it means for signs "to indicate." Heidegger is quite careful to distinguish between this indicating quality of sign and its functional properties. He goes so far as seeing that signs are not really "comprehended." But he still insists that "Signs address themselves to a specifically 'spatial' being-in-the-world. A sign is *not* really 'comprehended' when we stare at it and ascertain that it is an indicating thing that occurs." As to how exactly a sign continues to indicate despite the fact that we do not really "comprehend" it, Heidegger has this to say: "The sign applies to the circumspection of heedful association in such a way that the circumspection following its direction brings the actual aroundness of the surrounding world into an explicit 'overview' in that compliance" (ibid., 74), which is the Germanic English way of saying that there is a traffic cop in sight, either physically on the street corner or else in our mind, reminding us of the exam we took to obtain a driver's license. Because by the time a sign is made to indicate anything by virtue of its circumspection, or heedful association, or the actual aroundness of its surroundings, thus implicating us into compliance, a whole metaphysical culture of mutation has long been in operation. What is difficult even for the great philosopher of Dasein to acknowledge is that signs just are: "What is encountered is not a mere thing," he still insists. But a sign is nothing but a mere thing, if we dare to suspend our Christian Christological conception of it.

Consider the torn pocket of the young boy (Moshen Kafili) who comes to fetch his sister Razieh (Aida Mohammadkhani) in *The White Balloon*. Does it mean he was in a fight? Does it mean that his father beat him up? Does it mean that he has a careless mother who does not fix her child's torn pocket? What does that torn pocket mean? Maybe it means nothing. It is just there. If you put it next to his disheveled hair and slightly bruised face then you might head toward the conclusion that he has been in some sort of physical altercation with someone. Then if you place that conclusion next to the screaming father who is trying to take a shower in some subterranean bathroom, you may conjecture that his father has just beat him up. You see how many conjectures you have made in order to come out with a tentative conclusion? Even if you conclude that these are signs of violence, still you have no visible sign of the father. Where is he? You never see him (though you hear him scream, and the distance between the invisible sign and the audible scream further adds to the uncertainty of the sign). This is what I mean when I say that signs are let loose of their legislated semantics to mean, or indicate, or be useful in a logistics of cause and effect. Heidegger collapses the sign back to its *usefulness*, which is worse than demanding that it simply *indicate*. "Signs are not things which stand in an indicating relationship to another thing but are *useful things which explicitly bring a totality of useful things to circumspection so that the worldly character of what is at hand makes itself known at the same time*" (ibid.). It is obvious that "the actual surrounding world," or "circumspect association in the surrounding world," requires that "the conspicuousness" of signs be brought into consideration, but this is precisely where signs are mutated from their thingness into the charted binaries of time and space and made to sing and dance to specific tunes that cultures and their sneaky metaphysics demand of them. Ultimately the problem with Heidegger's semiology is its fundamentally Christian conception of sign that, seemingly unbeknownst to Heidegger himself (he was at one point going to become a priest), carries over into his ontology, whereby he cannot conceive of sign as inordinately meaning- (use- and indication-) less.

Heidegger believed that when a farmer considers the southern wind as a sign of rain, the wind, *ipso facto*, is not "already objectively present," and that it only comes into being when it is given birth to as a sign of pending rain. The fact that the wind in and of itself *means nothing* unless and until it is legislated to do so in a climatology of one sort or another does not persuade Heidegger altogether to come to peace with sign and its absolutely meaningless thingness. Contrary to Heidegger's fear, sign is that dangerous apparition that poses the debilitating question of "What to do with?" But there is no need to fear that indeterminacy. It is—if we overcome the Christological fear of accepting a sign that does not point to a higher authority—full of untapped, and untenable, possibilities. What is absolutely astonishing about Heidegger is the fact that he categorically recognizes that "sign can indicate many things of the most diverse sort," and yet when he uses the example of a "string on one's finger" as a sign he cannot attribute it to the circumspection of its surroundings and opts to argue that "the narrowness of intelligibility and use corresponds to the breadth of what can be indicated in such signs" (ibid., 76). As such the sign can become inaccessible, i.e. lose the narrowness of its intelligibility, and thus is in need of additional signs to supplement its accurately narrow intelligibility.

Now—do you remember the string that the old lady, Hura (Azizeh Seddighi), had on her finger in the third episode of Marziyeh Meshkini's *The Day I Became a Woman* (2000)? What did it mean? What had she forgotten? She never remembered. There is a sign for you that means nothing, and yet stays there and stares at you and at Hura like there is no tomorrow. A "string on one's finger," left to its own devices, means nothing before it is narrowly forced, by the sheer might of a memorial culture, to signify one thing or another. Heidegger comes closest to this recognition when he realizes that "the knot which cannot be used as a sign does not thus lose its sign character, but rather acquires the disturbing obtrusiveness of something near at hand." If Heidegger were freed of his Christology he would be capable of seeing that once shorn of its forced signification, the knot that has lost its significance as a reminder has lost its character as a signifier, and it is now nothing but a sign that, disturbingly for Heidegger (gloriously for me), signates, having just stormed the Bastille of metaphysical signification. But to see that Heidegger would have had to accept, in the immediate memory of his Christology, that the face of the Son does not point to the fact of the Father, and that the sign of Christ, in and of itself, is a referent-less bundle of signation, and that the face of Christ is not the hidden face of God revealed.

To camouflage his Christology, but with the result of revealing it even further, Heidegger turns to what he calls "the extensive use of signs," such as fetishism and magic, in primitive Dasein—namely a state of Being-in-time that is not (in) the European time. He denies these primitives any "theoretical speculation" about their signs, and believes them to be operating "within an 'immediate' Being-in-the-world." Contrary to the civilized Germans (namely Christianized Germans, for the idea of "Europe" is coterminous with Christianity) who have theorized their signs and distinguished between them and what they refer to, the primitives have remained at the infantile stage of taking the signs for what they are supposed to refer to. "This remarkable coincidence of the sign with what is indicated does not, however, mean that the sign-thing has already undergone a certain 'objectification,' has been experienced as a pure thing, and been transposed together with what is signified to the same region of being of objective presence." Quite to the contrary, all this primitive bondage of sign in its referents means is that "the sign has not yet become free from that for which it is a sign" (ibid., 76). This in fact is an accurate description of Christology, which in the disguise of phenomenological semiology has conspired to sustain the unexamined claim of the metaphysics of signification on signs. By assuming them to be significatory, signs are incarcerated in what they are supposed to be the sign of. Whereas left to their own devices, they have no such claim, care, or consideration whatsoever.

Heidegger's semiology (which is very useful for us to know, though we must converse with it through our own visual language) ultimately argues three simultaneous things, as he himself enumerates them: (1) That there is "a possible concretion of the what-for of serviceability," from which the *indicating* schemata of signs find their reasons for being; (2) This "indicating of signs belongs to a totality of useful things, to a referential context";and (3) That "signs are not just at hand along with other useful things but rather in their handiness the surrounding world becomes explicitly accessible to circumspection" (*Being and Time*, 76). He is ultimately ready to acknowledge that "signs are something ontically at hand," but this is as far as he is willing to go before he frantically adds without even closing the sentence that "this definite useful thing functions at the same time as something which indicates the ontological structure of handiness, referential totality, and worldliness." Signs, though, are far removed from their status of indefinite and useless dysfunctionality when they are subjected to such harassments. Signs indicate nothing. The "ontological structure of handiness" has both its feet inside the tyrannical metaphysics of meaningful usefulness. "Referential totality" is the very metanarrative of a semiology that does not take signs seriously but begins to read them only at the moment of their mutation into signifiers. Signs are far worldlier, if the world is taken for the sign of its own indeterminacy, than Heidegger is ready to see them.

All I am trying to say, as I appear to be chasing my own tail, is that signs signate invisible visions—this is what I have learned from watching so many (Iranian) films. Left to their own devices, signs signate visions that haunt our captured imagination, and thus give rise to the poetry of sight and sound. At its best, the cinema of Kiarostami (which also, in part, sustains Panahi's cinema and with it a major force in this visual imagining) emanates visions out of the gently de-signified signs. Kiarostami is fond of saying that his is an incomplete cinema, that his audience completes his films. If we are to take this assertion at all seriously, we have to account for it from the heart of his cinematic presence, wherein reality is brought to a surreal summation of itself and then de-signified to its formative signs. Kiarostami's meandering characters carry our sight into the familiarity of their surroundings, and are let loose there in order to de-familiarize those surroundings beyond recognition. Ahmad in *Where Is the Friend's House?*, Ali Sabziyan/Mohsen Makhmalbaf in *Close-Up* (1990), the director in *And Life Goes On*, Hossein in *Through the Olive Trees*, Mr. Badii in *Taste of Cherry* (1996), and ultimately the director in *The Wind Will Carry Us* (2000) are all the personifications of Kiarostami's camera, the medium that guides us through the labyrinth of their worldly simulation of the real. Before we know it, and in a way that defines the *cinema of assignation* that Kiarostami has made possible, things begin to lose their inherited meanings and expose their concealed and unsheltered signations.

Kiarostami's cinema of de-assignation—a reassigning of the sign to its signatory defiance of laws, legislations, semantics, and such—quietly appoints by disquietly disappointing. He achieves that paradoxical verve of his cinema through characters and plots that are all but entirely incidental to his films. What matters is always the visual constitution of the world that these characters unravel. As Kiarostami vividly demonstrated in one of his earliest masterpieces, *Fellow Citizen* (1983), he can make an entire feature film with perfect magic through an extreme close-up of a "character" (a traffic cop in this case) at the center of a suggestive sign of a non-story. Incidental to their plot and narrative, Kiarostami's characters are his crafted alter egos that carry his camera on their shoulders, as it were, through the maze of the familiar worlding of the world, and begin a gentle reassignation of signs that lets go of their histories and traditions of signification. Under Kiarostami's caring gaze, de-signified signs exude their presential (circumstantial, worldly, or being-at-hand, as Heidegger would say) energy with such ease and grace, patience and perseverance, that we do not recognize when exactly it is that our world has been de-worlded right before our own eyes. It is from the bosom of that kind of *actual* realism that Panahi's generation of *visual* realism begins to take these signs to their inconclusive festivities.

Almost all Kiarostami's characters, from the most innocent-looking Ahmad in *Where Is the Friend's House?* to the most sardonic Hossein in *Through the Olive Trees* to the most pernicious director in *The Wind Will Carry Us,* are flat-faced meanderers who seem not to know if they are coming or going. Badii's face in *Taste of Cherry* is the *locus classicus* of these de-faced faces. They signify nothing. They are poker-faced voids. The flat-facedness of Kiarostami's lead characters (*kaqaz-e espid-e na-ben-veshteh,* as Rumi once called it, "a blank page of un-written paper") is the prelude and the postscript of a de-worlded world: The human face, the first place in a film where you look for some sort of sign, reveals nothing with Kiarostami. Thus de-worlded, we become party to the appearance of signs in all their bewildering glory, as the imposed prison of their signification begins to fade out. The protagonists of Kiarostami's films are the mobile universes of signation that he manages to tease out of their captivity. In *Taste of Cherry,* we really don't care by the end if Mr. Badii is going to commit suicide or not. Through his flat-faced gaze we have already seen the signs coming out from under their tightly controlled significations. The world that emerges from under that gaze is utterly miasmatic, supple, surreal. By the time Ahmad in *Where Is the Friend's House?* has (not) found his friend's house, on his innocently bewildered gaze the world exposes the fictive transparency of its reality. By the time Hossein rushes up the hill after a distantly private conversation with Tahereh in *Through the Olive Trees* it does not really matter if she has said yes or no to his requests to marry him. The world has been stripped totally naked of its suffocating airs and a refreshing breeze of hope of the unknown gently graces it. Now nothing means anything anymore, and everything begins to make perfect sense. It is into that world that Panahi's generation of filmmakers is born (with silver spoons in their mouths), without even knowing it—and that precisely is the beauty of it.

It is a world in need of no metaphysics to make it signify, hermeneutics to extract its hidden meanings, aesthetics to theorize its claims to the beautiful and the sublime. Reality in its nakedly signating glory begins to sing and dance and thus make its infinite possibilities evident. That is where and when signs are released from the historical bondage of their tyrannical significations and suggest visions otherwise undreamt in our tyrannically legislated complacency. Kiarostami is by disposition political only in this counter-metaphysical sense, and he is utterly apolitical when it comes to the specific articulation of visions that his photographic exposure of signs makes possible. He has (from Forugh Farrokhzad through Sohrab Shahid Sales to Amir Naderi now in the very marrow of his bones) released the signs and set them free upon the world. He has taken his audience to the fountainhead of the infinite possibilities that are inherent in signs, and he holds them there to marvel at what they have missed. But he stops short of forcing the slightest assignation upon a recognizable sign that points to the vision that the texture of his cinema has made miraculously possible. Would that make him an apolitical filmmaker? No. That makes him an artist of ingenious possibilities who could not have but emerged from the ground-zero impossibilities of a counter-metaphysics of morals to end all morality in order to inaugurate an ethical life.

Visions, if you follow my argument, are invisible—that is to say, they are hidden to the naked eye. "Methinks I see my father, Horatio," says Hamlet. "Where, my lord?" Horatio wants to know, for he has just seen an apparition of the murdered king. "In my mind's eye," Hamlet clarifies. The ghost that appears on top of Elsinore is a vision identical to what appears to Hamlet in his "mind's eye"—vision instigated by an agitating sign. Arrested by significations, signs secretly inform our visions of their incarceration and plead with them to aid and rescue them and let them free. Visions are thus the signal indices of signs having been tyrannically imprisoned by one or another culture and its metaphysics, handcuffed and booked to mean one thing or another. Too visible to be seen, signs signate visions that are invisible and in need of detection. The logic of the invisible visions leading to visible signs is inverted because that's the only way that their blinded insights can become visible. The project of deciphering invisible visions back to the visible signs that have made them possible is tantamount to trying to see the possibilities of those invisible visions through the impossibilities of these visible signs. Had he been slightly more alert to his own Judaic tradition and slightly less European, Emmanuel Levinas would have seen through this release and not been diverted by a mere, futile, reversal of I-based signification. The Other is incomprehensible, as Self is always an Other, not because of the incongruity of the two, but because both have always already been mutated from explosive signation into tame signification.

Let me explain why I believe what Levinas has done in his ethical philosophy—dismantling the ethical neutrality of the whole history of European ontology—is quite critical for that European locality, but rather tangential to ours (this argument is along the same lines as one that I have always told you—how our poets and artists are our contemporary philosophers: different people think in different terms). Levinas exchanges *alterity* for *identity*, which is good enough as a post-Holocaust Judaic rebuttal to the Christological assignation of sign as signifier, underlying the I-based confidence of Husserl's phenomenology, but not good enough to prevent an even further ossification of the ipseity of signification, entirely forgetting that signifiers rest on otherwise defiant signs. Levinas reversed the central proposition of the Husserlian phenomenology and tried to make it Other-conscious rather than I-centered. Levinas went so far as proposing the utter incomprehensibility of the Other, but only as a rhetorical charge to undermine the quintessentially I-consciousness of the Husserlian phenomenology. Slightly closer to his own Judaic consciousness, he might have seen the plain sight of the absolute signness of the sign. But as a European he could not see the face of Christ as the always already signified face of the Other as the point of his departure. He started one step too short. He concluded one step too late. He was too good a European philosopher to be a groundbreaking Jewish semiotician.

Levinas' semiology is constitutional to his phenomenology, both of which are underlined by a post-Holocaust wish to see the face of God-the-unseen. He placed the *present* of consciousness against a Kantian supposition of autonomy emerging from heteronomy, and against a Hegelian auto-affection of self-consciousness, and squarely within an unrecoverable *past*. This *past* is not a chronological locus but an epistemological focus, an *a priori* supposition that makes all conscious propositions possible, an always distant diachrony that synchronizes the present. This always irretrievable past is the absolute Other that Levinas argued ought to inform, sustain, disturb, and, as all of these, subject the Self. He thus took the entire history of the European Enlightenment to task—that subjection is not the extraction of autonomy out of heteronomy as Kant thought, or auto-affection as self-consciousness as Hegel proposed. Rather, he argued, it is only through Other-based hetero-affection that the subject can come to un-learn itself in order to become itself. With a deeply mystical bent to his ontology, Levinas thought that the subject is not constituted by itself, but constituted by its infinitely unknowable Other. Levinas sought to place this Other, in its absolutely incomprehensible Otherness, at the center of the Self, always there to agitate, animate, and subject it, but never there to be grasped, comprehended, understood.

Could it be that the infinitely incomprehensible Other at the center of the Levinasian Self is none Other than Yahweh, the Hebrew God, having come back to help theorize a Jewish phenomenology in the anxiogeneric state of post-Holocaust European Jewry? Is that why Levinas rejects Martin Buber? Frightened by the terror that the Holocaust perpetrated on European Jewry, Levinas wants to de-center European phenomenology from its phobia of heteronomy, fear of anarchy, and its simultaneous proclivity toward absolutist autonomy, and redirect it from auto-affection toward hetero-affection. He rightly sees the horrors of the Holocaust coming to haunt Europe precisely because of its sustained history of denouncing and dismissing the Other, either in the confines of incarcerated madness (this is what Michel Foucault discovered) or else in the exoticized Orient (what Edward Said argued). Levinas wishes to return the Other to the center of the European Self. That is to say the European philosopher postulates an absolutely unknowable Biblical God as the irretrievable past, there in the heart of the present, agitating and animating it in fear and trembling, apprehensive of the world it inhabits.

The genius of Levinas' philosophical project is in his successfully relocating the presence of the infinitely unknowable, or the immanently irretrievable past, onto "the face of the Other." The reason for this relocation is very simple. The infinitely unknowable Other that Levinas wishes to place at the center of the living historical Self does not have a face. He places and locates that infinitely unknowable Other right on the face of the Other, which he has borrowed from Sartre and weds to his own concerns. His question from that point forward is entirely rhetorical, because he has already given the answer: "What then can be this relationship with an absence radically withdrawn from disclosure and from dissimulation?" he asks. "And what is this absence that renders visitation possible—an absence not reducible to hiddenness, since it involves a signifyingness—a signifyingness in which the other is not converted into the same." (Emmanuel Levinas, "The Trace of the Other," in *Deconstruction in Context: Literature and Philosophy*, edited by Mark C. Taylor, 1986: 35).

With this question, Levinas has already established the irretrievably absent—its being absolutely withdrawn from disclosure or dissimulation—and it is from these two premises that the visitation of the absence on the naked face is made possible. The naked face, thus, is anything but naked—it is the Transcendental Signified personified. The phrase "since it [the irretrievably absent Other that makes the present Self possible] involves a signifyingness—a signifyingness in which the other is not converted into the same" is precisely the moment when Levinas wants to have his cake and eat it too. The absolutely Other must perforce signify in order to make the face of the Other possible. But the Other will yield and signify *without* ever condescending to be converted into the Same.

Levinas goes about articulating the possibility of the absolutely Other animating the Same and subjecting it via the constitution of a *trace* as the simulacrum of the *sign*, through a process he calls "illeity." How does this *trace* work? The "signifyingness of a trace consists in signifying without making appear" ("The Trace of the Other," 356). *Trace* is a shadow of the *sign* that Levinas creates to have it signify phenomenologically without being implicated in its Sameness. He has to make this stipulation because he must place the trace, as a simulacrum of the sign, outside the provenance of phenomenology. "A trace does not belong to phenomenology," Levinas writes in this essay. He insists that "a trace is not a sign like any other," and yet he is adamant that "every trace also plays the role of a sign; it can be taken for a sign." But why insist on the difference between the trace and the sign? The answer is quite obvious: "When a trace is thus taken as a sign, it is exceptional with respect to other signs in that it signifies outside of every intention of signaling and outside of every project of which it would be the aim." So *trace* signals without deigning to be a mortal sign, sustaining its immortality because it emanates from the absolutely Other. So as the *trace* deigns to signal, while remaining just a *trace*, it is not stopped from doing its worldly deed, because "a *trace* in the strict sense disturbs the order of the world. It occurs by overprinting." Ultimately, "in this sense every sign is a *trace*. In addition to what the sign signifies, it is the past of him who delivered the sign." This is as much as Levinas can do in having the sign approximated to an absolutist Other so it can signify without being implicated in a systematic project of phenomenology. His point of departure is the political assertion of a post-Holocaust anxiety. The ultimate result, though, is the implication of sign yet again into a Christological signification, via the operation of a *trace*, which is and is not a sign. Covered under a Judaic gloss over a Christological enforcement of sign to signify is still buried the defiant sparkle of the sign to do nothing but signate incessantly, envision visions, and disturb the peace of law-abiding signifiers.

We need to learn from these extraordinary and sustained attempts at what the nature of our visual encounter with reality is by way of coming to terms with the misbehaving sign. In Iranian cinema, we have a rare and unprecedented occasion to think through things we have never thought through—for we are altogether too verbal in our memory and have just begun to learn how to see. I believe that in Panahi's generation of Iranian filmmakers we have finally come to a complete semiotic conclusion, where we can confidently say that signs are too visible to be seen, or that signs do not signify, or that signs are made to signify by the violent metaphysics of the culture that has captured and incarcerated them. "You red light! You stand here and you mean 'Stop!'" But signs do not just sit there quietly as law-abiding citizens of the republic of semiotic fear to which they have been force-migrated. Signs signate, we can now confidently conclude. They signate incessantly, without meaning anything. Stories that signs are made to tell are ruses. In and of themselves, signs signate visions. Too visible to be seen, signs give rise to invisible visions. We can see these visions only in our mind's eye. Visions, of prophets and poets, of filmmakers and photographers, have subterranean access to signs. Signs have agitated, animated, and informed visions to come and rescue them from any culture of semiotic bondage that errs in thinking to have incarcerated them.

Signs are the surface of things we call *reality*, and it is precisely in the surface of their signness that they demand our attention and defy their enforced signification. On our face is carved our name, and yet on the surface of the sign of our face that name loses its authorial power and eponymic reference. Signs are too visible to be seen, but the surface of the signs of things, called *reality*, exudes alluring suggestions—and then all it takes is a piercing set of eyes to see them and let them loose. That allure is particularly poignant at critical moments of inventive vitality, when a culture implodes internally and its artists explode creatively. In a revolutionary cinematic career that has now lasted over two decades, Mohsen Makhmalbaf has persistently done precisely that and tested the patience of settled signifiers, forcing them to remember their repressed but not forgotten signs. In his mature cinema, Makhmalbaf has achieved a *virtual* realism that has now successfully mutated into a poetic surrealism and categorically reconstituted what we ordinarily designate and thus dismiss as reality. At the height of his poetic realism, Makhmalbaf reaches a point where reality becomes entirely miasmatic, and the metaphysics of the real totally loses its grasp on the violence it perpetrates on the all-but-evident. The real is the intermediary evidence before the all-but-evident has totally yielded its unruly freedom to the tyranny of the metaphysics of authenticity that garbs itself as reality. Panahi's generation of Iranian filmmakers no longer take that reality seriously—or as I have always said, they take it too seriously to take it seriously.

At his best, Makhmalbaf learns and teaches how we should not be fooled by the bogus claims of reality to truth, of signifiers to signs, and through the instrumental facility of *the real* gets close, without being afraid, to the all-but-evident, where signs give an intimation of their whereabouts. This simple and elegant insight is the soul of Makhmalbaf's poetic surrealism. *A Moment of Innocence*, *Gabbeh*, and *Silence* are three successive moments in which the factual evidence of *the real* has been joyously emancipated from the violent grip of any metaphysical claim on its authenticity. These films enter the vicinity of the all-but-evident, the surface of the sign of things, before reality has any signifying claim on them. His confident, caring, and creative camera steals the light of freedom from the incarcerated heart of tyrannical darkness—where reality used to have a claim to authenticity. Having himself arisen from the heart of that darkness, Makhmalbaf knows exactly where to look for the light: Not in the Platonic Beyond casting its shadow on a cave wall, not in the Aristotelian Reason placed beyond the reach of human means, not even in an Enlightenment Modernity that has categorically denied him agency—but light in the very heart of darkness. All-but-evident in the midst of the real, the real in the heart of reality, reality authenticated in and by the metaphysical violence of any claim to authenticity that gives it its aura of truth.

These three masterpieces of the mature Makhmalbaf lead to an orchestral revelation of signs beyond their immediate invisibility. *A Moment of Innocence* remembers Makhmalbaf's youthful indiscretion as an occasion of cultural forgetfulness, a recollection of guilt writ forgivingly large. The last frozen shot of the film, the open invitation of the young woman's face, graced by a flowerpot (instead of the police officer's gun) and a piece of bread (instead of the young Makhmalbaf's knife), is the variegated field of a poetically surreal salutation to life. The factual evidence of Makhmalbaf's biography here begins gradually to loosen its signature grip on reality and morph into the liquidly real, from there to deliquesce into the all-but-evident, and from there continue to thaw into the irreducible surface of the signs of things. That visual vocabulary is now axiomatic to Panahi's generation of Iranian filmmakers—they speak it eloquently because they don't remember its grammar.

Gabbeh does for sight what *A Moment of Innocence* does for guilt—frees it from the controlled tyranny of the real, as it blesses it with the emancipatory force of the surreal. As a love story, *Gabbeh* is more a celebration of color in an Islamic Republic of fear and darkness than a mere tapestry of the emotive universe it seeks to reverse. The protagonist of *Gabbeh* is neither the young girl nor the object of her affection, neither the carpet nor its story. It is color. The galaxy of shades, shapes, and shimmering sensations that colors create and convolute to stir (e)motion constitutes the text and texture of *Gabbeh*. The scene in which the teacher pushes his fist out of the camera's frame and reaches for the blue in the sky, the green in the pasture, the red of the flowers, and the yellow of the wheat field are nothing short of cinematic genius. There Makhmalbaf has his hands on the very pulse of the all-but-evident, right before *the real* has any claim on it, way ahead of that definitive moment when reality has unleashed its metaphysical claim on its authenticity. Makhmalbaf is elemental in that moment, his frame throbbing with the beat of life before it is narrated, theorized, pigeonholed into one metaphysics or another. Signs are teased to reveal themselves, as if tickled by the fantasy of their own memory of themselves.

Silence does for sound what *Gabbeh* does for sight—frees it from the controlled tyranny of the evident, as it blesses it with the emancipatory grace of the possible. In *Silence*, Makhmalbaf blinds the sight in order to hear the sound. *Silence* will not only have to be heard with the blind boy's perfectly pitched ears but also seen with his totally darkened sight. *Silence* is extraordinarily beautiful to look at because it is imagined from within a blind boy's mind—Makhmalbaf's camera planted in his head. Add to that the archaic Persian of the Tajiki dialect that is pure poetry to an Iranian pair of ears, and the result is the idyllic lyricism of elemental sounds in *Silence* echoing the elemental colors of *Gabbeh*. Cut down to its primeval forces, the bare site of the evident is now the open field of the possible, and we are at the primordial pulse of simply being-in-the-world, where all symbolic orderings of the universe dissolve into their originary significations, long, very long, before they are acculturated into a violent metaphysical claim. In *Silence*, Khorshid (Tahmineh Normativa) imagines the world anew, with his blind insights and his hearing of the super-sonic sound of the real, to which the rest of the world is deaf. He is blind, but in his mind he sees for the world its alternatives. He has perfect pitch and in his ears is echoed the melodic harmony of a universe. His singular mission in life is to restore the cacophonic confusion of the world to that perfect harmony that he sees in his mind's eye. This is Makhmalbaf the religious visionary, turning his blindness into insight, his musical infirmity to visual strength, his metaphysical malady to cultural cure. When he was a young child walking by a record store, his grandmother would tell him to stick his fingers into his ears so he would not hear the sinful music. That tyrannical inhibition of forbidden music is sublimated into a restoration of harmonic order to an inherited universe of emotive dissonance. The conclusion of *Silence* is an orchestral celebration of cacophonic dissonances collectively contributing to the creation of a harmonic melody—a vision that does not demand categorical conformity, but that fuses differential discord into creative concord. Signs in *Silence* have become audile, sounds visual, and in the course of that metamorphic conversion, reality has lost all its claims to authenticity—and that is how you produce a cinematic diction that filmmakers like Panahi can speak without even having to learn it.

The visual subconscious of Panahi's *Crimson Gold* is inundated with signs that haunt the cultures (in plural—Islamic, Iranian, patriarchal, colonial) that have hunted them down for millennia, since time immemorial. These signs—a blank and emptied face, dancing shadows from a distance, the bare suggestions of an impending violence—signate visions to haunt the cultures that have defined and dismissed them. Signs, though, are in the habit of tricking the cultures that have tamed and tampered with them, and continue to remain defiant, signating visions and smuggling them into active and creative imaginings, visions, and apparitions that come out at night, when the traffic cops are asleep, and ambush the world order of things. We are in the bizarre habit of buying a ticket, going into a darkened room, and calling for the projectionist to please turn on his magic box and let the glorious undecidability of signs loose— we go to the movies.

Let me give you an example from a filmmaker who is in the same generation as Panahi's to make the case even more clear. What Marziyeh Meshkini achieves in her stunning debut, *The Day I Became a Woman*

(2000), echoes and extends, as I just explained in some detail, what previous filmmakers had done in crafting a parabolic manner of storytelling. In the case of *The Day I Became a Woman*, the de-signification of signs assumes a creative splitting of the body. The repressive life of a woman in an Islamic Republic is here partitioned into three moments: a girl at the age of nine who is about to "become a woman," a young woman in her early twenties, who is married, and an old lady in her seventies, who is now single. The drama begins in the first episode of the film with the young girl, "Hava," being prohibited from playing with her male friend on her ninth birthday. It continues with her, now called "Ahu," riding a bicycle against her horse-riding husband's will and being summarily divorced, and it concludes with her being called "Hura" in her old age, single and suave, semi-senile and entirely rambunctious. The singular signification of a body is here split into three, with different names, ages, and circumstances, suggesting singularity but effecting multiplicity. The splitting of the body de-centers and disperses the subject and dodges repressive identities. Body as sign escapes from one signification to another, from Hava to Ahu, from Ahu to Hura, who always thinks that she has forgotten something. To remind herself of that thing she has a piece of cloth wrapped around her finger (remember Heidegger's reading of the "string on one's finger"), but she never remembers what exactly that thing is. That piece of cloth is now a sign with no significance attached to it, just some bizarre, uncomfortable, anxiety-provoking *thing* that stubbornly persists in reminding Hura that she has forgotten something but never signifying what exactly that thing is. In the "Hura" episode both "Ahu" and "Hava" are quoted, so as to turn her into an anamnesis of them both, so we know that it is one sign that has been split into three signifiers, escaping from one into the other. But for this anamnesis not to coagulate and bring the three pseudo-signifiers of Hava, Ahu, and Hura together and suggest one person, the strategically ingenious piece of cloth on Hura's finger casts the sign indefinitely into the future, and thus the image of her boarding a phantasmagoric boat and sailing into infinity, with no hope or fear of its ever meaning anything. That little rag, a sign restored to its gloriously chaotic meaninglessness, is now haunting the metaphysical culture of signification that has historically forced it to mean one thing or another. Freed and setting sail on the open sea, it will perpetually signate, mean nothing, and make a mockery of every culture that ever forced any sign to mean anything, and of women in particular as signs, condemned to mean subjugation—let alone a republic made to mean "Islamic."

On 15 April 2001, Jafar Panahi flew from Hong Kong, where he was attending a film festival, to Buenos Aires, Argentina, in order to participate in another film festival. The grueling thirty-hour trip had a stopover at New York's JFK Airport before Panahi was to board his next plane to Montevideo, Uruguay. Before he left Hong Kong, he made sure to ask the staff of the Hong Kong Film Festival to ascertain if he needed a US transit visa. They assured him he did not. This is the rest of the story in Panahi's own words:

> As soon as I arrived at JFK Airport, the American police took me to an office and wanted to take my fingerprints and photographs because of my nationality. I refused and I showed them my invitations to the festivals. They threatened to put me in jail if I would not agree to the fingerprinting. I asked for an interpreter and to make a phone call. They refused. Then, they chained me like a medieval prisoner and put me in a police patrol car and took me to another part of the airport. There were many people there, women and men from different countries. They chained my feet and locked my chain to the others, all of us locked to a very dirty bench. For ten hours, no questions and answers, I was forced to sit on that bench, pressed to the others. I could not move. I was suffering from an old illness, but nobody noticed. Again, I asked to call someone in New York, but they refused. They not only ignored my request but also that of a boy from Sri Lanka who wanted to call his mom. Everybody was moved by the crying of the boy, people from Mexico, Peru, Eastern Europe, India, Pakistan, Bangladesh, and I was thinking that every country has its own laws, but I could not understand these inhuman acts.
>
> At last, I saw the next morning. Another policeman came to me and said that they had to take my photograph. I said never. I showed them my personal photos. They said no, they had to take my photo (the way photographs of criminals are taken) and do the fingerprinting. I refused. An hour later, two other men came to me and tried to threaten me to submit to the fingerprinting and photography and again I refused and I asked for a phone. At last, they accepted and I called Jamsheed Akrami, the Iranian film professor, and I explained to him the whole story. I asked him to convince them that I am not a guy who would do what they were looking for.

Two hours later, a policeman came to me and took my photo. They chained me again and took me to a plane, a plane that was going back to Hong Kong.

From the window of the plane I could see New York. I knew my film *The Circle* had been released there for two days and I was told the film was very well received. I thought that the audiences would understand my film better if they knew that its director was chained up at the same time. They would accept my belief that the circle of human limits do exist in all parts of this world but with different ratios. I saw the Statue of Liberty and I unconsciously smiled. I tried to draw the curtain and there were marks from the chain on my hand. I could not stand the other travelers gazing at me and I just wanted to stand up and cry that I'm not a thief! I'm not a murderer! I'm not a drug dealer! I...I am just an Iranian, a filmmaker. But how I could say this, in what language? In Chinese, Japanese, or in the mother tongues of those people from Mexico, Peru, Russia, India, Pakistan, and Bangladesh...or in the language of that young boy from Sri Lanka? Really, in what language?

I had not slept for sixteen hours and I had to spend another fifteen hours on my way back to Hong Kong. It was torture among all those watching eyes. I closed my eyes and tried to sleep. But I could not. I could just see the images of those sleepless women and men who were still chained.

I wish to use this incident to bring to your attention what happens when artists cross borders, refuse to obey orders, and to top it all let loose among a global audience platoons of misbehaving signs—long shots and close-ups put together and called a "film."

The dissolution of the (tyrannically sustained) symbolic orders of reality is not limited to the realm of cinematic aesthetic or theoretical reflection on it. The destruction of that symbolic order, and the emancipation of misbehaving signs from regimented symbols, now corresponds to the systematic dismantling of the nation-state as the site of cinematic production, distribution, and spectatorship. It is by now quite evident that what I just mapped out for you and termed the cinematic emancipation of signs from legislated symbolics corresponds to a mode and manner of the atomization of individuals and the mutation of our inherited geography along the two disenfranchising axes of East and West and

North and South into a globalized planetary geography with a whole different (counter-)metaphysical underpinning.

Restoring to signs their unruly behavior is quite unsettling—not just for censors, but also for the US (or any other) Immigration and Naturalization, Customs, and Homeland Security officers. You need a visa to enter the United States, even if you are passing through it, when you travel on an Iranian passport. That is the letter of the law, demanded and exacted at the cost of chaining one of the most distinguished filmmakers in the world to a chair and flying him back to where he came from, if he does not do as he is told. But Panahi does not do as he is told—in fact he has made a successful career in not doing as he is told. He refuses to be photographed, fingerprinted, or leave innocent but disturbing signs incarcerated within the cultural control of their manufactured authority. All artists, by definition, are anarchists. They do not leave the world be—they see something deeply disturbing about the world, the way it is, the way the infinite number of possibilities that exist to order the world are forfeited for one particular way they deem unacceptable, troubling, traumatic.

The experience of Panahi at JFK Airport in New York is symptomatic of something much larger in its normative implications. The US authorities at the airport were blocking the passage of something far more than a filmmaker on his way from one festival to another. The localized insecurities of the border police are now threatened with something far beyond their control—the unleashed imaginings of a global audience whose dreams have been forever agitated by a number of globe-trotting artists who refuse to abide by the rules and regulations of legislated symbolisms, of Islamic Republics, of a globalized US empire, of signs incarcerated inside a solitary cell of meaning, significance, sense, connotation, intonation, or "having-something-in-mind." Artists, poets, anyone who pauses for a minute and thinks—they are all homeless people. They are nowhere at home. "My home is a cloud," Nima Yushij once said in a poem, "and the whole world is cloudy with it." "It is part of morality," Theodor Adorno said, "not to be at home in one's home." "[I am] the outlander," added C. Wright Mills, "not only regionally, but down bone deep and for good…my Texas grandfather has something to do with that." All artists are outlanders, for they have seen the abyss, looked into the bottomless pit of the jubilant crowd of signs who could not care less to mean anything.

I remember, in an interview in anticipation of the premiere of Samira Makhmalbaf's *At Five in the Afternoon* at the Cannes Film Festival, she was asked by a reporter why she had opted to shoot a film in Afghanistan and about the fate of Afghan women. "There are doctors without borders," she responded, "why not artists without borders?" The global celebration of Iranian cinema over the last quarter of a century has marked a critical passage in our cultural history. There are two historical antecedents to the current rise of an aspect of Iranian art to global attention—one was when Goethe published his *Westöstliche Divan* in 1819 on the basis of his readings and impressions of Hafez, and second was when Edward FitzGerald published his *Rubaiyat of Omar Khayyam* in 1859, based on similar impressions from another Persian poet. Goethe and FitzGerald heralded a global celebration of Persian poetry that until the rise of Iranian cinema to similar attention during the last two decades of the twentieth century no other Persian art had enjoyed. The difference, however, between Goethe and FitzGerald's renditions of Hafez and Omar Khayyam, respectively, into German and English and the current global celebration of Iranian cinema is the difference between the means of communication in the nineteenth and those at the threshold of the twenty-first century. Today, the celebration of Iranian cinema at Cannes and a myriad of other festivals in four corners of the world means the commencement of its global dissemination all around the planet. To a considerable degree, the momentum of Iranian cinema is due to its visual vocabulary—the fact that it easily transcends linguistic and other cultural barriers. The border-crossing now contingent on the visual subconscious of Iranian cinema, unleashing an army of misbehaving signs, is by far the most subversive intrusion of a globalized national cinema into the peace and prosperity of settled signifiers and the tyranny of the order they wish to impose on a defiant world. Panahi can be stopped and chained at the border, but as he reflected from his airplane flying over Manhattan, his visual agitations were in motion down in the innermost souls of his eager audiences.

Today Iranian artists are no longer limited to the artificial borders drawn for them and their neighbors by colonial powers—the Russians and the British in particular—in the heyday of nineteenth-century anti-colonial nationalism. Major Iranian filmmakers have trespassed these borders and engaged a larger territorial claim for their art. Before shooting *At Five in the Afternoon* in Afghanistan, Samira had made her second feature film, *Blackboard* (2001), in the Kurdish mountains between Iran and Iraq—thus making one of the few films extant about a stateless people that by virtue of their historical predicament make a mockery of the entire project of (anti)colonial nationalism. Mohsen Makhmalbaf had also transgressed the national boundaries of cinema by making a film in Turkey (*A Time for Love*), one in Tajikistan (*Silence*), and another two (*Kandahar* and *Afghan Alphabet*) set in Afghanistan, and now *Sex and Philosophy*, again in Tajikistan. His *Cyclist* is also about the fate of Afghan refugees in Iran—thus turning his camera away from a national and toward an international concern. Hasan Yektapanah's *Jomeh* (2001) also attended the fate of Afghan refugees in Iran, as did Majid Majidi's *Baran*

(2002). In an almost total absence of any film production in Afghanistan, Iran became the site of an Afghani surrogate cinema. Surrogate cinemas, homeless filmmakers, digital film, transnational audiences, globalized spectatorship, privatized viewings, cross-national productions, and commercial distribution—Iranian cinema today is symptomatic of a seismic shift in the very notion of cinema as an art form. The arrest, incarceration, and humiliation of Jafar Panahi at JFK Airport are an entirely irrelevant personal ignominy, with no consequence to a reality much larger than a talented filmmaker and a bureaucratic insecurity.

With the appearance of Bahman Qobadi, Iranian cinema witnessed its first major Kurdish filmmaker. Qobadi's *A Time for Drunken Horses* (2001), *Marooned in Iraq* (2003), and *Turtles Can Fly* (2004) gave the Iranian Kurds their own voice and vision—and with these three films at the forefront of world attention the plight of millions of Kurds in Iran, Iraq, Syria, and Turkey assumed a semblance of its global significance. Before Qobadi, another great Kurdish filmmaker from Turkey, Yilmaz Güney, in *Yol* (1983), had already brought global attention to the predicament of his people. There are other Iranian Kurdish filmmakers who are as active as Qobadi—if not as internationally noted. Put together, they represent a Kurdish cinema that at the same time confirms and negates the colonial boundaries artificially drawn between nations and their collective sentiments. The semiotic dismantling of a visual subconscious at the creative center of Iranian cinema thus corresponds with a rapid meltdown of artificial and contested national boundaries that have divided nations in order to rule them better—while generating an internal relation of power between minoritized masses and a privileged elite—in this case the racialized "Persians" over the disenfranchised Kurds.

While the Iranian attention to Afghanistan made for a cinema of a multiethnic nation colonially carved by the British in early nineteenth century to protect the northern borders of their South Asian interests, the simultaneous attention that Iranian filmmakers have paid to the Kurdish predicament simulated a mono-ethnic but stateless nation in search of sovereignty. The Afghans have a state despite the multiplicity of their ethnicities challenging its claim to nationhood; Kurds lack a state despite their single ethnic, linguistic, and cultural claim to nationhood. One became while the other withered by the meandering whims of colonialism. The simultaneous attention of Iranian filmmakers to both the Afghan and the Kurdish predicaments has begun to corrode the fabric of the nation-state as the natural boundary of artistic creativity—particularly when Abbas Kiarostami made a film about AIDS in Africa: *ABC Africa* (2001). Makhmalbaf in Afghanistan, Kiarostami in Africa, Hatami-Kia in Bosnia, Qobadi in Iraq, Naderi in New York, Shahid Sales in Germany, Parviz Sayyad in Los Angeles, Susan Taslimi in Sweden, Shirin Neshat living in New York and shooting in Turkey and Morocco—artists without borders, filmmakers transgressing the fabricated national borders of their aesthetic visions, mirroring Turkish filmmakers in Germany, North Africans in France, the French in North Africa, South Asians in England. The dismantling of the nation-state as the site of cinematic perspective corresponds to the semiotic deconstruction of signifiers to their hitherto incarcerated, now emancipated signs.

Why did Panahi refuse to be photographed and fingerprinted by the US officials? For those officials, this was a bureaucratic procedure mandated by the will of a nation-state to safeguard its borders against potential terrorists. For Panahi this was the reduction of a decent, respectable, and celebrated artist to the status of a potential criminal. Two opposing symbolic orders colliding on the signatorial sites of a fingerprint and a photograph, occasioned by an imaginative release of a cinematic will to celebrate the glory of emancipated signs. Border-crossing might be prohibited for sign-makers, but his emancipated signs are wholeheartedly bought and jubilantly celebrated under the feet (and over the heads) of those very custom officials. This is much more than a simple alienation of a work of art from the artist who made it possible. This is the mutation of the work of art into a de-authored source of emancipation. Globalization is a double-edged sword, and (changing the metaphor) its antidote is in its poison.

In this trans-regional reach of their artistic creativity, Iranian artists had a historical antecedent in the literary and poetic disposition of the Persian language, which has never been confined to the current borders of their homeland. From the Ottoman Empire (1300–1918) in the eastern Mediterranean to the Mughal Empire (1526–1857) on the Indian subcontinent, and the Safavids (1502–1737) between them, the Persian language—poetry and prose—was the *lingua franca* of poets and prose stylists across borders and throughout centuries. The artificial nationalization of Persian literary history began only in the late nineteenth century as a major component of colonial nationalism. What today is happening in Iranian cinema is in fact a creative recapitulation of the trans-regional texture and disposition of its literary predecessor.

This transnational proclivity of Iranian cinema is equally evident in a series of short films that were directed by some prominent filmmakers on Kish island, in the Persian Gulf. Films such as Makhmalbaf's *Door* (1999) or Dariush Mehrjui's *The Cousin Is Lost* (2000) are all set on this nondescript island that could be *anywhere* but *nowhere* in particular and thus the *somewhere* of a cinematic invention. One of the most successful films made on Kish is Babak Payami's *Secret Ballot* (2001), based on a script by Makhmalbaf, which has the transgressive visions endemic to a *nameless* land and yet none of the habitually anthropological gaze of

Tehran-based artists looking down at provincial sites. These films, shot and set on Kish, are all in fact dreamt and delivered in the imaginative geography of a nowhere that becomes the cinematic *locus memorandum* of a complete remapping of the imagination—which itself is still agitated by the avalanche of visions created by runaway signs.

Beyond their immediate homeland and region, Iranian artists have ventured out into the wider world, a move that has reflected their global reception back to their global vision. The most spectacular case of an Iranian artist leaving his homeland for a second round of struggle to make it in an entirely foreign context is that of Amir Naderi. A pioneering figure in the rise of Iranian cinema to global significance, Naderi left his homeland in the early 1980s and began a second artistic career in New York, where he succeeded in launching an entirely new phase of his illustrious career. Panahi has met with Naderi on occasion and (like most other young Iranian filmmakers) thinks himself deeply indebted to Naderi's work. Consider the creative conversation between Panahi and Naderi, from the two complementary ends of what has happened in Iranian cinema from its immediate nativist origin to its thematically globalized imaginative geography!

Immediately related to the case of Naderi is the work of another Iranian artist, Shirin Neshat, who has also opted to make New York the principal site of her artistic career. Born and raied in Iran and educated in the United States, Neshat's daring photography and video installations have captured the attention of the world over the last two decades. Her "The Last Word" (2003) premiered at the second Tribeca Film Festival, moving Neshat's oeuvre in a more ambitiously cinematic direction. Integral to the visual aspect of Neshat's work has been the vocal and compositional gift of Sussan Deyhim. A vocalist with an astonishing range and depth, a brilliant composer, and a performer and actress with a versatile screen and stage presence, Deyhim's most spectacular achievement has been her leading role as Hoopoe in Neshat's adaptation of the medieval Persian poetic masterpiece *Logic of the Birds* (2001). Independent of Neshat, Deyhim has had her own shining career as a vocalist, attracting the attention of the legendary Bill Laswell, who produced Deyhim's album *Madman of God* (2002)—along the same lines that he produced the works of Miles Davis, Bob Marley, and Carlos Santana. In one of Neshat's most recent video works, "Tooba" (2002), she collaborated with the celebrated cinematographer Darius Khondji. After having worked with Bernardo Bertolucci, Lars von Trier, Roman Polanski, Alan Parker, and David Fincher (among many others), Khondji lent his perceptive camera to Neshat's eyes. Having begun his initial work with Neshat, Shoja Azari has also emerged as a gifted filmmaker. His *K* (2002) is a triptych based on three short stories by Franz Kafka, expanding the repertoire of Iranian cinema into the masterpieces of world literature.

New York was the scene of another great Iranian artist—Reza Abdoh (1963–95), who before his premature and tragic death from AIDS revolutionized experimental and site-specific theater in such works as *Tight Right White* (1994). In 1992, Abdoh also made a film from a suggestion of Sadeq Hedayat's literary masterpiece—to this day the crowning achievement of modern Persian fiction—*The Blind Owl*. A homosexual who came to erotic awakening and artistic prominence in Iran soon after the Islamic revolution of 1979, Abdoh had a thunderbolt of a creative career, leaving a permanent mark on the world theater scene. Two other Iranian artists living in New York—Nikzad Nodjoumi and Ardeshir Mohasses—have not yet succeeded in attracting global attention to their work on the scale and magnitude they so richly deserve. Born and raised in Iran and having moved to New York after the revolution, Nodjoumi's painting mixes sharp political satire with an awareness of his émigré status. Over the last two decades, Nodjoumi has exhibited his work extensively and art critics in the United States have started taking note. Equally important is the bitingly satirical work of Mohasses, by far the most successful Iranian cartoonist of his generation. His work evolved into a bitter and piercing indictment of political power on a universal scale soon after he moved to New York. To Chicago, meanwhile, immigrated another great Iranian artist, Sohrab Shahid Sales (1944–98), a pioneering figure in Iranian cinema whose two masterpieces, *A Simple Incident* and *Still Life*, have had an enduring impact on the rest of Iranian cinema, while his extensive work in German cinema remains relatively unknown.

Europe has also been a significant site of Iranian artists trespassing their national borders in search of a more global stage for their art. Hossein Zenderoudi was born in Iran in 1937 and in 1961 he moved to Paris, where he has been exceptionally prolific as a painter. Zenderoudi's work began with a creative adaptation of Islamic visual and performative leitmotifs and then extended into a style of abstract painting of luminous virtuosity. More recently, Susan Taslimi, born in 1946 and once an actress of exceptional talents in Iranian cinema and theater, is now a promising director living in Sweden. (Remind me once to tell you the hilarious story of Susan Taslimi, Arby Ovanessian, and I watching a Danish play in Oslo, while we were all attending a conference on Ibsen—Taslimi began whispering into Ovanessian's ear a Swedish translation of the Danish dialogue! You should have seen the look on Arby's face!) Taslimi made her directorial debut with *All Hell Let Loose* in 2002. Vahed Khakdan, another accomplished painter, has lived and made an illustrious artistic career in Germany. Meanwhile, Parviz Tanavoli, a celebrated contemporary sculptor who revolutionized modern Iranian figurative art, moved to Vancouver, British Columbia, in Canada, where he continues to break new ground in his work.

Altogether, visual, vocal, and performing artists have had a much better chance of working in their new environment than those whose literary and poetic output has remained linguistically limited to their expatriate Iranian audience. Nader Naderpour (d. 2000), one of the most celebrated poets of his time, died in Los Angeles with little notice except among Iranians of the Los Angeles persuasion. Esmail Khoi, an even more prominent poet, continues to write the most potent political poetry of his career, but his readership has remained limited to Iranians. Ebrahim Golestan in London and until recently Shahrokh Meskoob (d. 2004) in Paris are the best examples of towering literary figures who have dwindled to anonymity in their adopted lands. Sadeq Chubak (d. 1998), one of the most accomplished novelists of his generation, died in exile in California, barely noticed by anyone but the expatriate Iranian community, as did Gholamhossein Saedi in Paris in 1985. As Mahshid Amirshahi in Paris and Shahrnush Parsipur in New York remained relatively unknown to anyone but their Iranian readers, a generation of young Iranian artists like Ramin Bahrani in New York and Marjane Satrapi in Paris began to give a whole new and quite complicated meaning to the very notion of the term "Iranian artist." While the expatriate poets and novelists have remained in the deep background, the wings of Iranian visual and performing arts open ever more widely around the globe.

What we see and note outside Iran is of course only half of the story. Despite the fact that a considerable number of Iranian artists have left their homeland physically or by reputation, still the overwhelming majority remain inside Iran, and are barely noted outside. Major novelists like Mahmoud Dowlatabadi and, until his death in 2000, Houshang Golshiri, and prominent filmmakers such as Ebrahim Hatami-Kia are not well known outside Iran. Neither are visual artists such as Aydin Aghdashloo, Parviz Kalantari, Farshid Mesqali, Farah Ossuli, and Hossein Khosrojerdi, or sculptors and painters like Maryam Salour and Jazeh Tabatabai, or photographers like Bizhan Bani-Ahmad. Needless to say, no complete picture of Iranian art is possible without a simultaneous attention to the massive work produced inside Iranian borders for a specifically Iranian audience. But this knowledge will have to be produced in a language and through a lens that do not recklessly anthropologize Iranian art for a presumed foreign—colonially code-named "Western"—audience. The political borders artificially separating artists—Iranian or otherwise—can no longer be guarded as tightly as the US Immigration and Naturalization officers chaining Jafar Panahi to a chair are led to believe.

The global exposition of Iranian art is an exceptionally important development that has had a catalytic effect on the texture and disposition of artistic creativity around the world. People of all cultural temperaments and aesthetic dispositions converse with Iranian art in terms domestic to their own aesthetic sensibilities, and irrespective of the larger context of its immediate origin and historical heritage. Embedded in every aspect of Iranian art—poetic, visual, or performative—is a worldly conversation with the best of the rest of the world. Iranian artists who have crossed their national boundaries in language or by location—in spirit or in site—have in effect facilitated a new register in that worldly conversation. Living inside or outside Iran is no longer the measure of this creative engagement. There are artists like Kiarostami who have been born and raised entirely within the current borders of Iran and yet their art has crossed cultural boundaries east and west of their birthplace—and then there are filmmakers like Parviz Sayyad or painters like Mahmoud Farshchian who have physically moved outside Iran and yet their art caters almost exclusively to a hermetically sealed exilic community—with almost no organic connection to the material evidence of their physical environment. The antidote to that isolationism is the rich and robust cinema of Naderi, the beguiling seduction of Neshat's photography and video installations—and above all the rousing salutation of Iranian cinema as it welcomes the world in its expansive embrace.

Iranian artists are now conversing with the world with their own Persian accent. Artists around the world in turn are picking up that accent and communicating with their respective art with a Persian intonation. One can today arguably speak of an *Iranian cinema*—where Kiarostamiesque realism has become a staple of world cinema. "Iranian cinema is now produced from all over the globe," Naderi once told me after serving as a juror in an international film festival. Iranian cinema no longer belongs to Iranians alone—its thematic and aesthetic language is now freely quoted, creatively adapted, and fruitfully assimilated into other cinematic traditions—precisely in the same way that Iranian cinema itself borrowed freely, unequivocally, and with ingenious results from other cinematic traditions. People are now paying homage to Iranian cinema by imitating it—sometimes better, sometimes worse than the originals—precisely the same way Persian carpet designs are produced much less expensively in Pakistan, or Shiraz wine is produced in Australia (as you well know Sa'di and Hafez were great Australian poets). The result is an artistic tradition that expresses the best hopes of a world now in dire despair. After the catastrophic events of 9/11, the havoc that the United States wrought in Afghanistan and Iraq signals the commencement of a new imperial design for the world at large. As the world is dangerously moving toward a mono-polar empire, and with the United

States aggressively pursuing a predatory form of global imperialism, Iranian art projects an exemplary case for a polyfocal vision of our planet as one poignant form of resisting the delusions of that empire. The catastrophic looting of human cultural heritage in Iraq, and before that in Afghanistan, is a clear indication that this predatory empire has no claim to cultural hegemony and sees the world as a source of natural resources and a global marketplace—oilfields and supermarkets with colorful flags on them. Places like Iran and the entirety of the region it represents mean nothing to the ideologues of this warlike empire except a mixed network of lucrative retail outlets and potential security threat. Often ruled and represented alternatively by corrupt potentates or medieval tyrants, countries like Iran have no recourse to alternative self-representations except through their globally celebrated artists who have defied their colonially construed borders and crafted a vision beyond our current despair and toward our future hopes.

With Kiarostami, Makhmalbaf, and the culmination of generations of parabolic narratives in Meshkini's cinema, Iranian cinema in general has finally rested its case and reached an epistemic closure—the middle of its own nowhere. Filmmakers like Jafar Panahi are now the beneficiaries of a creative unconscious not totally aware of its own whereabouts. By the time Panahi picked up his camera and made his very first film, in him was already invested a visual subconscious. In the chaotic creativity of that visual subconscious the jubilant crowds of signs of our culture are all let loose and emancipated from their symbolic cells. This chaotic, creative eruption of signs now corresponds to the globalization of Iranian cinema, and the collapse of nation-state as the principal site of the creative unconscious of our (or any other) cinema. Like slaves running away from a citadel, we are frightened by the storm we face, reluctant and yet anxious to go back and knock at the door of our prisons to let us back in—just the way Shamlu described us in a poem. But behind that door there remains no prison. It's just a door, a heavy gate, constructed in the middle of a desert. It leads to nothing—to a void.

An Epistolary Conclusion

I HAVE ONE LAST STORY TO TELL YOU. Soon after the conclusion of Cannes in late May 1998, a nonprofit organization based in Washington, DC, called Search for Common Ground had planned to arrange a meeting between major Iranian and American filmmakers as part of its continued efforts to facilitate a rapprochement—as they call it—between the Iranian and the American *people*, as opposed to their respective governments, a second-track diplomacy of a sort. Richard Peña—the director of programming at the Film Society of Lincoln Center, in New York, and also my colleague in the Film division of the School of the Arts here at Columbia—and I were asked to moderate this meeting. Mohsen Makhmalbaf was to represent the Iranian delegation. John Marks, the president of Search for Common Ground, and Godfrey Cheshire, an American film critic, had come up with the idea when they met in Tehran when Marks had taken an American wrestling team to Iran and Cheshire was there researching Iranian cinema. Cheshire told us that a number of

American filmmakers, including Robert Redford and Oliver Stone, had expressed interest in the idea.

After months of negotiations and preparation, mostly facilitated by Cheshire, the meeting fell through and did not materialize at the scale that he had envisioned it. Cheshire ended up putting together a much smaller version of the meeting at the very last minute, alas with no enduring effect. It was a noble idea, but was lost in petty rivalries of various sorts. Makhmalbaf did not participate in that meeting. Instead, he, his two children Samira and Meysam, and I drove north from Cannes to Yssingeaux, a small provincial town near Lyon.

That summer the World Cup was in France. The Iranian national team had made it to the World Cup and was hosted in this small town in central France. Apparently, the dear and distinguished residents of Yssingeaux were not quite happy that, of all the nifty national teams they could have hosted from around the world, they were slotted for a certain Islamic Republic with a notorious record of nasty things to its credit. A number of local Iranian residents of Yssingeaux had come together and met with the mayor of the village and a few other local dignitaries and sought to remedy the situation. Their task, as they sorted out their options, was to give a cultural boost to the trademark "Iran" in order to facilitate a more hospitable environment for the Iranian national team. This objective was made much easier by the picture of Samira Makhmalbaf having been splashed all over glossy journals in Europe earlier that summer, and to add icing on the cake, by the fact that Mohsen Makhmalbaf's *Gabbeh*, a visual homage to the Persian carpet, so far as the critical apparatus of rug merchants in Yssingeaux could tell, had been recently released in France.

Once again Iranian cinema was sought to join forces with another aspect of Iranian national pride in order to whitewash the atrocities of the theocracy that rudely rules over Iran's destiny. And so it was that the good citizens of Yssingeaux had put their minds and resources together, contacted the ever-resourceful Mamad Haghighat in Paris, and arranged to come to Cannes and pick us up and take us to their beautiful village. At precisely nine o'clock on Monday morning, 25 May 1998, I remember quite vividly, we were all met by a delegation of delightful ladies from Yssingeaux, all dressed in their Sunday best and led by the wife of the mayor in the parking lot behind the Grand Hotel in Cannes. They were quite brisk and joyous early that morning. *"Je m'appelle Madame Martin,"* or some such name—*"Comment allez-vous?"*

Samira, Mohsen, Meysam, and I sat comfortably in the back of a Citroen station wagon, and were then driven quite ceremoniously through Cannes to a crowded highway, and before we could say a proper goodbye to the great Salle Lumière, we were on a wide and inviting highway driving north to our destination. The mayor's wife was driving us with the full posture and purpose of a maharani, while her friends in the front row were keeping her dutifully entertained, and we in the back seats were left to our own devices to manage for ourselves during what appeared like a blissfully long but pleasant journey.

The countryside was freshly green, dotted with occasional wineries, scattered industrial sites, small villages, and divided by a long and patiently gray highway. My mind, I remember, at that time was still on a conversation Mohsen and I had begun the night before we left Cannes. The reason the collective articulation of our historical agency has always taken on the shape of a *movement* rather than an incidental event was that it has in fact been in creative conversation with intellectual and artistic trends of the same purpose and proportion—poetry, film, and fiction in particular—that had marked Iran's colonial encounter with European modernity. Cultural conversations that each generation of Iranian artists and intellectuals have initiated with previous generations have themselves assumed the status and momentum of movements in their own rights. What has happened in Iranian cinema of the last half century, I was convinced, is also a *movement*—and not a simple aggregation of brilliant filmmakers—by virtue of its creative conversation with all its preceding and adjacent literary, poetic, and aesthetic events.

By far the most definitive moment of all such movements has been the categorical predicament of much of the world, Iran included, being born as nation-states into the globalizing project of European modernity through the gun barrel of colonialism. This has been the most enduring existential fact of the post-Enlightenment condition: that the whole world was born into the contemporaneity of its self-consciousness as the colonial extension of a self-universalizing modernity, the philosophical articulation of which it (the world outside Western Europe) had absolutely no share. The European project of modernity was self-universalizing because only through a global expansion of its epistemic assumptions could it assume overriding legitimacy—a legitimacy that it otherwise lacked in religious or mythic assumptions, and thus it had to cast itself in universal and absolutist terms in order to feign that legitimacy. There has been no social or artistic movement in Iran, or any other culture in its immediate and distant vicinity, over the last two hundred years that has not been directly related to the paradoxical predicament of colonially facilitated modernity. Put very simply, the European project of modernity was dispatched to the four corners of the world through the intermediary mechanism of colonialism. That simple fact has given a paradoxical disposition to all facets of modernity in all its colonial contexts, because the colonial subject was denied agency precisely at the moment that he was told he was in charge of his own destiny. As the colonial officer slapped the native in the face, and the Christian missionary in the company told him or her to turn the other cheek, the native also began to learn of European modernity that was telling the world that people were now free of their medieval bondage, and that now they had to dare to think. The world at large was made into a colonial site of conquest at the very moment that European modernity announced itself. Nowhere in the world could a creative consciousness announce itself in return, without ipso facto engaging that colonial project, unless it assumed the revolutionary disposition of a *movement*. There were beautiful vineyards around the highway, as we drove south toward Lyon.

The colonially militated modernity de-subjected the world at large, and precisely in that paradox denied it agency even as it was creating itself. A contradiction in terms, a walking denial of itself, the asphyxiation of its own breathing, the colonial subject, whether collectively rising in arms against colonialism or else obsequiously in compliance with it, could not but be, breathe, and exist in terms received or postulated through colonial modernity—a modernity whose claims to the Enlightenment were articulated not in a benign neglect but in a malign dismissal of the colonial subject. From Hegel's teleological constitution of a history for it, to Kant's articulation of a philosophy for its critical operation, to the French encyclopedist going on a normative rampage in propagating it, to the British utilitarian expansion of it into a colonizing project, the Enlightenment posited and privileged a European subject at the massive expense of the non-European world, turning it into an object of its colonizing gaze and imperial conquest.

"*Est-ce-que vous voulez boire quelque chose? Ou peut-etre allez a la toilette?*" Our distinguished driver needed to get some gas and do some additional refurbishing—so we had a short stop at a gas station, where we went to the restroom and also bought some God-awful instant coffee from a vending machine. We sat down for a while and I remember telling Mohsen how I thought no political act of resistance or compliance to colonialism could have altered the self-contradictory state of the colonial subject. Collective acts of insurrectionary counter-colonialism, whether they were launched in nationalist, socialist, or nativist (Islamist) terms, have categorically confirmed and paradoxically corroborated the terms of colonial modernity. Both nationalism and socialism were the flowering achievements of the European project of modernity. Their colonial adaptations even *against* European colonialism in effect implicated the colonials in a project that in its very inception had deliberately excluded them. Nativist movements were even worse. They were launched in apparent opposition to colonial domination but in effect turned out to confirm and authenticate a monumentally pernicious concoction called "the West." The oppositional presumption of "Islam" and "the West" mutated the ancestral faith of a multifaceted culture into the singular site of ideological resistance to colonialism and called it "Islam," while confirming and consolidating an equally dominant fallacy called "the West," the codified supposition of a civilizational superiority that Enlightenment modernity bequeathed to "Europe" and then to the US, as the military and cultural headquarters of its colonizing project. There is a reason, I remember I added, that such grand strategist and ideologues of the US empire like Bernard Lewis have spent a lifetime writing book after book about "Islam and the West," for in the very supposition of that binary Muslims, which here stand for the entirety of the colonized world, always get the shorter end of the stick.

What I was trying to say over that plastic cup of coffee was that whether they fought their European colonizers or joined them in their plunder, the colonized did so in terms dictated by a mode of modernity that denied them historical agency. The result was a categorical crisis of the colonial subject that in all its political acts positively or paradoxically confirmed the superiority of *the knowing Western subject* and the inferiority of *the knowable rest*. The entire project of Orientalism can in fact be read as the positing of *the knowing European subject* up against discovering Islam as *the knowable world*. Orientalists were foot soldiers of Immanuel Kant, but did not know it.

In about half an hour we were back on the road. I was thinking to myself on that flat, straight, and snoozy highway: Suppose we, as the overwhelming majority of the people of this planet, were not born to the dubious privilege of European modernity. Dubious I say because it was squarely predicated on the fact and phenomenon of the disenfranchised multitude it had to dismiss as colonial in order to assure itself of its capital significance. What then? Here I was reminded of a story of the medieval mystic Bayazid Bastami. Once a man asked the great Bayazid, "What is the best thing that can happen to a person?" "That he be born fortunate!" Bayazid responded. "If not?" the man wondered.

> *He should then have a knowing heart!*
> If not?
> *A pair of eyes that can see well!*
> If not?
> *A pair of ears that can hear well!*
> If not?
> *Just an urgent death!*

The world at large, I thought to myself after this story, was in effect left to its own devices—a knowing heart, two perceptive eyes, two sensitive ears, and only death to fear or expect. With the political act so constitutionally compromised—meaning no matter how loudly we protested and how violently we revolted we in fact dug deeper our own grave inside a binary that in its very epistemic fact denigrated the whole world to privilege those who were after conquering it—it was up to our insurrectionary aesthetics to release and set us free from this paradoxical predicament and restore in us a critically potent and creatively defiant agency. In insurrectionary aesthetics—not in being critically counter-colonial but in being creatively non-colonial (pay very close attention to that difference)—historical agency was restored to the de-subjected colonial. In their acts of creative insurrection, the colonial subjects have in fact bypassed colonial de-subjection by moving into the colonial condition itself, there to steal the light of freedom from the heart of darkness, to de-legislate the *socius* in a colonially conceived society—by releasing the *signum* (the mother of all signs) from its scripted incarceration in a metaphysically mandated semantics.

"*Nous sommes presque là,*" was quite a welcomed announcement coming from our merciful maharani at the wheel. We were all getting quite weary of the road. But we were soon off the main highway and on the narrow and winding roads to our destination. Yssingeaux is a small village of some 7,000 inhabitants, about an hour from Lyon and half an hour from Saint Etienne. It is a quiet little village, with rows of stone walls giving it a surreptitious, medieval look. We were driven by our delegated ladies straight to the mayor's residence, a fifteenth-century chateau, right in the middle of the village, which along with a Roman chapel were the main two edifices welcoming the visitors. "*J'éspère que vous n'avez pas trop fatigués!*" But we were. A small camera crew was waiting to interview Mohsen and Samira as we arrived, as was the mayor and an entourage of his associates.

After the interview was over in the backyard of the mayor's château, Samira, Mohsen, Meysam, and I were guided into a reception area inside. The mayor had invited half of the village, it seemed, for a supreme supper of baguettes, an avalanche of French cheese, and cold cuts of unfathomable variety. We were finally seated, fed, watered, and for those who cared to join, wined, with guests coming to the Makhmalbafs for some felicitous pleasantries. A special screening of Mohsen's *Gabbeh* had been arranged that night in a quite unceremonious hall that looked like their chamber of commerce or some bureaucratic outlet like that. We were all driven to this location, where Mohsen introduced his film, thanked his audience, and expressed his gratitude for their graciously hosting the Iranian national soccer team. People of Yssingeaux seemed moderately reassured, if not totally convinced, that the Iranian soccer team would not turn into ghostly goblins in the middle of the night and devour all their hidden stores of *fromage et jambon*. We were then driven back to the mayor's chateau and guided to the second floor of the building, where in what appeared like a renovated attic we were each given a comfortable bed and the collective promise of a good night's sleep.

I remember I was dead tired but could not sleep. Mohsen and I chatted for a while about the following day, when we were supposed to be driven by a local Iranian to Paris. Soon Mohsen and his children were all sound asleep. I was quite tired too but could not asleep for I was still stuck somewhere in the early nineteenth century in Tabriz, thinking about the succession of these literary and artistic *movements* that had preoccupied me between Cannes and Yssingeaux. Thinking about Tabriz in Yssingeaux—what sort of madness is this? But here I was—and I could not go to sleep.

In one political rebellion after another against colonialism and its local cronies we have failed—even, or particularly, when we have succeeded. Defeating colonialism politically means ideologically falling into its global worldview. The only way out for us—the only time that we have escaped the trap of colonial de-subjection—has been in and through our art. But how does it exactly work?

Is it not surprising, I thought (though I was really tired), that the very first genre of literary prose that appeared early in the course of our colonial encounter with European modernity was in fact travel writing by students, merchants, and diplomats who in one way or another found their way to Europe and then made a record of what they saw in the heart of the colonial powers—and what needed to be done in their neck of the woods. Mir Seyyed Abd al-Latif Shushtari was a merchant who in 1788 traveled to India as a business partner to his brother who was stationed in Basra. He wrote his *Tuhfat al-Alam* by way of an introductory commentary on who these British colonial officers were and what they were doing in India. As a merchant he had a penchant for the commercial consequences of colonialism, and the fact that he sat down and wrote an account of his thoughts is a clear indication of the overwhelming power of colonial modernity in his environment. His prose is sweet and simple, his observations innocent, but nevertheless his text exposes a very sensitive and alert awareness to what was new, what was coming, and the magnetic allure of power—in its specifically colonial configuration.

It is only apt that the first encounter of an Iranian with colonialism in fact took place in India, the site of its most visible presence. It is also from India that Mirza Abu Taleb Makki, a close friend of Mir Seyyed Abd al-Latif, in 1804 traveled to Europe and wrote his *Masir-e Talebi*, an elaborate travelogue in which he recorded details of his social and political observations. As an employee of the East India Company, Mirza Abu Taleb Makki was already exposed to what was happening around him while still in India. But his physical encounters with Europe, and per-haps even more poignantly his sitting down and writing an account of his observations, gave a narrative authenticity to what he experienced.

Many other Iranians traveled to Europe, the principal site of Enlightenment modernity, and wrote down their observations. The most elaborate and critically consequential travelogue was written in 1819, when Mirza Saleh Shirazi, an Iranian student deeply interested in contemporary politics and philosophy, traveled to Europe and recorded his *Safar-nameh*. His trip, begun in 1815, coincided with extraordinary events in European colonial history, to which Mirza Saleh was a shrewd and insightful observer. Napoleon was courting the Qajars in order to gain access to India and create trouble for the British. The British soon moved to outmaneuver him, offering to train the Qajar army to fight against the Russians. A few Iranian students at the court of Crown Prince Abbas Mirza became the beneficiaries of this arrangement and were sent to England to study various military sciences. Among them was this Mirza Saleh who convinced the crown prince to allow him to study lan-guages, philosophy, and history. His travelogue from this trip became an exemplary model of a simplified Persian prose, suited to address the predicament of the emerging nation-state in the throes of colonial modernity. From England, Mirza Saleh also brought back to Iran the first printing machine and established the first newspaper. His travelogue is among the first documents in which an Iranian intellectual directly engages with institutional changes necessary to address the problems of a counter-colonial nation-state.

By this time the genre of travel narratives had been solidly estab-lished. Europe was now emerging as the principal site of power—to the extent that in 1873 even the reigning monarch, Nasir al-Din Shah, made the first of many trips to Europe. Writing about Europe was a narrative mode of trying to come to terms with its political power. When in 1888 Haji Pirzadeh wrote his *Safar-nameh* about his travels in Iran, India, North Africa, and Europe, travel literature was universally recognized as the paramount mode of critical and creative encounter with colonial modernity. Even Nasir al-Din Shah kept a daily record of his obser-vations. When Hajj Mirza Muhammad Ali Mo'in al-Saltaneh wrote, in 1892, about his journey to Chicago, the United States also became incorporated into the colonial imagination of observant Iranians. *Seya-hat-nameh-ye Ebrahim Beik*, written by Zeyn al-Abedin Maraghei in 1903, brings this genre to a narrative closure. An Iranian living abroad, Mara-ghei returned to Iran and wrote a fictive description of his homecoming with one of the most critical accounts of political decay and social atro-phy that he observed in his homeland.

What comes after travel literature? With the travel literature Iran effectively opened up the world to the universe of power that encircled it. Exhausting the knowledge of Europe available in Persian, Iranians required more information about Europe, on its own terms. Thus began a massive movement to translate works from European languages into Persian. The translations of the time were haphazard and random, but they still reflect a vibrant and agitated imagination. Early in the nineteenth century and beginning with Abbas Mirza, the single most enlightened prince in the entire clan of corrupt Qajar monarchs, Iranians who were exposed to European literatures began to translate them into Persian. Abbas Mirza was particularly interested in historical accounts and novels. Edward Gibbon's *The Decline and Fall of the Roman Empire* was among the first books translated for Abbas Mirza by Mirza Reza Mohanddes, a student he had sent to England. The most prolific translators of the Qajar period were Mohammad Taher Mirza and Mohammad Hasan Khan I'temad al-Saltaneh. Alexandre Dumas (both Dumas *père* and Dumas *fils*) and Molière were the most popular authors in nineteenth-century Qajar Iran. But these translations were not limited to historical and literary sources. For instance, Descartes' "Discourse on Method" was translated into Persian in 1862. But by and large translators selected their texts with an eye toward the particular colonial predicament of their homeland. The translation of books on revolutionary movements, from fifteenth-century Bohemia to the Russian Revolution of 1905, testifies to the agitated mood of the time and its fears and aspirations.

Now Iranians needed to disseminate both an awareness and a critique of these ideas and practices, and what they meant for the colonial condition. The economic consequences of colonial modernity were creating major demographic changes in Iran. Neither literacy nor political concern about the fate of the nation was any longer limited to the royal court, the religious seminaries, or the mosque. Thus emerged a major movement in newspaper publishing, disseminating critical ideas on a range of political and social issues on an unparalleled scale.

The same Mirza Saleh Shirazi who had written an influential travel narrative of his European sojourns published the first Persian newspaper and simply called it *Kaghaz-e Akhbar*, or "News Paper." But this auspicious beginning did not last long. With the death of Abbas Mirza and the end of Fath Ali Shah's monarchy in 1834, many such early reforms came to an almost complete stop during the reign of Mohammad Shah (1834–48). It was well after the commencement of Nasir al-Din's monarchy in 1848 that the condition of colonialism and the increasing presence of the British and the Russians in Iran occasioned the rise of critical intervention by expatriate Iranian intellectuals. We may consider the execution of Ali Mohammad Bab in 1850 as the critical point of the last medieval revolutionary movement. The Babis, although having finally failed to dismantle the Qajars, pushed the colonial encounter of Iranians at large with European modernity into a critical stage. Soon after, an avalanche of Persian newspapers commenced publication, many of them based outside Iran, published by expatriate Iranian intellectuals, but with a sizable circulation inside the country.

The rise of the Iranian press in the early nineteenth century had a revolutionary impact on our collective awareness of the world at large. Usually, our neighboring countries were the launching pad for these periodicals. *Akhtar*, for example, was founded in 1875 in Istanbul, by a reform-minded publisher named Aqa Mohammad Taher Qazvini. He was joined by many Iranian expatriate intellectuals, chief among them Mirza Aqa Khan Kermani and Sheykh Ahmad Ruhi, two of the sharpest critical minds Iran has ever produced and whom Nasir al-Din Shah brutally murdered. Mirza Aqa Khan Kermani in fact made his living in Istanbul by writing for *Akhtar*. Another influential paper of the period was *Habl al-Matin*, published in Calcutta. *Habl al-Matin* was the chief organ of the Iranian constitutionalist revolutionaries, gathering momentum to curb the absolutist reign of the Qajars. Meanwhile in Cairo another newspaper began publication in 1898: *Sorayya* was published by Mirza Ali Mohammad Khan Kashani, an expatriate with very radical views on necessary revolutionary changes in Iran. Mirza Mohammad soon left *Sorayya* and established *Parvaresh* in 1900, where he continued to write critically on the political fate of his homeland. From London, Mirza Malkam Khan started *Qanun* in 1890, a journal almost exclusively dedicated to its publisher's revolutionary ideas on the necessity of constitutional government. Now consider the fact that the Tobacco Revolt of 1891, against the concession of the tobacco industry to a British company, and the subsequent assassination of Naser al-Din Shah in 1896, occurred exactly at this point and you will realize the significance of this early rise of the Iranian press in the articulation of our colonial encounter with European modernity.

As all these developments were well underway—our esteemed ancestors traveling to Europe and writing their observations, translating European literature, and publishing newspapers—something exceptionally important was also taking place. Almost as a subtext to these important developments, Persian prose, plagued by centuries of obtuse formalism, stylistic complication, syntactical convolution, and morphological madness, began to be radically simplified, cured of its endemic discursive diseases, made ready for purposeful writing. If I were to recommend one text for you to read regarding this crucial development it would be Zeyn al-Abedin Maraghe'i's *Seyahat-namah-ye Ebrahim Beik*, written in 1903. This exceptionally influential book opened up the political discourse of the time beyond anything achieved before—to the point that it became the defining text of the Constitutional Revolution of 1906–11. Maraghe'i's text, however, has an equally important status in the rise of modern Persian prose—to the point that it is impossible to imagine the rise of Persian fiction over the last century without the seminal presence of *Seyahat-namah-ye Ebrahim Beik*. This book is the story of a young Iranian expatriate who returns to his homeland after having been raised and educated abroad. This narrative ploy gives Maraghe'i an occasion to reflect critically on the backward condition of his homeland and severely criticize the Qajar dynasty for its criminal negligence of the nation at large. The significance of the book, however, is in its exceedingly simple and straightforward prose, a critical diction that has run away from the opiate language of the Qajar court and is breathing freely the healthy air of the outside world.

I cannot remember when exactly I fell asleep that night in Yssingeaux. But I have a clear memory of Mohsen waking me up the following day, of having breakfast and then all of us being driven to Paris. From Paris that June I took the train to London—the very first time that I crossed the channel through the newly constructed tunnel—where my son Kaveh was vacationing, and brought him with me back to Paris to spend a few more days with Mohsen and his children. That train ride is one of the most comfortable rides I ever had. I took a cab from our hotel to Gare du Nord in Paris and took a train to London. The train ride was so smooth, so silent, just like a dream. I sat in a comfortable seat by the window and placed the coffee I had just purchased in the train station on a small table in front of me. I love trains. They are life in motion.

As the train began to pull out of the station in Paris, I remember thinking to myself how a succession of literary and artistic movements began to develop, all contingent on these groundbreaking events in the course of the nineteenth century: a body of insightful travel narratives, the appearance of the Persian translation of European sources (fiction, history, and philosophy in particular), the gradual rise of a creative and critical press, and above all perhaps the simplification of Persian prose. The gradual writing of political memoirs, contemporary historiography, and social essays were chief among these emerging forms of addressing the current predicament of the nascent state. One text stands out as a solid account of these developments by a participant observer, and that is *Tarikh-e Bidari-ye Iranian* (*The History of the Iranians' Awakening*, 1910), composed by Nazem al-Islam Kermani (1863–1918). Nazem al-Islam was a close friend and associate of some of the leading public intellectuals and political activists of the late nineteenth century, and his *History* is the exemplary conclusion of the rise of the critical discourse that emerged in response to colonial modernity. If you ever get to read this book (there is a wonderful critical edition of it by the late Ali Akbar Sa'idi Sirjani), which I hope you will, notice the contemporary urgency with which Nazem al-Islam has written it; it is the summation of the most ambitious political hopes and aspirations of his generation. I very much like this book because it perfectly sums up the political culture of the nineteenth century, and you can see how between nationalism, socialism, and Islamism, the collective struggles of Iranians against both colonialism and its complacent Qajar aristocracy ultimately concluded with a constitutional revolution that (all the heroic struggle that went into its making notwithstanding) gave Iranians neither any enduring democratic institution nor any autonomous mode of critical thinking conducive to an agential presence in its own history.

What seems to have happened in Iran beginning with the Constitutional Revolution of 1906–11 is a succession of literary and artistic movements coterminous with our national struggle for rule of law and the establishment of democratic institutions. Between 1900 and 1930, for example, poetry was the single most important cultural mode of engagement with our contemporary issues. Here what you must keep in mind is that the discovery of oil in Masjid Soleiman in 1908 opened a whole new chapter in the history of colonial interest in Iran—a predicament well represented in the collective consciousness of the spectrum of illustrious poets who came of age in the early twentieth century. These poets gave voice to the defining ideas and sentiments of our collective self-awareness, hopes, and aspirations, fears and adversities. The moral trajectory of this poetry—best represented by Mirzadeh Eshqi (1893–1924), Iraj Mirza (1874–1925), Aref Qazvini (1879–1937), and Farrokhi Yazdi (1888–1939), chief among many others—picked up where the initial encounter with colonial modernity had left off with the Constitutional Revolution of 1906–11 (note the date and see how these poets were all at their best during the revolutionary period). A systematic articulation of a poetic modernity, a defiance of the classical Persian prosody, and a direct (at once critical and creative) engagement with the political consequences of a colonial encounter with European Enlightenment are the principal parameters of our cultural disposition at the threshold of the twentieth century.

I would strongly urge you to read at least one of these seminal poets very closely—say Iraj Mirza. More than anything else notice the felicity of his lyrical language and the elegance of his poetic diction. Do not let the liberality of his politics amaze, distract, or bar you from accessing the bounty of his far more creative imagination. Most of his readers are enchanted by the brilliance of his wit and the bite of his satire. But I want you to let his voice guide you further into the fertile land of his poetic imagination, which successfully departs from the prosaic limitations of his political age and its contingent ideological blinders. While you are at it, also note how the poetic language has already assumed a reality sui generis by the time of Iraj Mirza—that not even the poet himself is in full control of all the poetic implications of the universe he invokes. This is a very crucial development, for by now the creative disposition of a defiant postcolonial subject is taking shape and finding a domain for its insurrectionary urges. It is the *formal* and *stylized* dimensions of this poetry that are of utmost significance here, and not merely its politically progressive disposition, which by and large distracts our literary critics and historians from seeing something far more significant.

Over the next three decades, between 1930 and 1960, poetry continued to be the defining model of cultural production, though now it had the added momentum of New Poetry ("Sher-e No"), championed by Nima Yushij and announced in his groundbreaking "Afsaneh," published in 1922. But fiction now joined the scene in full throttle. Although Mohammad Baqer Mirza Khosravi had published his *Shams va Toghra* in 1906, it was not until the publication of Mohammad Ali Jamalzadeh's *Once upon a Time* in 1922 in Berlin that the new Persian fiction commenced in earnest. In 1941 (after its initial publication in 1937 in India), Sadeq Hedayat published his masterpiece, *The Blind Owl*, and in 1957 appeared Ahmad Shamlu's collection of poetry *Fresh Air*—two seminal works that consolidated the formation of a new literary fiction and poetry as the joint cultural forces of the post-Constitutional period. Between 1930s and 1960s, thus Persian poetry and fiction joined force in defining the terms of our literary modernity—the critical site and the creative terms of our collective defiance of our colonial de-subjection. In this fiction and in this poetry, we had begun articulating the terms of a mode of being-in-the world beyond the reach of any colonial officer denying or circumventing it.

Beginning with the early 1960s and all the way to the Islamic revolution of 1979, poetry and fiction continued to lead the cultural scene—and now to it was added with a panoramic rainbow of colorful possibilities the Iranian cinema. Although as early as the 1930s, Iran was producing silent films, it was not until Forough Farrokhzad's *The House Is Black* (1962), Ebrahim Golestan's *Mud Brick and Mirror* (1965), and ultimately Daryush Mehrjui's *Cow* (1969) that Iranian cinema joined forces with poetry and fiction to form the creative triumvirate of our cultural modernity. What I wish to emphasize here is the succession of artistic movements—from poetry to fiction and now to cinema—that both successively and simultaneously alternate and navigate a creative disposition in crafting agential authority in matters at once cultural and political. Please pay close attention here that while our *mode* of cultural expression changes and modulates among poetry, fiction, and cinema, constant remains the *formal* aesthetics within which our artists are experimenting with new and unprecedented formalism. In the vast and variegated domain of this aesthetic stylization of our material condition we can be actively imaginative and creatively combatant, at a time when political expression in Iran was almost impossible except through violent and militant ways.

The bizarre thing about this development is that both poetic and literary creativity came to an abrupt end in the aftermath of the Islamic revolution of 1979. While both Ahmad Shamlu (d. 2000) and Mehdi Akhavan Sales (d. 1990) were still alive after the revolution, as was Houshang Golshiri (d. 2000) and is Mahmoud Dolatabadi, none of them published a significant poem or a work of fiction beyond what they had already achieved. Beginning with the 1980s, cinema remained the sole cultural product of the time—and it has remained that way well into the first decade of the current century.

These successive movements—at once social and cultural, commencing their active formation early in the nineteenth century and coming to complete fruition late in the twentieth—have now culminated in cinema, which has in turn achieved a global presence. Throughout these artistic movements, literature, poetry, and film have been in the active pursuit of the constitution of an "Iranian" subject and an articulation of historical agency—a stealing of light from the heart of darkness. Against the background of a material absence to our institutional achievements in liberty and democratic ideals, artistic movements have been the substitutional simulacrum of creative agency sustaining our normative behaviour, informing our social consciousness, and projecting our political agency. The more disembodied has been the material basis of our achieving democratic agency, the more full-bodied has become the agential autonomy of our creative disposition in crafting an aesthetic domain in which we can imagine ourselves otherwise.

As a movement, our cinema has neither been linked to its cultural antecedents nor read in its global context. Its global audience thinks it local, while its local audience thinks it global. Well it used to be local, and it is now global. But the two attributes require a thematic link. If we were to connect them, what would we see? What does it mean for a cinema that commenced as the artistic continuation of our century-long attempt at articulating a counter-colonial agency and then went global?

I spent a few days in London before taking the same train back with my son, Kaveh, to Paris. I remember the day when Mohsen, his children Samira and Meysam, and his friend Mr. Ashrafi, Kaveh, and I all went for a walk by the Seine. It was early in the afternoon and the river was muddy and yet exuding a strange sense of peace and serenity. What has happened in Iranian cinema, I have concluded, is a movement integral to other similar cultural movements in our history—from critical essays, to poetry, to fiction, and now to cinema. Iranian cinema is not a mere aggregation of brilliant filmmakers. There have always been master film-makers all over the world. But they have not always been integral to a national cinema. What is definitive to Iranian cinema is akin but irre-ducible to Russian formalism, Italian Neorealism, French New Wave, German New Cinema, or Cuban revolutionary cinema. These multiple schools of filmmaking and other individual masters like Kurosawa and Hitchcock have had a lasting influence on Iranian cinema but are not the defining origin of its aesthetic texture or political disposition.

So what exactly is the defining moment of the Iranian cinema? Call-ing it just "Iranian cinema" categorizes it as yet another national cinema, similar to, say, Lebanese or Turkish cinema. This categorization is, of course, accurate, but also quite lazy and dismissive—quite non-descriptive in fact. On occasions, Iranian cinema has been called Iranian Neoreal-ism, perhaps in deference to Italian Neorealism and its obvious influence. But this will not do because the French and (to a lesser degree) Germans have also had an influence on Iranian cinema, and so have the Americans and other masters from around the world—from Tarkovsky to Kurosawa. Moreover, we don't call the French New Wave "French cinema" or Italian Neorealism "Italian cinema" or German New Cinema "German cinema." New Wave, New Realism, and New Cinema are thematic descriptions, theoretical proposals. The same is true about what is now called "Iranian cinema." It needs a definitive attribute, a qualifying description, a theo-retical proposal. A simple "wew" or "realism" means nothing.

There is a realism in Iranian cinema, but it is a peculiar kind of realism, a realism rooted in the particularity of our cultural modernity. Kiarostami's realism is entirely *actual*, taking the momentum of actual reality and then dismantling it, to the point that reality is stripped of all its inherited significance, so that it begins to exude its untapped and yet-to-be-navigated possibilities. Makhmalbaf's realism, on the other hand, is *virtual*. He is a visual minimalist, with an uncanny ability to reduce reality to its virtual matter-of-factness, where it cannot be any more indexical, thus teasing reality out of its convoluted habit of crowding its bare necessities. Meanwhile, Meshkini's realism is *parabolic* in the man-ner of its storytelling, and yet *fable-like* in the tonality of its abbreviated referentiality. She is committed to the factual evidence of the real with-out ever allowing it to perform its beguiling magic of a claim either to actuality or virtuality. All these realisms are deeply rooted in their visual ancestry—in Farrokhzad's *poetic*, Golestan's *affective*, Mehrjui's *psychedelic*, Ovanessian's *spatial*, Farmanara's *narrative*, Shahid Sales' *transparent*, Naderi's *visual*, and Beizai's *mythical* cinemas. These are the specifics of Iranian cinema. They represent a kind of signal rebellion against the incarceration of a received reality. It's about time we paid these visual poets their due respect and not lump them together, dismissing them with one easy term, Iranian neorealism. The water of the Seine is quite muddy and thick. But still when I look back, I have a vivid memory of Samira, Meysam, and my son, Kaveh, following me, Mohsen, and Mr. Ashrafi on the sunset of a quiet and calm afternoon.

Only a sweet and soft memory of that summer is left me, all else is now pale and fading, all except the conclusions I reached. My conclusion is that Iranian cinema, as indeed much of world cinema, is thoroughly indebted to its European antecedents, as well as to many non-European masters—but that it has something else, something definitive to its aesthetics, rooted in its historical reflection of a people and their destiny. Cinematic influences mostly come in the form of master practitioners of it (Kiarostami, for example, today has had an influence on contemporary world cinema quite independent of his place in an Iranian context). Indebted to these masters and traditions as Iranian cinema is, as a movement it has its own unique character. Iranian cinema has an immediate social context, and is integral to a succession of other literary, poetic, and artistic movements. What Iranian cinema of the last half century seems to have brought to fruition is not a *neorealism* but a *pararealism*, a take on realism that goes above, beyond, beside, and around reality, there and then, by and by, to frame and force it to yield its hidden alternatives, its undelivered promises. Iranian pararealism, as a result, is neither neorealism nor surrealism. It remains constitutionally bound by its awareness of reality; and yet it takes reality too seriously to take it too seriously. Iranian pararealism is frivolous with reality.

Iranian pararealism takes reality for a ride, into the neighborhood of the real, in the vicinity of all but evident, while poking at its isn't-it-obvious, tickling the soft sides of its I-could've-sworn. By the time Iranian pararealism is done with reality, reality is dizzy with a giddy and deliciously nauseous kind of joy. It doesn't know which way is up and which way is down, whether it's going or coming. But it is the same reality. Iranian pararealism pours Persian wine onto the porous surface of reality and gets it blissfully drunk. *Masti-o-Rasti*, we say in Persian, "Drunkenness and Truth." You tell the truth when you are drunk. Iranian pararealism teaches reality how to drink and be truthful, and thus to reclaim critical agency, to remake the subject against its active de-subjection in the course of Iran's colonial encounter with European modernity. Taking its clues from our fiction and poetry, Iranian cinema is not merely anti-colonial. It is non-colonial. It has found, carved, cultivated, and sustained a space in which we have found a mode of agential autonomy that is not articulate against any figment of imagination called "the West." In

Iranian cinema Kurosawa is as important as Ford, Godard as influential as Ray, Tarkovsky as pathbreaking as Ozu—and one can never tell (and that is the glory of it) who is from the East and who is from the West in that pantheon of divine revelations.

Despite some magnificent work of critical journalism and scholarship (particularly in Persian and by Iranians inside Iran), the study of Iranian cinema is in a very early stage and will remain that way until a generation or two from now, when we will have produced enough accounts of our immediate and memorial impressions of it so that a new generation of critical thinking will pick up the task where we left off. This is the case in no insignificant degree because what we see in Iranian cinema, from its very inception, is the tip of an iceberg the proportions of which, submerged in the Iranian collective subconscious, we may never fully see or measure. What I am merely suggesting here is the panoramic perspective of a two-hundred-year spectrum, from the earliest moments of our colonial encounter with European modernity to the age of globalization, where our poets and writers, artists and critics, have been at work in articulating, narrating and visualizing, a mode of agential authority for us through and by virtue of which we can stand up and say "I" without a British or French colonial officer pointing a gun at us—one way or another—forcing us either to fight back or to surrender.

If there is one thing I have learned as an illegal immigrant in the field of cinema studies, smuggling myself into it, as it were, it is that filmmakers the world over borrow (steal) creatively from each other in broad daylight. But they do this creative borrowing so ingeniously that it no longer matters that someone else before them did something similar. What matters, instead, is the domestic location of their aesthetics, which prompted and provoked by a visual repertoire external to the memorial evidence of their culture and character gives an ipso facto globality to their vision. It is critical to note how it is that cultures as widely different as Akira Kurosawa's Japan, Satyajit Ray's India, Vittorio de Sica's Italy, Abbas Kiarostami's Iran, Ingmar Bergman's Sweden, Theo Angelopoulos' Greece, or Youssef Chahine's Egypt can convey sentiments and ideas at once local to their concerns and yet global in the range of empathy they invoke. Master practitioners of their occupied sentiments, these artists are firmly grounded in their own culture and yet conversant with iconic figures from others. Cinematic "glocality," you can call it, and that was long before cultural globalization was even a term to demand any attention.

Iranian filmmakers, as all other filmmakers, have placed their cameras right in the middle of two critical locations: the fictive *socius* that holds their real society together, and the pregnant *signum* that pulls it apart. This attractive tension between the *socius* and the *signum* results in the signature of Iranian cinema, which is its pararealism—taking reality too seriously to take it seriously. Thus crafted to restore agency to a people, the pararealism of Iranian cinema is fundamental to its creative reconstitution of the Iranian subject in the face of its colonial de-subjection. One could easily argue that the French reception of Iranian cinema is to a large degree a response to what Julia Kristeva has accurately termed the "crisis of the (European) subject." Crisis of the subject at the heart of a power that had successfully imagined itself the center of the universe is indeed tantamount to a global crisis of subject at locations imagining themselves peripheral to that center. Thus the European crisis of the subject is the crisis of the subject in the whole geography radiating outward from that fictive center. Iranian cinema, just like any other cinema (Cuban, Chinese, Chilean, or Palestinian) born out of a national trauma, is, ipso facto, the dismantling of that dangerous delusion at the heart of European colonialism (now wedded to the American empire) and the terror and tyranny it has perpetrated on the face of the earth. A cinema that has emerged as a critically creative response to the colonially militated crisis of the subject has now become globally significant because that colonial denial of a people's agency has come home to roost—reminding Europe that it was never the center of anything other than its own creative delusions, perturbed imagination, code-named "the West." Crisis of the European subject became globally evident and up and about for the whole world to see in the Paris suburb of Argenteuil, where French Interior Minister Nicolas Sarkozy, welcomed with stones and bottles, said these neighborhoods ought to be "cleaned with a power hose" and describes its residents as "gangrene" and "rabble." The crisis of the European subject dwells in the ashes of Zyed Benna and Bouna Traore, two teenagers who were electrocuted in the Paris suburb of Clichy-sous-Bois—and upon which travesty hell broke loose and the very birthplace of Enlightenment modernity, from one end of France to another, went up in smoke. Clichy-sous-Bois was the Hurricane Katrina of Europe—the return of their repressed, the public embarrassment of their collectively denied. The crisis of the European subject, the implosion of the obscenity called "the West," and the dismantling of the very epistemic foregrounding of historically raising "the West" and simultaneously lowering the rest are all the promising signals of a global emancipation from the terror of a term that systematically separated the fate of people, for one tiny minority of them to call themselves "Westerners" and thus to rule and plunder the rest. In restoring creative agency to a segment of that rest, Iranian cinema was a Trojan horse. The French had no clue what they were celebrating at Cannes.

In the history of world cinema, Iranian pararealism is the heir of a succession of major national cinemas. If you begin with the Soviet Social

Realism of the 1920s and 1930s, you note that the first major national cinema was embedded in a mode of realism that emerged in the immediate aftermath of the Russian Revolution of 1917. During the 1920s, a major cinematic culture emerged in the Soviet Union, which in turn gave rise to the aesthetic conception of Russian formalism. A radical social revolutionary project, Russian cinema generated the astonishing aesthetic proposition that no revolutionary art was possible without a radical formalist revolution. Sergei Eisenstein emerged as the principal visionary and theorist of Soviet cinema. His style of montage became by far the most influential aesthetic legacy of this Russian cinematic formalism. In one cinematic masterpiece after another—from *Strike* (1924) to *Battleship Potemkin* (1925), *October* (1927), *The General Line* (1928), *Alexander Nevsky* (1938), and *Ivan The Terrible* (1942–46)—Eisenstein mapped out the contours of a revolutionary cinema at once politically engaged and aesthetically adventurous.

It seems that at a time of major national trauma, cinema (or any other art form) becomes far more integral to a people's social and cultural aspirations. The cinema that emerged in the immediate aftermath of the Russian revolution presents such an example. From the historical materialism of Karl Marx to the psychoanalytical theories of Freud, Eisenstein's cinema expanded the normative and moral texture of Soviet cinema—a phenomenon that later became definitive to the rest of world cinema. This thematic expansion corresponded to the immediate revolutionary project serving the peasantry and the proletariat in whose name it had articulated its thematic and aesthetic ideals. A committed Marxist revolutionary, Eisenstein gave to montage, his cinematic forte, an almost spontaneous dialectical force—fully at the service of the Socialist revolution. His preference for nonprofessional actors, who were asked to draw on their own emotional experiences rather than fake that of others, anticipated much that would later happen in various forms of realism. Eisenstein's visionary aesthetics soon left behind his political limitations, angering Stalin, while remaining true to his own vision.

After Soviet formalism emerged Italian Neorealism, in the 1940s and 1950s, with far-reaching influences beyond Italian cinema proper. In the immediate aftermath of World War II, a significant body of films were produced in Italy that gradually became a globally influential cinema. Real locations shot in realistic long takes, with non-actors given improvisatory liberty to enrich the fantasy of filmmaking with the fact of lived experiences, and a full-bodied topography of the moral and economic problems that postwar Italy faced became the hallmark of Italian Neorealism. The occupation of Cinecittà during the war had forced Italian filmmakers to shoot their scenes on location, forcing the prevalent cinaesthetics toward a far more realistic cinema than was possible in studio filmmaking. Italian Neorealism connected to the literary realism of nineteenth–century Italian culture—particularly to the literary *verismo* of Giovanni Verga—and thus crafted a new kind of *verismo* that was visually pertinent to Italian realities.

By and large, most masterpieces of Italian Neorealism have their roots in the national trauma of postwar anxieties. Roberto Rossellini's *Roma, città aperta* (*Rome, Open City*, 1945) is a testimony to Italian hostility toward the Gestapo. Italian Neorealism is perhaps the best example of a national trauma giving rise to a cinematic vision unprecedented in its immediate context. De Sica's *Sciuscià* (*Shoeshine*, 1946) claims the post-liberation Rome for a future Italy through a depiction of its downtrodden youth; and yet it manages to be a celebration of freedom in the midst of chaos and corruption. The film is at once jubilant, realistic, and hopeful. De Sica portrays Italy—from its anarchic city to the munificent peace of its countryside (all with the intrusion of the US army cashing in on its defeat of German Nazism for its future confrontation with Soviet socialism)—as a homeland that can now forget its pain and suffering and remember itself in peace and purpose. An absolute masterpiece example of Italian Neorealism, the six episodes of Rossellini's *Paisà* (*Paisan*, 1946) narrates the adventures of the Italian liberation forces in expelling the Nazi occupation of their homeland. In a stroke of genius, Rossellini began the momentous occasion of extracting life out of the brutalities of a national trauma—thus helping to imagine a living memory out of the death and destruction of Italian fascism.

After Italian Neorealism came German New Cinema in the 1950s and 1960s. Filmmakers like Rainer Maria Fassbinder, Wim Wenders, Werner Herzog, and Margarethe von Trotta brought to full fruition a cinematic adventure in Germany that sought to exorcise the ghost of post-Holocaust German soul-searching, brought on by one of the most devastating national traumas of modern history. Then came the French New Wave in the 1960s. The French New Wave emerged during the course and immediate aftermath of the Algerian war of independence, a national liberation movement that deeply divided French society, forced it to face its brutal colonial legacy, and ultimately led to the massive social uprisings of 1968. From the intellectual core of the magazine *Cahiers du Cinema* gradually emerged the most prominent young directors of this movement—Francois Truffaut and Jean-Luc Godard—and with them the idea of *auteur* filmmaking was born.

Can we then associate the rise of national cinemas with the occurrence of major traumatic experiences in the life of a nation? Consider the Cuban cinema of the 1960s, which was coterminous with the Cuban revolution of 1959. In both its revolutionary aspirations and its decidedly anti-Hollywood thematic and aesthetic thrust, Cuban cinema reflected the hopes and aspirations of the newly liberated nation. The rise of Tomás Gutiérrez Alea and Humberto Solás as two major revolutionary filmmakers placed Cuban cinema on the world map. As a revolutionary art arisen from the revolutionary trauma of a people, the significance of Cuban cinema was not limited to that country alone and soon assumed both symbolic and catalytic impact throughout Latin America. The Cuban Institute of Art and Film Industry emerged as the principal organ of the new Cuban cinema almost immediately after the collapse of Batista. The cinematic education of Tomás Gutiérrez Alea in Rome in the 1950s brought the gift of Italian Neorealism directly to the fertile imagination of revolutionary Cuba. Thus Cuban cinema—represented by luminary filmmakers like Gutiérrez Alea, Santiago Álvarez, Humberto Solás, Manuel Octavio Gómez, Sara Gómez, and Sergio Giral—became the single most significant site of collective revolutionary sentiment among countries or peoples fomenting revolution.

The same argument can be made for the Palestinian cinema, perhaps the most exciting emerging national cinema around these days. In this case, Palestinian cinema is still squarely rooted in the national trauma of a people historically denied their own homeland. The central trauma of "the Catastrophe" (or the Nakba, as the Palestinians themselves call it) remains definitive to Palestinian cinema, from the pioneering generation of Mustafa Abu Ali to the global celebration of such filmmakers as Michel Khleifi, and now down to its most astounding manifestations in the cinema of Elia Suleiman, Hany Abu Assad, Rashid Mashharawi, May Masri, Nizar Hassan, Tawfiq Abu Wael, Muhammad Bakri—having already given rise to the younger generation of Annemarie Jacir, Raed al-Hilou, and Sameh Zoabi. Consider the fact that the Palestinian Nakba is so central to this cinema that not a single Palestinian filmmaker has so far done a film on it, and yet every film they make is pointing to it. The only film that specifically addressed the Palestinian dispossession of their homeland is Yousry Nasrallah's *Gate of the Sun* (2004), a film directed by an Egyptian filmmaker on the basis of a novel by Elias Khouri, who is a Lebanese novelist—which fact of course points to the larger Arab context of the Palestinian national trauma.

This also seems to me what has happened in Iranian cinema, a national art form predicated on its literary and poetic antecedents and deeply rooted in the national trauma of a people facing the ravages of a predatory colonial history. That prolonged national trauma is yet to be completely exorcized from our collective psyche.

The origins of Iranian cinema are as old as cinema itself, and yet its first serious filmmakers are still mostly alive and well, active and with us. Where they came from no longer seems to matter. What they have done does. "*Kashefan-e forutan-e shokaran*," Ahmad Shamlu would call them, "The humble discoverers of hemlock"; "*Joyandegan-e shadi dar mejri atashfeshanha*": "Those who look for happiness in the mouths of volcanoes." Is that why the world did not take note of Iranian cinema until Iranians as a people exposed their guts for the whole world to see during the revolution—its battles fought, its dreams betrayed—and after that until the terror of the treacherous Iran-Iraq War was visited upon them and the Iraqis alike. Iranian cinema does not belong to Iranians alone. The perished Iraqis have a share in it—as do the Iraqi mothers whose sons were buried, Iraqi sisters deprived and widowed, and Iraqi children left orphaned. Iranian cinema is theirs too. Iranian cinema may speak Persian, but it has a sweet, sorrowful, Arabic accent to it. I know that accent very well. The Persian language—listen to it carefully. Can you hear its Afghan accent? Do you detect its Tajiki diction? Have you noticed how Panahi has restored dignity to the Turkish accent, Qobadi glory to Kurdish poetry? It deeply saddens me when Iranian cinema becomes the subject of useless theoretical speculation by anthropologists, thinking the best Iranians (or any other people) have produced is there to amuse and entertain their speculative banalities. But never mind that. Nothing, I assure you, of those ponderous prognostications will remain. Iranian cinema will.

What is Mohsen Makhmalbaf doing in India right now, in that Nirvanic neighborhood of his own wandering soul? Why do the Japanese love Iranian cinema so much? Do you know in Osaka I once saw Samira Makhmalbaf's *Blackboard* being sold in a supermarket? What have Koreans detected in it, and have you read what the Spaniards and the Portuguese think of it—so eloquently, persuasively? I once read a beautiful review of Samira's *Apple* by a woman from Brazil—no one famous or important, just a regular human being who had purchased the film from Amazon.com and sat down and wrote her noble thoughts. A Jordanian woman in Sharjah once told me she loved Marziyeh Meshkini's films. A Syrian filmmaker in Damascus once stopped in the middle of a sentence to tell me how much he admired Amir Naderi's cinema. Once in Beirut I sat at the side of a soothing sea and I sang Forugh Farrokhzad to eager ears. I once saw a Jamaican filmmaker who said he was going to remake all of Kiarostami's films, but set them in the Caribbean. Mohsen Makhmalbaf once refused to pull his films from an Israeli film festival, saying if Israeli people wanted to see his films, he was honored, and if the Israeli government wanted to abuse his cinema, it was not any worse than what the Islamic Republic did regularly. Do you know that in the Noble Sanctuary in Jerusalem, I once stood shoulder to shoulder with Palestinians and remembered my forgotten faith in the language I had learned from our ancestors' blasphemous pieties? In Dolores Hidalgo in Mexico, a half-Irish, half-Cuban wanderer offered me good wine in exchange for a chat on Kiarostami's use of long takes. Right here in New York, soon after 9/11, I screened Mohsen's *Kandahar* to thousands of New Yorkers, seeking to sooth their fears by having them think of the terror coming to others. *"Miveh bar shakheh shodam, sang pareh dar kaf-e kudak"*—again Shamlu: "I became fruit on a branch of a tree, and a stone in the palm of a child." Iranian cinema (not religion) is the heart of a heartless world, for it is the vision of silent nights, and in it we pray through the long winter we have endured to remain human, all too human.

Snapped and smuggled shots of a forgotten but stubborn dream— that's how I think of Iranian cinema...

ACKNOWLEDGMENTS

The publication of this book is made possible by two generous grants from the University Seminar Fund and the Committee on Asian and Middle Eastern Studies at Columbia University. I am grateful to my distinguished colleagues Professors Robert Belknap and William Theodore de Bary, and their respective committees, for their endorsement of my work.

My thanks to Mohammad Batmanglij go far beyond the ordinary gratitude of an author to an editor. He has been the principal interlocutor of a much more elongated series of conversations, of which with patience, grace, and panache he has masterfully carved out what you have read in this book. To Mohammad and Najmieh Batmanglij goes my sincerest gratitude for the grace of their company and the generosity of their open arms. Other than these words I have no other way of showing them how absolutely delighted I am they have included me among their friends and authors in one of the most beautiful and praiseworthy publishing events in contemporary Iranian studies.

My former student Tahereh Hadian went through immense trouble in Tehran locating for me the copies of the photos we have used as illustrations in this book. To her and to Houshang Golmakani, the distinguished editor of *Film* magazine, go my sincere thanks. I am equally grateful to Mani Petgar for his generous permission to use the photo from Amir Naderi's *The Runner* for the cover.

To Mohsen Makhmalbaf, Amir Naderi, Nikzad Nodjoumi, and Shirin Neshat I owe a particular note of gratitude for the privilege of their company, which has been the inspiration for my vision of what is sublime and beautiful.

As always, my children, Kaveh and Pardis, my wife and colleague, Golbarg Bashi, and my friends and colleagues at Columbia University in New York are the principal sources of my hopes and aspirations—the generosity and grace of their patience with me the clearest signs of what is good about the world.

Hamid Dabashi
New York
December 2006